Restoration of the Great Pyramids and Other Tomb Monuments in the Ancient Cemetery of Gizeh, Egypt. (After Hoelscher)

These royal tombs (pyramids) belonged to the leading kings of the early part of the Pyramid Age (about 3000 to 2500 B.C.). The Great Pyramid, the tomb of King Khufu (Greek *Cheops*), is on the right. Next in size is that of King Khafre (Greek *Chephren*) on the left. On the east side (front) of each pyramid is a temple (see also Fig. 11), where the dead king received food, drink, and clothing for the life hereafter. These temples, like the pyramids, were built on the desert plateau above, while the royal town was in the valley below on the right. For convenience, therefore, the temple was connected with the town below by a covered gallery, or causeway, of stone. This causeway may be seen descending in a straight line from the pyramid and temple of King Khafre and terminating below, just beside the Sphinx, in a large oblong building of stone, called a valley-temple, to distinguish it from the pyramid-temple on the plateau above. It was a splendid structure of granite, serving not only as a temple but also as the entrance to the causeway from the royal city. This valley-temple was adorned with magnificent statues of the king, a number of which were discovered at the bottom of a well in the valley-temple, where they had at some time been hurled by enemies. They now adorn the great Museum at Cairo; the head of the finest of them may be seen in Fig. 12. Here beside his valley-temple we see another great statue of King Khafre, which he had carved as a colossal portrait of himself, with the body of a lion. It is commonly called the Great Sphinx. It is the largest portrait figure ever executed: the head is sixty-five feet high, the body is about one hundred and eighty-seven feet long, and the face is about fourteen feet across. The pyramids are surrounded by the tombs of the queens and the great lords of the age. At the lower left-hand corner is an unfinished pyramid showing the inclined ascents up which the stone blocks were dragged. These ascents (called ramps) were built of sun-baked brick and are therefore darker in color than the white limestone of the pyramid against which they were built. They were taken down and removed after the pyramid was finished. These pyramid cemeteries mark for us the coming of earliest civilization after a long struggle with barbarism. They show us many of the most important things that made up civilization in the beginning, like the art of stone masonry, architecture with the earliest columns and colonnades (Fig. 11), art (especially sculpture, Fig. 12), the earliest seagoing ships, the incoming use of metal, and great progress in industries (Fig. 9). Besides these visible things, early civilization also included some things *not* visible, like the great government controlling all the people who did these wonderful things, and, especially, also belief in right living, in kindness to others, and that a good life here was the best way to gain happiness in the next world

HISTORY OF EUROPE

ANCIENT AND MEDIEVAL

EARLIEST MAN, THE ORIENT, GREECE
AND ROME

BY

JAMES HENRY BREASTED

EUROPE FROM THE BREAK-UP OF
THE ROMAN EMPIRE TO THE
FRENCH REVOLUTION

BY

JAMES HARVEY ROBINSON

GINN AND COMPANY

BOSTON · NEW YORK · CHICAGO · LONDON
ATLANTA · DALLAS · COLUMBUS · SAN FRANCISCO

The Athenæum Press
GINN AND COMPANY · PRO-
PRIETORS · BOSTON · U.S.A.

PREFACE

General European history is one of the most perplexing subjects to deal with in the high school. It seems absolutely essential that boys and girls should have some knowledge of *the whole past* of mankind ; without that they can have no real understanding of the world in which they live, for the simple reason that the present can only be explained by the past. The older historical manuals were, in the main, short accounts of past *events* ; but it is really past *conditions* and past *institutions* and past *ideas* that are best worth knowing about. The older books tended, moreover, to give too much attention to the remote past and too little information in regard to recent history, so that there was little chance of the pupil's realizing the vital bearing of the past on the present.

The aim of these two volumes is to avoid the defects of the older books, first, by frankly subordinating the mere happenings of the past to a clear statement of the conditions under which men lived for long periods, of the ideas which they held, and of the manner in which conditions and ideas have undergone great changes in man's slow rise from his original savage estate ; secondly, by devoting about half of the work, namely, "Our Own Times," to the past hundred and fifty years, which concern us most immediately.

The arrangement of the volumes is novel in a number of respects. Each chapter is divided into several *topical* sections, as will be seen by consulting the Contents. The topics are, of course, arranged with strict attention to chronology, but the writers have always before them a particular subject which they aim to make plain under each section heading. In short, each section is a *discussible topic and not a fragment of chronology.* The authors hope that this plan of presentation will serve to make the books more useful and teachable than the older method of arrangement.

These volumes are based on the authors' "Outlines of European History," but Chapters I–XX have been completely rewritten, simplified, and condensed ; and more space has been given to Roman history and less to that of the ancient Orient. Hearty thanks are due to Dr. T. G. Allen and Professor Carl F. Huth for reading the proofs of this portion and for revising the bibliographies. As for the rest of the work, much condensation has been effected and the details of presentation have been reconsidered from beginning to end.

Not only have the illustrations been carefully chosen with a view of corroborating and vivifying the text but under each picture a sufficiently detailed legend is given to explain its significance, and this often adds materially to the information given in the letterpress. The pictures consequently give a sort of parallel narrative and furnish a helpful supplement and corrective to the text itself. Everything which does not obviously bear upon the chief matters under consideration is sedulously excluded. (See "Outlines of European History," Part I, p. v, for acknowledgments of the authors in this important matter.)

These volumes meet the growing demand for a *two*-year course in European history in the earlier years of the high school and in the preparatory schools. The great achievements of the oriental peoples and of the Greek and Roman periods are brought into immediate relation with later European development, without devoting a whole year's study to them. English history, if somewhat briefly treated, is given its proper association with that of the neighboring nations on the Continent. By devoting the whole second year to the history of the tremendous changes which have overtaken the world since the middle of the eighteenth century, the student will be in a position to grasp the more immediate causes of the World War and the perplexing conditions in the midst of which we live.

J. H. B.
J. H. R.

CONTENTS

Contents

LIST OF COLORED PLATES

LIST OF COLORED MAPS

HISTORY OF EUROPE: ANCIENT AND MEDIEVAL

BOOK I. EARLIEST MAN

CHAPTER I

EARLIEST MAN IN EUROPE

I. THE PROGRESS OF EARLIEST MAN

1. Early Inventions and the Progress of Man. We all know that our fathers and mothers never saw an aëroplane when they were children, and very few of them had ever seen an automobile. Their fathers lived during most of their lives without electric lights or telephones in their houses. Their grandfathers, our great-grandfathers, were obliged to make all long journeys in stagecoaches drawn by horses, and some of them died without ever having seen a locomotive.

Each invention has grown out of earlier inventions, and each would have been impossible without the discoveries which preceded it. Thus, if we went back far enough, we should reach a point where no one could build a stagecoach or a wagon, because no one had invented a wheel or tamed a wild horse. Earlier still there were no ships and no travel or commerce by sea. There were no metal tools, for no one had ever seen any metal. It was impossible to write, for no one had invented writing, and so there were no books nor any knowledge of science ; and such institutions as schools and churches or even laws and government did not yet exist. This book is intended to tell the story of how mankind gained all these and many other things, and thus built up great nations which struggled among themselves for leadership, then weakened and fell. The earlier part of this story forms what we call ancient history.

2. The First Steps and the Earliest Ages of Human Progress. If we go back far enough in the story of man, we reach a time when he possessed nothing whatever but his bare hands with which to protect himself, satisfy his hunger, and meet all his other needs. He must have been without speech and unable even to build a fire. There was no one to teach him anything. The earliest men who began in this situation had to learn everything for themselves by slow experience and long effort, and every tool, however simple, had to be invented.

We cannot now trace all the different stages in his earliest progress; but this earliest progress brought to man two things without which he could have made no progress: the ability to speak and the means of kindling a fire (see *Ancient Times*, Fig. 1). After this he gained a third invention of the greatest assistance to him. He sometimes found a broken stone and used its ragged edge to aid him in hacking off his meat or shaping his wooden club. He then found that he could improve the form of such a stone, and thus he gradually learned to shape a rude stone tool or weapon (*Ancient Times*, Fig. 2). At this point he entered what we now call the Stone Age, more than fifty thousand years ago.

From this point on we can hold in our hands the very stone implements which early men used. We can distinguish, in the examples of their handiwork which still survive, three successive ages, which we may call the Early Stone Age, the Middle Stone Age, and the Late Stone Age.

II. THE EARLY STONE AGE

3. The Life of Early Stone Age Men. European savages entered the Early Stone Age over fifty thousand years ago — perhaps much earlier. In order to secure their food they followed the life of hunters, roaming about in the great forests which covered much of western Europe. In that distant age Europe possessed a tropical climate, and tropical animals filled its forests. Huge beasts like the hippopotamus wallowed along the banks of the rivers in the region which is now France and England. The fierce rhinoceros charged through the jungles. As the hunter fled before them he caught glimpses of gigantic elephants plunging through the thick tropical growth. At night he had no hut or shelter in which he might take refuge. He slept on the ground wherever he happened to be overtaken by darkness.

4. Earliest Flint Weapons and their Preservation. These early hunters gradually improved their first rough stone weapons and tools. They finally succeeded in producing what we now call a *fist-hatchet* (Fig. 1). It was a roughly shaped piece of flint, with a ragged edge sharp enough to use for cutting and chopping. Sometimes such stone weapons were lost on river banks and were gradually covered by sand, gravel, and soil which has since collected there. Thus buried they are found to-day in large numbers along the rivers of England, Belgium, and France. Along with them are often found the bones of the huge tropical animals we have mentioned, which long ago disappeared from their European haunts.

FIG. 1. A FLINT FIST-HATCHET OF THE EARLY STONE AGE

Rough flint flakes older than the fist-hatchet still survive to show us man's earliest efforts at shaping stone. But the fist-hatchet is the earliest well-finished type of tool produced by man. The original is about nine inches long, and the drawing reduces it to less than one third. Either end might be used as the cutting edge, but it was usually grasped in the fist by the narrower part, and never had any handle. Handles of wood or horn do not appear until much later (cf. Fig. 6, *4*, *5*).

5. The Coming of the Ice. For thousands of years the life of the hunter went on with little change. He slowly improved his rough stone fist-hatchet, and he probably learned to make additional implements of wood, but of these last we know nothing. Then he began to notice that the air of his forest home was losing its tropical warmth. Geologists have not yet found out why, but as the centuries passed, the ice, which all the year round still overlies the region of the North Pole and the summits of the Alps, began to descend. The northern ice crept further and further southward until it covered England as far south as the Thames. The glaciers of the Alps pushed down the Rhone valley as far as the spot where the city of Lyons now stands. On our own continent of North America the southern edge of the ice is marked by lines of bowlders carried and left there by the ice. Such lines of bowlders are found, for example, as far south as Long Island and westward along the valleys of the Ohio and the Missouri.[1] The hunter saw the glittering blue masses of ice, with their crown of snow, pushing through the green of his forest abode and crushing down vast trees in many a sheltered glen or favorite hunting ground. Gradually these savage men of early Europe were forced to accustom themselves to a colder climate, and many of the animals familiar to the hunter retreated to the warmer south, never to return.

III. The Middle Stone Age

6. Remains of Middle Stone Age Man in Caverns. The hunters were unable to build themselves shelters from the cold. They therefore took refuge in limestone caves, where they and their descendants continued to live for thousands of years. This period we call the Middle Stone Age. Century after century the sand and earth continued to blow into these caverns, and fragments of rock fell from the ceiling. Thus masses of rubbish accumulated

---

[1] Geologists have now shown that the ice advanced southward and retreated to the north again no less than four times. Following each advance of the ice a warm interval caused its retreat. There were four warm intervals, and we are now living in the fourth. The evidence now indicates that men began to make stone implements in the third warm interval. The last advance of the ice therefore took place between us and them. It is perhaps some thirty thousand years ago that the ice began to come south for the last time. See map and diagram in *Ancient Times*, p. 8.

on the cavern floor, and in one case it was as much as forty feet
deep. To-day we find among all this rubbish also many layers of
ashes and charcoal from the cave-dweller's fire (see *Ancient Times*,
Fig. 9), besides nu-
merous tools, weapons,
and implements which
he used. These things
disclose man's further
progress, step by step,
and show us that he
had now left the old
fist-hatchet far behind
and become a real
craftsman.

**7. The Industries
of Middle Stone Age
Man.** The tiny flint
chips still found at the
door of his cave show
us how the hunter
must have sat there
carefully chipping the
edges of his flint tools.
By this time he had
a considerable list of
tools from which he
could select. At his
elbow were knives,
chisels, drills and ham-
mers, polishers and
scrapers, all of flint
(Fig. 2). He could
now produce such a

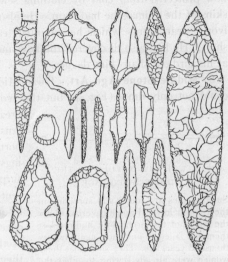

Fig. 2. Flint Tools and Weapons of
the Middle Stone Age

From right to left they include knives, spear-
and arrow-points, scrapers, drills, and various
edged tools. They show great skill and preci-
sion in flaking. The fine edges have all been
produced by chipping off a line of flakes along
the margin, seen especially in the long piece at
the right. This chipping was done by *pressure*.
The brittleness of flint is such that if a hard
piece of bone is pressed firmly against a flint
edge, a flake of flint, often reaching far back
from the edge, will snap off in response to
increasing pressure. This was a great improvement over the earliest method by striking,
or *percussion* (see Fig. 1 and *Ancient Times*, Fig. 2)

fine cutting edge by chipping (see *Ancient Times*, § 15) that
he could work ivory, bone, and especially reindeer horn.
With his enlarged list of tools he was able to shape pins,

needles, spoons, and ladles, all of ivory or bone, and carve them with pictures of the animals he hunted in the forest (Fig. 4). The fine ivory needles (Fig. 3) show that the hunter's body was now protected from cold by clothing sewed together out of the skins of the animals he had slain. He also fashioned keen barbed ivory spear points which he mounted, each on a long wooden shaft. He had also discovered the bow and arrow, and he carried at his girdle a sharp flint dagger.

8. Middle Stone Age Art. These Middle Stone Age hunters could not only draw (Fig. 4) but they could also paint with the greatest skill. In the caverns of southern France and northern Spain their paintings have been found in surprising numbers in recent years. Long lines of bison, deer, or wild horses cover the walls and ceilings of these caves. Sometimes they are only carved on the rock wall (Fig. 4, *2*) ; but many are painted in colors.

FIG. 3. IVORY NEEDLE OF THE MIDDLE STONE AGE

Such needles are found still surviving in the rubbish in the French caverns, where the wives of the prehistoric hunters lost them and failed to find them again twenty thousand years ago. They show that these women were already sewing together the skins of wild animals as clothing

They are all startling in their lifelikeness and vigor. These paintings,—made at least ten thousand years ago,—together with the carvings on the hunter's ivory and bone weapons (Fig. 4, *1, 3, 4*), form the earliest art in the whole career of man, in so far as we know.

IV. THE LATE STONE AGE

9. Last Retreat of the Ice ; the Late Stone Age. At length the climate again grew warmer and became what it is to-day. The traces left by the ice would lead us to think that it withdrew northward for the last time probably some ten thousand years ago. Men of a different race from those of the Early and Middle Stone Ages had meantime invaded western Europe. These men had learned that it was possible to *grind* the edge of a stone ax or chisel (Fig. 6, *4*) as we now do with tools of metal. They were also able to drill a hole in the stone ax head and insert a handle (Fig. 6, *5*). The common use of the *ground* stone ax, after the retreat of the ice, brings in the Late Stone Age. Traces of the

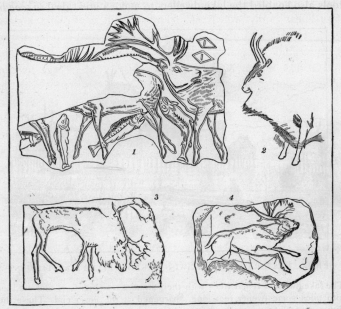

FIG. 4. DRAWINGS CARVED BY MIDDLE STONE AGE MAN ON IVORY

1, marching line of reindeer with salmon in the spaces — probably a talisman to bring the hunter and fisherman good luck; *2*, a bison at bay (not on ivory but incised in the rock of a cavern wall; over one hundred and fifty caverns containing such paintings and carvings are known in France and Spain); *3*, a grazing reindeer; *4*, a running reindeer. See *Ancient Times*, Figs. 9, 10

villages and settlements of Late Stone Age man have been found throughout all Europe, except in the extreme north.

10. Progress of Late Stone Age Man. The life of Late Stone Age man gradually made progress in a number of very important matters. *First,* with their *ground* stone axes, hatchets, and chisels (Fig. 6) men could now build *wooden huts.* These wooden dwellings of the Late Stone Age (Fig. 5) are the earliest such shelters found in Europe. Sunken fragments of these houses are found all along the shores of the Swiss lakes, lying at the bottom, among the piles which supported the houses of the village. *Second,* such tools also enabled the lake-dwellers to make a great deal of *wooden*

FIG. 5. RESTORATION OF A SWISS LAKE-DWELLER'S SETTLEMENT

The lake-dwellers felled trees with their stone axes (Fig. 6, *5*) and cut them into piles some twenty feet long, sharpened at the lower end. These they drove several feet into the bottom of the lake, in water eight or ten feet deep. On a platform supported by these piles they then built their houses. The platform was connected with the shore by a bridge, which may be seen here on the right. A section of it could be removed at night for protection. The fish nets seen drying at the rail, the "dugout" boat of the hunters who bring in the deer, and many other things have been found on the lake bottom in recent times

furniture. Pieces of stools, chests, carved dippers, spoons, and the like, all of wood, show that these houses were equipped with all ordinary wooden furniture. *Third,* the householder had also learned that clay will harden in the fire, and he was making handy jars, bowls, and dishes of *burned clay* (Fig. 6). Although roughly made without the use of the potter's wheel and unevenly burned without an oven, they added much to the equipment of his dwelling.

Fourth, the lake-dweller had somewhere gained knowledge of *flax*.[1] Before his door the women sat spinning flaxen yarn, and the rough skin clothing of his ancestors had given way to garments of woven stuff. *Fifth*, the lake-dwellers had already received one of the greatest possessions gained by man in his slow

FIG. 6. PART OF THE EQUIPMENT OF A LATE STONE AGE LAKE-DWELLER SEEN IN FIG. 5.

This group contains the evidence for three important inventions made or received by the men of the Late Stone Age: *first*, pottery jars, like *2* and *3*, with rude decorations, the oldest baked clay in Europe, and *1*, a large kettle in which the lake-dwellers' food was cooked; *second*, ground-edged tools like *4*, stone chisel with ground edge (§ 9), mounted in a deerhorn handle like a hatchet, or *5*, stone ax with a ground edge and pierced with a hole for the ax handle (the houses of Fig. 5 were built with such tools); and *third*, weaving, as shown by *6*, a spinning "whorl" of baked clay, the earliest spinning wheel. When suspended by a rough thread of flax eighteen to twenty inches long, it was given a whirl which made it spin in the air like a top, thus rapidly twisting the thread by which it was hanging. The thread when sufficiently twisted was wound up, and another length of eighteen or twenty inches was drawn out from the unspun flax to be similarly twisted. One of these earliest spinning wheels has been found in the Swiss lakes with a spool of flaxen thread still attached. (From photograph lent by Professor Hoernes)

advance toward civilization. This was the food grains which we call *cereals*, especially wheat and barley. The seeds of the wild grasses, which their ancestors once gathered, these Late Stone

[1] Flax, grain, and cattle-breeding were without doubt introduced into Europe from the Orient.

Age men had learned to cultivate. Thus wild grain was domesticated, and *agriculture* was introduced. *Sixth,* these Late Stone Age men possessed *domestic cattle.* On the green uplands above were now pasturing the creatures which Middle Stone Age man had once pursued through the wilds (*Ancient Times,* Fig. 12). For the mountain sheep and goats and the wild cattle had now learned to dwell near man and submit to his control. Indeed, the wild ox bowed his neck to the yoke and drew the plow across the forest-girt field where he had once wandered in unhampered freedom. Fragments of wooden wheels in the lake-villages show that he was also drawing the wheeled cart, the earliest in Europe.

11. Earliest Communities Organized. Wooden houses, agriculture, and the possession of domestic animals resulted in a more settled and less roaming life. Communities were formed. Groups of massive tombs still surviving, built of enormous blocks of stone, required the united efforts of large numbers of men. Also, the driving of fifty thousand piles for the lake-village at Wangen in Switzerland shows that men were learning to work together.

Friendly intercourse between these communities was also known. The amber from the north and the wide distribution of a certain kind of flint found in only one mine of France tell us of the beginnings of commerce between the prehistoric communities of Europe.

12. Summary of European Man's Progress down to about 3000 B.C. Let us now look back for a moment and see how much early man had gained in over fifty thousand years of slow progress. Before his first stone weapon he had learned to speak, then to kindle fire, and after that came his earliest efforts to work stone. For ages afterward (*Early Stone Age*) his progress consisted chiefly of improvements in his stone weapons. Then after the ice came down (*Middle Stone Age*) he learned to use ivory, bone, and reindeer horn, including ivory needles for sewing together skin clothing. He even painted wonderful animal figures on the walls of his cavern home and carved the same animals on his weapons. Later, as the ice retreated (*Late Stone Age*), and he learned to grind the edge of his stone tools, he could build wooden dwellings and fill them with wooden utensils and furniture.

He was also able to make pottery, spin and weave flax for clothing, cultivate grain, and follow agriculture. Then he learned to keep the once wild creatures, like cattle and sheep, as tamed domestic animals. At the same time Stone Age men had learned to lead a settled life in towns and villages.

13. Late Stone Age Barbarism all around the Mediterranean. Thus far we have followed man's advance only in *Europe*. Similar progress had also been made by Stone Age men all around the Mediterranean; that is, about 4000 B.C., not only in Europe but in Asia, and especially in northern Africa, mankind had reached about the same stage of advancement.

14. Rise of Civilization in Egypt (4000–3000 B.C.). But civilization cannot arise or exist at all without the following three things: the use of *metals*, the possession of *writing*, and the control of men by an organized *government*. Nowhere around the entire Mediterranean did the world of Late Stone Age barbarism as yet possess these things, nor did Europe ever gain them for itself unaided. Europe borrowed them. Hence we must now turn elsewhere to see where these and many other things that help to make up civilization first appeared.

In the southeast corner of the Mediterranean (see map, p. 176) the valley of the river Nile formed a home for men so well supplied with everything needful for human life and so favorably situated that the Late Stone Age men of Egypt, as the lower Nile valley is called, began to make more rapid progress than the Late Stone Age men of Europe. The Egyptians, emerging from the Late Stone Age, invented a system of writing, discovered metal, and learned to use it. Thus in the thousand years between 4000 and 3000 B.C. the Egyptians of the Late Stone Age advanced to a great and wonderful civilization, while the Europeans still remained in barbarism.

In the sailing ships which the Egyptians learned to build, the things like metal and writing, so important in civilization, began to pass from the dwellers along the Nile to the Late Stone Age Europeans about 3000 B.C. Barbarian Europe was thus discovered by civilized people crossing the Mediterranean, just as barbarian America was later discovered by civilized men who crossed the Atlantic. Hence in order to understand the further history of Europe we must turn to Egypt and the Near Orient,[1] of which Egypt is a part. There we shall take up the Egyptians just as they had reached the end of the Late Stone Age, and we shall follow them as they gained civilization and became the first great civilized nation.

15. Prehistoric (to 4000 B.C.) and Historic (after 3000 B.C.) Periods. It was not until man invented *writing* and began to produce written documents and monuments bearing inscriptions that the *Historic Period* began. All that we know about men of the Stone Age we have to learn from their surviving weapons, tools, implements, buildings, and other works of their hands, bearing no writing. The age before the appearance of written records we call the *Prehistoric Period*. The transition from the Prehistoric to the Historic Period did not take place suddenly, but was a slow process. The Historic Period began in the Orient during the thousand years between 4000 and 3000 B.C.,[2] as barbarism slowly gave way to civilization and writing became more common.

16. The Orient and Europe. The transition from the Prehistoric to the Historic Period took place in the Orient because civilization arose there. Civilization there is over five thousand years old. It long flourished in the Orient, where it arose, and there great and powerful nations held the leadership for over three thousand years. The barbarians of Late Stone Age Europe, however, long continued without metals and writing. Then, as they slowly acquired these things, leadership in civilization at length passed from the Orient to Europe in the sixth century B.C. We must now, therefore, turn to the Orient to see how man struggled up out of the age of stone tools and weapons into civilization and to follow three thousand years of oriental leadership in civilized life.

[1] The word "Orient" is used to-day to include Japan, China, and India. These lands make up a *Far* Orient. There is also a *Near* Orient, consisting of the lands around the eastern end of the Mediterranean, that is, Egypt and Western Asia, including Asia Minor. We shall use the word "Orient" in this book to designate the *Near* Orient.

[2] Notice that dates before Christ (B.C.) are numbered backward; that is, as time *advances* the numbers *decrease*. Thus 3000 B.C. is *later* than 4000 B.C.; 1800 B.C. is *later* than 1900 B.C.

QUESTIONS [1]

I. What progress in invention have you noticed in your own lifetime? Was there a time when man possessed none of these things? What three ages did earliest man pass through?

II. Describe man's earliest tools. How did he live, and what was Europe then like? What do we call this age? What great change brought it to an end?

III. Where did man then take refuge? Describe his progress and list his new inventions. What art did he possess?

IV. When did the ice withdraw for the last time? What new treatment of his edged tools did man then discover? Make a list of his new possessions in this age. What remains of its towns and communities still survive? Did civilization arise in Europe? Whence did it come to Europe? Contrast the Prehistoric and Historic Periods.

[1] The numerals at the beginnings of the paragraphs indicate the numbered subdivisions of the text of the chapter in which the answers to the questions may be found.

NOTE. The following necklace, of blue glazed beads, made in Egypt was found in a grave of the Late Stone Age in England.

BOOK II. THE ORIENT

CHAPTER II

THE STORY OF EGYPT

I. Egypt and the Rise of the Earliest Civilization

17. Egypt of To-day. We are to begin our study of the early Orient in Egypt. The traveler who visits Egypt at the present day lands in a very modern-looking harbor at Alexandria (see map, p. 176). He is presently seated in a comfortable railway car, in which we may accompany him as he is carried across a low flat plain covered with green fields and dotted with little villages of dark mud-brick huts and scattered palm groves.

Wandering through this verdure is a network of irrigation canals (Fig. 7). Brown-skinned men of slender build, with dark hair, are seen at intervals along the banks of these canals, lifting irrigation buckets attached to simple devices (Fig. 7) exactly like the "well sweeps" of our grandfathers in New England. The irrigation trenches are thus kept full of water for about a hundred days until the grain ripens. It is the best of evidence that Egypt enjoys no rain.

The black soil we see is unexcelled in fertility, for it is enriched each year by the overflow of the river. The roily waters rise above the river banks every summer, spread far over the flats, and stand there long enough to deposit a very thin layer of rich earthy sediment. This sediment, deposited through ages, has built up the Delta, which we are now crossing. The Delta and the valley above, as far as the First Cataract, together form Egypt (see map, p. 42). It contains over ten thousand square miles of cultivable soil, or somewhat more than the state of Vermont.

18. The Most Favorable Situation for the Rise of Civilization. As our train approaches the southern point of the Delta we begin to see heights on either side of the valley. These heights (Fig. 17) are the plateau of the Sahara Desert, through which the Nile has cut a vast, deep trench as it winds its way northward from inner Africa. This trench, or valley, is seldom more than thirty miles wide, while the strip of soil on each side of the river rarely exceeds ten miles in width. With the exception of the Delta, therefore, Egypt lies at the bottom of a vast trench. Protected by the uninhabited desert on each side, this valley formed a sheltered home, provided with water, a rich soil, a mild climate, and plentiful supplies of raw material of nearly all kinds. Nowhere else on the Mediterranean was there a situation so favorable for the progress of early men ; and nowhere else have the works of their hands, revealing their life in intimate detail, survived in such great numbers.

FIG. 7. AN EGYPTIAN *SHADOOF*, THE OLDEST OF WELL SWEEPS, IRRIGATING THE FIELDS

The man below stands in the water, holding his leather bucket (*A*). The pole (*B*) of the sweep is above him, with a large ball of dried Nile mud on its lower end (*C*) as a lifting weight, or counterpoise, seen just behind the supporting post (*D*). This man lifts the water into a mud basin (*E*). A second man (in the middle) lifts it from this first basin (*E*) to a second basin (*F*), into which he is just emptying his bucket; while a third man (*G*) lifts the water from the middle basin (*F*) to the uppermost basin (*H*) on the top of the bank, where it runs off to the left into trenches spreading over the fields. The low water makes necessary three successive lifts (to *E*, to *F*, to *H*) without ceasing night and day for one hundred days while the crops are growing. Lack of rain is thus atoned for by the Nile

As we journey into the Nile valley, therefore, we soon realize that it can tell us a story of human progress through successive ages such as we can find nowhere else. The first age was that from about 4000 to 3000 B.C., during which man for the first time passed out of barbarism into civilization.

The Nile-dweller's more fortunately situated home enabled him to outstrip in progress all other Late Stone Age peoples around the Mediterranean. The contents of prehistoric graves (see *Ancient Times*, Fig. 25) when examined in one cemetery after another show us gradually improving workmanship, which is evidence of this progress.

19. Life of the Earliest Nile-Dwellers. These earliest Egyptians, like the earliest Europeans, had once been only hunters living on the wild game in the Nile jungles. Wheat and barley found in their graves show that they were already cultivating grain,—the grain that later passed to Europe. A fragment of linen in a grave tells us also whence Europe derived its flax. The peasant at the bottom of this grave was therefore watering his fields of flax and grain down on the fertile soil of the valley over six thousand years ago, just as the brown men whom the traveler sees from the car windows to-day are still doing.

The villages of low mud-brick huts which flash by the car windows furnish us also with an exact picture of those vanished prehistoric villages, the homes of the early Nile-dwellers who are still lying in the graves on the desert margin. In such a village, over six thousand years ago, lived the local chieftain who controlled the irrigation-canal trenches of the district. To him the peasant was required to carry every season a share of the grain and flax which he gathered from his field ; otherwise the supply of water for his crops would stop, and he would receive an unpleasant visit from the chieftain, demanding instant payment. These were the earliest taxes.

20. Pictorial Records and Phonetic Signs. Such transactions led to scratching a rude picture of the basket grain-measure and a number of strokes on the mud wall of the peasant's hut, indicating the number of measures of grain he had paid. In this and many other ways the peasant's dealings with his neighbors or with the chieftain led him to make picture records, and these are the earliest writing known (see *Ancient Times*, Fig. 28).

Gradually each picture gained a fixed sound, for which it always stood. Let us imagine for convenience that Egyptian contained the English word "leaf." It might be written thus: ✑. The Egyptian would in course of time come to look upon the leaf as the sign for the syllable "leaf" wherever it might occur. By the same process 𒀭 might become the sign for the syllable "bee" wherever found. Having thus a means of writing the syllables "bee" and "leaf," the next step was to put them together thus, 𒀭 ✑, and they would together represent the word "belief." Notice, however, that in the word "belief" the sign 𒀭 suggests no longer the idea of a bee but only the *syllable* "be." That is to say, 𒀭 has become a *phonetic* sign. In this way early man could write many names of things of which you cannot make pictures. It is impossible to make a picture of "belief," as you can of a jar or a knife. Thus the Egyptians gradually gained many phonetic signs.

21. Advantage of Phonetic Signs. If the writing of the Egyptian had remained merely a series of pictures, such words as "belief," "hate," "love," "beauty," and the like could never have been written. But when a large number of his pictures had become phonetic signs, each representing a syllable, it was possible for the Egyptian to write any word he knew, whether the word meant a thing of which he could draw a picture or not. This possession of *phonetic* signs is what makes real writing for the first time. It arose among these Nile-dwellers earlier than anywhere else in the ancient world. Indeed, the Egyptian went still further, for he finally possessed a series of signs, each representing only *one* letter; that is, *alphabetic* signs, or real letters. There were twenty-four letters in this alphabet, which was known in Egypt long before 3000 B.C. It was thus the earliest alphabet known and the one from which our own has descended (see *Ancient Times*, §§ 51–56 and Figs. 29–30, where the reader will find the Egyptian alphabet).

22. Invention of Writing Materials. The Egyptians early found out that they could make an excellent paint or ink by thickening water with a little vegetable gum and then mixing in a little soot from the blackened pots over the fire. By dipping a pointed reed into this mixture one could write very well. They also learned that they could split a kind of river reed, called *papyrus*, into thin strips and make large sheets by pasting the strips together with overlapping edges. They thus produced a smooth, tough, pale-yellow paper, the earliest paper known. In this way arose pen, ink, and paper (see Fig. 8). All three of these inventions have descended to us from the Egyptians, and "paper" still bears its ancient name, "papyrus," but slightly changed. With the invention of phonetic writing and writing materials civilization was about to begin, and with its advance the *written records* would begin to be made, which meant the end of the Prehistoric Period and the beginning of the Historic Period (§ 15).

23. Egyptian Invention of our Calendar (4241 B.C.). The Egyptians at the same time found it necessary to measure time, for the peasant needed to know when he ought to go into the town for the next religious feast or how many days still remained before he must pay his neighbor the grain he borrowed last year. Like all other early peoples he found the time from new moon to new moon a very convenient rough measure. But the moon-month varies in length from twenty-nine to thirty days, and it does not evenly divide the year. The Egyptian scribe early discovered this inconvenience, and he decided to use the moon no longer for dividing his year. He would have twelve months and he would make his months all of the same length; that is, thirty days each. Then he would celebrate five feast days, a kind of holiday week five days long, at the end of the year. This gave him a year of 365 days. He was not yet enough of an astronomer to know that every four years he ought to have a leap year, of 366 days, although he discovered this fact later. This convenient Egyptian calendar was devised in 4241 B.C., and its introduction is the earliest dated event in history. Furthermore, this calendar is the very one which has descended to us, after more than six thousand years. Unfortunately, it has meantime suffered awkward alterations in the lengths of the months, alterations for which the Egyptians were not responsible (see p. 240).

24. Discovery of Metal (at least 4000 B.C.). Meantime the Egyptians were also making great progress in other matters. It was probably in the peninsula of Sinai (see map, p. 42) that some Egyptian, wandering thither, once happened to bank his camp fire with pieces of copper ore lying on the ground about the camp. The charcoal of his wood fire mingled with the hot fragments of ore piled around to shield the fire, and thus the ore was "reduced," as the miner says ; that is, the copper in metallic form was released from the lumps of ore. Next morning as the Egyptian stirred the embers he discovered a few glittering globules, now hardened into beads of metal. He drew them forth and turned them admiringly as they glittered in the morning sunshine. Before long, as the experience was repeated, he discovered whence these strange shining beads had come. He produced more of them, at first only to be worn as ornaments by his women. Then he learned to cast the metal into a blade to replace the flint knife which he carried in his girdle.

25. Dawning of the Age of Metal. Without knowing it this man stood at the dawning of a new era, the Age of Metal. The little disk of shining copper which he drew from the ashes might have reflected to this Egyptian wanderer a vision, could he have seen it, of steel buildings, Brooklyn bridges, huge factories roaring with the noise of thousands of machines of metal, and vast stretches of steel roads along which thunder hosts of rushing locomotives. For these things of our modern world, and all they signify, would never have come to pass but for the little bead of metal which the Egyptian held in his hand for the first time on that eventful day so long ago. Since the discovery of fire over fifty thousand years earlier (§ 2) man had made no conquest of the things of the earth which could compare in importance with this discovery of metal.

26. First Glimpse of the Pyramids. Such are the thoughts which occupy the mind of the well-informed traveler as his

train carries him southward across the Delta. The train rounds
a bend, and through an opening in the palms the traveler is
fairly blinded by a burst of blazing sunshine from the western
desert, in the midst of which he discovers a group of noble
pyramids rising above the glare of the sands. It is his first
glimpse of the great pyramids of Gizeh, and it tells him better
than any printed page what the Egyptian builders with copper
tools in their hands were able to do. A few minutes later his
train is moving among the modern buildings of Cairo, and the
very next day will surely find him taking the seven-mile drive
from Cairo out to Gizeh.

II. The Pyramid Age

27. The Pyramids as Royal Tombs. No traveler ever forgets
his first drive to the pyramids of Gizeh, as he sees their giant
forms rising higher and higher above the crest of the western
desert (frontispiece). These pyramids are tombs, in which the
kings of Egypt were buried. Other tombs of masonry, much
smaller in size, cluster about the pyramids in great numbers
(frontispiece). Here were buried the relatives of the king, and the
great men of his court who assisted him in the government of the
land (Fig. 8). Such mighty buildings reveal many things about
the men who built them. In the first place, they show that
the Egyptians believed in a life after death and that to obtain
such life they thought it necessary to preserve the body from
destruction. They built these tombs to protect the body after
death. From this belief came also the practice of "embalming,"
by which the body was preserved as a mummy (Fig. 20).

28. The Gods of Egypt: Re and Osiris. The Egyptians had
many gods, but there were two whom they worshiped above all
others. The Sun, which shines so gloriously in the cloudless
Egyptian sky, was their greatest god, and their most splendid
temples were erected for his worship. Indeed, the pyramid was
a symbol sacred to the Sun-god. They called him Re (pron. *ray*).
The other great power which they revered as a god was the

shining Nile. The great river and the fertile soil he refreshes, and the green life which he brings forth—all these the Egyptian thought of *together* as a single god, Osiris, the imperishable life of the earth which revives and fades every year with the changes of the seasons.

29. Rapid Progress from the Earliest Stone Masonry to the Great Pyramid. But this vast cemetery of Gizeh tells us of many other things besides the religion of the Egyptians. As we look up at the colossal pyramids behind the Sphinx (frontispiece) we can hardly grasp the fact of the enormous forward stride taken by the Egyptians since the days when they used to be buried with their flint knives in a pit scooped out on the margin of the desert. It was chiefly the use of metal which carried them so far. That Egyptian in Sinai who noticed the first bit of metal (§ 24) lived over a thousand years before these pyramids were built. He was buried in a pit like that of the earliest Egyptian peasant. By the thirty-fourth century B.C. the Egyptians were building the tombs of their kings of sun-baked brick. Such a royal tomb was merely a chamber in the ground, roofed with wood and covered with a mound of sand and gravel. Similar tombs continued to be built until about 3000 B.C., only a century before the Great Pyramid of Gizeh.

Meantime some skillful workmen found out that with their copper tools they could cut blocks of limestone and line the burial chamber with these stone blocks in place of the soft bricks. This was the first piece of *stone* masonry ever put together in so far as we know. It was built not more than fifty years before 3000 B.C. In the course of the next century and a half or less the first tombs of pyramidal form were erected, and by 2900 B.C. the king's architect was building the Great Pyramid of Gizeh. Most of this amazing progress was made during the thirtieth century B.C.; that is, between 3000 and 2900 B.C. (see diagram, *Ancient Times*, Fig. 38). Such rapid progress in control of mechanical power can be found in no other period of the world's history until the great development of machinery in the nineteenth century, which has just passed.

30. Vast Size of the Great Pyramid. It helps us to realize this progress when we know that the Great Pyramid covers thirteen acres. It is a solid mass of masonry containing 2,300,000 blocks of limestone, each weighing on an average two and a half tons; that is, each block is as heavy as a large wagonload of coal. The sides of the pyramid at the base are seven hundred and fifty-five feet long (that is, about a block and three quarters, counting twelve city blocks to a mile), and the building was nearly five hundred feet high. An ancient story tells us that a hundred thousand men were working on this royal tomb for twenty years (see frontispiece).

31. Length and Date of the Pyramid Age. From the summit of the Great Pyramid there is a grand view southward, down a long line of pyramids rising dimly as far as one can see on the southern horizon. Each pyramid was a royal tomb, and each such tomb therefore means that a king lived, ruled, and died. The line is over sixty miles long, and its oldest pyramids represent the first great age of Egyptian civilization after the land was united under one king.[1] We may call it the Pyramid Age, and it lasted about five hundred years—from about 3000 until after 2500 B.C.

32. Government in the Pyramid Age. Such a great piece of work as a pyramid shows the immense progress of the Egyptians in *government*. We perceive at once that it must have required a very skillful ruler and a great body of officials to manage and to feed a hundred thousand workmen around the Great Pyramid. The king who controlled such vast undertakings was no longer a local chieftain (§ 19), but he now ruled a united Egypt, the earliest great unified nation, having several millions of people. He had his *local* officials collecting taxes all over Egypt. It was also their business to try all cases at law wherever they arose, and every judge had before him the written law which bade him judge justly. Even those accused of treason received proper trials.

---

[1] Before this, little kingdoms scattered up and down the valley had long existed but were finally united into one kingdom, under a single king. The first king to establish this union permanently was Menes, who united Egypt under his rule about 3400 B.C.

The king's huge *central* offices, occupying low sun-baked brick buildings, sheltered an army of clerks with their reed pens and their rolls of papyrus (§ 22), keeping the king's records and accounts. The taxes received from the people here were not paid in money, for coined money did not yet exist. Such payments were made in produce : grain, live stock, wine, honey, linen, and the like.

33. The Royal City. The villas (Fig. 10) of the officials who assisted the king in all this business of government, with their gardens, formed a large part of the royal city. The chief quarter, however, was occupied by the palace of the king and the luxurious parks and gardens which surrounded it. Thus the palace and its grounds, the official villas, and the offices of the government made up the capital of Egypt, the royal city which once extended along the foot of the Gizeh pyramid cemetery and stretched far away southward over the valley plain. It was later called Memphis. But the city was all built of sun-baked brick and wood, and it has therefore vanished.

34. Earliest Seagoing Ships. In the Pyramid Age the Pharaoh, as the ruler was called, was powerful enough to seek wealth beyond the boundaries of Egypt. A few surviving blocks from a fallen pyramid-temple (Fig. 11) south of Gizeh bear carved and painted reliefs showing us the ships which he ventured to send beyond the shelter of the Nile mouths far across the end of the Mediterranean to the coast of Phœnicia (see map, p. 42). This was in the middle of the twenty-eighth century B.C., and this relief contains the oldest known picture of a seagoing ship (see *Ancient Times*, Fig. 41). Yet at that time the Pharaoh had already been carrying on such over-sea commerce for centuries.

35. Agriculture, Cattle-raising, and Beasts of Burden. A stroll among the tombs clustering so thickly around the pyramids of Gizeh (frontispiece) is almost like a walk among the busy communities of this populous valley in the days of the pyramid-builders, for the stone walls are often covered from floor to ceiling with carved scenes, beautifully painted, picturing the daily life on the great estate of which the buried noble had been lord (Figs. 8

and 9). The tallest form in all these scenes on the walls is that of the dead noble. He stands looking out over his fields and inspecting the work going on there (Fig. 8). These fields where the oxen draw the plow and the sowers scatter the seed are the oldest scene of agriculture known to us. Here too are the herds, long lines of sleek fat cattle. While they graze in the pasture, the milch cows are led up and tied to be milked. These cattle are also beasts of burden; we have noticed the oxen drawing the plow, and the donkey too is everywhere, for it would be difficult to harvest the grain without him. But we find no horses in these tombs of the Pyramid Age, for the horse was then unknown to the Egyptian.

FIG. 8. RELIEF SCENE FROM THE CHAPEL OF A PROMINENT NOBLE'S TOMB IN THE PYRAMID AGE

The tall figure of the noble stands at the right. A piece has fallen out of the wall, immediately before his face and figure. He is inspecting three rows of cattle and a row of fowl brought before him. Note the two scribes who head the two middle rows. Each is writing with a pen on a sheet of papyrus, and one carries two pens behind his ear. Such reliefs after being carved were colored in bright hues by the painter (see § 43)

36. The Coppersmith. On the next wall we find again the tall figure of the noble overseeing the booths and yards where the craftsmen of his estate are working. Yonder is the smith. This man could make excellent copper[1] tools of all sorts. The tool which demanded the greatest skill was the long, flat ripsaw, which the smith knew

---

[1] Before the end of the Pyramid Age the coppersmiths had learned how to *harden* their tools by melting a small amount of tin with the copper. This produced a mixture of tin (usually not more than 10 per cent) and copper, called bronze, which is much harder than copper. It is not yet certain where the first tin was obtained, or who made the first bronze, but it may have come from the north side of the Mediterranean (*Ancient Times*, § 336).

how to hammer into shape out of a broad strip of copper sometimes five or six feet long. Such a saw may be seen in use in Fig. 9.

37. The Lapidary, Goldsmith, and Jeweler. On the same wall we find the lapidary holding up for the noble's admiration splendid stone bowls cut from diorite. Although this kind of stone is as hard as steel, the bowl is ground to such thinness that the sunlight glows through its dark-gray sides. The booth of the goldsmith is filled with workmen and apprentices weighing gold and costly stones, hammering and casting, soldering and fitting together richly wrought jewelry which can hardly be surpassed by the best goldsmiths and jewelers of to-day (see *Ancient Times*, frontispiece and Fig. 47).

38. The Potter's Wheel and Furnace : Earliest Glass. In the next space on this wall we find the potter no longer building up his jars and bowls with his fingers alone, as in the Stone Age. He now sits before a small horizontal *wheel*, upon which he deftly shapes the vessel as it whirls round and round under his fingers. When the soft clay vessels are ready, they are no longer unevenly burned in an open fire, as among the Late Stone Age potters in the Swiss lake-villages (Fig. 6), but in closed furnaces.

Here we also find the craftsmen making *glass*. This art the Egyptians had discovered centuries earlier. They spread the glass on tiles in gorgeous glazes for adorning house and palace walls (see *Ancient Times*, plate, p. 164). Later they learned to make charming many-colored glass bottles and vases, which were widely exported.

39. Weavers and Paper-makers. Yonder the weaving women draw forth from the loom a gossamer fabric of linen. The picture on this wall could not tell us of its fineness, but fortunately pieces of such material have survived, wrapped around the mummy of a king of this age. These specimens of royal linen are so fine that it requires a magnifying glass to distinguish them from silk, and the best work of the modern *machine* loom is coarse in comparison with this fabric of the ancient Egyptian *hand* loom.

In the next space on the wall we find huge bundles of papyrus reeds, which barelegged men are gathering along the edge of the Nile marsh. These reeds furnish piles of pale-yellow paper in long sheets (§ 22). The ships which we have followed on the Mediterranean will add bales of this Nile paper to their cargoes and carry it to the European world.

40. Shipbuilders, Carpenters, and Cabinetmakers. We seem almost to hear the hubbub of hammers and mauls as we approach the next section of wall, where we find the shipbuilders and

FIG. 9. CABINETMAKERS IN THE PYRAMID AGE

At the left a man is cutting with a chisel which he taps with a mallet; next, a man "rips" a board with a copper saw; next, two men are finishing off a couch; and at the right a man is drilling a hole with a bow-drill. Scene from the chapel of a noble's tomb. Compare a finished chair belonging to a wealthy noble of the Empire (Fig. 19)

carpenters. Here is a long line of curving hulls, with workmen swarming over them like ants, fitting together the earliest seagoing ships. Beside them are the busy cabinetmakers (Fig. 9), fashioning luxurious furniture for the noble's villa (Fig. 10). The finished chairs and couches for the king or the rich are overlaid with gold and silver, or inlaid with ebony and ivory, and upholstered with soft leathern cushions (Fig. 19).

41. Traffic in Goods; Circulation of Precious Metals. Here on the wall is a picture of the market place. We can watch the cobbler offering the baker a pair of sandals as payment for a cake, or the carpenter's wife giving the fisherman a little wooden box to pay for a fish. We see therefore that the people have *no coined money* to use, and that in the market place trade is

actual exchange of goods, commonly called barter, or traffic.
Such was the business of the common people. If we could see the
large transactions in the palace, we should find there heavy rings of

FIG. 10. VILLA OF AN EGYPTIAN NOBLE

The garden is inclosed with a high wall. There are pools on either side
as one enters, and a long arbor extends down the middle. The house at
the rear, embowered in trees, is crowned by a roof garden shaded with
awnings of tapestry

gold of a standard weight, which circulated like money. Rings
of copper also served the same purpose. Such rings were the
forerunners of the earliest coins (Fig. 36).

42. Three Classes of Society in the Pyramid Age. These people in the market place painted on the chapel wall are the common folk of Egypt in the Pyramid Age. Some of them were *free men*, following their own business or industry. Others were *slaves*, working the fields on the great estates. Neither of these

Fig. 11. Court of a Pyramid-Temple containing the Earliest Known Colonnades (Twenty-eighth Century b.c.)

Notice the pyramid rising behind the temple (just as in frontispiece also). The center of the court is open to the sky; the roof of the porch all around is supported on columns, the earliest known in the history of architecture. From such Egyptian colonnaded courts those of later Europe were copied (see Fig. 60). Each column represents a palm tree, the capital being the crown of foliage. Thirteen hundred feet of copper piping, the earliest known plumbing, was installed in this building

humble classes owned any land. Over them were the *landowners*, the Pharaoh and his great lords and officials, like the owner of this tomb (Fig. 8).

43. Life and Art in the Pyramid Age. Here on this chapel wall again we see its owner seated at ease in his palanquin, borne upon the shoulders of slaves. He is returning from the inspection of his estate, where we have been following him. His bearers carry him into the shady garden before his house (Fig. 10), where they set down the palanquin and cease their song. This garden is the noble's paradise. Here he may recline for an hour of leisure with his family and friends, playing at draughts, listening to the music of harp, pipe, and lute, watching his women in the slow and stately dances of the time, while his children are sporting about among the arbors, splashing in the pool as they chase the fish, playing with ball, doll, and jumping jack, or teasing the tame monkey, which takes refuge under their father's ivory-legged stool.

The portrait sculptor was the greatest artist of this age. His statues were carved in stone or wood and colored in the hues of life ; the eyes were inlaid with rock crystal, and they still shine with the gleam of life (Fig. 13). More lifelike portraits have never been produced by any age, although they are the earliest portraits in the history of art. Such statues of the kings are often superb (Fig. 12). They were set up in the Pharaoh's pyramid temple (frontispiece and Fig. 11). In size the most remarkable statue of the Pyramid Age is the Great Sphinx, which stands here in this cemetery of Gizeh. The head is a portrait of Khafre, the king who built the second pyramid of Gizeh (see frontispiece), and was carved from a promontory of rock which overlooked the royal city. It is the largest portrait ever wrought. (On architecture see Fig. 11.)

III. THE FEUDAL AGE

44. The Barons of the Feudal Age. The Pyramid Age lasted until after 2500 B.C. (see § 31). It was not the end of civilization on the Nile ; other great periods were to follow. Along the palm-fringed shores far away to the south we shall find the buildings, tombs, and monuments which will tell us of two more great ages on the Nile—the Feudal Age and the Empire. We board a Nile boat and steam steadily southward. As we scan the scarred and weatherworn cliffs we discover many a tomb-door cut in the face of the cliff and leading to tomb-chapels excavated in the rock.

These cliff-tombs looking down upon the river belonged to the Feudal Age of Egyptian history. The men buried in these tombs succeeded in gaining greater power than their ancestors. They were granted lands by the king under arrangements which in later Europe we call feudal (Chap. XXIV). They were thus powerful barons, living like kings on their broad estates, made up of the fertile fields upon which these tomb-doors now look down. This Feudal Age lasted for several centuries and was flourishing by 2000 B.C.

45. The Libraries of the Feudal Barons. We know more about this Feudal Age because some of its books have escaped destruction. Fragments from the libraries of these feudal barons—the oldest libraries in the world—have fortunately been discovered in their tombs. These oldest of all surviving books are in the form of rolls of papyrus. Here are the most ancient story-books in the world : tales of wanderings and adventures in Asia ; tales of shipwreck at the gate of the unknown ocean beyond the Red Sea—the earliest "Sindbad the Sailor" (see a page from this story in *Ancient Times*, Fig. 58); and tales of wonders wrought by ancient wise men and magicians. Some of these stories set forth the sufferings of the poor and the humble and seek to stir the rulers to be just and kind in their treatment of the weaker classes.

Very few papyrus rolls were needed to deal with the science of this time. The largest and the most valuable of all contained what they had learned about medicine and the organs of the human body. This oldest medical book, when unrolled, is to-day about sixty-six feet long and has recipes for all sorts of ailments. Some of them are still good and call for remedies which, like castor oil, are still in common use ; others represent the ailment as due to demons, which were long believed to be the cause of disease. There are also rolls containing the simpler rules of arithmetic, based on the decimal system which we still use ; others treat the beginnings of geometry and elementary algebra.

46. Pharaoh's Commerce by Sea. While conditions *at home* made great progress, at the same time these rulers of the Feudal Age reached out by sea for the wealth of *other lands*. Their fleets sailed over among the Ægean islands and probably

FIG. 13. HEAD OF A ROYAL STATUE OF BRONZE IN THE PYRAMID AGE

It represents King Pepi I (nearly 2600 B.C.). It was hammered into shape over a wooden form. The metal is incrusted with rust, but owing to the eyes, of inlaid rock crystal, the portrait is very lifelike

FIG. 12. PORTRAIT OF KING KHAFRE, BUILDER OF THE SECOND PYRAMID OF GIZEH

Found in his valley-temple (Frontispiece). It is carved in excessively hard stone, called diorite. The falcon with protecting wings outstretched is a symbol of the great god Horus (twenty-ninth century B.C.)

FIG. 14. THE COLOSSAL COLUMNS OF THE NAVE IN THE GREAT
HALL OF KARNAK

These are the columns of the middle two rows in the nave (Fig. 16).
The human figures below show by contrast the vast dimensions of the
columns towering above them (§ 50)

controlled the large island of Crete (§§ 123–125). They dug a canal from the north end of the Red Sea westward to the nearest branch of the Nile in the eastern Delta (see map, p. 42). The Pharaoh's Mediterranean ships could sail up the easternmost mouth of the Nile, then enter the canal and, passing eastward through it, reach the Red Sea. Thus the Mediterranean and the Red Sea were first connected by this predecessor of the Suez Canal four thousand years ago. The power and prosperity of the Feudal Age did much to prepare Egypt to rule other nations, as mistress of a great empire.

IV. THE EMPIRE

47. Monuments of Thebes and Arrival of the Horse in Egypt. The monuments along the river banks have thus far told us the story of two of the three periods, or ages,[1] into which the career of this great Nile people falls. After we have left the tombs of the Feudal Age and have continued our journey over four hundred miles southward from Cairo, all at once we catch glimpses of vast masses of stone masonry and lines of tall columns rising among the palms on the east side of the river. They are the ruins of the once great city of Thebes, which will tell us the story of the third period, the Empire.

Here we find not only a vast cemetery but also great temples (see plan, *Ancient Times*, p. 81). A walk around the colossal temple of Karnak[2] at Thebes is as instructive to us in studying the Empire as we have found the Gizeh cemetery to be in studying the Pyramid Age. We find the walls of this immense temple covered with enormous sculptures in relief, depicting the wars of the Egyptians in Asia. We see the giant figure of the Pharaoh as he stands in his war chariot, scattering the enemy before his plunging horses. The Pharaohs of the Pyramid Age had never seen a horse (§ 35), and this is the first time we have met the

---

1 These three ages are (1) Pyramid Age, about 3000–2500 B.C. (pp. 20–29); (2) Feudal Age, flourishing 2000 B.C. (pp. 29–31); (3) the Empire, about 1580–1150 B.C. (pp. 31–37).

2 A view of the great Karnak temple taken from an aëroplane will be found in *Ancient Times*, Fig. 64. Karnak is the name of a tiny modern village near the great temple.

horse on the ancient monuments. After the close of the Feudal Age this animal began to be imported from Asia ; the chariot, the first wheeled vehicle in Africa, came with him, and Egypt learned warfare on a scale unknown before.

FIG. 15. PORTRAIT OF THE NAPOLEON OF ANCIENT EGYPT, THUT-MOSE III (FIFTEENTH CENTURY B.C.)

Carved in granite and showing the great conqueror (§ 49) wearing the tall crown of Upper Egypt, with the sacred asp forming a serpent-crest above his forehead. Such portraits in the Empire can be compared with the actual faces of these Egyptian emperors as we have them in their mummies (Fig. 20), and they are thus shown to be good likenesses. See *Ancient Times*, Fig. 63

48. The Empire (1580–1150 B.C.). The Pharaohs were now great generals with a well-organized standing army. With these forces the Pharaohs conquered an empire which extended from the Euphrates in Asia to the Fourth Cataract of the Nile in Africa (see map, I, p. 58). By an empire in ancient times we mean a group of nations subdued and ruled over by some more powerful nation. When government first arose, it began with tiny city-states independent of each other (see *Ancient Times*, § 38). Then a group of such city-states would gradually unite into a nation ; but the organization of men had now reached the point where *many nations* were combined into an empire, including a large part of the early oriental world. The Egyptian Empire, during which the Pharaohs were really emperors, lasted from the early sixteenth century to the twelfth century B.C.—somewhat over four hundred years.

49. Campaigns of Thutmose III. During all this period the greatest of these emperors as a soldier and leader was Thutmose III (Fig. 15). This Napoleon of Egypt, as we may call him, ruled for over fifty years, beginning about 1500 B.C. He was the first great general in history. On the temple walls at Karnak we can read the story of nearly twenty years of warfare, during which Thutmose crushed the cities and kingdoms of Western

Asia and united them into an enduring empire. At the same time he gave great attention to sea power. He built the first great navy in history. His war fleet carried his power even to the Ægean Sea, and one of his generals became governor of the Ægean islands.

V. THE HIGHER LIFE OF THE EMPIRE AND ITS FALL

50. The Empire Temples. The wealth which the Pharaohs captured in Asia and Nubia during the Empire brought them

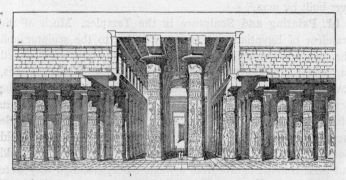

FIG. 16. RESTORATION OF THE GREAT HALL OF KARNAK, ANCIENT THEBES — LARGEST BUILDING OF THE EGYPTIAN EMPIRE

With the wealth taken in Asia the Egyptian conquerors of the Empire enabled their architects to build the greatest colonnaded hall ever erected by man. It is three hundred and thirty-eight feet wide and one hundred and seventy feet deep, furnishing a floor area about equal to that of the cathedral of Notre Dame in Paris, although this is only a single room of the temple. There are one hundred and thirty-six columns in sixteen rows. See *Ancient Times*, Fig. 271

power and magnificence unknown to the world before. All this was especially shown in their vast and splendid buildings. A new period in the history of art and architecture began. The temple of Karnak, which we have visited, contains the greatest colonnaded hall ever erected by man. The columns of the central aisle (Fig. 16) are sixty-nine feet high. The vast capital forming the summit of *each* column is large enough to contain a group of a hundred men standing crowded upon it at the same time.

European architects later borrowed many ideas from these buildings of Egypt (*Ancient Times,* Fig. 271).

Such temples as these at Thebes were seen through the deep
green of clustering palms, among towering obelisks and colossal
statues of the Pharaohs (Fig. 17). The whole was bright with
color, flashing at many a point with gold and silver. Mirrored
in the unruffled surface of the temple lake, it made a picture
of such splendor as the ancient world had never seen before.
Thus grew up at Thebes the first great "monumental city"
ever built by man.[1]

51. Painting and Sculpture in the Temples. Much of the
grandeur of Egyptian architecture was due to the sculptor and
the painter. The colonnades, with flower capitals, were colored
to suggest the plants they represented. The vast battle scenes,
carved on the temple wall, were painted in bright colors. The
portrait statues of the Pharaohs, set up before these temples, were
often so large that they rose above the towers of the temple
front itself,—the tallest part of the building,—and they could
be seen for miles around (Figs. 17 and 18). The sculptors could
cut these colossal figures from a single block, although they were
sometimes eighty or ninety feet high and weighed as much as a
thousand tons. This is a burden equal to a great transcontinental
train of eleven steel sleeping cars each weighing ninety tons.
Unlike the train, however, the statue was not cut up into smaller
units, but had to be handled as a single vast burden. Nevertheless, the engineers of the Empire moved many such gigantic
figures for hundreds of miles.[2] It is in works of this massive,
monumental character that the art of Egypt excelled.

52. Life and Art of the Empire. Just as at Gizeh, so the
cemetery at Thebes tells much of the life of the times which produced it. In the majestic western cliffs (Fig. 17) are cut hundreds
of tomb-chapels belonging to the great men of the Empire. Here
were buried the able generals who marched with the Pharaohs on

---

[1] City plans which treat a whole city as a symmetrical and harmonious unit are now
beginning to be made in America.

[2] On the moving of such great burdens, see *Ancient Times,* Fig. 61.

FIG. 17. GIGANTIC PORTRAIT STATUES OF A PHARAOH OF THE EMPIRE AT THEBES (1400 B.C.)

They are seventy feet high and adorned the front of a temple which once stood behind them. The right-hand figure bears many inscriptions of eminent Greek and Roman visitors (see § 408). In the cliffs behind is the vast cemetery of Thebes (§§ 52–53), and in a valley behind these cliffs are the royal tombs in which the Pharaohs of the Empire were buried (Fig. 20)

FIG. 18. COLOSSAL PORTRAIT FIGURE OF RAMSES II AT ABU SIMBEL
IN EGYPTIAN NUBIA

Four such statues, seventy-five feet high, adorn the front of this temple.
They are better preserved than those in Fig. 17, and show us that such vast
figures were portraits. The face of Ramses II here really resembles that
of his mummy. Grand view of the Nubian Nile, on which the statues have
looked down for thirty-two hundred years (see § 50). View taken from the
top of the crown of one of the statues. (Photograph by The University of
Chicago Expedition)

their campaigns in Asia and in Nubia. Here lay the gifted artists and architects who built the vast monuments we have just visited. Here in these tomb-chapels we may read their names and often long accounts of their lives. Here, for example, is the story of the general who saved Thutmose III's life in a great elephant hunt in Asia by rushing in and cutting off the trunk of an enraged elephant which was pursuing the king.

These tombs are wonderful treasuries of Egyptian art, for the very furniture which these great men used in their houses was put into their tombs. Many beautiful things, like chairs covered with gold and silver and provided with soft cushions of leather (Fig. 19), bedsteads of sumptuous craftsmanship, jewel boxes and perfume caskets of the ladies, or even the gold-covered chariot in which the Theban noble took his afternoon airing thirty-three or thirty-four hundred years ago, have been found in these tombs. They may now be seen in the National Museum at Cairo.

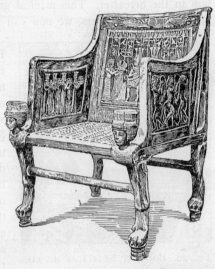

FIG. 19. ARMCHAIR FROM THE HOUSE OF AN EGYPTIAN NOBLE OF THE EMPIRE

This chair with other furniture from his house was placed in his tomb at Thebes in the early part of the fourteenth century B.C. There it remained for nearly thirty-three hundred years, till it was discovered in 1905 and removed to the National Museum at Cairo (§ 52)

53. Religion of the Empire. These tombs show us also how much farther the Egyptian had advanced in religion since the days of the pyramids of Gizeh. Each of these great men buried in the Theban cemetery looked forward to a judgment in the next world, where Osiris (§ 28) was the great judge and king.

Every good man might rise from the dead as Osiris had done, but in the presence of Osiris he would be obliged to see his soul weighed in the balances over against the symbol of truth and justice. The dead man's friends put into his coffin a roll of papyrus containing prayers and magic charms intended to aid him in the hereafter. This magical guidebook of the hereafter, with its varied contents, we now call the "Book of the Dead."

FIG. 20. BODY OF SETI I AS HE LIES IN HIS COFFIN IN THE NATIONAL MUSEUM AT CAIRO

Some of the leading Egyptians of the Empire finally gained the belief in a single god to the exclusion of all others. Such a belief we call monotheism (see § 112). Ikhnaton, the most unique of their kings, endeavored to make this belief in one god the religion of the whole Empire, but the opposition of the priests and the people was too strong, and he perished in the attempt.

54. Decline and Fall of the Egyptian Empire (1150 B.C.). Serious religious conflicts at home had thus greatly weakened Egypt by the middle of the fourteenth century (1350) B.C. After it had recovered itself somewhat, the great Pharaohs Seti I (Fig. 20) and his son Ramses II (Fig. 18) partially restored the old splendor. Their two reigns covered almost a century (ending about 1225 B.C.). They fought great wars in Asia, but they were unable to restore the Empire to its former extent and power. Their most powerful enemies were at first the Hittites of Asia Minor (§§ 128 and 129).

Then more dangerous foes arose. We find them pictured in the temple reliefs, and it is interesting to discover that these new enemies are many of them Europeans from the northern Mediterranean lands, where we left them (§ 12) in the Late Stone Age. These northerners finally entered Egypt in such numbers after 1200 B.C. that the weakened Egyptian Empire fell (about 1150 B.C.). Egypt never again recovered her old power and leadership.

55. Summary of the Story of Egypt. Thus ends the story of the Empire at Thebes. Our visit to Egypt has told us the story of how man passed from Stone Age barbarism to a civilization possessed of metal, writing, and government (pp. 14–20). The pyramids, tombs, and temples along the Nile have told us the history of civilized Egypt in three epochs : the pyramids of Gizeh and the neighboring cemeteries of Memphis have told us about the *Pyramid Age* (pp. 20–29) ; the cliff-tombs, which we found on the Nile voyage, have revealed the history of the *Feudal Age* (pp. 29–31) ; and the temples and cliff-tombs of Thebes have given us the story of the *Empire* (pp. 31–37). Thus the Nile has become for us a book of history, with its introduction giving us the rise of civilization, continued in three great chapters.

We should remember, moreover, that the three great chapters did not end the story ; for Egyptian institutions and civilization continued far down into the Christian Age and greatly influenced later history in Europe (§§ 379 and 418).

56. Decipherment of Egyptian. Finally, our Nile voyage has also shown us how we gain knowledge of ancient men and their deeds from the monuments and records which they have left behind. We have also noticed how greatly the use of the earliest *written* documents aids us in putting together the story. If we had made our journey up the Nile a hundred years ago, however, we should have had no one to tell us what these Egyptian records meant. For the last man who could read Egyptian hieroglyphs died over a thousand years ago. A hundred years ago, therefore, no one understood the curious writing which travelers found covering the great monuments along the Nile. It was not until 1822 that the ability to read Egyptian hieroglyphics was recovered. In that year a young French scholar named *Champollion* announced that he had learned how to read Egyptian writing.[1] Thus

---

[1] An account of Champollion's great feat will be found in *Ancient Times*, pp. 96–98.

the monuments of the Nile gained a voice and have told us their wonderful story of man's conquest of civilization.

57. Transition to Asia. In a similar way the monuments discovered along the Tigris and Euphrates rivers in Asia have been deciphered and made to tell their story. They show us that, following the Egyptians, the peoples of Asia emerged from barbarism, gained industries, learned the use of metals, devised a system of writing, and finally rose to the leading position of power in the ancient world. We must therefore turn, in the next chapter, to the story of the early Orient in Asia.

QUESTIONS

I. Where is Egypt? What are the shape and character of the country? What is the adjoining country like? How did the Stone Age Egyptians live? How did they originate writing? writing materials? Describe the origin of the calendar. Whence came *our* calendar? Describe the probable manner of the discovery of copper.

II. What was a pyramid used for? Explain the chief gods of Egypt. What kinds of tombs preceded the pyramids? In what century did most of this progress fall? Describe the Great Pyramid. Give the date and length of the Pyramid Age. Date and describe the earliest known seagoing ships. Write an account of the industries and the social life of the Pyramid Age. Describe its art.

III. How does the Nile voyage continue the story of the Egyptians? Give an account of the feudal barons. What kind of progress was being made?

IV. Through what ages has the voyage up the Nile carried us? Give the date and extent of the Egyptian Empire. Who was its greatest conqueror?

V. Describe the great buildings of the Empire. Describe the painting and sculpture in the Empire temples. Give an account of the cemetery at Thebes. What does it reveal of Egyptian civilization? Did Egyptian civilization continue after the fall of the Empire?

CHAPTER III

WESTERN ASIA: BABYLONIA, ASSYRIA, AND CHALDEA

I. THE LANDS AND RACES OF WESTERN ASIA

58. Geography of Western Asia. The westernmost portions of Asia are bounded by the Caspian and Black seas on the north, the Mediterranean and the Red Sea on the west, and the Indian Ocean and the Persian Gulf on the south and east. It is a region consisting chiefly of mountains on the north and desert on the south. The earliest home of men in Western Asia was the borderland between the desert and mountains and also between desert and sea,—the fertile fringe of the desert, shaped like a crescent, having the mountains on one side and the desert on the other. (See map, p. 42.)

This fertile crescent is approximately a semicircle, with the open side toward the south, having the west end at the southeast corner of the Mediterranean, the center directly north of Arabia, and the east end at the north end of the Persian Gulf. At the western end is Palestine, Assyria makes up a large part of the center, while at the eastern end is Babylonia. This great semicircle, for lack of a name, we shall refer to as the Fertile Crescent.[1]

After the meager winter rains large portions of the northern desert are covered with scanty grass, and spring thus turns the region for a short time into grasslands. *The history of Western Asia may be described as an age-long struggle between the mountain peoples of the north and the desert wanderers of these grasslands for the possession of the Fertile Crescent.* We shall first consider the invasions of the Fertile Crescent by the peoples of the desert.

[1] There is no general name, either geographical or political, which includes all of this great semicircle (see map, p. 42). Hence we are obliged to coin a term and call it the "Fertile Crescent."

59. The Arabian Desert and the Semitic Nomads. Arabia is totally lacking in rivers and enjoys but a few weeks of rain in midwinter ; hence it is a desert very little of which is habitable. Its people are and have been from the remotest ages a great white race called Semites, made up of many peoples and tribes. With two of the Semitic peoples we are familiar,— the Arabs and the Hebrews (many of whose descendants dwell among us). They all spoke and still speak slightly differing dialects of the same tongue. Hebrew was one of these dialects. For ages they have moved up and down the habitable portions of the Arabian world, seeking pasturage for their flocks and herds. Such wandering herdsmen are called *nomads*.[1]

From the earliest times, when the spring grass of the northern wilderness has gone, the nomads have been tempted to drift from the sandy waste into the Fertile Crescent. If they could secure a fitting place to live there, they slowly made the change from the *wandering* life of the desert nomad to the *settled* life of the agricultural peasant. We can follow this process going on for thousands of years. Among such movements we are familiar with one important example,— the passage of the Hebrews from the desert into Palestine, as described in the Bible ; and we shall later learn of a much more extensive example (Chapter XXII), the invasions of the Arab hosts of Islam, which even reached Europe. But it took many centuries for the long line of Semitic settlements to creep slowly westward along the north coast of Africa until it reached the Atlantic, and we must begin with the Semites in the desert.

60. Life of the Semitic Nomads. Out on the wide reaches of the desert there were no boundaries. The pasturage was as free as air to the first comer. No man of the tribe owned land. The wandering herdsmen possessed only scanty, movable property, chiefly flocks and herds. They knew no law ; they were unable to write. They were practically without industries, and thus the desert tribesmen led a life of unhampered freedom. Their needs obliged them to traffic now and then in the towns, and these desert

[1] On the origin of nomads see *Ancient Times*, §§ 35–36.

wanderers often became the common carriers of the settled communities, fearlessly leading their caravans across the wastes of the desert-bay, especially between Syria-Palestine and Babylonia.

The wilderness was the nomad's home. His imagination peopled the far reaches of the desert with invisible and hostile creatures, who inhabited every rock and tree, hilltop and spring. These creatures became his gods. He believed that each one of these beings controlled only a little corner of the desert ; thus such a being became the nomads' *tribal* god. The thoughts of the desert wanderers about their god were crude and barbarous, and their religious customs were often savage, leading them to sacrifice not only their animals but even their children to appease the angry god. On the other hand, the nomads had a dawning sense of justice and of right. Such feelings at last became lofty moral vision, which made the Semites the religious teachers of the civilized world. At the same time these Semites had practical gifts, especially in business, which made them the greatest merchants of the ancient world, as their Hebrew descendants among us still are at the present day.

61. The Western Semites on the West End of the Fertile Crescent. As early as 3000 B.C. they were drifting in from the desert and settling in Palestine, on the *western* end of the Fertile Crescent, where we find them in possession of walled towns by 2500 B.C. Here they were the predecessors of the Hebrews, and were called Canaanites ; farther north settled a powerful tribe known as Amorites. Later came the Arameans, who grew to be the greatest merchants throughout Western Asia.[1] Along the Mediterranean shores of north Syria some of these one-time desert wanderers took to the sea and became the Phœnicians. By 2000 B.C. all these settled communities of the Semites were in possession of much "town civilization," drawn for the most part from Egypt and Babylonia.

62. The East End of the Fertile Crescent. At the same time we can watch similar movements of the nomads at the *eastern*

---

[1] On the remarkable achievements of the Arameans, especially how they spread the alphabet, see *Ancient Times*, §§ 203-208.

end of the Fertile Crescent, along the lower course of the Tigris and Euphrates, which we shall often speak of as the "Two Rivers." They rise in the northern mountains (see map, p. 42), whence they issue to cross the Fertile Crescent and to cut obliquely southeastward through the northern bay of the desert (§ 58). On these two great rivers of Western Asia developed the earliest civilization anywhere known in Asia. Just as on the Nile, so here on the Two Rivers we shall find three great chapters in the story.

63. The Plain of Shinar (or Babylonia). As on the Nile, so also in Tigris-Euphrates history the earliest of the three chapters will be found in the lower valley near the rivers' mouths. This earliest chapter is the story of Babylonia.[1] As the Two Rivers approach most closely to each other, about one hundred and sixty or seventy miles from the Persian Gulf,[2] they emerge from the desert and enter a low plain of fertile soil, formerly brought down by the rivers. This plain, lying at the eastern end of the Fertile Crescent, is best known as Babylonia. But during the first thousand years of its known history, the city of Babylon, from which it was afterward named, either did not yet exist or was only an insignificant village (§ 69).

This plain was originally called Shinar. It was rarely more than forty miles wide and contained probably less than eight thousand square miles of cultivable soil — roughly equal to the area of New Jersey. It lies in the Mediterranean belt of rainy winter and dry summer, but the rainfall is so scanty (less than three inches a year) that irrigation of the fields is required in order to ripen the grain. When properly irrigated the Plain of Shinar is prodigiously fertile, and the chief source of wealth in ancient Shinar was agriculture. This plain was the scene of the most important and long-continued of those frequent struggles between the mountaineer and the nomad, of which we have spoken.

---

[1] The other two chapters of Tigris-Euphrates history were Assyria and the Chaldean Empire.

[2] This was the distance in ancient Babylonian and Assyrian times. But the rivers have since then filled up the Persian Gulf for one hundred and fifty to sixty miles (see note under scale on map, p. 42, and see map, *Ancient Times*, p. 106).

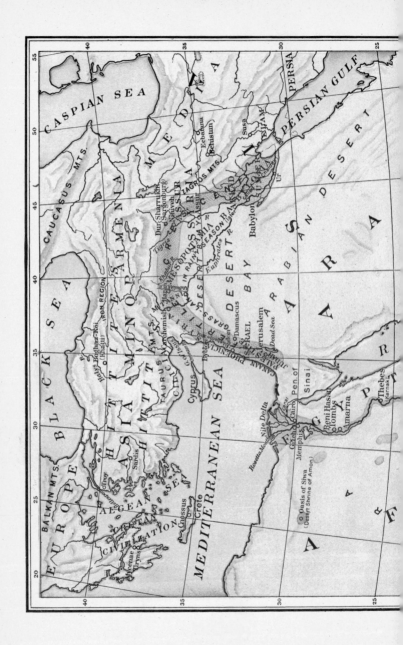

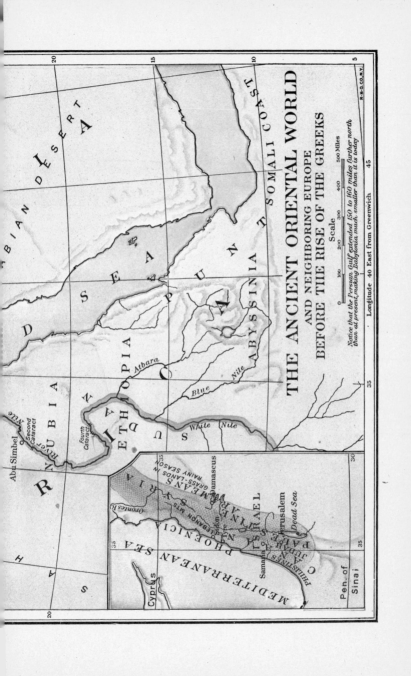

THE ANCIENT ORIENTAL WORLD

AND NEIGHBORING EUROPE
BEFORE THE RISE OF THE GREEKS

Scale

0   100   200   300   400   500 Miles

*Notice that the Persian Gulf extended 150 to 160 miles further north
than at present, making Babylonia much smaller than it is today*

Longitude 40 East from Greenwich   45

R.&G.CO.N.Y.

ARABIAN DESERT

A

RED SEA

NUBIA

Abu Simbel

Nile

Second Cataract

Fourth Cataract

River

ETHIOPIA

Atbara

Blue   Nile

White   Nile

SUDAN

PUNT

ABYSSINIA

COAST

SOMALI COAST

MEDITERRANEAN SEA

Cyprus

PHOENICIA

SYRIA

Orontes R.

Damascus

Lebanon Mts.

Anti-Lebanon Mts.

Hermon

GRASS-LANDS IN
RAINY SEASON

ISRAEL

JUDAH

Jerusalem

Dead Sea

Samaria

Jordan R.

PHILISTINES

Pen. of
Sinai

35   35   30

20

II. The Earliest Babylonians and the Rise of Civilization in Asia

64. Sumerian Mountaineers in Shinar and their Civilization.
We can find no relationship in race between the mountaineers
and the Semitic nomads of the Arabian desert. We find the
mountaineers shown on monuments of stone as having shaven
heads and wearing heavy woolen kilts, and we know that they
were a white race called Sumerians. Long before 3000 B.C. they
had entered the Plain of Shinar and had reclaimed the marshes
around the mouths of the Two Rivers. The southern section of
the Plain of Shinar therefore came to be called Sumer, after the
Sumerians.

Their settlements of low mud-brick huts soon crept northward
along the Euphrates. Gradually they learned to dig irrigation
trenches and to reap large harvests of barley and wheat. They
already possessed cattle, sheep, and goats. The ox drew the plow ;
the donkey pulled *wheeled* carts and chariots, and the wheel as a
burden-bearing device appeared here for the first time.[1] But the
horse was still unknown. The smith had learned to fashion
utensils of copper, but he did not at first know how to harden
the copper into bronze by an admixture of tin (p. 24, n. 1).

Trade and government led these people to make records,
scratched in rude pictures with the tip of a reed on a flat piece
of soft clay. Speed in writing simplified these pictures into
groups of *wedge-shaped* marks, once the lines of the picture
(Fig. 21). Hence these signs are called cuneiform, meaning
"wedge-form," writing (Latin *cuneus,* "wedge"). This writing
was phonetic, but did not possess alphabetic signs.

The Sumerian system of numerals was not based on tens, but
had the unit sixty as a basis. A large number was given as so
many sixties, just as we employ a score (fourscore, fivescore).
From this unit of sixty has descended our division of the circle
(six sixties) and of the hour and minute.

---

[1] Probably earlier than the wheel in the Swiss lake-villages of the Late Stone
Age (§ 10).

65. The Sumerian Temple-Towers, Houses, and Towns.

Almost in the center of the Plain of Shinar rose a tall tower. It was of sun-dried brick, for there was no stone in all Babylonia.

FIG. 21. EARLY SUMERIAN CLAY TABLET WITH CUNEIFORM, OR WEDGE-FORM, WRITING (TWENTY-EIGHTH CENTURY B.C.)

This tablet was written toward the close of the early period of the city-kings (§ 66), a generation before the accession of Sargon I (§ 67). It contains business accounts. The scribe's writing-reed, or *stylus*, was usually square-tipped. He pressed a corner of this square tip into the soft clay for *each line* of the picture sign. Lines so produced tended to be broad at one end and pointed at the other, that is, wedge-shaped. Each picture sign thus became a group of wedges, as shown in *Ancient Times*, Fig. 80. When the clay dried it was hard enough to make the tablet a fairly permanent record. Such tablets were sometimes baked and thus became as hard as pottery.

(By permission of Dr. Hussey)

It was the dwelling of Enlil, the great Sumerian god of the air. The tower served as an artificial mountain, probably built in memory of some ancient temple on a hilltop in the former mountain home of the Sumerians. Similar towers became common in the Plain of Shinar, and it was such a temple-tower in Babylon which later gave rise to the story of the "Tower of Babel" among the Hebrews. The Sumerian temple-tower was the ancestor of our church steeple (*Ancient Times*, Fig. 272).

Around the temple extended the houses of the townspeople. They were bare rectangular dwellings of sun-dried brick (Fig. 22). The towns were small and to-day are mounds of earth and crumbled sun-dried brick, in which lie buried the clay-tablet records of the ancient community which once lived there. When

we dig out such a mound we therefore find it a rich storehouse of things which tell us much about ancient Babylonian civilization (see *Ancient Times*, §§ 158–160, and Figs. 83, 84).

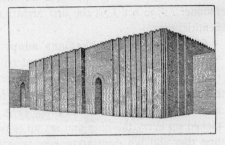

FIG. 22. RESTORATION OF AN EARLY BABYLONIAN HOUSE. (AFTER KOLDEWEY)

66. Sumerian City-Kingdoms of about 3050–2750 B.C. These clay tablets tell us about a class of free, landholding citizens working their lands with slaves and trading with caravans and small boats up and down the river. Over both these classes, free and slave, there was a numerous body of officials and priests— the aristocrats of the town. They were ruled, along with all the rest, by a priest-king. Such a community owned the fields for a few miles round about the town. The whole, that is, the town and its fields, formed a *city-kingdom*. Sumer as a whole consisted of a number of such small city-kingdoms, and this earliest Sumerian period may be called the Age of the City-Kingdoms. These little states were more skilled in war than the Egyptians and were constantly fighting each with its neighbors. These struggles among themselves so seriously weakened the Sumerians that in spite of their better organization and discipline they found it hard to cope with the incoming Semites of the desert.

67. Sargon of Akkad—Earliest Semitic Supremacy (about 2750 B.C.). The Semitic tribesmen from the desert had early begun to migrate into the Plain of Shinar, north of Sumer. By the middle of the twenty-eighth century B.C. they had established a kingdom there known as Akkad. This region comprised the narrow strip of land where the Two Rivers approach each other most closely (see map, p. 42). The men of Akkad, or Akkadians, under a bold and able leader named Sargon, descended the Euphrates and conquered the Sumerians. Thus arose the first *Semitic* kingdom of importance in history, and Sargon I, its founder (2750 B.C.), is the first great name in the history of the Semitic race.

68. The Semitic Akkadians adopt Sumerian Civilization. Sargon's conquests forced his nomad tribesmen (the Akkadians) to make a complete change in their manner of life. We may best picture the change if we say that they forsook their desert tents and built houses of sun-dried brick (Fig. 22), which could not be picked up every morning and set up somewhere else at night. At first they did not even know how to write, and they had no industries. Some of them now learned to write their Semitic tongue by using the Sumerian wedge-form signs for the purpose. Then it was, therefore, that a *Semitic language* began to be written for the first time. The Akkadians likewise learned Sumerian art, especially sculpture (Fig. 23), in which they far surpassed their Sumerian teachers. Thus the Akkadians took over and adapted the civilization of the Sumerians whom they had conquered.

III. The Age of Hammurapi and After

69. Hammurapi—the Second Semitic Supremacy. Centuries of struggle between the Sumerians and Semites ensued. Not long before 2200 B.C. a tribe of Amorites (§ 61) came in from the west and seized the little town of Babylon. Hammurapi, one of their later kings, fought for thirty years and conquered all Babylonia (about 2100 B.C.). Again the desert won, as this *second great Semitic ruler*, Hammurapi, raised

FIG. 23. A KING OF AKKAD STORMING A FORTRESS — THE EARLIEST
GREAT SEMITIC WORK OF ART (ABOUT 2700 B.C.)

King Naram-Sin of Akkad, one of the successors of Sargon I (§ 67), has
pursued the enemy into a mountain stronghold. His heroic figure towers
above his pygmy enemies, each one of whom has fixed his eyes on the conqueror, awaiting his signal of mercy. The sculptor, with fine insight, has
depicted the dramatic instant when the king lowers his weapon as the sign
that he grants the conquered their lives

Babylon, thus far a small and unimportant town, to be the leading city in the Plain of Shinar. Beginning with Hammurapi we may more properly call the plain "Babylonia."

FIG. 24. THE LAWS OF HAM-MURAPI, THE OLDEST SURVIV-ING CODE OF LAWS (2100 B.C.)*

Hammurapi brought in order and system where before all had been confusion. He collected all the older laws and customs of business, legal, and social life and issued these in a great *code of laws*. He had these laws engraved upon a stone shaft, which has survived to our day, the oldest preserved code of ancient law (Fig. 24). On the whole it is a surprisingly just code and shows much consideration for the poor and defenseless classes.

70. Expansion of Babylonian Commerce. Thus regulated, Babylonia prospered as never before. Her merchants penetrated far and wide into the surrounding countries. The Babylonian writing of the clay-tablet bills (Fig. 21) which accompanied the heavily loaded caravans had to be read by many a

* A shaft of stone (diorite), nearly eight feet high, on which the laws are engraved. They extend entirely around the shaft, occupying over thirty-six hundred lines. Above is a fine relief showing King Hammurapi standing at the left, receiving the laws from the Sun-god seated at the right. The flames rising from the god's shoulders indicate who he is. The flames on the left shoulder are commonly shown in the current textbooks as part of a staff in the god's left hand. This is an error. This scene is an impressive work of Semitic art, six hundred years later than Fig. 23.

merchant in the towns of Syria and behind the northern mountains. Thus the wedge-writing of Babylonia gradually spread through Western Asia. There was as yet no coined money, but lumps of silver of a given weight circulated so commonly (p. 67) that values were given in *weight* of silver. Loans were common, and the rate of interest was twenty per cent. Business was the chief occupation and was carried on even in the temples.

71. Higher Life of Babylonia. A journey through Babylonia to-day could not tell us such a story as we found among the monuments on our voyage up the Nile, for the Babylon of Hammurapi has perished utterly. There seems to have been no painting ; the sculpture of the Semites is in one instance (Fig. 23) powerful and dramatic, but the portrait sculptor was scarcely able to make one individual different from another. Of architecture little remains. There were no colonnades and no columns. The main lines were all *straight* verticals and horizontals, but the *arch* was used over front doorways (Fig. 22). All buildings were of brick, as Babylonia had no stone. The beautiful gem-cutting of the Babylonians, as we find it in their seals, was their greatest art (see *Ancient Times*, Fig. 106, *A*). There were schools where boys could learn to write cuneiform, and a schoolhouse of Hammurapi's time still survives, though in ruins (*Ancient Times*, Fig. 95).

72. Stagnation of Babylonian Civilization. After Hammurapi's death his kingdom swiftly declined. Barbarians from the mountains poured into the Babylonian plain. The most important thing about them was that they brought with them the horse, which then appeared for the first time in Babylonia (twenty-first century B.C.). They divided and soon destroyed the kingdom of Hammurapi. After him there followed more than a thousand years of complete stagnation in Babylonia. Progress in civilization entirely stopped, and there was no revival until the triumph of the Chaldeans (pp. 56–58).

73. Summary of Early Babylonian History. As we look back over this first chapter of early human progress along the Two Rivers, we see that it lasted about a thousand years, beginning a generation or two before 3000 B.C. The Sumerian mountaineers laid the foundations of civilization in Shinar and began a thousand-year struggle with the Semites of the desert. The Semites triumphed twice under two great leaders, Sargon (2750 B.C.) and Hammurapi (2100 B.C.). The Sumerians then disappeared, and the language of Babylonia became Semitic. The reign of Hammurapi marked the highest point and the end of the thousand-year development — the conclusion of the first great chapter of history along the Two Rivers.

IV. THE ASSYRIAN EMPIRE (ABOUT 750 TO 606 B.C.)

74. The Beginnings of Assur. The *second chapter of history along the Two Rivers* carries us up the river valley from Babylonia to the northeast corner of the desert (see map, p. 42). In this region, as early as 3000 B.C., a tribe of desert Semites had founded a little city-kingdom called Assur. This is the earliest form of our word "Assyria." Assur was an upland country with many fertile valleys and an agricultural population. In climate it was cooler and more invigorating than the hot Babylonian plain.

The Assyrians spoke a Semitic dialect (§ 59) differing only very slightly from that of Babylonia. Having given up their wanderings as herdsmen, they learned *town* life from the Sumerians, and received their earliest civilization from Sumer. Hence they learned to write their language with Babylonian cuneiform signs (Fig. 21). They were constantly obliged to defend their frontiers against both their own kindred of the desert on one side and the mountaineers on the other. Thus the Assyrians were toughened by the strain of frequent wars.

75. Foundation of the Assyrian Empire, Eighth Century B.C. Gradually the Assyrians conquered much additional territory all around their formerly small city-kingdom. By 1100 B.C. their peasant militia had beaten the western kings in Syria, where the Egyptian Empire had fallen two generations earlier (§ 54). There Assyrian soldiers for the first time saw the Mediterranean. Although often repulsed, Assyria had firmly established herself along the Mediterranean by the middle of the eighth century B.C. She had also subdued Babylonia, so that the Assyrian Empire finally held the entire Fertile Crescent, and the mountains on the north of it, almost to the Black and the Caspian seas. It conquered even Egypt (in 670 B.C.) and held it for a short time.

FIG. 25. RESTORATION OF THE PALACE OF SARGON II OF ASSYRIA
(722–705 B.C.)

The city (*GGG*) was inclosed by a wall (*HH*) and was a mile square, with room for eighty thousand people. The palace building, covering twenty-five acres, stood partly inside and partly outside of the city wall (*HH*) on a vast elevated platform (*CCCC*) of brick masonry, to which an inclined road-way (*B*) and stairways (*A*) rise from the *inside* of the city wall. The king could thus drive up in his chariot from the streets of the city below (*GGG*) to the palace pavement above (*CCCC*). The rooms and halls are clustered about a number of courts (*EF*) open to the sky. The main entrance (*D*, with stairs (*A*) before it leading down to the city) is adorned with massive towers and arched doorways built of richly colored glazed brick and embellished with huge human-headed bulls and reliefs like Fig. 26, all carved of alabaster. The pyramidal tower (*J*) behind the great court was inherited from Babylonia (§ 65). A better view of such a tower will be found in *Ancient Times*, p. 170. It was a sacred dwelling-place of the god, and his temple (with two others) stands just at the foot of the tower on the left (*K*)

Thus the once feeble little city of Assur gained the lordship over Western Asia, as head of an *empire*: a great group of conquered and vassal nations (§ 48). It was the most extensive empire the world had thus far seen (see map, II, in *Ancient Times*, p. 188).

76. Sargon II of Assyria (722–705 B.C.). In 722 B.C. one of the leading Assyrian generals usurped the throne, and as king he took the name of Sargon, the first great Semite of Babylonia, who had reigned two thousand years earlier (§ 67). As Sargon II he raised Assyria to the height of her grandeur and power as a military empire. His descendants were the great emperors of Assyria.[1] On the northeast of Nineveh (§ 77) he built a new royal residence (Fig. 25) on a vaster scale and more magnificent than any Asia had ever seen before. Babylonia in her greatest days had never possessed a capital like this.

77. Sennacherib (705–681 B.C.) ; **Nineveh, the Capital.** The grandeur of Sargon II was even surpassed by his son Sennacherib, one of the great statesmen of the early Orient. He devoted himself to the city of Nineveh, north of Assur, and it now became the far-famed capital of Assyria. Along the Tigris the vast palaces (like Fig. 25) and imposing temple-towers of the Assyrian emperors arose, reign after reign. The lofty and massive walls of Nineveh which Sennacherib built stretched two miles and a half along the banks of the Tigris, marked at the present day by a great group of mounds (*Ancient Times*, Fig. 203). Here in his gorgeous palace he ruled the Western Asiatic world with an iron hand and collected tribute from all the subject peoples.

78. Organization of the Assyrian Empire. To maintain the army was the chief work of the Assyrian State. The State was therefore a vast military machine, more terrible than any mankind had ever yet seen. We shall understand this situation if we imagine that our war department were the central office in Washington, and that our government should devote itself chiefly to supporting it.

79. The Assyrian Army and Military Equipment. An important new fact aided in bringing about this result. From the Hittites (see map, p. 42) iron had been introduced among the

---

[1] The leading Assyrian emperors of the dynasty of Sargon II are as follows :

Sargon II	722–705 B.C.
Sennacherib	705–681 B.C.
Esarhaddon	681–668 B.C.
Assurbanipal (called Sardanapalus by the Greeks)	668–626 B.C.

Assyrians. The Assyrian forces were therefore *the first large armies equipped with weapons of iron.* A single arsenal room of Sargon II's palace was found to contain two hundred tons of iron implements.

The bulk of the Assyrian army was composed of archers, supported by heavy-armed spearmen and shield bearers. Besides these, the famous horsemen and chariotry of Nineveh became the scourge of the East (Fig. 26). For the first time, too, the Assyrians employed powerful siege machinery, especially the battering-ram. This machine was the earliest "tank," for it ran on wheels and carried armed men (see *Ancient Times*, p. 140). The sun-dried-brick walls of the Asiatic cities could thus be battered down,

FIG. 26. AN ASSYRIAN KING HUNTING LIONS

and no fortified place could long repulse the assaults of the fierce Assyrian infantry. The Assyrian soldiers, moreover, displayed a certain inborn ferocity which held all Western Asia in abject terror. Wherever the terrible Assyrian armies swept through the land, they left a trail of ruin and desolation behind, and there were few towns of the Empire which escaped being plundered.

80. Civilization of the Assyrian Empire. While this plundered wealth was necessary for the support of the army, it also served higher purposes. As we have seen, the Assyrian palaces were now imposing buildings, suggesting by their size and splendor the far-reaching power of their builders. In the hands of the Assyrian architects the arch, inherited from Babylonia, for the

first time became an imposing monumental feature of architecture. The impressive triple arches of the Assyrian palace entrance (Fig. 25, *D*) were the ancestor of the Roman triumphal arches. They were faced with glazed brick in gorgeous colors, and on either side were vast human-headed bulls wrought in alabaster. Thus the architects of the Assyrian emperors produced the first magnificent monumental buildings that appeared in Asia.

Within the palace were hundreds of feet of pictures cut in alabaster (see Fig. 26). They display especially the great deeds of the emperor in war and hunting wild beasts. The human figures are monotonously alike—hard, cold, and unfeeling. Nowhere is there a human form which shows any trace of feeling, either joy or sorrow, pleasure or pain. The Assyrian sculptor's wild beasts, however, are sometimes magnificent in the animal ferocity which they display (see *Ancient Times*, Fig. 106, *B*).

81. Assurbanipal's Library. Assurbanipal, grandson of Sennacherib, and the last great Assyrian emperor, boasted that his father had instructed him not only in riding and shooting with bow and arrow but also in writing on clay tablets and in all the wisdom of his time. A great collection of twenty-two thousand clay tablets was discovered in Assurbanipal's fallen library rooms at Nineveh, where they had been lying on the floor covered with rubbish for twenty-five hundred years. They are now in the British Museum (see *Ancient Times*, Fig. 109). In this library the religious, scientific, and literary works of past ages had been systematically collected by the emperor's orders. They formed the earliest library known in Asia.

82. Economic and Agricultural Decline. Like many later rulers, however, the Assyrian emperors made a profound mistake in their method of governing their empire. The industries were destroyed and the farms left idle in order to supply men for a great *standing* army. Even so, the Empire had grown so large that the army was unable to defend it. As reports of foreign invasions and new revolts came in, the harassed ruler at Nineveh forced the subjects of his foreign vassal kingdoms to enter the army. With an army made up to a dangerous extent of such

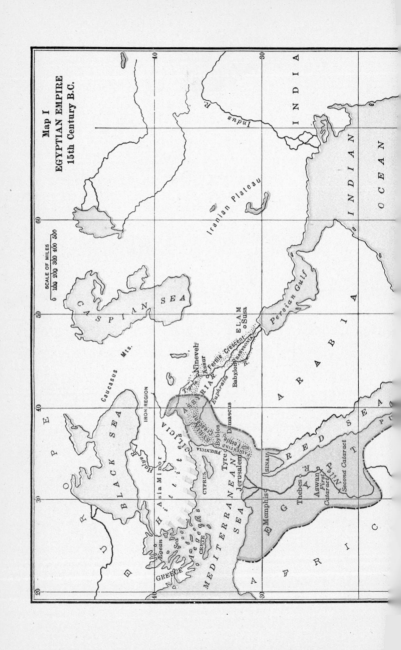

Map I
EGYPTIAN EMPIRE
15th Century B.C.

SCALE OF MILES
0 100 200 300 400 500

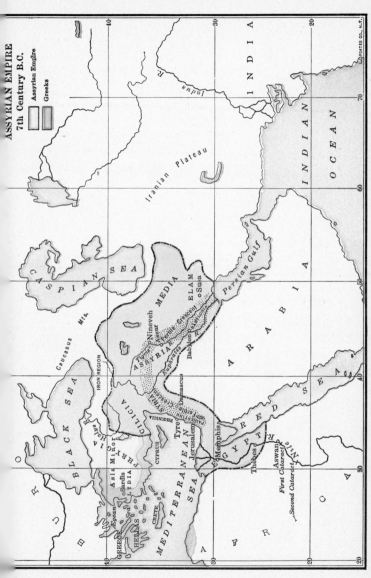

ASSYRIAN EMPIRE
7th Century B.C.

☐ Assyrian Empire
▨ Greeks

SEQUENCE MAP SHOWING EXPANSION OF THE ORIENTAL EMPIRES FOR A THOUSAND YEARS (FROM ABOUT 1500 TO 500 B.C.). IN FOUR PARTS. (See Map III and Map IV following)

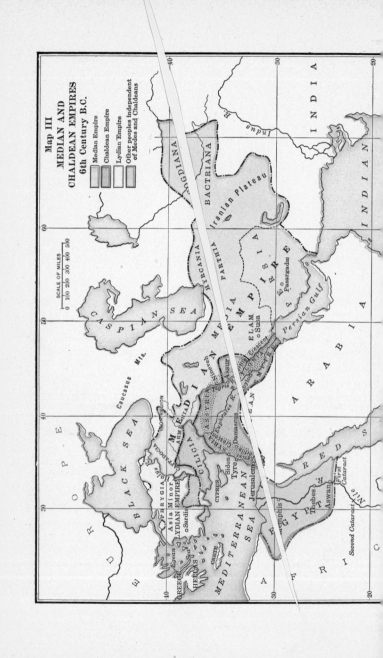

Map III
MEDIAN AND
CHALDEAN EMPIRES
6th Century B.C.

Median Empire
Chaldean Empire
Lydian Empire
Other peoples independent
of Medes and Chaldeans

SCALE OF MILES
0 100 200 300 400 500

EUROPE

BLACK SEA

Caucasus Mts.

CASPIAN SEA

SOGDIANA

BACTRIANA

Iranian Plateau

HYRCANIA

PARTHIA

MEDIAN EMPIRE

PERSIA

Pasargadae

Persian Gulf

ELAM
Susa

ARMENIA
IRON REGION

CILICIA

CAPPADOCIA
PHRYGIA
LYDIAN EMPIRE
Sardis
Asia Minor

CYPRUS

Nineveh
Assur
ASSYRIA
Tigris R.
Euphrates R.
SYRIA
Damascus
BABYLONIA
Babylon
Fertile Crescent

Sidon
Tyre
Jerusalem

MEDITERRANEAN SEA

GREECE
HELLAS
Aegean
CRETE

EGYPT
Memphis
Thebes
Aswan
First Cataract
Second Cataract

NILE R.

RED SEA

ARABIA

INDIA

Indus

INDIAN

AFRICA

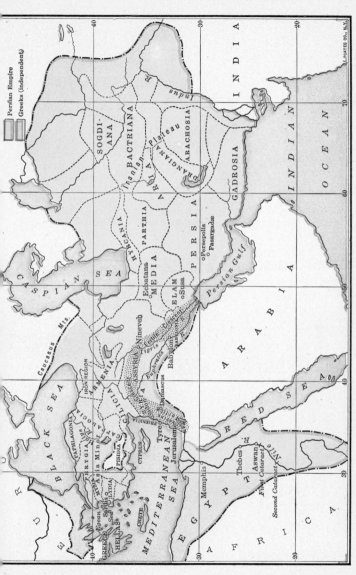

SEQUENCE MAP SHOWING EXPANSION OF THE ORIENTAL EMPIRES FOR A THOUSAND YEARS (FROM ABOUT 1500 TO 500 B.C.). IN FOUR PARTS. (See Map I and Map II preceding)

foreigners, with the commerce of the country also in the hands of foreigners, with no industries, and with fields lying idle,—under these conditions the Assyrian nation fast lost its inner strength.

83. Fall of Assyria; Destruction of Nineveh (606 B.C.). In addition to such weakness within, there were the most threatening dangers from without. These came, as of old, from both sides of the Fertile Crescent. Especially dangerous was a desert tribe whom we know as the Chaldeans. They had been for centuries creeping slowly around the head of the Persian Gulf and settling along its shores at the foot of the eastern mountains. The Chaldeans mastered Babylonia and then assailed the walls of Nineveh.

Weakened by a generation of decline within, and struggling vainly against assaults from without, the mighty city of the Assyrian emperors fell (606 B.C.). In the voice of the Hebrew prophet Nahum (ii, 8, 13, and iii entire) we hear an echo of the exulting shout which resounded from the Caspian to the Nile as the nations discovered that the terrible scourge of the East had at last been laid low. Its fall was forever, and when two centuries later Xenophon and his ten thousand Greeks marched past the place (§ 237) the Assyrian nation was but a vague tradition, and Nineveh, its great city, was a vast heap of rubbish, as it is to-day (see *Ancient Times,* Fig. 203). The second great chapter of history on the Two Rivers was ended, having lasted but a scant century and a half (about 750 to 606 B.C.).

84. Summary of Progress by the Assyrian Empire. The Empire of Assyria had greatly altered the nations of Western Asia. The rule of a single sovereign had been forced upon the whole great group of nations around the eastern end of the Mediterranean, and the methods of organizing such an empire had been much improved, leading over to the much greater Persian Empire which was built up (pp. 64–65) sixty years after the fall of Assyria. In spite of its often ferocious harshness, the Assyrian rule had furthered civilization. We have seen that the building of the magnificent palaces in and near Nineveh formed the first chapter in great architecture in Asia. At the same time Nineveh also possessed the first libraries as yet known there.

V. The Chaldean Empire: the Last Semitic Empire

85. Rise of the Chaldean Empire (606 B.C.). After the fall of Assyria the brief career of the Chaldean Empire formed the third great chapter of history on the Two Rivers.[1] The Chaldeans made their capital at Babylon and gave their name to the land, so that we now know it as Chaldea. They were the last Semitic lords of Babylonia in ancient times.

86. Reign of Nebuchadnezzar (604-561 B.C.). At Babylon, Nebuchadnezzar, the greatest of the Chaldean emperors, began a reign of over forty years,—a reign of such power and magnificence, especially as narrated in the Bible, that he has become one of the great figures of oriental history. It was he who carried away many Hebrews from Palestine to Babylonia as captives and destroyed Jerusalem, their capital (586 B.C.).

Copying much from Assyria, Nebuchadnezzar was able to surpass even his Assyrian predecessors in the splendor of the great buildings which he now erected at Babylon (see plan, *Ancient Times*, p. 165). High over all towered the temple-mount which rose by the temple of their greatest god, Marduk,—a real "Tower of Babel" (see § 65). Masses of rich tropical verdure, rising in terrace above terrace, crowned the roof of the gorgeous imperial palace, forming lofty roof gardens. Here in the ·cool shade of palms and ferns the great king might enjoy his idle hours, looking down upon the splendors of his city. These roof gardens were the mysterious "Hanging Gardens" of Babylon, whose fame spread far into the West, until they were numbered by the Greeks among the Seven Wonders of the World. The city was immensely extended by Nebuchadnezzar, and enormous fortified walls were built to protect it. It was this Babylon of Nebuchadnezzar which

---

[1] The three great chapters of history on the Two Rivers are:

1. Early Babylonia (thirty-first century to twenty-first century B.C.; Sargon I about 2750 B.C., Hammurapi about 2100 B.C.). See pp. 43–50.

2. The Assyrian Empire (about 750 to 606 B.C.). See pp. 51–55.

3. The Chaldean Empire (about 606 to 539 B.C.). See pp. 56–58.

With the exception of parts of the first, these three epochs were periods of *Semitic* power. To these we might in later times add a *fourth* period of Semitic supremacy, the triumph of Islam in the seventh century of our era, after the death of Mohammed (pp. 322–329).

has become familiar to all Christian peoples as the great city of the Hebrew captivity (§§ 110–111). So little survives of all the glories which made it world-renowned in its time (see tailpiece, p. 77) that nearly twenty years of excavation have recovered almost no standing buildings.

87. Civilization of Chaldean Babylon. The Chaldeans seem to have adopted the civilization of Babylonia in much the same way as other earlier Semitic invaders of this ancient plain (§ 68). Science made notable progress in one important branch — astronomy. This was really at that time only what we call "astrology," namely, a study of the movements of the heavenly bodies with a view of forecasting the future. But it was now very systematically pursued and was slowly becoming astronomy. The equator was divided into 360 degrees, and for the first time the Chaldean astrologers laid out the twelve groups of stars which we call the "Twelve Signs of the Zodiac." Thus the sky and its worlds began to be mapped out.

The five planets then known (Mercury, Venus, Mars, Jupiter, and Saturn) were regarded as the powers especially controlling the fortunes of men, and as such the five leading Babylonian divinities were identified with these five heavenly bodies. The names of these Babylonian divinities have therefore descended to us as the names of the planets. But on their way to us through Europe the ancient Babylonian divine names were translated into Roman forms. So the planet of Ishtar, the goddess of love, became Venus, while that of Marduk, the great god of Babylon, became Jupiter, and so on. The celestial observations made by these Chaldean "astrologers," as we call them, slowly became sufficiently accurate so that the observers could already foretell an eclipse. These observations when inherited by the Greeks formed the basis of the science of astronomy, which the Greeks carried so much further (§ 178). The practice of astrology has survived to our own day ; we still unconsciously recall it in such phrases as "his lucky star" or "an ill-starred undertaking."

88. Decline of the Old Oriental Lands. The reign of Nebuchadnezzar was the high-water mark of Chaldean civilization.

After his death (561 B.C.) the old civilized lands of the Orient seem to have lost most of their former power to go forward and to make fresh discoveries and new conquests in civilization, such as they had been making during three great ages on the Nile and three similar ages on the Two Rivers. Indeed, the leadership of the Semitic peoples in the early world was drawing near its close, and they were about to give way before the advance of new peoples of the Indo-European race (pp. 59–62). The nomads of the southern desert were about to yield to the hardy Indo-European peoples of the northern and eastern mountains, and to these we must now turn.

QUESTIONS

I. Summarize the history of the Fertile Crescent. Describe the nomads' life; their religion. Describe the Babylonian plain, giving size, climate, and products.

II. Describe Sumerian civilization. Tell about the earliest Semites in Babylonia and their first great leader. How did these Semites gain civilization; for example, writing?

III. Who was Hammurapi? Give an account of his laws. Describe Babylonian commerce in his age. How can we summarize Babylonian history?

IV. Locate Assyria on the Fertile Crescent. Whence did its people receive their civilization? What did the Assyrian Empire at its largest chiefly include? Give some account of Assyrian civilization. Outline the causes of the fall of Assyria.

V. Who were the Chaldeans? Describe Chaldean Babylon; its chief buildings. Discuss Chaldean astronomy.

NOTE. Huge winged bulls, like this one below, with human head were set up to adorn the entrances of Assyrian palaces (Fig. 25, *D*). They were carved in alabaster.

CHAPTER IV

WESTERN ASIA: THE MEDO-PERSIAN EMPIRE AND THE HEBREWS

I. The Indo-European Peoples and their Dispersion [1]

89. The Northern Grasslands. We have seen that the Arabian desert has been a great reservoir of unsettled peoples, who were continually leaving the grasslands on the margin of the desert and shifting over into the towns to begin a settled life (§ 59). Corresponding to these grasslands of the *South,* there are similar grasslands in the *North* (Fig. 27). These Northern grasslands stretch from the lower Danube eastward along the north side of the Black Sea through southern Russia and far into Asia north and east of the Caspian. In ancient times they always had a wandering shepherd population; and time after time, for thousands of years, these Northern nomads have poured forth over Europe and Western Asia, just as the desert Semites of the South have done over the Fertile Crescent (§ 59).

90. The Two Lines—Indo-European and Semitic. These nomads of the North were from the earliest times a great white race, the ancestors of the present peoples of Europe (and since our forefathers came from Europe, these same nomads were also our own ancestors). These nomads of the *Northern* grasslands, from whom most Americans have sprung, began to migrate in very ancient times, moving out along diverging routes. They at last extended in an imposing line from the frontiers of India on the

1 Pages 59–62 should be carefully worked over by the teacher with the class before the class is permitted to study this section alone. The diagram (Fig. 27) should be put on the blackboard and explained in detail by the teacher, and the class should then be prepared to put the diagram on the board from memory. This should be done again when the study of the Greeks is begun (§ 131), and a third time when Italy and the Romans are taken up.

east, westward across all Europe to the Atlantic, as they do to-day (Fig. 27). They are called, therefore, the *Indo-European* race. This great northern Indo-European line was confronted on the south by a similar line of Semitic peoples, extending from Babylonia on the east, through Phœnicia and the Hebrews westward along North Africa to Carthage and similar Semitic settlements of Phœnicia in the western Mediterranean (§ 59).

The history of the ancient world, as we are now to follow it, was often centered in the struggle between this *southern Semitic* line which issued from the Southern grasslands and the *northern Indo-European* line which came forth from the Northern grasslands. The result of the long conflict was the complete triumph of our ancestors, the Indo-European line, which conquered along the center and both wings and gained the leadership throughout the Mediterranean world under the Greeks and Romans (Chapters V to XVII).

91. The Indo-European Parent People and its Dispersion. It is probable that the original home of the Indo-European people was on the great grassy steppe in the region east and northeast of the Caspian Sea. Here, then, probably lived the parent people of all the later Indo-European race. Before they dispersed, probably about 2500 B.C., the parent people were still in the Stone Age for the most part, though copper was beginning to come in. Divided into numerous tribes, they wandered at will, seeking pasture for their flocks, for they already possessed domestic animals, including cattle and sheep. But chief among their domesticated beasts was the *horse*, which, as we recall, was still entirely unknown to the civilized oriental nations until after Hammurapi's time (see § 72). They employed him both for riding and for drawing wheeled carts. Some of the tribes had adopted a settled life and cultivated grain, especially barley. Being without writing, they possessed little government and organization. But they were the most gifted and the most highly imaginative people of the ancient world.

As their tribes wandered farther and farther apart they lost contact with each other. While they all at first spoke the same language, differences in speech gradually arose and finally became

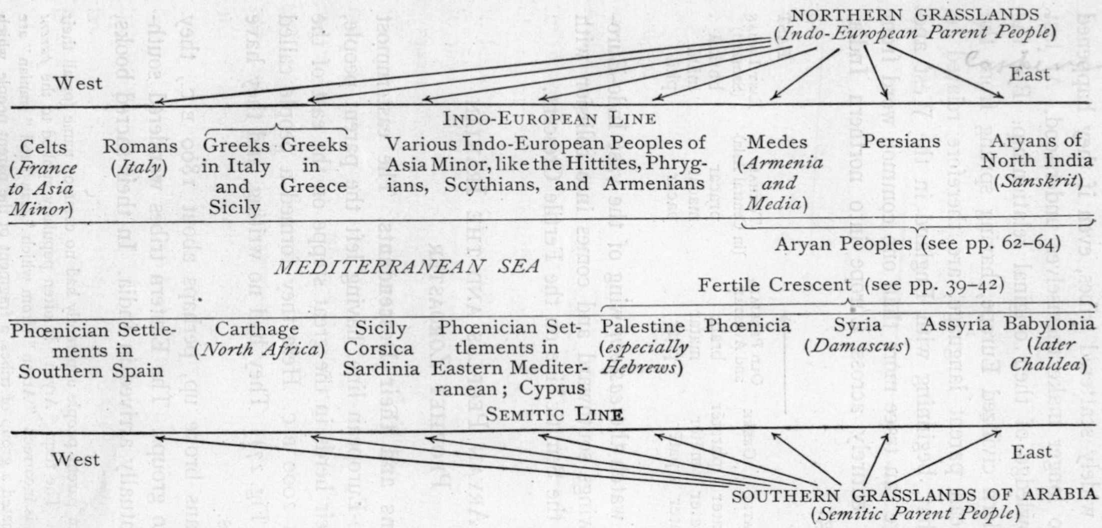

NORTHERN GRASSLANDS
(*Indo-European Parent People*)

INDO-EUROPEAN LINE

West					East
Celts (*France to Asia Minor*)	Romans (*Italy*)	Greeks in Italy and Sicily	Greeks in Greece	Various Indo-European Peoples of Asia Minor, like the Hittites, Phrygians, Scythians, and Armenians	Medes (*Armenia and Media*) Persians Aryans of North India (*Sanskrit*)

Aryan Peoples (see pp. 62–64)

Fertile Crescent (see pp. 39–42)

MEDITERRANEAN SEA

SEMITIC LINE

West					East
Phoenician Settlements in Southern Spain	Carthage (*North Africa*)	Sicily Corsica Sardinia	Phoenician Settlements Eastern Mediterranean; Cyprus	Palestine (*especially Hebrews*) Phoenicia Syria (*Damascus*)	Assyria Babylonia (*later Chaldea*)

SOUTHERN GRASSLANDS OF ARABIA
(*Semitic Parent People*)

FIG. 27. DIAGRAM SUGGESTING THE TWO LINES OF SEMITIC AND INDO-EUROPEAN DISPERSION

The actual lines along which these peoples lie are of course not straight. The lines sometimes overlie each other, as in Sicily, mentioned in both lines. Egypt, which geographically belongs in the southern line, has been omitted because it is not purely Semitic, although closely related to the Semites. Notice also that in the West the two races face each other for the most part across the Mediterranean; in the East they confront each other along the Fertile Crescent (pp. 39–42). The Hittites, included above among the Indo-European peoples, became so in language, though evidently not originally so in blood

so great that the widely scattered tribes, even if they happened to meet, could no longer make themselves understood. At last they lost all knowledge of their original relationship. But the languages of modern civilized Europe, having sprung from the same Indo-European parent language, are therefore related to each other; so that, beginning with England in the West and going eastward, we can trace more than one common word from people to people entirely across Europe into northern India. Note the following:

WEST ⟶ EAST

ENGLISH	GERMAN	LATIN	GREEK	OLD PERSIAN and AVESTAN	TOKHAR (in Central Asia)	EAST INDIAN (Sanskrit)
brother	bruder	frater	phratēr	brata	pracar	bhrātā
mother	mutter	mater	mētēr	matar	macar	mātā
father	vater	pater	patēr	pitar	pacar	pitā

We are now to watch the *eastern* wing of the vast Indo-European line as it swings southward and comes into collision with the right wing of the Semitic line on the Fertile Crescent.

II. THE ARYAN PEOPLES AND THE IRANIAN PROPHET ZOROASTER

92. The Aryans and their Descendants. The easternmost tribes of the Indo-European line, having left the parent people, were pasturing their herds in the great steppe on the east of the Caspian by about 2000 B.C. Here they formed a people called the Aryans[1] (see Fig. 27). They had no writing, and they have left no monuments.

When the Aryans broke up, perhaps about 1800 B.C., they separated into two groups. The Eastern tribes wandered south-eastward and eventually arrived in India. In their sacred books,

[1] The Indo-European parent people apparently had no common name for all their tribes as a great group. The term "Aryan" is often popularly applied to the *parent* people, but this custom is incorrect. "Aryan" (from which "Iran" and "Iranian" are later derivatives) designated a group of tribes, a fragment of the parent people, which detached itself and found a home for some centuries just east of the Caspian Sea. The Aryans, then, were *Eastern* descendants of the Indo-European parent people, as we are *Western* descendants of the parent people. The Aryans are our distant cousins but not our ancestors.

which we call the Vedas, written in Sanskrit, there are echoes
of the days of Aryan unity, and they furnish many a hint of
the ancient Aryan home on the east of the Caspian.

The other group, whose tribes kept the name "Aryan" in
the form "Iran," also left this home and pushed westward and
southwestward into the mountains bordering the Fertile Crescent.
We call them Iranians, and among them were two powerful tribes,
the Medes and the Persians.

93. The Median (Indo-European) Empire threatens Chaldean (Semitic) Babylonia. By 600 B.C., just after the fall of
Assyria (§ 83), the Medes had established a powerful Iranian
empire in the mountains east of the Tigris. It extended from
the Persian Gulf, where it included the Persians, northwestward
in the general line of the mountains to the Black Sea region. The
front of the Indo-European eastern wing was thus roughly parallel
with the Tigris at this point, but its advance was not to stop
here. Nebuchadnezzar (§ 86) and the Chaldean masters of
Babylon looked with anxious eyes at this dangerous Median
power. The Chaldeans on the Euphrates represented the leadership of men of Semitic blood from the *Southern* pastures. Their
leadership was now to be followed by that of men of Indo-
European blood from the *Northern* pastures (§ 90).

94. The Religion of the Iranians and the Spread of Zoroastrianism. All of these Iranians possessed a beautiful religion inherited from old Aryan days. Somewhere in the eastern mountains,
perhaps as far back as 1000 B.C., an Iranian named Zoroaster began to look out upon the life of men, which he studied in an effort
to find a new religion fitted to meet the needs of man. He watched
the ceaseless struggle between Good and Evil which met him
wherever he turned. The Good became to him a divine person,
whom he called Mazda, or Ahuramazda, which means "Lord of
Wisdom," and whom he regarded as God. Ahuramazda was surrounded by a group of helpers much like angels, of whom one of
the greatest was the Light, called "Mithras." Opposed to Ahuramazda and his helpers was an evil group led by a great Spirit of
Evil named Ahriman. It was he who later became the Satan of
the Jews and Christians.

Thus the faith of Zoroaster called upon every man to stand on one side or the other ; to fill his soul with the Good and the Light or to dwell in the Evil and the Darkness. Whatever course a man pursued, he must expect a judgment hereafter. This was the earliest appearance in Asia of belief in a last judgment. Zoroaster maintained the old Aryan veneration of fire as a visible symbol of the Good and the Light. The new faith had gained a firm footing before the prophet's death, and before 700 B.C. it was the leading religion among the Medes in the mountains along the Fertile Crescent. Thus Zoroaster became the first great founder of a noble religious faith.

95. The *Avesta*, the Persian Bible. As in the case of Mohammed, it is probable that Zoroaster could neither read nor write, for the Iranians possessed no system of writing in his day (see § 92). Besides a few hymns, fragments of his teaching have descended to us in writings put together over a thousand years after the prophet's death. They form a book known as the *Avesta*. This we may call the Bible of the Persians.

III. RISE OF THE PERSIAN EMPIRE : CYRUS

96. The Emergence of the Persians. No people became more zealous followers of Zoroaster than the group of Iranian tribes known as the Persians. At the fall of Nineveh (606 B.C.) (§ 83) they had already been long settled in the region at the south-eastern end of the Zagros Mountains, just north of the Persian Gulf. Here the Persians occupied a district some four hundred miles long. They were a rude mountaineer peasant folk, leading a settled agricultural life, with simple institutions, and possessing no art, writing, or literature.

97. Cyrus of Anshan and his Conquests. They acknowledged themselves vassals of the Empire of their kinsmen the Medes (§ 93). One of their tribes dwelling in the mountains of Elam (see map, p. 42) was organized as a little kingdom. About fifty years after the fall of Nineveh this little kingdom of Anshan was ruled over by a Persian named Cyrus. He succeeded in uniting the other tribes of his kindred Persians into a nation. Thereupon Cyrus at once rebelled against the rule of the Medes. He gathered his peasant soldiery and within three years defeated the Median king and made himself master of the Median territory (§ 93). The extraordinary career of Cyrus was now a spectacle upon which all eyes in the West were fastened with wonder and alarm.

With a powerful Persian army Cyrus marched far to the west, into Asia Minor, and conquered the kingdom of Lydia. He captured its capital, Sardis, and took prisoner its king, the wealthy and powerful Crœsus (546 B.C.). Within five years the power of the little Persian kingdom in the mountains of Elam had thus swept across Asia Minor to the Mediterranean and had become the leading state in the oriental world. Turning eastward again, Cyrus had no trouble in defeating the Chaldean army led by the young crown prince Belshazzar, whose name in the Book of Daniel (see Dan. v) is a household word throughout the Christian world. In spite of the vast walls erected by Nebuchadnezzar to protect Babylon (§ 86), the Persians entered the great city in 539 B.C., seemingly without resistance.

98. Persia Supreme ; Death of Cyrus (528 B.C.). Thus the Semitic East completely collapsed before the advance of the Indo-European power, only sixty-seven years after the Chaldean conquest of Nineveh (§ 83). Some ten years later Cyrus fell in battle (528 B.C.). His body was reverently laid away in a massive tomb of impressive simplicity, which still survives (see *Ancient Times*, Fig. 115). Thus passed away the first great conqueror of Indo-European blood.

All Western Asia was now subject to the Persian kings ; then in 525 B.C., only three years after the death of Cyrus, his son Cambyses conquered Egypt. This conquest of the only remaining ancient oriental power rounded out the Persian Empire to include the whole civilized Orient from the Nile Delta around the entire eastern end of the Mediterranean to the Ægean Sea, and from this western boundary eastward almost to India (see map, IV, p. 58). The great task had consumed just twenty-five years since the overthrow of the Medes by Cyrus.

IV. THE CIVILIZATION OF THE PERSIAN EMPIRE
(ABOUT 530 TO 330 B.C.)

99. Persia absorbs Civilization. The Persians found Babylon a great and splendid city, with the vast fortifications and magnificent buildings of Nebuchadnezzar visible far across the Babylonian plain (§ 86). The city was the center of the commerce of Western Asia and the greatest market in the early oriental world. Along the Nile, also, the Persian emperors now ruled the splendid cities whose colossal monuments we have visited. Such things as these, and the civilized life which the Persians found along the Nile and the Euphrates, soon influenced them greatly.

In order to carry on business and government the Persians, formerly without writing, soon devised an alphabet, of thirty-nine *cuneiform* signs (§ 64), which they employed for writing Persian on clay tablets. They also used it when they wished to make records on large monuments of stone.

100. Organization of the Persian Empire by Darius. The organization of this vast empire, stretching from the Indus River to the Ægean Sea (almost as long as the United States from east to west) and from the Indian Ocean to the Caspian Sea, was a colossal task. Though begun by Cyrus, it was carried through by Darius the Great (521–485 B.C.). His organization remains one of the most remarkable achievements in the history of the ancient Orient, if not of the world. For the system introduced by Darius was not only attempting government on a larger scale than the world had ever seen before but it was government controlled by *one man.*

Darius did not desire further conquests, but he planned to maintain the Empire as he had inherited it. He caused himself to be made actual king in Egypt and in Babylonia, but the rest of the Empire he divided into twenty provinces, each called a "satrapy." Each such province was under the control of a governor called a "satrap," who was appointed by the "Great King," as the Persian sovereign came to be called. The subject nations, or provinces, enjoyed a good deal of independence in their own local matters as long as they paid regular tribute and furnished recruits for the Great King's army.

In the East this tribute was paid, as of old, in produce (§§ 32 and 70). In the West, chiefly Lydia and the Greek settlements in western Asia Minor, the coinage of metal was common by 600 B.C. (§ 163), and there this tribute was paid in *coined money.* Thus the great commercial convenience of coined money issued by the State began to come into the Orient during the Persian period under Darius.

101. Darius makes Persia the Earliest Great Sea Power in Asia. Nothing shows the wise statesmanship of Darius the Great more clearly than his remarkable efforts to make Persia a great sea power. He sent a skillful Mediterranean sailor by the name of Scylax

FIG. 28. COLONNADES OF THE PERSIAN PALACE AT PERSEPOLIS

This sumptuous and ornate architecture of the Persians is made up of patterns borrowed from other peoples

to explore the course of the great Indus River in India, and then to sail along the coast of Asia from the mouth of the Indus westward to the Isthmus of Suez. Scylax was the first Western sailor who is known to have sailed along this south coast of Asia, so little known at that time (about 500 B.C.). At Suez, Darius restored the ancient but long filled-up canal of the Egyptians connecting the Nile with the Red Sea (§ 46; see *Ancient*

Times, § 271).　This gave him a sea route all the way from the Persian coast to the Mediterranean.　Unlike the Assyrians, Darius treated the Phœnician cities with kindness and succeeded in organizing a great Phœnician war fleet in the eastern Mediterranean. Thus the more enlightened Persian kings accomplished what the Assyrian emperors never achieved, and Persia became the first great sea power in Asia.　From end to end of the vast Empire the Persian emperors laid out a system of excellent roads, on which royal messengers maintained a regular postal system.

102. Summary of Persian History and Decline of Persia. For the oriental world as a whole, Persian rule meant about two hundred years of peaceful prosperity (ending about 333 B.C.). It showed men how a vast group of nations might be forced to yield to the power of a single sovereign and to accept his rule as if it were a permanent right.　Such an enormous empire, extending as it did from India to the shores of Europe, at the Hellespont, exerted a tremendous influence on Europe, as we shall see.　The Persian kings, however, as time went on, were no longer as strong and skillful as Cyrus and Darius.　They loved luxury and ease and left much of the task of ruling to their governors and officials.　This meant corrupt and ineffective government ; the result was weakness and decline.

The later world, especially the Greeks, often represented the Persian rulers as cruel and barbarous oriental tyrants.　This unfavorable opinion is not wholly justified.　For there can be no doubt that the Persian Empire, the largest the ancient world had thus far seen, enjoyed a government far more just and humane than any that had preceded it in the East.

The religious beliefs of the Persians spread among other peoples and even into Europe ; but far more important than Zoroastrianism for the Western world was the religion of the Hebrews.　We must therefore now glance briefly at the little Hebrew kingdom among the Persian vassals in the West, which was destined to influence the history of man more profoundly than any of the great empires of the early world.

V. The Hebrews

103. Hebrew Invasion of Palestine (about 1400 to 1200 B.C.).
The Hebrews were all originally men of the Arabian desert,[1]
wandering with their flocks and herds. For two centuries,
beginning about 1400 B.C., they were slowly drifting over into
their final home in Palestine, along the west end of the Fertile
Crescent.[2] When they entered it the Hebrews were nomad shepherds (see § 59) and possessed very little civilization. A southern group of their tribes had been slaves in Egypt, but had been
induced to flee by their heroic leader Moses, a great national
hero whose achievements they never forgot. He led them out of
Egypt.

On entering Palestine the Hebrews found the Canaanites (§ 61)
dwelling there in flourishing towns with massive walls. The
Canaanites had learned from Egypt the manufacture of many
valuable articles of commerce ; from Babylonia the caravans had
brought in bills and lists written on clay tablets (Fig. 21), and
the Canaanites had thus learned to use Babylonian cuneiform
writing. The Hebrews settled on the land around the towns of
the Canaanites and slowly mingled with them until the two
peoples, Hebrew and Canaanite, had become one. By this process
the Hebrews gradually adopted the civilization of the Canaanites.

104. Rise of the Hebrew Kingdom (about 1025 to 930 B.C.).
Even after the Hebrews had set up a king the old nomad customs
were still strong ; for Saul, the first king (about 1025 B.C.), had
no fixed home but lived in a tent. His successor, David, saw the
importance of a strong castle as the king's permanent home. He
therefore seized the old Canaanite fortress of Jerusalem. From
Jerusalem as his residence David extended his power far and
wide and made the Hebrews a strong nation. His people never
forgot his heroic deeds as a warrior nor his skill as a poet and

---

[1] The student should here carefully reread the account of the Arabian desert and the
Semitic nomads—their life, customs, and religion—in §§ 58–60. It was from this desert
and its life that the Hebrews all originally came.

[2] For an account of Palestine and its people before the Hebrews settled there, see
Ancient Times, pp. 197–200.

singer. Centuries later they revered him as the author of many of their religious songs or "psalms."

105. Solomon and the Division of the Kingdom (about 930 B.C.). David's son, Solomon, delighted in oriental luxury and display. To support his extravagance he weighed down the Hebrews with heavy taxes. The discontent was so great that when Solomon died the Northern tribes withdrew from the nation and set up a king of their own. Thus the Hebrew nation was divided into two kingdoms before it was a century old.

There was much hard feeling between the two Hebrew kingdoms, and sometimes fighting. Israel, as we call the Northern kingdom, was rich and prosperous; its market places were filled with industry and commerce; its fertile fields produced plentiful crops. Israel displayed the wealth and success of town life. On the other hand, Judah, the Southern kingdom, was poor; her land was meager. Besides Jerusalem, the capital, she had no large and prosperous towns. Many of the people still wandered with their flocks. The South thus remained largely nomad.

These two methods of life came into conflict in many ways, but especially in religion. Every old Canaanite town had for centuries worshiped its "baal," or lord, as its local god was called. These had never died out. The Hebrew townsmen found it very natural to worship these gods of their neighbors, the Canaanite townsmen. They were thus unfaithful to their old Hebrew God Yahveh (or Jehovah).[1] To some devout Hebrews, therefore, and especially to those in the South, the Canaanite gods seemed to be the protectors of the wealthy class in the towns, with their luxury and their injustice to the poor. On the other hand, Yahveh appeared to be the guardian of the simpler shepherd life of the desert, and therefore the protector of the poor and needy.

106. The Unknown Historian, Earliest Writer of History (Eighth Century B.C.). Thoughtful Hebrews began to feel the injustices of town life. They saw among the rich townsmen

---

[1] The Hebrews pronounced the name of their God "Yahveh." The pronunciation "Jehovah" began less than six hundred years ago and was due to a misunderstanding of the pronunciation of the word "Yahveh."

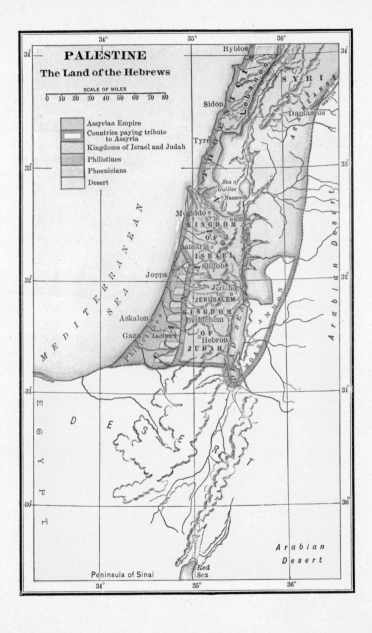

PALESTINE

The Land of the Hebrews

SCALE OF MILES

0 10 20 30 40 50 60 70 80

- Assyrian Empire
- Countries paying tribute to Assyria
- Kingdoms of Israel and Judah
- Philistines
- Phoenicians
- Desert

Byblos

Sidon

Damascus

SYRIA

Lebanon

PHOENICIA

Tyre

Sea of Galilee

Nazareth

Megiddo

Gilboa

KINGDOM OF ISRAEL

Samaria

Shiloh

Joppa

Jericho

JERUSALEM

KINGDOM OF JUDAH

Bethlehem

Askalon

Hebron

Gaza

Lachish

Philistines

MEDITERRANEAN SEA

DEAD SEA

MOAB

AMMON

Arabian Desert

EGYPT

DESERT

Peninsula of Sinai

Red Sea

Arabian Desert

showy clothes, fine houses, beautiful furniture, and cruel hard-heartedness toward the poor. These were things which had been unknown in the simple nomad life of the desert. Men who chafed under such injustices of town life turned fondly back to the grand old days of their shepherd wanderings out yonder on the broad reaches of the desert, where no man "ground the faces of the poor." It was a gifted Hebrew[1] of this kind who now put together a simple narrative history of the Hebrew forefathers— a glorified picture of their shepherd life. He told the immortal tales of the Hebrew patriarchs, of Abraham and Isaac, of Jacob and Joseph. These tales, preserved to us in the Old Testament, are among the noblest literature which has survived from the past.[2] They are the earliest example of historical writing in prose which we possess among any people, and their nameless author, whom we might call the Unknown Historian, is the earliest historian known in the ancient world.

107. Amos and the Prophets. Other men were not content merely to tell tales of the good old days. Amos, a simple herds-man clad in sheepskin, who came from the South, entered the towns of the wealthy North and denounced their showy clothes, fine houses, beautiful furniture, and above all their corrupt lives and hard-heartedness toward the poor, whose lands they seized for debt and whose labor they gained by enslaving their fellow Hebrews. By such addresses as these Amos, of course, endangered his life, but he thus became the first social reformer known in Asia. We apply the term "prophet" to these great Hebrew lead-ers, who pointed out the way toward unselfish living, brotherly kindness, and a higher type of religion.

108. The Hebrews learn to Write. While all this had been going on the Hebrews had been learning to write. The peoples of Western Asia were now abandoning the clay tablet (Fig. 21) and beginning to write on papyrus with the Egyptian pen and ink. The Hebrews borrowed their alphabet from the Phœnician

---

[1] Unfortunately we do not know his name, for the Hebrews themselves early lost all knowledge of his name and identity and finally associated the surviving fragments of his work with the name of Moses.

[2] The student should read these tales, especially Gen. xxiv, xxvii, xxviii, xxxvii, xxxix–xlvii, 12.

and Aramean merchants (§ 61). The rolls containing the Unknown Historian's tales of the patriarchs or the teachings of such men as Amos were the first books which the Hebrews produced — their first literature (see *Ancient Times*, Fig. 131). But literature remained the only art the Hebrews possessed. They had no painting, sculpture, or architecture, and if they needed these things they borrowed from their great neighbors, Egypt, Phœnicia (§ 139), Damascus, or Assyria.

109. Destruction of the Northern Kingdom by Assyria (722 B.C.). While the Hebrews had been deeply stirred by their own conflicts *at home,* such men as Amos had also perceived and proclaimed the dangers coming from *abroad,* from beyond the borders of Palestine, especially from Assyria. As Amos had foreseen, the Assyrians crushed the kingdom of Israel, and Samaria, its capital, was captured by them in 722 B.C. Many of the unhappy Northern Hebrews were carried away as captives, and Israel was destroyed after having existed as a separate kingdom for a little over two centuries.

The national hopes of the Hebrews were now centered in the helpless little kingdom of Judah (see map, p. 70), which still struggled on for over a century and a quarter. More helpless than Belgium in 1914, Judah was now entangled in a great world conflict, in which Assyria was the irresistible champion. Thus far the Hebrews had been accustomed to think of their God as dwelling and ruling in Palestine only. Did he have power also over the vast world arena where all the great nations were fighting? But even if so, was not Assur, the great god of victorious Assyria, stronger than Yahveh, the God of the Hebrews? A wonderful deliverance of Jerusalem from the cruel Assyrian army of Sennacherib (701 B.C.) enabled the great prophet Isaiah to teach the Hebrews that Yahveh, their God, controlled the great world arena, where *He,* and not Assur, was the triumphant champion.

110. Destruction of the Southern Kingdom by Chaldea (586 B.C.). A century later Jerusalem beheld and rejoiced over the fall of Assyria and the destruction of Nineveh (§ 83). But it had only exchanged one foreign lord for another, and Chaldea followed Assyria in control of Palestine (§ 85). Then their unwillingness to submit brought upon the men of Judah the same fate which their kindred of Israel had suffered. In 586 B.C. Nebuchadnezzar, the Chaldean king of Babylonia, destroyed Jerusalem and carried away the people to exile in Babylonia.

111. The Great Unknown Prophet answers Hebrew Doubts. Forced to dwell in a strange land the Hebrews were more than ever faced by the hard question: Was Isaiah right? Or did Yahveh dwell and rule in Palestine only? We hear the echo of their grief and their uncertainty in some of their surviving songs.

> By the rivers of Babylon,
> There we sat down, yea, we wept,
> When we remembered Zion [Jerusalem].
> Upon the willows in the midst thereof
> We hanged up our harps. (Psalms cxxxvii, 1-2)

Had they not left Yahveh behind in Palestine? And then arose an unknown voice[1] among the Hebrew exiles, and out of their centuries of affliction gave them the answer. In a series of triumphant speeches this greatest of early Hebrews declared Yahveh to be the creator and sole God of the universe.

112. Monotheism reached by the Hebrews in Exile. Thus had the Hebrew vision of Yahveh slowly grown from the days of their nomad life. Then they had seen him only as a fierce tribal war god, having as they thought no power beyond the corner of the desert where they lived. But now they had come to regard him as a kindly father and a righteous ruler of all the earth. This was *monotheism*, which is a Greek word meaning "one-god-ism." They had reached it only through a long development, which carried them through suffering and disaster. It had been a discipline lasting many centuries. Just as the individual to-day, especially a young person, learns from his mistakes and

---

[1] This unknown voice was that of a great poet-preacher, a prophet of the exile, whose name has been lost. But his addresses to his fellow exiles are preserved in sixteen chapters embedded in the Old Testament book now bearing the name of Isaiah (chaps. xl–lv, inclusive). We may call him the Unknown Prophet.

develops character as he suffers for his own errors, so the suffering Hebrews had outgrown many imperfect ideas. They thus illustrated the words of the greatest of Hebrew teachers, "First the blade, then the ear, then the full grain in the ear."[1] By this rich and wonderful experience of the Hebrews in religious progress the whole world was yet to profit.

113. Restoration of the Exiled Hebrews by the Persian Kings. When the victorious Cyrus entered Babylon (§ 97) the Hebrew exiles there greeted him as their deliverer. His triumph gave the Hebrews a Persian ruler. With great humanity the Persian kings allowed the exiles to return to their native land. Some had prospered in Babylonia and did not care to return. But at different times enough of them went back to Jerusalem to rebuild the city on a very modest scale and to restore the temple.

114. The Old Testament our Legacy in Hebrew Religion. These returned exiles arranged and copied the ancient writings of their fathers, such as the stories of the patriarchs or the speeches of Amos (§§ 106–107). They also added other writings of their own. All these writings, in Hebrew, form the Bible of the Jews at the present day. It has also become a sacred book for all Christians and, as part of the Christian Bible, is called the Old Testament. It forms the most precious legacy which we have inherited from the older Orient before the coming of Christ. It tells the story of how a rude shepherd folk issued from the wilds of the Arabian desert to live in Palestine and to go through experiences there which made them the religious teachers of the civilized world. And we should further remember that, crowning all their history, there came forth from them in due time the founder of the Christian religion (§ 419).

VI. Estimate of Oriental Civilization

115. Summary of the Achievements of the Orient: Inventions, Art, Religion. Persia was the last of the great oriental powers. We recall how the Orient passed from the discovery of

---

[1] The words of Jesus; see Mark iv, 28.

metal and the invention of writing, through three great chapters of history on the Nile (about 3000 to 1150 B.C.) and three more on the Two Rivers (thirty-first century to 539 B.C.). When the six great chapters were ended, the East finally fell under the rule of the incoming Indo-Europeans, led by the Persians (from 539 B.C. on).

What did the Ancient Orient really accomplish for the human race in the course of this long career? It gave the world the first highly developed *practical arts*, like metal work, weaving, glass-making, paper-making, and many other similar industries. To distribute the products of these industries among other peoples and carry on commerce, it built the earliest seagoing ships equipped with sails. It first was able to move great weights and undertake large building enterprises—large even for us of to-day. The early Orient therefore brought forth the first great group of inventions, surpassed in importance only by those of the modern world.

The Orient also gave us the earliest architecture in stone masonry, including the colonnade, the arch, the clerestory, and the tower, or spire. It produced the earliest refined sculpture, from the wonderful portrait figures and colossal statues of Egypt to the exquisite seals of early Babylonia. It gave us writing and the earliest alphabet. In literature it brought forth the earliest known tales in narrative prose, poems, historical works, social discussions, and even a drama. It gave us the calendar we still use. It gave us our weights and measures and founded the world's methods of commerce and business. It made a beginning in mathematics, astronomy, and medicine. It first produced government on a large scale, whether of a single great nation or of an empire made up of a group of nations.

Finally, in religion the East developed the earliest belief in a sole God and his fatherly care for all men, and laid the foundations of a religious life from which came forth the founder of the leading religion of the civilized world to-day. For these things, accomplished—most of them—while Europe was still undeveloped, our debt to the Orient is enormous.

116. Lack of Freedom, Political and Mental, in the Ancient Orient. There were some very important things, however, which the Orient had not yet gained. The Orient had always accepted as a matter of course the rule of a king. It had never occurred to anyone there that the *people* should have something to say about how they should be governed. No one had ever gained the idea of a free citizen, a man feeling what we call patriotism and under obligations to vote and to share in the government. Liberty as we understand it was unknown, and the rule of the people, which we call "democracy," was never dreamed of in the Orient. Such responsibilities as that of thinking about public questions and then voting, or of serving as a soldier to defend the nation, are duties which quicken the mind and force men to action, and they were among the strongest influences in producing great men in Greece and Rome.

Just as the Orientals accepted the rule of *kings* without question, so they accepted the rule of the *gods*. It was a tradition which they and their fathers had always accepted. This limited their ideas of the world about them. They thought that every storm was due to the interference of some god, and that every eclipse must be the angry act of a god or demon. Hence the Orientals made little inquiry into the *natural* causes of such things. In general, then, they suffered from a lack of freedom of the mind — a kind of intellectual bondage to religion and to old ideas. Under these circumstances natural science could not go very far, and religion was much darkened by superstition.

117. Transition to Europe. There were, therefore, still boundless things for mankind to do in government, in thought about the natural world, in gaining deeper views of the wonders and beauties of nature, as well as in art, in literature, and in many other lines. This future progress was to be made in Europe — that Europe which we left, at the end of our first chapter, in the Late Stone Age. To Europe, therefore, we must now turn, to follow across the eastern Mediterranean the course of rising civilization, as it passed from the Orient to our forefathers in early Europe four to five thousand years ago.

QUESTIONS

I. (See map, p. 100.) Diagram the two racial lines, Indo-European and Semitic. From which line are we descended? Give some account of the Indo-European parent people. Discuss its dispersion.

II. Locate the Aryan tribes on the map. What Indo-European people first invaded the Fertile Crescent, and when? Who was Zoroaster? What peoples adopted the religion he taught?

III–IV. Who was Cyrus? Where did his people live? What great ancient city did Cyrus finally conquer? What other ancient land did the *son* of Cyrus conquer? What was then the extent of the Persian Empire? Who organized it? Describe Persian rule.

V. What kind of life did the Hebrews originally lead? Where is Palestine? What was the final result of the Hebrew invasion? What kind of great men arose under the two Hebrew kingdoms? What happened to the two kingdoms? What happened to the surviving Hebrews? Who allowed some of the exiles to return to Palestine? Trace the growth of the Hebrews' idea of God.

VI. What were the most important things which the Orient contributed to human life? Did the people there ever have any voice in government? Were there any citizens? What was the attitude of the Orientals toward the gods? How did this attitude affect science? To what region do we now follow the story of early man?

NOTE. The lion figure below adorned the wall of the throne-room in the palace of Nebuchadnezzar at Babylon (§ 86). It is made of glazed brick in the brightest colors, which produced a gorgeous effect as architectural adornment. This art arose in Egypt, passed thence to Assyria and Babylonia, and was then adopted by the Persians.

BOOK III. THE GREEKS

CHAPTER V

THE DAWN OF EUROPEAN CIVILIZATION AND THE RISE OF THE EASTERN MEDITERRANEAN WORLD

I. THE DAWN OF CIVILIZATION IN EUROPE

118. Stone Age Europe and the Orient. We have already studied the life of earliest man in Europe, where we followed his progress step by step through some fifty thousand years (pp. 1–13 ; reread §§ 12–16). At that point we were obliged to leave him and to pass over from Europe to the Orient, to watch there the birth and growth of civilization, while all Europe remained in the barbarism of the Late Stone Age.

The inland villages of this age in Europe were already receiving occasional visits from the traders who came from the coast settlements along the Mediterranean. Such a trader's wares were always eagerly inspected, but the interest was greatest when he exhibited a few shining beads or neck rings of a strange, heavy, gleaming, reddish substance, so beautiful that the villagers trafficked eagerly for them. Most desired of all, however, was the dagger or ax head made of the same unfamiliar substance. Thus inner Europe made its first acquaintance with copper.

With rapt attention and awe-struck faces the Late Stone Age Europeans listened to the trader's tales, telling of huge ships which made the rude European dugouts (Fig. 5) look like tiny chips. These mighty vessels had sailed out of the vast river of Egypt, greater than any other river in the world, said the trader. They were heavily loaded with the products of the Egyptian workshops which we have visited (§§ 36–40) ; and these things they carried across the Mediterranean to the islands and coasts of southeastern

Europe or neighboring Asia. Thus at the dawn of history barbarian Europe looked across the Mediterranean to the great civilization of the Nile, as our own North American Indians fixed their wondering eyes on the first Europeans who landed in America and listened to like strange tales of great and distant peoples.

119. Backwardness of Continental Europe after receiving Metal (3000–2000 B.C.). Slowly Europe learned the use of metal.[1] In spite of much progress in craftsmanship and a more civilized life in general, the possession of metal did not enable the peoples of Europe to advance to a high type of civilization. They still remained without writing, without architecture in hewn-stone masonry, and without large sailing ships for commerce. In that portion of Europe nearest to Egypt, however, we find that civilization developed most rapidly ; namely, around the Ægean Sea, to which we must now turn.

II. The Ægean World: the Islands

120. The Ægean World. The Ægean Sea is like a large lake, almost completely encircled by the surrounding shores of Europe and Asia Minor, while the long island of Crete on the south lies like a breakwater, shutting off the Mediterranean from the Ægean Sea (see map, p. 42). From north to south this sea is at no point more than four hundred miles in length, while its width varies greatly. Its coast is deeply indented with many bays and harbors, and it is so thickly sprinkled with hundreds of islands that it is often possible to sail from one island to another in an hour or two. This sea, with its islands and the fringe of shores around it, formed a region by itself, which we may call the Ægean world.

It enjoys a mild and sunny climate ; for this region of the Mediterranean lies in the belt of rainy winters and dry summers. Here and there the bold and beautiful shores (plate, p. 84)

---

1 As we shall see, the Stone Age was only very gradually succeeded by the Copper or Bronze Age. Metal reached southeastern Europe not long after 3000 B.C., but in western and northern Europe it was almost 2000 B.C. before the beginning of the Copper Age, which soon merged into the Bronze Age.

are varied by river valleys and small plains descending to the water's edge. On these *lowlands* wheat and barley, grapes and olives, may be cultivated without irrigation. Hence bread, wine, and oil were the chief food, as among most Mediterranean peoples to this day. Wine is their tea and coffee, and oil is their butter.

121. People of the Ægean World. We call the earliest inhabitants of the Ægean world Ægeans. They were inhabiting this region when civilization dawned there (about 3000 B.C.), and they continued to live there for many centuries before the race known to us as the Greeks entered the region. These Ægeans, the predecessors of the Greeks in the northern Mediterranean, belonged to a great and gifted white race having no connection with the Greeks. They were, and their descendants still are, widely distributed along the northern shores of the

Fig. 29. A Colonnaded Hall and Stair-case in the Cretan Palace at Cnossus

The columns and roof of the hall are modern restorations

Mediterranean. We call them the Mediterranean race, but whence they came and their relationships with other peoples are questions as yet little understood.

122. Nearness of the Ægean World to the Orient. A map of the Mediterranean (p. 42) shows us that the islands of south-eastern Europe are not far from the Nile mouths, and that Asia and Europe face each other across the waters of the Ægean. Asia Minor with its trade routes was therefore also a link which connected the Ægean world with the Fertile Crescent. We see here, then, that the older oriental civilizations were connected with the Ægean by two routes: first and earliest, by ship across the Mediterranean from Egypt; second, by land through Asia Minor from the Euphrates world.

123. Rise of Cretan Civilization under Egyptian Influence (3000-2000 B.C.). Because of their nearness to Egypt, it was on the Ægean *islands* and not on the *mainland* of Europe that the earliest high civilization on the north side of the Mediterranean grew up. From the beginning the leader in this island civilization of the Ægeans was Crete. The little sun-dried-brick villages, forming the Late Stone Age settlements of Crete, received copper from the ships of the Nile by 3000 B.C. They soon learned to make bronze, and thus the Bronze Age began in Crete after 3000 B.C. While the great pyramids of Egypt were being built, the Cretan craftsmen were learning from their Egyptian neighbors the use of the potter's wheel, the closed oven for burning pottery (§ 38), and many other important things. For some time the Cretans had been employing rude picture records. Under the influence of Egypt these picture

FIG. 30. ONE OF THE LARGE DEC-ORATED CRETAN JARS, NEARLY FOUR FEET HIGH, FOUND AT ANCIENT CNOSSUS

signs gradually developed into real phonetic writing, the earliest in the Ægean world (about 2000 B.C.). (*Ancient Times*, Fig. 135.)

By 2000 B.C. the Cretans had become a highly civilized people. At Cnossus, not far from the middle of the northern coast (see map, p. 90), there grew up a Cretan kingdom which may finally have included a large part of the island. These kings rapidly learned the art of navigation from the Egyptians. Their ships, the earliest sailed by Europeans, were so numerous that these rulers are often called the "sea kings of Crete." Ruins of their earliest palace are still standing at Cnossus.

124. The Grand Age in Crete (about 1600 to 1500 B.C.). A few centuries of such development carried Cretan civilization to its highest level, and the Cretans entered upon what we may call their Grand Age (about 1600 to 1500 B.C.). The older palace of Cnossus (§ 123) gave way to a larger and more splendid building with a colonnaded hall, fine stairways, and impressive open areas. This building represented the first real architecture in the northern Mediterranean. Its walls were painted with fresh and beautiful scenes from daily life, all aquiver with movement and action. After learning the Egyptian art of glass-making the Cretans also adorned their buildings with glazed figures attached to the surface of the wall. Noble vases (Fig. 30) were painted or modeled in relief with grand designs drawn from plant life or often from the life of the sea, where the Cretans were now more and more at home. This wonderful pottery belongs among the finest works of decorative art ever produced by any people. (See also *Ancient Times*, §§ 341–342 and Figs. 136–141.)

125. Summary and Historical Position of Ægean Civilization. Beside the *two older centers* of civilization on the Nile and the Two Rivers in this age, there thus grew up here in the eastern Mediterranean, as a *third* great civilization, this splendid world of Crete and the Ægean Sea. It was this *third* great civilization, the first to arise in Europe, which formed the earliest link between the civilization of the Orient and the later progress of man in Greece and western Europe.

III. THE ÆGEAN WORLD: THE MAINLAND

126. Cretan Civilization on the European Mainland; Mycenæan Age (about 1500 to 1200 B.C.). As yet the mainland, both in Europe and in Asia Minor, had continued to lag behind the advanced civilization of the islands. Nevertheless, the fleets of Egypt and of Crete maintained commerce with the mainland of Greece. These ships naturally entered the southern bays, and especially the Gulf of Argos, which looks southward directly toward Crete (see map, p. 90). In the plain of Argos (plate, p. 84), Ægean chieftains were sufficiently civilized after 1500 B.C. to build the massive strongholds of Tiryns (Fig. 31) and Mycenæ (Fig. 32). They imported works of Cretan and Egyptian art in pottery and metal, which are to-day the earliest tokens of a life of higher refinement on the continent of Europe (see *Ancient Times*, § 364).

127. Civilization on the Asiatic Mainland: Troy (about 3000 to 1200 B.C.). Along the Asiatic side of the Ægean Sea we find much earlier progress than on the European side. In the days when metal was first introduced into Crete (after 3000 B.C.) there arose at the northwest corner of Asia Minor a shabby little Late Stone Age trading station known as Troy. Though

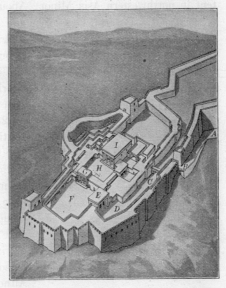

FIG. 31. RESTORATION OF THE CASTLE AND PALACE OF TIRYNS. (AFTER LUCKENBACH)

Unlike the Cretan palaces this dwelling of an Ægean prince is massively fortified. A rising road (*A*) leads up to the main gate (*B*), where the great walls are double. An assaulting party bearing their shields on the *left* arm must here (*C, D*) march with the exposed *right* side toward the city. By the gate (*E*) the visitor arrives in the large court (*F*) on which the palace faces. The main entrance of the palace (*G*) leads to its forecourt (*H*), where the excavators found the place of the household altar of the king (§ 145). Behind the forecourt (*H*) is the main hall of the palace (*I*). This was the earliest castle in Europe with outer walls of stone. The villages of the common people clustered about the foot of the castle hill. The whole formed the nucleus of a city-state (§ 137) in the plain of Argos (see plate, p. 84) several times destroyed (Fig. 33), it was rebuilt and continued to flourish, until it finally controlled a kingdom of considerable extent in northwestern Asia Minor. About 1500 B.C. the splendid and cultivated city of Troy (Fig. 33) was a powerful stronghold which had grown up as a northern rival of that flourishing Cnossus we have seen in the south.

128. Asia Minor and the Hittites. Inland from Troy and the Ægean world, across the far-stretching hills and mountains of Asia Minor, were the settlements of a great group of white peoples who were kindred of the Ægeans in civilization, though not in blood. We call them Hittites. Although the larger part of their land lay outside of the Ægean world, nevertheless one end of it formed the eastern shores of the Ægean Sea. Asia Minor, their land, is a vast peninsula from six hundred and fifty to seven hundred miles long and from three to four hundred miles wide, being about as large as the state of Texas. It is capable of supporting a large and prosperous population. Especially important were the rich deposits of iron at the northeastern corner. The Hittites thus became the earliest distributors of iron when it began to displace bronze in the Mediterranean world and the East (§ 79).

FIG. 32. THE MAIN ENTRANCE OF THE CASTLE OF MYCENÆ, CALLED THE "LION GATE"

A good example of the heavy stone masonry of the two cities of the Ægean Grand Age, Tiryns and Mycenæ, built on the plain of Argos (plate, p. 84, and map, p. 90). Above the gate is a large triangular relief showing two lions grouped on either side of a central column, the whole doubtless forming the emblem of the city or the "arms" of its kings

THE PLAIN OF ARGOS AND THE SEA VIEWED FROM THE CASTLE OF TIRYNS

A typical Greek landscape with plain and mountain and sea. Before us is one of the harbors of Argos, which looked southward directly upon Crete, whence came the first civilization that reached the mainland of Europe and created the cities of Tiryns and Mycenæ

The Hittites first received civilization from their contact with the Fertile Crescent at the east end of Asia Minor. Babylonian traders brought in business documents in the form of cuneiform tablets, and in this way the Hittites learned to write their own language with cuneiform signs. At the same time the Hittites, by studying Egyptian hieroglyphics, invented a similar system of

FIG. 33. THE MOUND OF ANCIENT TROY (ILIUM)

This mound was first dug into by Heinrich Schliemann (see *Ancient Times*, §§ 362–364). When he first visited it (see map, p. 42) in 1868, it was about one hundred and twenty-five feet high, and the Turks were cultivating grain on its summit. He excavated a pit like a crater in the top of the hill, passing downward through nine successive cities built each on the ruins of its predecessors (see *Ancient Times*, Fig. 150). At the bottom of his pit (about fifty feet deep) Schliemann found the original once bare hilltop about seventy-five feet high, on which the men of the Late Stone Age had established a small settlement of sun-baked-brick houses about 3000 B.C. (First City). Above the scanty ruins of this Late Stone Age settlement Schliemann found, in layer after layer, the ruins of the later cities, with the Roman buildings at the top. The entire depth of about fifty feet of ruins represented a period of about thirty-five hundred years from the lowest or First City (Late Stone Age) to the Ninth City (Roman) at the top. The Second City contained the earliest copper found in the series; the Sixth City was that of the Trojan War and the Homeric songs (§§ 142–143)

phonetic signs. In art and in architecture the Hittites likewise learned much both from the Nile and the Two Rivers.[1] They and their country formed a connecting link by which influences from the Fertile Crescent passed westward to the Ægean world.

129. The Hittite Empire (about 1450 to 1200 B.C.). By about 1450 B.C. the Hittites had succeeded in building up a powerful empire which included a large part of Asia Minor. They

[1] A fuller account of the civilization of the Hittites and of the important part they played as a link between the Fertile Crescent and the peoples of the Ægean, carrying many things of importance from Babylonia to the Greek world, will be found in *Ancient Times*, §§ 351–360.

played a vigorous part in the great group of nations around the eastern end of the Mediterranean, after Egypt had established the first empire there (§§ 48–49), and they finally aided in the overthrow of the Egyptian Empire (§ 54). The Hittite Empire lasted from about 1450 to 1200 B.C. While Hittite civilization was inferior to that of Egypt and Babylonia, it occupied a very important place in the group of civilizations forming the oriental neighbors of the Ægeans.

130. Summary of the Northeast Mediterranean World. As we look at the map (p. 42), we see that Greece and the Ægean, together with Troy and Asia Minor, formed a great civilized world on the north of the Mediterranean at its eastern end. We have seen that this civilized world had received civilization from the Orient on the south and east. Farther *north*, however, there were still numerous uncivilized peoples. From behind the Balkan mountains and the Black Sea they were migrating toward the Mediterranean (Fig. 27). Some of these uncivilized Northerners were the Greeks. They were soon to overwhelm the eastern Mediterranean, and with these Northern intruders we must begin a new chapter in the history of the eastern Mediterranean world.

IV. The Coming of the Greeks

131. Southward Advance of the Indo-European Line in Europe. The people whom we call the Greeks were a large group of tribes belonging to the Indo-European race. We have already followed the migrations of the Indo-European parent people until their wanderings finally ranged them in a line from the Atlantic Ocean to northern India (§ 91 and Fig. 27). While their eastern kindred were drifting southward on the east side of the Caspian the Greeks on the west side of the Black Sea were likewise moving southward from their pastures in the grasslands along the Danube (see map, p. 100).

Driving their herds before them, with their families in rough carts drawn by horses, the rude Greek tribesmen must have looked out upon the fair pastures of Thessaly, the snowy summit of Olympus, and the blue waters of the Ægean not long after 2000 B.C. The Greek peninsula which they had entered contains about twenty-five thousand square miles.[1] It is everywhere cut up by mountains and inlets of the sea into small plains and peninsulas, separated from each other either by the sea or by the mountain ridges (Fig. 41).

132. Barbarian Greek Herdsmen invade the Ægean World. These barbarian Greek herdsmen from the Northern grasslands (§ 89 and Fig. 27) had formerly led a *wandering* pastoral life like that which we have seen also in the Southern grasslands. But now they were entering upon a *settled* life among the Ægean towns, like Tiryns and Mycenæ (§ 126). As the newcomers looked out across the waters, they could dimly discern the islands where flourishing towns were carrying on busy industries in pottery and metal, which the ships of Egypt and the Ægeans (§ 123) were distributing far and wide.

It was to be long, however, before these inland Greek shepherds would themselves venture timidly out upon the great waters which they were viewing for the first time. Under the influences of the Orient the Greeks were now to go forward toward the development of a civilization higher than any the Orient had produced — the highest, indeed, which ancient man ever attained.

133. Greeks take Possession of the Ægean World. Gradually their vanguard (called the Achæans) pushed southward into the Peloponnesus, and doubtless some of them mingled with the dwellers in the villages which were grouped under the walls of Tiryns and Mycenæ (Figs. 31 and 32). But our knowledge of the situation in Greece is very meager because the peoples settled there could not yet write and therefore have left no written documents to tell the story. It is evident, however, that a second wave of Greek nomads (called the Dorians) reached the Peloponnesus by 1500 B.C. and gradually subdued and absorbed their

---

[1] It is about one sixth smaller than South Carolina — so small that Mount Olympus on the northern boundary of Greece can be seen over a large part of the peninsula. From the mountains of Sparta one can see from Crete to the mountains north of the Corinthian Gulf (see Fig. 41), a distance of two hundred and twenty-five miles.

earlier kinsmen (the Achæans) as well as the Ægean townsmen, the original inhabitants of the region.

The Dorians did not stop at the southern limits of Greece, but, learning a little navigation from their Ægean predecessors, soon passed over to Crete, where they must have arrived by 1400 B.C. Cnossus, unfortified as it was, must have fallen an easy prey to the invading Dorians. They conquered the island and likewise seized the other southern islands of the Ægean. Between 1300 and 1000 B.C. the several tribes now established in Greece took the remaining islands and the coast of Asia Minor, — the Dorians in the south, the Ionians in the middle, and the Æolians in the north. Here a memorable Greek expedition in the twelfth century B.C., after a long siege, captured and burned the prosperous city of Troy (§ 127), a feat which the Greeks never after forgot (§ 142). Thus during the thousand years between 2000 and 1000 B.C. the Greeks took possession not only of the whole Greek peninsula but likewise of the entire Ægean world.

134. Flight of the Ægeans and Fall of their Civilization (by 1200 B.C.). The northern Mediterranean all along its eastern end was thus being seized by invading peoples of Indo-European blood coming in from the north. The result was that both the Ægeans and their Hittite neighbors in Asia Minor were overwhelmed by the advancing Indo-European line (Fig. 27). The Hittite Empire (§ 129) was crushed, and the leading families among the Ægeans fled by sea, chiefly to the south and east. In only one place were they able to land in sufficient numbers to settle and form a nation. This was on the coast of southern Palestine (see map, p. 70), where a tribe of Cretans called Philistines founded a nation which proved very dangerous to the Hebrews. Palestine is still called after the Philistines, of which the word "Palestine" is a later form. By 1200 B.C., therefore, the splendid Ægean towns and their wonderful civilization (§§ 123–125) had been completely crushed by the incoming Greek barbarians.

The Ægean civilization, the earliest that Europe had gained, thus almost disappeared. But much of the Ægean population had not fled. Remaining in their old homes, they feebly carried on the old Ægean industries, and these formed part of the foundation on which the barbarian Greeks were destined to build up the highest civilization of the ancient world. These Ægeans mingled with their Greek conquerors. This commingling of Ægeans and Greeks produced a mixed race, the people known to us as the Greeks of history. Although the Ægeans thus survived, they lost their language; Greek, the language of the conquerors, became the speech of this mixed race, and so it has remained to this day.

V. THE NOMAD GREEKS MAKE THE TRANSITION TO THE SETTLED LIFE

135. Earliest Institutions of the Greeks. Long after the Greeks had seized the Ægean world they remained a barbarous people of flocks and herds. We remember that the nomads along the Fertile Crescent possessed no organized government, for there was no public business which demanded it. Such was exactly the condition of the nomad Greeks when they began a settled life in the Ægean world. From their old wandering life on the grasslands they carried with them the loose groups of families known as tribes. Within each tribe was an indefinite number of smaller groups of more intimate families called "brotherhoods." A "council" of the old men ("elders") occasionally decided matters in dispute or questions of tribal importance. Probably once a year, or at some important feast, an "assembly" of all the weapon-bearing men of the tribe might be held, to express its opinion of a proposed war or migration. These are the germs of later European political institutions and even of our own in the United States to-day.[1]

It was perhaps after the Greeks had found kings over such Ægean cities as Mycenæ (§ 126) that Greek kings began to

[1] Compare the House of Lords (= the above "council") and the House of Commons (= the above "assembly") in England, or the Senate (derived from the Latin word meaning "old man") and the House of Representatives in the United States.

appear. Thus the old-time nomad leaders whom they had once followed in war, religion, and the settlement of disputes became rude shepherd kings of the tribes.

136. Greeks begin Agriculture. Meantime the Greek shepherds slowly began the cultivation of land. This forced them to give up a wandering life, to build houses, and live in permanent homes. Nomad instincts and nomad customs were not easily rooted out, however, for flocks and herds continued to make up the chief wealth of the Greeks for centuries after they had taken up agriculture.

As each Greek tribe settled down and became a group of villages, the surrounding land was divided among the families by lot. Private ownership of land by families gradually resulted. As a consequence there arose disputes about boundaries, about inheritances in land (§ 158), and much other legal business. The settlement of such business tended to create a government. During the four centuries from 1000 to 600 B.C. we see the Greeks struggling with the problem of learning how to transact the business of settled landholding communities.

137. Rise of Greek Civilization in the Age of the Kings (1000–750 B.C.). No one had ever yet written a word of the Greek language in this age when the Greeks were adopting the settled agricultural life. Cretan writing (§ 123) had perished. This lack of writing among the Greeks greatly increased the difficulties as government transactions began and could not be recorded.

In course of time the group of villages forming the nucleus of a tribe grew together and merged at last into a city. This was the most important process in Greek political development; for the *organized city* became the only nation which the Greeks ever knew. Each city-state was a nation; each had its own laws, its own army and gods, and each citizen felt a patriotic duty toward his own city and no other. Overlooking the city from the heights in its midst was the king's castle (Fig. 31), which we call the "citadel," or "acropolis." Eventually, the houses and the market below were protected by a wall. The king had now

GREECE
IN THE FIFTH CENTURY B.C.

SCALE OF MILES

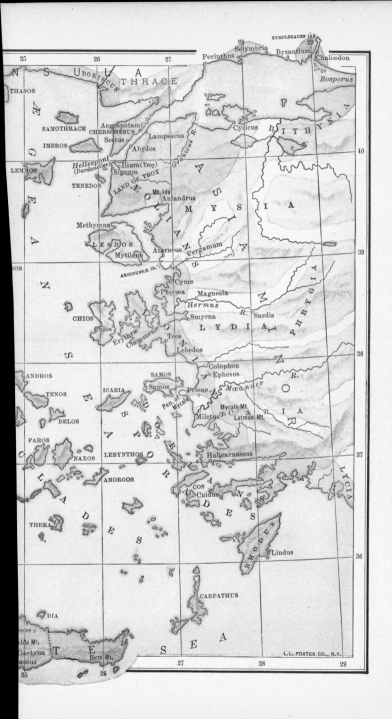

SYMPLEGADES IS.

Selymbria
Perinthus
Byzantium
Chalcedon

25   26   27

Bosporus

U D O R I S C U S

T H R A C E

THASOS

SAMOTHRACE
CHERSONESUS
Aegospotami
Lampsacus
Cyzicus
B I T H Y N I A

IMBROS
Sestus
Abydos

40

LEMNOS

Hellespont
(Dardanelles)
Ilium (Troy)
Sigeum
TENEDOS
LAND OF TROY

Granicus R.

M Y S I A

Mt. Ida
Antandrus

Methymna

L E S B O S
Atarneus
Pergamum

39

Mytilene

ARGINUSÆ IS.

Cyme
Phocæa
Magnesia

Hermus
R. Sardis

CHIOS

Smyrna

L Y D I A

P H R Y G I A

Chios
Erythræ
Clazomenæ
Teos
Lebedos

38

Colophon
Ephesus

R.

ANDROS

SAMOS

TENOS

ICARIA
Samos
Priene
Mæander

Pen. of
Mycale
Mycale Mt.
Latmos Mt.

DELOS

Miletus
C A R I A

PAROS

LEBYNTHOS
Halicarnassus

37

NAXOS

AMORGOS

Cos
Cnidus

THERA

R H O D U S
Lindus

36

CARPATHUS

DIA

Ida Mt.
Gortyna

C R E T E
Dicte Mt.

S E A

25   26   27   28   29

become a revered and powerful ruler of the city and guardian of the worship of the city gods. King and Council sat all day in the market and adjusted the business and the disputes between the people. These continuous sessions for the first time created a State and an uninterrupted government.

There were soon hundreds of such Greek city-states. Indeed, the entire Ægean world came to be made up of such tiny nations. It was while the Greeks were thus living in these little city-kingdoms under kings that Greek civilization arose, especially during the last two and a half centuries of the rule of the kings (1000–750 B.C.).

VI. Greek Civilization in the Age of the Kings

138. The Dawn of Greek Civilization. Long after 1000 B.C. the life of the Greeks continued to be rude and even barbarous. Here and there memories of the old Ægean splendor still lingered, as in the plain of Argos. Above the Greek village at Mycenæ still towered the massive stone walls (Fig. 32) of the ancient Ægean princes, who had long before passed away. To these huge walls the Greeks looked up with awe-struck faces and thought that they had been built by vanished giants called Cyclops. Without any skill in craftsmanship, the Greek shepherds and peasants were slow to take up building, industries, and manufacturing on their own account. They made a beginning at pottery, using the same methods employed by the Ægean potters in producing their fine ware in Crete a thousand years earlier (Fig. 30).

139. Oriental Influences carried by Phœnician Merchants. When we remember how civilization arose among the Ægeans (§§ 122–123), we perceive that the Greeks were now exposed to the same oriental influences which had first brought civilized life to the Ægean peoples. The Greek townsmen had to buy all the ordinary conveniences,—which they were still unable to manufacture for themselves. All these things came to them from across the sea. In the harbor they found Phœnician ships loaded with gorgeous clothing; perfume flasks made of glass and alabaster; porcelain, bronze, and silver tableware wrought with splendid decorative patterns; polished ivory combs, and plentiful jewelry (*Ancient Times,* Figs. 157–158).

We see, then, that after the fall of the Egyptian Empire and the destruction of the Ægean towns the ships of both the Egyptians and the Ægeans, the first traders in the Mediterranean, had disappeared. The Phœnicians (§ 61) on the west end of the Fertile Crescent, along the Syrian coast, were therefore taking advantage of this opportunity. They became the greatest merchants of the Mediterranean for several centuries after 1000 B.C. They pushed westward beyond the Ægean and were the discoverers of the western Mediterranean. Their colony of Carthage in north Africa (see map, p. 100) became the most important commercial state in the western Mediterranean, and they even planted settlements as far away as the Atlantic coast of Spain. Thus the Phœnicians were carrying the art and industries of the Orient throughout the Mediterranean.

140. Phœnicians carry the First Alphabet to Europe. But the Phœnicians brought to the Greeks a crowning gift of far more value than manufactured goods. Before 1000 B.C. the Phœnician merchants had given up the inconvenient clay tablet of Babylonia (Fig. 21), used all along the Fertile Crescent, and they were writing on imported Egyptian papyrus paper. They likewise invented their own system of twenty-two signs for writing their own language. These signs were alphabetic letters, the first system containing no word-signs or syllable-signs (§§ 20–21). The Greeks soon became familiar with the Phœnician tradesman's sheets of pale-yellow paper, bearing his bills and receipts, and at last they began to write Greek words by using the Phœnician letters. Thus an alphabet appeared in Europe for the first time. By 700 B.C. the Greek potters had begun to write their names on the jars which they painted (Fig. 34), and writing was shortly afterward common among Greeks of all classes. From the alphabet which the Phœnicians thus brought to the Greeks, all the alphabets of the civilized world have been derived, including our own.

Along with the alphabet the equipment for using it—that is, pen, ink, and paper—for the first time came into Europe. The Greeks received all their paper from Egypt through the Phœnicians; hence our word "paper," derived from "papyrus" (§ 22). The Greeks also called papyrus "byblos" after the Phœnician city of Byblos, from which they received it. Thus

FIG. 34. VASE-PAINTING CONTAINING THE EARLIEST EXAMPLE OF GREEK WRITING

Aristonothos, the artist who made this vase-painting, has inserted his name over the standard at the right, in the lower row, where the letters run to the right and drop down. It reads, "Aristonothos made it." This is not only the earliest signed vase (§ 140) but it is likewise the earliest signed work of art, crude though it may be, in Europe

arose the Greek word "biblia" for books, and from this word has come our word "Bible." This English word "Bible," once the name of a Phœnician city, is a living evidence of the origin of books and the paper of which they are made in the ancient Orient, from which the Greeks received so much.[1]

[1] A fuller account of the remarkable achievements of the Phœnicians will be found in *Ancient Times*, §§ 394–405.

141. Warfare and Weapons. The Greek nobles of this age loved war and were devoted to fighting and plundering. Their protective armor was of bronze, but their weapons were at this time commonly of iron (§§ 79, 128). It was only men of some wealth who possessed a fighting outfit like this. They were the leading warriors. The ordinary troops, lacking armor, were of little consequence in battle, which consisted of a series of single combats, each between two heroes. Thus each man's individual skill, experience, and daring won the battle, rather than the discipline of drilled masses.

142. Rise of the Hero Songs. Men delighted to sing of valiant achievements on the field of battle and to tell of the stirring deeds of mighty heroes. In the pastures of Thessaly, where the singer looked up at the cloud-veiled summit of Mount Olympus, the home of the gods, there early grew up a group of such songs telling many a story of the feats of gods and heroes, the earliest literature of the Greeks. Into these songs were woven also vague memories of remote wars which had actually occurred, especially the war in which the Greeks had captured and destroyed the splendid city of Troy (§ 133). Probably by 1000 B.C. some of these songs had crossed to the coasts and islands of Ionia on the Asiatic side of the Ægean Sea.

Here arose a class of professional bards who graced the feasts of king and noble with songs of battle and adventure recited to the music of the harp. Framed in exalted and ancient forms of speech, and rolling on in stately measures,[1] these heroic songs resounded through many a royal hall — the oldest literature born in Europe. After the separate songs had greatly increased in number, they were finally woven together by the bards into a connected whole — a great epic series, especially clustering about the traditions of the Greek expedition against Troy. They were not the work of one man, but a growth of several centuries, the work of generations of singers, some of whom were still living even after 700 B.C. It was then that they were first written down (§ 140).

---

[1] These were in hexameter; that is, six feet to a line. This Greek verse is the oldest literary form in Europe.

143. Homer. Among these ancient singers there seems to have been one of great fame whose name was Homer (see *Ancient Times*, Fig. 161). His reputation was such that he was supposed to have been the author of two great series of songs: the *Iliad*,[1] the story of the Greek expedition against Troy; and the *Odyssey*, or the tale of the wanderings of the hero Odysseus on his return from Troy. These are the only two series of songs that have entirely survived; even the ancient world had its doubts about Homer's authorship of the Odyssey.

These ancient bards not only gave the world its greatest epic in the Iliad, but they were, moreover, the earliest Greeks to put into permanent written form their thoughts regarding the world of gods and men. They gave to the disunited Greeks a common literature and the inspiring belief that they had once all taken part in a common war against Asia.

144. Homeric Songs and Greek Religion. At that time the Greeks had no other sacred books, and the Homeric songs became the veritable Bible of Greece. Just as devout Hebrews were taught much about their God by the beautiful tales of Him in the narrative of the great Unknown Historian (§ 106), so the wonderful Homeric songs brought vividly before the Greeks the life of the Gods. Homer became the religious teacher of the Greeks.

In the Homeric songs and in the primitive tales about the gods, which we call myths, the Greeks heard how the gods dwelt in veiled splendor among the clouds on the summit of Mount Olympus. There, in his cloud palace, Zeus, the Sky-god, with the lightning in his hand, ruled the gods like an earthly king. Apollo, the Sun-god, whose beams were golden arrows, was the deadly archer of the gods. But he also shielded the flocks of the shepherds and the fields of the plowman, and he was a wondrous musician. Above all he knew the future ordained by Zeus, and when properly consulted at his shrine at Delphi (Fig. 38) he could tell anxious inquirers what the future had in store for them. These qualities gave him a larger place in the hearts of all Greeks

---

[1] So named after Ilium, the Greek name of Troy.

than Zeus himself, and in actual worship he became the most beloved god of the Greek world.

Athena, the greatest goddess of the Greeks, seems to have been a warrior goddess, and the Greeks loved to think of her with shining weapons, protecting the Greek cities. But she held out her protecting hand over them also in times of peace, as the potters shaped their jars, the smiths wrought their metal, or the women wove their wool. Thus she became the wise and gracious protectress of the peaceful life of industry and art. Of all her divine companions she was the wisest in counsel, and an ancient tale told how she had been born in the very brain of her father Zeus, from whose head she sprang forth full-armed. These three then, Zeus, Apollo, and Athena, became the leading divinities of the Greek world.

There was a further group of great gods, each controlling some special realm. In a brazen palace deep under the waters Poseidon ruled the sea. The ancient Earth Mother, whom they called Demeter, brought forth the produce of the soil. At the same time they looked also to another earth god, Dionysus, for the fruit of the grapevine, and they rejoiced in the wine which he gave them. Hermes was the messenger of the gods, with winged feet, doing their bidding, but he was also the patron of the intercourse of men, and hence the god of trade and commerce. The Semitic goddess of love, whom we have met on the Fertile Crescent as Ishtar (§ 87), had now passed over from the Syrian cities to become likewise the Greek goddess of love, whom the Greeks called Aphrodite.

145. The Greek Gods, their Conduct and Worship. All these divinities the Greeks pictured in human form, and they thought of them as possessing human traits, both good and bad. Homer pictures to us the family quarrels between the august Zeus and his wife Hera, just as such things must have occurred in the household life of the Greeks. Such gods were not likely to require anything better in the conduct of men.[1]

---

[1] Greek religion was the result of a long development, which began on the grasslands, and also among the Ægeans, some of whose beliefs the Greeks inherited. This development continued far down in Greek history. See *Ancient Times*, §§ 412–423

One reason why the Greeks did not yet think that the gods required right conduct of men was their notion of life after death. They believed that all men passed at death into a gloomy kingdom beneath the earth (Hades), where the fate of good men did not differ from that of the wicked. As a special favor of the gods, the heroes, men of mighty and godlike deeds, were granted immortality and permitted to enjoy a life of endless bliss in the beautiful Elysian Fields or in the Islands of the Blest, somewhere far to the west, toward the unexplored ocean.

The symbols of the great gods were set up in every house, while in the dwelling of the king there was a special room which served as a kind of shrine for them. There was also an altar in the forecourt where sacrifices could be offered under the open sky. In so far as the gods had any dwellings at all, we see that they were in the houses of men, and there probably were no temples as yet.

146. Summary of the Age of the Kings. In this period the Greeks gradually completed the change from a wandering shepherd life to a settled life in and around small towns. Thus arose the little *city-kingdoms,* the most important thing in the organized life of the Greeks. At the same time, with the rise of the hero songs and the adoption of an oriental alphabet, the Greeks produced the earliest European literature which has survived. In general, then, the Age of the Kings saw the barbarian Greek shepherds forming civilized states, with government, writing, and literature (1000–750 B.C.).

QUESTIONS

I. How did Europe first receive metal and whence? How did it cross the Mediterranean? At what point? In what part of Europe did civilization first take root?

II. Describe the Ægean world in geography, climate, and products. Tell of its earliest inhabitants. Near what civilized world did the Ægean lie? As a result, how was it influenced? Where was this influence first felt? What civilized things did Crete first receive? What city was leader of Cretan civilization? What name have its kings received? Why?

Had Europe ever had sailing ships before? When did the Grand Age begin in Crete? Tell of its architecture and decorative art. After the rise of Crete how many great centers of civilization were there? Name them.

III. How did Cretan civilization influence the mainland of Europe? Where did the European mainland first feel the influence of Cretan civilization? Indicate on the map why this was. What two towns sprang up in Greece? Point them out on the map. Describe the castle of Tiryns and draw a plan of its main parts. Had there been any such stone buildings in Europe before this?

Where did a similar town arise on the Asiatic side of the Ægean? Give its name. When did it reach a highly flourishing state? Describe the remains of the city (Fig. 33). Who "excavated" it? When was it destroyed by the Greeks?

What people lived inland from Troy? Whence did they receive their civilization? When did their empire flourish? What did it include? What important metal did they first begin to mine and distribute in commerce? What barbarous people threatened the new civilization on the north side of the Mediterranean?

IV. To what great race do the Greeks belong? Whence did their ancestors come? How did they enter Greece? Were they nomads or townsmen? Who were two of the earliest Greek peoples? What became of the old Ægean people of Greece? What happened to Crete? What Ægean lands did the Greeks finally hold?

V. Describe the transition of the Greeks from nomad to settled life. Describe their government and its different institutions. What problems did their new settled life create? What about writing among them? What kind of Greek states arose?

VI. Did the Greeks take up civilization quickly? Did they receive much from the Ægeans? To what other civilized influences were the Greeks exposed after settling in the Ægean? Who brought such influences to the Greeks? How? What was the greatest thing the Phœnicians brought to the Greeks? How did it finally benefit *us*?

Describe warfare in this age. What songs arose? Who was their reputed author? Tell about the leading Greek gods. What can you say of their early places of worship?

CHAPTER VI

THE AGE OF THE NOBLES AND GREEK EXPANSION IN THE MEDITERRANEAN

I. The Disappearance of the Kings and the Leadership of the Nobles

147. Geographical Influences against a Union of All Greeks in One Nation. We have seen Greek civilization beginning under oriental influences. In matters of *government,* however, the Greek world showed striking differences from what we have seen in the Orient. There we watched each group of early city-states finally uniting into a large and powerful nation, like Egypt on the Nile or Babylonia on the Two Rivers. In Greece, however, there were influences which tended to prevent such a union of the Greek city-states into one nation. In the first place, the country was cut up by mountain ridges and deep bays, so that the different communities were quite separated. Moreover, the cities of Greece on the one hand were likewise separated from their kindred in the islands and in Asia Minor on the other hand.

Furthermore, the Greeks had by this time acquired permanent local habits and local dialects, showing more differences than those between our own Louisiana and New England. Each Greek community displayed such intense devotion to its own town and its own local gods that we find in Greece after 1000 B.C. scores of little city-states; including the islands and Asia Minor there must have been several hundred of them (§ 137).

148. The Four Unions. Four regions on the mainland of Greece, each forming a pretty clearly outlined geographical whole, like the peninsula of Laconia or that of Attica (see map, p. 90), permitted the union of city-states into a larger nation. The oldest of these was formed in the plain of Argos (map, p. 90). Here the towns of Argos gradually absorbed the ancient strongholds of Mycenæ and Tiryns (Figs. 31 and 32) and others in the vicinity, forming the nation of Argos and giving its name to the plain (plate, p. 84). In the same way the kings of Sparta conquered the two peninsulas on the south of them and finally also the land of the Messenians on the west. The two kingdoms of Argos and Sparta thus held a large part of the Peloponnesus.

In the Attic peninsula, likewise, the little city-kingdoms were slowly absorbed by Athens, which at last gained control of the entire peninsula. On the northern borders of Attica the region of Bœotia fell under the leadership of Thebes, but the other Bœotian cities were too strong to be wholly subdued. Elsewhere no large and permanent unions were formed. Sparta and Athens led the two most important unions among all the Greeks. Let it be borne in mind that such a nation remained a city-state in spite of its increased territory. The nation occupying the Attic peninsula was called Athens, and every peasant in Attica was called an Athenian. The city government of Athens covered the whole Attic peninsula.

149. The Greek State and the Struggle toward Democracy. In the matter of governing such a little city-state the Greeks entered upon a new stage of their development about 750 B.C., as the common people began the struggle to better their lot. As we shall see, this long and bitter struggle finally resulted in giving the people in some Greek states so large a share in governing that the form of the government might be called *democracy*. This is a word of Greek origin, meaning "the rule of the people," and the Greeks were the first people of the ancient world to gain it.

The cause of this struggle was not only the corrupt rule of the kings but also the oppression of the wealthy *nobles*. We have watched these men of wealth buying the luxuries of the Phœnician merchants (§ 139). By fraud, unjust seizure of lands, union of families in marriage, and many other influences, the strong men of ability and cleverness were able to enlarge their lands. Thus there had arisen a class of nobles whom we call

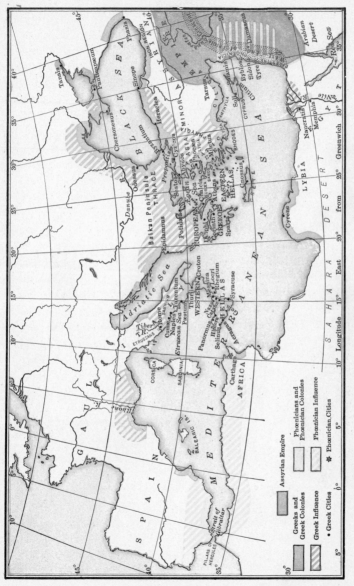

COLONIAL EXPANSION OF THE GREEKS AND PHŒNICIANS DOWN TO THE SIXTH CENTURY B.C.

hereditary, because they inherited their wealth and rank. These large landholders and men of wealth were also called *eupatrids*.

Their fields stretched for some miles around the city and its neighboring villages. In order to be near the king or secure membership in the Council (§§ 135, 137) and thus control the government, these men often left their lands and lived in the city. Such was the power of the eupatrids that the Council finally consisted only of men of this class. Wealthy enough to buy costly weapons, with leisure for continual exercise in the use of arms, these nobles had also become the chief protection of the State in time of war (§ 141).

150. Misery and Weakness of the Peasants. Thus grew up a sharp distinction between the city community and the peasants living in the country. The country peasant was obliged to divide the family lands with his brothers. His fields were therefore small, and he was poor. He went about clad in a goatskin, and his labors never ceased. Hence he had no leisure to learn the use of arms, nor any way to meet the expense of purchasing them. He and his neighbors were therefore of small account in war (§ 141). Indeed, he was fortunate if he could struggle on and maintain himself and family from his scanty fields. Many of his neighbors sank into debt, lost their lands to the noble class, and themselves became day laborers for more fortunate men, or, still worse, they sold themselves to pay their debts and thus became slaves. These day laborers and slaves had no political rights and were not permitted to vote in the Assembly.

Intimidated by the powerful nobles, the meager Assembly, which had once included all the weapon-bearing men of the tribe (§ 135), became a feeble gathering of a few peasants and lesser townsmen with little political power. The peasant therefore was less and less inclined to attend the Assembly at all.

151. Triumph of the Nobles ; Fall of the Kings (750–650 B.C.). By 750 B.C. the office of the king had in some states become merely a name. While the king was in some cases violently overthrown, in most states the nobles established from among themselves certain *elective officers* to take charge of matters formerly controlled by the king.

Thus in Athens they appointed a noble to be leader in war, while another noble was chosen as *archon*, or ruler, to assist the king in attending to the increasing business of the State. The Athenian king was thus gradually but peacefully deprived of his powers. In Sparta the power of the king was checked by the appointment of a second king, and on this plan Sparta continued to retain her kings. Elsewhere in the century between 750 and 650 B.C. the kingship quite generally disappeared. The result of the political and social struggle was thus the triumph of the nobles, who were henceforth in control in many states.

II. Greek Expansion in the Age of the Nobles

152. Rise of Commerce and Shipbuilding among the Greeks. The Age of the Nobles witnessed another great change in Greek life. The Greek merchants gradually took up sea trade. Among the Asiatic Greeks it was the Ionian cities which led in this commerce. The Ægean waters gradually grew familiar to the Greek communities, until the sea routes became far easier lines of communication than the country roads.

153. Greek Colonies. At this point the poverty of the peasants (§ 150) became an important influence, leading the Greek farmers to seek new homes and new lands beyond the Ægean world. Greek merchants were not only trafficking with the northern Ægean but their vessels had penetrated the great northern sea, which they called the "Pontus," known to us as the Black Sea (see map, p. 100). Before 600 B.C. they girdled the Black Sea with their towns and settlements, reaching the broad grainfields along the lower Danube and the iron mines of the old Hittite country (§ 128 and map, p. 42).

In the East, along the southern coasts of Asia Minor, Greek expansion was stopped by the Assyrian Sennacherib (§ 77). In the South they met a friendly reception in Egypt. Here they founded a trading station in the Delta and colonized Cyrene (map, p. 100).

It was the unknown West, however, which became the America of the early Greek colonists. Looking westward from the western coast of Greece the seamen could discover the shores of the heel of Italy, only fifty miles distant. When they had once crossed to it, they coasted around Sicily and far into the West. Here was a new world. Although the Phœnicians were already there (§ 139), its discovery was as momentous for the Greeks as that of America for later Europe (see map, p. 100).

By 750 B.C. their colonies appeared in this new Western world, and within a century they fringed southern Italy from the heel to a point well above the instep, north of Naples. Hence this region of southern Italy came to be known as "Great Greece" (see map, p. 192). As the Greeks were by this time superior in civilization to all the native dwellers in Italy, *the civilized history of that great peninsula begins with the settlement of the Greeks there.* They were the first to bring into Italy such things as writing, literature, architecture, and art (§§ 298–301 and head-piece, p. 189).

The Greek colonists also crossed over to fertile Sicily (plate, p. 106), where they drove out the Phœnician trading posts except at the western end of the island. Syracuse, at its southeast, became very soon the most cultivated, as well as the most powerful, city of the Greek world. At Massilia (Marseilles), on the coast of later France, the Western Greeks founded a town which controlled the trade up the Rhone valley. Thus, under the rule of the nobles, the Greeks expanded till their settlements stretched from the Black Sea along the north shore of the Mediterranean almost to the Atlantic.

III. GREEK CIVILIZATION IN THE AGE OF THE NOBLES

154. Influences leading toward Greek Unity. We have already noticed the tendencies which kept the Greek states apart (§ 147). There were now, on the other hand, influences which tended toward unity. Among such influences were the Greek contests in arms and their athletic games. There finally came to be held at stated seasons in honor of the gods. As early as 776 B.C. such contests were celebrated as public festivals at Olympia.[1] Repeated every four years, they finally aroused the interest and participation of all Greece.

Religion also became a strong influence toward unity, because there were some gods at whose temples *all* the Greeks worshiped. The different city-states therefore formed several religious councils, made up of representatives from the various Greek cities concerned. They came together at stated periods, and in this way each city had a voice in such joint management of the temples. These councils were perhaps the nearest approach to representative government ever devised in the ancient world. The most notable of them were the council for the control of the Olympic games, another for the famous sanctuary of Apollo at Delphi (Fig. 38), and also the council for the great annual feast of Apollo in the island of Delos.

These representatives spoke various Greek dialects at their meetings. They could understand each other, however, and their common language helped to bind together the people of the many different Greek cities. A sentiment of unity also arose under the influence of the Homeric songs (§ 143) with which every Greek was familiar—a common inheritance depicting all the Greeks united against the Asiatic city of Troy.

155. Barbarians and Hellenes. Thus bound together by ties of custom, religion, language, and common traditions, the Greeks gained a feeling of race unity, which set them apart from other races. They called all men not of Greek blood "barbarians," but this was not originally a term of reproach for the non-Greeks. Then the Greek sense of unity found expression in the first all-inclusive term for *themselves*. They gradually came to call themselves "Hellenes" and found pleasure in the belief that they had all descended from a common ancestor called Hellen. Connected with this word is also the name "Hellas," often applied to Greece. But it should be clearly understood that this new designation did

[1] Every schoolboy knows that these Olympic games have been revived in modern times as an international project.

not represent a Greek *nation* or state, but only the *group* of Greek-speaking peoples or states, often at war with one another. The most fatal defect in Greek character was the inability of the various states to forget their local differences and jealousies and to unite in a common federation or great nation including all Greeks.[1]

156. Architecture and Sculpture. In spite of oriental luxuries, like gaudy clothing and rich tableware (§ 139), Greek life in the Age of the Nobles was still rude and simple. The Greek cities of which we have been talking were groups of dingy sun-dried-brick houses, with narrow wandering streets which we should call alleys. On the height where the palace or castle of the king had once stood was an oblong building of brick, like the houses of the town below. In front it had a porch with a row of wooden posts, and it was covered by a "peaked" roof with a triangular gable at each end. This rude building was the earliest Greek temple. As for sculpture in this age, the figure of a god consisted merely of a wooden post with a rough-hewn head at the top. When draped with a garment it could be made to serve its purpose.

157. Rise of a New Literature. While there were still very few who could read, there was here and there a man who owned and read a written copy of Homer. The Greeks were beginning to think about human conduct. The old Greek word for *virtue* no longer meant merely valor in war but also kindly and unselfish conduct toward others. Duty toward a man's own country was now beginning to be felt in the sentiment we call patriotism. Right conduct, as it seemed to some, was even required by the gods.

Under these circumstances it was natural that a new literature should arise, as the Greeks began to discuss *themselves* and *their own* conduct. The old Homeric singers never referred to themselves; they never spoke of their *own* lives. They were absorbed in describing the valiant deeds of their heroes who had died long before. Meanwhile the problems of their own *present* began to

[1] We may recall here how slow were the thirteen colonies of America to suppress local pride sufficiently to adopt a constitution uniting all thirteen into a nation. It was local differences similar to those among the Greeks which afterward caused our Civil War.

press hard upon the minds of men ; the peasant farmer's distressing struggle for existence (see § 150) made men conscious of very present needs. Their *own* lives became a great and living theme.

158. Hesiod and the Earliest Cry for Social Justice in Europe (750-700 B.C.). The voices that once chanted the hero songs therefore died away, and now men heard the first voice raised in Europe on behalf of the poor and the humble. Hesiod, an obscure farmer, sang of the dreary and hopeless life of the peasant — of his *own* life as he struggled on under a burden too heavy for his shoulders. We even hear how his brother Persis seized the lands left by their father and then bribed the judges to confirm him in their possession.

This was the earliest European protest against the injustices committed by the rich in wealthy town life. It was raised at the very moment when across the corner of the Mediterranean the once nomad Hebrews were passing through the same experience (see §§ 106-107). The voice of Hesiod raising the cry for social justice in Greece sounds like an echo from Palestine. But we should notice that in Palestine the cry for social justice finally resulted not in altered government but in a *religion* of brotherly kindness ; whereas in Greece it resulted in altered government, in democratic *institutions,* — the rule of the people who refused longer to submit to the oppressions of the few and powerful. In the next chapter we shall watch the progress of the struggle by which the rule of the people came about.

159. Summary of the Age of the Nobles. *At home* the outstanding change in this age was the appearance of a noble class, produced largely by the incoming of landownership, with the result that the kings were overthrown and largely disappeared. In the eighth century B.C. a struggle between the nobles and the common people also began. At the same time the little Greek states showed no ability to suppress their differences and unite into a nation of all the Greeks. *Abroad* the Greeks of this age took to the sea and established colonies and new states along the entire northern coast of the Mediterranean from Asia Minor to the coast of later France (750-600 B.C.).

From a painting by C. Scott White

THE GREEK THEATER AT TAORMINA, WITH ITS ROMAN ADDITIONS

The Greek colony of Tauromenium (modern Taormina) was on the east coast of Sicily. We here look down from the seats of the theater, across the stage below, where a gap in the Roman colonnade behind the stage reveals a long vista of the beautiful Sicilian shore; while in the distance towers the majestic volcano of Etna (nearly 11,000 feet high), often displaying a wisp of smoke above its crown of snow

QUESTIONS

I. What geographical influences tended to prevent a union of all the Greeks? What leading unions did take place? Describe their situation. What is democracy? Discuss the power of the Greek nobles. What was the situation of the peasants financially? politically? What happened to the Greek kings?

II. Discuss the rise of Greek sea trade. Trace the spread of Greek colonies. What can you say of this movement as a racial matter? What racial contest arose?

III. Mention the several influences leading toward Greek unity. What names arose for Greeks and non-Greeks? Discuss the architecture and sculpture of this age; its literature, especially Hesiod. What resulted from the discontent of the poor?

NOTE. The buildings below are two Greek temples still standing at Pæstum (Greek, *Poseidonia*), one of the early Greek colonies in Italy in the vicinity of Naples. The temple of Neptune (Poseidon), the finest of the group, is the best-preserved Greek temple outside of Attica. It was built in the Age of the Tyrants, not long before 500 B.C., and is one of the noblest examples of archaic Greek architecture (§ 175).

CHAPTER VII

THE INDUSTRIAL REVOLUTION AND THE AGE OF
THE TYRANTS

I. THE INDUSTRIAL AND COMMERCIAL REVOLUTION

160. Growth of Greek Commerce and Industry. The remarkable spread of the Greek colonies, together with the growth of industries in the home cities, led to profound changes. The new colonies not only had needs of their own but they also had dealings with the inland, which finally opened up extensive regions of Europe as a market for Greek wares. The home cities at once began to meet this demand for goods of all sorts. The Ionian cities at first led the way as formerly. Then the islands also, and finally the Greek mainland, especially Corinth and Athens, began to share in the growing Greek trade. Ere long the commercial fleets of Hellas were threading their way along all the coasts of the northern, western, and southeastern Mediterranean, bearing to distant communities Greek metal work, woven goods, and pottery.

They brought back either raw materials and foodstuffs, such as grain, fish, and amber, or finished products like the magnificent utensils in bronze from the cities of the Etruscans in northern Italy (§ 298 and Fig. 53). At the yearly feast and market on the island of Delos the Greek householder found the Etruscan bronzes of the West side by side with the gay carpets of the Orient.

To meet the increasing demands of trade the Greek craftsman was obliged to enlarge his small shop, once perhaps only large enough to supply the wants of a single estate. Unable to find the necessary workmen, the proprietor who had the means bought slaves and trained them to the work. He thus enlarged his little stall into a factory with a score of hands. Henceforth industrial *slave labor* became an important part of Greek life.

161. Expansion of Athenian Commerce. When Athens entered the field of industry she won victories not less decisive than her later triumphs in art, literature, philosophy, or war. Her factories must have grown to a size before quite unknown in the Greek world, until they filled a large quarter at Athens (see plan, p. 138). Their output is found in distant regions even to-day ; for the ancient peoples bought the beautiful Athenian vases to put in the tombs of their dead. There they are still found. It is very impressive to see the modern excavator opening tombs far toward the interior of Asia Minor and taking out vases bearing the signature of the same **Athenian painter of vases** whose name you may also read on vases dug out of the Nile Delta in northern Africa or taken from tombs in cemeteries of the Etruscan cities of Italy (Fig. 35).

FIG. 35. AN ATHENIAN PAINTED VASE OF THE EARLY SIXTH CENTURY B.C.

This magnificent work (over thirty inches high) was found in an Etruscan tomb in Italy (see map, p. 192), whither it had been exported (§ 161) by the Athenian makers in the days of Solon

162. Improvement and Enlargement of Ships. Soon the Greek shipbuilder, responding to the growing commerce, began to build craft far larger than the old "fifty-oar" galleys. The new "merchantmen" were driven by sails, an Egyptian invention of ages before. They were so large that they could no longer easily be drawn up on the strand as before. Hence sheltered harbors were necessary.

The protection of these merchant ships demanded more effective warships, and the distinction gradually arose between a "man-o'-war," or battleship, and a "merchantman." Corinth is credited with producing the first decked warships, a great improvement, which gave the warriors above more room and better footing and protected the oarsmen below. For warships must be independent of the wind, and hence they were still driven by oars. The oarsmen were now arranged in three rows, and the power of an old "fifty-oar" thus multiplied by three without essentially increasing the ship's size. Battleships having the oars in three rows were called "triremes." These innovations were in common use by 500 B.C.

FIG. 36. SPECIMENS ILLUSTRATING THE BEGINNING OF COINAGE

163. Adoption of Coinage by the Greeks (Early Seventh Century B.C.).

Meantime Greek business life had entered upon a new epoch, due to the introduction of coined money. Not long after 700 B.C. the kings of Lydia in Asia Minor, following oriental custom (§ 70), began to cut up silver into lumps of a fixed weight. These they stamped with some symbol of the king or State to show that the State guaranteed their value, and such pieces formed the earliest-known coins (Fig. 36).

This great convenience was quickly adopted by the Greeks. Thus the Athenians began to use as their commonest coin a lump of silver weighing the hundredth part of a Babylonian *mina* (our pound). It was worth from eighteen to twenty cents. It still survives in large sections of Europe as the French *franc*. The

Athenians called this coin a *drachma*. The purchasing power of a drachma was in such ancient times very much greater than in our day. For example, a sheep cost one drachma, an ox five drachma, and a landowner with an income of five hundred drachmas ($100) a year was considered a wealthy man.

164. Rise of a Capitalistic Class. Greek wealth had formerly consisted of lands and flocks, but now men began to accumulate capital in *money*. Loans were made, and the use of interest came in from the Orient. The usual rate was 18 per cent yearly. Men who could never have hoped for wealth as farmers were now growing rich. There arose a prosperous industrial and commercial *middle class* which demanded a voice in the government. They soon became a political power of much influence, and the noble class were obliged to listen to them. At the beginning of the sixth century B.C. even a noble like Solon could say, "Money makes the man" (§ 168).

II. Rise of the Democracy and the Age of the Tyrants

165. Increased Power of the People. While a prosperous "capitalistic" class was thus arising, the condition of the peasant on his lands grew steadily worse. But other enemies now opposed the noble class. In the first place, the new men of fortune (§ 164) were bitterly hostile to the nobles; in the second place, the improvement in Greek industries had so cheapened all work in metal that it was possible for the ordinary man to purchase weapons and a suit of armor. This added to the importance of the ordinary citizen in the army and therefore greatly increased the power of the lower classes in the State.

166. Disunion among Nobles and Rise of Tyrants. At the same time the nobles were far from united. Serious feuds between the various noble families often divided them into hostile factions. The leader of a faction among the nobles often placed himself at the head of the dissatisfied people in real or feigned sympathy with their cause. Thus supported, he was able to

overcome and expel his rivals among the noble class and to gain
undisputed control of the State. In this way he became the ruler
of the State.

Such a ruler was in reality a king; but the new king differed
from the kings of old in that he had no royal ancestors and had
seized the control of the State by violence. The people did not
reverence him as of ancient royal lineage. His position always
remained insecure. The Greeks called such a man a "tyrant,"
which was not at that time a term of reproach as it is with us.
Nevertheless, the instinctive feeling of the Greeks was that they
were no longer free under a prince of this kind, and the slayer of
a "tyrant" was regarded as a hero and savior of the people. In
spite of public opinion about the tyrants, they were the first
champions of democracy. Many of them looked after the rights
of the people and gave much attention to public monuments, art,
music, and literature. By 650 B.C. such rulers had begun to
appear, but it was especially the sixth century (from 600 to
500 B.C.) which we may call the Age of the Tyrants.

167. Earliest Written Greek Codes of Law. Hitherto all
law, so long ago reduced to writing in the Orient (Fig. 24), had
been a matter of oral tradition in Greece. It was very easy for
a judge to twist oral law to favor the man who gave him the
largest present (§ 158). The people were now demanding that
the inherited oral laws be put into writing (see *Ancient Times,*
Fig. 166). After a long struggle the Athenians secured such a
written code, arranged by a man named Draco, about 624 B.C.
It was an exceedingly severe code — so severe, in fact, that the
adjective "Draconic" has passed into our language as a synonym
for "harsh."

168. Solon's Reforms. But writing down the law did not
meet all needs nor quiet unrest in Athens, and in 594 B.C. a noble
named Solon was chosen as archon (§ 151). He was given full
power to improve the evil condition of the peasants. He declared
void all mortgages on land and all claims of creditors which endangered the liberty of a citizen, and he set a limit to the amount
of land which a noble might hold.

Solon also made a law that anyone who, like Hesiod (§ 158), had lost a lawsuit could appeal the case to a jury of citizens over thirty years of age selected by lot. This change and some others greatly improved a citizen's chance of securing justice. Solon's laws were all written, and they formed the first Greek code of laws by which all free men were given equal rights in the courts. Some of these laws have descended to our own time and are still in force.

Furthermore, Solon proclaimed a new constitution which gave to all a voice in the control of the State. It made but few changes. It recognized four classes of citizens, graded according to the amount of their income. The wealthy nobles were the only ones who could hold the highest offices, and the peasants were permitted to hold only the lower offices. The government thus remained in the hands of the nobles, but the humblest free citizen could now be assured of the right to vote in the assembly of the people.

Solon was the earliest great Greek statesman about whom we have reliable information. The leading trait of his character was moderation, combined with unfailing decision. When all expected that he would make himself " tyrant " he laid down his expiring archonship without a moment's hesitation and left Athens for several years, to give his constitution a fair chance to work.

169. Pisistratus, Tyrant of Athens (540-528 B.C.), **and his Sons.** Nevertheless, Pisistratus, a member of one of the powerful noble families, finally gained control of the Athenian State as tyrant. He ruled with great sagacity and success, and many of the Athenians gave him sincere support. Athenian manufactures and commerce flourished as never before, and when Pisistratus died (in the same year as Cyrus the Persian, 528 B.C.) he had laid a foundation to which much of the later greatness of Athens was due.

170. Fall of the Sons of Pisistratus. In spite of their great ability, the sons of Pisistratus, Hipparchus and Hippias, were unable to overcome the prejudice of the Athenians against a ruler on whom the people had not conferred authority. One of the earliest exhibitions of Greek patriotism is the outburst of enthusiasm at Athens when two youths, Harmodius and Aristogiton (Fig. 37), at the sacrifice of their own lives, struck down one of the tyrants (Hipparchus). Hippias, the other one, was eventually obliged to flee. Thus, shortly before 500 B.C., Athens was freed from her tyrants.

171. The Reforms of Clisthenes. The people were now able to gain new power against the nobles by the efforts of Clisthenes, a noble friendly to the lower classes. He broke up the old tribal divisions on the basis of blood relationship and established purely *local* lines of division. He thus cut up the old noble clans and assigned the fragments to different local divisions, where the nobles would be in the minority. This prevented them from acting together and broke their power.

In order to avoid the rise of a new tyrant, Clisthenes established a law that once a year the people might by vote declare any prominent citizen dangerous to the State and banish him for ten years. To cast his vote against a man, a citizen had only to pick up one of the pieces of broken pottery lying about the market place, write upon it the name of the citizen to be banished, and deposit it in the voting urn. Such a bit of pottery was called an "ostracon" (tailpiece, p. 120), and to "ostracize" a man (literally to "potsherd" him) meant to banish him. By these and other means Athens had (about 500 B.C.) gained a form of government giving the people a high degree of power.

172. Expansion of Sparta. Meantime Sparta also had greatly increased in power. Long before 500 B.C. the Spartans had forced the neighboring states into a combination, called the "Spartan League," which included nearly the whole of the Peloponnese. As the leader of this league Sparta was the most powerful state in Greece. It had no industries, and it therefore did not possess the prosperous commercial class which had elsewhere done so much to overthrow the nobles and bring about the rise of the tyrants. Sparta was also opposed to the rule of the people and looked with a jealous eye on the rising democracy of Athens.

III. Civilization in the Age of the Tyrants

173. The Nobles as the Social Leaders. In spite of the growing power of the people the nobles continued to be the leaders, especially in all those matters which we call social. They created the social life of the time, and they were the prominent figures on all public occasions. The multitudes which thronged to the public games looked down upon the best-born youths of Greece contesting for the prizes in the athletic matches (§ 154), and the wealthier nobles put the swiftest horses into the chariot races.

Although noble youths might be found spending the larger part of the day practicing in the public inclosure devoted to athletic exercises, yet they usually also learned to write. It was in the Age of the Tyrants that the music of Greece rose to the level of a real art. A system of writing musical notes, meaning for music what the alphabet meant for literature, now arose (Fig. 44, *B*). The flute and the lyre were the favorite instruments, either of which might be played as the accompaniment of song, or both together, with choruses of boys and girls.

174. Literature, Music, and the Drama. Music had a great influence on the literature of the age, for the poets now began to write verses to be sung to the music of the lyre. Therefore such verses are called "lyric" poetry. The poets now put into songs their momentary moods, longings, dreams, hopes, and fiery storms of passion. Each in his way found a wondrous world within *himself*, which he thus pictured in short songs. Probably the greatest of these poets was Pindar of Thebes (see *Ancient Times*, § 482). Another great lyric singer of the age was the poetess Sappho, the earliest woman to gain undying fame in literature.

Another favorite form of song was the "chorus," with which the country folk loved to celebrate their rustic feasts. The singers as they marched in rustic procession wore goatskins, and their faces were concealed by masks. Some of the songs were sung responsively by the chorus and their leader. For the diversion of the listening peasants the leader would illustrate with gestures the story told in the song. He thus became to some extent an actor, the forerunner of the actors on our own stage. When a second leader was introduced, dialogue between the two was possible, though the chorus continued to recite most of the narrative. Thus arose a form of musical play, or drama, the action and narrative of which were carried on by the chorus and two actors. The Greeks called such a play a tragedy, which means "goat's

Fig. 37. Monument of the Tyrant Slayers of Athens, Harmo- dius and Aristogiton

On the slopes of the Areopagus (see plan, p. 138, and Fig. 43), overlooking the market place, the Athenians set up this group, depicting at the moment of attack the two heroic youths who lost their lives in an attempt to slay the two sons of Pisistratus and to free Athens from the two tyrants (514 B.C., § 170). Our illustration is an ancient copy in marble, the lost original having been made of bronze

play," perhaps because of the rustic disguise as goats which the chorus had always worn. These out-of-door feasts furnished the beginnings of the Greek theater (see Fig. 46).

175. Architecture. The tyrants were so devoted to building that architecture made very important advances. The older rough Greek temples of sun-dried brick (§ 156) were rebuilt in limestone by the tyrants. At no other time before or since were so many temples erected as in the Greek world in the Age of the Tyrants. In Sicily and southern Italy a number of the noble temples of

Doric Columns

this age still stand, to display to us the beauty and simplicity of Greek architecture when it was still at an undeveloped stage (tailpiece, p. 107). Instead of the *wooden* posts of the Age of the Nobles (§ 156), these temples were surrounded by lines of *stone* columns (colonnades) in a style called *Doric* (see Fig. 44, *A* and *B*). The idea of these columns was derived from Egypt (see *Ancient Times*, Fig. 167). Like those on the Nile, these Greek temples were also painted in bright colors.

176. Sculpture and Painting. Sculpture also made great progress. Moved by patriotic impulses the Athenian sculptors now wrought a wonderful monument for the market place of Athens. It was a memorial group of two bronze statues (Fig. 37), representing the two heroic youths who endeavored to free Athens from the sons of Pisistratus (§ 170). The work showed remarkable progress in ability to represent the human body in free and vigorous action. Similar progress was made by the painters of the age. Their painted vases are a wonderful treasury of beautiful scenes from Greek life (tailpiece, p. 149).

177. Growing Sense of Right and Wrong. Literature and painting show us that the Greeks of this age were intensely interested in the life of their own time. In the first place, they were thinking more deeply than ever before about conduct, and they were better able to distinguish between right and wrong. Men now felt that even Zeus and his Olympian divinities must do the right. Mortals too must do the same, for men had now come to believe that in the world of the dead there was punishment for the evildoer.

Likewise it was believed that there must be a place of blessedness for the good in the next world. Accordingly, in the temple at Eleusis scenes from the mysterious earth life of Demeter and Dionysus, to whom men owed the fruits of the earth, were presented by the priests in dramatic form before the initiated. Anyone who viewed these "mysteries," as they were called, received immortal life and might be admitted into the Islands of the Blessed.

178. Thales and the Prediction of a Solar Eclipse (585 B.C.). On the other hand, some thoughtful men were rejecting many old beliefs, especially regarding the world and its control by the gods. At Miletus, the leader of the Ionian cities, there was an able statesman named Thales, who had traveled widely and received from Babylonia a list of observations of the heavenly bodies. With these lists in his hands Thales could calculate when the next eclipse would occur. He therefore told the people of Miletus that they might expect an eclipse of the sun before the end of a certain year. When the promised eclipse (585 B.C.) actually occurred as he had predicted, the fame of Thales spread far and wide.

The prediction of an eclipse, a feat already accomplished by the Babylonians (§ 87), was not so important as the *consequences* which followed in the mind of Thales. Hitherto men had believed that eclipses and all the other strange things that happened in the skies were caused by the momentary angry whim of some god. Now, however, Thales boldly proclaimed that the movements of the heavenly bodies were in accordance with *fixed laws*. Other Ionian Greeks like Thales, especially Pythagoras, studied mathematics and the physics of musical tones. They wrote the first geographies, and one of them discovered that the earth is a sphere. They therefore became the forerunners of natural scientists and philosophers. They had entered what was for them a new world,—the world of science and philosophy, a world which the greatest minds of the early Orient had not discovered. This step, taken by Thales and the great men of the Ionian cities, remains and will forever remain the greatest achievement of the human intellect.

179. Summary and End of the Age of the Tyrants. The Age of the Tyrants was therefore one of the great epochs of the world's history, when the Greeks overtook and passed the Orient in civilization.[1] It saw the rise of manufactures among the Greeks, the spread of their commerce, the introduction of coinage, and the resulting appearance of wealthy business men. A new middle class, thus created, aided in overturning the nobles, and the world's

---

[1] A fuller account of the remarkable civilization of this age will be found in *Ancient Times*, §§ 479–496.

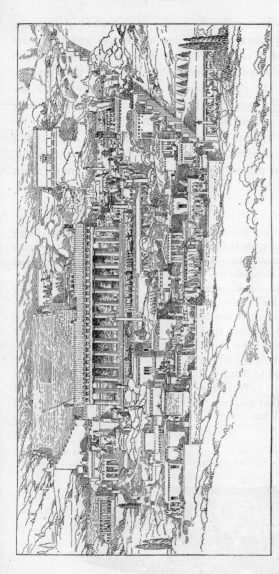

FIG. 38. THE BUILDINGS OF DELPHI RESTORED. (AFTER HOMOLLE-TOURNAIRE)

Beginning with the seventh century B.C. this place became a national sanctuary of the Greeks, where all Greece and many foreigners came to hear the oracles of the revered Apollo (§ 144). His temple, many times rebuilt, was a Doric structure, the largest colonnaded building which we see rising in the middle of the inclosure. A zigzag way passed up from the lower right-hand corner of this inclosure, and on each side of this way were ranged the treasuries containing the votive offerings of the Greeks to the great god — the statues and victorious trophies, many of them of gold and silver, presented by states, kings, and individuals

earliest democracies began. As a group the leaders of this age, many of them tyrants, made lasting impression, and they were called "the Seven Wise Men." They were the earliest statesmen and thinkers of Greece. The people loved to quote their sayings, such as "Know thyself," a proverb which was carved over the door of the Apollo temple at Delphi (Fig. 38) ; or Solon's wise maxim "Overdo nothing." After the fall of the sons of Pisistratus, however, the tyrants were disappearing, and although a tyrant here and there survived, especially in Asia Minor and Sicily, Greece thereupon passed out of the Age of the Tyrants (about 500 B.C.).

QUESTIONS

I. How did the new colonies of the Greeks influence manufacturing at home ? What can you tell of commerce and manufactures ? Discuss the effect upon shipbuilding. How did coinage arise ? How did it affect business and the accumulation of wealth ? What new class arose ?

II. How did the Greek farmer now fare as to wealth ? in military and political power ? How did the Greeks regard tyrants ? What law code was made at Athens ? What did Solon accomplish ? What did Pisistratus and his sons do ? How did Clisthenes aid the people ?

III. Describe the social position of the nobles. What can you say of education in this age ? Who were the leading lyric poets ? How did festal choruses lead to drama ? In what style of architecture were the temples now erected ? What progress does the monument of the tyrant slayers show ? What progress was made in ideas of conduct ? What did Thales do ? What can you say of the Age of the Tyrants as a whole ?

NOTE. This tailpiece shows the name of Themistocles scratched on a fragment of pottery (*ostracon*, § 171) by some citizen probably in 472 B.C.

CHAPTER VIII

THE REPULSE OF PERSIA AND THE RISE OF THE ATHENIAN EMPIRE

I. THE COMING OF THE PERSIANS

180. The Persian Advance to the Ægean (546 B.C.). In order to understand the coming chapters in the story of Greece we must now recall that in the middle of the Age of the Tyrants Cyrus the Persian marched westward to the Ægean (§ 97). The vast Persian Empire which he founded thus became a close neighbor of the Greeks directly on their east in Asia Minor. In the midst of their remarkable progress in civilization (§§ 173–179), the Ionian Greek cities of Asia Minor suddenly lost their liberty and actually became subjects of Persia.

As we have already learned, the Persians represented a high civilization and an enlightened rule ; but Persian supremacy in Greece would nevertheless have seriously checked the advance of the Greeks in civilization. There seemed little prospect that the tiny Greek states, even if they united, could successfully resist the vast oriental empire, controlling as it did all the countries of the ancient East, which we have been studying. Nevertheless the Ionian cities revolted against their Persian lords.

181. First Persian Invasion of Europe. During the struggle with Persia which followed this revolt the Athenians sent twenty ships to aid their Ionian kindred. This act brought a Persian army of revenge, under Darius, into Europe. The long march of the Persians across the Hellespont and through Thrace cost them many men, and the fleet which accompanied the Persian advance was wrecked in trying to round the high promontory of Mount Athos (492 B.C.). This advance into Greece was therefore abandoned for a plan of invasion by water across the Ægean.

182. Second Persian Invasion. In the early summer of 490 B.C. a considerable fleet of transports and warships bearing the Persian host put out from the island of Samos, sailed straight across the Ægean, and entered the straits between Eubœa and Attica (see map, p. 90). The Persians finally landed on the shores of Attica, in the Bay of Marathon (see map, p. 138), intending to march on Athens.

All was excitement and confusion among the Greek states. The defeat of the revolting Ionian cities, and especially the Persian sack of Miletus, had made a deep impression throughout Greece. Now this Persian foe who had crushed the Ionian cities was camping behind the hills only a few miles northeast of Athens. After dispatching messengers in desperate haste to seek aid in Sparta the Athenian citizens turned to contemplate the seemingly hopeless situation of their beloved city.

183. The Armies and Greek Leadership. Thinking to find the Athenians unprepared, Darius had not sent a large army. The Persian forces probably numbered no more than twenty thousand men, but at the utmost the Athenians could not put more than half this number into the field. Fortunately for them there was among their generals a skilled commander named Miltiades. As the citizen-soldiers of Attica flocked to the city at the call to arms, Miltiades was able to induce the leaders not to await the assault of the Persians at Athens but to march across the peninsula (see map, p. 138) and block the Persian advance among the hills overlooking the eastern coast and commanding the road to the city. This bold and resolute move roused courage and enthusiasm in the downcast ranks of the Greeks.

Nevertheless, when they issued between the hills and looked down upon the Persian host encamped upon the Plain of Marathon, flanked by a fleet of hundreds of vessels, misgiving and despair chilled the hearts of the little Attic army. But Miltiades held the leaders firmly in hand, and the arrival of a thousand Greeks from Platæa revived the courage of the Athenians.

184. The Battle of Marathon (490 B.C.). Unable to lure the Greeks from their advantageous position, the Persians, after several days' waiting, at length attempted to march along the road to Athens. Miltiades was familiar with the Persian custom of massing troops in the center. He therefore massed his own troops on both wings, leaving his center weak. It was a battle between bow and spear. The Athenians undauntedly faced the storm of Persian arrows (see § 97), and then both wings pushed boldly

FIG. 39. MOUND RAISED AS A MONUMENT TO THE FALLEN GREEKS AT MARATHON

The mound is nearly fifty feet high. Excavations undertaken in 1890 disclosed beneath it the bodies of the one hundred and ninety-two Athenian citizens who fell in the battle (§ 184). Some of their weapons and the funeral vases buried with them were also recovered and are now in the National Museum at Athens

forward to the line of shields behind which the Persian archers were kneeling. In the meantime the Persian center, finding the Greek center weak, had pushed it back, while the two Greek wings closed in on either side and thrust back the Persian wings in confusion. The Asiatic army crumbled into a broken multitude between the two advancing lines of the Greek wings. The Persian bow was useless, and the Greek spear everywhere spread death and terror. As the Persians fled to their ships they left over six thousand dead upon the field, while the Athenians lost less than two hundred men (Fig. 39). When the Persian commander sailed around the Attic peninsula and appeared with his fleet before the port of Athens, he found it unwise to attempt a landing, for the victorious Athenian army was already encamped beside the city.

II. The Greek Repulse of Persians and Phœnicians

185. Rise of Themistocles. Among the men who stood in the Athenian ranks at Marathon was Themistocles, the ablest statesman in Greece, a man who had already occupied the office of archon, the head of the Athenian state. He was convinced of the necessity of building up a strong navy, and as archon he had therefore striven to show the Athenians that the only way in which Athens could hope to meet the assault of Persia was by making herself undisputed mistress of the sea. He had failed in his effort. But now the Athenians had seen the Persians cross the Ægean with their fleet and land at Marathon. It was evident that a powerful Athenian navy might have stopped them. The Athenians therefore began to listen to the counsels of Themistocles to make Athens the great sea power of the Mediterranean.

186. Accession of Xerxes; Leadership and Plans of Themistocles. Darius the Great, whose remarkable reign we have studied (§§ 100–101), died without having avenged the defeat of his army at Marathon. His son and successor, Xerxes, therefore took up the unfinished task. The Greeks made ready to meet the new Persian assault. They soon saw that Xerxes' commanders were cutting a canal behind the promontory of Athos, to secure a short cut and thus to avoid all risk of such a wreck as had overtaken their former fleet in rounding this dangerous point. When the news of this operation reached Athens Themistocles was at last able to induce the Athenian Assembly to build a great fleet of probably a hundred and eighty triremes (§ 162). The Greeks were then able for the first time to meet the Persian advance by both sea and land.

Themistocles' masterly plan of campaign corresponded exactly to the plan of the Persian advance. The Asiatics were coming in combined land and sea array, with army and fleet moving near together down the east coast of the Greek mainland. The design of Themistocles was to meet the Persian fleet *first*, with full force, and fight a decisive naval battle as soon as possible. If victorious the Greek fleet commanding the Ægean would then be able to sail up the eastern coast of Greece and threaten the communications and supplies of the Persian army. There must be no attempt of the small Greek army to meet the vast land forces of the Persians, beyond delaying them as long as possible at the narrow northern passes, which could be defended with a few men. An effort to unite *all* the Greek states against the Persian invasion was not successful. Indeed, Themistocles was able to induce the Spartans to unite with Athens and to accept his plan only on condition that Sparta be given command of the allied Greek fleets.

187. Battles of Thermopylæ and Artemisium. In the summer of 480 B.C. the Asiatic army was approaching the pass of Thermopylæ, just opposite the westernmost point of the island of Eubœa (see map, p. 138). Their fleet moved with them. The Asiatic host must have numbered over two hundred thousand men, with probably as many more camp followers, while the enormous fleet contained presumably about a thousand vessels, of which perhaps two thirds were warships. Of the latter the Persians lost a hundred or two in a storm, leaving probably about five hundred warships available for action. The Spartan king Leonidas led some five thousand men to check the Persians at the pass of Thermopylæ, while the Greek fleet of less than three hundred triremes was endeavoring to hold together and strike the Persian navy at Artemisium, on the northern coast of Eubœa. Thus the land and sea forces of both contestants were face to face.

After several days' delay the Persians advanced to attack on both land and sea. The Greek fleet made a skillful and creditable defense against superior numbers, and all day the dauntless Leonidas held the pass of Thermopylæ against the Persian host. Meantime the Persians were executing two flank movements by land and by sea—one over the mountains to strike Leonidas in the rear, and the other with two hundred ships around the island of Euboea to take the Greek fleet likewise from behind. A storm destroyed the flanking Persian ships, and a second combat between the two main fleets was indecisive. The flank movement by sea therefore failed; but the flanking of the pass was successful. Taken in front and rear, the heroic Leonidas died fighting at the head of his small force, which the Persian host completely annihilated. The death of Leonidas stirred all Greece. With the defeat of the Greek land forces and the advance of the Persian army the Greek fleet, seriously damaged, was obliged to withdraw to the south. It took up its position in the Bay of Salamis (see map, p. 138, and Fig. 40), while the main army of the Spartans and their allies was drawn up on the Isthmus of Corinth, the only point at which the Greek land forces could hope to make another defensive stand.

188. Persians invade Attica and burn Athens. As the Persian army moved southward from Thermopylæ the undaunted Themistocles gathered together the Athenian population and carried them in transports to the little islands of Salamis and Ægina and the shores of Argolis (see map, p. 138, and plate, p. 84). Meantime the Greek fleet had been repaired and, with reënforcements, numbered over three hundred battleships. Nevertheless the courage of many Greeks at Salamis was shaken as they looked northward, where the far-stretching Persian host darkened the coast road, while in the south they could see the Asiatic fleet drawn up off the old port of Athens at Phalerum (see map, p. 138). High over the Attic hills the flames of the burning Acropolis showed red against the somber masses of smoke that obscured the eastern horizon and told them that the homes of the Athenians lay in ashes. With masterly skill Themistocles held together the irresolute Greek leaders, while he induced Xerxes to attack by means of a false message that the Greek fleet was about to slip out of the bay.

189. Battle of Salamis (480 B.C.). On the heights overlooking the Bay of Salamis the Persian king, seated on his throne, in the midst of his brilliant oriental court, took up his station to watch the battle. The Greek position between the jutting headlands of Salamis and the Attic mainland (see map, p. 138, and Fig. 40) was too cramped for the maneuvers of a large fleet. Crowded by the narrow sea room the huge Asiatic fleet soon fell

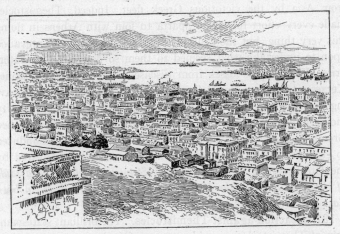

FIG. 40. PIRÆUS, THE PORT OF ATHENS, AND THE STRAIT AND ISLAND OF SALAMIS

The view shows the very modern houses and buildings of this flourishing harbor town of Athens (see map, p. 138). The mountains in the background are the heights of the island of Salamis, which extends also far over to the right (north), opposite Eleusis (see map, p. 138). The four steamers at the right are lying at the place where the hottest fighting in the great naval battle here (§ 189) took place. The Persian fleet advanced from the left (south) and could not spread out in a long front to enfold the Greek fleet because of the little island just beyond the four steamers, which was called Psyttaleia. The Greek fleet lying behind Psyttaleia and a long point of Salamis came into action from the right (north), around Psyttaleia. A body of Persian troops stationed by Xerxes on Psyttaleia were all slain by the Greeks

into confusion before the Greek attack. There was no room for retreat. The combat lasted the entire day, and when darkness settled on the Bay of Salamis the Persian fleet had been almost annihilated. The Athenians were masters of the sea, and it was impossible for the army of Xerxes to operate with the same freedom as before. By the creation of its powerful fleet Athens had saved Greece, and Themistocles had shown himself the greatest of Greek statesmen.

190. Retreat of Xerxes in the East ; Defeat of Carthage in the West. Xerxes was now troubled lest he should be cut off from Asia by the victorious Greek fleet. Indeed, Themistocles made every effort to induce Sparta to join with Athens in doing this very thing, but the cautious Spartans could not be prevailed upon to undertake what seemed to them so dangerous an enterprise. With many losses from disease and insufficient supplies Xerxes retreated to the Hellespont and withdrew into Asia, leaving his able general Mardonius with an army of perhaps fifty thousand men to winter in Thessaly. Meantime the news reached Greece that the army of Carthage, which Xerxes had induced to cross from Africa to Sicily, had been completely defeated by the Greeks under the leadership of Syracuse. *Thus the assault of the Asiatics upon the Hellenic world was beaten back in both East and West in the same year* (480 B.C.).

191. Reaction against Themistocles. The brilliant statesmanship of Themistocles, so evident to us of to-day, was not so clear to the Athenians as the winter passed and they realized that the victory at Salamis had not relieved Greece of the presence of a Persian army. It was evident that Mardonius would invade Attica with the coming of spring. Themistocles was removed from command by the factions of his ungrateful city. Nevertheless the most tempting offers from Mardonius could not induce the Athenians to forsake the cause of Greek liberty.

192. Final Defeat of Persia at Platæa (479 B.C.) **and by Sea.** As Mardonius in spring led his army again into Attica, the Athenians were again obliged to flee, this time chiefly to Salamis. Sparta, always reluctant and slow in a crisis, was finally induced to put her army into the field. When Mardonius saw the Spartan king Pausanias advancing through the Corinthian Isthmus he withdrew from Attica, having laid it waste a second time. With the united armies of Sparta, Athens, and other allies—some thirty thousand heavy-armed men—Pausanias followed Mardonius into

Bœotia. The armies met at Platæa. When Mardonius led his archers forward, and the Persians kneeling behind their line of shields rained deadly volleys of arrows into the compact Greek lines, the Hellenes never flinched, although their comrades were falling on every hand. With the gaps closed up the massive Greek lines pushed through the rows of Persian shields, and, as at Marathon, the spear proved victorious over the bow. In a heroic effort to rally his broken lines Mardonius himself fell. The Persian cavalry covered the rear of the flying Asiatic army and saved it from destruction.

Not only European Greece but Ionia too was saved from Asiatic despotism. For the Greek triremes crossed over to Asia Minor and drove out or destroyed the remnants of the Persian fleet. The Athenians now also seized the Hellespont and thus held the crossing from Asia into Europe. Thus the grandsons of the Greeks who had seen Persia advance to the Ægean (§ 97) blocked her further progress in the West and thrust her back from Europe. Indeed, no Persian army ever set foot in European Greece again.

III. The Rivalry with Sparta and the Rise of the Athenian Empire

193. Rivalry of Athens and Sparta. As the Athenians returned to look out over the ashes of what was once Athens, amid which rose the smoke-blackened heights of the naked Acropolis (Fig. 43), they began to realize the greatness of their deliverance and the magnitude of their victory. With the not too ready help of Sparta they had crushed the ancient power of Asia. They felt themselves masters of the world. The past seemed narrow and limited. A new and greater Athens dawned upon their vision.

This was all very different from the feeling of the stolid Spartans, whose whole State formed merely a military machine. Sparta was little more than a large military club or camp.[1] Living

---

[1] For a fuller account of the interesting life of the Spartan military class see *Ancient Times*, §§ 520–521.

in a group of straggling villages unworthy to be called a city, greatly attached to their own old customs, still using only iron money, and refusing to build a wall around their city, the old-fashioned Spartans looked with misgivings upon the larger world which was opening to Greek life. Although they desired to lead Greece in military power, they shrank from assuming the responsibilities of leadership. They represented the past and the privileges of the few (Fig. 41).

Athens, on the other hand, represented the future and the rights of the many. Thus Greece fell into two camps as it were : Sparta, the home of tradition and privileges granted only to the military class ; Athens, the champion of progress and the leadership of the people. And thus the sentiment of union born in the common struggle for liberty, which might have united the Hellenes into one Greek nation, was followed by an unquenchable rivalry between these two leading states, which went on for another century and finally cost the Greeks the leadership of the ancient world.

194. Themistocles, his Fortification of Athens ; the Athenian Fleet. Themistocles was now the soul of Athens and her policy of progress and expansion. He determined that Athens should no longer follow Sparta. He cleverly hoodwinked the Spartans and despite their obligations completed the erection of strong walls around a new and larger Athens. At the same time he fortified the Piræus, the Athenian port (see map, p. 138, and Fig. 40). When the Spartans, after the repulse of Persia, relinquished the command of the combined Greek fleets, the great Athenian navy, his own creation, was master of the Ægean.

195. Aristides and the Establishment of the Delian League (478–477 B.C.). As the Greek cities of Asia still feared the vengeance of the Persian king, it was easy for the Athenians to form a permanent defensive league with the cities of their Greek kindred in Asia and the Ægean islands. The wealthier of these cities contributed ships, while others paid a sum of money each year into the treasury of the league. Athens was to have command of the combined fleet and collect the money. She placed in charge of the important task of adjusting all contributions of the league and collecting the tribute money a patriotic citizen named

Aristides, who had distinguished himself at Salamis and Platæa. His friends called him "the Just" because of his honesty. Although he had formerly opposed Themistocles' naval plans, he

FIG. 41. THE PLAIN WHERE ONCE SPARTA STOOD

Olive groves now grow where the Spartans had their houses. The town was not walled until long after the days of Spartan and Greek power were over. From the mountains (nearly eight thousand feet high) behind the plain the visitor can see northeastward far beyond Athens and one hundred and twenty-five miles southward to the island of Crete

now did important service in vigorously aiding to establish the new naval league. The funds he collected were placed for protection in the temple of Apollo, on the little island of Delos. This new federation was known as the Delian League. It was completed within three years after Salamis. The transformation of such a league into an empire (§ 48), made up of states subject to Athens, could be foreseen as a very easy step. All this was therefore viewed with increasing jealousy and distrust by Sparta.

196. Rise of Cimon. Under the leadership of Cimon, the son of Miltiades (the hero of Marathon), the fleet of the League now drove the Persians out of the region of the Hellespont entirely. Cimon did not understand the importance of Athenian leadership in Greece, but favored a policy of friendship and alliance with Sparta. Hence political conflict arose at Athens over this question. Noble and wealthy and old-fashioned folk favored Cimon and friendship with Sparta, but progressive and modern Athenians followed Themistocles and his anti-Spartan plans.

197. Fall of Themistocles (472-471 B.C.). Themistocles was unable to win a majority of the Assembly; he was ostracized (tailpiece, p. 120), and at length, on false charges of treason, he was condemned and obliged to flee for his life. The greatest statesman in Athenian history spent the rest of his life in the service of the Persian king, and he never again saw the city he had saved from the Persians and made mistress of an empire.

198. Fall of Cimon; Growing Power of the People. In a final battle Cimon crushed the Persian navy on the coast of Asia Minor (468 B.C.) and returned to Athens covered with glory. Nevertheless, the Athenians disapproved of Cimon's friendly policy toward Sparta and ostracized him a few years later. Cimon was a noble, and his overthrow was a victory of the people against the nobles. The people now passed laws cutting off all the political power of the old councils (§ 135). Meanwhile a more popular council of five hundred paid members, which had grown up, gained the power to conduct almost all of the government business of Athens. At the same time the citizen juries introduced by Solon as a court of appeal (§ 168) were greatly enlarged. To enable the poorest citizens to serve on these juries the people passed laws granting pay for jury service. These juries, or citizen courts, were at last so powerful that they formed the final lawmaking body in the State, and, together with the Assembly of all the citizens, they made the laws. The people were indeed in control.

This control was aided by a new law that, with one exception, all the higher officers of the State should be chosen *by lot*.

199. Chief *Elective* Office and the Leadership of Pericles. There was, however, one kind of officer whom it was impossible to choose by lot, and that was the military commander, the general (*strategus*). The leader, or president, of the body of ten generals of Athens was the most powerful man in the State, and his office was elective. It thus became more and more possible for a noble with military training to make himself a strong and influential leader. If he was a man of persuasive eloquence he could lay out a definite series of plans for the nation, and by his oratory he could induce the Assembly of the Athenian citizens on the Pnyx (Fig. 42) to accept them.

After the fall of Cimon there came forward a handsome and brilliant young Athenian named Pericles, a descendant of one of the old noble families of the line of Clisthenes. He desired to build up the splendid Athenian Empire of which Themistocles had dreamed. He put himself at the head of the party of progress and of increased power of the people. He kept their confidence year after year and thus secured his continued reëlection as general. The result was that he became the actual head of the State in power, or, as we might say, he was the undisputed political "boss" of Athens from about 460 B.C. until his untimely death over thirty years later.

200. Superior Wealth and Power of Athens. The new Athens of which Pericles had become the head was rapidly becoming the leader of the Greek world. In this leadership commerce and money were coming to play a very large part.[1] A period of commercial prosperity followed the Persian wars. In her harbor town of Piræus, built by the foresight of Themistocles, the commerce of Athens flourished as never before. The population of Attica rose to probably over two hundred thousand, of whom over half lived at Athens. The State needed money far exceeding all its old needs. It required a hundred thousand dollars a year to pay

[1] A fuller statement of the growing importance of business and finance in the life of the Greek states will be found in *Ancient Times*, §§ 532–541.

the salaries of the jurymen and officials (§ 198). Large sums were needed for the new temples of marble; but the greatest expense was for war. A war fleet of two hundred triremes required

FIG. 42. THE PNYX, THE ATHENIAN PLACE OF ASSEMBLY

The speakers' platform, with its three steps, is immediately in the fore-ground. The listening Athenian citizens of the Assembly sat on the ground now sloping away to the left, but at that time probably level. The ground they occupied was inclosed by a semicircular wall, beginning at the further end of the straight wall seen here on the right, extending then to the left, and returning to the straight wall again behind our present point of view (see semicircle on plan, p. 138). This was an open-air House of Commons, where, however, the citizen did not send a representative, but came and voted himself as he was influenced from this platform by great Athenian leaders, like Themistocles, Pericles, or Demosthenes. Note the Acropolis and the Parthenon, to which we look eastward from the Pnyx (see plan, p. 138, and tailpiece, p. 157). The Areopagus is just out of range on the left (see Fig. 43)

nearly a hundred and twenty thousand dollars a month for wages of the sailors alone. The task of securing funds for running a government was a serious one.

The total income of the Athenian State at this time hardly reached three quarters of a million dollars. Small as this seems to us of modern times, no other Greek state could raise anything like so large an annual income. Sparta, clinging to her old-fashioned ways, without manufactures or commerce and issuing only her old-time iron coins, could not compete financially with Athens. This fact had military consequences, for Sparta could not maintain her full army in the field more than a few weeks because of the expense. In so far as war was a matter of money the commercial growth of Athens was giving her a growing superiority over all the other Greek states.

201. First War between Athens and Sparta (459–446 B.C.). Pericles had won favor with the people by favoring a policy of hostility to Sparta. Foreseeing the coming struggle with Sparta, Pericles greatly strengthened the defenses of Athens by inducing the people to connect the fortifications of the city with those of the Piræus harbor by two Long Walls, thus forming a road completely walled in, connecting Athens and her harbor (plan, p. 138).

Not long after Pericles gained the leadership of the people the war with Sparta broke out. It lasted nearly fifteen years, with varying fortunes on both sides. The Athenian merchants resented the keen commercial rivalry of Ægina, planted as the flourishing island was at the very front door of Attica (see map, p. 138). They finally captured the island after a long siege. Pericles likewise employed the Athenian navy in blockading for years the other great rival of Athens and friend of Sparta, Corinth, and thus ruined its merchants.

202. War with Persia ; the Egyptian Expedition. At the same time Athens dispatched a fleet of two hundred ships to assist Egypt, which had revolted against Persia. The Athenians were thus fighting both Sparta and Persia for years. The entire Athenian fleet in Egypt was lost. This loss so weakened the Athenian navy that the treasury of the Delian League was no longer safe in the little island of Delos against a possible raid by the Persians. Hence Pericles shifted the treasury from Delos to Athens, thus making the city still more the capital of an Athenian empire.

203. Peace with Sparta and Persia (445 B.C.). When peace was concluded (445 B.C.) all that Athens was able to retain was the island of Ægina, though at the same time she gained control of the large island of Eubœa. It was agreed that the peace should continue for thirty years. Thus ended what is often called the First Peloponnesian War, with the complete exhaustion of Athens as well as of her enemies in the Peloponnesus. Pericles had not shown himself a great naval or military commander in this war. The Athenians now also arranged a peace with Persia, over forty years after Marathon. But the rivalry between Athens and Sparta for the leadership of the Greeks was still unsettled. The struggle was to be continued in another long and weary Peloponnesian war. Before we proceed with the story of this fatal struggle we must glance briefly at the new and glorious Athens now growing up under the leadership of Pericles.

QUESTIONS

I. What great oriental power advanced to the east side of the Ægean? What did the Ionian cities of Asia do? What part did Athens take in their revolt? How did the Persians respond? Did the Athenians wait for the Persians at Athens? Who led the Athenians? Describe the Battle of Marathon.

II. What was Themistocles' policy for the future defense of Athens? Describe Themistocles' plan of campaign. Describe the first two battles; the Battle of Salamis. What did Xerxes then do? What was the result of the Greek failure to accept Themistocles' advice? What victory did the Greeks win in Sicily? Describe the final battle in Greece. What final results were obtained by the Greeks at sea?

III. What did Themistocles now do? What defensive arrangements did Athens now make with the eastern Greek cities? What differing policies did Cimon and Themistocles favor? What then happened to Themistocles? to Cimon? What new victories did the people gain? What new council arose?

How could a statesman still hold the leadership? Who now became the leader of the people's party? What were the chief expenses of the Athenian State? its chief sources of income? Could other states raise as much? Sketch the First Peloponnesian War.

CHAPTER IX

ATHENS IN THE AGE OF PERICLES

I. The Home, Education, and Training of Young Citizens

204. The New Athens and Athenian Houses. The hasty rebuilding of Athens after the Persians had burned it did not produce any noticeable changes in the houses, nor were there any of great size or splendor. There were still no beautiful houses anywhere in Europe, such as we found on the Nile (Fig. 10). The one-story front of even a wealthy man's house was simply a blank wall, usually of sun-dried brick. The door, commonly the only opening in the windowless front, led into a court open to the sky and surrounded by a porch with columns adopted from Egypt (Fig. 11). Here in the mild climate of Greece the family could spend much of their time as in a sitting room (Fig. 60). Around the court opened a number of doors leading to a living room, sleeping rooms, dining room, storerooms, and also a tiny kitchen.

The house lacked all conveniences. There was no chimney, and the smoke from the kitchen fire, though intended to drift up through a hole in the roof, often choked the room or floated out of the door. In winter gusty drafts filled the house, for many doorways were without doors, and glass in the form of panes for the windows (if there were any) was still unknown. The only stove was a pan of burning charcoal, called a brazier. Lacking windows, the ground-floor rooms depended for light entirely on the doors opening on the court. At night the dim light of an olive-oil lamp was all that was available. There was no plumbing or piping of any kind in the house, no drainage, and consequently no sanitary arrangements. The water supply was brought in jars by slaves from the nearest well or spring.

The simplicity and bareness of the house itself were in noticeable contrast with the beautiful furniture and pottery which the Greek craftsmen were now producing (tailpiece, p. 149).

The city was about a mile wide and somewhat more in length. The streets were merely lanes or alleys, narrow and crooked, winding between the bare mud-brick walls of the low houses. There was neither pavement nor sidewalk, and a stroll through the town after a rain meant wading through the mud. All the household rubbish and garbage were thrown directly into the street, and there was no system of sewerage.

205. Costume. The gorgeous oriental raiment of earlier days (§ 139) had now largely disappeared in Greece, as bright colors for men did among us in the days of our great-great-grandfathers. Nevertheless, the man of elegant habits gained a practiced hand in draping his white raiment and was proud of the gracefulness and the sweeping lines with which he could arrange its folds. The women were less inclined to give up the old finery, for unhappily they had little to think about but clothes and housekeeping (tailpiece, p. 149). For Greek citizens still kept their wives in the background, and they were more than ever mere housekeepers.

206. School, Education, and Military Service. There were therefore no schools for the girls, but when the boy was old enough he was sent to school in charge of an old slave called a *pedagogue* (a Greek word meaning "leader of a child"). There were no schools maintained by the State and no schoolhouses. School was conducted in his own house by some poor citizen, who was much looked down upon. He received his pay from the parents. Besides music and learning to read and write as of old (§ 173), the pupil learned by heart many passages from the old poets, and here and there a boy with a good memory could repeat the entire Iliad and Odyssey. On the other hand, the boys still escaped all instruction in mathematics, geography, or natural science.

When the Athenian lad reached the age of eighteen years and left school, he was received as a citizen, providing that both his parents possessed Athenian citizenship. At nineteen, after a year

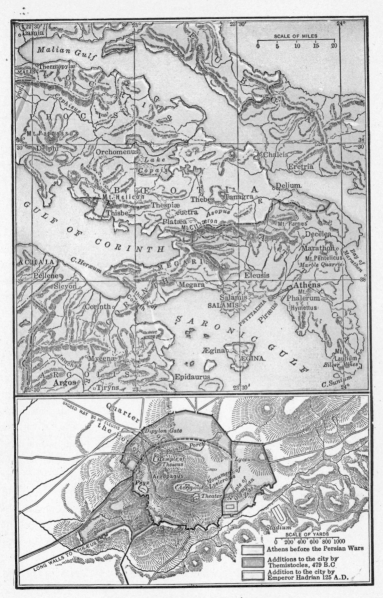

CENTRAL GREECE AND ATHENS

spent in garrison duty, the young recruits received spear and shield, given to each by the State. Thereupon they marched to the theater and entered the orchestra circle, where they were presented to the citizens of Athens before the play. Another year of garrison service on the frontier of Attica usually completed the young man's military service.

207. Athletics. If the wealth and station of his family permitted, the Athenian youth was then more than ever devoted to the new athletic fields. On the north of Athens, outside the Dipylon Gate, was the field known as the Academy. There was another similar athletic ground called the Lyceum on the east of the city. The later custom of holding courses of instructive lectures in these places (§ 286) finally resulted in giving the words "academy" and "lyceum" the associations they now possess for us. The earliest contest established at Olympia seems to have been a two-hundred-yard dash, which the Greeks called a *stadion* (six hundred Greek feet). The chief events were boxing, wrestling, running, jumping, casting the javelin, and throwing the disk. To these, other contests were afterward added, especially chariot and horse-back races. Some of the philosophers later severely criticized the Greeks for giving far too much of their time and attention to athletic pursuits.

II. Higher Education, Science, and the Training Gained by State Service

208. Higher Education Offered by the Sophists. On the other hand, there were serious-minded young men, who spent their time on worthier things. Many a bright youth who had finished his music, reading, and writing at the old-fashioned private school annoyed his father by insisting that such schooling was not enough and by demanding money to pay for a course of lectures delivered by more modern private teachers called *Sophists*, a class of new and clever-witted lecturers who wandered from city to city.

In the lectures of the Sophists a higher education was for the first time open to young men. In the first place, the Sophists taught rhetoric and oratory with great success; fathers who had no gift of speech had the pleasure of seeing their sons practiced public speakers. It was through the teaching of the Sophists also that the first successful writing of Greek prose began. They also taught mathematics and astronomy, and the young men of Athens for the first time began to learn a little natural science.

209. Intellectual Revolution; Difference between Young and Old. In these new ideas the fathers were unable to follow their sons. When a father of that day found in the hands of his son a book by one of the great Sophists which began with a statement questioning the existence of the gods, the new teachings seemed impious. The old-fashioned citizen could at least vote for the banishment of such impious teachers and the burning of their books. The revolution which had taken place in the mind of Thales (§ 178) was now taking place likewise in the minds of ever-increasing numbers of Greeks.

210. Progress in Science and Medicine. Science was advancing, although without the microscope or the assistance of chemistry. Among the sciences perhaps medicine made the most progress. In the first place, the Greek physicians rejected the older belief that disease was caused by evil demons and endeavored to find the natural causes of the ailment. To do this they sought

---

* In this view we stand inside the wall of Themistocles, near the Dipylon Gate in the Potters' Quarter (see plan, p. 138). In the foreground is the temple of Theseus, the legendary unifier of Attica, whom all Athenians honored as a god, and to whom this temple was long supposed (perhaps wrongly) to have been erected. It is built of Pentelic marble and was finished a few years after the death of Pericles; but now, after twenty-three hundred years or more, it is still the best-preserved of all ancient Greek buildings. Above the houses at the extreme right may be seen one corner of the hill called the Areopagus (see plan, p. 138), often called Mars' Hill. It was probably here that the apostle Paul (§ 419) preached in Athens (see Acts xvii). The buildings we see on the lofty Acropolis are all ruins of the structures erected after the place had been laid waste by the Persians (§ 188). The Parthenon (§ 215), in the middle of the hill (see plan, p. 138), shows the gaping hole caused by the explosion of a Turkish powder magazine ignited by a Venetian shell in 1687, when the entire central portion of the building was blown out. The space between the temple of Theseus, the Areopagus, and the Acropolis was largely occupied by the market place of Athens (§§ 213–214).

FIG. 43. THE SO-CALLED TEMPLE OF THESEUS, THE AREOPAGUS, AND THE ACROPOLIS OF ATHENS *

to understand the organs of the body. They discovered that the brain was the organ of thought, but the arterial system, the circulation of the blood, and the nervous system were still entirely unknown. The greatest physician of the time was Hippocrates, and he became the founder of scientific medicine.

211. Progress in History-Writing. Just at the close of Pericles' life, in the midst of national calamities, the historian Herodotus,—a great traveler,—who had long been engaged on a history of the world, finally published his famous work. The story was so told that the glorious leadership of Athens would be clear to all Greeks and would show them that to her the Hellenes owed their deliverance from Persia. Throughout Greece it created a deep impression, and so tremendous was its effect on Athens that the Athenians voted Herodotus a reward of ten talents, some twelve thousand dollars.

212. Educational Influence of Public Service and State Feasts. Besides the instruction received from the Sophists by many young men, their constant share in public affairs was giving them an experience which greatly assisted in producing an intelligent body of citizens. In the Council of Five Hundred (§ 198), citizens learned to carry on the daily business of the government. Every day also six thousand citizens were serving as jurors (§ 198). This service alone meant that one citizen in five was always engaged in duties which sharpened his wits and gave him some training in legal and business affairs.

Public festivals maintained by the State also played an important part in the lives of all Athenians. Every spring at the ancient feast of Dionysus the greatest play-writers each submitted three tragedies and a comedy to be played in the theater for a prize given by the State. The great State feast, called the Panathenæa, occurred every four years. A brilliant procession marched with music and rejoicing across the market place, carrying a beautiful new robe embroidered by the women of Athens for the goddess Athena. Following the procession the multitude ascended the Acropolis, where the robe was delivered to the goddess amid splendid sacrifices and impressive ceremonies.

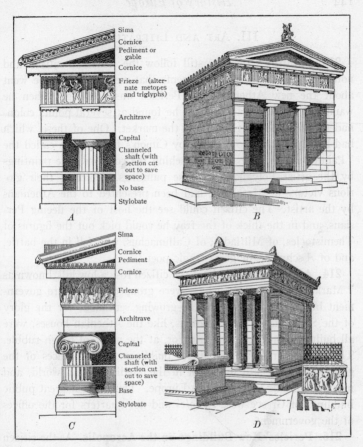

Sima
Cornice
Pediment or gable
Cornice
Frieze (alternate metopes and triglyphs)
Architrave
Capital
Channeled shaft (with section cut out to save space)
No base
Stylobate

A

B

Sima
Cornice
Pediment
Cornice
Frieze
Architrave
Capital
Channeled shaft (with section cut out to save space)
Base
Stylobate

C

D

FIG. 44. THE TWO LEADING STYLES OF GREEK ARCHITECTURE, THE DORIC (*A* AND *B*) AND THE IONIC (*C* AND *D*)

The little Doric building (*B*) is the treasury of the Athenians at Delphi (Fig. 38), containing their offerings of gratitude to Apollo. On the low base at the left side of the building were placed the trophies from the Battle of Marathon. Over them on the walls are carved hymns to Apollo with musical notes attached, the oldest musical notation surviving. The beautiful Ionic building (*D*) is a restoration of the temple of Victory on the Athenian Acropolis. Contrast its slender columns with the sturdier shafts of the Doric style, and it will be seen that the Ionic order is a more delicate and graceful style. *A* and *C* show details of both styles. (After Luckenbach)

III. ART AND LITERATURE

213. Painting. We can still follow the Athenian citizen and note a few of the noble monuments that met his eye as he went about the new Athens which Pericles was creating. When he wandered into the market place he found at several points colonnaded porches looking out upon the market. One of these, which had been presented to the city by Cimon's family, was called the "Painted Porch," for the wall behind the columns bore paintings by the artist Polygnotus. These paintings, depicting their glorious victory at Marathon, had been presented to the Athenians by the artist. The citizen could see the host of the fleeing Persians, and in the thick of the fray he could pick out the figures of Themistocles, of Miltiades, of Callimachus, who fell in the battle, and of Æschylus, the great tragic poet.

214. Architecture. Behind the citizen rose a low hill, known as "Market Hill," around which were grouped plain, bare government buildings. In spite of the growing sentiment for the glory of the State these plain buildings, like the Athenian houses, were all built of sun-dried-mud brick or, at the most, of rough rubble. The idea of great and beautiful buildings for the offices of the government was still unknown in the Mediterranean world, and no such building yet existed in Europe. Thus far the great public buildings of Greece were *temples* and not quarters for the offices of the government.

215. Pericles' New Buildings on the Acropolis. As the citizen turns from the Painted Porch the height of the Acropolis towers above him. There, on its summit, has always been the dwelling place of Athena, whose arm is ever stretched out in protection over her beloved Athens. Now at last Pericles has undertaken to replace the ancient shrines burned by the Persians, on a scale of magnificence and beauty before unknown anywhere in the Greek world. The tinkle of many distant hammers from the height above tells where the stonecutters are shaping the marble blocks for the still unfinished Parthenon, a noble temple dedicated to Athena (Figs. 43, 45, and plate, p. 144). There the people often see

© B. G. Teubner

A CORNER OF THE PARTHENON

Looking through the Doric colonnades at the southeast corner of the building to the distant hills of Hymettus. On the left is the base of the wall of the
interior, blown out by the explosion of a Turkish powder magazine. At the
top of this wall was the frieze of Phidias, extending around the inner part of
the building. From painting by Bethe-Löwe (Rhine Prints by B. G. Teubner,
Leipzig. The Prang Company, New York)

Pericles intently inspecting the buildings, as Phidias the sculptor and Ictinus the architect of the Parthenon follow him up and down the inclosure, explaining to him the progress of the work.

216. Phidias and the Parthenon Sculptures. Phidias was the greatest of the sculptors at Athens. In a long band of carved marble extending entirely around the Parthenon (plate, p. 144)

Fig. 45. Restoration of the Parthenon as it was in the Fifth Century b.c. (After Thiersch and Michaelis)

The gable ends of the temple each contained a triangular group of sculpture depicting the birth of Athena and her struggle with Poseidon, god of the sea, for possession of Attica. The wonderful frieze of Phidias (Fig. 47 and § 216) extended around the building inside the colonnades at the top of the wall

Phidias and his pupils portrayed the people of Athens moving in the stately procession (Fig. 47) of the Panathenaic festival (§ 212). Inside the new temple gleams the colossal figure of Athena, wrought by the cunning hand of Phidias in gold and ivory.

217. The Drama; Æschylus. In spite of the Sophists, the Athenian people still reverently believe that it was their gods who raised Athens to the powerful position she now occupies. All the citizens recall the story of the glorious victory of Salamis as Æschylus has told it in his great drama " The Persians." The play told them of the mighty purpose of the gods to save Hellas, just as the poet, who himself had fought the Persians (§ 213), might feel it.

As he skirts the foot of the Acropolis the citizen reaches the theater (see plan, p. 138, and Fig. 46), where he finds the people are already entering, for the spring feast of Dionysus (§ 212) has arrived. It is natural that the people should feel that the theater and all that is done there belong to them, especially as they look down upon the orchestra circle and recognize their friends and neighbors and their own sons in the chorus for the day's performance. The play would seem strange enough to us, for there is little or no scenery ; and the actors, who are always men, wear grotesque masks, a survival of old days (§ 174). The narrative is largely carried on in song by the chorus, but this is varied by the dialogue of the actors, and the whole is not unlike an opera.

218. Sophocles. A play of Sophocles is on, and the citizen's neighbor in the next seat leans over to tell him how as a lad many years ago he stood on the shore of Salamis, whither his family had fled, and as they looked down upon the destruction of the Persian fleet this same Sophocles, then a boy of sixteen, was in the crowd looking on with the rest. How deeply must the events of that tragic day have sunk into the boy's soul ! Because like Æschylus — the first great writer of tragedies — he too sees the will of the gods in all that happens to men. He uplifts his audience to worship Zeus, however dark the destiny which the great god lays upon men. For Sophocles is no friend of the Sophists, who scoff at the gods.

219. Euripides. But our citizen is inclined to distrust the new sensational plays of Euripides, the son of a farmer who lives on the island of Salamis (Fig. 40). He is a friend and companion of the Sophists, and in matters of religion his mind is troubled with doubts. His new plays are all filled with these doubts regarding the gods, and they have raised a great many questions and some doubts which the citizen has never been able to banish from his own mind since he heard them. Sophocles therefore suits all the old-fashioned folk, and it is very rarely that Euripides, in spite of his great ability, has been able to carry off the prize. The

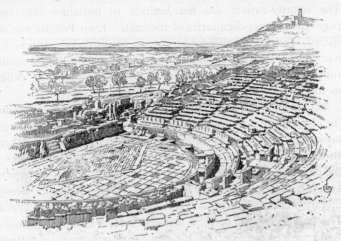

FIG. 46. THE THEATER OF ATHENS

This theater was the center of the growth and development of Greek drama, which began as a part of the celebration of the spring feast of Dionysus, god of the vine and the fruitfulness of the earth (§§ 144, 174, 212, 217). The temple of the god stood here, just at the left. Long before anyone knew of such a thing as a theater the people gathered at this place to watch the celebration of the god's spring feast, where they formed a circle about the chorus, which narrated in song the stories of the gods (§ 174). This circle (called the orchestra) was finally marked out permanently and seats of wood for the spectators were erected in a semicircle on one side, but the singing and action all took place in the circle on the level of the ground. On the side opposite the public was a booth, or tent (Greek *skēnē*, "scene") for the actors, and out of this finally developed the stage. From the seats, accommodating possibly seventeen thousand people, the citizens had a grand view of the sea with the island of Ægina, their old-time rival (§ 201), for orchestra and seats continued roofless, and a Greek theater was always open to the sky

citizen feels some anxiety as he realizes that his own son and most of the other young men of his set are enthusiastic admirers of Euripides. They constantly read his plays and talk them over with the Sophists.

220. Comedy. The great tragedies were given in the morning, and in the afternoon the people were ready for less serious entertainment, such as *comedy* offered. Out of the old-time country feasts the comedy had also developed into a stage performance. The comedy-writers did not hesitate to introduce into their plays the greatest dignitaries of the State. Even Pericles was not spared, and great philosophers or serious-minded writers like Euripides were represented on the stage and made irresistibly ridiculous, while the multitudes of Athens vented their delight in roars of laughter mingled with shouts and cheers.

221. Books and Reading. Thousands of citizens were reading the old plays that had already been presented. For now at length books had come to take an important place in the life of Athens. In our Athenian citizen's library were Homer and the works of the old classic poets. They were written on long rolls of papyrus as much as a hundred and fifty or sixty feet in length. Besides literary works, all sorts of books of instruction began to appear. The sculptors wrote of their art, and there was a large group of books on medicine, bearing the name of Hippocrates. Textbooks on mathematics and rhetoric circulated, and the Athenian housekeeper could even find a cookbook at the bookshop.

222. Summary of Periclean Athens. Under such influences there had grown up at Athens a whole community of intelligent men. They were the product of the most active interest in the life and government of the community. They constantly shared in its tasks and problems, and they were also in daily contact with the greatest works of art in literature, drama, painting, architecture, and sculpture. Very different from the old Athens of the days before the repulse of the Persians, the new Athens had thus become such a wonderful community as the ancient world had never seen before. It now remained to be seen whether the *people*, in complete control of the State, could guide her wisely and maintain her power. As we watch the citizens of Athens trying to furnish her with wise and successful guidance, we shall find another and sadly different side of the life of this wonderful community.

FIG. 47. PART OF THE FRIEZE OF PHIDIAS, SHOWING ATHENIAN YOUTHS RIDING IN THE PANATHENAIC FESTIVAL PROCESSION (see § 212)

Notice the marvelous dash and vigor of the horses; also the strength of the last youth, as he reins in his steed till the animal's jaw is drawn back to its neck. The reins and trappings were of metal, and have disappeared

FIG. 48. HERMES PLAYING WITH THE CHILD DIONYSUS

The uplifted right hand (now broken off) of the god probably held a bunch of grapes, with which he was amusing the child (§ 242). This wonderful work was wrought by the sculptor Praxiteles and is one of the few *original* works of the greatest Greek sculptors found in Greece. Nearly all such Greek originals have perished and we know them only in ancient Roman copies found in Italy (§ 408). This great work was dug out at Olympia

QUESTIONS

I. Describe an Athenian house of this age; its conveniences; its equipment; its decoration. What were the streets of Athens like? Describe Greek costume in this age. What was now the position of women? Describe the usual school and its teacher. What subjects were taught? What did a boy do when he left school? What were the chief events in athletics?

II. What did the Sophists teach? What did the fathers think about such teaching? What discoveries were made in medicine? in history-writing? How did government business train the citizens of Athens? What can you say about official State feasts at Athens?

III. Discuss the painting of Marathon in the Athenian market place. What buildings did Pericles erect? Describe the sculpture of Phidias. What play did Æschylus write about the war with Persia? Describe the theater at Athens. Describe a Greek play. What did Sophocles think about the gods and the Sophists? What did Euripides think about the gods? To which of these two men did the Athenians vote the most prizes? Tell about the comedies played at Athens. What books could a citizen find at the bookshop?

CHAPTER X

THE FALL OF THE ATHENIAN EMPIRE

I. The Second Peloponnesian War

223. Dangerous Hostility to Athens. While Athens under the guiding hand of Pericles had thus made herself the chief center of refined and civilized life in the Greek world, her political situation was becoming a serious one. When the danger from Persia seemed over, some of the island states of the Empire wished to withdraw. But Athens would not permit them to do so. She sent out her war fleet, conquered the rebellious islands, and forced them to pay money tribute instead of contributing ships. Often many of their citizens were driven out and their lands were divided among Athenian settlers. The people of the Empire outside of Attica were not allowed to become Athenian citizens. Athens in this way lost many loyal citizens which she might have gained among her subjects. At the same time Athens forced all the people of the Empire to come there to settle their legal differences. Much discontent resulted among the states of the Empire, and more than one of them sent secret messages to Sparta, with the purpose of throwing off Athenian control and going over to Sparta.

NOTE. The above headpiece shows us the lovely Porch of the Maidens built to adorn the temple on the Acropolis known as the Erechtheum.

While such was the state of affairs *within* the Athenian Empire, conditions *outside* were even more serious. To a backward military state like Sparta there were reasons for feeling jealous of Athens. Among these reasons were the outward splendor of Athens, her commercial prosperity, her not very conciliatory attitude toward her rivals, the visible growth of her power, and the example she offered of the seeming success of triumphant democracy. This feeling of unfriendliness toward Athens was not confined to Sparta but was quite general throughout Greece. The merchants of Corinth found Athenian competition a continuous vexation. When Athenian possessions in the north Ægean revolted and received support from Corinth and Sparta, the fact that hardly half of the thirty years' term of peace (§ 203) had expired did not prevent the outbreak of war.

224. Second Peloponnesian War (431 B.C.). It seemed as if all European Greece not included in the Athenian Empire had united against Athens, for Sparta controlled the entire Peloponnesus except Argos, and north of Attica Bœotia, led by Thebes, as well as its neighbors on the west, were hostile to Athens. The support of Athens consisted of the Ægean cities which made up her Empire and a few outlying allies of little power. She began the struggle with a large war fund and a fleet which made her undisputed mistress of the sea. But she could not hope to cope with the land forces of the enemy, which, some thirty thousand strong, had planned to meet on the Isthmus in the spring of 431 B.C.

Accordingly, Pericles' plan for the war was to undertake only naval enterprises and to make no effort to defend Attica by land. When Sparta led the Peloponnesian army into Attica, Pericles directed the country people to leave their homes and take refuge within the walls of Athens. Here they were placed in the open markets and squares, the sanctuaries, and especially between the Long Walls leading to the Piræus. To offset the devastation of Attica by the Spartan army, all that Athens could do was to organize destructive sea raids and inflict as much damage as possible along the coasts of the Peloponnesus or blockade and destroy Corinthian commerce as of old.

The masses of people crowded within the walls of Athens under the unsanitary conditions we have already described (§ 204) exposed the city to disease. A plague, brought in from the Orient, raged with intermissions for several seasons. It carried off probably a third of the population, and from this unforeseen disaster Athens never recovered. Constantly under arms for the defense of the walls, deprived of any opportunity to strike the enemy, forced to sit still and see their land laid waste, the citizens at last broke out in discontent.

225. Fall and Death of Pericles (429 B.C.). In spite of his undaunted spirit Pericles was unable to hold the confidence of a majority. He lost control, was tried for misappropriation of funds, and fined. The absence of his steadying hand and powerful leadership was at once felt by the people. There was no one to take his place, although a swarm of small politicians were contending for control of the Assembly. Realizing their helplessness, the people soon turned to Pericles again and elected him general. But the great days of his leadership were over; he was stricken with the plague and died soon after his return to power. Great statesman though he was, he had left Athens with a system of government which did not provide for the continuation of such leadership as he had furnished, and without such leadership the Athenian Empire was doomed.

226. Lack of Leaders after Pericles; Alcibiades. Men of the prosperous manufacturing class now came to the front. They possessed neither the high station in life, the ability as statesmen, nor the qualities of leadership to win the confidence and respect of the people. Moreover, these new leaders were not soldiers and could not command the fleet or the army as Pericles had done. The only notable exception was Alcibiades, a brilliant young man, a relative of Pericles and brought up in his house. If he had enjoyed the guidance of his foster father a few years longer, he might have become the savior of Athens and of Greece. As it happened, however, this young leader was more largely responsible than anyone else for the destruction of the Athenian Empire and the downfall of Greece.

Athens therefore completely lacked a strong and steadfast leader, whose well-formed plans might furnish a firm and guiding influence. Hence the management of Athenian affairs fell into confusion. It seemed impossible to regain steadfast leadership. Cleon, a tanner, one of the new leaders from among the common people, was a man of much energy, with a good deal of financial ability. As the war dragged on, the payment of army and fleet reduced Athenian funds to a very low state. Cleon then levied an income tax and raised the tribute of the Ægean cities.

227. Peace of Nicias (421 B.C.). Meantime there was really no *military* disaster of sufficient importance to cripple seriously either Sparta or Athens. It was the devastation wrought by the plague which had seriously affected Athens. Cleon having been killed in battle the leadership fell into the hands of Nicias, a man of no ability. After ten years of indecisive warfare a peace was arranged by Nicias to be kept for fifty years. Each contestant agreed to give up all new conquests and to retain only old possessions.

II. Third Peloponnesian War and Destruction of the Athenian Empire

228. Third Peloponnesian War ; Sicilian Expedition. Meanwhile serious difficulties arose in carrying out the conditions of the peace. The gifted and reckless Alcibiades, seeking opportunity for a brilliant military career, did all that he could to excite the war party in Athens. He was elected general and was soon able to carry the Assembly with him in his war plans. In this way Attica, exhausted by plague and warfare, was enticed by Alcibiades into a life-and-death struggle which was to prove final.

The war began with several years of ill-planned military and naval operations. For some years the Spartans did not respond with hostilities and sent no army into Attica. Alcibiades at length persuaded the Athenians to plan a great joint expedition of army and navy against Sicily, especially the mighty city of Syracuse, founded as a colony of Corinth. The Athenians placed Alcibiades and Nicias in command of this expedition.

229. Arrest of Alcibiades and his Flight to Sparta. Just as the fleet was about to sail certain sacred images in Athens were impiously mutilated, and the deed was attributed to Alcibiades. In spite of his demand for an immediate trial the Athenians postponed the case until his return from Sicily. When the fleet reached Italy, however, the Athenian people, with their usual inability to follow any consistent plan and also desiring to take Alcibiades at a great disadvantage, suddenly recalled him for trial. This procedure not only deprived the expedition of its only able leader but also gave Alcibiades an opportunity to desert to the Spartans, which he promptly did. His advice to the Spartans now proved fatal to the Athenians.

230. Incompetence of Nicias. The appearance of the huge Athenian fleet off their coast struck dismay into the hearts of the Syracusans, but Nicias entirely failed to see the importance of immediate attack before the Syracusans could recover and make preparations for the defense of their city. When, after much delay, Nicias was finally induced by the second general in command to begin the siege of the city, courage had returned to the Syracusans, and their defense was well organized.

On the advice of Alcibiades the Spartans sent an able commander with a small force to assist Syracuse, and the city was confident in its new ally. When Nicias made no progress in the siege Athens responded to his call for help with a second fleet and more land forces. No Greek state had ever mustered such power and sent it so far across the waters. All Greece watched the spectacle with amazement. Meantime the Syracusans too had organized a fleet. The Athenian fleet had entered the harbor, and in such narrow quarters they were unable to maneuver or take advantage of their superior seamanship. The fleet of Syracuse was finally victorious in several actions.

231. Capture of Athenian Fleet and Army at Syracuse (413 B.C.). With disaster staring them in the face, there was nothing for the Athenians to do but withdraw. But just at this point an eclipse of the moon occurred, and the superstitious Nicias insisted on waiting another month for a more favorable moon.

The Syracusans then blockaded the channel to the sea and completely shut up the Athenian fleet within the harbor, so that an attempt to break through and escape disastrously failed. The desperate Athenian army, abandoning sick and wounded too late, endeavored to escape into the interior, but was overtaken and forced to surrender. After executing the commanding generals the Syracusans took the prisoners, seven thousand in number, and sold them into slavery or threw them into the stone quarries of the city, where most of them miserably perished. Thus the Athenian expedition was completely destroyed (413 b.c.). This disaster, together with the earlier ravages of the plague, brought Athens near the end of her resources.

232. Distress of Athens. Sparta, seeing the unprotected condition of Athens, now no longer hesitated to undertake a campaign into Attica. On the advice of Alcibiades again, the Spartans occupied the town of Decelea, almost within sight of Athens. Here they established a permanent fort held by a strong garrison, and thus placed Athens in a state of perpetual siege. All agriculture ceased, and the Athenians lived on imported grain. The people now understood the folly of having sent away on a distant expedition the ships and the men that should have been kept at home to repel the attacks of a powerful and still uninjured foe.

To add still further to the Athenian distress, the powerful Persian satrap in western Asia Minor was helping the Spartans, though Athens also had tried to win his aid. The Greek islands and the cities of Asia Minor which had once united in the Delian League with Athens to throw off Persian rule were now combining with Sparta and Persia against Athens. Thus the former union of the Greeks in a heroic struggle against the Asiatic enemy had given way to a disgraceful scramble for Persian support.

233. Final Fall and Death of Alcibiades. Meantime the Athenians again turned to Alcibiades for help. In several conflicts, chiefly through his skill, the Peloponnesian fleet was finally completely destroyed, and Athens regained the command of the sea. Then Alcibiades returned in triumph to Athens and was elected general. It now needed only the abilities of such a leader as Alcibiades to bring about the union of the distracted Greek states and to found a great Greek nation. At this supreme moment, however, Alcibiades lacked the courage to seize the government, and the opportunity never returned. When he put to sea again a slight defeat, inflicted on a part of his fleet when he was not present, cost him the favor of the fickle Athenians. They failed to reëlect him general, and he retired to a castle which he had kept in readiness on the Hellespont. He never saw his native land again and died in exile, the victim of a Persian dagger.

234. Capture of the Athenian Fleet at Ægospotami (405 B.C.) and Fall of the Athenian Empire (404 B.C.). In spite of some success at sea Athens now suffered worse than ever before for lack of competent commanders. As a result the final disaster could not be long averted. The Attic fleet of a hundred and eighty triremes was lulled into false security in the Hellespont near the river called Ægospotami. Then as it lay drawn up on the beach it was surprised by the able Spartan commander Lysander and captured almost intact.

At last, twenty-seven years after Pericles had provoked the war with Sparta, the resources of Athens were exhausted. Not a man slept on the night when the terrible news of final ruin reached Athens. It was soon confirmed by the appearance of Lysander's fleet blockading the Piræus. The grain ships from the Black Sea could no longer reach the port of Athens. Starvation finally forced the stubborn democratic leaders to submit, and the city surrendered. The Long Walls and the fortifications of the Piræus were torn down, the remnant of the fleet was handed over to Sparta, all foreign possessions were given up, and Athens was forced to enter the Spartan League. These hard conditions saved the city from the complete destruction demanded by Corinth. Thus the century which had so gloriously begun for Athens with the repulse of Persia, the century which under the leadership of such men as Themistocles and Pericles had seen her rise to supremacy in all that was best and noblest in Greek life, closed with the annihilation of the Athenian Empire (404 B.C.).

QUESTIONS

I. How did Athens treat the subject states of her Empire? What was her policy regarding citizenship? regarding lawsuits in the subject states? How did these states now regard Athens? How did the states outside the Athenian Empire feel? What was the result? Who were the enemies of Athens in this war? What were her resources?

What was Pericles' plan of campaign? What disaster overtook Athens? How did this affect the fortunes of Pericles? What was the result? What young leader now came forward? What business man now tried to lead the nation? What was the result of ten years' war? Who arranged the peace? When?

II. Who was chiefly responsible for the reopening of the war? What great expedition did the Athenians plan? Who were the commanders? Tell the story of its expedition and its end. What did Sparta now do? What was now the internal condition of the Athenian Empire?

What part did Persia play in the war? What can you state of the restoration of Alcibiades to office? What was the result? How did the loss of her fleet affect Athens? What terms did Sparta make? Contrast the beginning and the end of the fifth century in Athenian history.

NOTE. This tailpiece is a view of the Parthenon temple on the Acropolis at Athens. It shows the better-preserved side of the building as it exists to-day. For a restoration see Fig. 45.

CHAPTER XI

THE FINAL CONFLICTS AMONG THE GREEK STATES AND THEIR HIGHER LIFE AFTER PERICLES

I. Spartan Leadership and the Decline of Democracy

235. Spartan Rule : Struggle of Oligarchy and Democracy. The long struggle of Athens for the political leadership of the Greek world had failed. It now remained to be seen whether her victorious rival, Sparta, was any better suited to undertake such leadership. Military garrisons commanded by Spartan officers were placed in many of the Greek cities, and Spartan control was maintained in a much more offensive form than was the old tyranny of Athens. In each city the Spartans established and supported by military force a government carried on by a small group of men from the noble or upper class. Such rule of a small group was called *oligarchy*, a Greek term meaning "rule of a few." By such violent means Sparta was able to repress the democracies which had everywhere been hostile to her. In some cities the oligarchies were guilty of the worst excesses, murdering or banishing their political opponents and seizing their fortunes. When the people regained power they retaliated in the same way and drove the oligarchs from the city.

236. Rise of Banking and Financial Experts. Athens was still the greatest city and the leading business center in the Mediterranean world. While farming declined, manufacturing and business flourished. Wealthy men combined their capital to form the first Greek banks at Athens. Athens thus became the financial center of the ancient world, as New York and London are of the modern world, and her bankers became the proverbially wealthy men of the time. At the same time the finances of a nation became more and more a matter of special training, and it was more difficult for the average citizen without experience to conduct the financial offices of the government.

237. Rise of Professional Soldiers. The same thing was true of military affairs. The long Peloponnesian Wars had kept large numbers of Greeks so long in the army that many of them remained in military life and became *professional soldiers*. Such soldiers serving a foreign state for pay are called "mercenaries." The Greek youths who could find no opportunities at home were therefore enlisting as soldiers in Egypt, in Asia Minor, and in Persia, and the best young blood of Greece was being spent to strengthen foreign states instead of building up the power of the Greeks.

During the Peloponnesian Wars *military leadership* had also become a profession. Athens produced a whole group of professional military leaders ; the most talented among these was Xenophon. About 400 B.C. he took service in Asia Minor with Cyrus, a young Persian prince. In a famous retreat from Babylon Xenophon led ten thousand Greek troops up the Tigris past the ruins of Nineveh and through the mountains until they reached the Black Sea and finally returned home in safety. Of this extraordinary raid into the Persian Empire Xenophon has left a modest account called the "Anabasis" ("up-going"), one of the great books which have descended to us from ancient times.

The Mediterranean, which had so long ago received the arts of *peace* from the Orient, was now also learning from the same sources the use of war machinery, like movable towers and battering rams. At the same time larger warships were constructed, some having as many as five banks of oars, and the old triremes with three banks could no longer stand against these new and powerful ships.

238. Greek States war against Sparta (395–387 B.C.) ; the King's Peace (387 B.C.). The rule of Sparta finally caused such dissatisfaction that the Greeks, led by Athens, began to revolt. Athenian successes against Sparta at length led the Persians to fear lest Athens should again be strong enough to endanger Persian control in Asia Minor. The Spartans, who had been fighting

Persia, therefore found it easy to arrange a peace with the Persians. The Greek states fighting Sparta were equally willing to come to terms, and when peace was at last established in Greece, it was under the humiliating terms of a treaty accepted by Hellas at the hands of a Persian king. It is known as the King's Peace (387 B.C.). It did not end the leadership of Sparta over the Greek states, and the Greek cities of Asia Minor were shamefully abandoned to Persia.

II. THE FALL OF SPARTA AND THE LEADERSHIP OF THEBES

239. Thebes and a New League against Sparta (378 B.C.). The Spartans were finally more hated than Athens had ever been. At Thebes a group of fearless and patriotic citizens succeeded in slaying the oligarchs. The Spartan garrison at Thebes surrendered, and a democracy was set up which gained the leadership of all Bœotia. Athens and Thebes then led another combination against Sparta. The Spartans met disaster on land, and when this was followed by the defeat of their fleet by Athens they were ready for peace.

To arrange this peace all the Greek states met at Sparta, and such meetings gave them experience in the united management of their common affairs for the welfare of all Hellas. By giving every state a voice in the control of Hellas, Sparta might still have finally united the Greeks into a great nation. But this was not to be. When the conditions of peace were being decided upon, the Spartans refused to allow Thebes to speak for the whole of Bœotia. The Thebans refused to enter the compact on any other terms, and the peace was concluded without them. This left Sparta and Thebes still in a state of war.

240. Battle of Leuctra and Fall of Sparta (371 B.C.). All Greece now expected to see the Thebans crushed by the heavy Spartan phalanx,[1] which had so long proved irresistible. But

---

[1] The action and effect of an advancing Greek phalanx are described in *Ancient Times*, § 637. For plan of the Battle of Leuctra see ibid. p. 403.

owing to the military skill of the Theban commander, a gifted and patriotic citizen named Epaminondas, the Thebans were most unexpectedly victorious in the decisive conflict which took place at Leuctra, in southern Bœotia (see map, p. 138). Over half of the Spartans engaged were slain and with them their king. The long-invincible Spartan army was at last defeated, and the charm of Spartan prestige was finally broken. After more than thirty years of leadership (since 404 B.C.) Spartan power was ended (371 B.C.).

241. Fall of Thebes and Political Prostration of the Whole Greek World. It then remained to be seen whether Thebes, the new victor, could accomplish what Athens and Sparta had failed in doing and could create a Greek nation. But the supremacy of the Thebans was based upon the genius of a single man, and when Epaminondas fell in a final battle with Sparta at Mantinea (362 B.C.), the power of Thebes collapsed.

Thus the only powerful Greek states which might have welded the Hellenic world into a nation had crushed each other. Hellas was therefore doomed to fall helplessly before a conqueror from the outside. Yet in spite of their political decline during the two generations since Pericles, the Greeks, and especially the Athenians, had been achieving things in art, architecture, literature, philosophy, and science which made this period perhaps the greatest in the history of man.

III. Sculpture and Painting

242. The Sculpture of Praxiteles. Sculpture had made notable progress since the days of Pericles. The great Athenian sculptor Praxiteles led the way. His native city being without the money for large monumental works, Praxiteles wrought individual figures of life size. Unlike the majestic, cold, and godlike figures of Phidias, the gods of Praxiteles seem near to us. They at once appeal to us as being human like ourselves, interested in a life like ours, and doing things which we should like to do ourselves. As they stand at ease in attitudes of repose, we find in them a beauty and sheer human appeal unattained by any earlier sculpture of the Greeks (Fig. 48).

243. Painting and Discovery of how to paint Light and Perspective. The introduction of portable paintings on wooden tablets made it possible for people of wealth to set up paintings in their own houses, and in this way private support of art increased and painting made more rapid progress than ever before or since. An Athenian painter named Apollodorus now began to notice that the light usually fell on an object from one side, leaving the unlighted side so dark that but little color showed on that side, while on the lighted side the colors came out very brightly. When he painted a woman's arm in this way, lo, it looked round and seemed to stand out from the surface of the painting; whereas up in the Painted Porch all the human limbs in the old painting of Marathon (§ 213) looked perfectly flat. By representing figures in the background of his paintings as smaller than those in front, Apollodorus also introduced what we now call *perspective*.

IV. Religion, Literature, and Thought

244. Age of Conflict after the Death of Pericles. Any young Athenian born at about the time of Pericles' death found himself in an age of conflict wherever he went : an age of conflict *abroad* on the field of battle as he stood with spear and shield in the Athenian ranks in the long years of warfare between Athens, Sparta, and Thebes ; an age of conflict *at home* in Athens amid the tumult and even bloodshed of the streets and markets of the city as the common people, the democracy, struggled with the nobles for the leadership of the State ; and finally an age of conflict *in himself* as he felt his own faith in old things struggling to maintain itself against new views which were coming in (§ 209).

He recalled the childhood tales of the gods, which he had heard at his nurse's knee. When he had asked her how the gods looked she had pointed to a beautiful vase in his father's house. There were the gods on the vase in human form, and so he had long thought of them as people like those of Athens. Later at school he had memorized long passages of the Homeric poems and learned more about the gods' adventures on earth. Then he had begun to go to the theater, where he was much delighted with the comedies of Aristophanes, the greatest of the comedy writers (§ 220). Aristophanes made ridiculous such men as Euripides and the Sophists, who doubted the existence of the gods.

245. Victory of Doubt; Triumph of Euripides. Then when this young Athenian left his boyhood teacher behind and went to hear the lectures of a noted Sophist (§ 208), he was told that no one knew with any certainty whether the gods existed, nor what they were like. Whatever the gods might be like, the Sophist was sure they were not such beings as he found pictured in the Homeric poems. The youth and his educated friends were all reading the splendid plays of Euripides (§ 219), with their uncertainties, struggles, and doubts about life and the gods. Euripides, to whom the Athenians had rarely voted a victory during his lifetime (§ 219), had now triumphed; but his triumph meant the defeat of the old beliefs, the rejection of the old ideas of the gods, and the incoming of a new age in thought and religion.

FIG. 49. PORTRAIT OF SOCRATES

This is not the best of the numerous surviving portraits of Socrates, but it is especially interesting because it bears under the philosopher's name nine inscribed lines containing a portion of his public defense as reported by Plato in his *Apology*

246. Socrates. The citizen was reminded of another source of doubt as he passed on the street the rude figure of a poor Athenian named Socrates, whose ill-clothed figure and ugly face (Fig. 49) had become familiar in the streets to all the folk of

Athens since the outbreak of the second war with Sparta. He was accustomed to stand about the market place all day long, engaging in conversation anyone he met and asking a great many questions very hard to answer. Socrates' questions left most people in a very confused state of mind, for he seemed to throw doubt on everything which the Athenians had once regarded as settled.

Yet the familiar and homely figure of this stonecutter's son was the personification of the best and highest things in Greek genius. Without desire for office or a political career, Socrates' greatest interest nevertheless was the State. He believed that the State, made up as it was of citizens, could be purified and saved only by the improvement of the *individual citizen* through the education of his mind to recognize virtue and right.

Inspired by this belief, Socrates went about in Athens engaging all his fellow citizens in discussion, convinced that he might thus lead each citizen in turn to a knowledge of the leading virtues. He firmly believed that the citizen who had once recognized these virtues would shape every action of his life by them. While Socrates made no appeal to religion as an influence toward good conduct, he nevertheless showed himself a deeply religious man, believing with devout heart in the gods, although they were not exactly those of the fathers, and even feeling, like the Hebrew prophets, that there was a divine voice within him calling him to his high mission.

247. Public Opinion of Socrates. Socrates' fame spread far and wide, and when the Delphian oracle (§ 144) was asked who was the wisest of the living it responded with the name of this greatest of Greek teachers. A group of pupils gathered about him, among whom the most famous was Plato. But the aims and noble efforts of Socrates were misunderstood. His keen questions seemed to throw doubt upon all the old beliefs.

248. The Trial and Death of Socrates (399 B.C.). So the Athenians summoned Socrates to trial for corrupting the youth with all sorts of doubts and impious teachings. He might easily have left Athens when the complaint was lodged against him. Nevertheless he appeared for trial, made a powerful and dignified defense, and, when the court voted the death penalty, passed his last days in tranquil conversation with his friends and pupils, in whose presence he then quietly drank the fatal hemlock poison. Thus the Athenian democracy, which had so fatally mismanaged the affairs of the nation in war, brought upon itself much greater reproach in condemning to death the greatest and purest soul among its citizens.

The undisturbed serenity of Socrates in his last hours, as pictured to us in Plato's story of the scene, profoundly affected the whole Greek world and still forms one of the most precious possessions of humanity. He was the greatest Greek, and in him Greek civilization reached its highest level.

249. Scientific Writing of History. The change in Greek belief was also evident in a new and remarkable history. Its author was Thucydides, the first scientific writer of history. A generation earlier Herodotus' history (§ 211) had represented the fortunes of nations as due to the will of the gods ; but Thucydides, with an insight like that of modern historians, traced historical events to their *earthly* causes in the world of men where they occur. There stood the two books, Herodotus and Thucydides, side by side in the citizen's library. There were only thirty years or so between them, but how different the beliefs of the two historians, the old and the new ! Thucydides' history has been one of the world's greatest prose classics ever since.

250. Isocrates and the Rise of the Science of Government. The success of Thucydides' work shows that the interest of the Athenians was no longer in poetry but in the new and more youthful art of prose. The teachers of rhetoric at Athens, the successors of the old Sophists (§ 208), became world-renowned, and they made the city the center of education for the whole Greek world. The leader among them was Isocrates. He chose as his theme the great political questions of his time. He was not a good speaker, and he therefore devoted himself especially to the *writing* of his speeches, which he then published as political essays. Throughout Greece these remarkable essays were read, and Isocrates finally became the political spokesman of Athens, if not of all Greece. In such discussions there arose a new science, the *science of government*.

Plato, the most gifted pupil of Socrates, was deeply interested in these new discussions. He published much of his beloved master's teaching in the form of dialogues, supposedly giving the discussions of the great teacher himself. Convinced of the hopelessness of democracy in Athens, he reluctantly gave up all thought of a career as a statesman, to which he had been strongly drawn, and settled down at Athens to devote himself to teaching. His school was in the grove of the Academy (§ 207).

In a noble essay entitled *The Republic* Plato presented a lofty vision of his ideal state and government. It was the self-contained, self-controlling city-state as it had in times past supposedly existed in Greece. He failed to perceive that the vital question for Greece now was *the relation of these city-states to each other*. He did not discern that the life of a cultivated state unavoidably passes beyond its own borders and by its needs and its contributions affects the life of surrounding states. It cannot be confined within its *political* borders, for its *commercial* borders lie as far distant as transportation can carry its produce.

251. Growth of a Hellenized World. Thus boundary lines cannot separate nations ; their life overlaps and mingles with the life round about them. It was so within Greece, and it was so far beyond the borders of Greek territory. There had thus grown up a *civilized world* which was reading Greek books, using Greek utensils, fitting up its houses with Greek furniture, decorating its house interiors with Greek paintings, building Greek theaters, learning Greek tactics in war — a great eastern Mediterranean and oriental world made up of many peoples bound together by commerce, travel, and common business interests. For this world, as a coming *political* unity, the lofty idealist Plato, in spite of much travel, had no eyes.

252. Disunion the End of Greek Political Development. Men in practical life, like Isocrates, clearly understood the situation at this time. Isocrates urged the Greeks to bury their petty differences and enlarge their purely *sectional* patriotism into loyalty toward a great nation which should unite the *whole Greek world*. He told his countrymen that so united they could easily overthrow the decaying Persian Empire and make themselves lords of the world, whereas now, while they continued to fight among themselves, the king of Persia could do as he pleased with them. To all Greeks who had read Xenophon's story of the march of his Ten Thousand (§ 237) the weakness of the Persian Empire was evident. Every motive toward unity was present.

Nevertheless, no Greek city was willing to submit to the leadership of another. *Local* patriotism, like the sectionalism which brought on our Civil War, prevailed everywhere, and *unalterable disunion was the end of Greek political development*. As a result the Greeks were now to become subjects of an outside power (§ 254), which had never had any share in advancing Greek culture.

253. Estimate of Greek Achievement after Pericles. But in spite of this final and melancholy collapse of Greek political power, what an incomparably glorious age of Greek civilization was this which we have been sketching! The rivalries which proved so fatal to the political leadership of the Greeks had been a constant incentive spurring them all on, as each city strove to surpass its rivals in art and literature and all the finest things in civilization. Great as the age of Pericles had been, the age that followed was still greater. The tiny Athenian state, with an area not larger than that of our little state of Delaware, and having at best twenty-five or thirty thousand citizens, had furnished in this period a group of great names in all lines of human achievement such as never in all the history of the world arose elsewhere in an area and a population so limited. Their names to-day are among the most illustrious in human history, and the achievements which we link with them form the greatest chapter in the higher life of man. Furthermore, Greek genius was to go on to many another future triumph, in spite of the loss of that political leadership which we are now to see passing into other hands.

QUESTIONS

I. Describe Sparta's rule over the Greeks. What is an oligarchy? What can you say of banking and finance? Discuss the military men of this time. In what did the rule of Sparta result?

II. What did the Thebans do? What was the result of the war? Tell about the peace congress at Sparta. What was the result? Who planned the Battle of Leuctra? What state was then leader of Greece? What was the outcome? Was there any other state capable of uniting and leading the Greeks?

III. Who was now the leading Greek sculptor? What progress did his work show? What form did painting now take? Who was the leading painter? What progress did his work show?

IV. In what ways was the age after Pericles one of conflict? How did an Athenian boy gain his ideas about the gods? How did doubts arise in his mind? What did he read? How did this affect his doubts? Who was Socrates and how did he teach? What was his chief interest? How did he attempt to improve the State? What was the people's impression about him? How did they finally treat him?

What progress was made in history-writing? By whom? What can you say of Isocrates? Tell about the views of Plato. Describe the Hellenized world. What was the result of Greek political development?

NOTE. This tailpiece shows the Oasis of Siwa in the Sahara (see § 268).

CHAPTER XII

ALEXANDER THE GREAT AND THE HELLENISTIC AGE

I. The Rise of Macedonia

254. Uncultivated States of the Balkan Peninsula. The backward and barbarous Northern peoples in Thrace and Macedonia spoke Indo-European tongues akin to Greek, but their Greek kindred of the South could not understand them. A little Greek civilization began here and there to improve somewhat the rough and uncultivated life of the population of Macedonia. The Macedonian kings commenced to cultivate Greek literature and art, and the mother of Philip, king of Macedon, was grateful that she had been able to learn to write in her old age.

255. Philip of Macedon and his New Army. Philip himself had enjoyed a Greek education, and when he gained the power over Macedonia, in 360 B.C., he understood perfectly the weakness

NOTE. The headpiece above (on the right) is a pleasing example of the Alexandrian art of mosaic — the art of putting together brightly colored bits of glass or stone and forming figures or designs with them, as a child puts together a puzzle picture. It was an old Egyptian art (see scene at left), carried on by the Greeks at Alexandria, where they seem to have learned it and used it in making beautiful pavements (§ 279).

of the disunited Greek world. With the ability of a skilled statesman and an able soldier he planned to make himself master of the Greeks. Out of the peasant population of his kingdom Philip formed a permanent, or standing, army of professional soldiers. The infantrymen soon became famous as the "Macedonian phalanx." Heretofore horsemen had played but a small part in war in Europe. Philip now drilled a large body of riders to move about *together* and to attack in *a single mass*, either alone or with the phalanx, so that the whole combined force, infantry and cavalry, moved as one great unit, an irresistible machine in which every part worked together with all the others.

FIG. 50. PORTRAIT BUST OF DEMOSTHENES

256. Philip gains the Leadership of the Greeks (338 B.C.). Philip then steadily extended the territory of his kingdom eastward and northward until it reached the Danube and the Hellespont. His progress on the north of the Ægean soon brought him into conflict with the interests of the Greek states, which owned cities in this northern region. Two parties then arose at Athens. One of them was quite willing to accept Philip's proffered friendship and to recognize in him the uniter and savior of the Greek world. The leader of this party was Isocrates (§ 252), now an aged man. The other party, on the contrary, denounced Philip as a barbarous tyrant who was endeavoring to enslave the free Greek cities. The leader of this anti-Macedonian party was the great orator Demosthenes (Fig. 50). His *Philippics,* as his public speeches denouncing King Philip are called, are among the greatest and noblest specimens of Greek eloquence.

After a long series of hostilities Philip defeated the Greek forces in a final battle at Chæronea (338 B.C.) and firmly established his position as head of a league of all the Greek states except

Sparta, which still held out against him. He had begun operations in Asia Minor intended to set free the Greek cities there, when, two years after the Battle of Chæronea, he was stabbed by conspirators during the revelries at the wedding of his daughter (336 B.C.).

257. Education and Character of Alexander the Great. The power passed into the hands of Philip's son Alexander, a youth of only twenty years. Seven years before, when Alexander was thirteen years of age, his father had summoned to the Macedonian court the great philosopher Aristotle (§ 286), a former pupil of Plato, to be the teacher of the young prince. Under his instruction the lad learned to know and love the masterpieces of Greek literature, especially the Homeric songs. The deeds of the ancient heroes touched and kindled his youthful imagination and lent a heroic tinge to his whole character. As he grew older and his mind ripened, his whole personality was aglow with the splendor of Greek genius and Hellenic culture.

II. Campaigns of Alexander the Great

258. Alexander subjugates the Greek States. The Greek states were still unwilling to submit to Macedonian leadership, and they fancied they could easily overthrow so youthful a ruler as Alexander. They were soon to learn how old a head there was on his young shoulders. When Thebes revolted against Macedonia for the second time after Philip's death, Alexander captured and completely destroyed the ancient city of Thebes, sparing only the house of the great poet Pindar (§ 174). All Greece was thus taught to fear and respect his power, but learned at the same time to recognize his reverence for Greek culture. The Greek states, therefore, with the exception of Sparta, formed a league and elected Alexander as its leader and general. As a result they all sent troops to increase his army.

259. Alexander, the Champion of Hellas against Asia. The Asiatic campaign which Alexander now planned was to make it clear that he was the champion of Hellas against Asia. He thought to lead the united Greeks against the Persian lord of Asia, as the Hellenes had once made common cause against Asiatic Troy (§ 133). Leading his army into Asia Minor, he therefore stopped at Troy and camped upon the plain (Fig. 33, and map, p. 176) where the Greek heroes of the Homeric songs had once fought. Here he worshiped in the temple of Athena and prayed for the success of his cause against Persia. He thus contrived to throw around himself the heroic memories of the Trojan War, till all Hellas beheld the dauntless figure of the Macedonian youth as if he had stepped out of that glorious age which in their belief had long ago united Greek arms against Asia (§ 133).

260. Battle of the Granicus (334 B.C.) and Conquest of Asia Minor. Meantime the Great King had hired thousands of Greek heavy-armed infantry, and they were now to do battle against their own Greek countrymen. At the river Granicus, in his first critical battle, Alexander had no difficulty in scattering the forces of the western Persian satraps. Marching southward he took the Greek cities one by one and freed all western Asia Minor forever from the Persian yoke.

Alexander then pushed boldly eastward and rounded the northeast corner of the Mediterranean. Here, as he looked out upon the Fertile Crescent, there was spread out before him the vast Asiatic world of forty million souls, where the family of the Great King had been supreme for two hundred years. In this great arena he was to be the champion for the next ten years (333–323 B.C.).

261. Defeat of Darius III at the Battle of Issus (333 B.C.). At this important point, by the Gulf of Issus (see map, p. 176), Alexander met the main army of Persia, under the personal command of the Great King, Darius III, the last of the Persian line. The Macedonians swept the Asiatics from the field (see *Ancient Times*, Fig. 202), and the disorderly retreat of Darius never stopped until it had crossed the Euphrates. The Great King then sent a letter to Alexander desiring terms of peace and offering to accept the Euphrates as a boundary between them, all Asia west of that river to be handed over to the Macedonians.

262. Alexander's Decision after Issus. It was a dramatic picture, the figure of the young king standing with this letter in his hand. As he pondered it he was surrounded by a group of the ablest Macedonian youth, who had grown up around him as his closest friends; but likewise by old and trusted counselors upon whom his father before him had leaned. As he considered the letter of Darius III, therefore, his father's old general Parmenio proffered him serious counsel, and, pointing out across the Mediterranean, he bade Alexander remember the Persian fleet operating there in his rear and likely to stir up revolt against him in Greece. There was nothing to do, said Parmenio, but to accept the terms offered by the Great King.

In this critical decision lay the parting of the ways. Before the kindling eyes of the young Alexander there rose a vision of world empire controlled by Greek civilization — a vision to which the duller eyes about him were entirely closed. He waved aside his father's old counselors and decided to advance to the conquest of the whole Persian Empire. In this far-reaching decision he showed himself at once as the strong man who represented a new age.

263. Conquest of Phœnicia and Egypt. The danger from the Persian fleet was now carefully and deliberately met by a march southward along the eastern end of the Mediterranean. All the Phœnician seaports on the way were captured. Feeble Egypt, so long a Persian province, then fell an easy prey to the Macedonian arms. The Persian fleet, thus deprived of all its home harbors and cut off from its home government, soon scattered and disappeared.

264. Alexander Lord of the Ancient East (330 B.C.). Having thus cut off the hostile fleet in his rear, Alexander returned from Egypt to Asia, and, marching eastward along the Fertile Crescent, he crossed the Tigris close by the mounds which had long covered the ruins of Nineveh. Here, near Arbela, the Great King had gathered his forces for a last stand (see map, p. 176). Although greatly outnumbered, the Macedonians crushed the Asiatic army and forced the Persians into disgraceful flight. In a few days Alexander was living in the winter palace of Persia in Babylon.

As Darius III fled into the eastern mountains he was stabbed by his own treacherous attendants (330 B.C.). Alexander rode up with a few of his officers in time to look upon the body of the last of the Persian emperors, the lord of Asia, whose vast realm had now passed into his hands. Thus at last both the valley of the Nile and the Fertile Crescent, the homes of the two earliest civilizations, were now in the hands of a *European* power and under the control of a newer and higher civilization. Less than five years had passed since the young Macedonian had entered Asia. He continued eastward through the original little kingdom of the Persians, whence Cyrus, the founder of the Persian Empire, had victoriously come forth over two hundred years before (see § 97).

265. Alexander's Campaigns in the Far East (330-324 B.C.) and his Return to Babylon (323 B.C.). In the course of the next five years, while the Greek world looked on in amazement, the young Macedonian seemed to disappear in the mists on the far-off eastern fringes of the known world. He marched his army in one vast loop after another through the heart of the Iranian plateau (see map, p. 176), northward across the Oxus and the Jaxartes rivers, southward across the Indus and the frontiers of India, into the valley of the Ganges, where at last the complaints of his weary troops forced him to turn back.

He descended the Indus and even sailed the waters of the Indian Ocean. Then he began his westward march again along the shores of the Indian Ocean, accompanied by a fleet which he had built on the Indus. The return march through desert wastes cost many lives as the thirsty and ill-provisioned troops dropped by the way. Over seven years after he had left the great city of Babylon, Alexander entered it again. He had been less than twelve years in Asia, and he had carried Greek civilization into the very heart of the continent. At important points along his line of march he had founded Greek cities bearing his name and had set up kingdoms which were to be centers of Greek influence on the frontiers of India. Never before had East and West so interpenetrated as in these amazing marches and campaigns of Alexander.

III. INTERNATIONAL POLICY OF ALEXANDER: ITS PERSONAL CONSEQUENCES

266. Alexander's Endeavor to merge European and Asiatic Civilization. Meantime Alexander had been applying himself constantly to the organization and administration of his vast conquests. He believed in the power and superiority of Greek culture. He was determined to Hellenize the world and to unite Asia with Europe by transplanting colonies of Greeks and Macedonians. On the other hand, he also felt that he could not rule the world as a Macedonian, but must make concessions to the Persian world (plate, p. 182). He therefore appointed Persians to high offices and set them over provinces as satraps. He even adopted Persian raiment in part. Finally he married Roxana, an Asiatic princess, and at a gorgeous wedding festival he obliged his officers and friends also to marry the daughters of Asiatic nobles.

267. His Plans to conquer the Western Mediterranean. In the midst of all this he carefully worked out a plan of campaign for the conquest of the *western* Mediterranean. The plan included instructions for the building of a fleet of a thousand battleships with which to subdue Italy, Sicily, and Carthage. It also included the construction of a vast roadway along the northern coast of Africa, to be built at enormous expense, to furnish a highway for his army from Egypt to Carthage and the Atlantic.

268. Deification of Alexander. What was to be his own position in this colossal world-state of which he dreamed? Many a great Greek had come to be recognized as a god, and there was in Greek belief no sharp line dividing gods from men. Alexander found in this attitude of the Greek mind the solution of the question of his own position. He would have himself lifted to a place among the gods. As a god he might impose his will upon the Greek cities without offense. This solution was the more easy because it had for ages been customary to regard the king as divine in Egypt, where he was a son of the Sun-god, and the idea was a common one in the Orient.

In Egypt therefore, seven years before, he had taken the time to march with a small following far out into the Sahara Desert to the Oasis of Siwa, where there was a famous shrine of Amon. The oracles of Amon at Siwa enjoyed the respect of the whole Greek world. Here in the vast solitude Alexander entered the holy place alone. No one knew what took place there, but when he came out he was greeted by the high priest of the temple as the son of the god Amon. Alexander took good care that Greece should hear of this remarkable event (see tailpiece, p. 168).

Four years later the young king found that this divinity which he claimed lacked outward and visible signs. He adopted oriental usages, among which was the requirement that all who approached him on official occasions should bow down to the earth and kiss his feet. He also sent formal notification to all the Greek cities that the league of which he had been head was disbanded, that he was henceforth to be officially numbered among the gods of each city, and that as such he was to receive the State offerings which each city presented. Thus were introduced into Europe absolute monarchy and the divine right of kings.

269. Personal Consequences suffered by Alexander. This superhuman station of the world-king Alexander was gained at tragic cost to Alexander the Macedonian youth and to the old friends and followers about him. They could not comprehend the necessity for measures which strained or snapped entirely those bonds of friendship which linked together comrades in arms. And then there were the Persian intruders, given high offices and treated like the equals of his personal friends (plate, p. 182) or even placed over them! Differences about these things caused the death of many of Alexander's old-time friends. Indeed, in a fit of rage, he himself murdered Clitus, who in the battle of the Granicus had saved his life, and who now had dared to reproach him openly. Thereupon, as we see the king in abject remorse sitting for three days in his tent, speechless with grief, refusing all food, and restrained only by his officers from taking his own life, we gather some slight impression of the terrible personal cost of Alexander's state policy.

270. Death of Alexander (323 B.C.) and Some of its Consequences. As Alexander was preparing for a campaign to subjugate the Arabian peninsula and leave him free to carry out his great plans for the conquest of the western Mediterranean, he fell sick, probably as the result of a drunken debauch, and after a few days died (323 B.C.). He was thirty-three years of age and had reigned thirteen years.

Alexander has been well termed "the Great." Few men of genius, and certainly none in so brief a career, have left so indelible a mark upon the course of human affairs. By his remarkable conquests he gave to the Greeks that *political* leadership which the triumph of their *civilization* had never before gained for them. His death in the midst of his colossal designs was a fearful calamity, for it made impossible forever the unification of Hellas and of the civilized world of that day by the power of that gifted race which was then civilizing the world. But his amazing conquests had placed the Orient under Western, that is, European, leaders, and from that day to this—with some intervals—the effort to force Western leadership on the Orient has continued.

IV. The Heirs of Alexander's Empire

271. Division of Alexander's Realm; the Ptolemies in Egypt. After a generation of exhausting wars by land and sea, Alexander's empire fell into three main parts,—in Europe, Asia, and Africa,—with one of his generals, or one of their successors, at the head of each. In Europe, Macedonia was in the hands of Antigonus, grandson of Alexander's commander of the same name. He endeavored also to maintain control of Greece. In Asia most of the territory of the former Persian Empire was under the rule of Alexander's general Seleucus; while in Africa, Egypt was held by Ptolemy, one of the cleverest of Alexander's Macedonian leaders. He gradually made himself king and became the founder of a dynasty or family of kings, whom we call the Ptolemies. Ptolemy at once saw that he would be constantly obliged to draw Greek mercenary troops from Greece. With statesmanlike judgment he therefore built up a fleet which gave him the mastery of the Mediterranean. He took up his residence at the great harbor city of Alexandria, the city which Alexander had founded in the western Nile Delta. For nearly a century (roughly the third century B.C.) the eastern Mediterranean from Greece to Syria and from the Ægean to the Nile Delta was an Egyptian sea. Thus under Macedonian leaders arose an Egyptian empire in the eastern Mediterranean like that which we found nearly a thousand years earlier (§ 49).

272. The Asiatic Empire of the Seleucids. The Seleucids (as we call Seleucus and his descendants) were not as powerful as the Ptolemies. Nevertheless they were the chief heirs of Alexander, for they held the larger part of his empire, extending at first from the Ægean to the frontiers of India. Its boundaries were not fixed, and its enormous extent made it very difficult to govern and maintain. The fleet of the Ptolemies hampered the commercial development and prosperity of the Seleucids, who therefore found it difficult to reach Greece for trade, troops, or colonists. They gave special attention to Syria, the region around the northeast corner of the Mediterranean reaching to the Euphrates. This empire is therefore often called Syria. Here, on the lower Orontes, Seleucus founded the great city which he called Antioch (after his father, Antiochus). It finally enjoyed great prosperity and became the commercial rival of Alexandria and the greatest seat of commerce in the northern Mediterranean (see map, p. 176).

273. The Macedonian Empire of the Antigonids. Compared with her two great rivals in Egypt and Asia, Macedonia in Europe seemed small indeed. Here Antigonus II, grandson of Alexander's general, became king (277 B.C.). He built a war fleet at vast expense, and in a long naval war with the Ptolemies he twice defeated the Egyptian fleet, thereby freeing the eastern Mediterranean from the former control of Egypt.

274. Decline of Greece. Greece was no longer commercial leader of the Mediterranean. The victories of Alexander the Great had opened up the vast Persian Empire to Greek commercial colonists, who poured into all the favorable centers of trade. Not only did Greece decline in population but commercial prosperity and the leadership in trade passed eastward, especially to Alexandria and Antioch. As the Greek cities lost their wealth they could no longer support fleets or mercenary armies, and they soon became too feeble to protect themselves. Although they began to combine in alliances or federations for mutual protection, they were unable to throw off the Macedonian yoke. In spite of the political feebleness of the Greeks in this age, their civilization reached its highest level under the successors of Alexander.

V. The Civilization of the Hellenistic Age

275. The Hellenistic Age. The three centuries following the death of Alexander we call the Hellenistic Age, meaning the period in which Greek civilization spread throughout the ancient world, especially the Orient, and was itself much modified by the culture of the Orient. The Orientals now had Greek-speaking rulers whose government and affairs were carried on in the Greek language.[1] This was the Greek spoken in Attica. The Orientals transacted business with multitudes of Greek merchants; they found many Greek books, attracting them to read. Attic Greek thus gradually became the daily language of the great cities and of an enormous world stretching from Sicily (Fig. 69) and southern Italy eastward on both sides of the Mediterranean and thence far into the Orient.

Civilized life in the cities enjoyed more comfort and was better equipped than ever before. The citizen's house (Fig. 51) was more beautifully furnished and decorated (§ 279), and for the first time it now possessed its own water pipes connected with the town water supply. The streets also were equipped with drainage channels or pipes, a thing unknown in the days of Pericles.

276. Rise of Secular Public Buildings. In the public buildings also a great change had taken place. The architects of the

---

[1] For a fuller sketch of Hellenistic civilization see *Ancient Times*, §§ 727–768.

Hellenistic Age began to design the first large and splendid buildings to house the offices of the government. These stately public buildings were erected in the heart of the city, where in early Greek and oriental cities the castle of the king had once stood.[1]

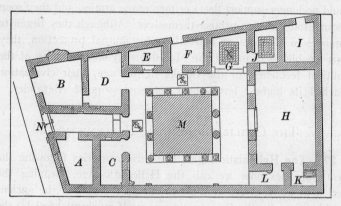

FIG. 51. GROUND PLAN OF THE HOUSE OF A WEALTHY GREEK BUILT IN THE HELLENISTIC AGE

The rooms are arranged around a central court (*M*) which is open to the sky. A roofed porch with columns (called a *peristyle*) surrounds the court (cf. Figs. 11 and 60). The main entrance is at *N*, with the room of the door-keeper on the right (*A*). At the corner is a shop (*B*). *C*, *D*, and *E* are for storage and housekeeping. *F* is a back-door entry through which supplies were delivered; it contained a stairway to the second floor. *G* was used as a small living room, with an inner living room (*J*) beside it. It had a built-in divan, and the entire side toward the peristyle was open. The finest room in the house was *H*, measuring about sixteen by twenty-six feet, with a mosaic floor, in seven colors, and richly decorated walls. It was lighted by a large door and two windows, and was accessible also by the passage *L*. *K* was a little bathroom, with a large marble bathtub. The sleeping rooms were all on the second floor, which cannot now be reconstructed. *I* was a second tiny shop. This house was excavated by the French on the island of Delos

277. Alexandria : its Commerce and Splendid Public Buildings.

In numbers, wealth, commerce, power, and in all the arts of civilization, Alexandria was now the greatest city of the whole ancient world. Along the harbors stretched the extensive Alexandrian docks, where ships which had braved the Atlantic storms

[1] For the interesting town of Priene see *Ancient Times*, pp. 460–461.

off the coasts of Spain and Africa moored beside oriental craft which had penetrated even to the gates of the Indian Ocean and gathered the wares of the vast oriental world beyond. From far across the sea the mariners approaching at night could catch the light of a lofty beacon shining from a gigantic lighthouse tower which marked the entrance of the harbor of Alexandria. This wonderful tower, the tallest building ever erected by a Hellenistic engineer, was a descendant of the old Babylonian temple-tower (see *Ancient Times*, p. 170 and Figs. 213 and 272), with which it was closely related.

From the deck of a great merchant ship of over four thousand tons the incoming traveler might look cityward past the lighthouse and beyond the great war fleet of the Ptolemies and see, embowered in the rich green masses of tropical verdure, the magnificent marble buildings of Alexandria : the royal palace, the museum, the gymnasiums, baths, stadiums, assembly hall, concert hall, market places, and basilicas, all surrounded by the residence quarters of the citizens. Unfortunately, not one of the splendid buildings of ancient Alexandria still stands.

278. Athenian Sculpture. We are more fortunate in the case of Pergamum (map, p. 90), another splendid city of this age which grew up under Athenian influences (Fig. 52). One of the kings of Pergamum defeated and beat off the hordes of Gauls who had come in from Europe. This achievement greatly stirred the Attic sculptors who were supported by the kings of Pergamum. They carved heroic marble figures of the Northern barbarians in the tragic moment of death in battle (Fig. 63 ; see also *Ancient Times*, Figs. 215 and 216). This same struggle with the Gauls was also suggested by an enormous band of relief sculpture depicting the mythical battle between the gods and the giants (Fig. 64). This vast work extended almost entirely around a colossal altar (Fig. 52, *A*) erected by the kings of Pergamum in honor of Zeus, to adorn the market place of the city. Among the best works of the Athenian sculptors of this age were also the reliefs on a wonderful marble sarcophagus, showing the great deeds of Alexander the Great (plate, p. 182).

279. Painting and Mosaic.

The great Greek painters of this age also loved to depict intensely dramatic and tragic incidents. Their original works have all perished, but copies of some of them have survived in the Italian city of Pompeii, painted on the walls as interior decorations of fine houses or worked out in mosaic as floor pavement (see headpiece and Note, p. 169).

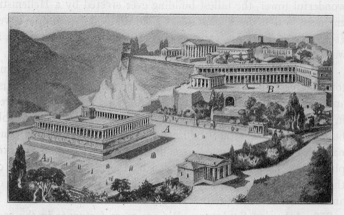

FIG. 52. RESTORATION OF THE PUBLIC BUILDINGS OF PERGAMUM, A HELLENISTIC CITY OF ASIA MINOR. (AFTER THIERSCH)

Pergamum, on the west coast of Asia Minor (see map, p. 90), became a flourishing city-kingdom in the third century B.C. under the successors of Alexander the Great (§ 271). The dwellings of the citizens were all lower down, in front of the group of buildings shown here. These public buildings stand on three terraces — lower, middle, and upper. The large *lower* terrace (*A*) was the main market place, adorned with a vast square marble altar of Zeus, having colonnades on three sides, beneath which was a long sculptured band (frieze) of warring gods and giants (Fig. 64). On the *middle* terrace (*B*), behind the colonnades, was the famous library of Pergamum, where the stone bases of library shelves still survive. The *upper* terrace (*C*) once contained the palace of the king; the temple now there was built by the Roman Emperor Trajan in the second century of the Christian era

280. Mechanical Progress; Archimedes and Science.

The keen and wide-awake intelligence of this wonderful age was everywhere evident, but especially in the application of science to the work and needs of daily life. It was an age of inventions; for example, the screw and the cogwheel were now invented. One of

GREEKS AND PERSIANS HUNTING LIONS WITH ALEXANDER THE GREAT

Alexander is out of range at the left. A Greek on horseback endeavors to pierce the wounded lion with his spear. A Persian friend or attendant of Alexander on foot wields an ax. Relief scene on a marble sarcophagus found at Sidon in 1881; the colors are exactly as on the original, now in the Museum at Constantinople. It was made not long after Alexander's death, and is one of the greatest works of Hellenistic art. (After Winter, *Alexandermosaik*)

the famous feats of the great scientist Archimedes was his arrangement of a series of pulleys and levers, which so multiplied power that the king was able by turning a light crank to move a large three-masted ship standing fully loaded on the dock and to launch it into the water. After witnessing such feats as this the people easily believed his proud boast, "Give me a place to stand on and I will move the earth." But Archimedes was far more than an inventor of practical appliances. He was a scientific investigator of the first rank, the discoverer of what science now calls specific gravity. Besides his skill in physics he was also the greatest of ancient mathematicians.

281. The Alexandrian Scientists. Although Archimedes lived in Syracuse he was in close correspondence with his friends in Alexandria, who formed the greatest body of scientists in the ancient world. They lived together at the *Museum*, where they were paid salaries and supported by the Ptolemies. They formed the first scientific institution founded and supported by a government. They became the founders of systematic scientific research, and their books were consulted as containing almost all the scientific knowledge of mankind for nearly two thousand years, until the revival of science in modern times.

The most famous mathematician among them was Euclid. His complete system of geometry was so logically built up that in modern England Euclid's geometry is still retained as a schoolbook — the oldest schoolbook in use to-day. Along with mathematics much progress was also made in astronomy. The Ptolemies built an astronomical observatory at Alexandria ; and although it was, of course, without telescopes, important observations and discoveries were made. An astronomer of little fame named Aristarchus, who lived on the island of Samos, even discovered that the planets revolve around the sun, though few people would believe him and his discovery was forgotten.

Astronomy had now greatly aided in the progress of geography. Eratosthenes, a great mathematical astronomer of Alexandria, very cleverly computed the approximate size of the earth. Much new information had also been gained regarding the extent and the character of the new regions reached by navigation and exploration in this age from the eastern coast of India to the British Isles. Eratosthenes was therefore able to write a more accurate geography than anyone before his time. It contained the first map bearing a cross-net of lines indicating latitude and longitude. He thus became the founder of scientific geography.

In the study of animal and vegetable life Aristotle and his pupils were the leaders, and the ancient world never outgrew their observations (§ 286). For the study of anatomy there was a laboratory in Alexandria, at the Museum, which the Ptolemies furnished with condemned criminals, on whom vivisection was practiced. In this way the nerves were discovered to be the lines along which sensations pass to the brain. Such research even came very near to discovering the circulation of the blood. Alexandria became the greatest center of medical research in the ancient world, and here young men studied to be physicians, much as they do in our medical schools to-day.

232. The Alexandrian Library and Book Publishing. Besides these natural sciences, there was now also much study of literature. The first library founded and supported by a Greek government had arisen during the childhood of Alexander the Great (not long before 350 B.C.). All such efforts were far surpassed by the Ptolemies at Alexandria, where their library finally contained over half a million rolls. The immense amount of hand copying required to secure good and accurate editions of famous works for this library gradually created the new science of editing and publishing correctly old and often badly copied works.[1] This naturally required much language study, and the Alexandrian scholars then began to write the first grammars and dictionaries.

233. Hellenistic Literature. Literature was to a large extent in the hands of such learned men as those of Alexandria. Forsaking war and tragedy, these scholars loved to picture such scenes as the shepherd at the spring, listening to the music of overhanging boughs, lazily watching his flocks, and dreaming the while of some winsome village maid who has scorned his devotion. In such

---

[1] See a page from the oldest surviving Greek book in *Ancient Times*, Fig. 223.

verse the greatest literary artist of the age was a Sicilian named Theocritus, whose idyls have taken a permanent place in the world's literature for two thousand years.

284. Education : Elementary Schools and Gymnasiums. In such a cultivated world education had made much progress. The elementary schools, once *private*, were now often *supported by the State*. When the lad had finished at the elementary school, his father allowed him to attend lectures on rhetoric, science, philosophy, and mathematics in the lecture rooms of the gymnasium building. Such an atmosphere was one to create great interest in study, and often a youth besought his father to allow him a few years of study at the Museum or in the schools of philosophy at Athens in preparation for a profession.

285. The Alexandrian Museum as a University. As the student strolled through the beautiful royal gardens of Alexandria and entered the Museum building, he found going on there lectures on astronomy, geography, physics, mathematics, botany, zoölogy, anatomy, medicine, or rhetoric, grammar, and literature.

286. The Schools of the University at Athens ; Aristotle. Athens was still the leading home of philosophy. The youth who went there to take up philosophical studies found the successors of Plato still continuing his teaching in the quiet grove of the Academy (§ 207), where his memory was greatly revered. Plato's pupil Aristotle, after having been the teacher of the young Alexander (§ 257), had returned to Athens, and he also had established at the Lyceum (§ 207) a school of his own known as the *Peripatetic* School, because it occupied a terrace called the "Walk" (Greek *peripatos*). With the help of groups of his more advanced students Aristotle put together a veritable encyclopedia of old and new facts in the different natural sciences, besides writing many treatises on other subjects, like logic, ethics, psychology, the drama, government, etc. The work was never completed, and many of the essays and treatises which it included have been lost. When Aristotle died, soon after the death of Alexander, his school declined. Aristotle's works formed the greatest attempt ever made in ancient times to collect and to state in a clear way the whole mass of human knowledge. The writings of no other man have ever enjoyed such widespread and unquestioned authority.[1]

But many Greeks desired some teaching which would lead them to a happy and contented frame of mind and guide men in their attempts to live successfully. To meet this desire two more schools of philosophy arose at Athens. The first, the *Stoic* School, taught that the great aim of life should be a fortitude of soul, which comes from virtue and is indifferent both to pleasure and to pain. Its followers were famous for their fortitude, and hence our common use of the word "stoicism" to indicate indifference to suffering. The Stoic School was very popular and finally became the greatest of the schools of philosophy. The second, the *Epicurean* School, founded by Epicurus in his own garden at Athens, taught that the highest good was pleasure, both of body and of mind, but always in moderation and in accordance with virtue. Its views were highminded but often misunderstood, hence even now we call a man devoted to pleasure, especially in eating, an "epicure." The school of Epicurus, like the Stoics, flourished and attracted many disciples.

These schools lived on the income of property left them by wealthy pupils and friends. We may regard Hellenistic Athens then (with its Academy, Lyceum, Stoic School, and Epicurean School) as possessing a university made up of four colleges, like an English university. The Museum of Alexandria was modeled on these Athenian organizations, and they have also become the model for academies of science and for universities ever since.

287. The Fall of the Old Greek Gods. For highly educated men the beliefs of Stoicism or Epicureanism served as their religion. Such men usually no longer believed in the gods in the old way. There was complete freedom of conscience — far more freedom than the Christian rulers of later Europe granted their subjects. The teachings of Socrates would no longer have caused his condemnation by his Athenian neighbors.

288. Increased Popularity of Oriental Gods. The great multitude of the common people had not the education to understand

[1] See *Outlines of European History*, Part I, p. 547.

philosophy nor the means to attend the philosophical schools. With the weakening of their faith in the old Greek gods many Greeks adopted the gods of the Orient, and these gods became more and more popular. Oriental beliefs and oriental symbols were everywhere. It was in an age like this that Christianity, an oriental religion, later passed easily from land to land (§420). More than ever the Orient exerted a steady pressure upon the life of the eastern Mediterranean, in commerce, government, customs, industry, art, literature, and religion.

289. The Larger World of the Hellenistic Age. In this larger world, with all its foreign, non-Greek life, the old Greek *city*-citizen, who had made Greek civilization what it was, played but a small part. The city-citizen had no share in guiding the affairs of the great nation or empire of which his city-state was a part. It was as if a citizen of Chicago might vote at the election of a mayor of his own city but had no right to vote at the election of a president of the United States. There was not even a name for the empire of the Seleucids, and their subjects, wherever they went, bore the names of their home cities or countries. The conception of "native land" in our sense was wanting, and patriotism did not exist.

A larger world had thus swallowed up the old Greek city-states. For while Greek civilization, with its language, its art, its literature, its theaters and gymnasiums, was *hellenizing the Orient*, the Orient in the same way was *orientalizing the eastern Mediterranean world*. But this world of the *eastern* Mediterranean, with its mixed Hellenic-oriental civilization, which had grown up as a result of Alexander's conquests, had by 200 B.C. reached a point when it was to feel the iron hand of a great new military power from the distant world of the *western* Mediterranean. At this point, therefore (200 B.C.), we shall be unable to understand the further story of the eastern Mediterranean until we have turned back and taken up the career of the western Mediterranean world. There in the West for some three centuries the city of Rome had been developing a power which was to unite both the East and the West into a vast empire including the *whole Mediterranean*.

QUESTIONS

I. Describe the new military arrangements of Philip of Macedon. What two parties arose at Athens? What was the result of the struggle between Philip and the Greeks? Who succeeded Philip and how was he educated?

II. How did Alexander deal with the Greeks? What great war did he then begin? Describe it until his arrival at the Gulf of Issus. What happened there? How was the danger from the Phœnician fleet met? What ancient land was thus conquered?

To what country did Alexander then march? What became of the Persian king after the Battle of Arbela? What was the result? What marches did Alexander then undertake? How did he establish Greek influences in the lands he traversed?

III. What was Alexander's policy regarding the relations of Asia and Europe? What further conquests did he plan? What was to be his own position as ruler? How did he endeavor to secure divine honors? How did this affect his friends? How did all this affect Alexander? What is the date of his death? Discuss the consequences of Alexander's death.

IV. What three empires resulted from the wars after Alexander's death? Discuss the empire of the Ptolemies; the empire of the Seleucids; the empire of the Antigonids. How did the fall of the Persian Empire affect Greece? How did the rise of Alexandria and Antioch affect Greek commerce? What were the consequences in Greece?

V. What is meant by the term "Hellenistic Age"? What improvements in houses appeared? What new kind of public buildings arose? Describe Alexandria; Pergamum and its sculpture; painting and mosaic. What can you say of inventive ability in the Hellenistic Age? Tell about Archimedes. What place do the Alexandrian scientists occupy in the history of science?

Discuss Alexandrian publishing and its influence; literature and education. What schools of philosophy arose? What happened to old Greek religion? Describe the civilization of the eastern Mediterranean world. What power was now about to lead?

BOOK IV. THE ROMANS

CHAPTER XIII

THE WESTERN MEDITERRANEAN WORLD AND THE ROMAN CONQUEST OF ITALY

I. THE WESTERN MEDITERRANEAN WORLD

290. The Mediterranean the Stage of Ancient History. The Mediterranean Sea is a very large body of water, almost as long as Europe itself. Its length is about twenty-four hundred miles, and laid out across the United States it would reach from New York over into California. A land bridge made up of Italy and Sicily extends almost across this great sea and divides it into two basins, which we may therefore conveniently call the

NOTE. The above headpiece shows an ancient bronze wolf (sixth century B.C.), wrought by Greek artists in Italy (§ 153), and illustrates the influence of Greek civilization in Rome even before 500 B.C. The two infants nourished by the she-wolf are later additions, put there in accordance with the tradition at Rome that the city was founded by these twin brothers, named Romulus and Remus. Their ancestor, so said the tradition, was Æneas (§ 387), one of the Trojan heroes, who had fled from Troy after its destruction (§ 133), and after many adventures had arrived in Italy. His son founded and became king of Alba Longa (§ 295). In the midst of a family feud among his descendants these twin boys, the sons of the War-god, Mars, were born, and after they had been set adrift in the Tiber by the ruling king, they gently ran aground at the base of the Palatine Hill, where a she-wolf found and nourished them. When they grew up they founded Rome. Similar legends formed all that the Romans knew of their early history through the period of the kings and far down into the Republic.

eastern and western Mediterranean worlds. Since we left pre-historic Europe (Chapter I) we have been following the story of civilized men in the *eastern* Mediterranean world; we must now turn back and take up the story of the *western* Mediterranean world also.

291. Italy : its Geography and Climate. The most important land in the western Mediterranean world in early times was Italy.

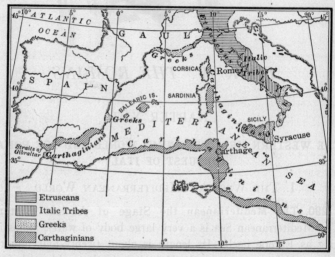

THE FOUR RIVAL PEOPLES OF THE WESTERN MEDITERRANEAN :
ETRUSCANS, ITALIC TRIBES, GREEKS, AND CARTHAGINIANS

It slopes westward in the main; it thus faces and belongs to the western Mediterranean world. The Italian peninsula (see map, p. 192) is nearly six hundred miles long. Italy is not only much larger than Greece but, unlike Greece, it is not cut up by a tangle of mountains into winding valleys and tiny plains. The main chain of the Apennines, though crossing the peninsula ob-liquely in the north, is nearly parallel with the coasts. There are larger plains for the cultivation of grain than we find anywhere in Greece ; and there is also much more room for upland pastur-age of flocks and herds. At the same time the coast is not so cut up and indented as in Greece; there are fewer good harbors. Hence agriculture and live stock developed much earlier than sea trade.

292. Western Indo-European Wing enters Italy. Probably not long after the Greeks had pushed southward into the Greek peninsula (§ 131), the western tribes of Indo-European blood had entered the Italian peninsula. The most important group, which settled in the central and southern parts of the peninsula, was the Italic tribes, the earliest Italians.

We remember that the Greeks, in conquering the Ægean, took possession of a highly civilized region on the borders of the Orient. This was not the case with the Indo-European invaders of Italy. They found the western Mediterranean world still without civilization. It had no architecture, no fine

FIG. 53. ETRUSCAN CHARIOT OF BRONZE

This magnificent work shows the ability of the Etruscans in the art of bronze-working (§ 298). The chariot was found in an Etruscan tomb in Italy; it is of full size and now belongs to the Metropolitan Museum of New York City

buildings, no fortified cities, only the rudest arts and industries, no writing, no literature, and no organized governments.

293. The Three Western Rivals confronting the Italic Tribes. After the Italic invaders three rival peoples gradually came into the western Mediterranean world. They all came from the *eastern* Mediterranean world. The *first* of these was a bold race of sea rovers whom we call the Etruscans. Their origin is still uncertain, but they probably had an earlier home in western Asia Minor. In any case the Etruscans had landed in Italy and were settled there by 1000 B.C. They finally gained full control of the west coast of Italy from the Bay of Naples almost to Genoa, and held the inland country to the Adriatic Sea and the Alps (see map, p. 192).

The Carthaginians were the *second* of the three rivals of the Italic tribes. We remember how the Phœnicians carried their commerce far into the western Mediterranean after 1000 B.C. (§ 139). On the African coast opposite Sicily they established a flourishing commercial city called Carthage. It soon became the leading harbor in the western Mediterranean. The Carthaginians finally held the northern coast of Africa westward to the Atlantic. Besides gaining southern Spain, they were also conquering the islands of the western Mediterranean, especially Sicily.

While the Carthaginians were endeavoring to make the western Mediterranean their own, the Italic peoples saw their *third* rivals invading the West. They were the Greeks. We have already followed the Greek colonies as they founded their city-states along the coast of southern Italy and in Sicily in the eighth century B.C. (§ 153). The strongest of all the western Greek cities was Syracuse, which took the lead more than once. We recall how the Athenians tried to conquer the West by capturing Syracuse (§§ 228–231).

294. Western Greek Colonies bring Civilization into the Western Mediterranean. Although the western Greeks, like those in the homeland, fought among themselves and failed to unite in a strong and permanent state, they brought the first civilization to Italy (§ 153). Thus fifteen hundred years after the barbarous Italic tribes had first settled in Italy there grew up on the south of them a wonderful world of Greek civilization, which went on developing, to reach its highest point in that Hellenistic culture which brought forth an Archimedes at Syracuse (§ 280). Let us now turn back to follow the career of the barbarous Italic tribes of central Italy under the leadership of Rome, and watch them slowly gaining organization and power and, finally, civilization, as they were influenced first by the Etruscans on their *north* and then by the Greeks on the *south* of them.

II. Earliest Rome

295. The Tribes of Latium. On the south or east bank of the Tiber, which flows into the sea in the middle of the west coast of Italy (see map, p. 192), there was a group of Italic tribes known as the Latins. In the days when the Etruscan sea raiders first landed on the shores north of the Tiber these Latin tribes had occupied a plain less than thirty by forty miles; that is, smaller than many an American county. They called it "Latium," whence their own name, "Latins." Like their Italic neighbors they lived scattered in small communities, cultivating grain and pasturing flocks on the upland. Their land was not very fertile, and the struggle for existence developed a strong and hardy people. Their center was a small town called Alba Longa, whose leadership the Latin tribes followed when they were obliged to unite and repel the attacks of their hostile neighbors on all sides. They watched very anxiously the growth of the flourishing Etruscan towns on the other (north) side of the Tiber, and they did what they could to keep the Etruscans from crossing to the Latin side.

296. The Emergence of Early Rome. When these Latin peasants needed weapons or tools they were obliged to carry their grain or oxen to a trading post on the south side of the Tiber, ten or twelve miles from its mouth (Fig. 54). Several neighboring hills bore straggling villages, and there was a stronghold on a hill called the Palatine. Here, stopped by the shoals, moored now and then an Etruscan ship which had sailed up the Tiber, the only navigable river in Italy. On the low marshy ground, encircled by the hills, was an open-air market, which they called the Forum, where the Latin peasants could meet the Etruscan traders and exchange grain or oxen for the metal tools or weapons they needed. Such must have been the condition of the group of villages called Rome about 1000 B.C.

297. Rome seized by Etruscans (about 750 B.C.). The Etrus-can invasion which the Latin tribes feared finally took place. Perhaps as early as 750 B.C. one of the Etruscan princes crossed the Tiber, drove out the last of the line of Latin chieftains, and took possession of the stronghold on the Palatine. From this place as his castle and palace he gained control of the villages on the hills above the Tiber, which then gradually merged into the

FIG. 54. THE TIBER AND ITS ISLAND AT ROME

The Tiber is not a large river, but when swollen by the spring freshets it still sometimes floods a large portion of Rome, doing serious damage. The houses which we see on the island are some of them old, but not as old as the ancient Rome we are to study. The bridges, however, are very old. The one on the right of the island was built of massive stone masonry in 62 B.C. It has been standing for over two thousand years. Many great Romans, like Julius Cæsar, whose names are familiar to us, must often have crossed this bridge

city of Rome. These Etruscan kings soon extended their power over the Latin tribes of the plain of Latium. The town of Alba Longa, which once led the Latins, disappeared. Thus Rome be-came a city-kingdom under an Etruscan king, like the other Etruscan cities which stretched from Capua far north to the harbor of Genoa (see map, p. 192). Although Rome was then ruled by a line of Etruscan kings for probably two centuries and a half, it must be borne in mind that the population of Latium which the Etruscan kings governed continued to be Latin and to speak the Latin tongue.

298. Etruscans receive Greek Civilization. The Etruscans had been trafficking in the Greek harbors since Mycenæan days. In time they learned to write their own language with Greek letters. Many tombs containing their inscriptions still survive in Italy. Although we know the letters and can pronounce the

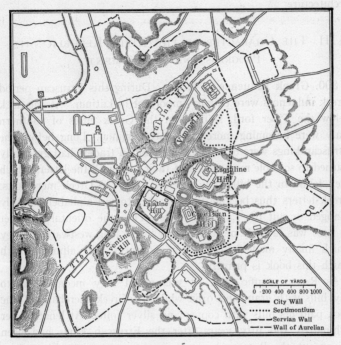

MAP OF EARLY ROME SHOWING THE SUCCESSIVE STAGES OF ITS GROWTH

Etruscan words, scholars are still unable to understand them. This intercourse with Greece also brought in many other products of Greek civilization, like the beautiful Greek vases (Fig. 35), until the Etruscans adopted much Greek civilization. They early produced such fine work in bronze (Fig. 53) that for a time it even excelled the metal work of the Greeks.

299. Expulsion of the Etruscan Kings of Rome (about 500 B.C.). The Etruscan kings introduced great improvements into Rome, but their cruelty and tyranny finally caused a revolt of their Latin subjects, and thus the kings of Rome were driven out. Thus about 500 B.C. the career of Rome under monarchs came to an end; but the two and a half centuries of Etruscan rule left their mark on Rome, always afterward discernible, especially in architecture.

III. The Character of the Early Republic: its Progress and Government

300. Greek Influence in Rome. During this Etruscan period Greek influences were equally important in Latium. At the dock below the Tiber ford, ships from the Greek cities of southern Italy were becoming more and more common. Long before the Etruscan kings were driven out the Roman traders had gradually learned to scribble memoranda of their own with the letters which they found in the bills they received from the Greek merchants. Greek letters thus became likewise the Roman alphabet, slightly changed to suit the Latin language. Thus the oriental alphabet (§ 140) was carried one step further in the long westward journey which finally made it (after some changes) the alphabet with which this book is printed.

As Roman traffic grew, it was found very inconvenient to pay bills with grain and oxen while the Greek merchant at the dock paid his bills with copper and silver coins. At length, over a hundred and fifty years after the Etruscan kings had been driven out, the Romans began to issue copper coins (Fig. 55).

But the Greeks also influenced other things besides Roman business. For the Roman peasant heard of strange gods of the Greeks, and he was told that they were the counterparts or the originals of his own gods. He was told that Venus was the Greek Aphrodite, Mercury was Hermes, Ceres was Demeter, and so on. For the Roman there was a god over each realm in nature and each field of human life: Jupiter was the great Sky-god and king of all the gods; Mars, the patron of all warriors; Venus, the queen of love; Juno, an ancient Sky-goddess, was protectress of women, of birth and marriage, while Vesta too watched over the household life ; Ceres was the goddess who maintained the fruitfulness of the earth, and especially the grainfields (compare English "cereal") ; and Mercury was the messenger of the gods, who protected intercourse and *merch*andising, as his name shows.

301. Mechanical Character of the Roman Mind. The rather coldly calculating Roman lacked the warm and vivid imagination of the Greeks which had created the beautiful Greek mythology.

A   *B*

FIG. 55. SPECIMENS OF EARLY ROMAN COPPER MONEY

In the time of Alexander the Great (second half of the fourth century B. C.) the Romans found it too inconvenient to continue paying their debts in goods, especially in cattle (§ 296). They therefore cast copper in blocks, each block with the figure of an ox upon it (see *A*, above), to indicate its value. The Roman word for cattle (*pecus*) was the origin of one of their frequent words for property (*pecunia*) and has descended to us in our common word "pecuniary." These blocks were unwieldy, and, influenced by the Greeks, the Romans then cast large disks of copper (*B*, above), which were also very ponderous, each weighing nearly a pound Troy. This coin was called an *as*. When two generations later (268 B. C.) the Romans began to coin silver (see Fig. 56), copper was no longer used for large payments and the *as* was reduced in size to one sixth its former weight

The Romans were better fitted for great achievements in political and legal organization than for new and original developments in religion, art, literature, or discoveries in science. Let us now see how Roman common sense and political wisdom developed the Roman State.

302. Establishment of the Roman Republic. When the Etruscan kings were driven out of Rome, about 500 B.C., the nobles, called *patricians*, were in control of the government. The patricians agreed that two of their number should be *elected* as heads of the State. These two magistrates, called *consuls,* were both to have the same powers, were to serve for a year only and then give way to two others. To choose them, annual elections were held in an assembly of the weapon-bearing men, largely under the control of the patricians. Nevertheless, we must call this new state a republic, of which the consuls were the presidents ; for the people had a voice in electing them. But as only patricians could serve as consuls, their government was very oppressive. The people (called the *plebs* ; compare our "plebeian"), especially among the Latin tribes, refused to submit to such oppression.

303. The Tribunes Defenders of the People. The patricians were unable to get on without the help of the people as soldiers in their frequent wars. They therefore agreed to give the people a larger share in the government, by allowing them in their own assembly to elect a group of new officials, called *tribunes.* The tribunes had the right to veto the action of any officer of the government — even that of the consuls themselves. When any citizen was treated unjustly by a consul he had only to appeal to one of the tribunes.

304. Growing Body of Government Officials. It gradually became necessary to create new officers for various kinds of business. To take care of the government funds, treasury officials called *quæstors* were appointed. Officials called *censors* were required to keep lists of the people, to look after their daily conduct and see that nothing improper was permitted. Our own use of the word "censor" is derived from these Roman officials. For the decision of legal cases a judge called a *prætor* was appointed to assist the consul, and the number of such judges slowly increased. In times of great national danger it was customary to appoint some revered and trustworthy leader as the supreme ruler of the State. He was called the Dictator, and he could hold his power for but a brief period.

305. The Senate and the Struggle of Plebs and Patricians. The consuls had great power and influence in all government matters, but they were much influenced by a council of patricians called the Senate (from Latin *senex*, meaning "old man"). The patricians enjoyed the exclusive right to serve as consuls, to sit in the Senate, and to hold almost all of the offices created to carry on the business of government (§ 304).

The tribunes, as we have seen (§ 303), could protect the people from some injustices, but they could not secure to the plebeian citizen the right to be elected as consul, or to become a senator, or to marry a patrician's daughter. The struggle of the common people to win their rights from the wealthy and powerful therefore continued. It was a struggle like that which we have followed in Athens and the other Greek states ; but at Rome it reached a much wiser and more successful settlement. The citizens of Rome manfully stood forth for their rights, and without fighting, civil war, or bloodshed they secured them to a large extent in the course of the first two centuries after the founding of the Republic.

306. Written Codes and New Laws. They insisted upon a record of the existing laws *in writing*, in order that they might know by what laws they were being judged. About fifty years after the establishment of the Republic the earliest Roman laws were reduced to writing and engraved upon twelve tablets of bronze (450 B.C.). But at the same time the people demanded the right to share in the making of *new* laws and to possess an assembly of the people, which might pass new laws.

307. Laws and Lawmaking Power. Having shaken off the legal power of the Senate to control their action, the assemblies of the people became the lawmaking bodies of the Roman State. In this way the people gradually secured a fairer share of the public lands and further social rights. Finally, and most important of all, these new laws increased the rights of the people to hold office. In the end Roman citizens elected their plebeian neighbors as censors and quæstors, as judges and at last even as consuls, and they saw men of the people sitting in the Senate.

308. New Nobility made up of Former Magistrates. Roman citizens had a deep respect for government and for its officials. There soon grew up a group of once plebeian families distinguished by the public service of its members, to whom the Roman citizens looked up with great respect. When the voters were called upon to select their candidates they preferred members of these eminent families, especially for the consulship. A new nobility was thus formed, made up of such illustrious families and the old patricians.

As a result of these changes this new nobility found its way into the Senate, which was thus made up of the three hundred men of Rome who had gained the most experience in government and in public affairs. Their combined influence was finally stronger than that of the consuls themselves, who were therefore obliged to carry on the government according to instructions from the Senate.

309. The Roman Senate Supreme Leader of the State. By far the larger part of the Roman citizens lived too far away to come up to the city and vote. Feeling, too, their own ignorance of public affairs, the Roman citizens were not unwilling that important public questions should be settled by the Senate. Thus the Roman Senate became a large committee of experienced statesmen, guiding and controlling the Roman State. They formed the greatest council of rulers which ever grew up in the ancient world, or perhaps in any age. They were a body of aristocrats, and their control of Rome made it an aristocratic state, in spite of its republican form. We are now to watch the steady development and progress of Roman power under the wise and stable leadership of the Senate.

IV. THE EXPANSION OF THE ROMAN REPUBLIC AND THE CONQUEST OF ITALY

310. Early Struggles of the Republic. It was a tiny nation which began its uncertain career after the expulsion of the Etruscan kings about 500 B.C. The territory of the Roman Republic thus far comprised only the city with the neighboring fields for a very few miles around. On the other side of the Tiber lived the dreaded Etruscans, and on the Roman side of the river, all around the little republic, lay the lands of the Latin tribes, only loosely united with Rome by treaty.

For two generations the new republic struggled for the preservation of its mere existence. Fortunately for the Romans, within a generation after the foundation of the Republic the Greek fleet of Syracuse utterly destroyed the Etruscan fleet (474 B.C.) (see tailpiece, p. 204). Later the Etruscans were attacked in the rear by the Gauls, who were at this time pouring over the Alpine passes into the valley of the Po and laying waste the Etruscan cities of the North. This weakening of the Etruscans probably saved Rome from destruction. By 400 B.C., or a little after, the Romans had conquered and taken possession of a fringe of new territory on all sides, which protected them from their enemies.

311. Roman Policy of Agricultural Expansion. In the new territory thus gained the Romans planted colonies of citizens, or they granted citizenship or other valuable privileges to the conquered population. Roman peasants, under obligation to bear Roman arms and having a voice in the government, thus pushed out into the new and enlarging Roman territory. We may call this plan a *policy of agricultural expansion*. It gave to Rome an ever-increasing body of brave and hardy citizen-soldiers. The Roman policy was thus in striking contrast with the narrow methods of the Greek republics, which jealously prevented outsiders from gaining citizenship. It was the steady expansion of Rome under this plan which in a little over two centuries after the expulsion of the Etruscan kings made the little republic on the Tiber mistress of all Italy (see map, p. 192).

312. Capture of Rome by the Gauls (382 B.C.). The second century of Roman expansion opened with a fearful catastrophe, which very nearly accomplished the complete destruction of the nation. In the first two decades after 400 B.C. the barbarian Gauls of the North (§ 310), who had been overrunning the territory of the Etruscans, finally reached the lower Tiber, defeated the Roman army, and entered the city. Unable, however, to capture the citadel on the Capitol Hill, the Gauls at length agreed to accept a ransom of gold and to return northward, where they settled in the valley of the Po. But they still remained a serious danger to the Romans.

313. Subjugation of the Latin Tribes (338 B.C.). As Rome recovered from this disaster it was evident that the city needed fortifications, and for the first time masonry walls (plan, p. 195) were built around it. Alarmed at its growing power, the Latin tribes now endeavored to break away from the control of the powerful walled city. In the two years' war which resulted the city was completely victorious (338 B.C.). Rome thus gained the undisputed leadership of the Latin tribes, which was at last to bring her the leadership of Italy.

The year 338 B.C., in which this important event took place, is a date to be well remembered, for it also witnessed the defeat of the Greek cities at the hands of Philip of Macedon (§ 256). In the same year, therefore, both the Greeks and the Latins saw themselves conquered and falling under the leadership of a single state — the Greeks under that of Macedonia, the Latins under that of Rome. In sixty-five years the Romans were now to gain the leadership of all Italy.

314. Samnite Wars (325–290 B.C.) **and the Battle of Sentinum** (295 B.C.). Meantime another formidable foe, a group of Italic tribes called the Samnites, had been taking possession of the mountains inland from Rome. They had gained some civilization from the Greek cities of the South, and they were able to muster a large army of hardy peasants, very dangerous in battle. By 325 B.C. a fierce war broke out between the Romans and the Samnites. It lasted with interruptions for a generation. The Romans lost several battles, and the Samnites succeeded in shifting their army northward and joining forces with Rome's enemies, the Etruscans and the Gauls. In the mountains midway between the upper Tiber and the eastern shores of Italy the Roman army met and crushed the combined forces of the allies in a terrible battle at Sentinum (295 B.C.). This victory not only gave the Romans possession of central Italy but it made them the leading power in the whole peninsula.

315. Rome Mistress of Central and Northern Italy. Henceforth the Etruscans were unable to maintain themselves as a leading power. One by one their cities were taken by the Romans, or they entered into alliance with Rome. The intruding Gallic barbarians were beaten off, though the settled Gauls continued to hold the Po valley. The northern boundary of the Roman conquests was therefore along the Arnus River, south of the Apennines. The Romans were then supreme from the Arnus to the Greek cities of southern Italy (see map, p. 192).

316. The War with Pyrrhus (280–275 B.C.) and Fall of the Greeks in Italy. The remaining three great rivals in the western Mediterranean world were now the Romans, the Greeks, and the Carthaginians. Four centuries of conflict among themselves had left the western Greek colonies (§ 153) still a disunited group of cities fringing southern Italy and Sicily. Alarmed at the threatening expansion of Roman power they endeavored to unite and sent an appeal for help to Pyrrhus, the vigorous and able king of Epirus, just across from the heel of Italy.

Leading a powerful army, Pyrrhus was a highly dangerous foe. His purpose was to form a great nation of the western Greeks in Sicily and Italy. He completely defeated the Romans in two battles, and he gained practically the whole island of Sicily. But the Carthaginians, seeing a dangerous rival rising only a few hours' sail from their home harbor, sent a fleet to assist the Romans against Pyrrhus. With a Carthaginian fleet at the mouth of the Tiber the Roman Senate resolutely refused to make peace so long as the army of Pyrrhus occupied Italian soil. At the same time the Greeks disagreed among themselves, as they always did at critical times. Pyrrhus, thus poorly supported, found himself unable to inflict a decisive defeat on the Romans, and returned to Epirus. One by one the helpless Greek cities of Italy then surrendered to the Roman army, and they had no choice but to accept alliance with the Romans. Thus ended all hope of a great Greek nation in the West.

317. Summary of Roman History down through the Conquest of Italy. Having freed itself from a long period of Etruscan tyranny the little Roman republic emerged about 500 B.C. to compete with three dangerous rival peoples, the Etruscans, Carthaginians, and Greeks, the first two of whom had brought the earliest civilization into the western Mediterranean. The Romans gradually developed their own government with remarkable skill, so that the nation was guided by a great council of their most experienced men, called the Senate. By a process of settling farmer colonists, that is, by *agricultural expansion*, the tiny republic on the Tiber gained the mastery of the entire Italian peninsula south of the Po valley. This long period of conquest extended over about two centuries and a quarter (500–275 B.C.). Thenceforward there were but two rivals in the western Mediterranean world — Rome and Carthage.

QUESTIONS

I. Discuss the geography of the western Mediterranean world; of Italy. Who were the Italic tribes? Name the four rival peoples of the western Mediterranean world and tell something of each.

II. Discuss early Latium. Describe its leading market town. What people furnished the first kings of Rome? Tell of their rule. What civilization did the Etruscans receive? Give examples. When were they expelled from Rome?

III. Tell about Greek influences among the Romans. Who took the place of the expelled Etruscan kings? What did the government of Rome become? How did the people gain power? the Senate?

IV. Describe the Roman policy of expansion. Discuss the wars with the Gauls; with the Latins; with the Samnites; with the Greeks and Pyrrhus. What was the result? What two rivals remained?

NOTE. This tailpiece shows an Etruscan helmet taken by the Syracusans in 474 B.C.

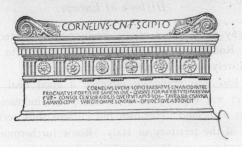

CORNELIVS·CN·F·SCIPIO

CORNELIVS·LVCIVS·SCIPIO·BARBATVS·CNAIVOD·PATRE
PROGNATVS·FORTIS·VIR·SAPIENSQVE·QVOIVS·FORMA·VIRTVTEI·PARISVMA
FVIT· CONSOL·CENSOR·AIDILIS·QVEI·FVIT·APVD·VOS· TAVRASIA·CISAVNA
SAMNIO·CEPIT· SVBIGIT·OMNE·LOVCANA·OPSIDESQVE·ABDOVCIT

CHAPTER XIV

THE ROMAN CONQUEST OF THE WESTERN MEDITERRANEAN WORLD

I. ITALY UNDER THE EARLY ROMAN REPUBLIC

318. The Problem of making Italy a Nation. After the leadership of Italy had been gained by Rome, there were men still living who could remember the Latin war (ended 338 B.C.), when Rome had for a time lost even the surrounding fields of little Latium. Now, less than sixty-five years later, the city on the Tiber was· mistress of *all Italy*. The new power over a large group of cities and states, thus gained within a single lifetime, was exercised by the Roman Senate with the greatest skill and success. The problem was to make Italy a nation, controlled by Rome. But if Rome had *annexed* all the conquered lands and endeavored to rule them from Rome as mere subjects, the population of Italy would have been dissatisfied and constant revolts would have followed.

The Romans accordingly granted the defeated cities a kind of citizenship, which entitled them to all the protection of the Roman State· in the courts and in carrying on business, but did not entitle them to vote. In distant communities, however, no one felt the lack of this privilege, for in order to vote it was necessary to go to Rome. Cities and communities controlled by Rome

NOTE. The above headpiece represents the beautiful stone sarcophagus of one of the early Scipios, found in the family tomb on the Appian Way. It is adorned with details of Greek architecture, which clearly show that it was done by a Greek artist (§ 320). Verses in early Latin, on the side of the sarcophagus, contain praises of the departed Scipio.

in this way were called *allies*. Enjoying the protection of the powerful Roman State, the allies were willing to place their troops entirely at the disposal of Rome.

Rome had also gradually *annexed* a good deal of territory to pay her war expenses and to supply her increasing numbers of citizens with land. Her own full citizens thus occupied about one sixth of the territory of Italy. Rome furthermore continued her policy of planting Roman colonies through the territory of the allies. All Italy was thus more or less dotted with such communities made up of citizens of the Roman Republic.

FIG. 56. A ROMAN DENARIUS OF SILVER

After the capture of the Greek cities of southern Italy, the Romans began the coinage of silver (268 B.C.) (see § 320). The large and inconvenient *as* (Fig. 55, *B*) was then displaced by silver for all large transactions. The value of this coin, called a *denarius*, was a little less than twenty cents, like the Athenian *drachma* (§ 163)

319. Lack of National Unity in Italy. Roman methods of organization had in this way created a kind of United States of Italy, which might in the course of time become merged into a nation. Meanwhile many of these peoples had no feeling of patriotism toward Rome. Having no common traditions like those of the Trojan War among the Greeks (§ 143), and speaking many different languages, they long remained quite distinct from each other and from Rome. Italy was therefore far from being a *nation*.

320. Italy Latin in Speech, but Greek in Civilization. In language the future nation was to be Latin, the tongue of the ruling city; geographically it comprised Italy; politically it was Roman.[1] When we consider Rome from the point of view of *civilization*, however, we are obliged to add a fourth name. For

---

[1] Compare the similar application of three names to our own country. Our language is English. Geographically we are commonly called America; politically we are the United States.

as time went on, Italy was to become in civilization more and more Greek. In the Greek cities of southern Italy the Romans for the first time saw beautiful temples (tailpiece, p. 107) and fine theaters (plate, p. 106); and they must have attended Greek plays also, of which they understood little or nothing. But the races and athletic games common in the Greek cities required no interpretation in order to be understood by the sturdy Roman soldiers who had fought Pyrrhus in the South.

In southern Italy the Romans had taken possession of the western fringe of the great Hellenistic world, whose wonderful civilization we have already studied (pp. 179–187). The Romans at once felt the superiority of this new world of cultivated life, which they had entered in the Greek South. It was as yet chiefly in commerce and in business that Greek influences were evident. Greek silver money appeared in greater quantities after the capture of the Greek cities, and not long after the war with Pyrrhus Rome issued her first silver coin (Fig. 56). Just as Athens had once done (§ 164), so Rome now began to feel the influence of money, and a moneyed class, largely merchants, arose. They were not manufacturers, as at Athens, and Rome never became a great industrial center.

II. The Rising Rivalry between Rome and Carthage

321. Roman Commercial Expansion Seaward. Roman ships issuing from the Tiber entered a triangular inclosure of the Mediterranean, called the Etruscan Sea. A glance at the map (p. 192) shows us how Rome and Carthage faced each other across this triangular sea, where both were now carrying on extensive business.

322. Carthaginian Commercial Expansion in Africa. As the trade of Carthage increased she had gradually gained control over the north African coast from the frontiers of the Greek city of Cyrene westward to the Atlantic (§ 139). She had become the commercial mistress of the western Mediterranean world. Her merchants seized southern Spain, with its profitable silver mines, and they gained control of the import of British tin by way of the Strait of Gibraltar. Outside of this strait their settlements extended both northward and southward far along the Atlantic coast. It was only the incoming of the Greeks (§ 153) which had prevented the Carthaginians from taking possession of all the western Mediterranean islands upon which their splendid harbor looked out, especially the island of Sicily. They closed the ports of the islands and the Strait of Gibraltar *to ships from all other cities*. Ships of other nations intruding in these waters were promptly rammed and sunk by Carthaginian warships.

323. Carthaginian Army and State Organization. Unlike Rome the military power of Carthage was built up entirely on a basis of money, with which she supported a large mercenary army. She had no farmers cultivating their own land, from whom she could draw an army of citizen-soldiers as did Rome. This was a serious weakness. The rulers of the city never trusted the army, made up as it was of hired foreigners. Carthage was governed by a group of merchant nobles, a wealthy aristocracy whose members formed a Council in complete control. They were energetic and statesmanlike rulers. Centuries of shrewd guidance on their part made Carthage a great state, far exceeding in power any of the Greek states that ever arose, not excluding Athens. The city of Carthage itself was luxurious and splendid, and in area it was three times as large as Rome.

324. Early Relations between Carthage and Rome. In the fourth century B. C., before Rome had gained the leadership of Italy, when the Roman merchants were still doing a small business, the Senate had made a treaty with Carthage, in which it was agreed that no Carthaginian ships should trade in the ports of Roman Italy and no Roman ships should enter the harbors of Sicily. With increasing vexation the merchants of Italy realized that Rome had gained the supremacy of Italy and pushed her frontiers to the southernmost tip of the peninsula, only to look across and find that the merchant princes of Carthage held the markets of Sicily and had made the western Mediterranean a Carthaginian sea. Indeed, should Carthage occupy Messina, it might cut off Rome from communication with even her own ports on the Adriatic side of Italy. For to reach them Roman ships must pass through the Strait of Messina, between Italy and Sicily.

325. War Strength of the Romans. The Roman Senate without doubt shared these apprehensions. But the Romans could put a *citizen* army of over three hundred thousand men into the field. Besides the troops made up of Roman citizens the principle was adopted of having each army include also about an equal number of troops drawn from the *allies* (§ 318). This plan, therefore, doubled the number of available troops. The Roman **army** consequently far exceeded in size any army ever before organized in the Mediterranean world.

In arms and tactics the Romans had been able to make some improvements on the Hellenistic art of war (§ 237). After hurling their spears into the ranks of the enemy, the Romans fought with their short swords, which were much more easily handled at close quarters than long spears (Fig. 57). At the same time the Romans had likewise improved the phalanx, which had thus far been a long massive line eight men deep, possessing no flexibility. It was one solid mass and had no joints. The Romans gave it joints

FIG. 57. A ROMAN SOL-
DIER OF THE LEGION

The figure of the soldier is carved upon a tombstone, erected in his memory by his brother. His offensive weapons are his spear (*pilum*), which he holds in his extended right hand with point upward, and his heavy short sword (*gladius*), which he wears girded high on his right side (see § 325). As defensive equipment he has a helmet, a leathern corselet stopping midway between the waist and knees, and a shield (*scutum*) made of wicker and heavy hide with metal trimming

and flexibility by cutting it up in both directions; that is, lengthwise and crosswise into small bodies of men, called *maniples*. As the Romans gradually learned to shift these smaller units more and more skillfully, the art of war entered upon a new chapter.[1] For purposes of mustering and feeding an army the Romans divided it into larger bodies, called *legions*, each containing usually forty-five hundred men.

III. The Struggle with Carthage: the Sicilian War, or First Punic War

326. Opening of the Sicilian War (First Punic War) (264 B.C.). The Romans soon discovered that the struggle with Carthage could not be avoided. A local war in Sicily gave a Carthaginian garrison opportunity to occupy the citadel of Messina, and the Carthaginians were then in command of the Strait of Messina (see map, p. 192, and § 324). The Romans now took a memorable step. A Roman army left the soil of Italy, crossed the sea for the first time in Roman history, and entered Sicily. The struggle with Carthage had begun (264 B.C.) (see map, I, p. 218).

327. Naval Victory of the Romans (241 B.C.). An alliance with Syracuse soon gave the Romans possession of eastern Sicily, but they were long hampered for lack of a fleet. In the fifth year of the war, however, the new Roman warships, which the Senate had caused to be built, put to sea for the first time. They numbered a hundred and twenty battleships.

In spite of inexperience, the Roman fleet was at first victorious. Then one newly built Roman fleet after another was destroyed by heavy storms at sea, and one of them was badly defeated by the Carthaginians. Year after year the struggle dragged on, while Hamilcar Barca, the Carthaginian commander, was plundering the coasts of Italy with his fleet. The treasury at Rome was empty, and the Romans were at the end of their resources; but by private contributions they succeeded in building another fleet,

---

[1] For a fuller explanation of these remarkable improvements, see *Ancient Times*, §§ 844-848, and Fig. 237.

which put to sea in 242 B.C. with two hundred battleships of five banks of oars. The Carthaginian fleet was defeated and broken up (241 B.C.), and as a result the Carthaginians found themselves unable to send reënforcements across the sea to their army in Sicily.

328. Peace after the Sicilian War (241 B.C.). The Carthaginians were therefore at last obliged to accept hard terms of peace at the hands of the Romans. They were to give up Sicily and the neighboring islands to Rome and to pay the Romans as war damages the sum of thirty-two hundred talents, over three and a half million dollars, within ten years. Thus in 241 B.C., after more than twenty-three years of fighting, the first period of the struggle between Rome and Carthage ended with the victory of Rome. For the first time Rome held territory outside the Italian peninsula, and from this step she was never able to withdraw.

IV. The Hannibalian War (Second Punic War) and the Destruction of Carthage

329. New Conquests of the Rivals. Both the rivals now devoted themselves to increasing their strength. In spite of protests from Carthage, only three years after the settlement of peace Rome took possession of both Sardinia and Corsica. She now possessed three island outposts against Carthage. At the same time the Romans conquered the Gauls and seized their territory in the Po valley. Thus Roman power was extended northward to the foot of the Alps, and the entire peninsula from the Alps southward was held by Rome (map, II, p. 218).

To offset this increase of Roman power the Carthaginian leaders turned toward Spain. There Hamilcar's gifted son Hannibal carried Carthaginian rule as far north as the Ebro River (map, II, p. 218), to which point Rome also extended her claims. Although only twenty-four years of age, Hannibal was already forming colossal plans for a bold surprise of Rome in her own territory, which by its unexpectedness and audacity should crush Roman power in Italy.

330. Opening of the Hannibalian War (218–202 B.C.). Hannibal speedily found opportunity for a frontier quarrel with Rome in Spain (219 B.C.). With a strong and well-drilled army of about forty thousand men he was soon marching northward along the east coast of Spain (map, *Ancient Times,* p. 538) with the purpose of crossing southern Gaul and invading Italy. Thus while the Roman Senate was planning to invade Spain and Africa Rome found its own land suddenly threatened from the north.

It was late autumn when Hannibal reached the Alps (218 B.C.). Overwhelmed by snowstorms; struggling over a steep and dangerous trail, sometimes so narrow that the rocks had to be cut away to make room for his elephants; looking down over dizzy precipices, or up to snow-covered heights where hostile natives rolled great stones down upon the troops, the discouraged army of Hannibal toiled on day after day, exhausted, cold, and hungry. At every point along the straggling line where help was most needed, the young Carthaginian was always present, encouraging and guiding his men. But when they issued from the Alpine pass and entered Italy in the upper valley of the Po, they had suffered such losses that they were reduced to some thirty-four thousand men.

With this little army the dauntless Carthaginian youth had entered the territory of the strongest military power of the time — a nation which could now call to her defense over seven hundred thousand men, citizens and allies. Hannibal, however, was thoroughly acquainted with the most highly developed methods of warfare, and the exploits of Alexander a century earlier were familiar to him. On the other hand, the Roman consuls, commanding the Roman armies, were simply magistrates like our mayors, often without much more knowledge of handling an army than has a city mayor in our time. They were no match for the crafty young Carthaginian.

By skillful use of his cavalry, in which the Romans were weak, Hannibal easily won two engagements in the Po valley. The Gauls of the region at once began to flock to his standards, but they were raw, undisciplined troops. Having successfully crossed the Apennines, Hannibal surprised the army of the unsuspecting consul, Flaminius, on the march. On the shores of Lake Trasimene he ambushed the Roman legions both in front and rear and cut to pieces the entire Roman army. The consul himself fell. Being only a few days' march from Rome, Hannibal might now have advanced directly against the city ; but he had no siege machinery (*Ancient Times*, p. 140), and his forces were not numerous enough to besiege so strong a fortress. He therefore desired a further victory in the hope that the allies of Rome would revolt and join him in attacking the city.

331. A Year of Delay and Preparation (217-216 B.C.). At this dangerous crisis the Romans appointed a Dictator, a stable old citizen named Fabius, whose plan was to wear out Hannibal by refusing to give battle and by using every opportunity to harass the Carthaginians. This policy of caution and delay did not meet with popular favor at Rome. The people called Fabius the Laggard (*Cunctator*), a name which ever afterward clung to him. The new consuls elected for 216 B.C. therefore recruited an army of nearly seventy thousand men and pushed southward toward the heel of the Italian peninsula to fight Hannibal. The battle took place at Cannæ (see map, p. 192).

332. The Battle of Cannæ (216 B.C.). Hannibal's stronger cavalry, forming his two wings, put to flight the horsemen forming the two Roman wings. Then these well-trained horsemen turned back to attack the heavy mass of the Roman center in the rear, and the Romans were caught between the Carthaginian center before them and the Carthaginian cavalry behind them. Only the sides of the trap were still open. Then two bodies of African reserves which Hannibal had kept waiting pushed quietly forward till they occupied positions on each side of the fifty-five thousand brave soldiers of the Roman center, who were thus inclosed on all sides.[1] What ensued was simply a slaughter of the doomed Romans, lasting all the rest of the day. When night closed in, the Roman army was annihilated. Ex-consuls, senators, nobles, thousands of the best citizens of Rome, had fallen in this frightful battle.

[1] See plan, *Ancient Times*, p. 540, and §§ 864-865.

Every family in Rome was in mourning. Of the gold rings worn by Roman knights as an indication of their rank Hannibal is reported to have sent a bushel to Carthage.

333. **Hannibal's Statesmanship versus Roman Power.** Thus this masterful young Carthaginian, the greatest of Semite generals, within two years after his arrival in Italy and before he was thirty years of age, had defeated his giant antagonist in four battles and destroyed three of the opposing armies. He might now count upon a revolt among the Roman allies. Within a few years southern Italy, including the Greek cities and even Syracuse in Sicily, forsook Rome and joined Hannibal. Only some of the southern Latin colonies held out against him.

In all this Hannibal was displaying the judgment and insight of a statesman combined with amazing ability to meet the constant demands of the military situation. But opposing him were the dogged resolution, the ripe statesmanship, the unshaken organization, and the seemingly inexhaustible numbers of the Romans. It was a battle of giants for the mastery of the world, for the victor in this struggle would without any question be the greatest power in the Mediterranean. In spite of Hannibal's victories, the steadiness and fine leadership of the Roman Senate held central Italy loyal to Rome. Although the Romans were finally compelled to place arms in the hands of slaves and mere boys, new armies were formed. With these forces the Romans proceeded to besiege and capture, one after another, the allied cities which had revolted against Rome. Even the clever devices of Archimedes (§ 280) during a desperate siege did not save Syracuse from being recaptured by the Romans (212 B.C.).

334. **Decline of Hannibal's Power.** As a last hope Hannibal marched upon Rome itself and with his bodyguard rode up to one of the gates of the great city, whose power seemed so unbroken. For a brief time the two antagonists faced each other, and many a Roman senator must have looked over the walls at the figure of the tremendous young Carthaginian who had shaken all Italy as with an earthquake. But they were not to be frightened into offers of peace in this way, nor did they send out any

message to him. His army was not large enough to lay siege to the greatest city of Italy. He had not been able to secure any siege machinery and he was therefore obliged to retreat without accomplishing anything.

When he had finally been ten years in Italy, Hannibal realized that unless powerful reënforcements could reach him his cause was hopeless. His brother Hasdrubal in Spain had gathered an army and was now marching into Italy to aid him. But Hasdrubal was met by a Roman army, completely defeated, and himself slain (207 B.C.). To the senators waiting in keenest anticipation at Rome, the news of the victory meant the salvation of Italy and the final defeat of an enemy who had all but accomplished the destruction of Roman power.

335. Defeat of Hannibal by Scipio (202 B.C.). For a few years more Hannibal struggled on in the southern tip of Italy. Meantime the Romans, taught by the defeat of their consuls, had given the command of their forces in Spain to Scipio, one of the ablest of their younger leaders and a trained soldier. He drove the Carthaginians entirely out of Spain, thus cutting off their chief supply both of money and of troops. In Scipio the Romans had at last found a general with the masterful qualities which make a great military leader. He demanded of the Senate that he be sent to Africa to invade the dominions of Carthage as Hannibal had invaded those of Rome.

By 203 B.C. Scipio had twice defeated the Carthaginian forces in Africa, and Carthage was forced to call Hannibal home. He had spent fifteen years on the soil of Italy, and the great struggle between the almost exhausted rivals was now to be decided in Africa. At Zama, inland from Carthage, the final battle of the war took place. The great Carthaginian was at last met by an equally great Roman, and Scipio won the battle.

336. Treaty ending the Hannibalian War (201 B.C.) ; **the Fate of Hannibal.** The victory over Carthage made Rome the leading power in the whole ancient world. In the treaty which followed the Battle of Zama the Romans forced Carthage to pay ten thousand talents (over $11,000,000) in fifty years and to surrender all her warships but ten triremes. But, what was worse, she lost her independence as a nation, and according to the treaty she could not make war anywhere without the consent of the Romans.

Hannibal escaped after his lost battle at Zama. He was one of the greatest and most gifted leaders in all history — a lion-hearted man, so strong of purpose that only a great nation like Rome could have crushed him. Rome still feared Hannibal and compelled the Carthaginians to expel him, and as a man of fifty he went into exile in the East, where we shall find him stirring up the successors of Alexander to combine against Rome (§ 340).

337. Destruction of Carthage (146 B.C.) : Third Punic War. Cato, a famous old-fashioned senator, was so convinced that Carthage was still a danger to Rome that he concluded all his speeches in the Senate with the words, "Carthage must be destroyed." For over fifty years more the merchants of Carthage were permitted to traffic in the western Mediterranean, and then the iron hand of Rome was laid upon the doomed city for the last time. To defend herself against the Numidians behind her, Carthage was finally obliged to begin war against them. This step, which the Romans had long been desiring, was a violation of the treaty with Rome. The Senate seized the opportunity at once and Carthage was called to account. In the three years' war (Third Punic War) which followed, the beautiful city was captured and completely destroyed (146 B.C.). Its territory was taken by Rome and called the Province of Africa. A struggle of nearly one hundred and twenty years had resulted in the annihilation of Rome's only remaining rival in the western Mediterranean world.

338. Summary of the Roman Conquest of the Western Mediterranean. While the Romans crowned their conquest of Italy by the skillful organization of their new Italian subjects, they received more and more of Greek civilization, including silver coinage. Only eleven years after they had conquered the Greek cities on their south they were involved in their first war with their remaining rival, Carthage (264 B.C.). Under the able leadership of the Senate, and in spite of the genius of Hannibal, the Romans were victorious in three great wars with Carthage (264–146 B.C.), and they destroyed the city in 146 B.C.

Thus the fourfold rivalry in the western Mediterranean, which had long included the Etruscans and Carthaginians, the Greeks and the Romans, had ended with the triumph of the once insignificant village on the Tiber. Racially, the western wing of the Indo-European line on the *north* side of the Mediterranean had proved victorious over that of the Semitic line on the *south* side (Fig. 27). The western Mediterranean world was now under the leadership of a single great nation, the Romans, as the eastern Mediterranean world had once been under the leadership of the Macedonians. We must now turn back and follow the dealings of Rome with the Hellenistic-oriental world of the eastern Mediterranean, which we left (pp. 179–187) after it had attained the most highly refined civilization ever achieved by ancient man (see map, II, p. 218).

QUESTIONS

I. What two kinds of communities did Rome organize in Italy? Was Italy therefore a nation? Why? What was Rome as to civilization? How did this happen?

II. Give the boundaries of the Etruscan Sea. What rival did Rome find there? Describe the power of Carthage. What early treaty did Rome make with Carthage? What important strait was threatened by Carthage? Discuss Roman power and ability in war.

III. What started the first war with Carthage? How were the Romans at first hampered? What was the result of the naval war? What terms did Rome force on Carthage?

IV. What islands did Rome next seize? What did the Carthaginians then do? What was the plan of Hannibal? Give an account of his great march and early victories. What was the policy of Fabius? Describe the Battle of Cannæ. Why did not Hannibal take Rome? What happened to Hannibal's reënforcements? What did the Roman leaders then do? What new leader did they appoint? What did he demand? What was the result?

What terms were forced on defeated Carthage? What became of Hannibal? What continued to be Roman feeling against Carthage? What resulted? How did Rome finally treat Carthage? Who was then leader of the western Mediterranean world?

CHAPTER XV

WORLD DOMINION AND DEGENERACY

I. The Roman Conquest of the Eastern Mediterranean World

339. Alexander's Successors all become Vassals of Rome (200-168 B.C.). While the heirs of Alexander were carrying on their ceaseless wars and alliances in the eastern Mediterranean, down to about 200 B.C. (pp. 177–179), the vast power of Rome had been slowly rising in the West. Hannibal had persuaded Macedonia into an alliance with him against Rome. This hostile step could not be overlooked by the Romans, and hence a year after the close of the Hannibalian War a later Philip of Macedon found himself face to face with a Roman army. On the field of Cynoscephalæ ("dog's heads"), in 197 B.C., the Macedonian army was disastrously routed, and the ancient realm of Alexander the Great became a vassal state under Rome. As allies of Rome (§ 318), the Greek states were then granted their freedom by the Romans.

This war with Macedon brought the Romans into conflict with Antiochus the Great, the Seleucid king, who held a large part of the vast empire of Persia in Asia. A war with this powerful Asiatic empire was not a matter which the Romans could view without great anxiety. Moreover, Hannibal, a fugitive from Carthage (§ 336), was with Antiochus, advising him. Nevertheless at Magnesia in Asia Minor the West led by Rome overthrew the East led by Antiochus (190 B.C.), and the lands of Asia Minor eastward to the Halys River submitted to Roman control. The treaty closed Asia Minor west of this river to Antiochus.

Within twelve years (200 to 189 B.C.) Roman arms had reduced to the condition of vassal states *two* of the three great empires which succeeded Alexander in the East—Macedonia and Syria (see map, III, p. 218). As for Egypt, the *third,* a little over thirty years after a Roman army had first appeared in the Hellenistic world, Egypt also acknowledged herself a vassal of Rome (168 B.C.).

340. Subjection of the Greeks. Although defeated, the eastern Mediterranean world, including the Greeks, long continued to give the Romans trouble. Then the Romans began harsh measures. The same year which saw the destruction of Carthage witnessed also the burning of Corinth by the Romans (146 B.C.). Greek liberty was ended, and while a city of such revered memories as Athens might be given greater freedom, those Greek states whose careers of glorious achievement in civilization we have followed were all reduced to the condition of Roman vassals.

341. Rome's Great Task of Imperial Organization. The Roman Senate had shown fine ability in conducting the great wars. But now Rome was faced by the problem of furnishing successful government for the vast dominions which she had conquered in three generations. In extent they would have reached entirely across the United States. To organize such an empire was a task like that which had been so successfully accomplished by Darius, the organizer of the Persian Empire (§ 100).

II. ROMAN GOVERNMENT AND CIVILIZATION IN THE AGE OF CONQUEST

342. Misgovernment of Roman Provinces. The Romans had at first no experience in governing their conquered lands. Most of the newly acquired countries were organized by them as provinces—each province under a Roman governor, who possessed unlimited power like that of an oriental king. He had complete control of all the taxes of the province, and could demand what he needed from its people to support his Roman troops and the expenses of his government. The governor was very often inexperienced in provincial government, but was eager to gain a fortune in his short term of office, usually a single year, and his rule thus often became a mere system of looting and robbery. The Senate soon found it necessary to have laws passed for the punishment of such abuses, but these laws were of little use in improving the condition of the provincials.

The evil effects of this situation were soon apparent. The provinces were filled with Roman business men whom we would call "loan-sharks." There were contractors called *publicans*, who were allowed to collect the taxes for the State at a great profit. We remember the common references to these publicans in the New Testament, where they are regularly classified with "sinners." These men of money plundered the provinces worse than the greedy Roman governors themselves.

343. Rise of a Wealthy Class at Rome. As these people returned to Italy, there grew up a wealthy class such as had been unknown there before. Their ability to buy resulted in a vast import trade to supply their demands. From the Bay of Naples to the mouth of the Tiber the sea was white with the sails of Roman ships converging on the docks of Rome. The men who controlled all this traffic became wealthy merchants. To handle all the money in circulation, banks were required. During the Hannibalian War the first banks appeared at Rome, occupying a line of booths on each side of the Forum. Under these influences Rome greatly changed.

When a returned governor of Africa put up a showy new house, the citizen across the way who still lived in his father's old house began to be dissatisfied with it. It was built of sun-dried brick, and, like the old settler's cabin of early America, it had but one room, called the *atrium* (Fig. 58). The Roman citizen of the new age had long before become familiar with the comfort, luxury, and beauty with which the Greek houses of southern Italy were filled (§§ 275, 279). He therefore soon added a colonnaded Hellenistic court (Figs. 59, 60), with adjoining dining room, bedrooms, library, rest rooms, and kitchen.

344. The New Luxury at Rome. Not long before the Carthaginian wars an ex-consul had been fined for having more than ten pounds' weight of silverware in his house. A generation later a wealthy Roman was using in his household silverware which weighed some ten thousand pounds. One of the Roman conquerors of Macedonia entered Rome with two hundred and fifty wagonloads of Greek statues and paintings. Even in so small a city as Pompeii, a citizen of wealth paved a handsome dining alcove with a magnificent mosaic picture of Alexander in battle, which had once formed a floor in a splendid Hellenistic residence in Alexandria (§ 275). The atrium thus became a large and stately reception hall where the master of the house could display his wealth in statues, paintings, and other works of art — the splendid trophies of war brought from the East.

Pipes for running water, baths, and sanitary conveniences were likewise quickly introduced. Some houses even had tile pipes conducting hot air for warmth, the earliest system of hot-air heating yet found. The kitchen was **furnished** with bronze utensils far better than those commonly found in our own homes.

FIG. 58. A ROMAN ATRIUM-HOUSE OF THE OLD DAYS

There was no attempt at beautiful architecture, and the bare front showed no adornment whatever. The opening in the roof, which lighted the atrium (§ 343), received the rainfall of a section cf the roof sloping toward it, and this water collected in a pool built to receive it in the floor of the atrium below (Fig. 59, *B*). The tiny area, or garden, shown in the rear was not common. It was here that the later Romans added the Hellenistic peristyle (Figs. 51, 59, and 60)

Such luxury required a great body of household servants. There was a doorkeeper at the front door (he was called "janitor" from the Latin word *janua*, meaning "door"), and from the front door inward there was a servant for every small duty in the house. Almost all these menials were slaves.

345. Influence of Greek Art and Literature in Rome.

While the effect of all this luxury introduced from the East was on the whole very bad, nevertheless the former plain, matter-of-fact life of the Roman citizen was stimulated and refined by the most beautiful works of Greek art. Hellenistic buildings were beginning to appear in Rome, and it was not long, too, before a Greek theater was erected, improved by the Romans with awnings, a stage curtain, and seats in the orchestra circle where once the Greek chorus had sung (plate, p. 102).

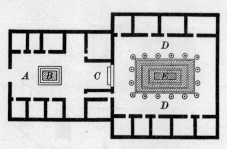

Fig. 59. Plan of a Roman House with Peristyle

The earliest Roman house had consisted of a single room, the atrium (*A*), with the pool for the rain water (*B*). Then a small alcove, or lean-to, was erected at the rear (*C*) as a room for the master of the house. Later the bedrooms on each side of the atrium were added. Finally, under the influence of Greek life (§ 343), the garden court (*D* and Fig. 60), with its surrounding colonnaded porch (peristyle; cf. Fig. 51) and a fountain in the middle (*E*), was built at the rear. Then a dining room, sitting room, and bedrooms were added, which opened on this court, and, being without windows, they were lighted from the court through the doors. In town houses it was quite easy to partition off a shop, or even a whole row of shops, along the front or side of the house, as in the Hellenistic house (Fig. 51). The houses of Pompeii (Fig. 60) were almost all built in this way

At the close of the Sicilian War (241 B.C.) a Greek slave from southern Italy named Andronicus was given his freedom by his master at Rome. Seeing the growing interest of the Romans in Greek literature, he translated the Odyssey (§ 143) into Latin as a schoolbook for Roman children. For their elders he likewise rendered into Latin the classic tragedies which we have seen in Athens (§ 217) and also a number of Attic comedies (§ 220). Through his work the materials and the forms of Greek literature began to enter Roman life.

The Romans had been accustomed to do very little in the way of educating their children. There were no schools at first, but

FIG. 60. PERISTYLE OF A POMPEIAN HOUSE (BELOW) AND ITS
EGYPTIAN ANCESTOR (ABOVE; SEE FIG. 11)

We must imagine ourselves standing with our backs toward the atrium (having immediately behind us the room *C* in Fig. 59). We look out into the court, the garden of the house (Fig. 59, *D*). The marble tables and statues and the marble fountain basin in the middle (Fig. 59, *E*), just as we see them here in the drawing, were all found by the excavators in their places, as they were covered by volcanic ashes over eighteen hundred years ago (Fig. 68). Here centered the family life, and here the children played about the court, brightened with flowers and the tinkling music of the fountains

the good old Roman custom had been for the father to instruct his own children. Gradually parents began to send their children to the schools which the freed Greek slaves of Rome were beginning to open there. Here and there a household possessed an educated Greek slave, like Andronicus, who became the tutor of the children, teaching his pupils to read from the new primer of Andronicus, as we may call his Latin translation of Homer.

346. Rise of Latin Literature and Literary Culture. Poets and writers of history now arose in Italy under the influence of Greek literature. Educated Romans could read of the great deeds of their ancestors in long epic poems modeled on those of Homer. In such literature were gradually recorded the picturesque legends of early Rome, like the story of Romulus and Remus and similar tales (p. 189, Note). Imitating the Greek comedies (§ 220), new Latin play-writers also produced very clever comedies caricaturing the society of Rome, to which the Romans listened with uproarious delight.

As the new Latin literature grew, papyrus rolls bearing Latin works were more and more common in Rome. One of the Roman conquerors of Macedon brought back the books of the Macedonian king and founded the first private library in Rome. Wealthy Romans of education were now providing library rooms in their houses (§ 343), and they spoke Greek almost as well as Latin.

III. Degeneration in City and Country

347. Corrupting Influences of the New Luxury. The new life of Greek culture and luxury brought with it many evils. Cato, one of the hardiest of the old-fashioned Romans, and other Romans like him, succeeded in passing law after law against expensive habits of many kinds, such as the growing love of showy jewelry among the women or their use of carriages where they formerly went on foot. But such laws could not prevent the slow demoralization of the people.

This was especially evident in the lives of the uneducated and poorer classes. Early in the wars with Carthage there had been introduced an old Etruscan custom of single combats between condemned criminals or slaves, who fought to honor the funeral of some great Roman. These fighters came to be called "swordsmen" (*gladiators*, from a Latin word *gladius*, meaning "sword") (see tailpiece, p. 229). Officials in charge of the various public feasts, without waiting for a funeral, used to arrange a long program of such combats, sure of pleasing the people, gaining their votes, and thus securing election to higher offices. These barbarous and bloody spectacles took place in a great stone structure called an amphitheater, because it was formed by placing two (*amphi*) theaters face to face (Fig. 71). Soon afterward combats between gladiators and wild beasts were introduced (see tailpiece, p. 229). The Romans also began to build enormous courses for chariot races, surrounded by seats for vast numbers of spectators. Such a building was called a *circus*.

348. Expenses of a Political Career. The common people of Rome were thus gradually debased. At the same time, as their poverty increased, the State arranged regular distributions of grain to the populace. A far greater evil was the bribery which the candidates for office now secretly practiced. Laws passed to prevent the practice were of slight effect. Henceforth we have only too often the spectacle of a Roman candidate trying to gain office in the government that ruled the world by bribing the little body of citizens who attended the Roman assemblies.

All these practices enormously increased the expenses of a political career. If elected the Roman politician received no salary, and in carrying on the business of his office he was obliged to meet heavy expenses, for he had to supply a staff of clerks for government business at his own expense. As a result the Roman politician now sought office chiefly in order that through it he might gain enough influence to finally obtain the governorship of a rich province. There he then would more than regain his expenses. When a retired provincial governor returned to Rome he was no longer the simple Roman of the good old days. He lived like a prince and surrounded himself with royal luxury.

349. Growth of Great Estates; Decline of Small Farms. The evils of the new wealth were not less evident outside of Rome. It was not thought proper for a Roman senator or noble to undertake commercial enterprises or to engage in any business. The most respectable form of wealth was lands. Hence the successful Roman noble or capitalist bought farm after farm, which he combined into a great estate or plantation. Only here and there were still to be found groups of little homestead farms of the good old Roman days. Large portions of Italy were in this condition. The small farm seemed in a fair way to disappear.

350. Slave Revolts and Disorders. It was impossible for a wealthy landowner to work these great estates with free, hired labor. Nor was he obliged to do so. From the close of the Hannibalian War onward the Roman conquests had brought to Italy great numbers of captives of war. These unhappy prisoners were sold as slaves. The estates of Italy were now filled with them. The life of such slaves on the great plantations which they worked was little better than that of beasts. When the supply of captives from the wars failed, slave pirates for many years carried on wholesale kidnaping in the Ægean and eastern Mediterranean.

Thus Italy and Sicily were fairly flooded with slaves. The brutal treatment which they received was so unbearable that at various places in Italy they finally rose against their masters. In central and southern Sicily the revolting slaves gathered some sixty thousand in number, slew their masters, captured towns, and set up a kingdom. It required a Roman consul at the head of an army and a war lasting several years to subdue them.

351. Destruction of Farm Life in Italy by War. Slave labor and the great wars were meantime further ruining the small farmers of Italy. Never has there been an age in which the terrible and desolating results of war have so tragically revealed the awful cost of military glory. Fathers and elder sons had been absent from home for years holding their posts in the legions, fighting the battles which had brought Rome her great position as mistress of the world. Home life and wholesome country influences were undermined and broken up. The mothers, left to bring up the younger children alone, saw the family scattered and drifting away from the little farm, till it was left forsaken.

352. Decline of Agriculture in Italy. Too often as the returning soldier approached the spot where he was born he no longer found the house that had sheltered his childhood. His family was gone, and his little farm, sold for debt, had been bought up by some wealthy Roman of the city and absorbed into a great plantation (§ 349). He cursed the wealth which had done all this and wandered up to the great city to look for free grain from the government, to enjoy the games and circuses, and to increase the poor class already there.

Or if he found his home and his little farm uninjured, he was soon aware that the hordes of slaves now cultivating the great plantations around him were producing grain more cheaply than he. When he had sold his harvest he had not received enough for it to enable him and his family to live. Forced to sell the little farm at last, he too wandered into Rome, where he found thousands upon thousands of his kind homeless, embittered, and dependent upon the State for food. These once sturdy farmer-citizens who were disappearing had made up the bulk of the citizenship of Rome, from whose ranks she had drawn her splendid armies.

353. Decline of Hellenistic Civilization. Nor was the situation any better in the most civilized portions of the Empire outside of Italy, and especially in Greece. Under the large plantation system the Greek farmers had disappeared, as those of Italy were now beginning to do. To this condition we must add, first, the robberies and extortions of the Roman taxgatherers and governors (§ 342) ; second, the continuous slave raids of the Ægean pirates, whose pillaging and kidnaping the Roman Republic criminally failed to prevent (§ 350) ; and third, the shift of Greek commerce eastward (§ 274). These were reasons enough for the destruction of business, of agriculture, and of prosperity in the Greek world. At the same time, that wondrous development of higher civilization which we found in the Hellenistic world (pp. 179–187) was likewise showing signs of decline.

354. Failure of Roman Government of the Mediterranean World. The failure of the Roman Senate to organize a successful government for the empire they had conquered,—a government even as good as that of Persia under Darius (§ 100),—this failure had brought the whole world of Mediterranean civilization dangerously near destruction. In the European background beyond the Alpine frontiers there were rumblings of vast movements among the Northern barbarians, threatening to descend as of old and completely overwhelm the civilization which for over three thousand years had been slowly built up by Orientals and Greeks and Romans in the Mediterranean world. It now looked very much as if the Roman State was about to perish, and with it the civilization which had been growing for so many centuries. Was civilized man indeed to perish from the earth ? or would the Roman State be able to survive and to preserve civilization from destruction ? Rome was a city-state. Among the Greeks this very form of state had outlived its usefulness and had over and over again proved its inability to organize and control successfully a larger world ; that is, an empire. Would the Roman Republic be able to transform itself into a great imperial State, with all the many offices necessary to give successful government to the peoples and nations surrounding the Mediterranean ?

355. The Difficulties confronting Rome after she had gained World Power. We stand at the point where the civilization of the Hellenistic world began to decline, after the destruction of Carthage and Corinth (146 B.C.). We are now to watch the Roman people struggling with three difficult and dangerous problems at the same time : *first,* the deadly internal hostility which we have seen growing up between rich and poor ; *second,* the organization of successful Roman government of the Mediterranean world while the dangerous internal struggle was going on ; and *third,* in the midst of these grave responsibilities, the invasions of the barbarian hordes of the North. In spite of all these threatening dangers we shall see Rome gaining the needed imperial organization which enabled the Roman State to hurl back the Northern barbarians, to hold the northern frontiers for five hundred years, and thus to shield and preserve the civilization which had cost mankind so many centuries of slow progress — the civilization which, because it was so preserved by the Roman Empire, has become our own inheritance to-day.

QUESTIONS

I. After the Hannibalian War what happened between Rome and Macedonia? between Rome and the Seleucid empire? What became of Egypt and the Greek states?

II. How did Rome organize the conquered lands? What kind of rule did she give them? Contrast the old and the new Roman houses. Discuss the new furnishings and conveniences; the incoming works of Greek art; of Greek literature. What was the result as to education? as to Latin literature? Discuss libraries at Rome.

III. Describe the effect of the new luxury on the Romans. What forms of public entertainment arose? Discuss treatment of the poor and expenses of a political career. What was the Roman politician's chief object? How did the new wealth affect landownership? Discuss slavery. What happened to the small farmers in Italy? in Greece? What great dangers now threatened Rome?

NOTE. The relief below, found in the Theater of Marcellus, built by Augustus, gives us a very vivacious glimpse of a battle between gladiators and wild beasts, just as the Romans saw it. The gladiators in this combat wear only a tunic and have no defensive armor except a helmet and a shield. Note the expression of pain on the face of the gladiator at the left, whose arm is being lacerated by the lion.

CHAPTER XVI

A CENTURY OF REVOLUTION AND THE END OF THE REPUBLIC

I. THE LAND SITUATION AND THE BEGINNING OF THE STRUGGLE BETWEEN SENATE AND PEOPLE

356. The Dangerous Situation to be met by the Senate. We must now take up the difficult problems demanding settlement by the Roman Senate. *In Italy* there was above all the perilous condition of the surviving small farmers (§§ 349–352) and the need of increasing in some way their numbers and their farms. Equally dangerous was the discontent of the Italian allies, who had never been given the vote or the right to hold office (§ 318). The problems *outside of Italy* were not less pressing. They were, likewise, two in number. There was first the need of a complete reform of provincial government and the creation of a system of honest and successful management of the great Roman Empire. And second there was the settlement of the frontier boundaries of the Empire and the repulse of the invading barbarians who were threatening to crush the Mediterranean world and its civilization, as the prehistoric Greeks had crushed Ægean civilization (§ 134).

357. Reforms of the Gracchi (133–121 B.C.). The crying needs of the farming class in Italy failed to produce any effect upon the blinded and selfish aristocrats of the Senate as a whole. The unselfish patriot who undertook to become the leader of the people against the Senate and to save Italy from destruction by restoring the farmer class was a noble named Tiberius Gracchus. He was a grandson of Scipio, the hero of Zama. Elected tribune (133 B.C.), he used to address the people with passionate eloquence and tell them of their wrongs: "The beasts that prowl about Italy have holes and lurking places, where they may make their beds. You who fight and die for Italy enjoy only the blessings of air and light. These alone are your heritage. Homeless, unsettled, you wander to and fro with your wives and children. . . . You fight and die to give wealth and luxury to others. You are called the masters of the world; yet there is no clod of earth that you can call your own."

As tribune, Tiberius Gracchus brought before the Assembly a law for the reassignment of public lands and the protection and support of the farming class. It was a statesmanlike and moderate law. In the effort to secure reëlection, that he might insure the *enforcement* of his law, Gracchus was slain by a mob of senators, who rushed out of the Senate house and attacked him and his supporters. This was the first murderous deed introducing a century of revolution and civil war (133–31 B.C.), which terminated in the destruction of the Roman Republic.

Ten years after the tribunate of Tiberius Gracchus his younger brother Gaius gained the same office (123 B.C.). He not only took up the struggle on behalf of the landless farmers but he made it his definite object to attack and weaken the Senate and thus reform the whole state. At the same time he proposed to give to the Italian allies the long-desired full citizenship — a proposal which angered the people as much as it did the Senate. His efforts finally resulted in a riot in which he was killed, as his brother had been (121 B.C.).

II. The Rise of One-Man Power: Marius and Sulla

358. The People resort to Army Leaders. The work of the Gracchus brothers had at least taught the people to look up to a leader. This tendency was the beginning of one-man power. But the leader to whom the people now turned was not a civil magistrate, as the Gracchus brothers had been, but a *military commander*. The misrule of the Senate abroad so angered the people that the Assembly passed a law appointing their own general to supersede a general appointed by the Senate in a foreign war. *The people by this action seized control of the army.*

359. Services of Marius, the People's Commander. The commander on whom the people relied was himself a man of the people, named Marius, who had once been a rough plowboy. He was fortunately an able soldier and Rome needed his abilities. Two powerful tribes of German barbarians, the Cimbrians and the Teutons, combined with some Gauls, had been shifting southward and crossing the northern frontiers of Rome. Six Roman armies, one after another, had been disastrously defeated. There was great anxiety in Rome ; the people repeatedly reëlected Marius consul and sent him against the terrible Northern barbarians. In two great battles in the North the people's hero not only defeated but almost destroyed the German hosts (102 B.C.). A soldier of the people had saved Rome.

Marius was not only an able soldier but he was also a great organizer. In order to secure sufficient men for the legions, he abolished the old custom of allowing only citizens of property to serve in the army, and he took in the poor and the penniless. Such men soon became professional soldiers. As once in Greece (§ 237), so now in Rome, the day of the citizen-soldier had passed.

But in spite of his ability as a soldier and as an army organizer, Marius was not a statesman. Having risen from the ranks, he was at heart a rough Roman peasant. As a political leader he failed completely, and the Senate gained the upper hand again. Then Marius retired in disgrace, but his leadership had revealed to the people how they might gain control over the Senate by combining on a *military* leader, whose power, therefore, did not consist in the peaceful enforcement of the laws and usages of the Roman State, but in the illegal application of military force.

360. Struggle between Rome and Italy : the Social War (90–88 B.C.). While the struggle between Senate and people was going on, there was increasing discontent among the Italian allies (§ 318). They had contributed as many troops to the army which conquered the Empire as had Rome herself, and now they were refused any voice in the control of that Empire or any just share in the immense wealth which they saw the Romans drawing from it. But the possession of this Empire had corrupted and blinded the Senate and the governing community at Rome.

There were, happily, some statesmanlike Roman leaders, who planned that the Italian allies should receive citizenship. Among them was a wealthy and popular noble named Drusus, who gained election as tribune and began to take measures leading to the enfranchisement of the Italian allies. But so fierce and savage was the opposition aroused, both in the Senate and among the people, that this great Roman statesman was stabbed in the street. Thereupon the leading Italian communities of central and southern Italy revolted and formed a new state and government of their own, with a capital which they impressively renamed Italica (90 B.C.).

Defeated at first in the war which followed (90–88 B.C.), the Romans tardily took action and granted the desired citizenship. The Italian communities then rejoined the Roman State. But the citizens residing in distant communities could not vote or take any part in the government unless they journeyed to Rome to do so. This situation was of course an absurdity, and again illustrated the inability of an ancient city-state to furnish the machinery of government for a large nation, not to mention a world empire. Nevertheless, Italy was now on the way to become a nation unified in government and in speech.

361. Sulla defies People's Laws with an Army. At the head of an army he had just been leading against the Italian allies was a former officer of Marius, named Sulla. The Senate now selected him to command in a war then coming on in Asia Minor. But the leaders of the people would not accept the Senate's appointment, and they passed a law electing Marius to this command. Now Marius had no army at the moment, but Sulla, being still at the head of his army, ignored the law passed by the people and marched with his troops on Rome. For the first time a Roman consul took possession of the city *by force*. The *Senate* was now putting through its will under military leadership, as the *Assembly* had before done (§ 358). Sulla forced a new law by which the Assembly would always be obliged to secure the consent of the Senate before it could vote on any measure. Having thus destroyed the power of the people legally to oppose the will of the Senate, Sulla marched off to his command in Asia Minor.

362. Revenge of Marius and his Death (86 B.C.). The Senate had triumphed, but with the departure of Sulla and his legions the people refused to submit. Marius, having entered Rome with troops, began a frightful massacre of the leading men of the senatorial party. The Senate, the first to sow seeds of violence in the murder of Tiberius Gracchus (§ 357), now reaped a fearful harvest. Marius was elected consul for the seventh time, but he died a few days after his election (86 B.C.). Meantime the leaders of the people ruled in Rome until the day of reckoning which was sure to come on the return of Sulla.

363. Sulla gives the Senate Supreme Leadership (82-79 B.C.). Having finished a victorious campaign in Asia Minor, Sulla returned. On the way the Roman army of Sulla defeated the Roman armies of the people, one after another, and Sulla entered Rome as master of the State, *without any legal power to justify such mastery*. By means of his army he forced his own appointment as Dictator (82 B.C.). His first action was to begin the systematic slaughter of the leaders of the people's party and the confiscation of their property. Then he forced the passage of a whole series of new laws which deprived the Assembly and the tribunes of their power and gave the supreme leadership of the State to the Senate.

III. THE OVERTHROW OF THE REPUBLIC: POMPEY AND CÆSAR

364. People elect Pompey Consul and regain Power (70 B.C.). Following the death of Sulla the people's party at once began agitation for the repeal of his hateful laws, which bound the people and the tribunes hand and foot. The people had now learned that they must have a *military* leader. They found him in a former officer of Sulla, named Pompey. He was elected consul (70 B.C.) chiefly because he agreed to repeal the obnoxious laws of Sulla.

He kept his promise, and this service to the people then secured to Pompey a military command of great importance.

365. Achievements of Pompey (67–62 B.C.). Such was the neglect of the Senate to protect shipping that the pirates of the East had overrun the whole Mediterranean (§ 350). They even appeared at the mouth of the Tiber, robbing and burning. Therefore, 67 B.C., the Assembly of the people passed a law giving Pompey supreme command in the Mediterranean. He quickly cleared the whole Mediterranean of pirates. When his command was enlarged to include Asia Minor and Syria, he crushed the remnant of the kingdom of the Seleucids (§ 272) and made Syria a Roman province. He entered Jerusalem and brought the home of the Jews under Roman control. Before he turned back, the legions under his leadership had marched along the Euphrates and had looked down upon the Caspian. There had been no such conquests in the Orient since the campaigns of the Great Macedonian, and to the popular imagination Pompey seemed a new Alexander marching in triumph through the East.

FIG. 61. BUST SAID TO BE A PORTRAIT OF JULIUS CÆSAR

The ancient portraits commonly accepted as those of Julius Cæsar are really of uncertain identity

366. Rise of Cæsar ; his Election as Consul (59 B.C.). Meantime a new popular hero had arisen at Rome. He was a nephew, of Marius, named Julius Cæsar (Fig. 61), born in the year 100 B.C. He took up the cause of Marius and thus quickly gained a foremost place among the leaders of the people.

Cæsar, however, met one serious setback. Catiline, a senator of evil reputation, whom Cæsar had supported for the consulship, was defeated. Catiline gathered about him a large body of dangerous followers and tried to seize the government. He failed because of the vigilance of the consul, the great orator Cicero (§ 386), and died fighting at the head of his outlawed followers. Cæsar was suspected of connection with this uprising of Catiline, and the suspicion seriously affected his political career.

When Pompey returned to Italy, hailed as the great conqueror of the Orient, he needed political influence to secure the Senate's formal approval of his actions in Asia Minor and a grant of land for his troops. For two years the Senate refused Pompey these concessions. Then Cæsar, to gain the help of Pompey, stepped forward in Pompey's support, and the two secured the adherence to their plans of a very wealthy Roman noble named Crassus. This private alliance of these three powerful men (called a "triumvirate") gave them the control of the situation. As a result Cæsar was elected consul for the year 59 B.C.

367. Cæsar's Achievements in Gaul (58–50 B.C.). The consulship was but a step in Cæsar's plans. Having fearlessly put through new land laws for the benefit of the people, Cæsar then provided for his own future career. It was clear to him that he must have an important military command in order to gain an army. He saw a great opportunity in the West, in the vast country now modern France, then occupied by the Gauls (see map, IV, p. 218). He had no difficulty in securing his appointment as governor of Gaul on both sides of the Alps for five years.

Cæsar took charge of his new province early in 58 B.C. and at once showed himself a military commander of surpassing skill. In eight years of march and battle he subdued the Gauls and conquered their territory from the ocean and the English Channel eastward to the Rhine. He even crossed the Channel and carried an invasion of Britain as far as the Thames. He added a vast dominion to the Roman Empire, comprising in general the territory of modern France and Belgium. We should not forget that his conquest brought Latin into France, as the ancestor from which French speech has descended (see map, IV, p. 218).

368. Cæsar's View of the Situation as a Statesman. Cæsar had shown himself at Rome a successful politician. In Gaul he proved his ability as a brilliant soldier. Was he also a great statesman, or was he, like Pompey, merely to seek a succession of military commands and to accomplish nothing to deliver Rome from being the helpless plaything of one military commander after another? Cæsar's understanding of the situation at Rome was perfectly clear. The old machinery of government furnished by the Republic possessed no means of preventing the rise in the provinces of one ambitious general after another to fight for control of the State, as Marius and Sulla had done. The old republican system could consequently never again restore order and stable government to Italy and the Empire.

The situation therefore demanded an able and patriotic commander with an army behind him, who should make himself the undisputed and permanent master of the Roman government and subdue all other competitors. Cæsar therefore steadily pursued this aim. One of his cleverest moves was the publication of a history of his campaigns in Gaul, which he had found time to write even in the midst of dangerous marches and critical battles. Although it is one of the greatest works of Latin prose, the book was really a political pamphlet, intended to tell the Roman people the story of the vast conquests which they owed to their governor in Gaul. It did not fail of its purpose. At present it is the best-known Latin reading book for beginners in that language.

369. Pompey supports the Senate. When Cæsar's second term as governor of Gaul drew near its end, his supporters in Rome, instructed by him, were arranging for his second election to the consulship. The Senate, dreading his return to Italy, were seeking another military leader like Sulla. The leading senators therefore made offers to Pompey, in spite of the fact that thus far he had been a leader of the people's party. He was no statesman and was simply looking for a command. The result was that he undertook to defend the cause of the Senate. What should have been a lawful political contest thus again became a military struggle between two commanding generals, Cæsar and Pompey, like that of Marius and Sulla a generation earlier.

370. Cæsar maneuvers Pompey out of Italy and is elected Consul (49 B.C.). Cæsar endeavored to compromise with the

Senate, but on receiving as their reply a summons to disband his army, he had no hesitation as to his future action. The professional soldiers who now made up a Roman army felt no responsibility as citizens, but were usually greatly attached to their commanding general. The veterans of Cæsar's campaigns in Gaul were unswervingly devoted to him. Before the Senate's message had been an hour in his hands Cæsar and his troops had crossed the Rubicon, the little stream which formed the boundary of his province, toward Rome (49 B.C.). Beyond this boundary Cæsar had no legal right to lead his forces. In crossing it he had taken a step which became so memorable that we still speak of any great decision as a "crossing of the Rubicon."

The swiftness of Cæsar's lightning blows was always one of the greatest reasons for his success. Totally unprepared for so swift a response on Cæsar's part, the Senate turned to Pompey, who informed them that the forces at his command could not hold Rome against Cæsar. As Pompey retreated the majority of the senators and a large number of nobles fled with him and his army. By skillful maneuvers Cæsar forced Pompey and his followers to forsake Italy and cross over to Greece. Being now in possession of Rome, Cæsar, after a brief dictatorship, was elected consul, and could then assume the rôle of lawful defender of Rome against the Senate and the army of Pompey.

371. Cæsar defeats Pompey and the Armies of the Senate (49–48 B.C.). Cæsar's position, however, was not yet secure. Pompey could muster all the peoples and kingdoms of the Orient against him. Furthermore, Pompey held the great fleet with which he had suppressed the pirates, and he was thus master of the sea. With all the East at his back he was improving every moment to gather and discipline an army with which to crush Cæsar. Furthermore, some of Pompey's officers held Spain. Cæsar was therefore obliged to reckon with the followers of Pompey on both sides, East and West. He determined to deal with the West first. With his customary swiftness he was in Spain by June (49 B.C.). Here, by cutting off their supplies, he forced Pompey's commanders to surrender without fighting a battle.

Having heard of Cæsar's departure into Spain, Pompey and his great group of senators and nobles were preparing at their leisure to cross over and again take possession of Italy. Before they could even begin the crossing, Cæsar had returned from Spain victorious, and to their amazement, notwithstanding the fact that they controlled the sea, he embarked at Brundisium, evaded their warships, and landed his army on the coast of Epirus (see map, p. 90). After some reverses, and in spite of his inferior numbers, Cæsar accepted battle with Pompey at Pharsalus, in Thessaly (48 B.C.). Pompey was crushingly defeated, and his army surrendered.

372. Cæsar completes the Conquest of the Mediterranean World (48–45 B.C.). Pompey then escaped into Egypt, where he was basely murdered. Cæsar, following Pompey to Egypt, found ruling there the beautiful Cleopatra, the last of the Ptolemies. The charms of this remarkable queen and the political advantages of her friendship met a ready response on the part of the great Roman. We know little of the campaign by which Cæsar next overthrew his opponents in Asia Minor. It was from there that he sent his famous report to the Senate : "I came, I saw, I conquered" (*veni, vidi, vici*). The only other obstacles to Cæsar's complete control of the empire of the world were all disposed of by March, 45 B.C., a little over four years after he had first taken possession of Italy with his army (map, IV, p. 218).

373. Cæsar's Reorganization of the State and Empire. Cæsar used his power with great moderation and humanity. From the first he had taken great pains to show that his methods were not those of the bloody Sulla. It is clear that he intended his own position to be that of a Hellenistic sovereign like Alexander the Great. Nevertheless, he was too wise a statesman to abolish at once the outward forms of the Republic. He made his power seem legal by having himself made Dictator for life, and he assumed also the powers of the other leading offices of the State.

Cæsar lived only five years (49–44 B.C.) after his first conquest of Italy (49 B.C.). Of this period, as we have seen, four years were almost wholly occupied by campaigns. Little time was therefore left him for the colossal task of reshaping the Roman State and organizing the vast Roman Empire, the task in which the Roman Senate had so completely failed. Cæsar did not abolish the Senate, but he greatly increased its numbers and filled it with his own friends and adherents, some of them provincials. He began far-reaching reforms of the corrupt Roman administration. In all this he was beginning the Roman Empire. He was in fact its first emperor, and only his untimely death prolonged the last struggles of the Republic for fifteen years more.

374. Cæsar's Vast Plans and his Death (44 B.C.). Cæsar sketched vast plans for the rebuilding of Rome ; he laid out great roads along the important lines of communication ; and he completely reformed the government of cities. He put an end to centuries of inconvenience with the Greco-Roman moon-calendar by introducing into Europe the more practical Egyptian calendar (§ 23), which we are still using, though with inconvenient later alterations.

But there were still men in Rome who were not ready to submit to the rule of one man. On the fifteenth of March, 44 B.C., three days before the date arranged for his departure on a great campaign beyond the Euphrates, these men struck down the greatest of the Romans. If some of his murderers, like Brutus and Cassius (headpiece, p. 244), fancied themselves patriots overthrowing a tyrant, they little understood how vain were all such efforts to restore the ancient Republic. World dominion and its military power had destroyed forever the Roman Republic, and the murder of Cæsar again plunged Italy and the Empire into civil war.

IV. The Triumph of Augustus and the End of the Civil War

375. Early Career of Cæsar's Nephew, Octavian (Augustus). Over in Illyria the terrible news from Rome found the murdered statesman's grand-nephew Octavian (Fig. 62), a youth of eighteen, quietly pursuing his studies. A letter from his mother, brought by a secret messenger, bade him flee far away eastward without delay, in order to escape all danger at the hands of his uncle's murderers. The youth's reply was to proceed without a moment's hesitation to Rome. This statesmanlike decision of character reveals the quality of the young man both as he then showed it and for years to follow.

On his arrival in Italy Octavian learned that he had been legally adopted by Cæsar and also made his sole heir. He was too young to be regarded as dangerous by Cæsar's enemies. But his young shoulders carried a very old head. He slowly gathered the threads of the tangled situation in his clever fingers, not forgetting the lessons of his adoptive father's career,— especially the necessity of military power. Then playing the game of politics, with several legions at his back, he showed himself a statesman no longer to be ignored. The murderers of Cæsar were defeated and slain in a great battle at Philippi (42 B.C.), and within ten years after Cæsar's assassination this youth of twenty-eight gained complete control of Italy and the West.

Fig. 62. Portrait of Augustus, now in the Boston Museum of Fine Arts

376. Octavian ends a Century of Revolution and Civil War (133–30 B.C.). Cæsar's friend and lieutenant, Antony, with whom Octavian had joined hands, had meantime shown that he had no ability as a serious statesman. His prestige was greatly dimmed by a disastrous campaign against the Parthians. Dazzled by the attractions of Cleopatra, Antony was now living in Alexandria and Antioch, where he ruled the East as far as the Euphrates like an oriental sovereign. He and Cleopatra cherished hopes of ruling Rome. The tales of all this reached Octavian and the Romans. Octavian soon saw that Antony must be overthrown. He easily induced the Senate to declare war on Cleopatra, and thus he was able to advance against Antony. As Cæsar and Pompey, representing the West and the East, had once before faced each other on a battlefield in Greece (§ 371), so now Octavian and Antony, the leaders of the West and the East, met at Actium on the west coast of Greece. The outcome was a sweeping victory for the heir of Cæsar.

The next year Octavian landed in Egypt and took possession of that ancient land. Antony, probably forsaken by Cleopatra, took his own life. The proud queen too, unwilling to grace Octavian's triumph at Rome, died by her own hand. She was the last of the Ptolemies (§ 271), the rulers of Egypt for nearly three hundred years, since Alexander the Great. Octavian therefore made Egypt Roman territory (30 B.C.). To the West, which he already controlled, Octavian had now added also the East. Thus he had restored the unity of Roman dominions. The lands under his control encircled the Mediterranean, and the entire Mediterranean world was under the power of a single ruler.

377. Summary of a Century of Revolution. The struggle between the rich and the poor which resulted in violence under the Gracchus brothers after 133 B.C. was accompanied by the rise of military leaders, who gained great power and wealth in the newly conquered possessions. They were then able to rule and control the State in defiance of the laws. A century of strife, including many years of civil war between the leaders of the people and the Senate, resulted in the overthrow of the Republic (about 30 B.C.). Octavian's success marked the final triumph of one-man power in the entire ancient world, as it had long ago triumphed in the Orient. The century of strife which Octavian's victory ended was now followed by two centuries of profound peace. These were the first two centuries of the Roman Empire, beginning in 30 B.C.[1] We shall now take up these two centuries of peace in the two following chapters.

[1] It should be noticed that these two centuries of peace did not begin with the Christian Era. They began thirty years before the first year of the Christian Era, and hence the two centuries of peace do not correspond exactly with the first two centuries of our Christian Era.

QUESTIONS

I. What dangers now threatened Rome in Italy? outside of Italy? Tell the story of the Gracchus brothers.

II. How did the people gain more enduring power? Mention the achievements of Marius; his failures. What caused disunion in Italy? How was it finally removed? How did the Senate now gain power? How did the people retaliate? Describe the triumph of Sulla.

III. How did the people regain power? Describe Pompey's campaigns. How did Cæsar rise? What did he accomplish as governor? What was his view of the political situation of Rome? What did he write? Recount his struggle with the Senate.

What happened to Pompey's army in Italy? in Spain? in Greece? Where did Cæsar go after the Battle of Pharsalus? What territory did he finally control (see map, IV, p. 218)? What did he accomplish after his triumph? When and how did he die?

IV. Describe the situation and first action of Octavian on hearing of his uncle's death. What did he achieve in the next ten years? Recount his struggle with Antony. What period did this victory end? What kind of rule and what period did it begin?

NOTE. The tailpiece below shows a restoration of a magnificent marble inclosure containing the "Altar of Augustan Peace," erected by order of the Senate in honor of Augustus. The inclosure was open to the sky, and its surrounding walls, of which portions still exist, are covered below by a broad band of ornamental plant spirals, very sumptuous in effect. Above it is a series of reliefs.

CHAPTER XVII

THE FIRST CENTURY OF PEACE: THE AGE OF AUGUSTUS AND THE SUCCESSORS OF HIS LINE

I. THE RULE OF AUGUSTUS (30 B.C.–A.D. 14) AND THE BEGINNING OF TWO CENTURIES OF PEACE

378. Octavian's Moderate Policy. When Octavian returned to Italy all classes rejoiced at the termination of a hundred years of revolution, civil war, and devastation. The great majority of Romans now felt that an individual ruler was necessary for the control of the vast Roman dominions. Octavian therefore entered upon forty-four years of peaceful effort to give to the Roman Empire the efficient organization and good government which it had so long lacked. His most difficult task was to alter the old form of the State so as to make legal the position in the government which he had taken by military force. Unlike Cæsar, Octavian felt a sincere respect for the institutions of the Roman Republic and did not wish to destroy them nor to gain for himself the throne of an oriental sovereign.

379. Organization of the Roman State by Octavian. Accordingly, on returning to Rome, Octavian did not disturb the Senate, but did much to improve its membership. Indeed, he voluntarily handed over his powers to the Senate and the Roman people in

NOTE. The above headpiece shows us the two sides of a coin issued by Brutus, one of the leading assassins of Julius Cæsar (§ 374). On one is the head of Brutus; on the other are two daggers, intended to recall the assassination of Cæsar, and between them appears the cap of liberty, to suggest the liberty which the Romans supposedly gained by his murder, while there appears, below, the inscription EID MAR, which means the Ides of March (the Roman term for the fifteenth of March), the date of Cæsar's murder.

January, 27 B.C. The Senate thereupon, fully aware of the strength of Octavian and realizing by past experience that it did not possess the organization for ruling the great Roman world, gave him officially the command of the army and the control of the most important frontier provinces. Besides these vast powers he held also the important rights of a tribune (§§ 303, 357), and on this last office he chiefly based his right to power.

At the same time the Senate conferred upon him the title of *Augustus,* that is, "the august"; but his chief official title was *Princeps,* that is, "the first," meaning the first of the citizens. Another title given the head of the Roman Empire was an old word for commander or general; namely, *Imperator,* from which our word "emperor" is derived. Augustus, as we may now call Octavian, regarded his position as that of an official of the Roman Republic, elected by the Senate and the people.

The Roman Empire, which here emerges, was thus under a double government of the Senate and of the Princeps, whom we commonly call the emperor. But this double power was not well balanced. The old authority of the Senate could not be maintained reign after reign, when the Senate controlled no army. The Princeps held too much power to remain a mere elected magistrate. He was the real ruler, because the legions were behind him, and the so-called republican State created by Augustus tended to become a military monarchy, as we shall see.

380. Peace Policy of Augustus. The Empire which Rome now ruled consisted of the entire Mediterranean world (map, I, p. 260). Back from the Mediterranean the frontier boundaries were a pressing question. There was a natural boundary in the south, the Sahara, and also in the west, the Atlantic; but on the north and east further conquests might be made. In the main Augustus adopted the policy of organizing and consolidating the Empire *as he found it,* without making further conquests. In the east his boundary thus became the Euphrates, and in the north the Danube and the Rhine.

For the defense of these vast frontiers it was necessary to maintain a large standing army. It probably contained, on the average, about two hundred and twenty-five thousand men. It was now recruited chiefly from the provinces, and the foreign soldier who entered the ranks received citizenship in return for his service. Thus the fiction that the army was made up of citizens was maintained. But the tramp of the legions was heard no more in Italy. Henceforth they were posted far out on the frontiers, and the citizens at home saw nothing of the troops who defended them excepting the emperor's bodyguard.

381. The Great Task of organizing the Provinces. Within these frontiers Augustus now undertook to organize government for the entire Mediterranean world. Great peoples and nations had to be provided for in the huge Empire and given honest and efficient government. Some of them had old and successful systems of government ; others had no government at all. Egypt, for example, had long before possessed the most highly organized administration in the ancient world, but regions of the West, like Gaul, had not yet been given a system of government. All this Augustus endeavored to do.

The appointment of a provincial governor now rested almost wholly with the emperor, and such a governor knew that he was responsible to him for wise and honest government of his territory. He also knew that if he proved successful he could hold his post for years or be promoted to a better one. There thus grew up under the permanent control of Augustus and his successors a body of experienced and efficient provincial administrators (contrast § 342).

382. The Mediterranean *World* becoming a Mediterranean *Nation*. The great Mediterranean world now entered upon a new age of prosperity and development such as the nations along its shores, long accustomed to fight each other in war after war, had never known before. A process of unification began which was to make the Mediterranean *world* a Mediterranean *nation*. The national threads of our historical narrative have heretofore been numerous, as we have followed the stories of the oriental nations, of Athens, Sparta, Macedonia, Rome, Carthage, and others. For a long time we have followed these narratives separately like individual strands ; but now they are to be twisted together into a single thread of national history, that of the Roman Empire. The great exceptions are the German barbarians in the North and the unconquered Orient east of the Euphrates.

II. THE CIVILIZATION OF THE AUGUSTAN AGE

383. The Work of Augustus on Behalf of Italy and Rome. In the new Mediterranean nation thus growing up it was the purpose of Augustus that Italy should occupy a leading position. He made a remarkable effort to restore the fine old days of Roman virtue, the good old Roman customs, the beliefs of the fathers. He also undertook to rebuild Rome and make it the leading art center of the ancient world. On the Palatine Hill he rebuilt several dwelling houses into a palace for his residence. From this royal dwelling on the *Palatine* arose our English word "palace."

The palace looked down upon an imposing array of new marble buildings surrounding the ancient Forum (§ 296). The finest of these was the magnificent business hall (basilica) erected by Cæsar, left unfinished and then damaged by fire. It was now restored and completed by Augustus (Fig. 65, *E*). On the north of the old Forum Cæsar had constructed another, called the Forum of Cæsar (Fig. 65, *N*) ; but the growing business of the city led Augustus to build a third forum, known as the Forum of Augustus (Fig. 65, *O*), which he placed next to that of Cæsar (see *Ancient Times,* Fig. 247). The first stone theater in Rome had been built by Pompey (plan, p. 248). Augustus erected a larger and more magnificent one.

384. Influence of Greece and the Orient on Roman Architecture. In this new architecture of Rome, Greek models were the controlling influence. Nevertheless, oriental influences also were very prominent. Greek architecture did not employ the arch so long used in the Orient, but the architects of Rome now gave it a place of prominence along with the colonnade, as the two leading features of their buildings. It was through these Roman buildings that the arch gained its important place in our own modern architecture. (See *Ancient Times,* p. 611.)

385. Weakness of Rome in Art and Science. There were no creative sculptors in Rome like those whom we have met in Athens. Neither did a single great painter arise there, and the painting which was practiced was chiefly that of wall decoration,

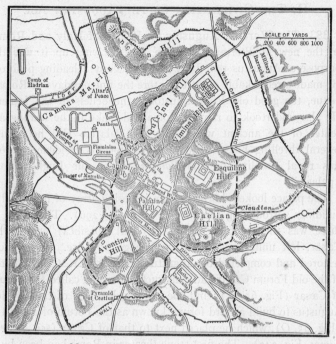

MAP OF ROME UNDER THE EMPERORS

in the Greek or Hellenistic manner as we find it in the houses of Pompeii (Fig. 68), which we are yet to visit.

If Rome was a borrower in art, she was even more so in science. Rome had no such men as Archimedes (§ 280) and Eratosthenes (§ 281). The leading geography of the time was written by a Greek living in Rome, named Strabo. Although it sadly lacked in scientific method, it was for many centuries the world's standard geography and may still be read with great pleasure and profit as an ancient book of travel.

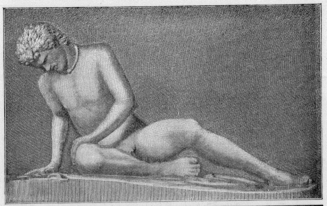

FIGS. 63 AND 64. SCULPTURES OF HELLENISTIC PERGAMUM

Above (Fig. 63) is a Gallic trumpeter, as he sinks in death with his trumpet at his feet (§ 278). Below (Fig. 64) is a part of the frieze around the great altar of Zeus at Pergamum (Fig. 52). It pictures the mythical struggle between gods and giants. A giant at the left, whose limbs end in serpents, raises over his head a great stone to hurl it at the goddess on the right (§ 278)

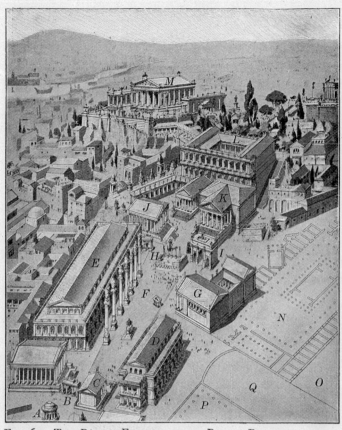

FIG. 65. THE ROMAN FORUM AND ITS PUBLIC BUILDINGS IN THE
EARLY EMPIRE. (AFTER LUCKENBACH)

We look across the ancient market place (*F*, § 296) to the Tiber with its
ships at the head of navigation. On each side of the market place (*F*),
where we see the buildings (*E, J,* and *D, G, I*), were once rows of little
wooden booths for selling meat, fish, and other merchandise. Especially
after the beginning of the Carthaginian wars these were displaced by fine
buildings like the basilica hall *D*, built not long after 200 B.C. Note the
Attic roofs and colonnades and the clerestory windows of the basilicas (*D, E*)
copied from the Hellenistic cities (§ 276), and originally from the Orient
(Fig. 16). It was soon to be adopted as a form for Christian church buildings.

See complete key on opposite page, footnote *

386. Leading Cultivated Men at Rome ; Cicero. Indifference to science at Rome was in marked contrast with Roman interest in literature. The leading Romans displayed in some cases an almost pathetic devotion to literary studies, even while weighed down with the heaviest responsibilities. Cæsar put together a treatise on Latin speech while crossing the Alps in a palanquin, when his mind must have been filled with the problems of his great wars in Gaul. Such men as these had studied in Athens or Rhodes and were deeply versed in Greek learning and literature. They spoke Greek every day among themselves, perhaps more than they did Latin.

The most cultivated man Rome ever produced was Cicero (§ 366). In the struggle to save the Republic, Cicero had failed as a statesman. Thereupon he devoted himself to his literary pursuits. As the greatest orator in Roman history he had already done much to perfect and beautify Latin prose in the orations which he delivered in the course of his career as a lawyer and a statesman. After his retirement he produced a group of remarkable treatises on duty, the gods, friendship, old age, and the like, and he left behind also several hundred letters which were preserved by his friends. As one of the last sacrifices of the civil wars, Cicero had fallen by the hands of Antony's brutal soldiery ; but his writings were to exert an undying influence. They made Latin speech one of the most beautiful instruments of human expression, and as an example of the finest literary style they have

---

* The Sacred Way (plan, p. 248) passed the little circular temple of Vesta (*A*) and reached the Forum at the Arch of Augustus (*B*) and the Temple of the Deified Julius Cæsar (*C*). On the right was the oldest basilica in the Forum (*D*) and on the left the magnificent new Basilica of Julius Cæsar (*E*) (§ 383). Opposite this, across the old Forum market place (*F*), was the new Senate House (*G*) planned by Julius Cæsar (§§ 374, 383). At the upper end of the Forum was the new speaker's platform (*H*) ; near it Septimius Severus (§ 430) later erected his crude arch (*I*). Beyond rises the Capitol, with the Temple of Saturn (*J*) and the Temple of Concord (*K*) at its base ; above, on its slope, is the Tabularium (*L*), a place of public records ; and on the summit of the Capitol the Temple of Jove (*M*). Julius Cæsar extended the Forum northward by laying out his new Forum (*N*) behind his Senate House (*G*). The subsequent growth of the emperors' Forums on this side may be seen in *Ancient Times*, Fig. 247, where the same lettering is repeated and continued.

influenced the best writing in all the various languages of Europe during the Middle Ages and in modern times.

387. Rise of Poetry in the Augustan Age; Horace and Virgil. Thus in the last days of the Republic, in spite of turbulence and civil war, Cicero and the men of his time had perfected Latin *prose*. On the other hand, the greatest of Latin *poetry* arose under the inspiration of the early Empire and the universal peace established by Augustus. Horace, the leading poet of the time, although only the son of a freedman of unknown race, had studied in Greece. He knew the old Greek lyric poets (§ 174) who had suffered danger and disaster as he himself had done in the long civil war. With the haunting echoes of old Greek poetry in his soul, he began to write of the men and the life of his own time. The poems of Horace will always remain one of the greatest legacies from the ancient world — a treasury of Roman life as pictured by a ripe and cultivated mind, unsurpassed even in the highly developed literature of the Greeks.

Virgil, the other great poet of the Augustan Age, spent much of his time in the quiet of his ancestral farm under the shadow of the Alps in the North. Here, as he looked out upon his own fields, the poet began to write verses like those of Theocritus (§ 283), reflecting to us in all its poetic beauty the rustic life of his time on the green hillsides of Italy. As time passed he gained an exalted vision of the mission of Rome, and especially of Augustus, as the restorer of world peace. Virgil then undertook the creation of a great epic poem, in which he pictured the wanderings of the Trojan hero Æneas escaping from burning Troy to Italy. There in the course of many heroic adventures Æneas founded the royal line of Latium (headpiece, p. 189). From him, according to the story, were descended the Julian family, the Cæsars, the ancestors of Augustus. Deeply admired by the age that produced it, the Æneid (as this poem is called after Æneas) has ever since been one of the leading schoolbooks of the civilized world and has had an abiding influence on the best literature of later times.

388. Death of Augustus (A.D. 14) and his Account of his Deeds. Augustus himself, when he was over seventy-five years old and felt his end approaching, put together a narrative of his career, which was engraved on bronze tablets and set up before his tomb. In this simple story the career of Augustus is unfolded with such grandeur as to make the document the most impressive brief record of a great man's life which has survived to us from the ancient world. Almost with his last breath Augustus penned the closing lines of this remarkable record, and on the nineteenth of August, the month which bears his name, in the fourteenth year of the Christian Era, the first of the Roman emperors died.

III. The Line of Augustus and the End of the First Century of Peace (A.D. 14–68)

389. The Four Successors of the Line of Augustus (A.D. 14–68). Augustus had been in supreme control of the great Roman world for nearly half a century. Four descendants of his family, either by blood or adoption, were to rule for more than another half century and thus to fill out the first century of peace. Augustus had never put forward a law providing for the appointment of his successors. Any prominent Roman citizen might have aspired to the office. Augustus left no son, and one after another his male heirs had died. He had finally been obliged to ask the Senate to associate with him his stepson Tiberius, his wife's son by an earlier marriage.

390. Tiberius (A.D. 14–37) and Caligula (A.D. 37–41). At the death of Augustus, the Senate, therefore, at once appointed Tiberius to all his stepfather's powers and without any limit as to time. He was an able soldier and an experienced man of affairs. He gave the provinces wise and efficient governors and showed himself a skilled and successful ruler. Tiberius no longer allowed the Roman rabble to go through the farce of voting on what the emperor had already decided, and even the appearance of a government by the Roman people thus finally disappeared forever.

As Tiberius had lost his son, the choice for his successor fell upon Gaius Cæsar, a great-grandson of Augustus, nicknamed Caligula ("little boot") by the soldiers among whom he was brought up. After a mad career of drunkenness and debauchery this mockery of a reign was brought to a sudden close by Caligula's own officers, who put an end to his life in his palace on the Palatine, when he had reigned only four years.

391. Claudius (A.D. 41-54). The imperial guards, ransacking the palace after the death of Caligula, found in hiding the trembling figure of a nephew of Tiberius and uncle of the dead

FIG. 66. THE AQUEDUCT OF THE EMPEROR CLAUDIUS

This wonderful aqueduct, built by the Emperor Claudius about the middle of the first century after Christ, is over forty miles long. About three fourths of it is subterranean, but the last ten miles consists of tall arches of massive masonry, as seen here at the left, supporting the channel in which the water flowed till it reached the palace of the emperor on the Palatine (plan, p. 248). Such ancient Roman aqueducts were so well built that four of them are still in use at Rome, and they convey to the city a more plentiful supply of water than any great modern city elsewhere receives

Caligula, named Claudius. Though now fifty years old, he had always been merely tolerated by his family as a man both physically and mentally inferior. But the guards hailed him as emperor, nevertheless, and the Senate was obliged to consent.

Nevertheless Claudius accomplished much for the Empire and devoted himself to its affairs (Fig. 66). He conducted in person a successful campaign in Britain and for the first time made its southern portion a province of the Empire. It was this conquest which probably even then began to bring elements of Latin speech into the English language, for Britain remained a Roman province for three and a half centuries.

392. The Infamy of Nero (A.D. 54-68). Agrippina, the last wife of Claudius, was able to push aside his son, Britannicus, and to obtain succession to the throne for her own son, Nero. Not only on his mother's side but also on his father's, Nero was descended from the family of Augustus. His mother had intrusted his education to the philosopher Seneca, and for the first five years of his reign, while Seneca was his chief minister, the rule of Nero was wise and successful. Then palace intrigues removed this able minister from the court. Nero's strong-minded mother, Agrippina, was also banished. Thereafter he cast aside all restraint and followed his own evil nature in a career of such vice and cruelty that the name of Nero has ever since been regarded as one of the blackest in all history.

Nero was devoted to art and wished personally to follow it. He even made a tour of Greece as a musician and composer. As the companion of actors, sportsmen, and prize fighters he even took part in gladiatorial exhibitions. His cowardly and suspicious nature led him to condemn his old teacher, Seneca, to death, and also to cause the assassination of the son of Claudius and of many other innocent and deserving men. In the same way he was persuaded to take the life of his wife, and, to crown his infamy, he even had his own mother assassinated.

A great disaster, meantime, took place in Rome. A huge fire broke out and destroyed a large portion of the city. Dark rumors ran through the streets that Nero himself had set fire to the city that he might rebuild it more splendidly, and gossip told how he sat watching the conflagration while reciting to the lyre a poem of his own on the destruction of Troy. There is no evidence to support these rumors. But under the circumstances Nero himself welcomed another version, which accused a new sect, the Christians, of having started the fire, and he executed a large number of them with horrible tortures.

393. Death of Nero and End of the First Century of Peace
(A.D. 68). The dissatisfaction at Rome, and Nero's treatment of
the only able men around him, deprived him of support there.
Then the provinces began to chafe under heavy taxation. This
discontent finally broke out in open revolt and rebellious troops
marched on Rome from several points. The cowardly Nero went
into hiding, and on hearing that the Senate had voted his death,
he theatrically stabbed himself and, attitudinizing to the last,
passed away uttering the words, "What an artist dies in me!"
Thus ended (A.D. 68) the last ruler of the line of Augustus, and
with him closed the first century of peace (31 B.C.–A.D. 68) ; for
several Roman commanders now struggled for the throne and
threatened to involve the Empire in another long civil war.

QUESTIONS

I. Describe the new state organized by Octavian. What was his
policy regarding conquests ? What can you say of his army ? Who
appointed the governors ? What was the result ?

II. What position did Augustus desire for Italy ? What did he do
for Rome ? Whence did Rome inherit her architecture ? her art and
science ? Discuss Roman interest in literature. Who was Rome's
most cultivated man ? What position does he hold in literature ?
What can you say about Horace ? about Virgil ? What did Augustus
write ? When did he die ?

III. How long did Augustus and the successors belonging to his
family reign ? Tell of the reigns of the first two who followed him.
What were the chief achievements of Claudius ? Tell the story of
Nero's reign. What century ended with his death ? When ?

CHAPTER XVIII

THE SECOND CENTURY OF PEACE AND THE CIVILIZATION OF THE EARLY ROMAN EMPIRE

I. THE EMPERORS OF THE SECOND CENTURY OF PEACE
(BEGINNING A.D. 69)

394. Advent of the Second Century of Peace (A.D. 69). For about a year after the death of Nero the struggle among the leading military commanders for the throne of the Cæsars continued. Fortunately Vespasian, a very able commander in the East, was victorious, and A.D. 69 he was declared emperor by the Senate. With him, therefore, began a second century of peace under a line of able emperors who brought the Empire to the highest level of prosperity and happiness.

NOTE. The above headpiece shows us the body of a citizen of Pompeii who perished when the city was destroyed by an eruption of Vesuvius, A.D. 79 (§ 404). The fine volcanic ashes settled around the man's body, and these rain-soaked ashes made a cast of his figure before it had perished. After the body had perished it left in the hardened mass of ashes a hollow mold, which the modern excavators poured full of plaster and thus secured a cast of the figure of the unfortunate man just as he lay smothered by the deadly ashes which overwhelmed him over eighteen hundred years ago.

395. Two Great Tasks of the Emperors. Two great tasks were accomplished by the emperors of the age we are discussing : *first*, that of perfecting the system of defenses on the frontiers ; and *second*, that of more fully developing the government and organization of the Empire. Let us look first at the frontiers. On the south the Empire was protected by the Sahara desert and on the west by the Atlantic, but on the north and east it was open to attack. The shifting German tribes constantly threatened the northern frontiers; while in the east the frontier on the Euphrates was continually made unsafe by the Parthians, the only civilized power still unconquered by Rome (see map, I, p. 260).

Owing to the pressure of the barbarians on the northern frontiers, Mediterranean civilization was still in constant danger of being overwhelmed from the North. The great problem for future humanity was whether the Roman emperors would be able to hold off the barbarians long enough to permit these rude Northerners to gain enough of Mediterranean civilization to respect it, and thus to preserve at least some of it for mankind in the future.

396. The Flavian Emperors and the Frontier Problem (A.D. 69-96). The Flavian family, as we call Vespasian and his two sons, Titus and Domitian, did much to make the northern frontiers safe. Domitian adopted the frontier lines laid down by Augustus and planned their fortification with walls wherever necessary. But on the lower Danube he failed to crush the dangerous power of the growing kingdom of Dacia (see map, I, p. 260).

397. Trajan (A.D. 98-117) **and his Wars.** This left the whole threatening situation on the lower Danube to be met by the brilliant soldier Trajan. He captured one stronghold of the Dacians after another, and in two wars finally destroyed their capital. Having built a massive stone bridge across the Danube, Trajan made Dacia a Roman province and sprinkled plentiful Roman colonies on the north side of the great river. The descendants of these colonies in the same region still call themselves *Rumanians* and their land *Rumania*, a form of the word " Roman."

Trajan then turned his attention to the eastern frontier, where a large portion of the boundary was formed by the upper

Euphrates River. Rome thus held the western half of the Fertile Crescent, but it had never conquered the eastern half, with Assyria and Babylonia (see map, I, p. 260), which was held by the powerful kingdom of the Parthians. Trajan, emulating Alexander, defeated the Parthians and added Armenia, Mesopotamia, and Assyria to the Empire as new provinces. Then a sudden rebellion in his rear forced him to a dangerous retreat. Weakened by

FIG. 67. RESTORATION OF THE ROMAN FORTIFIED WALL ON THE GERMAN FRONTIER

This masonry wall, some three hundred miles long, protected the northern boundary of the Roman Empire between the upper Rhine and the upper Danube, where it was most exposed to German attack. At short intervals there were blockhouses along the wall, and at points of great danger strongholds and barracks for the shelter of garrisons

sickness and bitterly realizing that this great expedition was a failure, he died in Asia Minor while returning to Rome (A.D. 117).

398. Hadrian (A.D. 117-138) completes the Frontier Defenses. Trajan's successor, Hadrian, was another able soldier, but he had also the judgment of a statesman. He made no effort to continue Trajan's conquests in the East. On the contrary, he wisely brought the frontier back to the Euphrates. But he retained Dacia and strengthened the whole northern frontier, especially the long barrier reaching from the Rhine to the Danube, where the completion of the continuous wall (Fig. 67) was largely due to him. He built a similar wall along the northern boundary across Britain. The line of both these walls is still visible. As a result of these wise measures and the impressive victories of Trajan, the frontiers were safe and quiet for a long time.

399. The Army under Trajan and Hadrian. Under Trajan and Hadrian the army which defended these frontiers was the greatest and most skillfully managed organization of the kind which the ancient world had ever seen. Drawn from all parts of the Empire, the army now consisted of many different nationalities, like the British army in the recent World War. A legion of Spaniards might be stationed on the Euphrates, or a group of youths from the Nile might spend many years in sentry duty on the wall that barred out the Germans. We are still able to hold in our hands the actual letters written from a northern post by a young Egyptian recruit in the Roman army to his father and sister in a distant little village on the Nile.[1] Such posts were equipped with fine barracks and living quarters for officers and men, and the discipline necessary to keep the troops always ready to meet the barbarians outside the walls was never relaxed.

400. Improvements in Government. Meantime the Empire had been undergoing important changes within. The emperors developed a system of *government departments*, headed by efficient ministers, such as we have in modern states. It was the wise and efficient Hadrian who accomplished the most in perfecting this organization of the government business. Thus after Rome had been for more than three centuries in control of the Mediterranean world, it finally possessed a well-developed government organization. With the complete control of these departments entirely in his own hands, the power of the emperor was much increased.

Among many changes, one of the most important was the abolition of the system of "farming" taxes; that is, allowing them to be collected by private individuals for profit—a system which had caused both the Greeks and the Romans (§ 342) much trouble. Government tax collectors now everywhere gathered in the taxes of the great Mediterranean world.

---

[1] See *Ancient Times*, Fig. 253 and p. 631, footnote.

401. Rise of a System of Law for the Whole Empire. Not only did the subjects of this vast State pay their taxes into the same treasury but they were now controlled by the same laws. The lawyers of Rome under the emperors we are now discussing were the most gifted legal minds the world had ever seen. They altered the narrow *city*-law of Rome that it might meet the needs of the whole Mediterranean world. In spirit these laws of the Empire were most fair, just, and humane. Antoninus Pius, the kindly emperor who followed Hadrian, maintained that an accused person must be held innocent until proved guilty by the evidence, a principle of law which has descended to us and is still part of our own law. These laws did much to unify the peoples of the Mediterranean world into a single nation ; for they were now regarded by the law not as different nations but as subjects of the same great State, which extended to them all the same protection of justice, law, and order.

402. Close Attention to the Provinces by the Emperors. Able and conscientious governors were now controlling affairs all over the Empire. Emperors like Trajan and Hadrian relieved the communities of much responsibility for their own affairs. Hence the local communities inclined more and more to depend upon the emperor, and their interest in public affairs and ability to manage them declined. This was eventually a serious cause of general decay, as we shall see.

II. THE CIVILIZATION OF THE EARLY ROMAN EMPIRE : THE PROVINCES

403. The Peoples of the Roman Empire. Here was a world of sixty-five to a hundred million souls encircling the entire Mediterranean. We might have stood at the Strait of Gibraltar, and, if human vision had been able to penetrate so far, we might have surveyed these peoples as our eyes swept along the Mediterranean coasts out through Africa and back through Asia and Europe to the Strait again. On our right in Africa would have been Moors, North Africans, and Egyptians ; in the eastern background,

Arabs, Jews, Phœnicians, Syrians, Armenians, and Hittites; and as our eyes returned through Europe, Greeks, Italians, Gauls, and Iberians (Spaniards) ; while north of these were the Britons and some Germans within the frontier lines. All these people were of course very different from one another in native

Fig. 68. A Street in Ancient Pompeii as it appears To-day

The pavement and sidewalk are in perfect condition, as when they were first covered by the falling ashes (§ 404). At the left is a public fountain, and in the foreground is a street crossing. Of the buildings on this street only half a story still stands, except at the left, where we see the entrances of two shops, with the tops of the doors in position and the walls preserved to the level of the second floor above

manners, clothing, and customs, but they all enjoyed Roman protection and rejoiced in the far-reaching Roman peace. For the most part, as we have seen, they lived in cities, and the life of the age was prevailingly a city life, even though many of the cities were small.

404. Pompeii. Fortunately one of the provincial cities has been preserved to us with much that we might have seen there if we could have visited it nearly two thousand years ago. The little city of Pompeii, covered with volcanic ashes in the brief reign of Titus (A.D. 79), still shows us the very streets and houses, the forum and the public buildings, the shops and the markets, and a host of other things, mirroring the very life of the people of this town as it was in the days when they were suddenly overwhelmed by the eruption of the volcano of Vesuvius (Fig. 68).[1] Pompeii was close beside the Greek cities of southern Italy, and we at once discover that the place was essentially Hellenistic in its life and art.

405. Improved Means of Intercourse. In some matters there had been great progress. This was especially true of intercourse and rapid communication. Everywhere the magnificent Roman roads, massively paved with smooth stone, like a town street, led straight over the hills and across the rivers by imposing bridges. Some of these bridges still stand and are in use to-day (Fig. 70). The speed of travel and communication was fully as high as that maintained in Europe and America a century ago, before the introduction of the steam railway, and the roads were better.

By sea, however, the chief difference was the freedom from the old-time pirates (§ 365), and the resulting regularity of over-sea communications. For example, a Roman merchant could send a letter to his agent in Alexandria in ten days. The huge government corn ships that plied regularly between the Roman harbors and Alexandria were stately vessels carrying several thousand tons. Good harbors had everywhere been equipped with docks, and lighthouses modeled on the Pharos at Alexandria guided the mariners into every harbor.

406. Wide Extent of Commerce. Under these circumstances business flourished as never before. The good roads led merchants to trade beyond the frontiers and to find new markets. There was a fleet of a hundred and twenty ships plying regularly across the Indian Ocean between the Red Sea and the harbors of India. The wares which they brought were shipped west from the docks of Alexandria, which still remained the greatest commercial city

[1] See *Ancient Times*, Figs. 197, 202, 243, and 256.

on the Mediterranean, the Liverpool of the Roman Empire. There was a proverb that you could get everything at Alexandria except snow. A vast network of commerce thus covered the ancient world from the frontiers of China and the coast of India on the east to Britain and the harbors of the Atlantic on the west.

407. Travel and Life in the Provinces. Both business and pleasure now made travel very common. The Roman citizen of means and education made his tour of the Mediterranean much as the modern sight-seer does. As he passed through the towns of the provinces, he found everywhere evidences of the generosity of the citizens. There were fountains, theaters, music halls, baths, gymnasiums, and schools, erected by wealthy men and given to the community. The boys and girls of these towns found open to them schools with teachers paid by the government, where all those ordinary branches of study which we have found in the Hellenistic Age were taught (Fig. 69). The boy who turned to business could engage a stenographer to teach him shorthand, and the young man who wished higher instruction could still find university teachers at Alexandria and Athens and also at a number of younger universities in both East and West.

408. The Roman Traveler in Greece and the Orient. To such a traveler wandering in Greece and looking back some six hundred years to the Age of Pericles or the Persian Wars of Athens, Greece seemed to belong to a distant and ancient world, of which he had read in the histories of Thucydides and Herodotus (§§ 211, 249). As the Roman visitor strolled through Athens or Delphi, he noticed many an empty pedestal, and he recalled how the villas of his friends at home were now adorned with the statues which had once occupied those empty pedestals (see § 344). The Greek cities which had brought forth such things were now poor and helpless commercially and politically.

As the traveler passed eastward through the flourishing cities of Asia Minor and Syria, he might feel justifiable pride in what Roman rule was accomplishing. In the western half of the Fertile Crescent, especially just east of the Jordan, where there had formerly been only a nomad wilderness (§ 58), there were now prosperous towns, with long aqueducts, with baths, theaters, basilicas, and imposing public buildings, of which the ruins even at the present day are astonishing. All these towns were not only linked together by the fine roads we have mentioned but they were likewise connected with Rome by other fine roads leading entirely across Asia Minor and the Balkan Peninsula.

Beyond the desert behind these towns lay the former empires of Babylonia, Assyria, and Persia, with the ruins of their once great cities, all held by the troublesome Parthian Empire. Trajan's effort to conquer that country having failed (§ 397), the Roman traveler made no effort to extend his tour beyond this point.

But he could take a great Roman galley at Antioch and cross over to Alexandria, where a still more ancient world awaited him. In the vast lighthouse, over four hundred years old and visible

Fig. 69. Scribblings of Sicilian Schoolboys on a Brick in the Days of the Roman Empire

In passing a brickyard these schoolboys of seventeen hundred years ago amused themselves in scribbling school exercises *in Greek* on the soft clay bricks before they were baked. At the top a little boy who was still making capitals carefully wrote the capital letter *S* (Greek Σ) ten times, and under it the similar letter *K*, also ten times. These he followed by the words "turtle" (ΧΕΛΩΝΑ), "mill" (ΜΥΛΑ), and "pail" (ΚΑΔΟΣ), all in capitals. Then an older boy, who could do more than write capitals, has pushed the little chap aside and proudly demonstrated his superiority by writing in two lines an exercise in tongue gymnastics (like "Peter Piper picked a peck of pickled peppers," etc.), which in our letters is as follows:

Nai neai nea naia neoi temon, hōs neoi ha naus

This means: "Boys cut new planks for a new ship, that the ship might float." A third boy then added two lines at the bottom. The brick illustrates the spread of the Greek language (§ 409) and of education in general in the provinces under the Roman Empire (§ 407)

for hours before he reached the harbor, he recognized the model of the Roman lighthouses he had seen. Here our traveler found himself among a group of wealthy Greek and Roman tourists on the Nile. As they left the magnificent buildings of Hellenistic Alexandria (§ 277), their voyage up the river carried them at once into the midst of an earlier world — the earliest world of which

FIG. 70. ROMAN BRIDGE AND AQUEDUCT AT NÎMES, FRANCE

This structure was built by the Romans about A.D. 20 to supply the Roman colony of Nemausus (now called Nîmes) in southern France with water from two excellent springs twenty-five miles distant. It is nearly nine hundred feet long and one hundred and sixty feet high, and carried the water over the valley of the river Gard. The channel for the water is at the very top, and one can still walk through it. The miles of aqueduct on either side of this bridge and leading up to it have almost disappeared (§ 409)

they knew. All about them at Memphis and Thebes were buildings which were thousands of years old before Rome was founded. On these monuments we still find their scribblings at the present day (Fig. 17).

409. Ancient Civilization in the East : Later Roman in the West. The eastern Mediterranean was regarded by the Romans as *their* ancient world. There the Roman traveler found Greek everywhere as far west as Sicily (Fig. 69). But when he entered the western Mediterranean he found that the language of civilized intercourse was Latin, the language of Rome. In the western Mediterranean civilization was a recent matter, just as it is in America. In that age western Europe had for the first time been building cities; but it was under the guidance of Roman architects, and their buildings looked like those at Rome. We can still visit and study massive bridges, spacious theaters, imposing public monuments, sumptuous villas, and luxurious public baths—a line of Roman ruins stretching from Britain through southern France and Germany to the northern Balkans (Fig. 70). Similarly in North Africa between the desert and the sea, west of Carthage, the ruins of whole cities with magnificent public buildings, and also of extensive Roman frontier posts, still survive to show us how Roman civilization developed there.

410. The Whole Mediterranean World Highly Civilized. All these Roman buildings, still encircling the Mediterranean, reveal to us the fact that as a result of all the ages of human progress which we have studied, the whole Mediterranean world, West as well as East, had now gained a high civilization. The Roman legions and their military stations stretched on the north of the Mediterranean from Britain to Jerusalem and on its south from Jerusalem to Morocco, like a dike restraining the stormy sea of barbarians outside, which would otherwise have poured in and overwhelmed the results of centuries of civilized development.

III. THE CIVILIZATION OF THE EARLY ROMAN EMPIRE: ROME

411. New Public Buildings of Rome. As for Rome itself, a visitor at the close of the reign of Hadrian found it the most magnificent monumental city in the world of that day. It had by that time quite surpassed Alexandria in size and in the number and splendor of its public buildings. It was especially in and alongside the old Forum that the grandest structures of the Empire had grown up. There Vespasian erected a vast amphitheater for gladiatorial combats, now known as the Colosseum (Fig. 71). Along the north side of the old Forum the emperors built three new forums which surpassed in magnificence anything which the Mediterranean world had ever seen before (§ 383).[1]

In these buildings of Trajan and Hadrian the architecture of Rome reached its highest level of splendor and beauty, and also in workmanship. Sometime in the Hellenistic Age architects had begun to employ increasing quantities of cement concrete.

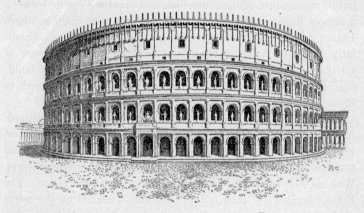

FIG. 71. THE VAST FLAVIAN AMPHITHEATER AT ROME, NOW CALLED THE COLOSSEUM. (AFTER LUCKENBACH)

Such buildings for witnessing gladiatorial combats (§ 347) were at first temporary "grand stands" of wood. This enormous building, one of the greatest in the world, was an oval arena surrounded by rising tiers of seats, accommodating nearly fifty thousand people. We see here only the outside wall, as restored. It was built by the emperors Vespasian and Titus (§ 411) and was completed A.D. 80. Every Roman town of any size had such an arena. The one at Pola, in Dalmatia, a town of forty thousand people, still stands, and could seat about twenty thousand spectators. A fine one still stands in Verona, Italy. In these places the emperors threw thousands of barbarian prisoners to the wild beasts

The domed roof of Hadrian's Pantheon is a single enormous concrete cast, over a hundred and forty feet across. The Romans, therefore, eighteen hundred years ago were employing concrete on a scale which we have only recently learned to imitate, and after all this lapse of time the roof of the Pantheon seems to be as safe

[1] See *Ancient Times*, Fig. 247.

and stanch as it was when Hadrian's architects first knocked away the posts which supported the wooden form for the great cast.[1]

412. Roman Sculpture and Painting. In the *relief* sculpture adorning all these monuments Roman art is at its best. The reliefs still covering Trajan's column are a wonderful picture book of his campaigns (§ 397). Of *statue* sculpture, however, the vast majority of the works produced in this period were copies of the masterpieces of the great Greek sculptors. However, *portrait* sculptors produced busts of the leading Romans which are among the finest of such works ever wrought (Fig. 72).

In painting, the wall decorators were almost the only surviving practicers of the art. They merely copied the works of the great Greek masters of the Hellenistic Age. Portrait painting, however, flourished, and the hack portrait artist at the street corner, who painted your picture quickly for you on a tablet of wood, was almost as common as our own portrait photographer.[2]

FIG. 72. PORTRAIT OF AN UNKNOWN ROMAN

This terra-cotta head is one of the finest portraits ever made (§ 412). It represents one of the masterful Roman lords of the world, and shows clearly in the features those qualities of power and leadership which so long maintained Roman supremacy

413. Decline of Literature; Plutarch's *Lives*. There was now a larger educated public at Rome than ever before, and the splendid libraries maintained by the State were open to all. Authors and literary men were also liberally supported by the emperors. Nevertheless, even under these favorable circumstances

[1] See *Ancient Times*, Fig. 264.
[2] See examples of Roman sculpture and painting in *Ancient Times*, Figs. 197, 251, and plate, p. 654, and read footnote, ibid. p. 631.

not a single genius of great creative imagination arose. Just as in sculpture and painting, so now in literature, the leaders were content to imitate or copy the great works of the past. Real progress in literature therefore ceased. But in this age of Latin literature at least one immortal work was written by a Greek — Plutarch's remarkable series of lives of the greatest men of Greece and Rome. The book forms an imperishable gallery of heroes, which has held the interest and the admiration of the world for eighteen centuries.

414. Lack of Scientific Attainments at Rome. In science the Romans were always merely collectors of the knowledge gained by the Greeks. During a long and successful official career Pliny devoted himself with great industry to scientific studies. He made a vast collection of the facts then known in science and found in books, chiefly Greek. He put them all together in a huge work which he called *Natural History* — really an encyclopedia. He was so deeply interested in science that he lost his life in the great eruption of Vesuvius, as he was trying both to study the tremendous event at short range and (as admiral of the fleet) to save the fleeing people of Pompeii (§ 404). But Pliny's *Natural History* did not contain any new facts of importance discovered by the author himself, and it was marred by many errors in matters which Pliny misunderstood. Nevertheless, for hundreds of years, until the revival of science in modern times, Pliny's work was, next to Aristotle, the standard authority referred to by all educated Europeans. Thus men fell into an indolent attitude of mind and were satisfied merely to learn what earlier discoverers had found out. This attitude never would have led to the discovery of the size of the earth as determined by Eratosthenes (§ 281) or in modern times to X-ray photographs or wireless telegraphy.

415. End of Investigative Science at Alexandria. A great astronomer and geographer of Alexandria, named Ptolemy, who flourished under Hadrian and the Antonines, was *the last of the famous scientists of the ancient world*. He wrote among other works a handbook on astronomy, mostly taken from the works

of earlier astronomers. In it he unfortunately adopted the conclusion that the sun revolved around the earth as a center. His
book became a standard work, and hence this mistaken view of
the solar system, called the *Ptolemaic system*, was everywhere
accepted by the later world. It was not until four hundred years
ago that the real truth, already long before discovered by the
Greek astronomer Aristarchus of Samos (§ 281), was rediscovered
by the Polish astronomer Copernicus.[1]

416. Cosmopolitan Life of Rome. Educated Greeks at Rome
were now holding important positions in the government or
as teachers and professors paid by the government. The
city was no longer Roman or Italian; it had become Mediterranean. Men of all the world elbowed each other and talked
business in the banks and countinghouses of the magnificent new
forums; they filled the public offices and administrative departments of the government, and discussed the hand-copied daily
paper published by the State; they sat in the libraries and lecture
halls of the Roman university, and they crowded the lounging
places of the public baths and the vast amphitheater. We call
such all-inclusive, widely representative life "cosmopolitan"—
a word of Greek origin meaning "world-cityish."

This inflow of all the world at Rome was evident in the luxuries
now enjoyed by the rich. Roman ladies were decked with dia-
monds, pearls, and rubies from India, and they robed themselves
in shining silks from China. The tables of the rich were bright
with peaches, which they called "Persian apples," and with
apricots, both now appearing for the first time in the Roman
world. Roman cooks learned to prepare rice, formerly an oriental delicacy prescribed for the sick. Instead of sweetening their
dishes with honey as formerly, Roman households began to find
a new product in the market place known as "sakari"; for so
the report of a venturesome oriental sailor of the first century
of our era calls the sirup of sugar cane, which he brought by sea

[1] Knowledge of the spherical form of the earth as shown by Ptolemy and earlier Greek
astronomers was never lost. It was passed down to the travelers and navigators of later
Europe and finally led Columbus to undertake the voyage to India and the East *westward* — the voyage which resulted in the discovery of America.

from India into the Mediterranean for the first time. This is the earliest mention of sugar in history. These new things from the Orient were beginning to appear in Roman life just as the potatoes, tobacco, and Indian corn of America found their way into Europe after the voyages of Columbus had disclosed a new Western world.

IV. Popularity of Oriental Religions and the Spread of Early Christianity

417. Decline of Intellectual Life and Roman Religion. The life of the Orient was at the same time continuing to bring into the Mediterranean other things less easily traced than rice or sugar, but much more important in their influence on the Roman world. These were the oriental religions. The intellectual life of the Empire was steadily declining, as we have seen indicated by literature and science. Thoughtful Romans read the Greek philosophy of the Stoics and Epicureans (§ 286) in the charming treatises of Cicero (§ 386). Such readers had given up the old Roman gods and accepted as their religion the precepts of daily conduct which they found in the Stoic or Epicurean philosophy. But such teaching was only for the highly educated and the intellectual class.

418. Oriental Religions in Europe. Multitudes, including even the educated, yielded to the fascination of the mysterious religions coming in from the East. Many took refuge in the faith of the Egyptian Isis, and temples of Isis were to be found in all the larger cities. To-day tiny statuettes and other symbols of the Egyptian goddess are found even along the Seine, the Rhine, and the Danube.

In the army the Persian Mithras, a god of light (§ 94), was a great favorite, and many a Roman legion had its underground chapel where its members celebrated his triumph over darkness and evil. These and other oriental faiths all had their "mysteries," consisting chiefly of dramatic presentations of the career of the god, especially his submission to death, his triumph over it, and his ascent to everlasting life (§ 53). It was believed that to witness these things and to undergo certain holy ceremonies of initiation would enable one to share in the pure and endless life of the god and to dwell with him forever.

The old Roman faith had little to do with conduct and held out to the worshiper no such hopes of future blessedness. Little wonder that the multitudes were irresistibly attracted by the comforting promises of these oriental faiths and the blessed future to be gained in their "mysteries."

The Jews, too, since their temple in Jerusalem had been destroyed by the Romans, were to be found in increasing numbers in all the larger cities. Strabo, the geographer, said of them, "This people has already made its way into every city, and it would be hard to find a place in the habitable world which has not admitted this race and been dominated by it." The Roman world was becoming accustomed to their synagogues ; but the Jews refused to acknowledge any god besides their own, and this brought them disfavor and trouble with the government.

419. Rise of Christianity. Among all these faiths of the Orient the common people were more and more inclining toward one whose teachers told how their Master, Jesus, a Hebrew, was born in Palestine, the land of the Jews, in the days of Augustus. Everywhere they told the people of his vision of human brotherhood and of divine fatherhood. This faith he had preached for a few years, till he incurred the hatred of his countrymen, and in the reign of Tiberius they had put him to death.

A Jewish tentmaker of Tarsus named Paul, a man of passionate eloquence and unquenchable love for his Master, passed far and wide through the cities of Asia Minor and Greece, and even to Rome, proclaiming his Master's teaching. He left behind him a line of devoted communities stretching from Palestine to Rome. Certain letters which he wrote in Greek to his followers were circulating widely among them and were read with eagerness. At the same time a narrative of the Master's life had also appeared and was now widely read by the common people. There were finally *four* leading biographies of Jesus in Greek, which came to be regarded as authoritative, and these we call the Four Gospels. Along with the letters of Paul and some other writings they were later put together in a Greek book now known in the English translation as the New Testament.

420. Superiority of Christianity. The other oriental faiths, in spite of their attractiveness, could not offer to their followers the consolation and fellowship of a life so exalted and beautiful, so full of brotherly appeal and human sympathy as that of the new Hebrew Teacher. The slave and the freedman, the artisan and the craftsman, the humble and the despised in the huge barracks which sheltered the poor in Rome, eagerly listened to this new "mystery" from the East, as they thought it to be. As time passed, multitudes learned of the new gospel and found joy in the hopes which it awakened. In the second century of peace Christianity was rapidly outstripping the other religions of the Roman Empire.

421. Roman Persecution of the Early Christians. The government officials often found these early converts, like the Jews, not only refusing to sacrifice to the emperor as a god, as all good Roman citizens were expected to do, but also openly prophesying the downfall of the Roman State. While the Roman government was usually very tolerant in matters of religion, the early Christians were therefore frequently called upon to endure cruel persecution. Their religion seemed to interfere with good citizenship, since it forbade them to show the usual respect for the emperor and the government. Nevertheless their numbers steadily grew.

V. Marcus Aurelius and the End of the Second Century of Peace

422. End of the Second Century of Peace (about A.D. 167). In spite of outward prosperity, Mediterranean civilization was declining in the second century of peace. This became noticeable in the reign of Hadrian. Then the noble Emperor Marcus Aurelius (A.D. 161–180) was called upon to face a very serious situation. His ability and enlightened statesmanship are undoubted. Indeed, they were only equaled by the purity and beauty of his personal life. Amid the growing anxieties of his position, even as he sat in his tent and guided the operations of the legions in the forests of what is now Bohemia, he found time to record his thoughts and leave to the world a little volume of meditations written in Greek, which many people still read with great pleasure and profit.

After his army had been seriously reduced in numbers by a four years' war with the Parthians and by a terrible plague, the barbarian hordes in the German North broke through the frontier defenses (Fig. 67), and for the first time in two centuries they poured down into Italy (A.D. 167). The two centuries of peace were ended. With little intermission, until his death (A.D. 180), Marcus Aurelius maintained the struggle against the Germans in the region of modern Bohemia. In spite of victory over the barbarians, he was unable to sweep them entirely out of the northern regions of the Empire. He finally took the very dangerous step of allowing some of them, in return for military service, to remain permanently as farmer colonists on lands assigned to them *inside of the frontier*. This policy, as we shall see, resulted in very serious consequences to the Empire.

423. Summary of the Two Centuries of Peace. The remarkable forty-four years of the peaceful reign of Augustus had ushered in a century of peace which was completed by the four succeeding reigns of the Julian line, ending (A.D. 68) with the death of the infamous Nero. The second century of peace which began soon afterward was made up for the most part by the reigns of a group of very able emperors, especially Trajan and Hadrian. These men expanded the once local government and laws of the former city-state of Rome until they fitted the needs of a vast state including the whole Mediterranean world. At this time Christianity was spreading very rapidly. Internal decay was going on, however, and under Marcus Aurelius, about A.D. 167, the two centuries of peace ended. We now pass on, therefore, to a fearful century of revolution, civil war, and anarchy, from which a very different Roman world emerged.

QUESTIONS

I. What two great tasks were to be accomplished by the emperors of the second century of peace? Discuss the wars of Trajan. What did Hadrian do for the defenses? Describe the army. Tell about important developments in the internal organization of the Empire; in its laws; in the emperor's attention to the provinces.

II. Indicate the extent and mention the chief peoples of the Roman Empire. Tell the story of Pompeii. Describe the communications and commerce of the eastern Mediterranean; the life of the provincial towns, especially education. What was the language of the West? Describe its surviving monuments. What do the Roman buildings still show regarding the position and the extent of the Roman Empire?

III. Tell about the buildings of the emperors at Rome; sculpture and painting; literature and science; the cosmopolitan life of Rome; its oriental luxuries.

IV. What was the state of religion in the Empire? What was the situation of the oriental religions among the Romans? Mention the leading ones and give an account of them, especially Christianity. How did its sacred book arise? What danger threatened the early Christians?

V. What was the state of civilization in the second century of peace? What brought this period to an end? Under whom? What dangerous step did he take? Describe his character and writings. What followed the two centuries of peace?

NOTE. This tailpiece shows the model of a part of the ruins of a former fashionable Roman watering place at Bath, England.

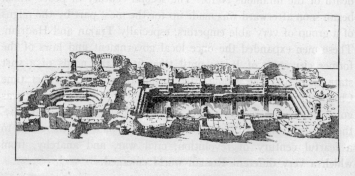

CHAPTER XIX

A CENTURY OF REVOLUTION AND THE DIVISION OF THE EMPIRE

I. INTERNAL DECLINE OF THE ROMAN EMPIRE

424. Signs of Inner Decay. We have seen good government, fine buildings, education, and other evidences of civilization more widespread in the second century of peace than ever before. Nevertheless, the great Empire which we have been studying was suffering from an inner decay. In the first place, the decline of farming, so noticeable before the fall of the Republic (§§ 351 ff.), had gone steadily on. This was partly due to the exhaustion of the soil and bad cultivation.

425. Decline of Farming and Agriculture. Land continued to pass over into the hands of the rich and powerful. A rich man's estate was called a *villa*, and the system of villa estates, having destroyed the small farmers of Italy (§§ 349–352), was now destroying them in the provinces likewise. Villas now covered not only Italy but also Africa, Gaul, Britain, Spain, and other leading provinces.

Unable to compete with the great villas, and finding the burden of taxes unbearable, most of the small farmers gave up the struggle. Such a farmer would often become the *colonus* of some wealthy villa owner. By this arrangement the farmer and his descendants were forever bound by law to the land which they worked, and they passed with it from owner to owner when it changed hands. While not actually slaves, they were not free to leave or go where they pleased. The great villas once worked by slaves were now cultivated chiefly by these *coloni* (plural of *colonus*), the forerunners of the medieval serfs (§ 525), while slaves had steadily diminished in numbers.

Multitudes of the country people, unwilling to become *coloni*, forsook their fields and turned to the city for relief. Great stretches of unworked and weed-grown fields were no uncommon sight. As the amount of land under cultivation decreased, the ancient world was no longer raising enough food to feed itself properly. The scarcity was felt most severely in the great centers of population like Rome, where prices had rapidly gone up. Our own generation is not the first to complain of the "high cost of living." The destruction of the small farmers formed the leading cause among a whole group of causes which brought about the decline and fall of this great Empire.

426. Decline of Population and Citizenship. The large families which country life favors were no longer reared, the number of marriages decreased, and the population of the Empire shrank. Debased by the life of the city, the once sturdy farmer lost his independence in an eager scramble for a place in the waiting line of city poor, to whom the government distributed free grain, wine, and meat. The city became a great hive of shiftless population supported by the State with money gained from taxes resting chiefly on the lessening number of struggling agriculturists. The same situation was in the main to be found in all the leading cities.

In spite of outward splendor, therefore, the cities too were declining. They had now learned to depend upon the emperors to care for them even in their own local affairs (§ 402). Responsible and actively interested citizenship, which does so much to develop the best among the people of any community and which had earlier so sadly declined in Greece, was passing away, never to reappear in the ancient world. .

427. Decline of Business. At the same time the business life of the cities was also deteriorating. The country communities no longer possessed a numerous purchasing population. Hence the city manufacturers could no longer dispose of their products in the country. They rapidly declined, and discharged their workmen, who began to increase the multitudes of the city poor.

For a number of reasons the government was unable to secure enough precious metals to coin the money necessary for the transaction of business. The emperors were obliged to begin mixing with their silver an increasing amount of less valuable metals and coining this cheaper alloy. A *denarius*, the common small coin worth when pure nearly twenty cents (Fig. 56), a century after the death of Marcus Aurelius was worth only half a cent.

428. Decline of the Army. It was impossible to maintain a paid army without money. As it became quite impossible to collect taxes *in money*, the government was obliged to accept grain and produce as payment of taxes. Here and there the army was then paid in grain. On the frontiers, for lack of other pay, the troops were assigned lands, which of course did them no good unless they could cultivate them. So they were allowed to marry and to live with their families in little huts on their lands near the frontier. As was to be expected they soon lost all discipline and became merely a feeble militia.

429. Demoralization caused by Lack of a Law of Succession. This degeneration of the army was much hastened by a serious imperfection in the organization of the Roman State, left there by Augustus. This was the lack of a legal and long-respected method of choosing a new emperor and thus maintaining from reign to reign without a break the supreme authority in the Roman State. The troops found that they could make a new emperor whenever the old emperor's death gave them an opportunity. For an emperor so made they had very little respect, and if he attempted to enforce discipline or did not heed their wishes, they put him out of the way and selected another. Rude and barbarous mercenary soldiers, few of whom were citizens, thus became the highest authority in the State.

Finally, the spread of civilization to the provinces had resulted in the feeling that they were the equals of Rome and Italy itself. When (A.D. 212) citizenship was granted to all free men within the Empire, the provincials gained more and more opportunity to compete for the leadership of the Empire.

II. A Century of Revolution

430. Beginning of a Century of Revolution (A.D. 180). These forces of decline were swiftly bringing on a century of revolution which was to shipwreck the civilization of the early world. This fatal period began with the death of Marcus Aurelius (A.D. 180). The assassination of his unworthy son Commodus, who reminds us of Nero, was the opportunity for a struggle among a group of military usurpers. From this struggle a rough but successful soldier named Septimius Severus emerged triumphant. He systematically filled the highest posts in the government with military leaders of low origin. Thus, both in the army and in the government, the ignorant and often foreign masses were gaining control.

When the line of Severus ended (A.D. 235), the storm broke. The barbaric troops in one province after another set up their puppet emperors to fight among themselves for the throne of the Mediterranean world. The proclamation of a new emperor would be followed again and again by news of his assassination. From the leaders of the barbaric soldier class, after the death of Commodus, the Roman Empire received eighty rulers in ninety years. Most of these so-called emperors were not unlike the revolutionary bandits who proclaim themselves presidents of Mexico.

431. Fifty Years of Anarchy; Collapse of Higher Civilization. For fifty years there was no public order, as the plundering troops tossed the scepter of Rome from one soldier emperor to another. Life and property were nowhere safe ; robbery and murder were everywhere. The disorder and fighting between rival emperors hastened the ruin of all business, till national bankruptcy ensued. In this tempest of anarchy during the third century of our era the civilization of the ancient world fell into final ruin. The leadership of mind and of scientific knowledge won by the Greeks in the *third century* B.C. (§ 281) yielded to the reign of ignorance and superstition in these disasters of the *third century of the Christian Era.*

Such turmoil sadly weakened the Roman army. The Northern barbarians were quick to perceive the helplessness of the Empire.

They crossed the frontiers almost at will and penetrated far into Greece and Italy ; in the West they overran Gaul and Spain, and some of them even crossed to Africa.

432. Rise of New Persia (A.D. 226) **under Sassanian Kings.** At the same time a new danger had arisen in the East. A renewal of patriotism among the old Persian population, coupled with a religious revival, had resulted in a vigorous restoration of their national life. Their leaders, a family called Sassanians (or Sassanids), overthrew the Parthians (A.D. 226) and furnished a new line of enlightened Persian kings. As they took possession of the Fertile Crescent and established their capital at Ctesiphon on the Tigris, close by Babylon, a new Orient arose on the ruins of seemingly dead and forgotten ages. The Sassanian kings organized a much more powerful State than that of the Parthians which they overthrew, and they regarded themselves as the rivals of the Romans for the Empire of the world. The old rivalry between the Orient and the West, as in the days of Greece and Persia, was now continued, with Rome as the champion of the West, and this New Persia as the leader of the East.

433. Aurelian (A.D. 270–275) **and Diocletian** (A.D. 284–305) **restore Order.** It now looked as if the Roman Empire were about to fall to pieces, when one of the soldier emperors, named Aurelian, defeated all his rivals and restored some measure of order and safety. But, in order to protect Rome from the future raids of the barbarians, he built entirely around the great city the massive wall (see plan, p. 248) which still stands,—a confession of the dangerous situation and terrible decline of Rome in the third century of our era. It was a little over a century after the death of Marcus Aurelius when the emperor Diocletian restored what looked like a lasting peace (A.D. 284).

434. Summary of Four Centuries of Roman Imperialism. If at this point we look back some four hundred years over the history of Rome since she had become mistress of the world, we discern three great periods. With the foundation of the Empire by Augustus there began two centuries of peace, and this period of peace was both preceded and followed by a century of revolution.

We have thus seen a century of revolution, which destroyed the Republic and introduced the Empire ; two centuries of peace under the Empire ; and then a second century of revolution which almost destroyed and completely altered the Empire. The first century of revolution led from the Gracchus brothers to the triumph of one-man power and the foundation of the Empire by Augustus (that is, from about 133 to 30 B.C.). The two centuries of peace beginning with the foundation of the Empire by Augustus continued down to the barbarian invasion in the reign of Marcus Aurelius (that is, from about 30 B.C. to nearly A.D. 170). The second century of revolution led from the enlightened reign of Marcus Aurelius to oriental despotism under Diocletian (that is, from about A.D. 180 to about 284). Thus four centuries of Roman imperialism, after bringing forth such masterful men as Sulla and Julius Cæsar, had passed through various stages of one-man power, to end in despotism. We are now first to examine that despotism and then to see how it was overwhelmed by two centuries of barbarian invasions from the North, while at the same time it was also crushed by the reviving power of the Orient, whose assaults were to last many centuries more (see map, p. 260).

III. The Roman Empire an Oriental Despotism

435. Diocletian ; the Roman Empire an Oriental Despotism (A.D. 284-305). The Roman world under Diocletian was a totally different one from that which Augustus and the Roman Senate had ruled three centuries before. Diocletian deprived the shadowy Senate of all power except that of governing the city of Rome. Reduced to a mere City Council, or Board of Aldermen, it then disappeared from the stage of history. The emperor thus became an absolute monarch with none to limit his authority. With the unlimited power of the oriental despot the emperor now assumed also its outward symbols,— the diadem, the gorgeous robe embroidered with pearls and precious stones, the throne and footstool, before which all who came into his presence must bow down to the dust.

Long regarded as a divinity, the emperor had now become an oriental Sun-god, and he was officially called the "Invincible Sun." His birthday was on the twenty-fifth of December. All were obliged as good citizens to join in the official sacrifices to the head of the State as a god. With the incoming of this oriental attitude toward the emperor, the long struggle for democracy, which we have followed through so many centuries of the history of early man, ended for a time in the triumph of oriental despotism.

436. Division of the Empire by Diocletian ; his Administration. War with New Persia, the new oriental enemy, carried the emperor much to the East. The result was that Diocletian resided most of the time at Nicomedia in Asia Minor (see map, II, p. 260). As a natural consequence he was unable to give close attention to the West. Following some earlier examples, Diocletian therefore appointed another emperor to rule jointly with himself, to give his attention to the West. It was not Diocletian's intention to divide the Roman Empire, any more than it had been the purpose to divide the Republic in electing two consuls. The final result was, nevertheless, the drifting apart of the Roman Empire into East and West.

The provinces of the Empire were by this time over a hundred in number. Diocletian and his successors organized the business of each province in the hands of a great number of local officials graded into many successive ranks and classes from high to low. The financial burden of this vast organization, together with the luxurious oriental court of the emperor, was enormous ; for this multitude of government and court officials and the clamorous army had all to be paid and supported by ever-increasing taxation.

437. Loss of Business Men ; Obligatory Practice of Occupations. When the scarcity of coin (§ 427) forced the government to accept grain and produce from the taxpayers, taxes had become a mere share in the yield of the lands. The Roman Empire thus sank to a primitive system of taxation already thousands of years old in the Orient. It was now customary to oblige a group of wealthy men in each city, mainly the members of the local city councils and their families, to become responsible for the payment of the entire taxes of the district each year, and if there was a deficit these men were forced to make up the lacking balance out of their own wealth. The penalty of wealth seemed to be ruin, and there was no motive for success in business when such prosperity meant ruinous overtaxation. As the Roman Empire had already lost its prosperous *farming class*, it now lost likewise its enterprising and successful *business men*. Diocletian therefore, chiefly in the interest of taxation, endeavored to force these classes to continue their occupations. He forbade any man to leave his lands or occupation and even tried to make craftsmanship hereditary by demanding that the sons follow the occupation of their father.

438. Disappearance of Liberty and Free Citizenship. Thus under this oriental despotism the liberty for which men had striven so long disappeared in Europe, and the once free Roman citizen had no independent life of his own. Even the citizen's wages and the prices of the goods he bought or sold were as far as possible fixed for him by the State. The emperor's innumerable officials, among them a regular organization of government agents who were little better than spies, kept an eye upon even the humblest citizen. They watched the grain dealers, butchers, and bakers, and saw to it that they properly supplied the public and never deserted their occupation. Even entrance into the clergy (§ 441) was closely supervised by the State, because every man becoming a priest or monk meant the loss of so much in taxes (§ 442). In a word, the Roman government now attempted to regulate almost every interest in life, and wherever the citizen turned he felt the irksome interference and oppression of the State.

Staggering under his burden of taxes, in a State which was practically bankrupt, the citizen now seemed like a mere cog in the vast machinery of the government. His whole life consisted of toil for the State, which always collected so much in taxes that he was fortunate if he could survive on what was left. As a mere toiler for the State he was finally just where the peasant on the Nile had been for thousands of years. The emperor had become a Pharaoh, and the Roman Empire a colossal Egypt of ancient days.

IV. The Division of the Empire and the Triumph of Christianity

439. Constantine (A.D. 324–337) and the Shift of Power from Italy to the Balkan Peninsula. Under Diocletian, Italy had been reduced to the position of a taxed province and had thus lost the last vestige of superiority over the other provinces of the Empire. During the century of revolution just past, the soldiers of the Balkan Peninsula had filled the army with the best troops and furnished more than one emperor, among them Diocletian. An emperor who had risen from the ranks of provincial troops in the Balkans felt little attachment to Rome. Rome had not only ceased to be the residence of an emperor, but the center of power had clearly shifted from Italy to the Balkan Peninsula.

Out of the struggles following Diocletian's death the Emperor Constantine the Great emerged victorious (A.D. 324). He did not hesitate to turn to the eastern edge of the Balkan Peninsula and establish there a New Rome as his residence. He chose the ancient Greek town of Byzantium, on the European side of the Bosporus, a magnificent situation overlooking both Europe and Asia and fitted to be a center of power in both. In placing his new capital here, Constantine established a city, the importance of which was equaled only by the foundation of Alexandria in Egypt. The emperor stripped many an ancient city of its great monuments in order to secure materials for the beautification of his splendid residence (Fig. 73). By A.D. 330 the new capital on the Bosporus was a magnificent monumental city, worthy to be the successor of Rome as the seat of the Mediterranean Empire. It was named Constantinople ("Constantine's city") after its founder.

440. The Separation of East and West. The transfer of the capital of the Roman Empire to the east side of the Balkan Peninsula meant the separation of East and West—the cutting of the Roman Empire in two. Although the separation did not take place abruptly, yet within a generation after Constantinople was founded, the Roman Empire had in fact if not in name become two states. The theory and ideal of unity persisted but was never more than temporarily realized hereafter.

441. The Churches a New Arena for the Rise of Able Men. Meantime the Christian churches had steadily increased in numbers. The management of the great Christian communities and

FIG. 73. ANCIENT MONUMENTS IN CONSTANTINOPLE

The obelisk in the foreground (nearly one hundred feet high) was first set up in Thebes, Egypt, by the conqueror Thutmose III (§ 49); it was erected here by the Roman Emperor Theodosius. The small spiral column at the right is the base of a bronze tripod set up by the Greeks at Delphi (Fig. 38) in commemoration of their victory over the Persians at Plataea (§ 192). The names of thirty-one Greek cities which took part in the battle are still to be read, engraved on this base. These monuments of ancient oriental and Greek supremacy stand in what was the Roman horse-race course when the earlier Greek city of Byzantium became the eastern capital of Rome (§ 439). Finally, the great mosque behind the obelisk, with its slender minarets, represents the triumph of Islam under the Turks, who took the city A.D. 1453

their churches called for increasing ability and experience. Public discussion and disputes in the Church meetings enabled gifted men to stand forth, and their ability brought them position and influence. The Christian Church thus became a new arena for the development of statesmanship, and Church statesmen were soon to be the leading influential men of the age, when the city democracies had long since ceased to produce such men.

These officers of the Church came to be distinguished from the other members and were called the *clergy*, while the people who made up the membership of the churches were called the *laymen*, or the *laity*. The old men who cared for the smaller country congregations were finally called merely *presbyters*, a Greek word meaning "old men," and our word "priest" is derived from this Greek term. Over the group of churches in each city a leading priest gained authority as *bishop*. In the larger cities these bishops had such influence that they became *archbishops*, or head bishops, having authority over the bishops in the surrounding cities of the province. Thus Christianity, once the faith of the weak and the despised, became a powerful organization, strong enough to cope with the government.

442. Christianity placed on a Legal Basis with Other Religions (A.D. 311). The Roman government therefore began to see the uselessness of persecuting the Christians. In the time of Diocletian his associate Galerius, feeling the dangers threatening Rome from *without* and the uselessness of the struggle against the Christians *within*, issued a decree (A.D. 311) by which Christianity was legally recognized in his territories. Its followers received the same legal position as the worshipers of the old gods. This decree was later maintained by Constantine for the whole Empire. Constantine and succeeding emperors went even further in their favor toward the Christians. They gradually abolished all other religions, they helped maintain the Christian Church, they granted its officials many striking privileges, such as freedom from taxation and the right of having their own law and courts.

443. Summary of the Age of Diocletian ; the Eclipse of the City of Rome. The century of revolution which ended in the despotic government set up by Diocletian completely destroyed the creative ability of ancient men in art and literature, as it likewise stopped all progress in business and affairs. In so far as the ancient world was one of *progress in civilization*, its history was ended with the accession of Diocletian. Besides the increasing invasions of the barbarians, the other outstanding events of the age were the foundation of an eastern capital, the resulting eclipse and increasing weakness of the city of Rome, and the triumph of Christianity. As the barbarians came in and the power of the Roman Empire waned, it had still a great mission before it in the preservation of at least something of the heritage of civilization, which it was to hand down through centuries of strife and trouble to us of to-day.

V. RETROSPECT

444. Summary of Ancient History. Besides the internal decay of Rome and the triumph of the Christian Church, the other great outstanding feature of the last centuries of the Roman Empire was the incoming of the barbarians, with the result that while Mediterranean civilization steadily declined, it nevertheless slowly spread northward, especially under the influence of the Church, till it transformed the ruder life of the North. At this point then we have returned to the region of western and northern Europe, where we first took up the career of man, and there, among the crumbling monuments of the Stone Age, Christian churches were soon to rise. What a vast sweep of the human career rises before our imagination as we picture the first church towers among the massive tombs of Stone Age man!

445. The Long Struggle of Civilization and Barbarism. We have watched the men of Europe struggling upward through thousands of years of Stone Age barbarism, while toward the end of that struggle civilization was arising in the Orient. Then on the borders of the Orient we saw the Stone Age Europeans of the Ægean receiving civilization from the Nile and thus developing a wonderful civilized world of their own. This remarkable Ægean civilization, the earliest in Europe, was overwhelmed and destroyed by the incoming of those Indo-European barbarians whom we call the *Greeks*. Writing, art, architecture, and shipbuilding, which had arisen on the borders of southeastern Europe, passed away, and civilization in Europe perished at the hands of the

Greek nomads from the Danube. Civilization would have been lost entirely had not the Orient, where it was born, now preserved it. Southeastern Europe, controlled by the Greeks, was therefore able to make another start, and from the Orient it again received writing, art, architecture, shipbuilding, and many other things which make up civilization. After having thus halted civilization in Europe for over a thousand years, the Greeks left behind their early barbarism, and, developing a noble and beautiful culture of their own, they carried civilization to the highest level it ever attained. Then, as the Indo-European barbarians (this time the *Germans*) again descended to the Mediterranean, Roman organization, as we shall see, prevented civilization from being destroyed for the second time. Thus enough of the civilization which the Orient and the Greeks had built up was preserved so that after long delay it rose again in Europe to become what we find it to-day. Such has been the long struggle of civilization and barbarism which we have been following. In the remaining chapters of this book we are to learn how Christian civilization triumphed and barbarism disappeared from Europe.

446. The Trail which we have Followed. To-day, marking the various stages of the long career of ancient man, which we have been following, the stone fist-hatchets lie deep in the river gravels of France ; the furniture of the pile-villages sleeps at the bottom of the Swiss lakes ; the majestic pyramids and temples announcing the dawn of civilization rise along the Nile ; the silent and deserted city-mounds by the Tigris and Euphrates shelter their myriads of clay tablets ; the palaces of Crete look out toward the sea they once ruled ; the noble temples and sculptures of Greece still proclaim the new world of beauty and freedom first revealed by the Greeks ; the splendid Roman roads and aqueducts assert the supremacy and organized control of Rome ; and the Christian churches proclaim the new ideal of human brotherhood. These things still reveal the trail along which our ancestors came, and in following that fascinating trail we have recovered the earliest chapters in the wonderful human story which we call Ancient History.

QUESTIONS

I. What had become of the small farmers in the Roman Empire? What system had resulted? What was happening to the cultivated lands? What was the effect on the food supply? on the great cities? on citizenship? on business? What happened to coined money? What was the effect on the army? What resulted?

II. What was the policy of Severus? How may we contrast the third century of our era with the third century B.C.? What did the Northern barbarians do? What happened in the Orient? What two men saved the Empire? When? Divide up into three great periods the first four centuries of Roman leadership of the Mediterranean world. To what had four centuries of Roman imperialism led?

III. What kind of State was organized by Diocletian? Where did Diocletian chiefly reside? What did he do with the West? Tell of his administrative organization and taxation. What happened to successful business men? How did Diocletian treat the various occupations? What thus became of the citizen?

IV. How did the emperors now regard Rome? What did Constantine do? How did this affect the Empire? Describe the development and organization of the Church. How did the Empire now treat the Church?

V. Where did mankind first gain civilization? Where did civilization first arise in Europe? What happened when the Greeks came in? Where was civilization then preserved? Who carried it to its highest level? By whom was it almost destroyed for the second time? What organization saved it for the second time?

BOOK V. THE MIDDLE AGES

CHAPTER XX

THE GERMAN INVASIONS AND THE BREAK-UP OF THE ROMAN EMPIRE

I. Founding of Kingdoms by Barbarian Chiefs

447. The Menace of the Barbarians. We must now describe the way in which the western portions of the Roman Empire were invaded by barbarous peoples from the North, who broke up the old Roman government and established in its stead kingdoms under their own rulers. These Germans, or "Barbarians" as the Romans called them, belonged to the same great group of peoples to which the Persians, Greeks, and Romans belonged — the Indo-European race (§§ 89–91). They were destined, as their relatives had earlier done, to take possession of the lands of others and help build up a different civilization from what they found.

The peoples of northern Europe had not advanced much in civilization since the Late Stone Age (§§ 9–11). They were a constant menace to the highly civilized countries on the Mediterranean to the south of them. It will be recalled that the Germans created great terror in Rome when they first advanced to the south and were with difficulty defeated by the skill of Marius (§ 359).

During the century of revolution after the reign of Marcus Aurelius, the old organization of the Roman army had so weakened that the barbarians raided the lands of the Empire with little opposition. After these earlier raids the barbarians commonly withdrew. By the time of Diocletian, however, the barbarians were beginning to form permanent settlements within the limits of the Empire, and there followed two centuries of barbarian migration, in the course of which they finally took possession of the entire western Mediterranean world.

448. The German Peoples at Home. The Germans were a fair-haired, blue-eyed race of men of towering stature and terrible strength, as it seemed to the Romans. In their native forests of the North each German tribe or nation occupied a very limited area, probably not over forty miles across. They lived in villages, each of about a hundred families, and there was a head man over each village. Their homes were but slight huts, easily moved or replaced. They had little interest in farming the fields around the village, much preferring their herds, and they shifted their homes often. They possessed no writing and very little in the way of industries, manufactures, or commerce.

449. The German Peoples in Migration and War. Hardened to wind and weather in their raw Northern climate, their native fearlessness and love of war and plunder often led them to wander about, followed by their wives and families in heavy wagons. An entire people might comprise some fifty villages, but each village group remained together, protected by its body of about a hundred warriors, the heads of the village families. When combined, these hundreds made up an army of five to six thousand men. Each hundred held together in battle, as a fighting unit. They all knew each other ; the village head man, the leader of the group, had always lived with them ; the warrior in the tumult of battle saw all about him his friends and relatives, the sons of his brothers, the husbands of his daughters. In spite of lack of discipline, these fighting groups of a hundred men, united by ties of blood and daily association, formed battle units as terrible as any ever seen in the ancient world. Their eager joy in battle and the untamed fierceness of their onset made them irresistible.

450. Whole German Peoples settle in the Empire and serve in the Army. The highly organized and carefully disciplined Roman legions, which had gained for Rome the leadership of the world, were now no more. Indeed, the lack of men for the army had long since led the emperors to hire the Germans as soldiers. A more serious step was the admission of *entire* German peoples to live in the Empire with all their old customs. The men were then received into the Roman army, but they remained under their own German leaders and they fought in their old village units. For it was only as the Roman army was made up of the German fighting units that it had any effectiveness. Barbarian life, customs, and manners were thus introduced into the Empire, and the Roman army as a whole was barbarian.

451. German Peoples gain Some Civilization. This constant commingling of the German peoples with the civilized communities of the Empire was gradually softening their Northern wildness and giving them not only familiarity with civilization but also a respect for it. Their leaders, who held office under the Roman government, came to have friends among highborn Romans. German generals sometimes married educated Roman women of rank, even relatives of the emperors. Some of them too were converted to Christianity. An educated German named Ulfilas translated the New Testament into Gothic, a dialect akin to German. As the Germanic peoples possessed no writing, he was obliged to devise an alphabet from Greek and Latin for writing Gothic. He thus produced the earliest surviving example of a written Germanic tongue and aided in converting the Northern peoples to Christianity.

452. Most Medieval Notions to be found in the Late Roman Empire. It would be a great mistake to suppose, however, that Roman civilization suddenly disappeared at this time as a result of the incoming barbarians. Long before the German conquest, art and literature had begun to decline toward the level that they reached in the Middle Ages. Many of the ideas and conditions which prevailed after the coming of the barbarians were common enough before. Even the ignorance and strange ideas which we associate particularly with the Middle Ages are to be found in the later Roman Empire.

The term "Middle Ages" will be used in this volume to mean, roughly speaking, the period of over a thousand years that elapsed between the fifth century, when the disorder of the barbarian invasions was becoming general, and the opening of the sixteenth century, when Europe was well on its way to recover all in the way of knowledge and skill that had been lost since the break-up of the Roman Empire.

453. The Huns force the Goths into the Empire. Previous to the year 375 the attempts of the Germans to penetrate into the Roman Empire appear to have been due to their love of adventure, their hope of plundering their civilized neighbors, or the need of new lands for their increasing numbers. But suddenly a new force appeared in the rear of the Germans which thrust some of them across the northern boundary of the Empire. The Huns, a Mongolian folk from central Asia, swept down upon the Goths, who were a German tribe settled upon the Danube, and forced a part of them to seek shelter across the river, within the limits of the Empire.

Here they soon fell out with the Roman officials, and a great battle was fought at Adrianople in 378 in which the Goths defeated and slew the Roman emperor, Valens. The Germans had now not only broken through the boundaries of the Empire but they had also learned that they could defeat the troops on which the Empire relied for protection. The battle of Adrianople may therefore be said to mark the beginning of the conquest of the western part of the Empire by the Germans. For some years, however, after the battle of Adrianople the various bands of West Goths—or *Visigoths*, as they are often called—were induced to accept the terms of peace offered by the emperor's officials, and some of the Goths agreed to serve as soldiers in the Roman armies.

454. Alaric takes Rome (410). Among the Germans who succeeded in getting an important position in the Roman army was Alaric, but he appears to have become dissatisfied with the treatment he received from the emperor. He therefore collected an army, of which his countrymen, the West Goths, formed a considerable part, and set out for Italy, and finally decided to march on Rome itself. The Eternal City fell into his hands in 410 and was plundered by his followers.

Although Alaric did not destroy the city, or even seriously damage it, the fact that Rome had fallen into the hands of an invading army was a notable disaster. The pagans explained it on the ground that the old gods were angry because so many people had deserted them and become Christians. St. Augustine, in his famous book, *The City of God*, took much pains to prove that the Roman gods had never been able on previous occasions to prevent disaster to their worshipers and that Christianity could not be held responsible for the troubles of the time.

455. West Goths settle in Southern Gaul and Spain; the Vandals. Alaric died before he could find a satisfactory spot for his people to settle upon permanently. After his death the West Goths wandered into Gaul and then into Spain. Here they came upon the Vandals, another German tribe, who had crossed the Rhine four years before Alaric had captured Rome. For three years they had devastated Gaul and then had moved down into Spain. For a time after the arrival in Spain of the West Goths there was war between them and the Vandals. The West Goths seem to have got the best of their rivals, for the Vandals determined to move on across the Strait of Gibraltar into northern Africa, where they established a kingdom and conquered the neighboring islands in the Mediterranean (see map, p. 296).

Having rid themselves of the Vandals, the West Goths took possession of a great part of the Spanish peninsula, and this they added to their conquests across the Pyrenees in Gaul, so that their kingdom extended from the river Loire to the Strait of Gibraltar.

It is unnecessary to follow the confused history of the movements of the innumerable bands of restless barbarians who wandered about Europe during the fifth century. Scarcely any part of western Europe was left unmolested; even Britain was conquered by German tribes, the Angles and Saxons.

456. Attila and the Huns. To add to the universal confusion caused by the influx of the German tribes, the Huns (the Mongolian people who had first pushed the West Goths into the Empire) now began to fill all western Europe with terror. Under their chief, Attila, this savage people invaded Gaul. But the

Romans and the German inhabitants joined together against the invaders and defeated them in the battle of Châlons, in 451. After this rebuff in Gaul, Attila turned to Italy. But the danger there was averted by a Roman embassy headed by Pope Leo the Great, who induced Attila to give up his plan of marching upon Rome. Within a year he died, and with him perished the power of the Huns, who never troubled Europe again.

457. The "Fall" of the Empire in the West (476). The year 476 has commonly been taken as the date of the "fall" of the Western Empire and of the beginning of the Middle Ages. What happened in that year was this. Most of the Roman emperors in the West had proved weak and indolent rulers. So the barbarians wandered hither and thither pretty much at their pleasure, and the German troops in the service of the Empire became accustomed to set up and depose emperors to suit their own special interest, very much in the same way that a boss in an American city often succeeds in securing the election of a mayor who will carry out his wishes. Finally, in 476, Odoacer, the most powerful among the rival German generals in Italy, declared himself *king* and banished the last of the emperors of the West.[1]

458. Theodoric establishes the Kingdom of the East Goths in Italy. It was not, however, given to Odoacer to establish an enduring German kingdom on Italian soil, for he was conquered by the great Theodorci, the king of the East Goths (or *Ostrogoths*). Theodoric had spent ten years of his early youth in Constantinople and had thus become familiar with Roman life and was on friendly terms with the emperor of the East.

The struggle between Theodoric and Odoacer lasted for several years, but Odoacer was finally shut up in Ravenna and surrendered, only to be treacherously slain a few days later by Theodoric's own hand (493).

Theodoric put the name of the emperor at Constantinople on the coins which he issued and did everything in his power to gain the emperor's approval of the new German kingdom. Nevertheless,

---

[1] The common misapprehensions in regard to the events of 476 are discussed by the author in *The New History*, pp. 154 ff.

although he desired that the emperor should sanction his usurpation, Theodoric had no idea of being really subordinate to Constantinople.

Theodoric greatly admired the Roman laws and institutions and did his best to preserve them. The old offices and titles were retained, and Goth and Roman lived under the same Roman law. Order was maintained and learning encouraged. In Ravenna, which Theodoric chose for his capital, beautiful buildings still exist that date from his reign (see tailpiece, p. 306).

459. Franks and Burgundians. While Theodoric had been establishing his kingdom in Italy in this enlightened way, Gaul, which we now call France, was coming under the control of the most powerful of all the barbarian peoples, the *Franks*, who were to play a more important rôle in the formation of modern Europe than any of the other German races (§§ 466–468).

Besides the kingdom of the East Goths in Italy and of the Franks in Gaul, the West Goths had their kingdom in Spain, the Burgundians had established themselves on the Rhone River, and the Vandals in Africa. Royal alliances were concluded between the various reigning houses, and for the first time in the history of Europe we see something like a family of nations, living each within its own boundaries and dealing with one another as independent powers (see map, p. 296). It seemed for a few years as if the new German kings who had divided the western portion of the Empire among themselves would succeed in keeping order and in preventing the loss of such civilization as remained.

But no such good fortune was in store for Europe, which was now only at the beginning of the turmoil which was to leave it almost completely barbarized, for there was little to encourage the reading or writing of books, the study of science, or attention to art, in a time of constant warfare and danger.

460. Cassiodorus and his Manuals. Theodoric had a distinguished Roman counselor named Cassiodorus (d. 575), to whose letters we owe a great part of our knowledge of this period, and who busied himself in his old age in preparing textbooks of the "liberal" arts,—grammar, rhetoric, logic, arithmetic, geometry,

MAP OF EUROPE IN THE TIME OF THEODORIC

It will be noticed that Theodoric's kingdom of the East Goths included a considerable part of what we call Austria to-day, and that the West Gothic kingdom extended into southern France. The Vandals held northern Africa and the adjacent islands. The Burgundians lay in between the East Goths and the Franks. The Lombards, who were later to move down into Italy, were in Theodoric's time east of the Bavarians, after whom modern Bavaria is named. Some of the Saxons invaded England, but many remained in Germany, as indicated on the map. The Eastern Empire, which was all that remained of the Roman Empire, included the Balkan Peninsula, Asia Minor, and the eastern portion of the Mediterranean. The Britons in Wales, the Picts in Scotland, and the Scots in Ireland were Celts, consequently modern Welsh, Gaelic, and Irish are closely related and belong to the Celtic group of languages

music, and astronomy. His treatment of these seven important subjects, to which he devotes a few pages each, seems to us very silly and absurd and enables us to estimate the low plane to which learning had fallen in Italy in the sixth century. Yet these and similar works were regarded as standard treatises and used as textbooks all through the Middle Ages, while the really great Greek and Roman writers of the earlier period were forgotten.

461. Disappearance of Books. Between the time of Theodoric and that of Charlemagne (§ 505) three hundred years elapsed, during which scarcely a person was to be found who could write out, even in the worst of Latin, an account of the events of his day. Everything conspired to discourage education. The great centers of learning — Carthage, Rome, Alexandria, Milan — had all been partially destroyed by the invaders. The libraries which had been kept in the temples of the pagan gods were often burned, along with the temples themselves, by Christian enthusiasts, who were not sorry to see the heathen books disappear with the heathen religion.

462. Code of Justinian. The year after Theodoric's death one of the greatest of the emperors of the East, Justinian (527–565), came to the throne at Constantinople. He employed a very able lawyer named Tribonian to gather together all the numerous laws which had grown up since the age of the Twelve Tablets (§ 306) a thousand years before. Justinian was the Hammurapi of the Roman Empire (§ 69), and the vast body of laws which he collected provided for almost every situation and every difficulty arising in social life, in business transactions, or in legal proceedings. The collection of decisions of famous Roman judges brought together in Justinian's Digest became the foundation of law for later ages and still greatly influences the laws of civilized peoples of to-day.

463. End of the Old Temples. Justinian did much to beautify his capital, Constantinople, but it was no longer for building the old temples of the gods or basilicas and amphitheaters that the ruler gave his wealth. The worship of the old gods had long before been prohibited by Christian emperors. After A.D. 400 the splendid temples which fringed the Mediterranean and extended far up the Nile were gradually forsaken by their worshipers, till finally they stood deserted and desolate as they are to-day or were converted into Christian churches. The last blow to what the

Church regarded as Greek paganism was now struck by Justinian, who closed the schools of philosophy at Athens, established centuries earlier by the followers of Plato and Aristotle and by the Stoics and Epicureans. These, as we have seen (§ 286), formed

FIG. 74. CHURCH OF ST. SOPHIA

This picture shows us the interior of the famous church of St. Sophia, built at Constantinople by Justinian from A. D. 532 to 537. Justinian's architects roofed the great church with a gigantic dome one hundred and eighty-three feet high at the center, sweeping clear across the audience room and producing the most imposing vaulted interior now surviving from the ancient world. Justinian is said to have expended eighteen tons of gold and the labor of ten thousand men in the erection of the building. Since the capture of Constantinople by the Turks (A. D. 1453) the vast church has served as a Mohammedan mosque. The Turks have whitewashed the gorgeous mosaics with which the magnificent interior is adorned, and large circular shields bearing the monogram of the Sultan have been hung against the walls

a sort of great university frequented by scholars from all parts of the Empire. The buildings to which the emperor now devoted his wealth were churches. Saint Sophia, which he built at Constantinople, still stands to-day, the most magnificent of the early churches of the East.

464. Justinian destroys Kingdoms of the Vandals and East Goths. Justinian undertook to regain for his empire the provinces in Africa and Italy that had been occupied by the Vandals and East Goths. His general, Belisarius, overthrew the Vandal kingdom in northern Africa in 534, but it was a more difficult task to destroy the Gothic rule in Italy. However, in spite of a brave resistance, the Goths were so completely defeated in 553 that they agreed to leave Italy with all their movable possessions. What became of the remnants of the race we do not know.

465. The Lombards occupy Italy. The destruction of the Gothic kingdom was a disaster for Italy, for the Goths would have helped defend it against later and far more barbarous invaders. Immediately after the death of Justinian the country was overrun by the Lombards, the last of the great German peoples to establish themselves within the bounds of the former Empire. They were a savage race, a considerable part of which was still pagan. The newcomers first occupied the region north of the Po, which has ever since been called "Lombardy" after them, and then extended their conquests southward. Instead of settling themselves with the moderation and wise statesmanship of the East Goths, the Lombards moved about the peninsula pillaging and massacring. They were unable, however, to conquer all of Italy. Rome, Ravenna, and southern Italy continued to be held by the emperors who succeeded Justinian at Constantinople. As time went on, the Lombards lost their wildness and adopted the habits and religion of the people among whom they lived. Their kingdom lasted over two hundred years, until it was conquered by Charlemagne (see below, § 508).

II. KINGDOM OF THE FRANKS

466. The Franks and their Method of Conquest. The various kingdoms established by the German chieftains were not very permanent, as we have seen. The Franks, however, succeeded in conquering more territory than any other people and in founding an empire far more important than the kingdoms of the West and East Goths, the Vandals, or the Lombards. We must now see how this was accomplished.

When the Franks are first heard of in history they were settled along the lower Rhine, from Cologne to the North Sea. Their method of getting a foothold in the Empire was essentially different from that which the Goths, Lombards, and Vandals had adopted. Instead of severing their connection with Germany and becoming an island in the sea of the Empire, they conquered by degrees the territory about them. However far they might extend their control, they remained in constant touch with their fellow barbarians behind them. In this way they retained the warlike vigor that was lost by the races who were completely surrounded by the luxuries of Roman civilization.

FIG. 75. FRANKISH WARRIOR

It is very hard to find illustrations for a chapter on the barbarian invasions, for this period of disorder was not one in which pictures were being painted or buildings erected. From the slight descriptions we have of the costume worn by the Frankish soldiers, we infer that it was something like that represented here. We know that they wore their hair in long braids and carried weapons similar to those in the picture

In the early part of the fifth century they had occupied the district which forms to-day the kingdom of Belgium, as well as the regions east of it. In 486, seven years before Theodoric founded his Italian kingdom, they went forth under their great king, Clovis (a name that later grew into Louis), and defeated the Roman general who opposed them. They extended their control over Gaul as far south as the Loire, which at that time formed the northern boundary of the kingdom of the West Goths. Clovis next enlarged his empire on the east by the conquest

THE DOMINIONS OF THE FRANKS UNDER THE MEROVINGIANS

This map shows how the Frankish kingdom grew up. Clovis while still a young man defeated the Roman general Syagrius in 486, near Soissons, and so added the region around Paris to his possessions. He added Alemannia on the east in 496. In 507 he made Paris his capital and conquered Aquitania, previously held by the West Goths. He also made a beginning in adding the kingdom of the Burgundians to his realms. He died in 511. His successors in the next half century completed the conquest of Burgundy and added Provincia, Bavaria, and Gascony. There were many divisions of the Frankish realms after the time of Clovis, and the eastern and western portions, called Austrasia and Neustria, were often ruled by different branches of the *Merovingians*, as Clovis's family was called

of the Alemanni, a German people living in the region of the Black Forest and north of the Lake of Constance.

467. Conversion of Clovis (496). The battle in which the Alemanni were defeated (496) is in one respect important above all the other battles of Clovis. Although still a pagan himself, his wife had been converted to Christianity. In the midst of the battle, seeing his troops giving way, he called upon Jesus Christ and pledged himself to be baptized in his name if he would help the Franks to victory over their enemies. When he won the battle he kept his word and was baptized, together with three thousand of his warriors.

468. Conquests of Clovis and his Successors. To the south of Clovis's new possessions in Gaul lay the kingdom of the West Goths; to the southeast that of another German people, the Burgundians. Clovis speedily extended his power to the Pyrenees and forced the West Goths to confine themselves to the Spanish portion of their realm, while the Burgundians soon fell completely under the rule of the Franks. Then Clovis, by a series of murders, brought portions of the Frankish nation itself, which had previously been independent of him, under his scepter.

When Clovis died in 511 at Paris, which he had made his residence, his four sons divided his possessions among them. Wars between rival brothers, interspersed with the most horrible murders, fill the annals of the Frankish kingdom for over a hundred years after the death of Clovis. Yet the nation continued to develop in spite of the unscrupulous deeds of its rulers.

The Frankish kings who followed Clovis succeeded in extending their power over pretty nearly all the territory that is included to-day in France, Belgium, and the Netherlands, as well as over a goodly portion of western Germany. Half a century after the death of Clovis their dominions extended from the Bay of Biscay on the west to a point east of Salzburg.

III. Results of the Barbarian Invasions

469. Fusion of the Barbarians and the Roman Population. As one looks back over the German invasions it is natural to ask upon what terms the newcomers lived among the old inhabitants of the Empire, how far they adopted the customs of those among whom they settled, and how far they clung to their old habits? These questions cannot be answered very satisfactorily. So little is known of the confused period of which we have been speaking that it is impossible to follow closely the mixing of the two races.

In the first place, we must be on our guard against exaggerating the numbers in the various bodies of invaders. The readiness with which the Germans appear to have adopted the language and customs of the Romans would tend to prove that the invaders formed but a small minority of the population. Since hundreds of thousands of barbarians had been absorbed during the previous five centuries, the invasions of the fifth century can hardly have made an abrupt change in the character of the population.

470. Contrast between Spoken and Written Latin. The barbarians within the old Empire were soon speaking the same conversational Latin which was everywhere used by the Romans about them. This was much simpler than the elaborate and complicated language used in books, which we find so much difficulty in learning nowadays. In the various countries of southern Europe the speech of the common people was gradually diverging more and more from the written Latin and finally grew into French, Spanish, Italian, and Portuguese. But the barbarians did not produce this change, for it had begun before they came and would have gone on without them. They did no more than contribute a few convenient words to the new languages.

The northern Franks, who did not penetrate far into the Empire, and the Germans who remained in what is now Germany and in Scandinavia, had of course no reason for giving up their native tongues; the Angles and Saxons in Britain also kept theirs. These Germanic languages in time became Dutch, English, German, Danish, Swedish, etc. Of this matter something will be said later (pp. 679–684).

471. The Roman and the German Law. The Germans and the older inhabitants of the Roman Empire appear to have had no dislike for one another except when there was a difference in religion.[1] Where there was no religious barrier the two races intermarried freely from the first. The Frankish kings did not hesitate to appoint Romans to important positions in the government and in the army, just as the Romans had long been in the

---

[1] The West and East Goths and the Burgundians were heretics in the eyes of the Catholic Church, for they had been taught their Christianity by missionaries who disagreed with the Catholic Church on certain points.

habit of employing the barbarians as generals and officials. In only one respect were the two races distinguished for a time— each had its particular law.

The West Goths were probably the first to write down their ancient laws, using the Latin language for the purpose. Their example was followed by the Franks, the Burgundians, and later by the Lombards and other peoples. These codes make up the "Laws of the Barbarians," which form our most important source of knowledge of the habits and ideas of the Germans at the time of the invasions. For several centuries following the barbarian conquests the members of the various German tribes appear to have been judged by the laws of the particular people to which they belonged. The older inhabitants of the Empire, on the contrary, continued to have their lawsuits decided according to the Roman law.

472. Medieval Trials. The German laws did not provide for trials, either in the Roman or the modern sense of the word. There was no attempt to gather and weigh evidence and base the decision upon it. Such a mode of procedure was far too elaborate for the simple-minded Germans. Instead of a regular trial, one of the parties to the case was designated to prove that his side of the case was right by one of the following methods:

1. He might solemnly swear that he was telling the truth, and get as many other persons of his own class as the court required, to swear that they believed that he was telling the truth. This was called *compurgation*. It was believed that God would punish those who swore falsely.

2. On the other hand, the parties to the case, or persons representing them, might meet in combat, on the supposition that Heaven would grant victory to the right. This was the so-called *wager of battle*.

3. Lastly, one or other of the parties might be required to submit to the *ordeal* in one of its various forms: He might plunge his arm into hot water or carry a bit of hot iron for some distance, and if at the end of three days he showed no ill effects, the case was decided in his favor. Or he might be ordered to walk over

hot plowshares, and if he was not burned, it was assumed that God had intervened by a miracle to establish the right. This method of trial is but one example of the rude civilization which displaced the refined and elaborate organization of the Romans.

473. The Ignorance and Disorder of the Early Middle Ages. The account which has been given of the conditions in the Roman Empire, and of the manner in which the barbarians occupied its western part, serves to explain why the following centuries — known as the early Middle Ages — were a time of ignorance and disorder. The Germans, no doubt, varied a good deal in their habits and character. The Goths differed from the Lombards, and the Franks from the Vandals; but they all agreed in knowing nothing of the art, literature, and science which had been developed by the Greeks and adopted by the Romans. The invaders were ignorant, simple, vigorous people, with no taste for anything except fighting, eating, and drinking. Such was the disorder that their coming produced that the declining civilization of the Empire was pretty nearly submerged. The libraries, buildings, and works of art were destroyed or neglected, and there was no one to see that they were restored. So the Western world fell back into a condition similar to that in which it had been before the Romans conquered and civilized it.

The loss was, however, temporary. The great heritage of skill and invention which had been slowly accumulated in Egypt and Greece, and which formed a part of the civilization which the Romans had adopted and spread abroad throughout their great Empire, did not wholly perish.

It is true that the break-up of the Roman Empire and the centuries of turmoil which followed set everything back, but we shall see how the barbarian nations gradually developed into our modern European states, how universities were established in which the books of the Greeks and Romans were studied. Architects arose in time to imitate the old buildings and build a new kind of their own quite as imposing as those of the Romans; and men of science carried discoveries far beyond anything known to the wisest of the Greeks and Romans.

QUESTIONS

I. How did the Germans first come into the Roman Empire, and for what reasons? What is meant by the barbarian invasions? Give some examples. Trace the history of the West Goths. Where did they finally establish their kingdom? Why has the year 476 been regarded as the date of the fall of the Roman Empire? Tell what you can of Theodoric and his kingdom. Contrast the Lombard invaders of Italy with the East Goths.

II. Who were the Franks, and how did their invasion differ from that of the other German peoples? What did Clovis accomplish, and what was the extent of the kingdom of the Franks under his successors?

III. On what terms do the Germans seem to have lived with the people of the Roman Empire? Why are the "Laws of the Barbarians" useful to the historian? Compare the ways in which the Germans tried law cases with those we use to-day in the United States. Tell as clearly as possible why the Middle Ages were centuries of disorder and ignorance as compared with the earlier period.

NOTE. The illustration below represents the tomb of Theodoric. Emperors and rich men were accustomed in Roman times to build handsome tombs for themselves. Theodoric followed their example and erected this two-storied building at Ravenna to serve as his mausoleum. The dome consists of a single great piece of rock thirty-six feet in diameter, weighing five hundred tons, brought from across the Adriatic. Theodoric was a heretic in the eyes of the Catholic Church, and not long after his death his remains were taken out of his tomb and scattered to the winds, and the building converted into a church. The picture represents the tomb as it probably looked originally; it has been somewhat altered in modern times, but is well preserved.

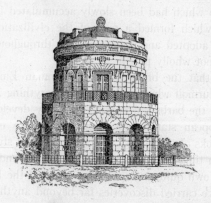

CHAPTER XXI

THE RISE OF THE PAPACY

I. The Christian Church

474. The Popes. Besides the emperors at Constantinople and the various German kings there grew up in Europe a line of rulers far more powerful than any of these, namely, the *popes* at Rome.

We have already seen how marvelously the Christian communities founded by the apostles and their fellow missionaries multiplied until, by the middle of the third century, people came to conceive of a "Catholic," or all-embracing, Church. We have seen how Emperor Constantine favored Christianity and how his successors worked in the interest of the new religion. The Justinian Code (§ 462) safeguarded the Church and the Christian clergy and harshly treated those who ventured to hold another view of Christianity from that approved by the government.

475. Contrast between Pagan and Christian Ideas. One great source of the Church's strength lay in the general fear of death and judgment to come, which Christianity had brought with it. The educated Greeks and Romans of the classical period usually thought of the next life, when they thought of it at all, as a very uninteresting existence compared with that on this earth. One who committed some great crime might suffer for it after death with pains similar to those of the hell in which the Christians believed. But the great part of humanity were supposed to lead in the next world a shadowy existence, neither sad nor glad. Religion, even to the devout pagan, was, as we have seen, mainly an affair of this life ; the gods were worshiped with a view to securing happiness and success in this world.

Christianity opposed this view of life with an entirely different one. It constantly emphasized man's existence after death, which it declared to be infinitely more important than his brief sojourn on earth. Under the influence of the Church this conception of life gradually supplanted the pagan one in the Roman world, and it was taught to the barbarians.

476. The Monks. The "other-worldliness" became so intense that thousands gave up their ordinary occupations altogether and devoted their entire attention to preparation for the next life. They shut themselves in lonely cells, and, not satisfied with giving up most of their natural pleasures, they inflicted bodily suffering upon themselves by hunger, cold, and other discomforts. They trusted that in this way they might avoid some of the sins into which they were apt to fall, and that, by self-inflicted punishment in this world, they might perchance escape some of that reserved for them in the next. (See next chapter.)

477. The Church claims to be One Means of Salvation. The barbarians were taught that their fate in the next world depended largely upon the Church. Its ministers never wearied of presenting the alternative which faced every man so soon as this short earthly existence should be over—the alternative between eternal bliss in heaven and perpetual, unspeakable torment in hell. Only those who had been duly baptized could hope to reach heaven; but baptism washed away only past sins and did not prevent new ones. These, unless their guilt was removed through the Church, would surely drag the soul down to hell.

478. Miracles. The divine power of the Church was, furthermore, established in the eyes of the people by the wonderful works which Christian saints were constantly performing. They healed the sick, made the blind to see and the lame to walk. They called down God's wrath upon those who opposed the Church and invoked terrible punishments upon those who treated her holy rites with contempt. To the reader of to-day the frequency of the miracles narrated by medieval writers seems astonishing. The lives of the medieval saints, of which hundreds and hundreds have been preserved, contain little else than accounts of them, and no one appears to have doubted their everyday occurrence.

479. The Early Churches. A word should be said of the early Christian church buildings. The Romans were accustomed to build near their market places a species of public hall, in which townspeople could meet one another to transact business and in which judges could hear cases and public officials attend to their duties. These buildings, as we have seen, were called *basilicas*. There were several magnificent ones in Rome itself, and there

FIG. 76. SANTA MARIA MAGGIORE

This beautiful church at Rome was built shortly after Constantine's time, and the interior, here shown, with its stately columns, above which are fine mosaics, is still nearly as it was in the time of St. Augustine, fifteen hundred years ago. The ceiling is of the sixteenth century

was doubtless at least one to be found in every town of considerable size. The roofs of these spacious halls were usually supported by long rows of columns ; sometimes there were two rows on each side, forming aisles. When, after Constantine had given his approval to Christianity, large, fine churches began to be built they were constructed like these familiar public halls and, like them, were called basilicas.

During the sixteen hundred years that have passed since Constantine's time naturally almost all the churches of his day have disappeared or been greatly altered. But the beautiful church of Santa Maria Maggiore in Rome (Fig. 76) was built only a hundred years later and gives us an excellent notion of a Christian basilica with its fine rows of columns and its handsome mosaic decorations. In general, the churches were plain and unattractive on the outside. A later chapter will explain how the basilica grew into the Gothic cathedral, which was as beautiful outside as inside.

480. The Church and the Roman Government. The chief importance of the Church for the student of medieval history does not lie, however, in its religious functions, vital as they were, but rather in its remarkable relations to the government. From the days of Constantine on, the Catholic Church had usually enjoyed the hearty support and protection of the government. But so long as the Roman Empire remained strong and active there was no chance for the clergy to free themselves from the control of the emperor, even if they had been disposed to do so. He made such laws for the Church as he saw fit, and the clergy did not complain. The government was, indeed, indispensable to them. It undertook to root out paganism by destroying the heathen shrines and preventing heathen sacrifices, and it punished severely those who refused to accept the teachings sanctioned by the Church.

But as the great Empire began to fall apart there was a growing tendency among the churchmen in the West to resent the interference of the new rulers whom they did not respect. Consequently they managed gradually to free themselves in large part from the control of the government.

481. The Church begins to perform the Functions of Government. The authority of the various barbarian kings was seldom sufficient to keep their realms in order. There were always many powerful landholders scattered throughout the kingdom who did pretty much what they pleased and settled their grudges against their fellows by neighborhood wars. Fighting was the main business as well as the chief amusement of this class. The king was unable to maintain peace and protect the oppressed, however anxious he may have been to do so.

Under these circumstances it naturally fell to the Church to keep order, when it could, by either threats or persuasion ; to see that contracts were kept, the wills of the dead carried out, and marriage obligations observed. It took the defenseless widow and orphan under its protection and dispensed charity ; it promoted education at a time when few laymen, however rich and noble, were able even to read. These conditions serve to explain why the Church was finally able so greatly to extend the powers which it had enjoyed under the Roman Empire, and why it undertook duties which seem to us to belong to the State rather than to a religious organization.

II. ORIGIN OF THE POWER OF THE POPES

482. Origin of Papal Power. We must now turn to a consideration of the origin and growth of the supremacy of the popes, who, by raising themselves to the head of the Western Church, became in many respects more powerful than any of the kings and princes with whom they frequently found themselves in bitter conflict.

There is little doubt that the bishop of Rome and his flock had almost from the very first enjoyed a leading place among the Christian communities. The Roman church was the only one in the West which could claim the distinction of having been founded by the immediate followers of Christ — the "two most glorious apostles, Peter and Paul."

483. Belief that Peter was the First Bishop of Rome. The New Testament speaks repeatedly of Paul's presence in Rome. As for Peter, there had always been an unquestioned tradition, accepted throughout the Christian Church, that he was the first bishop of Rome. This belief appears to have been generally accepted at least as early as the middle of the second century. There is, certainly, no conflicting tradition, no rival claimant. The belief itself, whether or not it corresponds with actual events, is a fact of the greatest historical importance. Peter enjoyed a preëminence among the other apostles and was singled out by Christ upon several occasions. In a passage of the New Testament (Matt. xvi, 18–19), which has affected history more profoundly than the edicts of the most powerful monarch, Christ says: "And I say also unto thee, That thou art Peter, and upon this rock I will build my church ; and the gates of hell shall not prevail against it. And I will give unto thee the keys of the kingdom of heaven : and whatsoever thou shalt bind on earth shall be bound in heaven ; and whatsoever thou shalt loose on earth shall be loosed in heaven." This the popes have always claimed as the divine sanction of the powers which they believed to be theirs.

484. The Roman Church the Mother Church. Thus it was natural that the Roman church should early have been looked upon as the "mother church" in the West. Its doctrines were considered the purest, since they had been handed down from its exalted founders. When there was a difference of opinion in regard to the truth of a particular teaching, it was natural that all should turn to the bishop of Rome for his view. Moreover, the majesty of Rome, the capital of the world, helped to exalt its bishop above his fellows. It was long, however, before all the other bishops, especially those in the large cities, were ready to accept unconditionally the authority of the bishop of Rome, although they acknowledged his leading position and that of the Roman community.

We know comparatively little of the bishops of Rome during the first three or four centuries of the Church's existence. It is only with the accession of Leo the Great (440–461) that our knowledge of the history of the papacy may, in one sense, be said to begin (§ 456).

485. Title of Pope. The name "pope" (Latin *papa*, "father") was originally and quite naturally given to all bishops, and even to priests. It began to be especially applied to the bishops of Rome, perhaps as early as the sixth century, but was not apparently confined to them until two or three hundred years later. Gregory VII (d. 1085; §§ 592–593, below) was the first to declare explicitly that the title should be used only for the bishop of Rome.

Not long after the death of Leo the Great, Odoacer put an end to the Western line of emperors. Then, as we know, Theodoric and his East Goths settled in Italy, only to be followed by still less desirable intruders, the Lombards. During this tumultuous period the people of Rome, and even of all Italy, came to

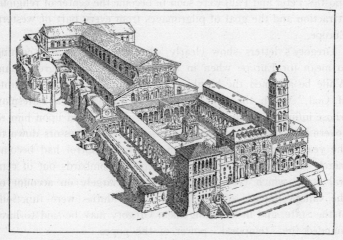

FIG. 77. THE ANCIENT BASILICA OF ST. PETER

Of the churches built by Constantine in Rome that in honor of St. Peter was, next to the Lateran, the most important. It was constructed on the site of Nero's circus, where St. Peter was believed to have been crucified. It retained its original appearance, as here represented, for twelve hundred years, and then the popes (who had given up the Lateran as their residence and come to live in the Vatican palace close to St. Peter's) determined to build the new and grander church one sees to-day (see pp. 456–457, below). Constantine and the popes made constant use in their buildings of columns and stones taken from the older Roman buildings, which were in this way demolished

regard the Pope as their natural leader. The Eastern emperor was far away, and his officers, who managed to hold a portion of central Italy around Rome and Ravenna, were glad to accept the aid and counsel of the Pope.

486. Gregory the Great (590–604). The pontificate of Gregory the Great, one of the half dozen most distinguished heads that the Church has ever had, shows how great a part the papacy

could play. When he was chosen Pope (in 590) and most reluctantly left his monastery, ancient Rome, the capital of the
Empire, was already transforming itself into medieval Rome, the
capital of Christendom. The temples of the gods had furnished
materials for the many Christian churches. The tombs of the
apostles Peter and Paul were soon to become the center of religious
attraction and the goal of pilgrimages from every part of western
Europe.

Gregory's letters show clearly what the papacy was coming
to mean for Europe when in the hands of a really great man.
While he assumed the humble title of "Servant of the servants
of God," which the popes still use, Gregory was a statesman
whose influence extended far and wide. It devolved upon him to
govern the city of Rome,— as it did upon his successors down to
the year 1870,— for the Eastern emperor's control had become
merely nominal. He had also to keep the Lombards out of central Italy, which they failed to conquer largely on account of
the valiant defense of the popes. These duties were functions
of the State, and in assuming them Gregory may be said to have
founded the "temporal" power of the popes.

487. Gregory's Missionary Undertakings. Beyond the borders of Italy, Gregory was in constant communication with the
emperor and the Frankish and Burgundian rulers. Everywhere
he used his influence to have good clergymen chosen as bishops,
and everywhere he watched over the interests of the monasteries.
But his chief importance in the history of the papacy is due to
the missionary enterprises he undertook, through which the great
countries that were one day to be called England, France, and
Germany were brought under the sway of the Roman church
and its head, the Pope.

As Gregory had himself been a devoted monk it was natural
that he should rely chiefly upon the monks in his great work of
converting the heathen. Consequently, before considering his
missionary achievements, we must glance at the origin and
character of the monks, who are so conspicuous throughout the
Middle Ages.

QUESTIONS

I. Why is it essential to know about the history of the Church in order to understand the Middle Ages? Compare the Christian idea of the importance of life in this world and the next with the pagan views. Describe a basilica. Mention some governmental duties that were assumed by the Church. Give the reasons why the Church became such a great power in the Middle Ages.

II. Why was the Roman church the most important of all the Christian churches? On what grounds did the bishop of Rome claim to be the head of the whole Church? Did the Christians in the eastern portion of the Roman Empire accept the bishop of Rome as their head? Why did the popes become influential in the governing not only of Rome but of Italy? Tell what you can of Gregory the Great.

NOTE. The Roman Emperor Hadrian (§ 398) built a great circular tomb at Rome, on the west bank of the Tiber, for himself and his successors. It was two hundred and forty feet across, perhaps one hundred and sixty-five feet high, covered with marble and adorned with statues. When Rome was besieged by the Germans in 537 the inhabitants used the tomb for a fortress and threw down the statues on the heads of the barbarians. When Gregory the Great prayed that Rome be delivered from a terrible pestilence he saw the archangel Michael sheathing his sword over Hadrian's tomb; and since then it has been called the Castle of the Holy Angel.

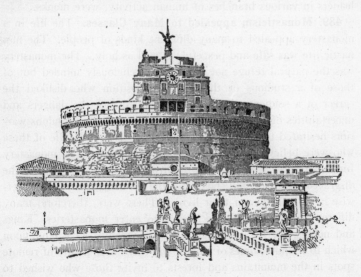

CHAPTER XXII

THE MONKS AND THEIR MISSIONARY WORK;
THE MOHAMMEDANS

I. Monks and Monasteries

488. Importance of the Monks. It would be difficult to over-estimate the influence that the monks exercised for centuries in Europe. The proud annals of the Benedictines, Franciscans, Dominicans, and Jesuits contain many a distinguished name. The most eminent philosophers, scientists, historians, artists, poets, and statesmen may be found in their ranks. Among those whose achievements we shall mention later are "The Venerable Bede," Boniface, Thomas Aquinas, Roger Bacon, Fra Angelico, Luther, Erasmus, Loyola—all these, and many others who have been leaders in various branches of human activity, were monks.

489. Monasticism appealed to Many Classes. The life in a monastery appealed to many different kinds of people. The monastic life was safe and peaceful, as well as holy. The monastery was the natural refuge not only of the religiously minded but of those of a studious or thoughtful disposition who disliked the career of a soldier and were disinclined to face the dangers and uncertainties of the times. Even the rude and unscrupulous warriors hesitated to destroy the property or disturb the life of those who were believed to enjoy God's special favor. The monastery furnished, too, a refuge for the friendless, an asylum for the disgraced, and food and shelter for the indolent, who would otherwise have had to earn their living. There were, therefore, many different motives which led people to enter monasteries. Kings and nobles, for the good of their souls, readily gave land upon which to found colonies of monks, and there were plenty of remote spots in the mountains and forests to invite those who wished to escape from the world and its temptations, its dangers or its cares.

490. Rule of St. Benedict. Monastic communities first developed on a large scale in Egypt in the fourth century. The idea, however, was quickly taken up in Europe. In the sixth century monasteries multiplied so rapidly in western Europe that it became necessary to establish definite rules for these communities which proposed to desert the ordinary ways of the world and lead a holy life apart. Accordingly St. Benedict drew up, about the year 526, a sort of constitution for the monastery of Monte Cassino, in southern Italy, of which he was the head. This was so sagacious, and so well met the needs of the monastic life, that it was rapidly accepted by the other monasteries and gradually became the "rule" according to which all the Western monks lived.[1]

The Rule of St. Benedict is as important as any constitution that was ever drawn up for a state. It is for the most part very wise and sensible. It provided that, since everyone is not fitted for the monk's life, the candidate for admission to the monastery should pass through a period of probation, called the *novitiate*, before he was permitted to take the solemn, final vows. The brethren were to elect the head of the monastery — the abbot, as he was called. Along with frequent prayer and meditation the monks were to do the necessary cooking and washing for the monastery and raise the necessary vegetables and grain. They were also to read and teach. Those who were incapacitated for outdoor work were assigned lighter tasks, such as copying books.

491. The Monastic Vows. The monk had to take the three vows of obedience, poverty, and purity. He was to obey the abbot without question in all matters that did not involve his committing a sin. He pledged himself to perpetual and absolute poverty, and everything he used was the property of the convent. He was not permitted to own anything whatsoever — not even a book or a pen. Along with the vows of obedience and poverty, he was also required to pledge himself never to marry; for not

[1] Benedict did not introduce monasticism in the West, as is sometimes supposed, nor did he even found an *order* in the proper sense of the word, under a single head, like the later Franciscans and Dominicans. Nevertheless, the monks who lived under his rule are ordinarily spoken of as belonging to the Benedictine Order.

only was the single life considered more holy than the married, but the monastic organization would have been impossible unless the monks remained single.

The influence of the Benedictine monks upon Europe is incalculable. From their numbers no less than twenty-four popes and forty-six hundred bishops and archbishops have been chosen. They boast almost sixteen thousand writers, some of great distinction. Their monasteries furnished retreats during the Middle Ages, where the scholar might study and write in spite of the prevailing disorder of the times.

492. How the Monks contributed to Civilization. The copying of books, as has been said, was a natural occupation of the monks. Doubtless their work was often done carelessly, with little heart and less understanding. But with the great loss of manuscripts due to the destruction of libraries and the general lack of interest in books, it was most essential that new copies should be made. Even poor and incorrect ones were better than none. Almost all the books written by the Romans disappeared altogether during the Middle Ages, but from time to time a monk would copy out the poems of Virgil, Horace, or Ovid, or the speeches of Cicero. In this way some of the chief works of the Latin writers have continued to exist down to the present day.

The monks regarded good hard work as a great aid to salvation. They set the example of careful cultivation of the lands about their monasteries and in this way introduced better farming methods into the regions where they settled. They entertained travelers at a time when there were few or no inns and so increased the intercourse between the various parts of Europe.

493. Arrangement of a Monastery. The home which the monks constructed for themselves was called a monastery or abbey. This was arranged to meet their particular needs and was usually at a considerable distance from any town, in order to insure solitude and quiet.[1] It was modeled upon the general plan of the Roman country house. The buildings were arranged around a court, called the *cloister*. On all four sides of this was a covered

[1] Later monasteries were sometimes built in towns or just outside the walls.

walk, which made it possible to reach all the buildings without exposing one's self to either the rain or the hot sun. Not only the Benedictines but all the orders which sprang up in later centuries arranged their homes in much the same way.

On the north side of the cloister was the *church*, which always faced west. As time went on and certain groups of monks were

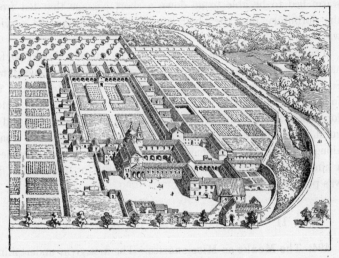

FIG. 78. MONASTERY OF VAL DI CRISTO

This monastery in southern Spain has two cloisters, the main one lying to the left. One can see how the buildings were surrounded by vegetable gardens and an orchard which supplied the monks with food. We know that we are viewing the monastery from the west, for the church faces us

given a great deal of property, they constructed very beautiful churches for their monasteries. Westminster Abbey was originally the church of a monastery lying outside the city of London, and there are in Great Britain many picturesque remains of ruined abbey churches which attract the attention of every traveler.

On the west side of the cloister were storerooms for provisions; on the south side, opposite the church, was the "refectory," or dining room, and a sitting room that could be warmed in cold weather. In the cloister, near the dining room, was a wash room where the monk could wash his hands before meals. To the east of the cloister was the "dormitory," where the monks slept. This always adjoined the church, for the Rule required that the monks should hold services seven times a day. One of these services, called vigils, came well before daybreak, and it was convenient when you were summoned in the darkness out of your warm bed to be able to go down a short passage that led from the dormitory into the choir of the church, where the service was held.

The Benedictine Rule provided that the monks should so far as possible have everything for their support on their own land. So outside the group of buildings around the cloister would be found the garden, the orchard, the mill, a fishpond, and fields for raising grain. There were also a hospital for the sick and a guest house for pilgrims or poor people who happened to come along. In the greater monasteries there were also quarters where a king or nobleman might spend a few nights in such comfort as was possible in those days.

II. Missionary Work of the Monks

494. The Monks as Missionaries. The first great undertaking of the monks was the conversion of those German peoples who had not yet been won over to Christianity. These the monks made not merely Christians but also dutiful subjects of the Pope. In this way the strength of the Roman Catholic Church was greatly increased. The first people to engage the attention of the monks were the heathen German tribes who had conquered the once Christian Britain.

495. Saxons and Angles conquer Britain. The islands which are now known as the kingdom of Great Britain and Ireland were, at the opening of the Christian Era, occupied by several Celtic peoples of whose customs and religion we know almost nothing. Julius Cæsar commenced the conquest of the islands (55 B.C.) (§ 367), and later the Emperor Claudius carried on the work (§ 391). But the Romans never succeeded in establishing their power beyond the wall which they built from the Clyde to the

Firth of Forth to keep out the wild tribes of the North. Even south of the wall the country was not completely Romanized, and the Celtic tongue has actually survived down to the present day in Wales.

At the opening of the fifth century the barbarian invasions forced Rome to withdraw its legions from Britain in order to protect its frontiers on the Continent. The island was thus left to be conquered gradually by the Germanic peoples, mainly Saxons and Angles, who came across the North Sea from the region south of Denmark. Almost all record of what went on during the two centuries following the departure of the Romans has disappeared. No one knows the fate of the original Celtic inhabitants of England. It was formerly supposed that they were all killed or driven to the mountain districts of Wales, but this seems unlikely. More probably they were gradually lost among the dominating Germans, with whom they merged into one people. The Saxon and Angle chieftains established small kingdoms, of which there were seven or eight at the time when Gregory the Great became Pope (§§ 486–487).

496. Conversion of Britain. Gregory, while still a simple monk, had been struck with the beauty of some Angles whom he saw one day in the slave market at Rome. When he learned who they were he was grieved that such handsome beings should still belong to the kingdom of the Prince of Darkness, and he wished to go as a missionary to their people, but permission was refused him. So when he became Pope he sent forty monks to England under the leadership of a prior named Augustine (who must not be confused with the church father of that name). The heathen king of Kent, in whose territory Augustine and his monks landed with fear and trembling (597), had a Christian wife, the daughter of a Frankish king. Through her influence the monks were kindly received and were given an ancient church at Canterbury, dating from the Roman occupation before the German invasions. Here they established a monastery, and from this center the conversion, first of Kent and then of the whole island, was gradually accomplished. Canterbury has always maintained its early preëminence and may still be considered the religious capital of England.

England thus became a part of the ever-growing territory embraced in the Roman Catholic Church and remained for nearly a thousand years as faithful to the Pope as any other Catholic country. The most distinguished writer of the seventh and early eighth centuries in Europe was the English monk Bæda (often called "The Venerable Bede," 673-735), from whose admirable history of the Church in England most of our information about the period is derived.

497. St. Boniface, the Apostle to the Germans. In 718 St. Boniface, an English monk, was sent by the Pope as a missionary to the Germans. He succeeded in converting many of the more remote German tribes who still clung to their old pagan beliefs. His energetic methods are illustrated by the story of how he cut down the sacred oak of the old German god Odin, at Fritzlar, in Hesse, and used the wood to build a chapel, around which a monastery soon grew up.

III. Mohammed and his Religion

498. Mohammed. Just at the time that Gregory the Great was doing so much to strengthen the power and influence of the popes in Rome, a young Arab camel driver in far-away Mecca was devising a religion which was destined to spread with astounding rapidity into Asia, Africa, and Europe and to become a great rival of Christianity. And to-day the millions who believe in Mohammed as God's greatest prophet are probably equal in number to those who are faithful to the Pope.

Before the time of Mohammed the Arabs (a branch of the great Semitic people) had played no great part in the world's history. The scattered tribes were constantly at war with one another, and each tribe worshiped its own gods, when it worshiped at all. Mecca was considered a sacred spot, however, and the fighting was stopped four months each year so that all could peacefully visit the *Kaaba*, a sort of temple, full of idols and containing in particular a black stone, about as long as a man's hand, which was regarded as specially worthy of reverence.

FIG. 79. INTERIOR OF THE GREAT MOSQUE OF CORDOVA (LATTER PART OF TENTH CENTURY)

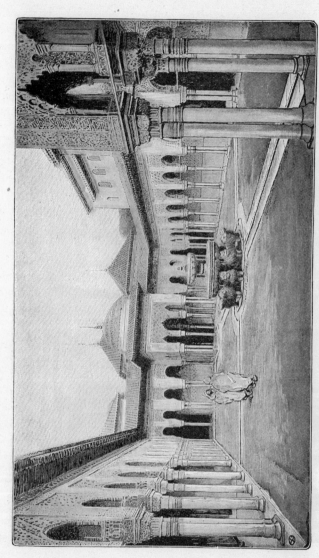

FIG. 80. COURT OF THE LIONS IN THE ALHAMBRA (BEGUN IN 1377)

As Mohammed traveled back and forth across the desert with his trains of camels heavily laden with merchandise he had plenty of time to think, and he became convinced that God was sending him messages which it was his duty to reveal to mankind. He met many Jews and Christians, of whom there were great numbers in Arabia, and from them he got some ideas of the Old and New Testaments. But when he tried to convince people that he was God's prophet, and that the Angel Gabriel had appeared to him in his dreams and told him of a new religion, he was treated with scorn.

Finally, he discovered that his enemies in Mecca were planning to kill him, and he fled to the neighboring town of Medina, where he had friends. His flight, which took place in the year 622, is called the *Hejira* by the Arabs. It was taken by his followers as the beginning of a new era—the year One, as the Mohammedans reckon time.

499. Islam and the Koran. A war followed between the people of Mecca and those who had joined Mohammed in and about Medina. It was eight years before his followers became numerous enough to enable him to march upon Mecca and take it with a victorious army. Before his death in 632 he had gained the support of all the Arab chiefs, and his new religion, which he called *Islam* (meaning "reconciliation"; by which he meant reconciliation to Allah, the sole God), was accepted throughout the whole Arabian peninsula. The new believers he called Muslims, or, as we spell it, Moslems, meaning "the reconciled." By us they are often called Mohammedans, after their prophet.

Mohammed could probably neither write nor read well, but when he fell into trances from time to time he would repeat to his eager listeners the words which he heard from heaven, and they in turn wrote them down. These sayings, which were collected into a volume shortly after his death, form the *Koran*, the Mohammedan Bible. This contains the chief beliefs of the new religion as well as the laws under which all good Mohammedans were to live.

The Koran announces a day of judgment when the heavens shall be opened and the mountains be powdered and become like flying dust. Then all men shall receive their reward. Those who have refused to accept Islam shall be banished to hell to be burned and tormented forever. "They shall not taste therein coolness or drink, save scalding water and running sores," and the scalding water they shall drink like thirsty camels.

Those, on the other hand, who have obeyed the Koran, especially those who die fighting for Islam, shall find themselves in

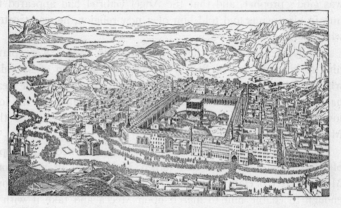

FIG. 81. A BIRD'S-EYE VIEW OF MECCA AND ITS MOSQUE

Mecca is one of the few towns in the barren Arabian peninsula, for by far the great majority of the Arabs live as roving shepherds (§ 60) and not in towns. Mecca had been a sacred place long before the time of Mohammed, and the people had been accustomed to come there as pilgrims to do homage to a sacred black stone called the Kaaba. Mohammed did not interfere with these customs. After his death the Moslems built a large court around the Kaaba. Over the Kaaba they erected a square shelter, which we see in the middle of the court. To this place the Moslem believers still come in great numbers as pilgrims every year

a garden of delight. They shall recline in rich brocades upon soft cushions and rugs and be served by surpassingly beautiful maidens, with eyes like hidden pearls. Wine may be drunk there, but "their heads shall not ache with it, neither shall they be confused." They shall be content with their past life and shall hear no foolish words; and there shall be no sin but only the greeting, "Peace, peace."

The religion of Mohammed was much simpler than that of the medieval Christian Church; it did not provide for a priesthood or for any great number of ceremonies. The Mohammedan mosque, or temple, is a house of prayer and a place for reading the Koran; no altars or images or pictures of any kind are permitted in it. The mosques are often very beautiful buildings, especially in great Mohammedan cities such as Jerusalem, Damascus, Cairo, and Constantinople. They have great courts surrounded by covered colonnades and are adorned with beautiful marbles and mosaics and delightful windows with bright stained glass. The walls are adorned with passages from the Koran, and the floors covered with rich rugs. They have one or more minarets, from which the call to prayer is heard five times a day.

500. Rise of the Oriental Empire of the Moslems. The Moslem leaders who succeeded to Mohammed's power were called *caliphs.* As rulers, they proved to

FIG. 82. A PAGE OF A MANUSCRIPT COPY OF THE KORAN, THE BIBLE OF THE MOSLEMS

This writing has descended from the ancient alphabet of the Phœnicians (§ 140), and, like the Phœnician writing, it is still written and read from right to left. The Arab writers love to give their letters decorative flourishes, producing a handsome page. The rich, decorative border is a good example of Moslem art. The whole page was done by hand. In such hand-written books as these the educated Moslems wrote out translations of the books of the great Greek philosophers and scientists, like Aristotle. At the same time the Moslems wrote their own treatises on algebra, astronomy, grammar, and other sciences in similar books. These books later came to the knowledge of Western Christian scholars, who learned much from them

FIG. 83. MOORISH MOSQUE TOWER, OR MINARET, IN SPAIN

This tower in Seville was built, not long before A.D. 1200, out of the ruins of Roman and West Gothic buildings found here by the Moors, and blocks bearing Latin inscriptions are to be seen in a number of places in its walls. After extensive alterations at the top by Christian architects, it was converted into the bell tower of a Christian church

be men of the greatest ability. They organized the untamed desert nomads, who now added a burning religious zeal to the wild courage of barbarian Arabs. This combination made the Arab armies of the caliphs irresistible. Within a few years after Mohammed's death they took Egypt and Syria from the feeble successors of Justinian at Constantinople. They thus reduced the Eastern Empire to little more than the Balkan Peninsula and Asia Minor. At the same time the Arabs crushed the empire of the New Persians (§ 432) and brought the Sassanian line of kings to an end (A.D. 640), after it had lasted a little over four hundred years. Thus the Moslems built up a great oriental empire, with its center at the east end of the Fertile Crescent.

501. The Nomad Arabs learn City Civilization along the Fertile Crescent. Just as the people of Sargon and Hammurapi took over the city civilization which they found along the lower Euphrates (§ 68), so now in the same region the Moslem Arabs of the desert took over the city civilization of the New Persians. With the ruins of Babylon looking down upon them, the Moslems built their splendid capital at Bagdad beside the New Persian royal residence of Ctesiphon. They built of course under the influence of the ancient structures

STREET SCENE IN CAIRO

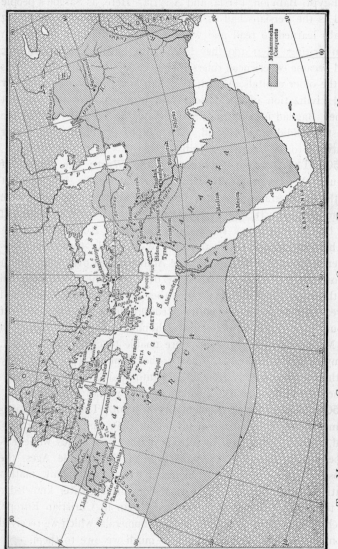

The Mohammedan Conquests at their Greatest Extent, about the Year 750

of Egypt, Babylon, Persia, and Assyria. Here, as Sargon's people and as the Persians had so long before done, the once wandering Arabs learned to read and write and could thus put the Koran into writing. Here too they learned the business of government and became experienced rulers. Thus beside the shapeless mounds of the older capitals, Akkad, Babylon, and Ctesiphon, the power and civilization of the Orient rose into new life for the last time. Bagdad became the finest city of the East and one of the most splendid in the world. The caliphs extended their power eastward to the frontiers of India.

502. The Moslem Advance to the West; the Battle of Tours. Westward the Moslems pushed along the African coast of the Mediterranean, as their Phœnician kindred had done before them (§ 139). It was the Moslem overthrow of Carthage and its bishop which now relieved the bishop of Rome (the Pope) of his only dangerous rival in the West. Only two generations after the death of Mohammed the Arabs crossed over from Africa into Spain (A.D. 711). Here they overthrew the feeble kingdom of the West Goths (§ 455) ; then they moved on into France and threatened to girdle the entire Mediterranean. At the battle of Tours (A.D. 732), however, just a hundred years after the death of Mohammed, the Moslems were unable to crush the Frankish army under their leader, Charles the Hammer (§ 504). They withdrew permanently from France into Spain, where they established a western Moslem kingdom, which we call Moorish.

503. Leadership of Moslem Civilization. The Moorish kingdom developed a civilization far higher than that of the Franks, and, indeed, the highest in Europe of that age. Thus while Europe was sinking into the ignorance of the Middle Ages, the Moslems were the leading students of science, astronomy, mathematics, and grammar. There was soon much greater knowledge of these matters among the Moslems than in Christian Europe. Such Arabic words as *algebra* and our numerals, which we received from the Arabs, suggest to us how much we owe to them.

Some of the buildings which they erected soon after their arrival still stand. Among these is the mosque at Cordova with its forest of columns and arches.[1]   They also erected a great tower at Seville (Fig. 83). This has been copied by the architects of Madison Square Garden in New York. The Mohammedans built beautiful palaces and laid out charming gardens. One of these palaces, the Alhambra, built at Granada some centuries after their arrival in Spain, is a marvel of lovely detail (Fig. 80). They also founded a great university at Cordova, to which Christians from the North sometimes went in search of knowledge.

Historians commonly regard it as a matter of great good luck that Charles the Hammer and his barbarous soldiers succeeded in defeating and driving back the Mohammedans at Tours. But had they been permitted to settle in southern France they might have developed science and art far more rapidly than did the Franks. It is difficult to say whether it was a good thing or a bad thing that the Moors, as the Mohammedans in Spain were called, did not get control of a portion of Gaul.

QUESTIONS

I. What various reasons led men to enter monasteries? When and where did Christian monasteries originate? Give some of the chief provisions of St. Benedict's Rule. Why did the monks sometimes devote part of their time to copying books? Describe the general plan of a monastery.

II. Tell about the conversion of the king of Kent. Did England become a part of the medieval Catholic Church?

III. Give a short account of Mohammed's life. Define *Kaaba, Islam, Koran*. What countries did the Mohammedans conquer during the century following Mohammed's death? Where is Mecca, Bagdad, Damascus, Cordova? Tell what you can of the Moorish buildings in Spain.

[1] The great mosque, which the Mohammedan rulers built at Cordova (Fig. 79) on the site of a Christian church of the West Goths, was second in size only to the Kaaba at Mecca (Fig. 81). It was begun about 785 and gradually enlarged and beautified during the following two centuries, with the hope that it would rival Mecca as a place of pilgrimage. The part represented in the illustration was built by Caliph Al-Hakim, who came to the throne in 961. The beautiful holy of holies (the entrance of which may be seen in the background) is richly adorned with magnificent mosaics. The whole mosque is five hundred and seventy by four hundred and twenty-five feet; that is, about the size of St. Peter's in Rome.

CHAPTER XXIII

CHARLEMAGNE AND HIS EMPIRE

I. Conquests of Charlemagne

504. How Pippin became King of the Franks (752). We have seen how the kings of the Franks, Clovis and his successors, conquered a large territory, including western Germany and what is called France to-day. As time went on, the king's chief minister, who was called the Mayor of the Palace, got almost all the power into his hands and really ruled in the place of the king. Charles the Hammer, who defeated the Mohammedans at Tours in 732 (§ 502), was the Mayor of the Palace of the western Frankish king. His son, Pippin the Short, finally determined to do away altogether with the old line of kings and put himself in their place. Before taking the decisive step, however, he consulted the Pope, who gave his approval. With this sanction from Rome (752) the Frankish counts and dukes, in accordance with the old German ceremony, raised Pippin on their shields, in somewhat the way college boys nowadays carry off a successful football player on their shoulders. He was then anointed king by St. Boniface, the apostle to the Germans, of whom we have spoken, and received the blessing of the Pope.[1]

It would hardly be necessary to mention this change of dynasty in so short a history as this were it not that the calling in of the Pope brought about a revolution in the ideas of kingship. The kings of the German tribes had hitherto usually been successful warriors who held their office with the consent of the people, or at least of the nobles. Their election was not a matter that concerned the Church at all. But when, after asking the Pope's

---

[1] The old line of kings which was displaced by Pippin is known as the Merovingian line. Pippin and his successors are called the Carolingian line.

opinion, Pippin had the holy oil poured on his head,—in accordance with an ancient religious custom of the Jews,—first by Bishop Boniface (§ 497) and later by the Pope, he seemed to ask the Church to approve his usurpation. As the historian Gibbon puts it, "A German chieftain was transformed into the Lord's anointed." The Pope threatened with God's anger anyone who should attempt to supplant the consecrated family of Pippin.

It thus became a *religious* duty to obey the king and his successors. He came to be regarded by the Church, when he had received its approval, as God's representative on earth. Here we have the beginning of the later theory of kings "by the grace of God," against whom it was a sin to revolt, however bad they might be. We shall see presently how Pippin's famous son Charlemagne received his crown from the hands of the Pope.

505. Charlemagne (ca. 742–814). Charlemagne, who became king of all the Frankish realms in 771, is the first historical personage among the German peoples of whom we have any satisfactory knowledge.[1] Compared with him, Theodoric, Clovis, Charles the Hammer, Pippin, and the rest are but shadowy figures.

Charlemagne's looks, as described by his secretary, so exactly correspond with the character of the king as exhibited in his reign that they are worthy of attention. He was tall and stoutly built; his face was round, his eyes were large and keen, his expression bright and cheerful. His voice was clear, but rather weak for his big body. He delighted in riding and hunting and was an expert swimmer. His excellent health and his physical endurance can alone explain the astonishing swiftness with which he moved about his vast realm and conducted innumerable campaigns against his enemies in widely distant regions in rapid succession.

Charlemagne was an educated man for his time, and one who knew how to appreciate and encourage scholarship. While at

[1] "Charlemagne" is the French form for the Latin *Carolus Magnus* (Charles the Great). We must never forget, however, that Charlemagne was not French; he talked a German language, namely Frankish, and his favorite palaces at Aix-la-Chapelle, Ingelheim, and Nimwegen were in German regions.

dinner he had someone read to him; he delighted especially in history. He tried to learn writing, which was an unusual accomplishment at that time for any except churchmen, but began too late in life and got no farther than signing his name. He called learned men to his court and did much toward reëstablishing a regular system of schools.

The impression which his reign made upon men's minds continued to grow even after his death. He became the hero of a whole series of romantic adventures which were as firmly believed for centuries as his real deeds. A study of Charlemagne's reign will make clear that he was truly a remarkable person, one of the greatest figures in the world's records and deservedly the hero of the Middle Ages.

506. Charlemagne's Idea of a Great Christian Empire. It was Charlemagne's ideal to bring all the German peoples together into one great Christian empire, and he was wonderfully successful in attaining his end. Only a small portion of what is now called Germany was included in the kingdom ruled over by Charlemagne's father, Pippin the Short. Frisia and Bavaria had been Christianized, and their rulers had been induced by the efforts of Charlemagne's predecessors and of the missionaries, especially Boniface, to recognize the overlordship of the Franks. Between these two half-independent countries lay the unconquered Saxons. They were as yet pagans and appear still to have clung to much the same institutions as those under which they had lived when the Roman historian Tacitus described them seven centuries earlier.

507. The Conquest of the Saxons. The Saxons occupied the region beginning somewhat east of Cologne and extending to the Elbe, and north to where the great cities of Bremen and Hamburg are now situated. They had no towns or roads and were consequently very difficult to conquer, as they could retreat, with their few possessions, into the forests or swamps as soon as they found themselves unable to meet an invader in the open field. Yet so long as they remained unconquered they constantly threatened the Frankish kingdom, and their country was necessary to the rounding out of its boundaries. Charlemagne never undertook, during his long military career, any other task half so serious as the subjugation of the Saxons, which occupied many years.

Charlemagne believed the Christianizing of the Saxons so important a part of his duty that he decreed that anyone should suffer death who broke into a church and carried off anything by force. No one, under penalty of heavy fines, was to make vows, in the pagan fashion, at trees or springs, or partake of any heathen feasts in honor of the demons (as the Christians termed the heathen gods), or fail to present infants for baptism before they were a year old.

These provisions are characteristic of the theory of the Middle Ages, according to which the government and the Church went hand in hand in ordering and governing the life of the people. Disloyalty to the Church was regarded by the State as quite as serious a crime as treason against itself.

Before the Frankish conquest the Saxons had no towns. Now, around the seat of the bishop, or about a monastery, men began to collect, and towns and cities grew up. Of these the chief was Bremen, which is still one of the most important ports of Germany.

508. Charlemagne King of the Lombards. Summoned by the Pope to protect him from his old enemies the Lombards (§ 465), Charlemagne invaded Lombardy in 773 with a great army and took Pavia, the capital, after a long siege. The Lombard king was forced to become a monk, and his treasure was divided among the Frankish soldiers. Charlemagne then took the extremely important step, in 774, of having himself recognized by all the Lombard dukes and counts as king of the Lombards.

509. Foreign Policy of Charlemagne. So far we have spoken only of the relations of Charlemagne with the Germans, for even the Lombard kingdom was established by the Germans. He had, however, other peoples to deal with, especially the Slavs on the east (who were one day to build up the kingdoms of Poland and Bohemia and the vast Russian empire, which is so important in world politics to-day). On the opposite boundary of his dominion there were the Mohammedan Moors in Spain (§ 503).

Against these it was necessary to protect his realms, and the second part of Charlemagne's reign was devoted to what may be called his foreign policy. A single campaign in 789 seems to have sufficed to subdue the Slavs, who lay to the north and east of the Saxons, and to force the Bohemians to acknowledge the supremacy of the Frankish king and pay tribute to him.

At an assembly that Charlemagne held in 777, ambassadors appeared before him from certain dissatisfied Mohammedans in Spain. They had fallen out with the emir of Cordova[1] and now offered to become the faithful subjects of Charlemagne if he would come to their aid. In consequence of this embassy he undertook his first expedition to Spain in the following year. After some years of war the district north of the Ebro was conquered by the Franks. In this way Charlemagne began that gradual expulsion of the Mohammedans from the peninsula, which was to be carried on by slowly extending conquests until 1492, when Granada, the last Mohammedan stronghold, fell (§ 718).

II. Establishment of a Line of Emperors in the West

510. Charlemagne crowned Emperor by the Pope. But the most famous of all the achievements of Charlemagne was his reëstablishment of the Western Empire in the year 800. It came about in this wise. Charlemagne went to Rome in that year to settle a dispute between Pope Leo III and his enemies. To celebrate the satisfactory settlement of the dispute the Pope held a solemn service on Christmas Day in St. Peter's. As Charlemagne was kneeling before the altar during this service the Pope approached him and set a crown upon his head, saluting him, amid the acclamations of those present, as "Emperor of the Romans."

The reasons for this extraordinary act, which Charlemagne insisted took him completely by surprise, are given in one of the

[1] The Mohammedan caliphate broke up in the eighth century, and the ruler of Spain first assumed the title of emir (about 756) and later (929) that of caliph. The latter title had originally been enjoyed only by the head of the whole Arab empire, who had his capital at Damascus and later at Bagdad.

Frankish histories, the *Chronicles of Lorsch*, as follows : "The name of Emperor had ceased among the Greeks, for they were under the reign of a woman [the Empress Irene], wherefore it seemed good both to Leo, the apostolic pope, and to the bishops who were in council with him, and to all Christian men, that they should name Charles, King of the Franks, as Emperor. For he held Rome itself, where the ancient Cæsars had always dwelt, in addition to all his other possessions in Italy, Gaul, and Germany. Wherefore, as God had granted him all these dominions, it seemed just to all that he should take the title of Emperor, too, when it was offered to him at the wish of all Christendom."

Charlemagne appears to have accepted gracefully the honor thus thrust upon him. Even if he had no right to the imperial title, it was obviously proper and wise to grant it to him under the circumstances. Before his coronation by the Pope he was only king of the Franks and of the Lombards ; but his conquests seemed to give him a right to a higher title which should include all his outlying realms.

511. Continuity of the Roman Empire. The empire thus reëstablished in the West was considered to be a continuation of the Roman Empire founded by Augustus. Charlemagne was reckoned the immediate successor of the emperor at Constantinople, Constantine VI, whom Irene had deposed and blinded. Yet it is hardly necessary to say that the position of the new emperor had little in common with that of Augustus or Constantine. In the first place, the Eastern emperors continued to reign in Constantinople for centuries, quite regardless of Charlemagne and his successors. In the second place, the German kings who wore the imperial crown after Charlemagne were generally too weak really to rule over Germany and northern Italy, to say nothing of the rest of western Europe. Nevertheless, the Western Empire, which in the twelfth century came to be called the Holy Roman Empire, endured for over a thousand years. It came to an end only in 1806, when the last of the emperors, wearied of his empty if venerable title, laid down the crown.

The assumption of the title of emperor was destined to make the German rulers a great deal of trouble. It constantly led them into unsuccessful efforts to keep control over Italy, which really lay outside their natural boundaries. Then the circumstances under which Charlemagne was crowned made it possible for the popes to claim, later, that it was they who had transferred the imperial power from the old eastern line of emperors to Charlemagne and his family, and that this was a proof of their right to dispose of the crown as they pleased. The difficulties which arose necessitated many a weary journey to Rome for the emperors, and many unfortunate conflicts between them and the popes. The long struggles between the German kings and the popes will be described in a later chapter (XXVI).

III. How Charlemagne carried on his Government

512. Difficulty of governing so Large an Empire. The task of governing his vast dominions taxed even the highly gifted and untiring Charlemagne ; it was quite beyond the power of his successors. The same difficulties continued to exist that had confronted Charles the Hammer and Pippin—above all, a scanty royal revenue and overpowerful officials, who were apt to neglect the interests and commands of their sovereign.

Charlemagne's income, like that of all medieval rulers, came chiefly from his royal estates, as there was no system of general taxation such as had existed under the Roman Empire. He consequently took the greatest care that his numerous plantations should be well cultivated, and that not even a turnip or an egg which was due him should be withheld. An elaborate set of regulations for his farms is preserved, which sheds much light upon the times.

513. Origin of Titles of Nobility. The officials upon whom the Frankish kings were forced to rely chiefly were the counts, the "hand and voice of the king" wherever he could not be in person. They were expected to maintain order, see that justice was done in their district, and raise troops when the king needed them. On the frontier were the counts of the "march,"[1] or margraves (marquises). These titles, together with that of duke, still exist as titles of nobility in Europe, although they are no longer associated with any governmental duties except in cases where their holders have the right to sit in the upper House of Parliament.

514. The Dark Century before Charlemagne. Charlemagne was the first important king since Theodoric to pay any attention to book learning. About 650 the supply of papyrus—the kind of paper that the Greeks and Romans used—had been cut off, owing to the conquest of Egypt by the Arabs, and as our kind of paper had not yet been invented, there was only the very expensive parchment to write upon. While this had the advantage of being more durable than papyrus, its high cost discouraged the copying of books. The eighth century—that immediately preceding Charlemagne's coronation—is commonly regarded as the most ignorant, the darkest, and the most barbarous period of the Middle Ages.

Yet, in spite of this dark picture, there was promise for the future. It was evident, even before Charlemagne's time, that Europe was not to continue indefinitely in the path of ignorance. Latin could not be forgotten, for that was the language of the Church, and all its official communications were in that tongue. Consequently it was absolutely necessary that the Church should maintain some sort of education in order that there might be persons who knew enough to write a Latin letter and conduct the church services. Some of those who learned Latin must have used it to read the old books written by the Romans. Then the textbooks of the later Roman Empire (§ 460) continued to be used, and these, poor as they were, contained something about grammar, arithmetic, geometry, astronomy, and other subjects.

515. Establishment of Schools. It seemed to Charlemagne that it was the duty of the Church not only to look after the education of its own officers but to provide the opportunity of at least an elementary education for the people at large. In

---

[1] This word meant territories on the boundaries of the Empire which were open to invasion.

accordance with this conviction he issued (789) an order to the clergy to gather together the children of both freemen and serfs in their neighborhood and establish schools "in which the boys may learn to read."

It would be impossible to say how many of the abbots and bishops established schools in accordance with Charlemagne's recommendations. It is certain that famous centers of learning existed at Tours, Fulda, Corbie, Orleans, and other places during his reign. Charlemagne further promoted the cause of education by the establishment of the famous "School of the Palace" for the instruction of his own children and the sons of his nobles. He placed the Englishman Alcuin at the head of the school and called distinguished men from Italy and elsewhere as teachers.

516. Decline in Education after Charlemagne's Time. The hopeful beginning that was made under Charlemagne in the revival of education was destined to prove disappointing in its immediate results. It is true that the ninth century produced a few noteworthy men who have left works which indicate ability and mental training. But the break-up of Charlemagne's empire, the struggles between his descendants, the coming of new barbarians, and the disorder caused by the unruly feudal lords, who were not inclined to recognize any master, all combined to keep Europe back for at least two centuries more. Indeed, the tenth century and the first half of the eleventh seem, at first sight, little better than the seventh and the eighth. Yet ignorance and disorder never were quite so prevalent after Charlemagne as they were before.

QUESTIONS

I. Explain the importance of the coronation of Pippin. Describe Charlemagne's appearance and character. How did Charlemagne forward the interests of the Church in his efforts to incorporate the Saxons in his empire?

II. What led to Charlemagne's becoming emperor? What modern countries did his empire include?

III. What were the chief sources of Charlemagne's revenue? How did titles of nobility originate in medieval Europe? What did Charlemagne do for education?

CHAPTER XXIV

THE AGE OF DISORDER; FEUDALISM

I. THE DISRUPTION OF CHARLEMAGNE'S EMPIRE

517. Division of Charlemagne's Empire. It was a matter of great importance to Europe whether Charlemagne's extensive empire held together or fell apart after his death in 814. He does not seem to have had any expectation that it would hold together, because some years before his death he arranged that it should be divided among his three sons. But as two of these died before he did, it fell into the hands of the only surviving son, Louis, who succeeded his august father as king of all the various parts of the Frankish domains and was later crowned emperor.

Louis, called "the pious," proved a feeble ruler. He tried all sorts of ways of dividing the Empire peaceably among his rebellious and unruly sons, but he did not succeed, and after his death they, and their sons as well, continued to fight over the question of how much each should have. It is not necessary to speak of the various temporary arrangements that were made. Finally it was agreed in 870, by the Treaty of Mersen, that there should be three states, a West Frankish kingdom, an East Frankish kingdom, and a kingdom of Italy. The West Frankish realm corresponded roughly with the present boundaries of France and Belgium. Its people talked dialects derived from the spoken Latin, which the Romans had introduced after their army, under the command of Julius Cæsar, conquered Gaul (§ 367). The East Frankish kingdom included the rest of Charlemagne's empire outside of Italy and was German in language and customs.

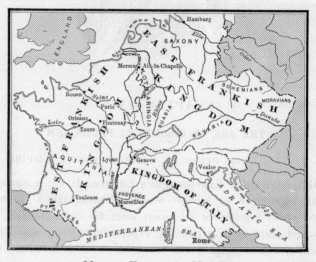

MAP OF TREATY OF MERSEN

This map shows the division of Charlemagne's empire made in 870 by his descendants in the Treaty of Mersen

518. Obstacles to maintaining Order. Each of the three realms established by the Treaty of Mersen was destined finally to grow into one of the powerful modern states which we see on the map of Europe to-day, but hundreds of years elapsed before the kings grew strong enough to control their subjects, and the Treaty of Mersen was followed by several centuries of constant disorder and local warfare. Let us consider the difficulties which stood in the way of peace.

In the first place, a king found it very hard to get rapidly from one part of his realms to another in order to put down rebellions, for the remarkable roads which the Romans had so carefully constructed to enable their armies to move about had fallen into disrepair, and floods had carried away the bridges.

In the East Frankish kingdom matters must have been worse than in the West Frankish realm, for the Romans had never conquered Germany and consequently no good roads had ever been constructed there.

Besides the difficulty of getting about quickly and easily, the king had very little money. This was one of the chief troubles of the Middle Ages. There are not many gold or silver mines in western Europe, and there was no supply of precious metals from outside, for commerce had largely died out. So the king had no treasury from which to pay the many officials which an efficient government finds it necessary to employ to do its business and to keep order. He had to give his officers — the counts, dukes, and margraves (§ 513) — *land* instead of *money*, and their land was so extensive that they tended to become rulers themselves within their own possessions.

519. New Invasions. In addition to the weakness and poverty of the kings there was another trouble, — and that the worst of all, — namely, the constant new invasions from all directions which kept all three parts of Charlemagne's empire, and England besides, in a constant state of terror and disaster. These invasions were almost as bad as those which had occurred before Charlemagne's time; they prevented western Europe from becoming peaceful and prosperous, and serve to explain the dark period of two hundred years which followed the break-up of Charlemagne's empire.

We know how the Mohammedans had got possession of northern Africa and then conquered Spain, and how Charles the Hammer had frustrated their attempt to add Gaul to their possessions (§ 502). But this rebuff did not end their attacks on southern Europe. They got control of the island of Sicily shortly after Charlemagne's death and then began to terrorize Italy and southern France. Even Rome itself suffered from them. The picture on page 342 shows how the people of Arles, in southern France, built their houses inside the old Roman amphitheater in order to protect themselves from these Mohammedan invaders.

On the east the German rulers had constantly to contend with the Slavs. Charlemagne had defeated them in his time, as mentioned above, but they continued to make much trouble for two centuries at least. Then there were also the Hungarians, a

FIG. 84. AMPHITHEATER AT ARLES IN THE MIDDLE AGES

The great Roman amphitheater at Arles (built probably in the first or second century) is about fifteen hundred feet in circumference. During the eighth century, when the Mohammedans were invading southern France, it was converted into a fortress. Many of the inhabitants settled inside its walls, and towers were constructed, which still stand. The picture shows it before the dwellings were removed, about 1830

savage race from Asia, who ravaged Germany and northern Italy and whose wild horsemen penetrated even into the West Frankish kingdom. Finally they were driven back eastward and settled in the country now named after them—Hungary.

520. The Northmen. Lastly there came the Northmen, bold and adventurous pirates from the shores of Denmark, Sweden, and Norway. These skillful and daring seamen not only attacked the towns on the coast of the West Frankish kingdom but made their way up the rivers, plundering and burning the villages and towns as far inland as Paris. In England we shall find them, under the name of Danes, invading the country and forcing Alfred the Great to recognize them as the masters of northern England.[1]

So there was danger always and everywhere. If rival nobles were not fighting one another, there were foreign invaders of some kind devastating the country, bent on robbing, maltreating, and enslaving the people whom they found in towns and villages and monasteries. No wonder that strong castles had to be built and the towns surrounded by walls ; even the monasteries, which were not of course respected by pagan invaders, were in some cases protected by fortifications.

521. Power and Independence of the Great Landowners. In the absence of a powerful king with a well-organized army at his back, each district was left to look out for itself. Doubtless many counts, margraves, bishops, and other great landed proprietors, who were gradually becoming independent princes, earned the loyalty of the people about them by taking the lead in defending the country against its invaders and by establishing fortresses as places of refuge when the community was hard pressed. These conditions serve to explain why such government as continued to exist during the centuries following the death of Charlemagne was necessarily carried on mainly not by the king and his officers but by the great landholders.

II. THE MEDIEVAL CASTLE

522. The Medieval Castle. As one travels through England, France, or Germany to-day he often comes upon the picturesque ruins of a medieval castle perched upon some rocky cliff and overlooking the surrounding country for miles. As he looks at the thick walls, often surrounded by a deep, wide trench once filled with water, and observes the great towers with their tiny windows, he cannot but wonder why so many of these forts were built and why people lived in them.

---

[1] These Scandinavian pirates are often called *vikings*, from their habit of leaving their long boats in the *vik*, which meant, in their language, " bay " or " inlet."

Obviously, whoever lived there was in constant expectation of being attacked by an army, for otherwise he would never have gone to the trouble and expense of shutting himself up in those dreary, cold, stone rooms, behind walls from ten to twenty feet thick. We can picture the great hall of the castle crowded with the armed followers of the master of the house, ready to fight for him when he wished to make war on a neighbor; or if he

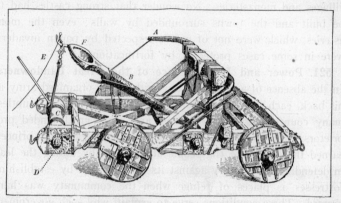

FIG. 85. MACHINE FOR HURLING STONES

This machine was a medieval device for throwing stones and bolts of iron, which were often heated red hot before they were fired. It consisted of a great bow (*A*) and the beam (*B*), which was drawn back by the windlass (*C*) turned by a crank applied at the point (*D*). Then a stone was put in the pocket (*F*) and the trigger pulled by means of the string (*E*). This let the beam fly up with a bang against the bumper, and the missile went sailing against the wall or over it among the defenders of the castle

himself were attacked they would rush to the little windows and shoot arrows at those who tried to approach, or pour lighted pitch or melted lead down on their enemies.

The Romans had been accustomed to build walls around their camps, and a walled camp was called *castra*; and in such names as Rochester, Winchester, Gloucester, Worcester, we have reminders of the fact that these towns were once fortresses. These camps, however, were all *government* fortifications and did not belong to private individuals.

But as the Roman Empire grew weaker and the disorder caused by the incoming barbarians became greater, the various counts and dukes and even other large landowners began to build forts for themselves, usually nothing more than a great round mound of earth surrounded by a deep ditch and a wall made of stakes interwoven with twigs. On the top of the mound was a wooden fortress, surrounded by a fence or palisade similar to the one at the foot of the mound. This was the type of "castle" that prevailed for several centuries after the death of Charlemagne. There are no remains of these wooden castles in existence, for they were not the kind of thing to last very long, and those that escaped being burned or otherwise destroyed rotted away in time.

FIG. 86. TOWER OF BEAUGENCY

This square donjon, not far from Orléans, France, is one of the very earliest square towers that survive. It is a reproduction in stone of the earlier wooden donjons. It was built about 1100, just after the First Crusade began. It is about seventy-six by sixty-six feet in area and one hundred and fifteen feet high

About the year 1100 these wooden buildings began to be replaced by great square stone towers. This was due to the fact that the methods of attacking castles had so changed that wood was no longer a sufficient protection. The Romans when they besieged a walled town were accustomed to hurl great stones and heavy, pointed stakes at the walls and over them. They had ingenious machines for this purpose. But the German barbarians who overran the Roman Empire were unaccustomed to these machines, which therefore had fallen into disuse. They were, however, introduced again from the Eastern Empire about the year 1100, and this is the reason why stone castles began to be built about that time.

A square tower (Fig. 86) can, however, be more easily attacked than a round tower, which has no corners, so a century later round towers became the rule and continued to be used until about the year 1500, when gunpowder and cannon had become so common that even the strongest castle could no longer be defended, for it could not withstand the force of cannon balls. The accompanying pictures (Figs. 87 and 88) give an idea of the stone castles built from about 1100 to 1450 or 1500. In Fig. 85 we can see how a stone-throwing machine, such as was used before the invention of cannon, was constructed and operated.

523. General Arrangement of a Castle. When the castle was not on a steep rocky hill, which made it very hard to approach, a deep ditch was constructed outside the walls, called the *moat*. This was filled with water and crossed by a bridge, which could be drawn up when the castle was attacked, leaving no way of getting across. The doorway was further protected by a grating of heavy planks, called the *portcullis*, which could be quickly dropped down to close the entrance (Fig. 87). Inside the castle walls was the great *donjon*, or chief tower, which had several stories, although one would not suspect it from its plain exterior. There was sometimes also a fine hall, as at Coucy (Fig. 88), and handsome rooms for the use of the lord and his family, but sometimes they lived in the donjon. There were buildings for storing supplies and arms, and usually a chapel.

III. The Serfs and the Manor

524. The Vil, or Manor. Obviously the owner of the castle had to obtain supplies to support his family and servants and armed men. He could not have done this had he not possessed extensive tracts of land. A great part of western Europe in the time of Charlemagne appears to have been divided into great estates or plantations.

These medieval estates were called *vils*, or *manors*, and closely resembled the Roman villas which had existed in former centuries. The peasants who tilled the soil were called *villains*, a word derived from *vil*. A portion of the estate was reserved by the lord for his own use ; the rest of the plowed land was divided among the peasants, usually in long strips, of which each peasant had several scattered about the manor.

525. Condition of the Serfs. The peasants were generally serfs, who did not own their fields, but could not, on the other hand, be deprived of them so long as they worked for the lord and paid him certain dues. They were attached to the land and went with it when it changed hands. The serfs were re-

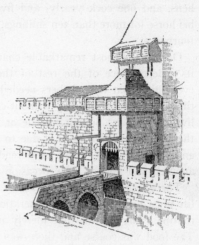

Fig. 87. Fortified Gate of a Medieval Castle

Here one can see the way in which the entrance to a castle was carefully protected: the moat (*A*); the drawbridge (*B*); the portcullis (*C*)

quired to till those fields which the lord reserved for himself and to gather in his crops. They might not marry without their lord's permission. Their wives and daughters helped with the indoor work of the manor house. In the women's buildings the women serfs engaged in spinning, weaving, sewing, baking, and brewing, thus producing clothes, food, and drink for the whole community.

We get our clearest ideas of the position of the serfs from the ancient descriptions of manors, which give an exact account of what each member of a particular community owed to the lord.

For example, we find that the abbot of Peterborough held a manor upon which Hugh Miller and seventeen other serfs, mentioned by name, were required to work for him three days in each week during the whole year, except one week at Christmas, one at Easter, and one at Whitsuntide. Each serf was to give the lord abbot one bushel of wheat and eighteen sheaves of oats, three hens, and one cock yearly, and five eggs at Easter. If he sold his horse for more than ten shillings, he was to give the said abbot fourpence.

One of the most remarkable characteristics of the manor was its independence of the rest of the world. It produced nearly everything that its members needed and might almost have continued to exist indefinitely without communication with those who lived beyond its bounds. Little or no money was necessary, for the peasants paid what was due to the lord in the form of labor and farm products. They also rendered the needful help to one another and found little occasion for buying and selling.

There was almost no opportunity to better one's condition, and life must have gone on for generation after generation in a weary routine. The life was not merely monotonous, it was wretched. The food was coarse and there was little variety, as the peasants did not even take pains to raise fresh vegetables. The houses usually had but one room, which was ill-lighted by a single little window and had no chimney.

526. Barter replaced by Money Transactions. The increased use of money in the twelfth and thirteenth centuries, which came with the awakening trade and industry, tended to break up the manor. The old habit of trading one thing for another without the intervention of money began to disappear. As time went on, neither the lord nor the serf was satisfied with the old system, which had answered well enough in the time of Charlemagne. The serfs, on the one hand, began to obtain money by the sale of their products in the markets of neighboring towns. They soon found it more profitable to pay the lord a certain sum instead of working for him, for they could then turn their whole attention to their own farms.

FIG. 88. COUCY-LE-CHÂTEAU

This castle of Coucy-le-Château was built by a vassal of the king of France in the thirteenth century. It was at the end of a hill and protected on all sides but one by steep cliffs. One can see the moat (*A*) and the double drawbridge and towers which protected the portal. The round donjon (*B*) was probably the largest in the world, one hundred feet in diameter and two hundred and ten feet high. At the base its walls were thirty-four feet thick. At the end of the inner court (*C*) was the residence of the lord (*D*). To the left of the court was a great hall and to the right were the quarters of the garrison. This ancient building was destroyed by the Germans during the recent World War

The landlords, on the other hand, found it to their advantage to accept money in place of the services of their tenants. With this money the landlord could hire laborers to cultivate his fields and could buy the luxuries which were brought to his notice as commerce increased. So it came about that the lords gradually gave up their control over the peasants, and there was no longer very much difference between the serf and the freeman who paid a regular rent for his land. A serf might also gain his liberty by running away from his manor to a town. If he remained undiscovered, or was unclaimed by his lord for a year and a day, he became a freeman.[1]

These manors served to support their lords and left them free to busy themselves fighting with other landowners in the same position as themselves.

IV. FEUDAL SYSTEM

527. Gradual Development of Feudalism. Landholders who had large estates and could spare a portion of them were accustomed to grant some of their manors to another person on condition that the one receiving the land should swear to be true to the giver, should fight for him on certain occasions, and should lend him aid when particular difficulties arose. It was in this way that the relation of *lord* and *vassal* originated. The vassal who received the land pledged himself to be true to his lord, and the lord, on the other hand, not only let his vassal have the land but agreed to protect him when it was necessary. These arrangements between vassals and lords constituted what is called the *feudal system*.

The feudal system, or feudalism, was not established by any decree of a king or in virtue of any general agreement between

[1] The slow extinction of serfdom in western Europe appears to have begun as early as the twelfth century. A very general emancipation had taken place in France by the end of the thirteenth century, though there were still some serfs in France when the Revolution came in 1789. Germany was far more backward in this respect. We find the peasants revolting against their hard lot in Luther's time (1524–1525), and it was not until the middle of the nineteenth century that all vestiges of serfdom disappeared in Prussia.

all the landowners. It grew up gradually and irregularly without any conscious plan on anyone's part, simply because it seemed convenient and natural under the circumstances. The owner of vast estates found it to his advantage to parcel them out among vassals, that is to say, men who agreed to accompany him to war, guard his castle upon occasion, and assist him when he was put to any unusually great expense. Land granted upon the terms mentioned was called a *fief*. One who held a fief might himself become a lord by granting a portion of his fief to a vassal upon terms similar to those upon which he held his lands of his lord, or *suzerain*. The vassal of a vassal was called a *subvassal*.

528. Homage and Fidelity. The one proposing to become a vassal knelt before the lord and rendered him homage[1] by placing his hands between those of the lord and declaring himself the lord's "man" for such and such a fief. Thereupon the lord gave his vassal the kiss of peace and raised him from his kneeling posture. Then the vassal swore an oath of fidelity upon the Bible, or some holy relic, solemnly binding himself to fulfill all his duties toward his lord. This act of rendering homage by placing the hands in those of the lord and taking the oath of fidelity was the first and most essential duty of the vassal (Fig. 89). For a vassal to refuse to do homage for his fief when it changed hands amounted to a declaration of revolt and independence.

529. Feudal Obligations. The obligations of the vassal varied greatly. He was expected to join his lord when there was a military expedition on foot, although it was generally the case that the vassal need not serve at his own expense for more than forty days.

Besides the military service due from the vassal to his lord, he was expected to attend the lord's court when summoned. There he sat with other vassals to hear and pronounce upon those cases in which his fellow vassals were involved.

Under certain circumstances vassals had to make money payments to their lord ; as, for instance, when the lord was put to extra expense by the necessity of knighting his eldest son or

1 " Homage" is derived from the Latin word *homo*, meaning "man."

providing a dowry for his daughter, or when he was captured by an enemy and was held for ransom. Lastly, the vassal might have to entertain his lord should he be passing his castle. There are amusingly detailed accounts in some of the feudal contracts of exactly how often the lord might come, how many followers he might bring, and what he should have to eat.

FIG. 89. CEREMONY OF HOMAGE

This is a modern picture of the way in which the ceremony of homage took place. The new vassal is putting his hands between those of his lord. To the left are retainers in their chain armor, and back of the lord and his lady is the jester, or court fool, whose business it is to amuse his master when he needs entertainment

530. Various Kinds of Fiefs. There were fiefs of all kinds and of all grades of importance, from that of a duke or count, who held directly of the king and exercised the powers of a practically independent prince, down to the holding of the simple knight, whose bit of land, cultivated by peasants or serfs, was barely sufficient to enable him to support himself and provide the horse upon which he rode to perform his military service for his lord.

It is essential to observe that the fief was not granted for a certain number of years, or simply for the life of the grantee, to go back at his death to the owner. On the contrary, it became *hereditary* in the family of the vassal and passed down to the eldest son from one generation to another. So long as the vassal remained faithful to his lord and performed the stipulated services, and his successors did homage and continued to meet the conditions upon which the fief had originally been granted, neither the lord nor his heirs could rightfully regain possession of the land.

The result was that little was left to the original owner of the fief except the services and dues to which the *practical* owner, the vassal, had agreed in receiving it. In short, the fief came really to belong to the vassal, and only the shadow of ownership remained in the hands of the lord. Nowadays the owner of land either makes some use of it himself or leases it for a definite period at a fixed money rent. But in the Middle Ages most of the land was held by those who neither really owned it nor paid a regular rent for it, and yet who could not be deprived of it by the nominal owner or his successors.

531. Subvassals of the King not under his Control. Obviously the great vassals who held directly of the king became almost independent of him as soon as their fiefs were granted to them and their descendants. Their vassals, since they had not done homage to the king himself, often paid little attention to his commands. From the ninth to the thirteenth century the king of France or the king of Germany did not rule over a great realm occupied by subjects who owed him obedience as their lawful sovereign, paid him taxes, and were bound to fight under his banner as the head of the State. As a feudal landlord himself, the king had a right to demand fidelity and certain services from those who were his vassals. But the great mass of the people over whom he nominally ruled, whether they belonged to the nobility or not, owed little to the king directly, because they lived upon the lands of other feudal lords more or less independent of him.

V. Neighborhood Warfare in the Middle Ages

532. War the Law of the Feudal World. One has only to read a chronicle of the time to discover that brute force governed almost everything outside of the Church. The feudal obligations were not fulfilled except when the lord was sufficiently powerful to enforce them. The oath of fidelity was constantly broken, and faith was violated by both vassal and lord.

We may say that war, in all its forms, was the law of the feudal world. War formed the chief occupation of the restless nobles who held the land and were supposed to govern it. An enterprising vassal was likely to make war, first, upon each of the lords to whom he had done homage ; secondly, upon the bishops and abbots with whom he was brought into contact, and whose control he particularly disliked ; thirdly, upon his fellow vassals ; and lastly, upon his own vassals. The feudal bonds, instead of offering a guarantee of peace and concord, appear to have been a constant cause of violent ill-feeling and conflict. Everyone was bent upon profiting to the full by the permanent or temporary weakness of his neighbor.

In theory, the lord could force his vassals to settle their disputes in an orderly manner before his court ; but often he was neither able nor inclined to bring about a peaceful adjustment, and he would frequently have found it hard to enforce the decisions of his own court. So the vassals were left to fight out their quarrels among themselves, and they found their chief interest in life in so doing.

533. Justs and Tourneys. Justs and tourneys were military exercises — play wars — to fill out the tiresome periods which occasionally intervened between real wars. They were, in fact, diminutive battles in which whole troops of hostile nobles sometimes took part. These rough plays called down the condemnation of the popes and even of the kings. The latter, however, were much too fond of the sport themselves not to forget promptly their own prohibitions.

534. The " Truce of God." The horrors of this constant fighting led the Church to try to check it. About the year 1000 several Church councils in southern France decreed that the fighters were not to attack churches or monasteries, churchmen, pilgrims, merchants, and women, and that they must leave the peasant and his cattle and plow alone. Then Church councils began to issue what was known as the " Truce of God," which provided that all warfare was to stop during Lent and various other holy days as well as on Thursday, Friday, Saturday, and Sunday of every week. During the truce no one was to attack anyone else. Those besieging castles were to refrain from any assaults during the period of peace, and people were to be allowed to go quietly to and fro on their business without being disturbed by soldiers.

If anyone failed to observe the truce, he was to be excommunicated by the Church — if he fell sick no Christian should dare to visit him, and on his deathbed he was not to receive the comfort of a priest, and his soul was consigned to hell if he had refused to repent and mend his ways. It is hard to say how much good the Truce of God accomplished. Some of the bishops and even the heads of great monasteries liked fighting pretty well themselves. It is certain that many disorderly lords paid little attention to the truce and found three days a week altogether too short a time for plaguing their neighbors.

535. The Kings finally get the Better of the Feudal Lords. Yet we must not infer that the State ceased to exist altogether during the centuries of confusion that followed the break-up of Charlemagne's empire, or that it fell entirely apart into little local governments independent of each other. In the first place, a king always retained some of his ancient majesty. He might be weak and without the means to enforce his rights and to compel his more powerful subjects to meet their obligations toward him. Yet he was, after all, the *king*, solemnly anointed by the Church as God's representative on earth. He was always something more than a feudal lord. The kings were destined to get the upper hand before many centuries in England, France, and Spain, and finally in Italy and Germany, and to destroy the castles behind whose walls their haughty nobles had long defied the royal power.

QUESTIONS

I. What led to the breaking up of Charlemagne's empire ? What is the importance of the Treaty of Mersen ? What were the chief obstacles that prevented a king in the early Middle Ages from really controlling an extensive realm ? What invasions occurred in western Europe after Charlemagne's time ? Tell what you can of the Northmen.

II. Describe the changes that took place during the Middle Ages in the method of constructing castles. Describe the arrangement of a castle.

III. What was a manor, and what Roman institution did it resemble ? What was a serf ? What were the chief services that a serf owed to his master? What effect did the increased use of money have upon serfdom?

IV. Define "lord," "vassal," "fief," "homage," "feudalism." What services did a vassal owe to his lord? What effects did feudalism have upon the power of the kings?

V. What is meant by neighborhood warfare? Why was it very common in the Middle Ages? What was the Truce of God?

NOTE. This castle of Pierrefonds, not very far from Paris, was built by the brother of the king of France, about 1400. It has been very carefully restored in modern times and gives one a good idea of the way in which the feudal lords of that period lived. Within the walls are a handsome central courtyard and magnificent apartments.

CHAPTER XXV

ENGLAND IN THE MIDDLE AGES

I. The Norman Conquest

536. Importance of England in the History of Western Europe. The country of western Europe whose history is of greatest interest to English-speaking peoples is, of course, England. From England the United States and the vast English colonies have inherited their language and habits of thought, much of their literature, and many of their laws and institutions. In this volume it will not, however, be possible to study England except in so far as it has played a part in the general development of Europe. This it has greatly influenced by its commerce and industry and colonies, as well as by the example it was the first to set in modern times of permitting the people to share with the king in the government.

The conquest of the island of Britain by the Angles and Saxons has already been spoken of, as well as the conversion of these pagans to Christianity by Augustine and his monks (§§ 494–496). The several kingdoms founded by the invaders were brought under the overlordship of the southern kingdom of Wessex by Egbert, a contemporary of Charlemagne.

537. The Danes and Alfred the Great (871–901). But no sooner had the long-continued invasions of the Angles and Saxons come to an end and the country been partially unified than the Northmen (or Danes, as the English called them), who were ravaging France (§ 520), began to make incursions into England. Before long they had conquered a large district north of the Thames and were making permanent settlements. They were defeated, however, in a great battle by Alfred the Great, the first English king of whom we have any satisfactory knowledge. He forced the Danes to accept Christianity and established, as the

boundary between their settlements and his own kingdom of
Wessex, a line running from London across the island to Chester.

**538. England from Alfred to the Norman Conquest
(901-1066).** But more Danes kept coming, and the Danish invasions continued for more than a century after Alfred's death
(901). Sometimes they were bought off by a money payment
called the *Danegeld*, which was levied on the people of England
like any other tax. But finally a Danish king (Cnut) succeeded
in making himself king of England in 1017. This Danish dynasty
maintained itself, however, for only a few years. Then a last
weak Saxon king, Edward the Confessor, reigned for twenty years.

Upon his death one of the greatest events in all English history
occurred. The most powerful of the vassals of the king of France
crossed the English Channel, conquered England, and made himself king. This was William, Duke of Normandy.

539. France in the Middle Ages. We have seen how Charlemagne's empire broke up, and how the feudal lords became so
powerful that it was difficult for the king to control them. The
West Frankish kingdom, which we shall hereafter call France,
was divided among a great many dukes and counts, who built
strong castles, gathered armies and fought against one another,
and were the terror alike of priest, merchant, and laborer. (See
above, §§ 517-521 and 532-534.)

In the tenth century certain great fiefs, like Normandy, Brittany, Flanders, and Burgundy, developed into little nations, each
under its line of able rulers. Each had its own particular customs
and culture, some traces of which may still be noted by the
traveler in France. These little feudal states were created by
certain families of nobles who possessed exceptional energy or
statesmanship. By conquest, purchase, or marriage they increased
the number of their fiefs, and they insured their control over their
vassals by promptly destroying the castles of those who refused
to meet their obligations.

540. Normandy. Of these subnations none was more important or interesting than Normandy. The Northmen had been the
scourge of those who lived near the North Sea for many years

SCENES FROM THE BAYEUX TAPESTRY

In the Norman town of Bayeux a strip of embroidery is preserved, some two hundred and thirty feet long and eighteen inches wide. It dates from the time of the Norman Conquest. Of the two scenes here given the upper one shows the Normans landing with their horses on the shores of England and starting for the battle of Hastings. The lower scene shows the battle itself, with the English on their hill trying to drive back the invaders. While the ladies who did the work could not draw very well, historians are able to get some ideas of the period from the pictures

before one of their leaders, Rollo (or Hrolf), agreed in 911 to accept from the West Frankish king a district on the coast, north of Brittany, where he and his followers might peacefully settle. Rollo assumed the title of Duke of the Normans and introduced the Christian religion among his people. For a considerable time the newcomers kept up their Scandinavian habits and language. Gradually, however, they appropriated such culture as their neighbors possessed, and by the twelfth century their capital, Rouen, was one of the most enlightened cities of Europe. Normandy became a source of infinite perplexity to the French kings when, in 1066, Duke William added England to his possessions and the title of "the Conqueror" to his name; for he thereby became so powerful that his overlord, the king of France, could hardly hope to control the Norman dukes any longer.

541. William lays Claim to England. William of Normandy claimed that he was entitled to the English crown, but we are somewhat in the dark as to the basis of his claim. There is a story that he had visited the court of Edward the Confessor and had become his vassal on condition that, should Edward die childless, he was to declare William his successor. However this may be, Harold of Wessex assumed the crown upon Edward's death and paid no attention to William's demand that he should surrender it.

William thereupon appealed to the Pope, promising that if he came into possession of England he would see that the English clergy submitted to the authority of the Roman bishop. Consequently the Pope, Alexander II, condemned Harold and blessed in advance any expedition that William might undertake to secure his rights. The conquest of England therefore took on the character of a sort of holy war, and as the expedition had been well advertised, many adventurers flocked to William's standard. During the spring and summer of 1066 ships were building in the various Norman harbors for the purpose of carrying William's army across the Channel.

542. Battle of Hastings (October, 1066). The English occupied the hill of Senlac, west of Hastings, and awaited the

FIG. 90. ABBAYE-AUX-DAMES, CAEN

William the Conqueror married a lady, Matilda, who was remotely related to him. This was against the rules of the Church, and he took pains to get the Pope's sanction to his marriage. But he and his queen were afraid that they might have committed a sin in marrying, so William built a monastery for men and Matilda a nunnery for women as a penance. The churches of these monasteries still stand in the Norman city of Caen. William was buried in his church. The picture represents the interior of Matilda's church and is a good example of what the English called the Norman style of architecture

coming of the enemy. They had few horses and fought on foot with their battle-axes. The Normans had horses, which they had brought across in their ships, and were supplied with bows and arrows. The English fought bravely and repulsed the Normans as they tried to press up the hillside. But at last the English were thrown into confusion, and King Harold was killed by a Norman arrow which pierced his eye.

William thus destroyed the English army in this famous battle of Hastings, and the rightful English king was dead. But the Norman duke was not satisfied to take possession of England as a conqueror merely. In a few weeks he managed to induce a number of influential nobles and several bishops to agree to accept him as king, and London opened its gates to him. On Christmas Day, 1066, he was chosen king by an assembly in Westminster Abbey and duly crowned.

543. William's Policy in England. William introduced the Norman feudalism to which he was accustomed, but took good care that it should not weaken his power. The English who had refused to join him before the battle of Hastings were declared to have forfeited their lands, but were permitted to keep them upon condition of receiving them back from the new king as his vassals. The lands of those who actually fought against him at Hastings, or in later rebellions, including the great estates of Harold's family, were seized and distributed among his faithful followers, both Norman and English, though naturally the Normans among them far outnumbered the English.

William declared that he did not propose to change the English customs but to govern as Edward the Confessor, the last Saxon king, had done. He maintained the Witenagemot, a council made up of bishops and nobles, whose advice the Saxon kings had sought in all important matters. But he was a man of too much force to submit to the control of his people. He avoided giving to any one person a great many estates in a single region, so that no one should become inconveniently powerful. Finally, in order to secure the support of the smaller landholders and to prevent combinations against him among the greater ones, he required every landowner in England to take an oath of fidelity *directly* to him, instead of having only a few great landowners as vassals who had their own subvassals under their own control, as in France (§ 531).

544. General Results of the Norman Conquest. It is clear that the Norman Conquest was not a simple change of kings, but that a new element was added to the English people. We cannot tell how many Normans actually emigrated across the Channel, but they evidently came in considerable numbers, and their influence upon the English habits and government was very great. A century after William's conquest the whole body of the nobility, the bishops, abbots, and government officials, had become practically all Norman. Besides these, the architects who built the castles and fortresses, the cathedrals and abbeys, came from Normandy. Merchants from the Norman cities of Rouen and

Caen settled in London and other English cities, and weavers from Flanders in various towns and even in the country. For a short time these newcomers remained a separate people, but by the year 1200 they had become for the most part indistinguishable from the great mass of English people amongst whom they had come. They had nevertheless made the people of England more energetic, active-minded, and varied in their occupations and interests than they had been before the conquest.

II. HENRY II AND THE PLANTAGENETS

545. Civil War ending in the Accession of Henry II (1154-1189). William the Conqueror was followed by his sons. Upon the death of these the country went through a terrible period of civil war, for some of the nobility supported the Conqueror's grandson Stephen, and some his granddaughter Matilda. After the death of Stephen, when Henry II, Matilda's son,[1] was finally recognized in 1154 by all as king, he found the kingdom in a melancholy state. The nobles had taken advantage of the prevalent disorder to erect castles without royal permission and to establish themselves as independent rulers, and many disorderly hired soldiers had been brought over from the Continent to support the rivals for the throne.

546. Henry II. Henry II at once adopted vigorous measures. He destroyed the illegally erected fortresses, sent off the foreign soldiers, and deprived many earls who had been created by Stephen and Matilda of their titles. Henry's task was a difficult one. He had need of all his tireless energy and quickness of mind to restore order in England and at the same time rule the wide realms on the Continent which he had either inherited or gained through his marriage with a French heiress.

In order to avoid all excuse for the private warfare which was such a persistent evil on the Continent, he undertook to improve and reform the law courts. He arranged that his judges should make regular circuits throughout the country, so that they might

[1] See genealogical table below, p. 365.

try cases on the spot at least once a year. We find, too, the beginning of our grand jury in a body of men in each neighborhood who were to be duly sworn in, from time to time, and should then bring accusations against such malefactors as had come to their knowledge.

547. Trial by Jury. As for the "petty," or smaller, jury of twelve, which actually tried the accused, its origin and history are obscure. The juries of Henry II left the verdict for Heaven to pronounce in the ordeal ; but a century later we find the jury of twelve itself rendering verdicts. The plan of delegating to twelve men the duty of deciding on the guilt or innocence of a suspected person was very different from the earlier systems. It resembled neither the Roman trial, where the judges made the decision, nor the medieval compurgation and ordeals (§ 472). The decisions of Henry's judges were mainly drawn from old English custom,

FIG. 91. NORMAN GATEWAY AT BRISTOL, ENGLAND

This beautiful gateway was originally the entrance to a monastery, begun in 1142. It is one of the finest examples of the Norman style of building to be seen in England

instead of from Roman law as in France, and they became the basis of the *common law* which is still used in all English-speaking countries.

548. Thomas Becket and Henry II. Henry's reign was embittered by the famous struggle with Thomas Becket, which illustrates admirably the peculiar dependence of the monarchs of his day upon the churchmen. Becket was born in London and became a churchman, but he grew up in the service of the king and

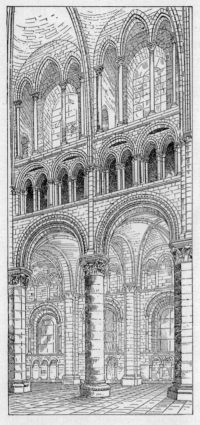

FIG. 92. CHOIR OF CANTERBURY
CATHEDRAL

The choir of Canterbury Cathedral was
destroyed by fire four years after Thomas
Becket was murdered there. The picture
shows how it was rebuilt under Henry II
during the years 1175–1184. The picture
shows a very important change that was
taking place in architecture. The two lower
rows of arches are the round kind that
had been used up to that time, while the
upper row shows how the pointed arch
was coming in (see below, §§ 656–658)

was able to aid Henry in
gaining the throne. It appeared to Henry that there
could be no better head for
the English clergy than this
loyal Becket ; he therefore
determined to make him
Archbishop of Canterbury.

In securing the election of
Becket as Archbishop of
Canterbury, Henry intended
to insure his own complete
control of the Church. He
proposed to punish churchmen who committed crimes,
like other offenders, to make
the bishops meet all the
feudal obligations, and to
prevent appeals to the Pope.
Becket, however, immedi-
ately gave up the gay life
he had previously led, and
opposed every effort of the
king to reduce the independence of the Church. After
a haughty assertion of the
supremacy of the Church
over the king's government
(see below, §§ 592–593),
Thomas fled from the wrath-
ful and disappointed mon-
arch to France and the
protection of the Pope.

In spite of a patched-
up reconciliation with the
king, Becket proceeded to

excommunicate some of the great English prelates and, as Henry believed, was conspiring to rob his son of the crown. In a fit of anger Henry exclaimed among his followers, "Is there no one to avenge me of this miserable churchman?" Unfortunately certain knights took the rash expression literally, and Becket was murdered in his own cathedral of Canterbury, whither he had returned. The king really had no wish to resort to violence, and his sorrow and remorse when he heard of the dreadful deed, and his terror at the consequences, were most genuine. The Pope proposed to excommunicate him. Henry, however, made peace with the papal legates by the solemn assertion that he had never wished the death of Thomas and by promising to return to Canterbury all the property which he had confiscated, to send money to aid in the capture of the Holy Sepulcher at Jerusalem, and to undertake a crusade himself.

549. The French Possessions of the Plantagenets. Although Henry II was one of the most important kings in English history, he spent a great part of his time across the Channel in his French possessions. A glance at the accompanying map will show that rather more than half of his realms lay to the south of the English Channel. He controlled more territory in France than the French king himself. As great-grandson of William the Conqueror[1] he inherited the duchy of Normandy and the suzerainty

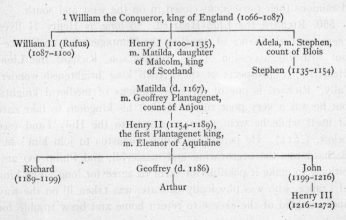

[1] William the Conqueror, king of England (1066–1087)

William II (Rufus) (1087–1100)

Henry I (1100–1135), m. Matilda, daughter of Malcolm, king of Scotland

Adela, m. Stephen, count of Blois

Stephen (1135–1154)

Matilda (d. 1167), m. Geoffrey Plantagenet, count of Anjou

Henry II (1154–1189), the first Plantagenet king, m. Eleanor of Aquitaine

Richard (1189–1199)

Geoffrey (d. 1186)

Arthur

John (1199–1216)

Henry III (1216–1272)

over Brittany. His mother, Matilda, had married the count of Anjou and Maine, so that Henry II inherited these fiefs along with those which had belonged to William the Conqueror. Lastly, he had himself married Eleanor, heiress of the dukes of Guienne, and in this way doubled the extent of his French lands. Henry II and his successors are known as the "Plantagenets," owing to the habit that his father, the count of Anjou, had of wearing a bit of broom (Latin *planta genista*) in his helmet.

So it came about that the French kings beheld a new State, under an able and energetic ruler, developing within their borders and including more than half the territory over which they were supposed to rule. A few years before Henry II died, an ambitious monarch, Philip Augustus, ascended the French throne and made it the chief business of his life to get control of his feudal vassals, above all, the Plantagenets.

Henry divided his French possessions among his three sons, Richard, Geoffrey, and John; but father and sons were engaged in constant disputes with one another, as none of them were easy people to get along with. Philip Augustus took advantage of these constant quarrels of the brothers among themselves and with their father. These quarrels were most fortunate for the French king, for had the Plantagenets held together they might have annihilated the royal house of France, whose narrow dominions their possessions closed in on the west and south.

550. Richard the Lion-Hearted. So long as Henry II lived there was little chance of expelling the Plantagenets from France; but with the accession of his reckless son, Richard the Lion-Hearted, the prospects of the French king brightened wonderfully. Richard is one of the most famous of medieval knights, but he was a very poor ruler. He left his kingdom to take care of itself while he went upon a crusade to the Holy Land (see below, § 611). He persuaded Philip Augustus to join him; but Richard was too overbearing and masterful, and Philip too ambitious, to make it possible for them to agree for long. The king of France, who was physically delicate, was taken ill on the way and was glad of the excuse to return home and brew trouble for

Map labels (reading across the image):

Legend
- Domain of the French King
- Fiefs held by other vassals than Henry II

0   50   100   200
Scale of Miles

R.Dee
R.Esk
Stirling   R.Forth
Edinburgh
R.Tweed
Newcastle
Solway Firth   Durham
ULSTER
Armagh
CONNAUGHT
York
R.Humber
The Wash
Dublin   Anglesey
Chester
LEINSTER   R.Dee
R.Shannon
Limerick
MUNSTER   Wexford
Waterford
Leicester
Oxford
London
R.Thames
Bristol   Runnymede   Canterbury
R.Severn   Clarendon   Dover   Calais
Salisbury   Hastings
Milford   Southampton   Winchester
Exeter

NORTH   SEA

Irish Channel

English Channel

Cherbourg   Havre   Rouen
Caen   Eves
Brest   Verdun
NORMANDY   PARIS
BRITTANY   R.Marne
Rennes   MAINE   CHAMPAGNE
Le Mans   Troyes
ANJOU   Blois
Angers   Orleans   BURGUNDY
Nantes   Tours   Berry
R.Loire   Fontevrault   R.Saone
Chinon
POITOU   Lyons   R.Rhone
MARCHE   R.Isere
Limoges   AUVERGNE
R.Garonne   AQUITAINE
(GUIENNE)   Avignon
Bordeaux   Arles   Provence
GASCONY   R.Rhone   Marseille
R.Adour   Toulouse
LANGUEDOC

BAY   OF   BISCAY

THE EMPIRE
Flanders
Bruges
Boulogne

M.-R. ENG., BUFFALO.

THE PLANTAGENET POSSESSIONS IN ENGLAND AND FRANCE

his powerful vassal. When Richard himself returned, after several years of romantic but fruitless adventure, he found himself involved in a war with Philip Augustus, in the midst of which he died.

551. John loses the French Possessions of his House. Richard's younger brother John, who enjoys the reputation of being the most despicable of English kings, speedily gave Philip a good excuse for seizing a great part of the Plantagenet lands. John was suspected of conniving at the brutal murder of his nephew Arthur (the son of Geoffrey [1]). He was also guilty of the less serious offense of carrying off and marrying a lady betrothed to one of his own vassals. Philip Augustus, as John's suzerain, summoned him to appear at the French court to answer the latter charge. Upon John's refusal to appear or to do homage for his continental possessions, Philip caused his court to issue a decree confiscating almost all of the Plantagenet lands, leaving to the English king only the southwest corner of France.

Philip found little difficulty in possessing himself of Normandy itself, which showed no reluctance to accept him in place of the Plantagenets. Six years after Richard's death the English kings had lost all their continental fiefs except Guienne. It should be observed that Philip, unlike his ancestors, was no longer merely *suzerain* of the new conquests, but was himself duke of Normandy and count of Anjou, of Maine, etc. The boundaries of his domain — that is, the lands which he himself controlled directly as feudal lord — now extended to the sea.

St. Louis, Philip's successor, arranged with John's successor in 1258 that the English king should do him homage for Guienne, Gascony, and Poitou, and should surrender every claim on all the rest of the former possessions of the Plantagenets. So it came about that the English kings continued to hold a portion of France for several hundred years.

552. John of England becomes a Vassal of the Pope. John not only lost Normandy and other territories which had belonged

---

[1] Geoffrey, John's next older brother, who would naturally have succeeded Richard, died in 1186.

to the earlier Norman kings but he actually consented to become the Pope's vassal, receive England as a fief from the papacy, and pay tribute to Rome. This strange proceeding came about in this wise : The monks of Canterbury had (1205) ventured to choose an archbishop — who was at the same time their abbot (§ 496) — without consulting King John. Their appointee hastened off to Rome to gain the Pope's confirmation, while the irritated John forced the monks to hold another election and make his treasurer archbishop. The Pope at that time was no less a person than Innocent III, one of the greatest of medieval rulers. Innocent rejected both the men who had been elected, sent for a new deputation of monks from Canterbury, and bade them choose Stephen Langton, a man of great ability. John then angrily drove the monks of Canterbury out of the kingdom.

Innocent replied by placing England under the *interdict* ; that is to say, he ordered the clergy to close all the churches and suspend all public services — a very terrible thing to the people of the time. John was excommunicated, and the Pope threatened that unless the king submitted to his wishes he would depose him and give his crown to Philip Augustus of France. As Philip made haste to collect an army for the conquest of England, John humbly submitted to the Pope in 1213. He went so far as to hand England over to Innocent III and receive it back as a fief, thus becoming the vassal of the Pope. He agreed also to send a yearly tribute to Rome.

III. The Great Charter and the Beginnings of Parliament

553. The Granting of the Great Charter (1215). We must now turn to another very important event in John's reign — the drawing up of the Great Charter of English liberties.

When, in 1213, John proposed to lead his English vassals across the water in order to attempt to reconquer his lost possessions in France, they refused to accompany him on the ground that their feudal obligations did not bind them to fight outside of their country. Moreover, they showed a lively discontent with John's tyranny and his neglect of those limits of the kingly power which several of the earlier Norman kings had solemnly recognized. In 1214 a number of the barons met and took a solemn oath that they would compel the king, by arms if necessary, to sign a charter containing the things which, according to English traditions, a king might *not* do. As John would not agree to do this, it proved necessary to get together an army and march against him. The insurgent nobles met him at Runnymede, not far from London. Here on the 15th of June, 1215, they forced him to swear to observe what they believed to be the rights of his subjects, which they had carefully written out.

554. Provisions of the Charter. The Great Charter is perhaps the most famous document in the history of government. The nobles who concluded this great treaty with a tyrannous ruler saw that it was to their interest to have the rights of the churchmen and of the small class of other freemen safeguarded as well as their own. The king promises to observe the rights of his vassals, and the vassals in turn agree to observe the rights of their vassals. The towns are not to be oppressed. The merchant is not to be deprived of his goods for small offenses, nor the farmer of his wagon and implements. The king is to impose no tax, besides the three feudal aids,[1] except with the consent of the Great Council of the nation. This was to include the prelates and greater barons and all the king's vassals.

There is no more notable clause in the Charter than that which provides that no *freeman* is to be arrested, or imprisoned, or deprived of his property, unless he be immediately sent before a court of his peers for trial. To realize the importance of this we must recollect that in France, down to 1789,—nearly six hundred years later,—the king exercised such unlimited powers that he could order the arrest of anyone he pleased and could imprison him for any length of time without bringing him to

---

[1] These three regular feudal dues were payments made when the lord knighted his eldest son, gave his eldest daughter in marriage, or had been captured and was waiting to be ransomed.

trial or even informing him of the nature of his offense. The Great Charter provided further that the king should permit merchants to move about freely and should observe the privileges of the various towns; nor were his officers longer to be allowed to exercise despotic powers over those under them.

It must be remembered, however, that the barons, who forced the Charter on the king, had their own interests especially in mind. The nobles, churchmen, merchants, and other freemen made up only about a sixth of the population, and the Charter had little or nothing to say of serfs or villains who formed the great mass of the English people at that time. They could still be victimized as before by their masters, the lords of the manor. But in later centuries, when the serfs had become free, the Charter could be appealed to in support of the commons in general against attempts of the ruler to oppress them.

555. Permanent Value of the Charter. In spite of his solemn confirmation of the Charter, John, with his accustomed treachery, made an unsuccessful effort to break his promises in the Charter; but neither he nor his successors ever succeeded in getting rid of the document. Later there were times when the English kings evaded its provisions and tried to rule as absolute monarchs. But the people always sooner or later bethought them of the Charter, which thus continued to form a barrier against permanent despotism in England.

556. Origin of the English Parliament. During the long reign of John's son, Henry III, Parliament began to grow up, an institution which has not only played a most important rôle in English history but has also served as the model for similar bodies in almost every civilized state in the world.

The Great Council of the Norman kings, like the older Witenagemot of Saxon times, was a meeting of nobles, bishops, and abbots, which the king summoned from time to time to give him advice and aid and to sanction important undertakings. During Henry III's reign its meetings became more frequent and its discussions more vigorous than before, and the name *Parliament* began to be applied to it.

In 1265 a famous Parliament was held, where a most important new class of members—the *commons*—were present, who were destined to give it its future greatness. In addition to the nobles and prelates, two simple knights were summoned from each county and two citizens from each of the more flourishing towns to attend and take part in the discussions.

Edward I (son of Henry III) definitely adopted this innovation. He doubtless called in the representatives of the towns because the townspeople were becoming rich and he wished to have an opportunity to ask them to make grants of money to meet the expenses of the government. He also wished to obtain the approval of all the upper classes when he determined upon important measures affecting the whole realm. Ever since the so-called " Model Parliament " of 1295 the commons, or representatives of the " freemen," have always been included along with the clergy and nobility when the national assembly of England has been summoned.

557. Growth of the Powers of Parliament. The Parliament early took the stand that the king must agree to "redress of grievances" before it would grant him any money. This meant that the king had to promise to remedy any acts of himself or his officials of which Parliament complained before it would agree to let him raise the taxes. Instead of following the king about and meeting wherever he might happen to be, the Parliament from the time of Edward I began to hold its sessions in the city of Westminster, now a part of London, where it still continues to meet.

Under Edward's successor, Edward II, Parliament solemnly declared in 1322 that important matters relating to the king and his heirs, the state of the realm and of the people, should be considered and determined upon by the king "with the assent of the prelates, earls and barons, and the commonalty [that is, commons] of the realm." Five years later Parliament showed its power by deposing the inefficient king, Edward II, and declaring his son, Edward III, the rightful ruler of England.

The new king, who was carrying on an expensive war with France, needed much money and consequently summoned Parliament every year, and, in order to encourage its members to grant him money, he gratified Parliament by asking its advice and listening to its petitions. He passed no new law without adding "by and with the advice and consent of the lords spiritual and temporal and of the commons."

558. House of Lords and House of Commons. At this time the separation of the two houses of Parliament took place, and ever since the "lords spiritual and temporal"—that is, the bishops and higher nobles—have sat by themselves in the House of Lords ; and the members of the House of Commons, including the country gentlemen (knights) and the representatives elected by the more important towns, have met by themselves. Parliament thus made up is really a modern, not a medieval, institution, and we shall hear much of it later.

IV. WALES AND SCOTLAND

559. Extent of the King of England's Realms before Edward I (1272–1307). The English kings who preceded Edward I had ruled over only a portion of the island of Great Britain. To the west of their kingdom lay the mountainous district of Wales, inhabited by that remnant of the original Britons which the Angles and Saxons had been unable to conquer (§ 495). To the north of England was the kingdom of Scotland, which was quite independent, except for an occasional recognition by the Scotch kings of the English kings as their feudal superiors. Edward I, however, succeeded in conquering Wales permanently and Scotland temporarily.

560. Edward I conquers Wales. For centuries a border warfare had been carried on between the English and the Welsh. When Edward I came to the throne he demanded that Llewellyn, Prince of Wales (as the head of the Welsh clans was called), should do him homage. Llewellyn, who was a man of ability and energy, refused the king's summons, and Edward marched into Wales. Two campaigns were necessary before the Welsh finally succumbed. Llewellyn was killed (1282), and with him expired the independence of the Welsh people. Edward divided the country into shires and introduced English laws and customs, but his policy of conciliation was so successful that there was but a single rising in the country for a whole century. He later presented his son to the Welsh as their prince, and from that time down to the present the title of " Prince of Wales" has usually been conferred upon the heir to the English throne.

561. Edward intervenes in Scotch Affairs. The conquest of Scotland proved a far more difficult matter than that of Wales. When the Angles and Saxons conquered Britain some of them wandered north as far as the Firth of Forth and occupied the so-called Lowlands of Scotland. The mountainous region to the north, known as the Highlands, continued to be held by wild tribes related to the Welsh and Irish and talking a language similar to theirs, namely, Gaelic. There was constant warfare between the older inhabitants themselves and between them and the newcomers from Germany, but both Highlands and Lowlands were finally united under a line of Scotch kings, who moved their residence down to Edinburgh, which, with its fortress, became their chief town.

It was natural that the language of the Scotch Lowlands should be English, but in the mountains the Highlanders to this day continue to talk the ancient Gaelic of their forefathers.

It was not until the time of Edward I that the long series of troubles between England and Scotland began. The dying out of the old line of Scotch kings in 1290 was followed by the appearance of a number of claimants to the crown. In order to avoid civil war Edward was asked to decide who should be king. He agreed to make the decision on condition that the one whom he selected should hold Scotland as a *fief* from the English king. This arrangement was adopted, and the crown was given to John Baliol. But Edward unwisely made demands upon the Scots which aroused their anger, and their king renounced his homage to the king of England. The Scotch, moreover, formed an alliance with Edward's enemy, Philip the Fair of France ; thenceforth, in all the difficulties between England and France, the English kings had always to reckon with the disaffected Scotch, who were glad to aid England's enemies on the other side of the English Channel.

562. Edward attempts to incorporate Scotland with England. Edward marched in person against the Scotch (1296) and speedily put down what he regarded as a rebellion. He declared that Baliol had forfeited his fief through treason, and that consequently the English king had become the real ruler of Scotland. He emphasized his claim by carrying off the famous Stone

FIG. 93. CONWAY CASTLE

Edward built this fine castle in 1284 on the north coast of Wales to keep the Welsh in check. Its walls are twelve to fifteen feet in thickness. There were buildings inside, including a great banqueting hall one hundred and thirty feet long

of Scone (now in Westminster Abbey), upon which the kings of Scotland had been crowned for ages. Continued resistance led Edward to attempt to incorporate Scotland with England in the same way that he had treated Wales. This was the beginning of three hundred years of intermittent war between England and Scotland, which ended only when a Scotch king, James VI, succeeded to the English throne in 1603 as James I.

That Scotland was able to maintain her independence was mainly due to Robert Bruce, a national hero who succeeded in bringing both the nobility and the people under his leadership. Edward I died, old and worn out, in 1307, when on his way north to put down a rising under Bruce, and left the task of dealing with the Scotch to his incompetent son, Edward II. The Scotch acknowledged Bruce as their king and decisively defeated Edward II in the great battle of Bannockburn (1314), the most famous conflict in Scottish history. Nevertheless, the English refused to acknowledge the independence of Scotland until forced to do so in 1328.

563. The Scotch Nation differs from the English. In the course of their struggles with England the Scotch people of the Lowlands had become more closely welded together, and the independence of Scotland, although it caused much bloodshed, first and last, served to develop certain permanent differences between the little Scotch nation and the rest of the English race. No Scotchman to the present day likes to be mistaken for an Englishman. The peculiarities of the language and habits of the people north of the Tweed have been made familiar to all readers of good literature by the novels of Sir Walter Scott and Robert L. Stevenson and by the poems of Robert Burns.

V. The Hundred Years' War

564. Edward III claims the French Crown. England and France were both becoming strong states in the early fourteenth century. The king in both of these countries had got the better of the feudal lords, and a parliament had been established in France as well as in England, in which the townspeople as well as the clergy and nobility were represented. But both countries were set back by a long series of conflicts known as the Hundred Years' War, which was especially disastrous to France. The trouble arose as follows:

It will be remembered that King John of England had lost all the French possessions of the Plantagenets except the duchy of Guienne (§ 551). For this he had to do homage to the king of France and become his vassal. This arrangement lasted for many years, but in the time of Edward III the old French line of kings died out, and Edward declared that he himself was the rightful ruler of all France because his mother, Isabella, was a sister of the last king of the old line.[1]

565. Edward III invades France. The French lawyers, however, decided that Edward had no claim to the French throne and that a very distant relative of the last king was the rightful heir to the crown (Philip VI). Edward, nevertheless, maintained that he was rightfully king of France. He added the French emblem of the lilies (fleur-de-lis) to the lions on the English coat of arms (Fig. 94). In 1346 he landed in Normandy with an English army, devastated the country, and marched up the Seine toward Paris. He met the troops of Philip at Crécy, where a celebrated battle was fought, in which the English with their long bows and well-directed arrows put to rout the French knights. Ten years later the English made another incursion into France and again defeated the French cavalry. The French king (John II) was himself captured and carried off to London.

[1] The French kings during the fourteenth and fifteenth centuries:

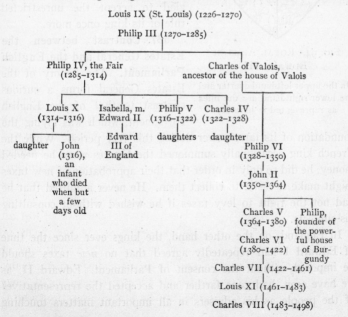

Louis IX (St. Louis) (1226–1270)

Philip III (1270–1285)

Philip IV, the Fair (1285–1314) — Charles of Valois, ancestor of the house of Valois

Louis X (1314–1316) — Isabella, m. Edward II — Philip V (1316–1322) — Charles IV (1322–1328)

daughter — John (1316), an infant who died when but a few days old

Edward III of England

daughters

daughter

Philip VI (1328–1350)

John II (1350–1364)

Charles V (1364–1380) — Philip, founder of the powerful house of Burgundy

Charles VI (1380–1422)

Charles VII (1422–1461)

Louis XI (1461–1483)

Charles VIII (1483–1498)

566. The French Parliament (Estates General). The French Parliament, commonly called the Estates General, came together to consider the unhappy state of affairs. The members from the towns were more numerous than the representatives of the clergy and nobility. A great list of reforms was drawn up. These provided among other things that the Estates General should meet regularly even when the king failed to summon them, and that the collection and expenditure of the public revenue should be no longer entirely under the control of the king but should be supervised by the representatives of the people. The city of Paris rose in support of the revolutionary Estates, but the violence of its allies discredited rather than helped the movement, and France was soon glad to accept the unrestricted rule of its king once more.

Fig. 94. Royal Arms of Edward III

On the upper left-hand quarter and the lower right-hand are the lilies as represented in heraldry

567. Contrast between the Estates General and the English Parliament. The history of the Estates General forms a curious contrast to that of the English Parliament, which was laying the foundation of its later power during this very period. While the French king occasionally summoned the Estates when he needed money, he did so only in order that their approbation of new taxes might make it easier to collect them. He never admitted that he had not the right to levy taxes if he wished without consulting his subjects.

In England, on the other hand, the kings ever since the time of Edward I had repeatedly agreed that no *new* taxes should be imposed without the consent of Parliament. Edward II, as we have seen, had gone farther and accepted the representatives of the people as his advisers in all important matters touching the welfare of the realm. While the French Estates gradually sank into insignificance, the English Parliament soon learned to grant no money until the king had redressed the grievances which it pointed out, and thus it insured its influence over the king's policy.

563. Edward III finds it Impossible to conquer France. Edward III found it impossible, however, to conquer France, and Charles V, the successor of the French king John II, managed before Edward died in 1377 to get back almost all the lands that the English had occupied.

For a generation after the death of Edward III the war with France was almost discontinued. France had suffered a great deal more than England. In the first place, all the fighting had been done on her side of the Channel, and in the second place, the soldiers, who found themselves without occupation, wandered about in bands maltreating and plundering the people.

569. The Bubonic Plague of 1348–1349 (the "Black Death"). The horrors of war had been increased by the deadly bubonic plague which appeared in Europe early in 1348. In April it had reached Florence ; by August it was devastating France and Germany ; it then spread over England from the southwest northward, attacking every part of the country during the year 1349. This disease, like other terrible epidemics, such as small-pox and cholera, came from Asia. Those who were stricken with it usually died in two or three days. It is impossible to tell what proportion of the population perished. Reports of the time say that in one part of France but one tenth of the people survived, in another but one sixteenth ; and that for a long time five hundred bodies were carried from the great hospital of Paris every day. A careful estimate shows that in England toward one half of the population died. At the Abbey of Newenham only the abbot and two monks were left alive out of twenty-six. There were constant complaints that certain lands were no longer of any value to their lords because the tenants were all dead.

570. Conditions of English Labor. In England the growing discontent among the farming classes may be ascribed partly to the results of the great pestilence and partly to the new taxes which were levied in order to prolong the disastrous war with France. Up to this time the majority of those who cultivated the land were villains, or serfs, who belonged to some particular manor, paid stated dues to their lord, and performed definite services for him. Hitherto there had been relatively few farm hands who might be hired and who sought employment anywhere that they could get it. The Black Death, by greatly decreasing the number of laborers, raised wages and served to increase the importance of the unattached laborer. Consequently he not only demanded higher wages than ever before but readily deserted one employer when another offered him more money.

This appeared very shocking to those who were accustomed to the traditional rates of payment, and the government undertook to keep down wages by prohibiting laborers from asking more than had been customary during the years that preceded the pestilence. Every laborer, when offered work at the established wages, was ordered to accept it on pain of imprisonment. The first "Statute of Laborers" was issued in 1351 ; but apparently it was not obeyed, and similar laws were enacted from time to time for a century.

571. Breaking up of the Manors. The old manor system (§§ 524–526) was breaking up. Many of the laboring class in the country no longer held lands as serfs but moved from place to place and made a living by working for wages. The villain, as the serf was called in England, began to regard the dues which he had been accustomed to pay to his lord as unjust. A petition to Parliament in 1377 asserts that the villains are refusing to pay their customary services to their lords or to acknowledge the obligations which they owe as serfs.

572. The Peasant Revolt of 1381. In 1381 the peasants rose in revolt against the taxes levied on them to carry on the hopeless war with France. They burned some of the houses of the nobles and of the rich bishops and abbots and took particular pains to see that the registers were destroyed which were kept by the various lords enumerating the obligations of their serfs.

573. Final Disappearance of Serfdom in England. Although the peasants met with little success, serfdom decayed rapidly. It became more and more common for the serf to pay his dues to the lord in money instead of working for him, and in this way he lost one of the chief characteristics of a serf. The landlord then either hired men to cultivate the fields which he reserved for his own use, or rented the land to tenants. These tenants were not in a position to force their fellow tenants on the manor to pay the full dues which had formerly been exacted by the lord. Sixty or seventy years after the Peasants' War the English rural population had in one way or another become free men, and serfs had practically disappeared.

574. Renewal of the Hundred Years' War (1415). The war between England and France almost ceased for nearly forty years after the death of Edward III. It was renewed in 1415, and the English king Henry V won another great victory at Agincourt, similar to that won at Crécy. Once more the English bowmen slaughtered great numbers of French knights. Fifteen years later the English had succeeded in conquering all of France north of the Loire River, but a considerable region to the south still continued to be held by King Charles VII of France. He was weak and indolent and was doing nothing to check the English victories. The English were engaged in besieging the great town of Orleans when help and encouragement came to the French from a most unexpected quarter. A peasant girl put on a soldier's armor, mounted a horse, and led the faint-hearted French troops to victory.

575. Joan of Arc. To her family and her companions Joan of Arc seemed only "a good girl, simple and pleasant in her ways," but she brooded much over the disasters that had overtaken her country, and a "great pity on the fair realm of France" filled her heart. She saw visions and heard voices that bade her go forth to the help of the king and lead him to Rheims to be crowned.

It was with the greatest difficulty that she got anybody to believe in her mission or to help her to get an audience with her sovereign. But her own firm faith in her divine guidance triumphed over all doubts and obstacles. She was at last accepted as a God-sent champion and placed at the head of some troops dispatched to the relief of Orleans. This city, which was the key to southern France, had been besieged by the English for some months and was on the point of surrender. Joan, who rode at the head of her troops, clothed in armor like a man, had now become the idol of the soldiers and of the people. Under the guidance and in-spiration of her courage, sound sense, and burning enthusiasm, Orleans was relieved and the English completely routed. The Maid of Orleans, as she was henceforth called, was now free to conduct the king to Rheims, where he was crowned in the cathe-dral (July 17, 1429).

The Maid now felt that her mission was accomplished and begged permission to return to her home and her brothers and sisters. To this the king would not consent, and she continued to fight his battles with success. But the other leaders were jealous of her, and even her friends, the soldiers, were sensitive to the taunt of being led by a woman. During the defense of Compiègne in May, 1430, she was allowed to fall into the hands of the Duke of Burgundy, who sold her to the English. They were not satisfied with simply holding as a prisoner that strange maiden who had so discomfited them; they wished to discredit everything that she had done, and so declared, and undoubtedly believed, that she was a witch who had been helped by the devil. She was tried by a court of clergymen, found guilty, and burned at Rouen in 1431. Her bravery and noble constancy affected even her executioners, and an English soldier who had come to triumph over her death was heard to exclaim, "We are lost—we have burned a saint." The English cause in France was indeed lost, for her spirit and example had given new courage and vigor to the French armies.

576. England loses her French Possessions. The English Parliament became more and more reluctant to grant funds when there were no more victories gained. From this time on the Eng-lish lost ground steadily. They were expelled from Normandy in 1450. Three years later the last vestige of their possessions in southern France passed into the hands of the French king. The Hundred Years' War was over, and, although England still retained Calais, the great question whether she should extend her sway upon the Continent was finally settled.

577. The Wars of the Roses (1455–1485); Retainers. The close of the Hundred Years' War was followed in England by the Wars of the Roses, between the rival families, Lancaster and York,[1] which were struggling for the crown. The badge of the house of Lancaster was a red rose, and that of York was a white one. Each party was supported by a group of the wealthy and powerful nobles whose conspiracies, treasons, murders, and executions fill the annals of England during the period which we have been discussing.

The nobles no longer owed their power as they had in previous centuries to *vassals* who were bound to follow them to war (§§ 527–532). Like the king, they relied upon *hired soldiers*. It was easy to find plenty of restless fellows who were willing to become the retainers of a nobleman if he would agree to clothe them and keep open house, where they might eat and drink their fill. Their master was to help them when they got into trouble, and they on their part were expected to intimidate, misuse, and even murder at need those who opposed the interests of their chief.

[1] Descent of the rival houses of Lancaster and York:

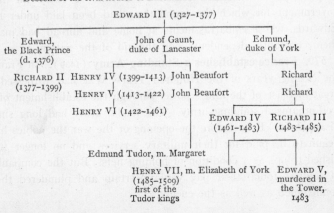

EDWARD III (1327–1377)

Edward, the Black Prince (d. 1376) — RICHARD II (1377–1399)

John of Gaunt, duke of Lancaster — HENRY IV (1399–1413) — HENRY V (1413–1422) — HENRY VI (1422–1461); John Beaufort — John Beaufort

Edmund, duke of York — Richard — Richard — EDWARD IV (1461–1483) RICHARD III (1483–1485)

Edmund Tudor, m. Margaret — HENRY VII, m. Elizabeth of York (1485–1509) first of the Tudor kings — EDWARD V, murdered in the Tower, 1483

578. The Despotism of the Tudors. It is needless to speak of the several battles and the many skirmishes of the miserable Wars of the Roses. These lasted from 1455, when the Duke of York set seriously to work to displace the weak-minded Lancastrian king (Henry VI), until the accession of Henry VII, of the house of Tudor, thirty years later (1485). (See table on page 383.)

The Wars of the Roses had important results. Nearly all the powerful families of England had been drawn into the war, and

a great part of the nobility, whom the kings had formerly feared, had perished on the battlefield or lost their heads in the ruthless executions carried out by each party after it gained a victory. This left the king far more powerful than ever before. He could now control Parliament, even if he could not do away with it. For a century and more after the accession of Henry VII the Tudor kings exercised almost

FIG. 95. PORTRAIT OF HENRY VII

despotic power. England ceased for a time to enjoy the free government for which the foundations had been laid under the Edwards, whose embarrassments at home and abroad had made them constantly dependent upon the aid of the nation.

579. France establishes a Standing Army (1439). In France the closing years of the Hundred Years' War had witnessed a great increase of the king's power through the establishment of a well-organized standing army. The feudal army had long since disappeared. Even before the opening of the war the nobles had begun to be paid for their military services and no longer furnished troops as a condition of holding fiefs. But the companies of soldiers found their pay very uncertain and plundered their countrymen as well as the enemy.

The Estates agreed in 1439 that the king should use a certain tax, called the *taille*, to support the troops necessary for the protection of the frontier. This was a fatal concession, for the king now had an army and the right to collect what he chose to consider a permanent tax, the amount of which he later greatly increased ; he was not dependent, as was the English king, upon the grants made for brief periods by the representatives of the nation assembled in Parliament.

580. The New Feudalism. Before the king of France could hope to establish a compact, well-organized state it was necessary for him to reduce the power of his vassals, some of whom were almost his equals in strength. The process of reducing the power of the nobles had, it is true, been begun. They had been forbidden to coin money, to maintain armies, and to tax their subjects ; and the powers of the king's judges had been extended over all the realm. But the task of consolidating France was reserved for the son of Charles VII, the shrewd and treacherous Louis XI (1461–1483).

FIG. 96. LOUIS XI OF FRANCE

581. Work of Louis XI. The most powerful and dangerous of Louis XI's vassals were the dukes of Burgundy, and they gave him a great deal of trouble. Of Burgundy something will be said in later chapters. Louis XI had himself made heir to a number of provinces in central and southern France,—Anjou, Maine, Provence, etc.,—which by the death of their possessors came under the king's immediate control (1481). He humiliated in various ways the vassals who in his early days had combined against him. Louis's aims were worthy, but his means were generally despicable. It sometimes seemed as if he gloried in being the most rascally among rascals, the most treacherous among the traitors.

582. England and France establish Strong National Governments. Both England and France emerged from the troubles and desolations of the Hundred Years' War stronger than ever before. In both countries the kings had overcome the menace of feudalism by destroying the power of the great families. The royal government was becoming constantly more powerful. Commerce and industry increased the people's wealth and supplied the monarchs with the revenue necessary to maintain government officials and a sufficient army to keep order throughout their realms. They were no longer forced to rely upon the uncertain fidelity of their vassals. In short, England and France were both becoming modern states.

QUESTIONS

I. Tell what you can about England before the Norman Conquest. How did Normandy come into existence? How did William of Normandy get possession of England? What was William's policy after he conquered England?

II. Mention some of the reforms of Henry II. Describe Henry's troubles with Thomas Becket. What was the extent of the possessions of the Plantagenets in France? In what way did the French king succeed in getting a considerable part of the Plantagenet possessions into his own hands? Describe the chief events in the reign of King John of England.

III. How was the Great Charter granted, and what were some of its main provisions? What is the English Parliament? When was it formed? What were its powers?

IV. When was Wales conquered by the English kings? What are the Highlands and the Lowlands of Scotland? Tell of the attempts of Edward I to get possession of Scotland.

V. Give the origin and general course of the Hundred Years' War under Edward III. Why did not the Estates General become as powerful as the English Parliament? Tell about the Black Death. What led to the disappearance of serfdom in England? Give an account of Joan of Arc. What were the great causes of disorder in England during the generation before the accession of Henry VII? What was accomplished by Louis XI?

CHAPTER XXVI

POPES AND EMPERORS

I. Origin of the Holy Roman Empire

583. Otto the Great (936-973). Charlemagne's successors in the German part of his empire found it quite as hard as did the kings of the western, or French, kingdom to keep control of their vassals. Germany, like France, was divided into big and little fiefs, and the dukes and counts were continually waging war upon each other and upon their king. The general causes of this chronic disorder in the Middle Ages have been described in a previous chapter.

The first German ruler whom we need to notice here was Otto the Great, who came to the throne in the year 936. He got as many of the great fiefs as possible into the hands of his relatives in the hope that they would be faithful to him. He put an end forever to the invasions of the Hungarians who had been ravaging Germany. He defeated them in a great battle near Augsburg and drove them out of his realms. As has already been said (see above, § 519), they finally settled in eastern Europe and laid the foundations of what was to become the important state of Hungary.

584. Otto the Great becomes King of Italy and Emperor (962). It would seem as if Otto had quite 'enough trouble at home, but he thought that it would make him and his reign more glorious if he added northern Italy to his realms. So in 951 he crossed the Alps and, without being formally crowned, was generally acknowledged as king of Italy. He had to hasten back to Germany to put down a revolt organized by his own son, but ten years later he was called to Rome by the Pope, who was seeking protection from the attacks of his enemies. Otto accepted the invitation, and the grateful Pope in return crowned him emperor, as Charlemagne's successor (962).

The coronation of Otto was a very important event in German history ; for, from this time on, the German kings, instead of confining their attention to keeping their own kingdom in order, were constantly distracted by the necessity of keeping hold on their Italian kingdom, which lay on the other side of a great range of mountains.

The succeeding German emperors had usually to make several costly and troublesome journeys to Rome,—a first one to be crowned, and then others either to depose a hostile Pope or to protect a friendly one from the oppression of neighboring lords. These expeditions were very distracting, especially to a ruler who left behind him in Germany a rebellious nobility that always took advantage of his absence to revolt.

585. The Holy Roman Empire. Otto's successors dropped their old title of king of the East Franks as soon as they had been duly crowned by the Pope at Rome, and assumed the magnificent and all-embracing designation, "Emperor Ever August of the Romans."[1] Their "Holy Roman Empire," as it came to be called later, which was to endure, in name at least, for more than eight centuries, was obviously even less like that of the ancient Romans than was Charlemagne's. As *kings* of Germany and Italy they had practically all the powers that they enjoyed as *emperors*. The title of emperor was of course a proud one, but it gave the German kings no additional power except the fatal right that they claimed of taking part in the election of the Pope. We shall find that, instead of making themselves feared at home and building up a great state, the German emperors wasted their strength in a long struggle with the popes, who proved themselves in the end far stronger, and eventually reduced the Empire to a mere shadow.

[1] Henry II (1002-1024) and his successors, not venturing to assume the title of emperor till crowned at Rome, but anxious to claim Rome as attached to the German crown, began to call themselves, before their coronation, " King of the Romans."

II. The Church and its Property

586. Lands of the Church draw it into the Feudal System. In order to understand the long struggle between the emperors and the popes, we must stop a moment to consider the condition of the Church in the early Middle Ages. It seemed to be losing all its strength and dignity and to be falling apart, just as Charlemagne's empire had dissolved into feudal bits. This was chiefly due to the fact that the churchmen held such vast tracts of land.

A king, or other landed proprietor, might grant fiefs to churchmen as well as to laymen. The bishops became the vassals of the king or of other feudal lords by doing homage for a fief and swearing fidelity, just as any other vassal would do. An abbot would sometimes secure for his monastery the protection of a neighboring lord by giving up his land and receiving it back again as a fief.

587. Fiefs held by Churchmen not Hereditary. One great difference, however, existed between the Church lands and the ordinary fiefs. According to the law of the Church the bishops and abbots could not marry and so could have no heirs to whom they might transmit their property. Consequently, when a land-holding churchman died, someone had to be chosen in his place who should enjoy his property and perform his duties. The rule of the Church had been, from time immemorial, that the clergy of the bishopric should choose the bishop, their choice being ratified by the people. As for the abbots, they were, according to the Rule of St. Benedict, to be chosen by the members of the monastery.

588. Investiture. In spite of these rules, the bishops and abbots had come, in the tenth and eleventh centuries, to be selected, to all intents and purposes, by the various kings and feudal lords. It is true that the outward forms of a regular election were usually permitted ; but the feudal lord made it clear whom he wished chosen, and if the wrong person was elected he simply refused to hand over to him the lands attached to the bishopric or abbey.

When a bishop or abbot had been duly chosen, the feudal lord proceeded to the *investiture*. The new bishop or abbot first became the "man" of the lord by doing him homage (§ 528), and then the lord transferred to him the lands and rights attached to the office. No careful distinction appears to have been made between the property and the religious powers. The lord often conferred both by bestowing upon a bishop the ring and the crosier (the bishop's pastoral staff), the emblems of religious authority. It seemed shocking enough that the king or feudal lord, who was often a rough soldier, should dictate the selection of the bishops; but it was still more shocking that he should assume to confer religious powers with religious emblems.

In Germany the king had found it convenient, from about the beginning of the eleventh century, to confer upon the bishops in many cases the authority of a count in the districts about them. In this way they might have the right to collect tolls, coin money, and perform other important governmental duties. To forbid the king to take part in the investiture was, consequently, to rob him of his authority over many of his government officials, since bishops, and sometimes even abbots, were often counts in all but name. He therefore found it necessary to take care who got possession of the important church offices.

589. The Marriage of the Clergy. Still another danger threatened the wealth and resources of the Church. During the tenth and eleventh centuries the rule of the Church prohibiting the clergy from marrying appears to have been widely neglected in Italy, Germany, France, and England. To the stricter people of the time this appeared a terrible degradation of the clergy, who, they felt, should be unencumbered by family cares and should devote themselves wholly to the service of God. The question, too, had another side. It was obvious that the property of the Church would soon be dispersed if the clergy were allowed to marry, since they would wish to provide for their children. Just as the feudal lands had become hereditary (§ 530), so the church lands would become hereditary unless the clergy were forced to remain unmarried.

590. Buying and Selling of Church Offices: Simony. Besides the feudalizing of its property and the marriage of the clergy, there was a third great and constant source of weakness and corruption in the Church at this period, namely, the temptation to buy and sell church offices. The revenue from a great church estate and the high rank that went with the office were enough to induce the members of the noblest families to vie with each other in securing church positions. The king or prince who possessed the right of investiture was sure of finding someone willing to pay something for important benefices.

The sin of buying or selling church offices was recognized as a most serious one. It was called "simony,"[1] a name derived from Simon the Magician, who, according to the account in the Acts of the Apostles, offered money to the Apostle Peter if he would give him the power of imparting the Holy Spirit to those upon whom he should lay hands.

It must be remembered, however, that when a king or lord accepted a gift from one for whom he procured a benefice, he did not regard himself as *selling* the office; he merely shared its advantages. No transaction took place in the Middle Ages without accompanying gifts and fees of various kinds.

The evil of simony (or "graft," as we should call it) spread downward and infected the whole body of the clergy. A bishop who had made a large outlay in obtaining his office naturally expected something from the priests, whom it was his duty to appoint. Then the priest, in turn, was tempted to exact too much for baptizing and marrying his parishioners and for burying the dead.

591. Nicholas II reforms Election of Popes (1059). So it seemed, at the opening of the eleventh century, as if the Church was to be dragged down by its property into the anarchy of feudalism described in a preceding chapter.

The popes had, therefore, many difficulties to overcome in the gigantic task which they undertook of making the Church a great international monarchy, like the Roman Empire, with

[1] Pronounced *sĭm'o-ny*. See Acts viii, 20.

its capital at Rome. The control exercised by kings and feudal lords in the selection of Church officials had to be done away with. The marriage of the clergy had to be checked, for fear that the property and wealth of the Church would go to their families and so be lost to the Church. Simony with its degrading effects had to be abolished.

The first great step toward the freeing of the Church from the control of the kings and feudal lords was taken by Pope Nicholas II. In 1059 he issued a remarkable decree which took the election of the head of the Church once for all out of the hands of both the emperor and the people of Rome and placed it definitely and forever in the hands of the *cardinals,* who represented the Roman clergy.[1]

The reform party which directed the policy of the popes now proposed to emancipate the Church as a whole from the base entanglements of earth: first, by strictly forbidding the clergy to marry; and secondly, by depriving the kings and feudal lords of their influence over the choice of the bishops and abbots. The magnitude of the task which the popes had undertaken first became fully apparent when the celebrated Gregory VII (often called Hildebrand) ascended the papal throne, in 1073.

592. The *Dictatus* of Gregory VII. Among the writings of Gregory VII there is a very brief statement, called the *Dictatus,* of the powers which he believed the popes to possess. Its chief claims are the following: The Pope enjoys a unique title; he is the only *universal* bishop and may depose and reinstate other bishops or transfer them from place to place. No council of the Church may be regarded as speaking for Christendom without his consent. The Roman Church has never erred, nor

---

[1] The word "cardinal" (Latin *cardinalis,* "principal") was applied to the priests of the various parishes in Rome, to the several deacons connected with the Lateran, — which was the cathedral church of the Roman bishopric, — and, lastly, to six or seven suburban bishops who officiated in turn in the Lateran. The title became a very distinguished one and was sought by ambitious foreign prelates and ecclesiastical statesmen, like Wolsey, Richelieu, and Mazarin. If their official titles were examined, it would be found that each was nominally a cardinal bishop, priest, or deacon of some Roman church. The number of cardinals varied until fixed, in 1586, at six bishops, fifty priests, and fourteen deacons.

will it err to all eternity. No one may be considered a Catholic Christian who does not agree with the Roman Church. No book is authoritative unless it has received the papal sanction.

Gregory does not stop with asserting the Pope's complete supremacy over the Church. He says that "the Pope is the only person whose feet are kissed by all princes"; that he may depose emperors and "absolve subjects from allegiance to an unjust ruler." No one shall dare to condemn one who appeals to the Pope. No one may annul a decree of the Pope, though the Pope may declare null and void the decrees of all other earthly powers; and no one may pass judgment upon his acts.

593. Gregory VII puts his Theories into Practice. Immediately upon his election as Pope, Gregory began to put into practice his high conception of the rôle that the religious head of Christendom should play. He explained, kindly but firmly, to William the Conqueror (§ 541) that the papal and kingly powers are both established by God as the greatest among the authorities of the world, just as the sun and moon are the greatest of the heavenly bodies. But the papal power is obviously superior to the kingly, for it is responsible for it. At the Last Day, Gregory would have, he urged, to render an account of the king as one of the flock intrusted to his care. The king of France was warned to give up his practice of simony, lest he be excommunicated and his subjects freed from their oath of allegiance. All these acts of Gregory appear to have been dictated not by worldly ambition but by a fervent conviction of their righteousness and of his heavy responsibility to God and toward all men.

III. The Long Struggle between Popes and Emperors

594. Struggle over Investiture between Henry IV and Gregory VII. The popes who immediately preceded Gregory had more than once forbidden the churchmen to receive investiture from laymen. Gregory reissued this prohibition in 1075. Investiture was, as we have seen (§ 588), the legal transfer by the king or other lord, to a newly chosen church official, of the lands and rights attached to the office. In forbidding investiture by laymen Gregory attempted nothing less than a revolution. The bishops and abbots were often officers of government, exercising in Germany and Italy powers similar in all respects to those of the counts. The German king not only relied upon them for advice and assistance in carrying on his government, but they were among his chief allies in his constant struggles with his vassals.

This act of Gregory's led to a long and bitter struggle between the popes and German rulers, lasting for two hundred years. Gregory's legates so irritated the young German king, Henry IV, that he had the Pope deposed as a wicked man (1076).

Gregory's reply to Henry and the German bishops who had deposed him was speedy and decisive. "Incline thine ear to us, O Peter, chief of the Apostles. As thy representative and by thy favor has the power been granted especially to me by God of binding and loosing in heaven and earth (compare § 483). . . . I withdraw, through thy power and authority, from Henry the King, who has risen against thy Church with unheard-of insolence, the rule over the whole kingdom of the Germans and over Italy. I absolve all Christians from the bonds of the oath which they have sworn, or may swear, to him ; and I forbid anyone to serve him as king."[1]

For a time after the Pope had deposed him everything went against Henry. Instead of resenting the Pope's interference, the discontented Saxons, and many other of Henry's vassals, believed that there was now an excellent opportunity to get rid of Henry and choose a more agreeable ruler.

595. Henry submits to the Pope at Canossa (1077). Henry was so discouraged that he hastened across the Alps in midwinter and appeared as a humble suppliant before the castle of Canossa,[2] whither the Pope had come on his way to Germany. For three days the German king presented himself before the closed door, barefoot and in the coarse garments of a pilgrim and a penitent, before the Pope consented to receive him. The spectacle of this

---

[1] See tailpiece at the end of this chapter.

[2] The castle of Canossa belonged to Gregory VII's ally and admirer, the Countess of Tuscany.

mighty prince of distinguished appearance, in tears before the little man who humbly styled himself the "servant of the servants of God," has always been regarded as most completely typifying the power of the Church and the potency of her curses against even the most exalted of the earth.

The famous scene at Canossa settled nothing, however, and the struggle went on. The Pope took sides with Henry's enemies in Germany, but the German king was able to march down into Italy later and drive Gregory from Rome. They both died in the midst of the conflict.

596. Concordat of Worms (1122). After a long succession of troubles between their successors a compromise was reached in the Concordat of Worms (1122) which put an end to the controversy over investitures in Germany. The emperor promised to permit the Church freely to elect the bishops and abbots and renounced his old claim to invest with the religious emblems of the ring and the crosier. But the elections were to be held in the presence of the king, and he was permitted, in a separate ceremony, to *invest* the new bishop or abbot with his fiefs and his governmental powers by a touch of the scepter. In this way the religious powers of the bishops were obviously conferred by the churchmen who elected them; and although the king might still practically invalidate an election by refusing to hand over the lands, nevertheless the actual appointment of the bishops and abbots was taken out of his hands.

597. Frederick I (Barbarossa) of Hohenstaufen (1152-1190). A generation after the matter of investitures had been arranged by the Concordat of Worms the most famous of German emperors, next to Charlemagne, came to the throne. This was Frederick I, commonly called Barbarossa (from his red beard). He belonged to the family of Hohenstaufen, so called from their castle in southern Germany. Frederick's ambition was to restore the Roman Empire to its old glory and influence. He regarded himself as the successor of the Cæsars, as well as of Charlemagne and Otto the Great. He believed his office to be quite as truly established by God himself as the papacy.

In his lifelong attempt to maintain what he thought to be his rights as emperor he met, quite naturally, with the three old difficulties. He had constantly to be fighting his rivals and rebellious vassals in Germany; he had to face the opposition of the popes, who never forgot the claims that Gregory VII had

ITALIAN TOWNS IN THE TWELFTH CENTURY

made to control the emperor as well as other rulers. Lastly, in trying to keep hold of northern Italy, which he believed to belong to his empire, he spent a great deal of time with but slight results.

598. The Attempt to conquer the Lombard Towns. One of the greatest differences between the early Middle Ages and Frederick's time was the development of town life. The towns had never decayed altogether in Italy, and by the time of Frederick

Barbarossa they had begun to flourish once more, especially in Lombardy. Such towns as Milan, Verona, and Cremona were practically independent states, often fighting one another.

But in spite of all the warfare and disorder the Italian cities became wealthy and, as we shall see later, were centers of learning and art similar to the ancient cities of Greece, such as Athens and Corinth. They were able to combine in a union known as the Lombard League to oppose Frederick, for they hated the idea of paying taxes to a German king from across the Alps. Frederick made several expeditions to Italy, but he only succeeded, after a vast amount of trouble, in getting them to recognize him as a sort of overlord. He was forced to leave them to manage their own affairs and go their own way.

599. Frederick II and Southern Italy. After some forty years of fighting in Germany and Italy, Frederick Barbarossa decided to undertake a crusade to the Holy Land and lost his life on the way thither. The grandson of Frederick Barbarossa, the famous Frederick II, continued the wearisome struggle between the emperors and popes. He was unable to bring any order into German affairs and devoted most of his attention to southern Italy. His mother, Constance, was heiress to the kingdoms of Naples and Sicily, and here Frederick built up the first well-regulated modern state. He was an unusually thoughtful man for a medieval king and appears to have rejected many of the opinions of his time. His enemies asserted that he was not even a Christian and that he declared that Moses, Christ, and Mohammed were all alike impostors. He nevertheless issued very harsh edicts against heretics and did all he could to discover and punish them.

We cannot stop to relate the romantic and absorbing story of his long struggle with the popes. They speedily discovered that he was bent upon establishing a powerful state to the south of them and upon extending his control over the Lombard cities in such a manner that the papal possessions would be held as in a vise. This, they felt, must never be permitted.

Frederick was denounced in solemn councils, and at last deposed by one of the popes. After his death (1250) his sons maintained themselves for a few years in the Sicilian kingdom; but they finally gave way before a French army, led by the brother of St. Louis, Charles of Anjou, upon whom the Pope bestowed the southern realms of the Hohenstaufens.

600. End of the Medieval Empire. With Frederick's death the medieval Empire may be said to have come to an end. It is true that after a period of "fist law," as the Germans call it, a new king, Rudolf of Hapsburg, was elected in Germany in 1273. The German kings continued to call themselves emperors. Few of them, however, took the trouble to go to Rome to be crowned by the Pope. No serious effort was ever made to reconquer the Italian territory for which Otto the Great, Frederick Barbarossa, and his grandson had made such serious sacrifices. Germany was hopelessly divided and its king was no real king. He had no capital city and no well-organized government. Such power as existed was mainly in the hands of the king's powerful vassals, — dukes, counts, bishops, and abbots.

By the middle of the thirteenth century it becomes apparent that neither Germany nor Italy was to be converted into a strong single kingdom like England and France. The map of Germany shows a confused group of duchies, counties, archbishoprics, bishoprics, abbacies, and free towns, each one of which asserted its practical independence of the weak king and emperor.

In northern Italy each town, including a certain district about its walls, had become an independent state, dealing with its neighbors as with independent powers. The Italian towns were destined to become the birthplace of our modern culture during the fourteenth and fifteenth centuries. Venice and Florence, in spite of their small size, came to be reckoned among the most important states of Europe (see §§ 661–668, below). In the central part of the peninsula the Pope maintained more or less control over his possessions, but he often failed to subdue the towns within his realms. To the south the kingdom of Naples, which the Hohenstaufens had lost, remained for some time under the French dynasty, which the Pope had called in, while the island of Sicily drifted into Spanish hands.

QUESTIONS

I. Describe the way in which the German kings gained the title of emperor. What do you understand by the Holy Roman Empire?

II. What was the effect of the vast landholdings of the Church? What was investiture, and why did it raise difficulties between the popes and emperors? Why did the Pope oppose the marriage of the clergy? How is the Pope elected? What is a cardinal? What was the *Dictatus*, and what claims did it make?

III. Describe the conflict between Henry IV and Gregory VII. What were the provisions of the Concordat of Worms? What new enemies did Frederick Barbarossa find in northern Italy? Narrate the struggle between Frederick II and the popes and its outcome. In what condition was Germany left after the extinction of the Hohenstaufens?

NOTE. The pictures below are taken from an illustrated manuscript written some decades after Gregory VII's death. In the one on the left Gregory is represented blowing out a candle and saying to his cardinals, "As I blow out this light, so will Henry IV be extinguished." In the one on the right is shown the death of Gregory (1085). He probably did not wear his crown in bed, but the artist wanted us to be sure to recognize that he was Pope.

CHAPTER XXVII

THE CRUSADES

I. Origin of the Crusades

601. Fascination of the Crusades. Of all the events of the Middle Ages the most romantic and fascinating are the Crusades, the adventurous expeditions to Syria and Palestine, undertaken by devout and warlike kings and knights with the hope of permanently reclaiming the Holy Land from the infidel Turks. All through the twelfth and thirteenth centuries each generation beheld at least one great army of crusaders gathering from every part of the West and starting toward the Orient. Each year witnessed the departure of small bands of pilgrims or of solitary soldiers of the cross.

For two hundred years there was a continuous stream of Europeans of every rank and station — kings and princes, powerful nobles, simple knights, common soldiers, monks, townspeople, and even peasants — from England, France, Germany, Spain, and Italy, making their way into Western Asia. If they escaped the countless dangers which beset them on the journey, they either settled in this distant land and devoted themselves to war or commerce, or returned home, bringing with them tales of great cities and new peoples, of skill, knowledge, and luxury unknown in the West.

602. The Holy Land conquered first by the Arabs and then by the Turks. Syria had been overrun by the Arabs in the seventh century, shortly after the death of Mohammed, and the Holy City of Jerusalem had fallen into the hands of the infidels (§ 500). The Arab, however, shared the veneration of the Christian for the places associated with the life of Christ and, in general, permitted the Christian pilgrims who found their way thither to worship unmolested. But with the coming of a new and ruder people, the Seljuk Turks, in the eleventh century, the pilgrims began to bring home news of great hardships. Moreover, the Eastern emperor was defeated by the Turks in 1071 and lost Asia Minor. The presence of the Turks, who had taken possession of the fortress of Nicæa, just across from Constantinople, was of course a standing menace to the Eastern Empire. When the energetic Emperor Alexius (1081–1118) ascended the throne he endeavored to expel the infidel. Finding himself unequal to the task, he appealed for assistance to the head of Christendom, Pope Urban II.

603. Urban II issues Call to First Crusade (1095). The first great impetus to the Crusades was the call issued by Urban at the celebrated church council which met in 1095 at Clermont in France. In an address which produced more remarkable immediate results than any other which history records, the Pope exhorted knights and soldiers of all ranks to give up their usual wicked business of destroying their Christian brethren in private warfare (see above, §§ 532–534) and turn, instead, to the succor of their fellow Christians in the East. He warned them that the insolent Turks would, if unchecked, extend their sway still more widely over the faithful servants of the Lord. Urban urged, besides, that France was too poor to support all its people, while the Holy Land flowed with milk and honey. "Enter upon the road to the Holy Sepulcher; wrest the land from the wicked race and subject it to yourselves."

When the Pope had finished, all who were present exclaimed, with one accord, "It is the will of God." This, the Pope declared, should be the rallying cry of the crusaders, who were to wear a cross upon their bosoms as they went forth, and upon their backs as they returned, as a holy sign of their sacred mission.

604. The Motives of the Crusaders. The Crusades are ordinarily represented as the most striking examples of the simple faith and religious enthusiasm of the Middle Ages. They appealed, however, to many different kinds of men. The devout, the romantic, and the adventurous were by no means the only classes that were attracted. Syria held out inducements to the discontented noble who might hope to gain a principality in the East, to the merchant who was looking for new enterprises, to the merely restless who wished to avoid his responsibilities at home, and even to the criminal who enlisted with a view of escaping the results of his past offenses.

It is noteworthy that Urban appeals especially to those who had been "contending against their brethren and relatives," and urges those "who have hitherto been robbers now to become soldiers of Christ." And the conduct of many of the crusaders indicates that the Pope found a ready hearing among these classes. Yet higher motives than a love of adventure and the hope of conquest impelled many who took their way eastward. Great numbers, doubtless, went to Jerusalem "through devotion alone, and not for the sake of honor or gain," with the sole object of freeing the Holy Sepulcher from the hands of the infidel.

To such as these the Pope promised that the journey itself should take the place of all penance for sin. The faithful crusader, like the faithful Mohammedan, was assured of immediate entrance into heaven if he died repentant. Later, the Church exhibited its extraordinary authority by what would seem to us an unjust interference with business contracts. It freed those who "with a pure heart" entered upon the journey from the payment of interest upon their debts and permitted them to mortgage property against the wishes of their feudal lords.

605. Peter the Hermit and his Army. The Council of Clermont met in November. Before spring (1096) those who set forth to preach the Crusade—above all, the famous Peter the Hermit, who was formerly given credit for having begun the whole crusading movement—had collected, in France and along the Rhine, an extraordinary army of the common folk. Peasants, workmen, vagabonds, and even women and children, answered the summons, all blindly intent upon rescuing the Holy Sepulcher, two thousand miles away. They were confident that the Lord would sustain them during the weary leagues of the journey, and that, when they reached the Holy Land, he would grant them a prompt victory over the infidel.

This great host was got under way in several divisions under the leadership of Peter the Hermit, and of Walter the Penniless and other humble knights. Many of the crusaders were slaughtered by the Hungarians, who rose to protect themselves from the depredations of this motley horde in its passage through their country. Part of them got as far as Nicæa, only to be slaughtered by the Turks. This is but an example, on a large scale, of what was going on continually for a century or so after this first great catastrophe. Individual pilgrims and adventurers, and sometimes considerable bodies of crusaders, were constantly falling a prey to every form of disaster—starvation, slavery, disease, and death—in their persistent endeavors to reach the far-away Holy Land.

II. The First Crusade

606. The First Crusade (1096). The most conspicuous figures of the long period of the Crusades are not, however, to be found among the lowly followers of Peter the Hermit, but are the knights, in their long coats of flexible armor. A year after the summons issued at Clermont great armies of fighting men had been collected in the West under distinguished leaders — the Pope speaks of three hundred thousand soldiers. Of the various divisions which were to meet in Constantinople the following were the most important : the volunteers from Provence under the papal legate and Count Raymond of Toulouse ; inhabitants of Germany, particularly of Lorraine, under Godfrey of Bouillon and his brother Baldwin, both destined to be rulers of Jerusalem ; and lastly, an army of French and of the Normans of southern Italy under Bohemond and Tancred.[1]

[1] For the routes taken by the different crusading armies see the accompanying map

Upon the arrival of the crusaders at Constantinople it quickly became clear that they had not much more in common with the "Greeks"[1] than with the Turks. Emperor Alexius ordered his soldiers to attack Godfrey's army, encamped in the suburbs of his capital, because their chief at first refused to take the oath of feudal homage to him. The emperor's daughter Anna, in her history of the times, gives a sad picture of the outrageous conduct of the crusaders. They, on the other hand, denounced the Greeks as traitors, cowards, and liars.

FIG. 97. KNIGHT OF THE FIRST CRUSADE

In the time of the Crusades knights wore a coat of interwoven iron rings, called a hauberk, to protect themselves. The habit of using the rigid iron plates, of which later armor was constructed, did not come in until the Crusades were over

The Eastern emperor had hoped to use his Western allies to reconquer Asia Minor and force back the Turks. The leading knights, on the contrary, dreamed of carving out principalities for themselves in the former dominions of the emperor and proposed to control them by right of conquest. Later we find both Greeks and Western Christians shamelessly allying themselves with the Mohammedans against each other.

607. Conquest of Jerusalem. The first real allies that the crusaders met with were the Christian Armenians, who gave them aid after their terrible march through Asia Minor. With their help Baldwin got possession of Edessa, of which he made himself prince. The chiefs induced the great body of the crusaders to postpone the march on Jerusalem, and a year was spent in taking the rich and important city of Antioch. Then Raymond of Toulouse set to work and conquered a principality for himself on the coast about Tripoli.

[1] The people of the Eastern Empire were called Greeks because the Greek language continued to be used in Constantinople.

In the spring of 1099 about twenty thousand warriors were at last able to move upon Jerusalem. They found the city well walled, in the midst of a desolate region where neither food nor water nor the materials to construct the siege apparatus necessary for the capture of the Holy City were to be found. However, the opportune arrival at Jaffa of galleys sent from Genoa furnished the besiegers with supplies, and, in spite of all the difficulties, the place was taken in a couple of months. The crusaders showed no mercy to the people of the city, but with shocking barbarity cruelly massacred the inhabitants. Godfrey of Bouillon was chosen ruler of Jerusalem and took the modest title of "Defender of the Holy Sepulcher." He soon died and was succeeded by his

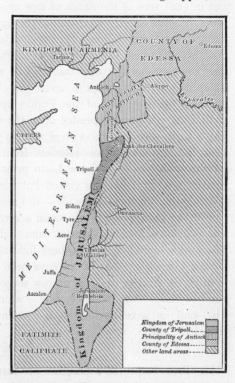

MAP OF THE CRUSADERS' STATES IN SYRIA

brother Baldwin, who left Edessa in 1100 to take up the task of extending the bounds of the kingdom of Jerusalem.

608. Founding of Latin Kingdoms in Syria. It will be observed that the "Franks," as the Mohammedans called all the Western folk, had established the centers of four principalities. These were Edessa, Antioch, the region about Tripoli conquered by Raymond, and the kingdom of Jerusalem. The last was further increased by Baldwin, who, with the help of the mariners from Venice and Genoa, succeeded in getting possession of Acre, Sidon, and a number of other smaller coast towns.

The news of these Christian victories quickly reached the West, and in 1101 tens of thousands of new crusaders started eastward. Most of them were lost in passing through Asia Minor, and few reached their destination. The original conquerors were consequently left to hold the land against the Saracens and to organize their conquests as best they could. This was a very difficult task —too difficult to accomplish under the circumstances.

The permanent hold of the Franks upon the eastern borders of the Mediterranean depended upon the strength of the colonies which their various princes were able to establish. It is impossible to learn how many pilgrims from the West made their permanent homes in the new Latin principalities. Certainly the greater part of those who visited Palestine returned home after fulfilling the vow they had made—to kneel at the Holy Sepulcher.

Still the princes could rely upon a certain number of soldiers who would be willing to stay and fight the Mohammedans. The Turks, moreover, were so busy fighting one another that they showed less energy than might have been expected in attempting to drive the Franks from the narrow strip of territory—some five hundred miles long and fifty wide—which they had conquered. The map on page 405 shows the extent and situation of the crusaders' states.

III. The Religious Orders of the Hospitalers and Templars

609. Military Religious Orders. A noteworthy outcome of the crusading movement was the foundation of several curious orders, of which the Hospitalers and the Templars were the most important. These orders combined the two great interests of the time, those of the monk and of the soldier. They permitted a man to be both at once; the knight might wear a monkish cowl over his coat of armor.

The Hospitalers grew out of a monastic association that was formed before the First Crusade for the succor of the poor and sick among the pilgrims. Later the society admitted noble knights to its membership and became a military order, at the same time continuing its care for the sick. This charitable association, like the earlier monasteries, received generous gifts of land in western Europe and built and controlled many fortified monasteries in the Holy Land itself. After the evacuation of Syria in the thirteenth century the Hospitalers moved their headquarters to the island of Rhodes, and later to Malta. The order still exists, and it is considered a distinction to this day to have the privilege of wearing its emblem, the cross of Malta.

FIG. 98. COSTUME OF THE HOSPITALERS

The Hospitaler here represented bears the peculiar Maltese cross on his bosom. His crucifix indicates his religious character, but his sword and the armor which he wears beneath his long gown enabled him to fight as well as pray, and to succor the wounded

610. The Templars. Before the Hospitalers were transformed into a military order a little group of French knights banded together in 1119 to defend pilgrims on their way to Jerusalem from the attacks of the infidel. They were assigned quarters in the king's palace at Jerusalem, on the site of the former Temple of Solomon; hence the name "Templars," which they were destined to render famous. The "poor soldiers of the Temple" were enthusiastically approved by the Church. They wore a white cloak adorned with a red cross, and were under a very strict monastic rule which bound them by the vows of obedience, poverty, and celibacy. The fame of the order spread throughout Europe, and the most exalted, even dukes and princes, were ready to renounce the world and serve Christ under its black and white banner.

The order was aristocratic from the first, and it soon became incredibly rich and independent. It had its collectors in all parts of Europe, who dispatched the "alms" they received to the Grand Master at Jerusalem. Towns, churches, and estates were given to the order, as well as vast sums of money. The Pope showered privileges upon the Templars. They were exempted from tithes and taxes and were brought under his immediate jurisdiction; they were released from feudal obligations, and bishops were forbidden to excommunicate them for any cause.

No wonder they grew insolent and aroused the jealousy and hate of princes and prelates alike. Early in the fourteenth century, through the combined efforts of the Pope and Philip the Fair of France, the order was brought to a terrible end. Its members were accused of the most abominable practices,—such as the worship of idols and the systematic insulting of Christ and his religion. Many distinguished Templars were burned for heresy; others perished miserably in dungeons. The once powerful order was abolished and its property confiscated.

IV. The Second and Later Crusades

611. The Second and Third Crusades. Fifty years after the preaching of the First Crusade, the fall of Edessa (1144), an important outpost of the Christians in the East, led to a second great expedition. This was forwarded by the great theologian, St. Bernard, who went about using his unrivaled eloquence to induce volunteers to take the cross. In a fierce hymn of battle he cried to the Knights Templars: "The Christian who slays the unbeliever in the Holy War is sure of his reward, the more sure if he himself be slain. The Christian glories in the death of the infidel, because Christ is glorified." The king of France readily consented to take the cross, but the emperor, Conrad III, appears to have yielded only after St. Bernard had preached before him and given a vivid picture of the terrors of the Judgment Day.

In regard to the less distinguished recruits, a historian of the time tells us that so many thieves and robbers hastened to take the cross that everyone felt that such enthusiasm could only be the work of God himself. St. Bernard himself, the chief promoter of the expedition, gives a most unflattering description of the "soldiers of Christ." "In that countless multitude you will find few except the utterly wicked and impious, the sacrilegious, homicides, and perjurers, whose departure is a double gain. Europe rejoices to lose them and Palestine to gain them; they are useful

FIG. 99. KRAK-DES-CHEVALIERS, RESTORED

This is an example of the strong castles that the crusaders built in Syria. It was completed in the form here represented about the year 1200 and lies halfway between Antioch and Damascus. It will be noticed that there was a fortress within a fortress. The castle is now in ruins (see headpiece of this chapter)

in both ways, in their absence from here and their presence there." It is unnecessary to describe the movements and fate of these crusaders; suffice it to say that, from a military standpoint, the so-called Second Crusade was a miserable failure.

In the year 1187, forty years later, Jerusalem was recaptured by Saladin, the most heroic and distinguished of all the Mohammedan rulers of that period. The loss of the Holy City led to the most famous of all the military expeditions to the Holy Land, in which Frederick Barbarossa (§ 599), Richard the Lion-Hearted of England (§ 550), and his political rival, Philip Augustus of

France, all took part. The accounts of this Third Crusade show that while the several Christian leaders hated one another heartily enough, the Christians and Mohammedans were coming to respect one another. We find examples of the most polite relations between the representatives of the opposing religions. In 1192 Richard concluded a truce with Saladin, by the terms of which the Christian pilgrims were allowed to visit the holy places in safety and comfort.

612. The Fourth and Subsequent Crusades. In the thirteenth century the crusaders began to direct their expeditions toward Egypt as the center of the Mohammedan power. The first of these was diverted in an extraordinary manner by the Venetians, who induced the crusaders to conquer Constantinople for their benefit. The further expeditions of Emperor Frederick II (§ 599) and St. Louis, king of France, need not be described. Jerusalem was irrevocably lost in 1244,

FIG. 100. TOMB OF A CRUSADER

The churches of England, France, and Germany contain numerous figures in stone and brass of crusading knights, reposing in full armor with shield and sword on their tombs

and although the possibility of recovering the city was long considered, the Crusades may be said to have come to a close before the end of the thirteenth century.

V. CHIEF RESULTS OF THE CRUSADES

613. Settlements of the Italian Merchants. For one class, at least, the Holy Land had great and permanent charms, namely, the Italian merchants, especially those from Genoa, Venice, and Pisa. It was through their early interest and by means of supplies from their ships that the conquest of the Holy Land had been rendered possible. The merchants always made sure that they were well paid for their services. When they aided in the successful siege of a town they arranged that a definite quarter should be assigned to them in the captured place, where they might have their market, docks, church, and all that was necessary for a permanent center for their commerce. This district belonged to the town from which the merchants came. Venice even sent governors to live in the quarters assigned to its citizens in the kingdom of Jerusalem. Marseilles also had independent quarters in Jerusalem, and Genoa had its share in the county of Tripoli.

614. Oriental Luxury introduced into Europe. This new commerce had a most important influence in bringing the West into permanent relations with the Orient. Eastern products from India and elsewhere—silks, spices, camphor, musk, pearls, and ivory—were brought by the Mohammedans from the East to the commercial towns of Palestine and Syria; then, through the Italian merchants, they found their way into France and Germany, suggesting ideas of luxury hitherto scarcely dreamed of by the still half-barbarous Franks.

615. Effects of the Crusades on Warfare. Moreover, the Crusades had a great effect upon the methods of warfare, for the soldiers from the West learned from the Greeks about the old Roman methods of constructing machines for attacking castles and walled towns. This led, as has been pointed out in a previous chapter (§§ 522–523), to the construction in western Europe of stone castles, first with square towers and later with round ones, the remains of which are so common in Germany, France, and England. The Crusades also produced heraldry, or the science of coats of arms. These were the badges that single knights or groups of knights adopted in order to distinguish themselves from other people.

616. Other Results of the Crusades. Some of the results of the Crusades upon western Europe must already be obvious, even from this very brief account. Thousands and thousands of Frenchmen, Germans, and Englishmen had traveled to the Orient by land and by sea. Most of them came from hamlets or castles where they could never have learned much of the great world beyond the confines of their native village or province. They suddenly found themselves in great cities and in the midst of unfamiliar peoples and customs. This could not fail to make them think and give them new ideas to carry home. The Crusade took the place of a liberal education. The crusaders came into contact with those who knew more than they did, above all the Arabs, and brought back with them new notions of comfort and luxury.

Yet in attempting to estimate the debt of the West to the Crusades it should be remembered that many of the new things may well have come from Constantinople, or through the Mohammedans of Sicily and Spain,[1] quite independently of the armed incursions into Syria. Moreover, during the twelfth and thirteenth centuries towns were rapidly growing up in Europe, trade and manufactures were extending, and the universities were being founded. It would be absurd to suppose that without the Crusades this progress would not have taken place. So we may conclude that the distant expeditions and the contact with strange and more highly civilized peoples did no more than hasten the improvement which was already perceptible before Urban made his ever-memorable address at Clermont.

QUESTIONS

I. What led to the Crusades ? Describe Urban's speech. What was the character of Peter the Hermit's expedition ?

II. Who were the leaders of the First Crusade ? Describe the capture of Jerusalem by the Crusaders.

III. Who were the Hospitalers ? What was the order of the Temple and what became of the Templars ?

IV. What was the Second Crusade ? Give some particulars in regard to the Third Crusade and its leaders.

V. Give as complete an account as you can of the chief results of the Crusades.

---

[1] The western Europeans derived many important ideas from the Mohammedans in Spain, as *Arabic* numerals, alchemy, algebra, and the use of paper.

BOOK VI. MEDIEVAL CIVILIZATION

CHAPTER XXVIII

THE MEDIEVAL CHURCH AT ITS HEIGHT

I. Organization and Powers of the Church

617. General Character of the Medieval Church. In the preceding pages it has been necessary to refer constantly to the Church and the clergy. Indeed, without them medieval history would become almost a blank, for the Church was incomparably the most important institution of the time, and the popes, bishops, and abbots were the soul of nearly every great enterprise. We have already learned something of the rise of the Church and of its head, the Pope, as well as the mode of life and the work of the monks as they spread over Europe. We have also watched the long struggle between the emperors and the popes, in which the emperors were finally worsted. We must now consider the Medieval Church as a completed institution at the height of its power in the twelfth and thirteenth centuries.

We have already had abundant proofs that the Medieval Church was very different from our modern churches, whether Catholic or Protestant.

1. In the first place, everyone was required to belong to it, just as we all must belong to some country to-day. One was not born into the Church, it is true, but he was ordinarily baptized into it when he was a mere infant. All western Europe formed a single religious association, from which it was a crime to revolt. To refuse allegiance to the Church, or to question its authority or teachings, was regarded as treason against God and was punishable with death.

2. The Medieval Church did not rely for its support, as churches usually must to-day, upon the voluntary contributions of its members. It enjoyed, in addition to the revenue from its vast tracts of lands and a great variety of fees, the income from a regular tax, the *tithe*. Those upon whom this fell were forced to pay it, just as we all must now pay taxes imposed by the government.

3. It is clear, moreover, that the Medieval Church was not merely a religious body, as churches are to-day. Of course it maintained places of worship, conducted devotional exercises, and cultivated the religious life ; but it did far more. It was, in a way, a *State*, for it had an elaborate system of law and its own courts, in which it tried many cases which are now settled in our ordinary courts.[1] One may get some idea of the business of the church courts from the fact that the Church claimed the right to try all cases in which a clergyman was involved or anyone connected with the Church or under its special protection, such as monks, students, crusaders, widows, orphans, and the helpless. Then all cases where the rites of the Church, or its prohibitions, were involved came ordinarily before the church courts, as, for example, those concerning marriage, wills, sworn contracts, usury, blasphemy, sorcery, heresy, and so forth. The Church even had its prisons, to which it might sentence offenders for life.

4. The Church not only performed the functions of a State, it had the organization of a State. Unlike the Protestant ministers of to-day, all churchmen and religious associations of medieval Europe were under one supreme head, the Pope (§§ 482–485, 592–593), who made laws for all and controlled every church officer, wherever he might be, whether in Italy or Germany, Spain or Ireland. The whole Church had one official language, Latin, in which all communications were written and in which its services were everywhere conducted.

---

[1] The law of the Church was known as the *canon law*. It was taught in most of the universities and practiced by a great number of lawyers. It was based upon the acts of the various church councils, from that of Nicæa (A.D. 325) down, and, above all, upon the decrees and decisions of the popes.

618. The Medieval Church a Monarchy. The Medieval Church may therefore properly be called a monarchy in its government. The Pope was its all-powerful and absolute head. He was the supreme lawgiver. He might set aside or repeal any law of the Church, no matter how ancient, so long as he did not believe it to be ordained by the Scriptures or by Nature. He might, for good reasons, make exceptions to all merely human laws ; as, for instance, permit cousins to marry, or free a monk from his vows. Such exceptions were known as *dispensations*.

The Pope was not merely the supreme lawgiver, he was the supreme judge. Anyone, whether clergyman or layman, in any part of Europe could appeal to him at any stage in the trial of a large class of cases. Obviously this system had serious drawbacks. Grave injustice might be done by carrying to Rome a case which ought to have been settled in Edinburgh or Cologne, where the facts were best known. The rich, moreover, always had the advantage, as they alone could afford to bring suits before so distant a court.

The control of the Pope over all parts of the Christian Church was exercised by his *legates*. These papal ambassadors were intrusted with great powers. Their haughty mien sometimes offended the prelates and rulers to whom they brought home the authority of the Pope,— as, for instance, when the legate Pandulf grandly absolved all the subjects of King John of England, before his very face, from their oath of fealty to him (§ 552).

The task assumed by the Pope of governing the whole Western world naturally made it necessary to create a large body of officials at Rome in order to transact all the multiform business and prepare and transmit the innumerable legal documents.[1] The cardinals and the Pope's officials constituted what was called the papal *curia*, or court.

619. Sources of the Pope's Income. To carry on his government, and to meet the expenses of palace and retinue, the Pope had need of a vast income. This he secured from various sources.

---

[1] Many of the edicts, decisions, and orders of the popes were called *bulls*, from the seal (Latin, *bulla*) attached to them.

Heavy fees were exacted from those who brought cases to his court for decision. The archbishops, bishops, and abbots were expected to make generous contributions when the Pope confirmed their election. In the thirteenth century the Pope himself began to fill many benefices throughout Europe, and he customarily received half the first year's revenues from those whom he appointed. For several centuries before the Protestants finally threw off their allegiance to the popes there was widespread complaint on the part of both clergy and laymen that the fees and taxes levied by the Roman *curia* were excessive.

620. The Archbishops and Bishops. Next in order below the head of the Church were the archbishops and bishops. An archbishop was a bishop whose power extended beyond the boundaries of his own diocese and who exercised a certain control over all the bishops within his province.

There is perhaps no class of persons in medieval times whose position it is so necessary to understand as that of the bishops. They were regarded as the successors of the apostles, whose powers were held to be divinely transmitted to them. They represented the Church Universal in their respective dioceses, under the supreme headship of their "elder brother," the Pope, the bishop of Rome, the successor of the chief of the apostles. Their insignia of office, the miter and crosier, are familiar to everyone (see tailpiece at end of this chapter). Each bishop had his especial church, which was called a cathedral and usually surpassed the other churches of the diocese in size and beauty.

In addition to the oversight of his diocese, it was the bishop's business to look after the lands and other possessions which belonged to the bishopric. Lastly, the bishop was usually a feudal lord, with the obligations which that implied. He might have vassals and subvassals, and often was himself a vassal, not only of the king but also of some neighboring lord.

621. The Parish Priest and his Duties. The lowest division of the Church was the parish. At the head of the parish was the parish priest, who conducted services in the parish church and absolved, baptized, married, and buried his parishioners. The priests were supposed to be supported by the lands belonging to the parish church and by the tithes. But both of these sources of income were often in the hands of laymen or of a neighboring monastery, while the poor priest received the merest pittance, scarcely sufficient to keep soul and body together.

622. Reasons for the Great Power of Clergymen in the Middle Ages. The influence of the clergy was greatly increased

FIG. 101. CANTERBURY CATHEDRAL

The bishop's church was called a cathedral, because in it stood the bishop's chair, or throne (Latin, *cathedra*). It was therefore much more imposing ordinarily than the parish churches, although sometimes the abbey churches belonging to rich monasteries vied with the bishop's church in beauty

by the fact that they alone were educated. For six or seven centuries after the break-up of the Roman Empire very few outside of the clergy ever dreamed of studying, or even of learning to read and write. Even in the thirteenth century an offender who wished to prove that he belonged to the clergy, in order that he might be tried by a church court, had only to show that he could read a single line; for it was assumed by the judges that no one unconnected with the Church could read at all.

It was therefore inevitable that all the teachers were clergymen, that almost all the books were written by priests and monks, and that the clergy was the ruling power in all intellectual, artistic, and literary matters — the chief guardians and promoters of civilization. Moreover, the civil government was forced to rely upon churchmen to write out the public documents and proclamations. The priests and monks held the pen for the king. Representatives of the clergy sat in the king's councils and acted as his ministers ; in fact, the conduct of the government largely devolved upon them.

The offices in the Church were open to all ranks of men, and many of the popes themselves sprang from the humblest classes. The Church thus constantly recruited its ranks with fresh blood. No one held an office simply because his father had held it before him, as was the case in the civil government.

623. Excommunication and Interdict. No wonder that the churchmen were by far the most powerful class in the Middle Ages. They controlled great wealth ; they alone were educated ; it was believed they held the keys of the kingdom of heaven and without their aid no one could hope to enter in. By excommunication they could cast out the enemies of the Church and could forbid all men to associate with them, since they were accursed. By means of the *interdict* they could suspend all religious ceremonies in a whole city or country by closing the church doors and prohibiting all public services.

II. The Heretics and the Inquisition

624. Rebels against the Church : Heresy. Nevertheless, in spite of the power and wonderful organization of the Church, a few people began to revolt against it as early as the time of Gregory VII, and the number of these rebels continued to increase as time went on. Popular leaders arose who declared that no one ought any longer to rely upon the Church for his salvation ; that all its elaborate ceremonies were worse than useless ; that its Masses, holy water, and relics were mere money-getting devices of a sinful priesthood and helped no one to heaven.

Those who questioned the teachings of the Church and proposed to cast off its authority were, according to the accepted view of the time, guilty of the supreme crime of heresy. Heretics were of two sorts. One class merely rejected the practices and some of the doctrines of the Roman Catholic Church while they remained Christians and endeavored to imitate as nearly as possible the simple life of Christ and the apostles.

625. The Waldensians. Among those who continued to accept the Christian faith but refused to obey the clergy the most important sect was that of the Waldensians, which took its rise about 1175. These were followers of Peter Waldo of Lyons, who gave up all their property and lived a life of apostolic poverty. They went about preaching the Gospel and explaining the Scriptures, which they translated from Latin into the language of the people. They made many converts, and before the end of the twelfth century there were great numbers of them scattered throughout western Europe.

626. The Albigensians. On the other hand, there were popular leaders who taught that the Christian religion itself was false. They held that there were two principles in the universe, the good and the evil, which were forever fighting for the victory. They asserted that the Jehovah of the Old Testament was really the evil power, and that it was, therefore, the evil power whom the Catholic Church worshiped. These heretics were often called Albigensians, a name derived from the town of Albi in southern France, where they were very numerous. Their teachings were, however, old, common before the break-up of the Roman Empire.

It is very difficult for us who live in a time of religious toleration to understand the universal and deep-rooted horror of heresy which long prevailed in Europe. But we must recollect that to the orthodox believer in the Church nothing could exceed the guilt of one who committed treason against God by rejecting the religion which had been handed down in the Roman Church from the immediate followers of his Son. Moreover, doubt and unbelief were not merely sin ; they were revolt against the most powerful social institution of the time, which, in spite of the sins of some of its officials, continued to be venerated by people at large throughout western Europe.

In southern France there were many adherents of both the Albigensians and the Waldensians, especially in the county of Toulouse. At the beginning of the thirteenth century there was in this region an open contempt for the Church, and bold heretical teachings were heard even among the higher classes.

Against the people of this flourishing land Pope Innocent III preached a crusade in 1208. An army marched from northern France into the doomed region and, after one of the most atrocious and bloody wars upon record, suppressed the heresy by wholesale slaughter. At the same time, the war checked the civilization and destroyed the prosperity of the most enlightened portion of France.

627. The Inquisition. The most permanent defense of the Church against heresy was the establishment, under the headship of the Pope, of a system of courts designed to ferret out secret cases of unbelief and bring the offenders to punishment. These courts, which devoted their whole attention to the discovery and conviction of heretics, were called the Holy Inquisition, which gradually took form after the Albigensian crusade. The unfairness of the trials and the cruel treatment of those suspected of heresy, through long imprisonment or torture,—inflicted with the hope of forcing them to confess their crime or to implicate others, —have rendered the name of the Inquisition infamous.

Without by any means attempting to defend the methods employed, it may be remarked that the inquisitors were often earnest and upright men, and the methods of procedure of the Inquisition were not more cruel than those used in the secular courts of the period.

The assertion of the suspected person that he was not a heretic did not receive any attention, for it was assumed that he would naturally deny his guilt, as would any other criminal. A person's belief had, therefore, to be judged by outward acts. Consequently one might fall into the hands of the Inquisition by mere accidental conversation with a heretic, by some unintentional neglect to show due respect toward the Church rites, or by the malicious testimony of one's neighbors. This is really the most terrible aspect of the Inquisition and its procedure.

If the suspected person confessed his guilt and abjured his heresy, he was forgiven and received back into the Church; but a penance of life imprisonment was imposed upon him as a fitting means of wiping away the unspeakable sin of which he had been guilty. If he persisted in his heresy he was "relaxed to the secular arm"; that is to say, the Church, whose law forbade it to shed blood, handed over the convicted person to the civil power, which burned him alive without further trial.

III. THE FRANCISCANS AND DOMINICANS

628. Founding of the Mendicant Orders. We may now turn to that far more cheerful and effective method of meeting the opponents of the Church, which may be said to have been discovered by St. Francis of Assisi. His teachings and the example of his beautiful life probably did far more to secure continued allegiance to the Church than all the harsh devices of the Inquisition.

We have seen how the Waldensians tried to better the world by living simple lives and preaching the Gospel. Owing to the disfavor of the Church authorities, who declared their teachings erroneous and dangerous, they were prevented from publicly carrying on their missionary work. Yet all conscientious men agreed with the Waldensians that the world was in a sad plight, owing to the negligence and the misdeeds of the clergy. St. Francis and St. Dominic strove to meet the needs of their time by inventing a new kind of clergyman, the begging brother, or "mendicant friar" (from the Latin *frater*, "brother"). He was to do just what the bishops and parish priests often failed to do — namely, lead a holy life of self-sacrifice, defend the Church's beliefs against the attacks of the heretics, and awaken the people to a new religious life. The founding of the mendicant orders is one of the most interesting events of the Middle Ages.

629. St. Francis of Assisi (1182-1226) **and his Order.** There is no more lovely and fascinating figure in all history than St. Francis. He was born (probably in 1182) at Assisi, a little town in central Italy. He was the son of a well-to-do merchant, and during his early youth he lived a very gay life, spending his father's money freely. He read the French romances of the time and dreamed of imitating the brave knights whose adventures they described. Although his companions were wild and reckless, there was a delicacy and chivalry in Francis's own make-up which made him hate all things coarse and heartless. When later he voluntarily became a beggar, his ragged cloak still covered a true poet and knight.

The contrast between his own life of luxury and the sad state of the poor early afflicted him. When he was about twenty, after a long and serious illness which made a break in his gay life and gave him time to think, he suddenly lost his love for the old pleasures and began to consort with the destitute, above all with lepers. His father does not appear to have had any fondness whatever for beggars, and the relations between him and his son grew more and more strained. When finally he threatened to disinherit the young man, Francis cheerfully agreed to surrender all right to his inheritance. Stripping off his clothes and giving them back to his father, he accepted the worn-out garment of a gardener and became a homeless hermit, busying himself in repairing the dilapidated chapels near Assisi.

He soon began to preach in a simple way, and before long a rich fellow townsman resolved to follow Francis's example — sell his all and give to the poor. Others soon joined them, and these joyous converts, free of worldly burdens, went barefoot and penniless about central Italy preaching the Gospel instead of shutting themselves up in a monastery.

When, with a dozen followers, Francis appealed to the Pope in 1210 for his approval, Pope Innocent III hesitated. He did not believe that anyone could lead a life of absolute poverty. Moreover, might not these ragged, ill-kempt vagabonds seem to condemn the Church by adopting a life so different from that of the rich and comfortable clergy? Yet if he disapproved the friars he would seem to disapprove at the same time Christ's directions to his apostles. He finally decided to authorize the brethren to continue their missions.

630. Missionary Work undertaken. Seven years later, when Francis's followers had greatly increased in numbers, missionary work was begun on a large scale, and brethren were dispatched to Germany, Hungary, France, Spain, and even to Syria. It was not long before an English chronicler was telling with wonder of the arrival in his country of these barefoot men, in their patched gowns and with ropes about their waists, who, with Christian faith, took no thought for the morrow, believing that their Heavenly Father knew what things they had need of.

631. Francis did not desire to found a Powerful Order. As time went on, the success of their missionary work led the Pope to bestow many privileges upon them. It grieved Francis, however, to think of his little band of companions being converted into a great and powerful order. He foresaw that they would soon cease to lead their simple, holy life and would become ambitious and perhaps rich. "I, little Brother Francis," he writes, "desire to follow the life and the poverty of Jesus Christ, persevering therein until the end; and I beg you all and exhort you to persevere always in this most holy life of poverty, and take good care never to depart from it upon the advice and teachings of anyone whomsoever."

After the death of St. Francis (1226) many of the order, which now numbered several thousand members, wished to maintain the simple rule of absolute poverty; others, including the new head of the order, believed that much good might be done with the wealth which people were anxious to give them. They argued that the individual friars might still remain absolutely possessionless even if the order had beautiful churches and comfortable monasteries. So a stately church was immediately constructed at Assisi to receive the remains of their humble founder, who in his lifetime had chosen a deserted hovel for his home; and a great chest was set up in the church to receive the offerings of those who desired to give.

632. The Founding of the Dominican Order. St. Dominic (b. 1170), the Spanish founder of the other great mendicant order, was not a simple layman like Francis. He was a churchman and took a regular course of instruction in theology for ten years in a Spanish university. He then (1208) accompanied his bishop to southern France on the eve of the Albigensian crusade and was deeply shocked to see the prevalence of heresy. His host at Toulouse happened to be an Albigensian, and Dominic spent the night in converting him. He then and there determined to devote his life to fighting heresy.

By 1214 a few sympathetic spirits from various parts of Europe had joined Dominic, and they asked Pope Innocent III to sanction their new order. The Pope again hesitated, but is said to have dreamed a dream in which he saw the great Roman Church of the Lateran tottering and ready to fall had not Dominic supported it on his shoulders. He interpreted this as meaning that the new organization might sometime become a great aid to the papacy, and gave it his approval. As soon as possible Dominic sent forth his followers, of whom there were but sixteen, to evangelize the world, just as the Franciscans were undertaking their first missionary journeys. By 1221 the Dominican order was thoroughly organized and had sixty monasteries scattered over western Europe.

"Wandering on foot over the face of Europe, under burning suns or chilling blasts, rejecting alms in money but receiving thankfully whatever coarse food might be set before the wayfarer, enduring hunger in silent resignation, taking no thought for the morrow, but busied eternally in the work of snatching souls from Satan and lifting men up from the sordid cares of daily life"—in this way did the early Franciscans and Dominicans win the love and veneration of the people.

The Dominicans were called the "Preaching Friars" and were carefully trained in theology in order the better to refute the arguments of the heretics. The Pope delegated to them especially the task of conducting the Inquisition. They early began to extend their influence over the universities, and the two most distinguished theologians and teachers of the thirteenth century, Albertus Magnus and Thomas Aquinas, were Dominicans. Among the Franciscans, on the other hand, there was always a considerable party who were suspicious of learning and who showed a greater desire to remain absolutely poor than did the Dominicans. Yet as a whole the Franciscans, like the Dominicans, accepted the wealth that came to them, and they too contributed distinguished scholars to the universities.

IV. Church and State

633. Chief Sources of Difficulty between Church and State. We have seen that the Medieval Church was a single great institution with its head, the Pope, at Rome and its officers in all the countries of western Europe. It had its laws, law courts, taxes, and even prisons, just like the various kings and other rulers. In general, the kings were ready to punish everyone who revolted against the Church. Indeed, the State depended upon the churchmen in many ways. It was the churchmen who wrote out the documents which the king required ; they took care of the schools, aided the poor, and protected the weak. They tried, by issuing the Truce of God (§ 534), to discourage neighborhood warfare, which the kings were unable to stop.

But as the period of disorder drew to an end and the kings and other rulers got the better of the feudal lords and established peace in their realms, they began to think that the Church had become too powerful and too rich. Certain difficulties arose of which the following were the most important :

1. Should the king or the Pope have the advantage of selecting the bishops and the abbots of rich monasteries ? Naturally both were anxious to place their friends and supporters in these influential positions. Moreover, the Pope, like the king, could claim a considerable contribution from those whom he appointed, and the king naturally grudged him the money (compare §§ 586–590).

2. How far might the king venture to tax the lands and other property of the Church ? Was this vast amount of wealth to go on increasing and yet make no contribution to the support of the government ? The churchmen usually maintained that they needed all their money to carry on the church services, keep

up the churches and monasteries, take care of the schools, and aid the poor, for the State left them to bear all these necessary burdens. The law of the Church permitted the churchmen to make voluntary gifts to the king when there was urgent necessity.

3. Then there was trouble over the cases to be tried in the church courts and the claim of churchmen to be tried only by clergymen. Worst of all was the habit of appealing cases to Rome, for the Pope would often decide the matter in exactly the opposite way from which the king's court had decided it.

4. Lastly there was the question of how far the Pope as head of the Christian Church had a right to interfere with the government of a particular state, when he did not approve of the way in which a king was acting. The powers of the Pope were very great, everyone admitted, but even the most devout Catholics differed somewhat as to just how great they were.

We have seen some illustrations of these troubles in the chapter on the Popes and Emperors.

634. Edward I and Philip the Fair propose to tax the Clergy. It was natural after a monarch had squeezed all that he could out of the Jews and the towns, and had exacted every possible feudal due, that he should turn to the rich estates of the clergy, in spite of their claim that their property was dedicated to God and owed the king nothing. The extensive enterprises of Edward I (§§ 559 ff.) led him in 1296 to demand one fifth of the personal property of the clergy.

Philip the Fair of France exacted one hundredth and then one fiftieth of the possessions of clergy and laity alike. This led to a bitter conflict between the French king and Pope Boniface VIII about the year 1300. The Pope at first forbade all such payments but was in the end forced to permit the clergy to pay their feudal dues and make loans to the king.

In spite of this setback the Pope never seemed more completely the recognized head of the Western world than during the first great jubilee, in the year 1300, when Boniface called together all Christendom to celebrate the opening of the new century by a great religious festival at Rome. It is reported that two millions of people, coming from all parts of Europe, visited the churches of Rome, and that in spite of widening the streets many were crushed in the crowd. So great was the influx of money into the papal treasury that two assistants were kept busy with rakes collecting the offerings which were deposited at the tomb of St. Peter.

635. The Babylonian Captivity of the Church. After the death of Boniface (1303) King Philip proposed to have no more trouble with popes. He arranged in 1305 to have the French Archbishop of Bordeaux chosen head of the Church, with the understanding that he should transfer the papacy from Rome to France. The new Pope accordingly summoned the cardinals to meet him at Lyons, where he was crowned under the title of "Clement V." He remained in France during his whole pontificate, moving from one rich abbey to another.

His successors took up their residence in the town of Avignon, just outside the French frontier of those days. There they built a sumptuous palace in which successive popes lived in great splendor for sixty years.

The prolonged exile of the popes from Rome, lasting from 1305 to 1377, is commonly called the Babylonian Captivity [1] of the Church, on account of the woes attributed to it. The popes of this period were for the most part good and earnest men; but they were all Frenchmen, and the proximity of their court to France led to the natural suspicion that they were controlled by the French kings. This, together with their luxurious court, brought them into discredit with the other nations, above all with the English and the Germans.

At Avignon the popes were naturally deprived of some of the revenue which they had enjoyed from their Italian possessions when they lived at Rome. This deficiency had to be made up by increased taxation, especially as the expenses of the splendid papal court were very heavy. The papacy was, consequently, rendered unpopular by the various new methods employed to raise money.

[1] The name recalled, of course, the long exile of the Jews from their land (see above, §§ 110–111).

636. Statute of Provisors (1352). The papal exactions met with the greatest opposition in England because the popes were thought to favor France, with which country the English were at war. A law was passed by Parliament in 1352, ordering that

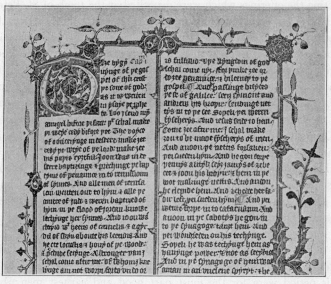

FIG. 102. PAGE FROM WYCLIFFE'S TRANSLATION OF THE BIBLE

This is the upper half of the first page of the Gospel according to Mark and contains verses 1-7 and 15-23. The scribe of the time made *i*, *y*, and *th* in something the same way. The page begins: " The bigynninge of the gospel of ihusu crist, the sone of god. As it is writen in isaie, the prophete, Loo, I send myn aungel bifore thi face, that schal make thi weie redi bifore thee. The voice of one crying in deseert, make thee redi the weie of the lord, make thee his pathis ryghtful. Joon was in deseert baptizinge and prechinge the baptism of penaunce in to remissioun of sinnes." While the spelling is somewhat different from ours it is clear that the language used by Wycliffe closely resembled that used in the familiar authorized version of the New Testament, made two centuries and a half later

all who procured a church office from the Pope should be outlawed, since they were enemies of the king and his realm. This and similar laws failed, however, to prevent the Pope from filling English benefices. The English king was unable to keep the money of his realm from flowing to Avignon, and at the meeting of the English Parliament held in 1376 a report was made to the effect that the taxes levied by the Pope in England were five times those raised by the king.

637. John Wycliffe. The most famous and conspicuous critic of the Pope at this time was John Wycliffe, a teacher at Oxford. He was born about 1320, but we know little of him before 1366, when Pope Urban V demanded that England should pay the tribute promised by King John when he became the Pope's vassal (§ 552). Parliament declared that John had no right to bind the people without their consent, and Wycliffe began his career of opposition to the papacy by trying to prove that John's agreement was void. About ten years later we find the Pope issuing bulls against the teachings of Wycliffe, who had begun to assert that the State might appropriate the property of the Church, if it was misused, and that the Pope had no authority except as he acted according to the Gospel. Soon Wycliffe went further and boldly attacked the papacy itself, as well as many of the Church institutions.

Wycliffe's anxiety to teach the people led him to have the Bible translated into English. An example of his language is given on the previous page. He also prepared a great number of sermons and tracts in English. He is the father of English prose, for we have little in English before his time, except poetry.

Wycliffe and his "simple priests" were charged with encouraging the discontent and disorder which culminated in the Peasants' Revolt, which occurred not long before his death (§ 572). Whether this charge was true or not, it caused many of his followers to fall away from him. But in spite of this and the denunciations of the Church, Wycliffe was not seriously interfered with and died peaceably in 1384. Wycliffe is remarkable as being the first distinguished scholar and reformer to repudiate the headship of the Pope and those practices of the Church of Rome which more than a century after his death were attacked by Luther in his successful revolt against the Medieval Church. This will be discussed in a later chapter.

QUESTIONS

I. In what ways did the Medieval Church differ from the modern churches with which we are familiar? In what ways did the Medieval Church resemble a State? What were the powers of the Pope? What were the duties of a bishop in the Middle Ages? Why was the clergy the most powerful class in the Middle Ages?

II. What were the views of the Waldensians? of the Albigensians? What was the Inquisition?

III. Narrate briefly the life of St. Francis. Did the Franciscan order continue to follow the wishes of its founder? Contrast the Dominicans with the Franciscans.

IV. What were the chief subjects of disagreement between the Church and the State? Describe the conflict between Boniface VIII and Philip the Fair. How did the Babylonian Captivity come about? What were some of the results of the sojourn of the popes at Avignon? What were the views of John Wycliffe?

NOTE. The tailpiece of this chapter represents an English bishop ordaining a priest and is taken from a manuscript of Henry II's time. The bishop is wearing his miter and holds his pastoral staff, the crosier, in his left hand while he raises his right, in blessing, over the priest's head.

CHAPTER XXIX

MEDIEVAL TOWNS — THEIR BUSINESS AND BUILDINGS

I. THE TOWNS AND GUILDS

638. Reappearance of Towns and their Importance. In discussing the Middle Ages we have hitherto dealt mainly with kings and emperors, and with the popes and the Church of which they were the chief rulers ; we have also described the monks and monasteries, the warlike feudal lords and their castles, and the hard-working serfs who farmed the manors ; but nothing has been said about the people who lived in the towns.

Towns have always been the chief centers of progress and enlightenment, for the simple reason that people must live close together in large numbers before they can develop business on a large scale, carry on trade with foreign countries, establish good schools and universities, erect noble public buildings, support libraries and museums and art galleries. One does not find these in the country, for the people outside the towns are too scattered and usually too poor to have the things that are common enough in large cities.

One of the chief peculiarities of the early Middle Ages, from the break-up of the Roman Empire to the time of William the Conqueror, was the absence of large and flourishing towns in western Europe, and this fact alone would serve to explain why there was so little progress.

The Roman towns were decreasing in population before the German inroads. The confusion which followed the invasions hastened their decline, and a great number of them disappeared altogether. Those which survived and such new towns as sprang up were of little importance during the early Middle Ages. During the long period from Theodoric to Frederick Barbarossa, over six centuries, by far the greater part of the population of England, Germany, and northern and central France were living in the country, on the great estates belonging to the feudal lords, abbots, and bishops.[1]

A great part of the medieval towns, of which we begin to have some scanty records about the year 1000, appear to have originated on the manors of feudal lords or about a monastery or castle (Fig. 103). The French name for town, *ville*, is derived from "vill," the name of the manor, and we use this old Roman word when we call a town Jackson*ville* or Harris*ville*. The need of protection was probably the usual reason for establishing a town with walls about it, so that the townspeople and the neighboring country people might find safety within it when attacked by neighboring feudal lords.

639. Compactness of a Medieval Town. The way in which a medieval town was built seems to justify this conclusion (see headpiece of this chapter—the German town of Siegen as it formerly looked). It was generally crowded and compact compared with its more luxurious Roman predecessors. Aside from the market place there were few or no open spaces. There were no amphitheaters or public baths as in the Roman cities. The streets were often mere alleys over which the jutting stories of the high houses almost met. The high, thick wall that surrounded it prevented its extending easily and rapidly as our cities do nowadays.

640. Townsmen originally Serfs. All towns outside of Italy (§ 598) were small in the eleventh and twelfth centuries, and, like the manors on which they had grown up, they had little commerce as yet with the outside world. They produced almost all

[1] In Italy and southern France town life was doubtless more general than in northern Europe.

that their inhabitants needed except the farm products which came from the neighboring country. There was likely to be little expansion as long as the town remained under the absolute control of the lord or monastery upon whose land it was situated. The townspeople were scarcely more than serfs, in spite of the fact

Fig. 103. A Castle with a Village below it

A village was pretty sure to grow up near the castle of a powerful lord and might gradually become a large town

that they lived within a wall and were traders and artisans instead of farmers. They had to pay irritating dues to their lord, just as if they still formed a farming community.

With the increase of trade (see below, §§ 643–648) came the longing for greater freedom. For when new and attractive commodities began to be brought from the East and the South, the people of the towns were encouraged to make things which they could exchange at some neighboring fair for the products of distant lands. But no sooner did the townsmen begin to engage in manufacturing and to enter into relations with the outside world than they became aware that they were subject to exactions and restrictions which rendered progress impossible.

Consequently, during the twelfth century there were many insurrections of the towns against their lords, and there was a general demand that the lords should grant the townsmen *charters* in which the rights of both parties should be definitely stated.

641. Town Charters. These charters were written contracts between the lord and the town government, which served at once as the certificate of birth of the town and as its constitution. The old dues and services which the townspeople owed as serfs (see above, § 525) were either abolished or changed into money payments.

As a visible sign of their freedom many of the towns had a belfry, a high building with a watchtower, where a guard was kept day and night in order that the bell might be rung in case of approaching danger (see headpiece of this chapter). It contained an assembly hall, where those who governed the town held their meetings, and a prison. In the fourteenth century the wonderful town halls began to be erected, which, with the exception of the cathedrals and other churches, are usually the most remarkable buildings which the traveler sees to-day in the old commercial cities of Europe.

642. The Guilds. The tradesmen in the medieval towns were at once manufacturers and merchants; that is, they made, as well as offered for sale, the articles which they kept in their shops. Those who belonged to a particular trade — the bakers, the butchers, the sword-makers, the armorers, etc.— formed unions or guilds to protect their special interests. The oldest statutes of a guild in Paris are those of the candle-makers, which go back to 1061. The number of trades differed greatly in different towns, but the guilds all had the same object — to prevent anyone from practicing a trade who had not been duly admitted to the union.

A young man had to spend several years in learning his trade. During this time he lived in the house of a "master workman" as

FIG. 104. STREET IN QUIMPER, FRANCE

None of the streets in even the oldest European towns look just as they did
in the twelfth and thirteenth centuries, but here and there, as in this town of
Brittany, one can still get some idea of the narrow, cramped streets and overhanging houses and the beautiful cathedral crowded in among them

an "apprentice," but received no remuneration. He then became a "journeyman" and could earn wages, although he was still allowed to work only for master workmen and not directly for the public. A simple trade might be learned in three years, but to become a goldsmith one must be an apprentice for ten years. The number of apprentices that a master workman might employ was strictly limited, in order that the journeymen might not become too numerous.

The way in which each trade was to be practiced was carefully regulated, as well as the time that should be spent in work each day. The system of guilds discouraged enterprise but maintained uniform standards everywhere. Had it not been for these unions the defenseless, isolated workmen, serfs as they had formerly been, would have found it impossible to secure freedom and municipal independence from the feudal lords who had formerly been their masters.

II. Business in the Later Middle Ages

643. Revival of Business. The chief reason for the growth of the towns and their increasing prosperity was a great development of trade throughout western Europe. Commerce had pretty much disappeared with the decline of the Roman roads and the general disorganization produced by the barbarian invasions. In the early Middle Ages there was no one to mend the ancient Roman thoroughfares. The great network of highways from Persia to Britain fell apart when independent nobles or poor local communities took the place of a world empire. All trade languished, for there was little demand for those articles of luxury which the Roman communities in the North had been accustomed to obtain from the South, and there was but little money to buy what we should consider the comforts of life; even the nobility lived uncomfortably enough in their dreary and rudely furnished castles.

644. Italian Cities trade with the Orient. In Italy, however, trade does not seem to have altogether ceased. Venice, Genoa, Amalfi, and other towns appear to have developed a considerable

Mediterranean commerce even before the Crusades (see map above, p. 396). Their merchants, as we have seen, supplied the destitute crusaders with the material necessary for the conquest of Jerusalem (§ 607). The passion for pilgrimages offered inducements to the Italian merchants for expeditions to the Orient, whither they transported the pilgrims and returned with the products of the East. The Italian cities established trading stations in the East and carried on a direct traffic with the caravans which brought to the shores of the Mediterranean the products of Arabia, Persia, India, and the Spice Islands. The southern French towns and Barcelona entered also into commercial relations with the Mohammedans in northern Africa.

645. Commerce stimulates Industry. This progress in the South could not but stir the lethargy of the rest of Europe. When commerce began to revive, it encouraged a revolution in manufacture. So long as the manor system prevailed and each man was occupied in producing only what he and the other people on the estate needed, there was nothing to send abroad and nothing to exchange for luxuries. But when merchants began to come with tempting articles, the members of a community were encouraged to produce a surplus of goods above what they themselves needed, and to sell or exchange this surplus for commodities coming from a distance. Merchants and artisans gradually directed their energies toward the production of what others wished as well as what was needed by the little group to which they belonged.

646. The Luxuries of the East introduced into Europe. The romances of the twelfth century indicate that the West was astonished and delighted by the luxuries of the East — the rich fabrics, oriental carpets, precious stones, perfumes, drugs, silks, and porcelains from China, spices from India, and cotton from Egypt. Venice introduced the silk industry from the East and the manufacture of those glass articles which the traveler may still buy in the Venetian shops. The West learned how to make silk and velvet as well as light and gauzy cotton and linen fabrics. The Eastern dyes were introduced, and Paris was soon imitating the tapestries of the Saracens. In exchange for those luxuries which they were unable to produce, the Flemish towns sent their woolen cloths to the East, and Italy its wines.

647. Important Commercial Centers. The Northern merchants dealt mainly with Venice and brought their wares across the Brenner Pass and down the Rhine, or sent them by sea to be exchanged in Flanders (see map). By the thirteenth century important centers of trade had come into being, some of which are still among the great commercial towns of the world. Hamburg, Lübeck, and Bremen carried on active trade with the countries on the Baltic and with England. Augsburg and Nuremberg, in the south of Germany, became important on account of their situation on the line of trade between Italy and the North. Bruges and Ghent sent their manufactures everywhere. English commerce was relatively unimportant as yet compared with that of the great ports of the Mediterranean.

648. Obstacles to Business. For various reasons it was very difficult indeed to carry on business on a large scale in the Middle Ages. In the first place, as has been said, there was little money, and money is essential to buying and selling, unless people confine themselves merely to exchanging one article for another. There were few gold and silver mines in western Europe, and consequently the kings and feudal lords could not supply enough coin. Moreover, the coins were crude, with such rough, irregular edges (Fig. 105) that many people yielded to the temptation to pare off a little of the precious metal before they passed the money on. "Clipping," as this was called, was harshly punished, but that did not stop the practice, which continued for hundreds of years. Nowadays our coins are perfectly round and often have "milled" edges, so that no one would think of trying to appropriate bits of them as they pass through his hands.

It was universally believed that everything had a "just" price, which was merely enough to cover the cost of the materials used in its manufacture and to remunerate the maker for the work he had put into it. It was considered outrageous to ask more than the just price, no matter how anxious the purchaser might be to obtain the article.

Every manufacturer was required to keep a shop in which he offered at retail all that he made. Those who lived near a town were permitted to sell their products in the market place within the walls on condition that they sold directly to the consumers. They might not dispose of their whole stock to one dealer, for fear that if he had all there was of a commodity he might raise the price above the just one. These ideas made all wholesale trade very difficult.

649. Payment of Interest on Money forbidden. Akin to these prejudices against wholesale business was that against taking interest. Money was believed to be a dead and sterile thing, and no one had a right to demand any return for lending it. Interest was considered wicked, since it was exacted by

FIG. 105. MEDIEVAL COINS

The two upper coins reproduce the face and back of a silver penny of William the Conqueror's reign, and below is a silver groat of Edward III. The same irregularities in outline will be noted in the ancient coins represented in Fig. 36

those who took advantage of the embarrassments of others. "Usury," as the taking of even the most moderate and reasonable rate of interest was then called, was strenuously forbidden by the laws of the Church. We find Church councils ordering that impenitent usurers should be refused Christian burial and have their wills annulled. So money lending, which is necessary to all great commercial and industrial undertakings, was left to the Jews, who were not required to obey the rules established by the Christian Church for its own members.

650. The Jews as Money Lenders. This ill-starred people played a most important part in the economic development of Europe, but they were terribly maltreated by the Christians, who held them guilty of the supreme crime of putting Christ to death. The active persecution of the Jews did not, however, become common before the thirteenth century, when they first began to be required to wear a peculiar cap, or badge, which made them easily recognized and exposed them to constant insult. Later they were sometimes shut up in a particular quarter of the city, called the Jewry. As they were excluded from the guilds, they not unnaturally turned to the business of money lending, which no Christian might practice. Undoubtedly this occupation had much to do in causing their unpopularity. The kings permitted them to make loans, often at a most exorbitant rate ; Philip Augustus allowed them to exact 46 per cent, but reserved the right to extort their gains from them when the royal treasury was empty. In England the usual rate was a penny a pound for each week.

651. The Lombards as Bankers. In the thirteenth century the Italians—Lombards, as the English called them [1]—began to go into a sort of banking business and greatly extended the employment of bills of exchange. They lent for nothing, but exacted damages for all delay in repayment. This appeared reasonable and right even to those who condemned ordinary interest.

652. Tolls and Other Annoyances. Another serious disadvantage which the medieval merchant had to face was the payment of an infinite number of tolls and duties which were demanded by the lords through whose domains his road passed. Not only were duties exacted on the highways, bridges, and at the fords, but those barons who were so fortunate as to have castles on a navigable river blocked the stream in such a way that the merchant could not bring his vessel through without a payment for the privilege.

The charges were usually small, but the way in which they were collected and the repeated delays must have been a serious source of irritation and loss to the merchants. For example, a

[1] There is a Lombard Street in the center of old London where one still finds banks.

certain monastery lying between Paris and the sea required that those hastening to town with fresh fish should stop and let the monks pick out what they thought worth three pence, with little regard to the condition in which they left the goods. When a boat laden with wine passed up the Seine to Paris, the agent of the lord of Poissy could have three casks broached, and, after trying them all, he could take a measure from the one he liked best. At the markets all sorts of dues had to be paid, such, for example, as fees for using the lord's scales or his measuring rod. Besides this, the great variety of coinage which existed in feudal Europe caused infinite perplexity and delay.

653. Pirates. Commerce by sea had its own particular trials, by no means confined to the hazards of wind and wave, rock and shoal. Pirates were numerous in the North Sea. They were often organized and sometimes led by men of high rank, who appear to have regarded the business as no disgrace. The coasts were dangerous and lighthouses and beacons were few. Moreover, natural dangers were increased by false signals which wreckers used to lure ships to shore in order to plunder them.

654. The Hanseatic League. With a view of reducing these manifold perils, the towns early began to form unions for mutual defense. The most famous of these was that of the German cities, called the Hanseatic League. Lübeck was always the leader, but among the seventy towns which at one time and another were included in the confederation we find Cologne, Brunswick, Danzig, and other centers of great importance. The union purchased and controlled settlements in London,— the so-called Steelyard near London Bridge,— at Wisby, Bergen, and the far-off Novgorod in Russia. They managed to monopolize nearly the whole trade on the Baltic and North Seas, either through treaties or the influence that they were able to bring to bear.[1]

The League made war on the pirates and did much to reduce the dangers of traffic. Instead of dispatching separate and defenseless merchantmen, their ships sailed out in fleets under the protection of a man-of-war. On one occasion the League

[1] The ships of the Hanseatic League were very small (see below, Fig. 152).

undertook a successful war against the king of Denmark, who had interfered with their interests. At another time it declared war on England and brought her to terms. For two hundred years before the discovery of America the League played a great part in the commercial affairs of western Europe; but it had begun to decline even before the discovery of new routes to the East and West Indies revolutionized trade.

655. Trade carried on by Towns not by Nations. It should be observed that, during the thirteenth, fourteenth, and fifteenth centuries, trade was not carried on between *nations*, but by the various *towns*, like Venice, Lübeck, Ghent, Bruges, Cologne. A merchant did not act or trade as an independent individual but as a member of a particular merchant guild, and he enjoyed the protection of his town and of the treaties it arranged. If a merchant from a certain town failed to pay a debt, a fellow-townsman might be seized if found in the town where the debt was due. At the period of which we have been speaking, an inhabitant of London was considered as much of a foreigner in Bristol as was the merchant from Cologne or Antwerp. Only gradually did the towns merge into the nations to which their people belonged.

The increasing wealth of the merchants could not fail to raise them to a position of importance which earlier tradesmen had not enjoyed. They began to build fine houses and to buy the various comforts and luxuries which were finding their way into western Europe. They wanted their sons to be educated, and so it came about that other people besides clergymen began to learn how to read and write. As early as the fourteenth century many of the books appear to have been written with a view of meeting the tastes and needs of the business class.

Representatives of the towns were summoned to the councils of the kings—into the English Parliament and the French Estates General, about the year 1300, for the monarch was obliged to ask their advice when he demanded their money to carry on his government and his wars (§ 557). The rise of the business class alongside of the older orders of the clergy and nobility is one of the most momentous changes of the thirteenth century.

FIG. 106. FAÇADE OF THE CATHEDRAL AT RHEIMS (THIRTEENTH CENTURY) AS IT APPEARED BEFORE THE WORLD WAR

FIG. 107. ROSE WINDOW OF RHEIMS CATHEDRAL, NEARLY FORTY FEET
IN DIAMETER, FROM THE INSIDE

This wonderful work of art was shattered by the German gunners during
the World War

Fig. 108. Interior of Exeter Cathedral (Early
Fourteenth Century)

Fig. 109. North Porch of Chartres Cathedral
(Fourteenth Century)

III. Gothic Architecture

656. Medieval Buildings. Almost all the medieval buildings
have disappeared in the ancient towns of Europe. The stone
town walls, no longer adequate in our times, have been removed,
and their place taken by broad and handsome avenues. The old

Fig. 110. Romanesque Church of Châtel-Montagne in the
Department of Allier, France

This is a pure Romanesque building with no alterations in a later style, such
as are common. Heavy as the walls are, they are reënforced by buttresses
along the side. All the arches are round, none of them pointed

houses have been torn down in order to widen and straighten the
streets and permit the construction of modern dwellings. Here
and there one can still find a walled town, but they are few in
number and are merely curiosities (see Fig. 131).

Of the buildings erected in towns during the Middle Ages only
the churches remain, but these fill the beholder with wonder and
admiration. It seems impossible that the cities of the twelfth and
thirteenth centuries, which were neither very large nor very rich,

could possibly find money enough to pay for them. It has been estimated that the bishop's church at Paris (Notre Dame) would cost at least five millions of dollars — at pre-war prices — to reproduce, and there are a number of other cathedrals in France, England, Italy, Spain, and Germany which must have been almost as costly. No modern buildings equal them in beauty and grandeur,

and they are the most striking memorial of the religious spirit and the town pride of the Middle Ages.

The construction of a cathedral sometimes extended over two or three centuries, and much of the money for it must have been gathered penny by penny. It should be remembered that everybody belonged in those days to the one great Catholic Church, so that the building of a new church was a matter of interest to the whole community — to men of every rank, from the bishop himself to the workman and the peasant.

657. The Romanesque Style. Up to the twelfth century churches were built in what is called the *Romanesque*, or Roman-like, style because they resembled the solid old basilicas referred to in earlier chapters (see §§ 383 and 479 above). These Romanesque churches had stone ceilings (see Figs. 90, 92, 110), and it was necessary to make the walls very thick and solid to support them. There was a main aisle in the center, called the *nave*, and a narrower aisle on either side, separated from the nave by massive stone pillars, which helped to hold up the heavy ceiling. These pillars were connected by round arches of stone above them. The tops of the small-ish windows were round, and the ceiling was constructed of round vaults, somewhat like a stone bridge, so the *round* arches form one of the striking features of the Romanesque style which distinguishes it from the Gothic style, that followed it. The windows had to be small in order that the walls should not be weakened, so the Romanesque churches are rather dark inside.

658. The Gothic Style. The architects of France were not satisfied, however, with this method of building, and in the twelfth century they invented a new and wonderful way of constructing churches and other buildings which enabled them to do away with the heavy walls and put high, wide, graceful windows in their place. This new style of architecture is known as the *Gothic*,[1] and its underlying

[1] The inappropriate name "Gothic" was given to the beautiful churches of the North by Italian architects of the sixteenth century, who did not like them and preferred to build in the style of the ancient Romans. The

FIG. 112. CROSS SECTION OF AMIENS CATHEDRAL

It will be noticed that there is a row of rather low windows opening under the roof of the aisle. These constitute the so-called *triforium* (E). Above them is the *clerestory* (F), the windows of which open between the flying buttresses. So it came about that the walls of a Gothic church were in fact mainly windows. The Egyptians were the first to invent the clerestory (see § 50 and Fig. 16)

Italians with their "classical" tastes assumed that only German barbarians — whom they carelessly and ignorantly called Goths — could admire a Gothic cathedral,

principles can readily be understood from a little study of the accompanying diagram (Fig. 112), which shows how a Gothic cathedral is supported, not by heavy walls but by *buttresses*.

The architects discovered in the first place that the concave stone ceiling, which is known as the *vaulting (A)*, could be sup-

ported by *ribs (B)*. These could in turn be brought together and supported on top of pillars which rested on the floor of the church. So far so good! But the builders knew well enough that the pillars and ribs would be pushed over by the weight and outward "thrust" of the stone vaulting if they were not firmly supported from the outside. Instead of erecting heavy walls to insure this support they had recourse to buttresses *(D)*, which they built quite outside the walls of the church and connected by means of "flying" buttresses

FIG. 113. FLYING BUTTRESSES OF NOTRE DAME, PARIS

The size of the buttresses and the height of the clerestory windows of a great cathedral are well shown here

(CC) with the points where the pillars and ribs had the most tendency to push outward. *In this way a vaulted stone ceiling could be supported without the use of a massive wall.* This ingenious use of buttresses instead of walls is the fundamental principle of Gothic architecture. It was discovered for the first time by the architects in the medieval towns and was apparently quite unknown to earlier builders.

The wall, no longer essential for supporting the ceiling, was used only to inclose the building, and windows could be built as high and wide as pleased the architect. By the use of *pointed* instead of *round* arches it was possible to give great variety to the windows and vaulting. So pointed arches came into general use, and the Gothic is often called the "pointed" style on this account, although the use of the ribs and buttresses, not the pointed arch, is the chief peculiarity of that form of architecture.

FIG. 114. GROTESQUE HEADS, RHEIMS CATHEDRAL

Here and there about a Gothic cathedral the stone carvers were accustomed to place grotesque and comical figures and faces. During the process of restoring the cathedral at Rheims a number of these heads were brought together, and the photograph was taken upon which the illustration is based

659. Church Windows. The light from the huge windows (those at Beauvais are fifty to fifty-five feet high) would have been too intense had it not been softened by the stained glass, set in exquisite stone tracery, with which they were filled (Fig. 107). The stained glass of the medieval cathedral, especially in France, where the glass workers brought their art to the greatest perfection, was one of its chief glories. By far the greater part of this old glass has of course been destroyed, but it is still so highly prized that every bit of it is now carefully preserved, for it has never since been equaled. A window set with odd bits of it pieced together like crazy patchwork is more beautiful, in its rich and jewel-like coloring, than the finest modern work.

660. Gothic Sculpture. As the skill of the architects increased they became bolder and bolder and erected churches that were marvels of lightness and delicacy of ornament, without sacrificing dignity or beauty of proportion. The façade of Rheims cathedral (Fig. 106) was—before its mutilation by German shells during the World War—one of the most famous examples of the best work of the thirteenth century, with its multitudes of sculptured figures and its gigantic rose window (Fig. 107), filled with exquisite stained glass of great brilliancy. The interior of Exeter cathedral (Fig. 108), although by no means so spacious as a number of the French churches, affords an excellent example of the beauty and impressiveness of a Gothic interior. The porch before the north entrance of Chartres cathedral (Fig. 109) is a magnificent example of fourteenth-century work.

One of the charms of a Gothic building is the profusion of carving—statues of saints and rulers and scenes from the Bible, cut in stone. The same kind of stone was used for both constructing the building and making the statues, so they harmonize perfectly. Here and there the Gothic stone carvers would introduce amusing faces or comical animals (Figs. 111, 114).

In the fourteenth and fifteenth centuries Gothic buildings other than churches were built. The most striking and important of these were the guild halls, erected by the rich corporations of merchants, and the town halls of important cities. But the Gothic style has always seemed specially appropriate for churches. Its lofty aisles and open floor spaces, its soaring arches leading the eye toward heaven, and its glowing windows suggesting the glories of paradise, fostered the faith of the medieval Christian.

IV. The Italian Cities of the Renaissance

661. The Renaissance. We have been speaking so far of the town life in northern Europe in the twelfth and thirteenth centuries. We must now see how the Italian towns in the following

two centuries reached a degree of prosperity and refinement un-
dreamed of north of the Alps. Within their walls learning and
art made such extraordinary progress that a special name is
often given to the period when they flourished — the *Renaissance*,[1] or new birth. The Italian towns, like those of ancient
Greece, were each a little state with its own peculiar life and
institutions. Some of them, like Rome, Milan, and Pisa, had
been important in Roman times; others, like Venice, Florence,
and Genoa, did not become conspicuous until about the time
of the Crusades.

The map of Italy at the beginning of the fourteenth century was
still divided into three zones, as it had been in the time of the
Hohenstaufens.[2] To the south lay the kingdom of Naples. Then
came the states of the Church, extending diagonally across the
peninsula. To the north and west lay the group of city-states to
which we now turn our attention.

662. Venice and its Relations with the East. Of these city-
states none was more celebrated than Venice, which in the history
of Europe ranks in importance with Paris and London. This
singular town was built upon a group of sandy islets lying in the
Adriatic Sea, about two miles from the mainland. It was protected from the waves by a long, narrow sand bar similar to those
which fringe the Atlantic coast from New Jersey southward. Such
a situation would not ordinarily have been chosen as the site
of a great city[3]; but it was a good place for fishermen, and its
very desolation and inaccessibility recommended it to those settlers
who fled from their homes on the mainland during the barbarian
invasions. As time went on, the location proved to have its advantages commercially, and even before the Crusades Venice had
begun to engage in foreign trade. Its enterprises carried it eastward, and it early acquired possessions across the Adriatic and in
the Orient. The influence of this intercourse with the East is

[1] This word, although originally French, has come into such common use that it is
quite permissible to pronounce it as if it were English, — *re-nā'sens*.

[2] See map above, p. 396.

[3] It is the sole surviving successor to the pile villages of the lake-dwellers who
wandered down the valley of the Po (§ 10).

plainly shown in the celebrated church of St. Mark, whose domes and decorations suggest Constantinople rather than Italy (Fig. 116).

663. Venice extends its Sway on the Mainland. It was not until early in the fifteenth century that Venice found it to her interest to extend her sway upon the Italian mainland. She

Fig. 115. A Scene in Venice

Boats, called gondolas, take the place of carriages in Venice; one can reach any point in the city by some one of the numerous canals, which take the place of streets. There are also narrow lanes along the canals, crossing them here and there by bridges, so one can wander about the town on foot

doubtless believed it dangerous to permit her rival, Milan, to get possession of the Alpine passes through which her goods found their way north. It may be, too, that she preferred to draw her food supplies from the neighborhood instead of transporting them across the Adriatic from her eastern possessions. Moreover, all the Italian cities except Venice already controlled a larger or smaller area of country about them.

About the year 1400 Venice reached the height of its prosperity. It had a population of two hundred thousand, which was very large for those days. It had three hundred seagoing vessels which went to and fro in the Mediterranean, carrying wares from the East to the West. It had a war fleet of forty-five galleys,

FIG. 116. ST. MARK'S AND THE DOGE'S PALACE IN VENICE

One sees the façade of St. Mark's to the left and that of the doge's palace beyond. The church, modeled after one in Constantinople, was planned before the First Crusade and is adorned with numerous colored marble columns and slabs brought from the East. The interior is covered with mosaics, some of which go back to the twelfth and the thirteenth century. The façade is also adorned with brilliant mosaics. St. Mark's "is unique among the buildings of the world in respect to its unparalleled richness of material and decoration." The doge's palace contained the government offices and the magnificent halls in which the senate and Council of Ten met. The palace was begun about 1300, and the façade we see in the picture was commenced about a hundred years later. It shows the influence of the Gothic style, which penetrated into northern Italy

manned by eleven thousand marines ready to fight the battles of the republic. But when Constantinople fell into the hands of the Turks (1453), and when, later, the route to India by sea was discovered (see below, §§ 673–674), Venice could not maintain control of the trade with the East, and while it remained an important city, it no longer enjoyed its former influence and power.

664. Government of Venice. Although Venice was called a republic, it was really governed by a very small group of persons. In 1311, after a rebellion, the famous Council of Ten was created as a sort of committee of public safety. The whole government,

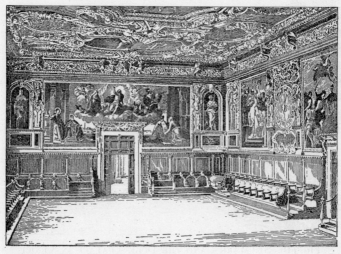

FIG. 117. SENATE CHAMBER IN THE DOGE'S PALACE

This is an example of the magnificent decoration of the rooms used by the Venetian government. It was adorned by celebrated painters in the sixteenth century, when Venice became famous for its artists

domestic and foreign, was placed in its hands, in conjunction with the senate and the *doge* (that is, duke), the nominal head of the republic. The government, thus concentrated in the hands of a very few, was carried on with great secrecy, so that public discussion, such as prevailed in Florence and led to innumerable revolutions there, was unheard of in Venice. The Venetian merchant was such a busy person that he was quite willing that the State should exercise its functions without his interference.

Venice often came to blows with other rival cities, especially Genoa, but its citizens lived quietly at home under the government of its senate, the Council of Ten, and the doge. The other Italian towns were not only fighting one another much of the time but their government was often in the possession of *despots*, somewhat like the old Greek tyrants, who got control of towns and managed them in their own interest.

665. Position of the Italian Despots. There are numerous stories of the incredible ferocity exhibited by the Italian despots. It must be remembered that they were very rarely legitimate rulers, but usurpers, who could hope to retain their power only so long as they could keep their subjects under control and could defend themselves against equally illegitimate usurpers

Fig. 118. Tomb of an Italian Despot

The family of the Visconti maintained themselves many years as despots of Milan. Gian Galeazzo Visconti began in 1396 a magnificent Carthusian monastery not far from Milan, one of the most beautiful structures in Italy. Here, long after his death, a monument was erected to him as founder of the monastery. The monument was begun about 1500 but not completed for several decades

in the neighboring cities. This situation developed a high degree of sagacity, and many of the despots found it to their interest to govern well and even to give dignity to their rule by patronizing artists and men of letters. But the despot usually made many bitter enemies and was almost necessarily suspicious of treason on the part of those about him. He was, ever conscious that at any moment he might fall a victim to the dagger or the poison cup.

666. The *Condottieri*. The Italian towns carried on their wars among themselves largely by means of hired troops. When a military expedition was proposed, a bargain was made with one of the professional leaders (*condottieri*), who provided the necessary force. As the soldiers had no more interest in the conflict than did those whom they opposed, who were likewise hired for the occasion, the fight was not usually very bloody ; for the object of each side was to capture the other without unnecessarily rough treatment.

667. Florence. The history of Florence, perhaps the most important of the Italian cities, differs in many ways from that of Venice and of the despotisms of which Milan was an example. Florence was a republic, and all classes claimed the right to interest themselves in the government. This led to constant changes in the constitution and frequent struggles between the different political parties. When one party got the upper hand it generally expelled its chief opponents from the city. Exile was a terrible punishment to a Florentine, for Florence was not merely his native city — it was his *country*, and loved and honored as such.

668. The Medici ; Lorenzo the Magnificent. By the middle of the fifteenth century Florence had come under the control of the great family of the Medici, whose members played the rôle of very enlightened political bosses. By quietly watching the elections and secretly controlling the selection of city officials, they governed without letting it be suspected that the people had lost their power. The most distinguished member of the house of Medici was Lorenzo the Magnificent (d. 1492) ; under his rule Florence reached the height of its glory in art and literature.

As one wanders about Florence to-day he is impressed with the contradictions of the Renaissance period. The streets are lined with the palaces of the noble families to whose rivalries much of the continual disturbance was due. The lower stories of these buildings are constructed of great stones, like fortresses, and

their windows are barred like those of a prison (Fig. 119) ; yet
within they were often furnished with the greatest taste and luxury.
For in spite of the disorder, against which the rich protected

themselves by mak-
ing their houses half
strongholds, the beau-
tiful churches, noble
public buildings, and
works of art which
now fill the museums
indicate that mankind
has never, perhaps,
reached a higher de-
gree of perfection in
the arts of peace than
amidst the turmoil of
this restless town (see
below, Figs. 126, 127).

**669. Rome, the
Capital of the Pa-
pacy.** During the same
period in which Venice
and Florence became
leaders in wealth and
refinement Rome, the
capital of the popes,
likewise underwent a
great change. After
the popes returned
from their seventy
years' residence in
France and Avignon

Fig. 119. The Palace of the Medici
in Florence

This palace was erected about 1435 by Cosimo
dei Medici, and in it Lorenzo the Magnificent conducted the government of Florence and entertained the men of letters and artists with whom he
liked best to associate. It shows how fortresslike
the lower portions of a Florentine palace were, in
order to protect the owner from attack

(§ 635) they found the town in a dilapidated state. For years
they were able to do little to restore it, as there was a long period
during which the papacy was weakened by the existence of a rival
line of popes who continued to live at Avignon. When the "great

FIG. 120. CATHEDRAL AND BELL
TOWER AT FLORENCE

The church was begun in 1296 and completed in 1436. The great dome built by the architect Brunelleschi has made his name famous. It is three hundred feet high. The façade is modern but after an old design. The bell tower, or campanile, was begun by the celebrated painter Giotto about 1335 and completed about fifty years later. It is richly adorned with sculpture and colored marbles and is considered the finest structure of the kind in the world

schism" was over, and all the European nations once more acknowledged the Pope at Rome (1417), it became possible to improve the city and revive some of its ancient glory. Architects, painters, and men of letters were called in and handsomely paid by the popes to erect and adorn magnificent buildings and to collect a great library in the Vatican palace.

670. St. Peter's and the Vatican. The ancient basilica of St. Peter's (Fig. 77) no longer satisfied the aspirations of the popes. It was gradually torn down, and after many changes of plan the present celebrated church with its vast dome and imposing approach (Fig. 121) took its place. The old palace of the Lateran, where the government of the popes had been carried on for a thousand years, had been deserted after the return from Avignon, and the new palace of the Vatican was gradually constructed to the right of St. Peter's. It has thousands of rooms, great and small, some of them adorned by the most distinguished of the Italian painters, and others filled with ancient statuary.

FIG. 121. ST. PETER'S AND THE VATICAN PALACE

St. Peter's is the largest church in the world. It is about seven hundred feet long, including the portico, and four hundred and thirty-five feet high, from the pavement to the cross on the dome. The reconstruction was begun as early as 1450, but it proceeded very slowly. Several great architects, Bramante, Raphael, Michael Angelo, and others, were intrusted with the work. After many changes of plan the new church was finally in condition to consecrate in 1626. It is estimated that it cost over $50,000,000. The construction of the vast palace of the popes, which one sees to the right of the church, was carried on during the same period. It is said to have no less than eleven thousand rooms. Some of them are used for museums and others are celebrated for the frescoes which adorn their walls, by Raphael, Michael Angelo, and other of Italy's greatest artists

As one visits Venice, Florence, and Rome to-day he may still see, almost perfectly preserved, many of the finest of the buildings, paintings, and monuments which belong to the period we have been discussing.

V. EARLY GEOGRAPHICAL DISCOVERIES

671. Medieval Commerce on a Small Scale. The business and commerce of the medieval towns was on what would seem to us a rather small scale. There were no great factories, such as have grown up in recent times with the use of steam and machinery, and the ships which sailed the Mediterranean and the North Sea were small and held only a very light cargo compared with modern merchant vessels. The gradual growth of a world commerce began with the sea voyages of the fifteenth century, which led to the exploration by Europeans of the whole globe, most of which was entirely unknown to the Venetian merchants and those who carried on the trade of the Hanseatic League. The Greeks and Romans knew little about the world beyond southern Europe, northern Africa, and western Asia, and much that they knew was forgotten during the Middle Ages. The Crusades took many Europeans as far East as Egypt and Syria.

672. Marco Polo. About 1260 two Venetian merchants, the Polo brothers, visited China and were kindly received at Pekin by the emperor of the Mongols. On a second journey they were accompanied by Marco Polo, the son of one of them. When they got back to Venice in 1295, after a journey of twenty years, Marco gave an account of his experiences which filled his readers with wonder. Nothing stimulated the interest of the West more than his fabulous description of the abundance of gold in Zipangu (Japan) and of the spice markets of the Moluccas and Ceylon.

673. The Discoveries of the Portuguese. About the year 1318 Venice and Genoa opened up direct communication by sea with the towns of the Netherlands. Their fleets, which touched at the port of Lisbon, aroused the commercial enterprise of the Portuguese, who soon began to undertake extended maritime expeditions. By the middle of the fourteenth century they had discovered the Canary Islands, Madeira, and the Azores. Before this time no one had ventured along the coast of Africa beyond the arid region of Sahara. The country was forbidding, there were no ports, and mariners were, moreover, discouraged by the general belief that the torrid region was uninhabitable. In 1445, however, some adventurous sailors came within sight of a headland beyond the desert, and, struck by its luxuriant growth of tropical trees, they called it Cape Verde (the green cape). Its discovery put an end once for all to the idea that there were only parched deserts to the south.

A MAP OF THE GLOBE IN THE TIME OF COLUMBUS

In 1492 a German mariner, Behaim, made a globe which is still preserved in Nuremberg. He did not know of the existence of the American continents or of the vast Pacific Ocean. It will be noticed that he places Japan (Cipango) where Mexico lies. In the reproduction many names are omitted and the outlines of North and South America are sketched in so as to make clear the misconceptions of Columbus's time

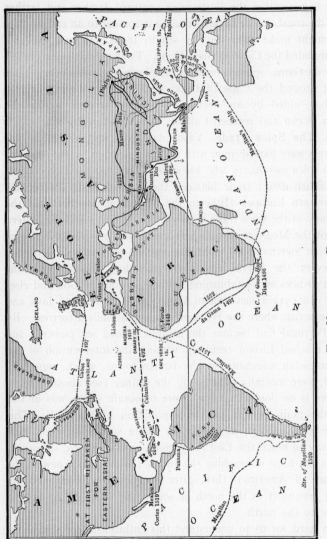

THE VOYAGES OF DISCOVERY

For a generation the Portuguese ventured farther and farther along the coast, in the hope of finding it coming to an end, so that they might make their way by sea to India. At last, in 1486, Diaz rounded the Cape of Good Hope. Twelve years later (1498) Vasco da Gama, spurred on by Columbus's great discovery, after sailing around the Cape of Good Hope and northward beyond Zanzibar, aided by an Arab pilot, steered straight across the Indian Ocean and reached Calicut, in Hindustan, by sea.

674. The Spice Trade. Vasco da Gama and his fellow adventurers were looked upon with natural suspicion by the Mohammedan spice merchants, who knew very well that their object was to establish *direct* trade between the Spice Islands (Moluccas) and western Europe. Hitherto the Mohammedans had had the monopoly of the spice trade between the Moluccas and the eastern ports of the Mediterranean, where the products were handed over to Italian merchants. The Mohammedans were unable, however, to prevent the Portuguese from concluding treaties with the Indian princes and establishing trading stations at Goa and elsewhere. In 1512 a successor of Vasco da Gama reached Java and the Moluccas, where the Portuguese speedily built a fortress. By 1515 Portugal had become the greatest among sea powers; and spices reached Lisbon regularly without the intervention of the Mohammedan merchants or the Italian towns, which, especially Venice, were mortally afflicted by the change (see above, § 663).

There is no doubt that the desire to obtain spices was at this time the main reason for the exploration of the globe. This motive led European navigators to try in succession every possible way to reach the East — by going around Africa, by sailing west in the hope of reaching the Indies (before they knew of the existence of America), then, after America was discovered, by sailing around it to the north or south, and even sailing around Europe to the north.

It is hard for us to understand this enthusiasm for spices, for which we care much less nowadays. One former use of spices was to preserve food, which could not then as now be carried rapidly, while still fresh, from place to place; nor did our conveniences

then exist for keeping it by the use of ice. Moreover, spice
served to make even spoiled food more palatable than it would
otherwise have been.

675. Idea of reaching the Spice Islands by sailing Westward.
It inevitably occurred to thoughtful men that the East Indies
could be reached by sailing *westward*. All intelligent people knew,

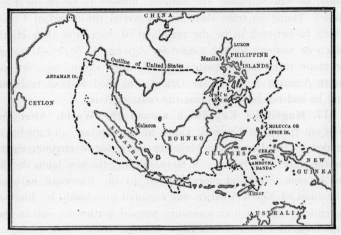

THE MALAY ARCHIPELAGO

The outline of the United States has been drawn in to make clear the vast
extent of the region explored by the Portuguese at the opening of the sixteenth century. It is not far from two thousand miles from Ceylon to Malacca
Strait, and as far from there on to the Spice Islands as from Denver to
Richmond, Virginia

all through the Middle Ages, that the earth was a globe. The
chief authority upon the form and size of the earth continued to be the ancient astronomer Ptolemy, who had lived about
A.D. 150. He had reckoned the earth to be about one sixth smaller
than it is ; and as Marco Polo had given an exaggerated idea of
the distance which he and his companions had traveled eastward,
and as no one suspected the existence of the American continents,
it was supposed that it could not be a very long journey from
Europe across the Atlantic to Japan.[1]

[1] See accompanying reproduction of Behaim's globe.

676. Columbus discovers America (1492). In 1492, as we all know, a Genoese navigator, Columbus (b. 1451), who had had much experience on the sea, got together three little ships and undertook the journey westward to Zipangu,—the land of gold,— which he hoped to reach in five weeks. After thirty-two days from the time he left the Canary Islands he came upon land, the island of San Salvador, and believed himself to be in the East Indies. Going on from there he discovered the island of Cuba, which he believed to be the mainland of Asia, and then Haiti, which he mistook for the longed-for Zipangu (§ 672). Although he made three later expeditions and sailed down the coast of South America as far as the Orinoco, he died without realizing that he had not been exploring the coast of Asia.

677. Magellan's Expedition around the World. After the bold enterprises of Vasco da Gama and Columbus, an expedition headed by the Portuguese Magellan succeeded in circumnavigating the globe. There was now no reason why the new lands should not become more and more familiar to the European nations. The coast of North America was explored principally by English navigators, who for over a century pressed northward, still in the vain hope of finding a northwest passage to the Spice Islands.

678. The Spanish Conquests in America. Cortes began the Spanish conquests in the western world by undertaking the subjugation of the Aztec empire in Mexico in 1519. A few years later Pizarro established the Spanish power in Peru. Spain now superseded Portugal as a maritime power, and her importance in the sixteenth century is to be attributed largely to the wealth which came to her from her possessions in the New World.

By the end of the century the Spanish main — that is, the northern coast of South America — was much frequented by adventurous seamen, who combined in about equal parts the occupations of merchant, slaver, and pirate. Many of these hailed from English ports, and it is to them that England owes the beginning of her commercial greatness.

It is hardly necessary to say that Europeans exhibited an utter disregard for the rights of the people with whom they came in contact and often treated them with contemptuous cruelty. The exploration of the globe and the conquest by European nations of peoples beyond the sea led finally to the vast colonization of modern times, which has caused many wars but has served to spread European ideas throughout the world. This creation of a greater Europe will be one of the most important subjects to be discussed in the next volume of this work.

QUESTIONS

I. Why are towns necessary to progress? How did the towns of the eleventh and twelfth centuries originate? What was the nature of a town charter? Describe the guild organization.

II. Describe the revival and extending of commerce in the Middle Ages. What were some of the obstacles to business? Describe the Hanseatic League.

III. What are the chief characteristics of Romanesque churches? What were the principles of construction which made it possible to build a Gothic church? Tell something about the decoration of a Gothic church.

IV. Describe the map of Italy in the fourteenth century. What are the peculiarities of Venice? Who were the Italian despots? Contrast Florence with Venice. Tell something of the buildings constructed in Rome.

V. What geographical discoveries were made before 1500? How far is it by sea from Lisbon to Calicut around the Cape of Good Hope? What was the importance of the spice trade? What led Columbus to try to reach the Indies by sailing westward?

CHAPTER XXX

BOOKS AND SCIENCE IN THE MIDDLE AGES

I. How the Modern Languages Originated

679. General Use of Latin in the Middle Ages. We should leave the Middle Ages with a very imperfect notion of them if we did not now stop to consider what people were thinking about during that period, what they had to read, and what they believed about the world in which they lived.

To begin with, the Middle Ages differed from our own time in the very general use then made of Latin, both in writing and speaking. The language of the Roman Empire continued to be used in the thirteenth century, and long after ; all books that made any claim to learning were written in Latin ;[1] the professors in the universities lectured in Latin, friends wrote to one another in Latin, and state papers, treaties, and legal documents were drawn up in the same language. The ability of every educated person to make use of Latin, as well as of his native tongue, was a great advantage at a time when there were many obstacles to intercourse among the various nations. It helps to explain, for example, the remarkable way in which the Pope kept in touch with all the clergymen of Western Christendom, and the ease with which students, friars, and merchants could wander from one country to another. There is no more interesting or important revolution than that by which the languages of the people in the various European countries gradually pushed aside the ancient tongue and took its place, so that even scholars scarcely ever think now of writing books in Latin.

In order to understand how it came about that two languages, the Latin and the native speech, were both commonly used in all

---

[1] In Germany the books published annually in the German language did not exceed those in Latin until after 1690.

the countries of western Europe all through the Middle Ages, we must glance at the origin of the modern languages. These all fall into two quite distinct groups, the *Germanic* and the *Romance*.

680. The Germanic Languages. Those German peoples who had continued to live *outside* of the Roman Empire naturally adhered to the language they had always used; namely, the particular Germanic dialect which their forefathers had spoken for untold generations. From the various languages used by the German barbarians, modern German, English, Dutch, Swedish, Norwegian, Danish, and Icelandic are largely derived.

681. The Romance Languages. The second group of languages developed *within* the territory which had formed a part of the Roman Empire, and includes modern French, Italian, Spanish, and Portuguese. It has now been clearly proved that these Romance languages were one and all derived from the *spoken* Latin, employed by the soldiers, merchants, and people at large. This differed considerably from the elaborate and elegant *written* Latin which was used, for example, by Cicero and Cæsar. It was undoubtedly much simpler in its grammar and varied a good deal in different regions; a Gaul, for instance, could not pronounce the words like a Roman. Moreover, in conversation people did not always use the same words as those employed in books. For example, a horse was commonly spoken of as *caballus*, whereas a writer would use the word *equus*; it is from *caballus* that the word for "horse" in Spanish, Italian, and French is derived (*caballo, cavallo, cheval*).

As time went on, the spoken language diverged farther and farther from the written. Latin is a troublesome speech on account of its complicated inflections and grammatical rules, which can be mastered only after a great deal of study. The people of the more remote Roman provinces and the incoming barbarians naturally paid very little attention to the niceties of syntax and found easy ways of saying what they wished.[1]

---

[1] Even the monks and others who wrote Latin in the Middle Ages often did not know enough to follow strictly the rules of the language. Moreover, they introduced many new words to meet the new conditions and the needs of the time, such as *imprisonare*, "to imprison"; *utlagare*, "to outlaw"; *baptizare*, "to baptize"; *foresta*, "forest"; *feudum*, "fief"; etc.

Yet several centuries elapsed after the German invasions before there was anything written in this conversational language. So long as the uneducated could understand the correct Latin of the books when they heard it read or spoken, there was no necessity of writing anything in their familiar daily speech. But by the time Charlemagne came to the throne the gulf between the spoken and the written language had become so great that he advised that sermons should be given thereafter in the language of the people, who, apparently, could no longer follow the Latin.

Although little was written in any German language before Charlemagne's time, there is no doubt that the Germans possessed an unwritten literature, which was passed down by word of mouth for several centuries before any of it was written out.

682. Ancient English, or Anglo-Saxon. The oldest form of English is commonly called Anglo-Saxon and is so different from the language which we use that, in order to be read, it must be learned like a foreign language. We hear of an English poet, as early as Bede's time, a century before Charlemagne. A manuscript of an Anglo-Saxon epic, called *Beowulf*, has been preserved which belongs perhaps to the close of the eighth century. King Alfred displayed great interest in the English language. He actually translated several old Latin works and encouraged the writing of the *Anglo-Saxon Chronicle*. This old form of our language prevailed until after the Norman Conquest; the *Anglo-Saxon Chronicle*, which does not close until 1154, is written in pure Anglo-Saxon. Here is an example:

"Here on thissum geare Willelm cyng geaf Rodberde eorle thone eorldom on Northymbraland. Da komon tha landes menn togeanes him & hine ofslogen, & ix hund manna mid him."[1] In modern English this reads: "In this year King William gave the Earl Robert the earldom of Northumberland. Then came the men of the country against him and slew him, and nine hundred men with him."

---

[1] In writing Anglo-Saxon two old letters are used for *th*, one (þ) for the sound in "thin" and the other (ð) for that in "father." The use of these old letters serves to make the language look more different from that of to-day than it is.

By the middle of the thirteenth century, two hundred years after the Norman Conquest, English begins to look somewhat familiar, as may be seen in the examples which follow:

> And Aaron held up his hond
> To the water and the more lond;
> Tho cam thor up schwilc froschkes here
> The dede al folc Egipte dere;
> Summe woren wilde, and summe tame,
> And tho hem deden the moste schame;
> In huse, in drinc, in metes, in bed,
> It cropen and maden hem for-dred. . . .

> And Aaron held up his hand
> To the water and the greater land;
> Then came there up such host of frogs
> That did all Egypt's folk harm;
> Some were wild, and some were tame,
> And those caused them the most shame;
> In house, in drink, in meats, in bed,
> They crept and made them in great dread. . . .

Chaucer (about 1340–1400) was the first great English writer whose works are now read with pleasure, although one is sometimes puzzled by his spelling and by certain words which are no longer used. This is the way one of his tales opens:

> A poure wydow somdel stope in age,
> Was whilom dwellyng in a narwe cotage,
> Bisyde a grove, stondyng in a dale.
> This wydwe of wichh I telle yow my tale,
> Syn thilke day that sche was last a wif,
> In pacience ladde a ful symple lyf.

683. French and Provençal. In the Middle Ages, however, French, not English, was the most important of the national languages of western Europe. In France a vast literature was produced in the language of the people during the twelfth and thirteenth centuries which profoundly affected the books written in Italy, Spain, Germany, and England.

Two quite different languages had gradually developed in France from the spoken Latin of the Roman Empire. To the north, French was spoken; to the south, Provençal.[1]

Very little in the ancient French language written before the year 1100 has been preserved. The West Franks undoubtedly began much earlier to sing of their heroes, of the great deeds of Clovis and Charles the Hammer. These famous rulers were, however, completely overshadowed later by Charlemagne, who became the unrivaled hero of medieval poetry and romance (§ 505). It was believed that he had reigned for a hundred and twenty-five years, and the most marvelous exploits were attributed to him and his knights. He was supposed, for instance, to have led a crusade to Jerusalem. Such themes as these — more legend than history — were woven into long epics, which were the first written literature of the Frankish people. These poems, combined with the stories of adventure, developed a spirit of patriotic enthusiasm among the French which made them regard "fair France" as the especial care of Providence.

684. Romances of King Arthur and the Knights of the Round Table. The famous *Song of Roland*, the chief character of which was one of Charlemagne's captains, was written before the First Crusade. In the latter part of the twelfth century the romances of King Arthur and his Knights of the Round Table begin to appear. These enjoyed great popularity in all western Europe for centuries, and they are by no means forgotten yet. Arthur, of whose historical existence no one can be quite sure, was supposed to have been king of Britain shortly after the Saxons gained a foothold in the island.[2]

---

[1] Of course there was no sharp line of demarcation between the people who used the one language or the other, nor was Provençal confined to southern France. The language of Catalonia, beyond the Pyrenees, was essentially the same as that of Provence. French was called *langue d'oïl*, and the southern language *langue d'oc*, each after the word used for "yes."

[2] Malory's *Mort d'Arthur*, a collection of the stories of the Round Table made in the fifteenth century for English readers, is the best place to turn for these famous stories.

Besides the long and elaborate epics, like *Roland*, and the romances in verse and prose, there were numberless short stories in verse (the *fabliaux*), which usually dealt with the incidents of everyday life, especially with the comical ones.

II. THE TROUBADOURS AND CHIVALRY

685. The Troubadours. Turning now to southern France, the beautiful songs of the *troubadours*, which were the glory of the Provençal tongue, reveal a gay and polished society at the courts of the numerous feudal princes. The rulers not merely protected and encouraged the poets — they aspired to be poets themselves and to enter the ranks of the troubadours, as the composers of these elegant verses were called. These songs were always sung to an accompaniment on some instrument, usually the lute. The troubadours traveled from court to court, not only in France but north into Germany and south into Italy, carrying with them the southern French poetry and customs. We have few examples of Provençal before the year 1100, but from that time on, for two centuries, countless songs were written, and many of the troubadours enjoyed an international reputation. The terrible Albigensian crusade (§ 626) brought misery and death into the sprightly circles which had gathered about the count of Toulouse and other rulers who had treated the· heretics too leniently.

686. Chivalry. For the student of history the chief interest of the long poems of northern France and the songs of the South lies in the insight that they give into the life and aspirations of this feudal period. These are usually summed up in the term *chivalry*, or *knighthood*, of which a word may properly be said here, since we should know little of it were it not for the literature of which we have been speaking. The knights play the chief rôle in all the medieval romances ; and, since many of the troubadours belonged to the knightly class, they naturally have much to say of it in their songs.

Chivalry was not a formal institution established at any particular moment. Like feudalism, with which it was closely connected, it had no founder, but appeared spontaneously throughout western Europe to meet the needs and desires of the period. When the youth of good family had been carefully trained to ride his horse, use his sword, and manage his hawk in the hunt, he was made a *knight* by a ceremony in which the Church took part, although the knighthood was actually conferred by an older knight.

687. Ideals of Knighthood. The knight was a Christian soldier, and he and his fellows were supposed to form, in a way, a separate order, with high ideals of the conduct befitting their class. Knighthood was not, however, membership in an association with officers and a definite constitution. It was an ideal, half-imaginary society — a society to which even those who enjoyed the title of king or duke were proud to belong. One was not born a knight as he might be born a duke or count, and could become one only through the ceremony mentioned above. Although most knights belonged to the nobility, one might be a noble and still not belong to the knightly order, and, on the other hand, one who was baseborn might be raised to knighthood on account of some valorous deed.

The knight must, in the first place, be a Christian and must obey and defend the Church on all occasions. He must respect all forms of weakness and defend the helpless wherever he might find them. He must fight the infidel Mohammedans ceaselessly, pitilessly, and never give way before the enemy. He must perform all his feudal duties, be faithful in all things to his lord, never lie or violate his plighted word. He must be generous and give freely and ungrudgingly to the needy. He must be faithful to his lady and be ready to defend her and her honor at all costs. Everywhere he must be the champion of the right against injustice and oppression. In short, chivalry was the Christianized profession of arms.

688. The German Minnesingers. The Germans also made their contribution to the literature of chivalry. The German poets of the thirteenth century are called *minnesingers*. Like the troubadours, whom they greatly admired, they usually sang of love, hence their name (German, *Minne*). The most famous of the Minnesingers was Walther von der Vogelweide (d. about 1228), whose songs are full of charm and of enthusiasm for his German fatherland.

III. MEDIEVAL SCIENCE

689. Medieval Ignorance of the Past. So long as all books had to be copied by hand, there were, of course, but few of them compared with those of modern times. The literature of which we have been speaking was not in general *read*, but was only *listened to*, as it was sung or recited by those who made it their profession. Wherever the wandering troubadour or minnesinger appeared he was sure of a delighted audience for his songs and stories, both serious and light. People unfamiliar with Latin could, however, learn little of the past, for there were no translations of the great classics of Greece and Rome, of Homer, Plato, Cicero, or Livy. All that they could know of ancient history was derived from the fantastic romances referred to above, which had for their theme the quite preposterous deeds ascribed to Alexander the Great, Æneas, and Cæsar. As for their own history, the epics relating to the earlier course of events in France and the rest of Europe were hopelessly confused. For example, the writers attributed to Charlemagne a great part of the acts of the Frankish kings from Clovis to Pippin.

690. Medieval Popular Science. Of what we should call scientific books there were practically none. It is true that there was a kind of encyclopedia in verse which gave a great deal of misinformation about things in general. Everyone continued to believe, as the Greeks and Romans had done, in strange animals like the unicorn, the dragon, and the phœnix, and in still stranger habits of real animals. A single example will suffice to show what passed for zoölogy in the thirteenth century.

"There is a little beast made like a lizard and such is its nature that it will extinguish fire should it fall into it. The beast is so cold and of such a quality that fire is not able to burn it, nor will trouble happen in the place where it shall be." This beast signifies the holy man who lives by faith, who "will never have hurt from fire nor will hell burn him. . . . This beast we name also by another name, salamander. It is accustomed to mount into apple-trees, poisons the apples, and in a well where it falls it poisons the water."

It will be noticed that the habits of the animals were supposed to have some moral or religious meaning and carry with them a lesson for mankind. It may be added that this and similar stories were centuries old and are found in the encyclopedias of the Romans. The most improbable things were repeated from generation to generation without its occurring to anyone to inquire if there was any truth in them.

From the Roman and early Christian writers the Middle Ages got the idea of strange races of men and manlike creatures of various kinds. We find the following in an encyclopedia of the thirteenth century : "Satyrs be somewhat like men, and have crooked noses, and horns in the forehead, and are like to goats in their feet. . . . Those be wonderful creatures that have heads as hounds, and seem beasts rather than men ; and some be called Cyclops, and have that name because each of them hath but one eye, and that in the middle of the forehead ; and some be all headless and noseless and their eyes be in the shoulders ; and some have plain faces without nostrils, and the lower lips of them stretch so that they veil therewith their faces when they be in the heat of the sun. Also in Scythia be some with so great and large ears, that they spread their ears and cover all their bodies with them, and these be called Panchios. . . ."

Two old subjects of study were revived and received great attention in Europe from the thirteenth century onwards until recent times. These were *astrology* and *alchemy*.

691. Astrology. Astrology (§ 87) was based on the belief that the planets influence the make-up of men and consequently their fate. Following an idea of the Greek philosophers, especially Aristotle, it was believed that all things were compounded of "the four elements"—earth, air, fire, and water. Each person was a particular mixture of these four elements, and the position of the planets at the time of his birth was supposed to influence his mixture or "temperament"—that is to say, his character.

By knowing a person's temperament one could judge what he ought to do in order to be successful in life, and what he should avoid. For example, if one were born under the influence of Venus he should be on his guard against violent love and should choose for a trade something connected with dress or adornment ; if he were born under Mars he might make armor or horseshoes or become a soldier. Many common words are really astrological terms, such as "ill-starred," "disastrous," "jovial," "saturnine," "mercurial" (derived from the names of the planets). Astrology was taught in the universities because it was supposed to be necessary for physicians to choose times when the stars were favorable for particular kinds of medical treatment.

692. Alchemy. Alchemy was chemistry directed toward the discovery of a method of turning the baser metals, like lead and copper, into gold and silver. The alchemists, even if they did not succeed in their chief aim, learned a great deal incidentally in their laboratories, and finally our modern chemistry emerged from alchemy. Like astrology, alchemy goes back to ancient times, and the people of the thirteenth century got most of their ideas through the Mohammedans, who had in turn got theirs from the Greek books on the subjects.

IV. MEDIEVAL UNIVERSITIES AND STUDIES

693. Origin of the Universities. All European countries now have excellent schools, colleges, and universities. These had their beginning in the later Middle Ages. With the incoming of the barbarian Germans and the break-up of the Roman Empire education largely disappeared and for hundreds of years there was nothing in western Europe, outside of Italy and Spain, corresponding to our universities and colleges.

But by the end of the twelfth century the teachers had become so numerous in Paris that they formed a union, or guild, for the advancement of their interests. This union of professors was called by the usual name for corporations in the Middle Ages, *universitas*; hence our word "university." The king and the Pope both favored the university and granted the teachers and students many of the privileges of the clergy, a class to which they were regarded as belonging, because learning had for so many centuries been confined to the clergy.

About the time that we find the beginnings of a university or guild of professors at Paris, another great institution of learning was growing up at Bologna. Here the chief attention was given not to theology, as at Paris, but to the study of the law, both Roman and church (canon) law. Students streamed to Bologna in greater and greater numbers. In order to protect themselves in a town where they were regarded as strangers, they also organized themselves into such powerful unions that they were able to force the professors to obey the rules they laid down.

The University of Oxford was founded in the time of Henry II, probably by English students and masters who had become discontented at Paris. The University of Cambridge, as well as numerous universities in France, Italy, and Spain, were founded in the thirteenth century. The German universities were established much later, most of them in the latter half of the fourteenth century and in the fifteenth. The northern institutions generally took the great mother university on the Seine as their model, while those in southern Europe usually adopted the methods of Bologna.

694. The Academic Degree. When, after some years of study, a student was examined by the professors, he was, if successful, admitted to the corporation of teachers and became a *master* himself. What we call a *degree* to-day was originally, in the medieval universities, nothing more than the right to teach; but in the thirteenth century many who did not care to become professors in our sense of the word began to desire the honorable title of *master* or *doctor* (which is only the Latin word for "teacher").[1]

[1] The origin of the bachelor's degree, which comes at the end of our college course nowadays, may be explained as follows: The bachelor in the thirteenth century was a student who had passed part of his examinations in the course in "arts," as the college course was then called, and was permitted to teach certain elementary subjects before he became a full-fledged master. So the A.B. was inferior to the A.M. then as now.

695. Simple Methods of Instruction. The students in the medieval universities were of all ages, from thirteen to forty, and even older. There were no university buildings, and in Paris the lectures were given in the Latin Quarter, in Straw Street (so called from the straw strewn on the floors of the hired rooms where the lecturer explained the textbook, with the students squatting on the floor before him). There were no laboratories, for there was no experimentation. All that was required was a copy of the textbook. This the lecturer explained sentence by sentence, and the students listened and sometimes took notes.

696. Veneration for Aristotle. The most striking peculiarity of the instruction in the medieval university was the supreme deference paid to Aristotle (§ 286). Most of the courses of lectures were devoted to the explanation of some one of his numerous treatises. The Latin translations were bad and obscure, and the lecturer had enough to do to give some meaning to them and to reconcile them to the teachings of Christianity.

The teachers of the thirteenth century were so fascinated by his logic and astonished at his learning that the great theologians of the time, Albertus Magnus (d. 1280) and Thomas Aquinas (d. 1274), did not hesitate to prepare elaborate commentaries upon all his works. He was called "The Philosopher"; and so fully were scholars convinced that it had pleased God to permit Aristotle to say the last word upon each and every branch of knowledge that they humbly accepted him, along with the Bible, the church fathers, and the canon and Roman law, as one of the unquestioned authorities which together formed a complete guide for humanity in conduct and in every branch of science.

697. Scholasticism. The name "scholasticism" is commonly given to the beliefs and method of discussion of the medieval professors. To those who later outgrew the fondness for logic and the supreme respect for Aristotle, scholasticism, with its neglect of Greek and Roman literature, came to seem an arid and profitless plan of education. Yet, if we turn over the pages of the wonderful works of Thomas Aquinas, we see that the scholastic philosopher might be a person of extraordinary insight and learning, ready to recognize all the objections to his position, and able to express himself with great clearness and cogency. The training in logic, if it did not increase the sum of human knowledge, accustomed the student to make careful distinctions and present his arguments in an orderly way.

698. Course of Study. No attention was given in the medieval universities to the great subject of history, nor was Greek taught. Latin had to be learned in order to carry on the work at all, but little time was given to the Roman classics. The new modern languages were considered entirely unworthy of the learned. It must of course be remembered that none of the books which we consider the great classics in English, French, Italian, or Spanish had as yet been written.

699. Petrarch tries to learn Greek. Although the medieval professors paid the greatest respect to the Greek philosopher Aristotle and made Latin translations of his works the basis of the college course, very few of them could read any Greek and none of them knew much about Homer or Plato or the Greek tragedians and historians. In the fourteenth century Petrarch (1304–1374) set the example in Italy of carefully collecting all the writings of the Romans, which he greatly admired. He made an unsuccessful effort to learn Greek, for he found that Cicero and other Roman writers were constantly referring with enthusiasm to the Greek books to which they owed so much.

700. Chrysoloras begins to teach Greek in Florence (1396). Petrarch had not the patience or opportunity to master Greek, but twenty years after his death a learned Greek prelate from Constantinople, named Chrysoloras, came to Florence and found pupils eager to learn his language so that they could read the Greek books. Soon Italian scholars were going to Constantinople to carry on their studies, just as the Romans in Cicero's time had gone to Athens. They brought back copies of all the ancient writers that they could find, and by 1430 Greek books were once more known in the West, after a thousand years of neglect.

701. The Humanists. In this way western Europe caught up with ancient times ; scholars could once more know all that the

Greeks and Romans had known and could read in the original
the works of Homer, Sophocles, Herodotus, Plato, Aristotle, Demosthenes, and other philosophers, historians, orators, and
tragedians. Those who devoted their lives to a study of the
literature of Greece and Rome were called *Humanists*. The name
is derived from the Latin word *humanitas*, which means "culture."
In time the colleges gave up the exclusive study of Aristotle and
substituted a study of the Greek and Latin literature, and in this
way what is known as our "classical" course of study originated.

V. Beginnings of Modern Inventions

702. Roger Bacon's Attack on Scholasticism. So long, however, as intellectual men confined themselves to studying the old
books of Greece and Rome they were not likely to advance beyond what the Greeks and Romans had known. In order to
explain modern discoveries and inventions we have to take account
of those who began to suspect that Aristotle was ignorant and
mistaken upon many important matters, and who set to work to
examine things about them with the hope of finding out more
than anyone had ever known before.

Even in the thirteenth century there were a few scholars who
criticized the habit of relying upon Aristotle for all knowledge.
The most distinguished faultfinder was Roger Bacon, an English
Franciscan monk (d. about 1290), who declared that even if
Aristotle were very wise he had only planted the tree of knowledge and that this had "not as yet put forth all its branches nor
produced all its fruits." "If we could continue to live for endless
centuries we mortals could never hope to reach full and complete
knowledge of all the things which are to be known. No one knows
enough of nature completely to describe the peculiarities of a
single fly and give the reason for its color and why it has just
so many feet, no more and no less."

703. Bacon foresees Great Inventions. Bacon declared that
if men would only study common things instead of reading the
books of the ancients, science would outdo the wonders which

people of his day thought could be produced by magic. He said that in time men would be able to fly, would have carriages which needed no horses to draw them and ships which would move swiftly without oars, and that bridges could be built without piers to support them.

All this and much more has come true, but inventors and modern scientists owe but little to the books of the Greeks and Romans, which the scholastic philosophers and the Humanists relied upon. Although the Greek philosophers devoted considerable attention to natural science, they were not much inclined to make long and careful experiments or to invent anything like the microscope or telescope to help them. Aristotle thought that the sun and all the stars revolved about the earth and that the heavenly bodies were perfect and unchangeable. He believed that heavy bodies fell faster than light ones and that all earthly things were made of the four elements—earth, air, water, and fire. The Greeks and Romans knew nothing of the compass, or gunpowder, or the printing press, or the uses to which steam can be put. Indeed, they had scarcely anything that we should call a machine.

704. Discoveries of the Thirteenth Century. The thirteenth century witnessed certain absolutely new achievements in the history of mankind. The compass began to be utilized in a way to encourage bolder and bolder ventures out upon the ocean. The lens was discovered, and before the end of the century spectacles are mentioned. The lens made the later telescope, microscope, spectroscope, and camera possible, upon which so much of our modern science depends. The Arabic numerals began to take the place of the awkward Roman system of using letters. One cannot well divide XLVIII by VIII, but he can easily divide 48 by 8. Roger Bacon knew of the explosive nature of a compound of sulphur, saltpeter, and charcoal, and a generation after his death gunpowder began to be used a little for guns and artillery. A document is still preserved referring to the making of brass cannon and balls in Florence in the year 1326. By 1350 powder works were in existence in at least three German towns, and French and English books refer now and then to its use.

At least a hundred and fifty years elapsed, however, before gunpowder really began to supplant the old ways of fighting with bows and arrows and axes and lances. By the year 1500 it was becoming clear that the old stone castles were insufficient protection against cannon, and a new type of unprotected castle began to be erected as residences of the kings and the nobility (see below, Fig. 130).

Gunpowder has done away with armor, bows and arrows, spears and javelins, castles and walled towns. It may be that sometime some such fearfully destructive compound may be discovered that the nations may decide to give up war altogether as too dangerous and terrible a thing to resort to under any circumstances.

FIG. 122. EFFECTS OF CANNON ON A MEDIEVAL CASTLE

705. Advantages of printing with Movable Type. The invention of the compass, of the lens, and of gunpowder have helped to revolutionize the world. To these may be added the printing press, which has so facilitated and encouraged reading that it is nowadays rare to find anybody who cannot read.

The Italian classical scholars of the fifteenth century succeeded, as we have seen (§§ 699–701, above), in arousing a new interest in the books of the Greeks as well as of the Romans. They carefully collected every ancient work that they could lay hands on, made copies of it, edited it, and if it was in Greek translated it into Latin. While they were in the midst of this work certain patient experimenters in Germany and Holland were turning their attention to a new way of multiplying books rapidly and cheaply by the use of lead type and a press.

706. Excellent Work of Medieval Copyists. The Greeks and Romans and the people of the Middle Ages knew no other method of obtaining a new copy of a book except by writing it out laboriously by hand. The professional copyists were incredibly dexterous with their quills, as may be seen in Fig. 123 — a page from a Bible of the thirteenth century which is reproduced in its original size.[1] The letters are as clear, small, and almost as regular as if they had been printed. The whole volume, containing the Old and New Testaments, is about the size of this history. After the scribe had finished his work the volume was often turned over to the *illuminator*, who would put in gay illuminated initials and sometimes page borders, which were delightful in design and color.[2] Books designed to be used in the Church services were adorned with pictures as well as with ornamented initials and decorative borders. Plate, p. 480, is a reproduction of a page from a Book of Hours in the library of Columbia University. It is the same size as the original.

The written books were, in short, often both compact and beautiful, but they were never cheap or easily produced in great numbers. When Cosimo, the father of Lorenzo the Magnificent, wished to form a library just before the invention of printing, he applied to a contractor who engaged forty-five copyists. By working hard for nearly two years they were able to produce only two hundred volumes for the new library.

---

[1] Fig. 123 is a reproduction, exactly the size of the original, of a page in a manuscript Bible of the thirteenth century (in Latin) belonging to the library of Columbia University. The page represented is taken from 1 Maccabees i, 56–ii, 65 (a portion of the Scriptures not usually included in the Protestant Bibles). It begins, "...ditis fugitivorum locis. Die quintadecima mensis Chalen, quinto quadragesimo et centesimo anno edificavit rex Antiochus abhominandum ydolum desolationis super altare Dei; per universas civitates Jude in circuitum edificaverunt aras et ante januas domorum, et in plateis incendebantur thura, et sacrificabant et libros Dei legis com-busserunt." The scribes used a good many abbreviations, as was the custom of the time, and what is transcribed here fills five lines of the manuscript.

[2] The word "miniature," which is often applied to them, is derived from *minium*, that is, vermilion, which was one of the favorite colors. Later the word came to be applied to anything small.

PAGE FROM A BOOK OF HOURS, FIFTEENTH CENTURY
(ORIGINAL SIZE)

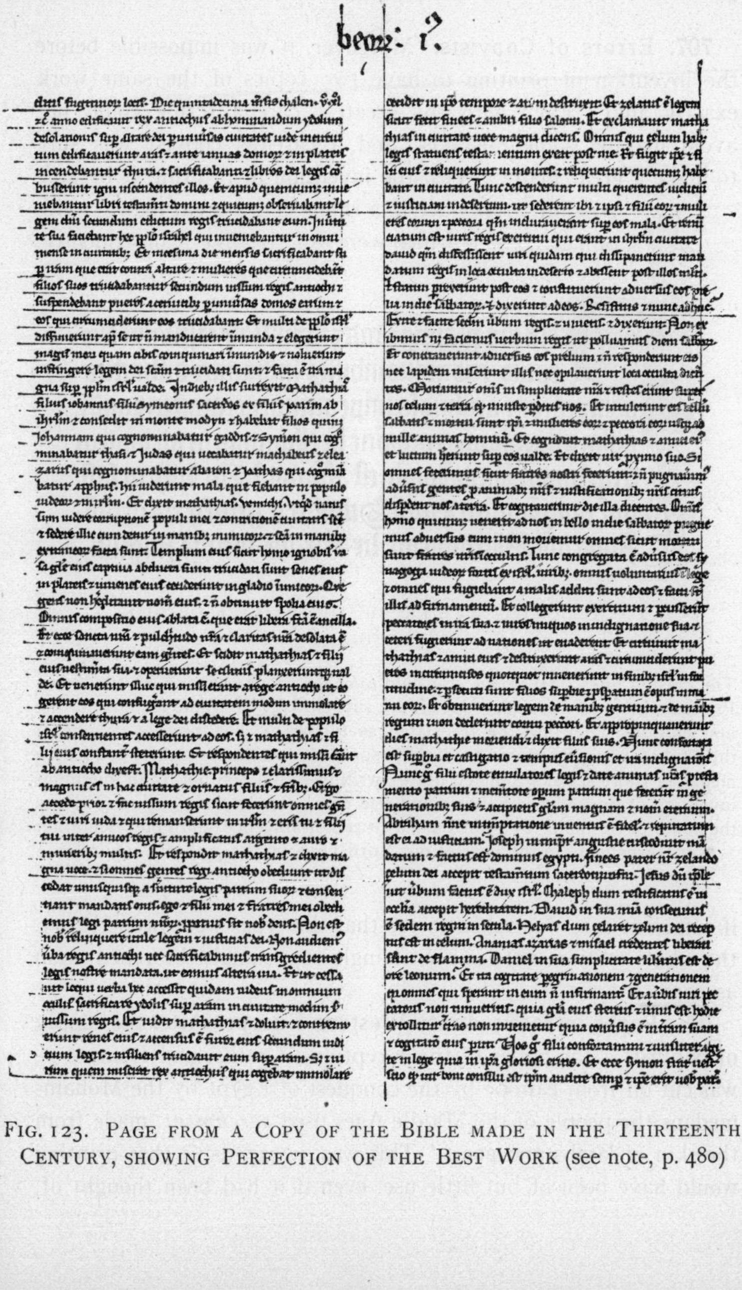

FIG. 123. PAGE FROM A COPY OF THE BIBLE MADE IN THE THIRTEENTH CENTURY, SHOWING PERFECTION OF THE BEST WORK (see note, p. 480)

707. Errors of Copyists. Moreover, it was impossible before the invention of printing to have two copies of the same work exactly alike. Even with the greatest care a scribe could not avoid making some mistakes, and a careless copyist was sure to make a great many. With the invention of printing it became possible to produce in a short time a great many copies of a given book which were exactly alike. Consequently,

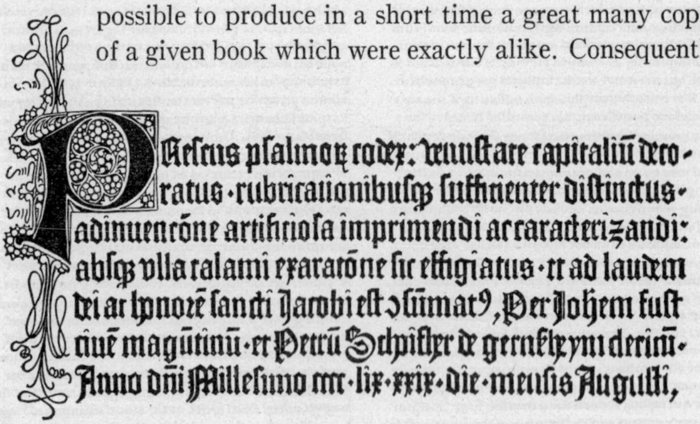

Ġßefeus pſalmoꝛ roꝺeꝛ: ꝛeuuſtare rapitaliū ꝺeco-
ꝛatus · rubricationibuſcꝫ ſuffꝛnenter ꝺiſtinctus·
aꝺinuentōne artiſitioſa imprimenꝺi arcaraĉterizanꝺi:
abſcꝫ vllaralami eꝛaratōne ſic effigiatus · et aꝺ lauꝺem
ꝺei arlpnoꝛe ſancti Jacobi eſt � ſūmat⁹, Ꝑer Jotꝫem fuſt
ciuē magūtinū · er Ꝑetrū Sctꝫifꝫer ꝺe gerneflꝫyni derinū·
Ꝑnno ꝺni Milleſimo cccc · liꝛ · ꝛꝛiꝛ · ꝺie · menſis Auguſti,

FIG. 124. CLOSING LINES OF THE PSALTER OF 1459
(MUCH REDUCED)

The closing lines (that is, the so-called *colophon*) of the second edition of the Psalter, which are here reproduced, are substantially the same as those of the first edition. They may be translated as follows : " The present volume of the Psalms, which is adorned with handsome capitals and is clearly divided by means of rubrics, was produced not by writing with a pen but by an ingenious invention of printed characters ; and was completed to the glory of God and the honor of St. James by John Fust, a citizen of Mayence, and Peter Schoifher of Gernsheim, in the year of our Lord 1459, on the 29th of August "

if sufficient care was taken to see that the types were properly set, the whole edition, not simply a single copy, might be relied upon as correct.

708. Paper introduced into Western Europe. After the supply of papyrus — the paper of the Egyptians, Greeks, and Romans — was cut off from Europe by the conquest of Egypt by the Mohammedans the people of the Middle Ages used *parchment*, made from the skin of lambs and goats. This was so expensive that printing would have been of but little use, even if it had been thought of,

before paper was introduced into Europe by the Mohammedans.[1]
Paper began to become common in the thirteenth and fourteenth
centuries and was already replacing parchment before the invention of printing.

709. The Earliest Printed Books. The earliest book of any
considerable size to be printed was the Bible, which appears to
have been completed at May-
ence in the year 1456. A year
later the famous Mayence
Psalter was finished, the first
dated book (Fig. 124). There
are, however, earlier examples
of little books printed with
engraved blocks and even with
movable types. In the German towns, where the art
spread rapidly, the printers
adhered to the style of letters
which the scribe had found it
convenient to make with his
quill — the so-called *Gothic*, or
black letter. In Italy, however, where the first printing
press was set up in 1466, a
type was soon adopted which
resembled the letters used in
ancient Roman inscriptions.
This was quite similar to the
style of letter commonly used

FIG. 125. AN OLD-FASHIONED
PRINTING OFFICE

Until the nineteenth century printing
was carried on with very little machinery. The type was inked by hand,
then the paper laid on and the form
slipped under a wooden press operated
by hand by means of a lever

to-day. The Italians also invented the compressed *italic* type,
which enabled them to get a great many words on a page. The
early printers generally did their work conscientiously, and the
very first book printed is in most respects as well done as any
later book.

[1] The Arabs seem to have derived their knowledge of paper-making from the
Chinese.

By the year 1500, after printing had been used less than half a century, there appear to have been at least forty printing presses to be found in various towns of Germany, France, Italy, the Netherlands, and England. These presses had, it is estimated, already printed eight millions of volumes. So there was no longer any danger of the old books being again lost, and the encouragement to write and publish new books was greatly increased. From that date our sources for history become far more voluminous than those which exist for the previous history of the world; we are much better informed in regard to events and conditions since 1500 than we ever can be respecting those of the earlier periods.

VI. THE ART OF THE RENAISSANCE

710. Development of Art in Italy. We have already described briefly the work of the medieval architects and referred to the beautiful carvings that adorned the Gothic cathedrals and to the pictures of saints and angels in stained glass which filled the great church windows. But in the fourteenth and fifteenth centuries art developed in a most astonishing manner in Italy and set new standards for all of western Europe.

Florence was the great center of artistic activity during the fifteenth century. The greatest sculptors and almost all of the most famous painters and architects of the time either were natives of Florence or did their best work there. During the first half of the century sculpture again took the lead. The bronze doors of the baptistery at Florence by Ghiberti, which were completed in 1452, are among the finest products of Renaissance sculpture (Fig. 126).[1]

Florence reached the height of its preëminence as an art center during the reign of Lorenzo the Magnificent, who was a devoted patron of all the arts. With his death (1492) this preëminence passed to Rome, which was fast becoming one of the great capitals

[1] Opposite the cathedral at Florence (Fig. 120) stands the ancient baptistery. Its northern bronze doors, with ten scenes from the Bible, surrounded by a very lovely border of foliage, birds, and animals, were completed by Lorenzo Ghiberti in 1452, after many years of labor. Michael Angelo declared them worthy to be the gates of heaven.

Courtesy of Braun et Cie

FIG. 126. GHIBERTI'S DOORS AT FLORENCE

FIG. 127. HOLY FAMILY BY ANDREA DEL SARTO

of Europe. The art-loving popes, Julius II and Leo X, took pains to secure the services of the most distinguished artists and architects of the time in the building and adornment of St. Peter's and the Vatican; that is, the papal church and palace (see above, § 670).

711. Height of Renaissance Art — Da Vinci, Michael Angelo, Raphael. During the sixteenth century the art of the Renaissance reached its highest development. Among all the great artists of this period three stand out prominently — Leonardo da Vinci, Michael Angelo, and Raphael. The first two not only practiced but achieved distinction in the three arts of architecture, sculpture, and painting.[1] It is impossible to give in a few lines any idea of the beauty and significance of the work of these great geniuses. Both Raphael and Michael Angelo left behind them so many and such magnificent frescoes and paintings, and in the case of Michael Angelo statues as well, that it is easy to appreciate their importance. Leonardo, on the other hand, left but little completed work. His influence on the art of his time, which was probably greater than that of either of the others, came from his many-sidedness, his originality, and his unflagging interest in the discovery and application of new methods. He was almost more experimenter than artist.

While Florence could no longer boast of being the art center of Italy, it still produced great artists, among whom Andrea del Sarto may be especially mentioned (Fig. 127). But the most important center of artistic activity outside of Rome in the sixteenth century was Venice. The distinguishing characteristic of the Venetian pictures is their glowing color. This is strikingly exemplified in the paintings of Titian, the most famous of all the Venetian painters.[2]

712. Painting in Northern Europe. It was natural that artists from the northern countries should be attracted by the renown of the Italian masters and, after learning all that Italy could teach them, should return home to practice their art in

[1] Leonardo was engineer and inventor as well.
[2] See Fig. 128.

their own particular fashion. About a century after painting began to develop in Italy two Flemish brothers, Van Eyck by name, showed that they were not only able to paint quite as excellent pictures as the Italians of their day, but they also discovered a new way of mixing their colors superior to that employed in Italy. Later, when painting had reached its height in Italy, Albrecht Dürer and Hans Holbein the Younger [1] in Germany vied with even Raphael and Michael Angelo in the mastery of their art. Dürer is especially celebrated for his wonderful woodcuts and copperplate engravings, in which field he has perhaps never been excelled.

When, in the seventeenth century, painting had declined south of the Alps, Dutch and Flemish masters—above all, Rubens and Rembrandt—developed a new and admirable school of painting. To Van Dyck, another Flemish master, we owe many notable portraits of historically important persons. [2] Spain gave to the world in the seventeenth century a painter whom some would rank higher than even the greatest artists of Italy, namely, Velasquez (1599–1660). His genius, like that of Van Dyck, is especially conspicuous in his marvelous portraits.

QUESTIONS

I. Why was Latin used by learned men, churchmen, scholars, and lawyers in the Middle Ages? What is the origin of the Germanic languages? of the Romance tongues? When does English become sufficiently modern for us to read it easily without special study? What is the character of the French romances of the Middle Ages?

II. Who were the troubadours? Describe chivalry and the ideal knight.

III. Why did people know little of history in the Middle Ages? Give some examples of the beliefs in regard to the habits of animals and the existence of strange races of men. What value was supposed to come from studying the habits of animals? Define astrology. What words do we use that recall the beliefs of the Middle Ages in regard to the influence of the stars on man? What was alchemy?

[1] See below, Fig. 132.
[2] See below, Figs. 146 and 148.

IV. What was a "university" originally? Mention some early universities. What was the origin of our degrees? What subjects were studied in a medieval university? Why was Aristotle so venerated by the medieval scholars? What was scholasticism? How and when were Greek books again brought into western Europe? Who were the Humanists? Why did not the Humanists make any discoveries?

V. Why did Roger Bacon criticize the enthusiasm for Aristotle? What great inventions did he foresee? What great new discoveries were made in the thirteenth century? What effects did the introduction of gunpowder have? How were books made before the invention of printing? What are the disadvantages of a book copied by hand? What is the earliest large printed book? How rapidly did printing spread? What do you consider the chief effects of the introduction of printing?

VI. Say something of the chief artists of the Renaissance in Italy and their work. Name some of the artists of the sixteenth and seventeenth centuries who lived outside of Italy.

BOOK VII. THE PROTESTANT REVOLT AND THE WARS OF RELIGION

CHAPTER XXXI

EMPEROR CHARLES V AND HIS VAST REALMS

I. EMPEROR MAXIMILIAN AND THE HAPSBURG MARRIAGES

713. Charles V's Empire. In the year 1500 a baby was born in the town of Ghent who was destined before he reached the age of twenty to rule, as Emperor Charles V, over more of Europe than anyone since Charlemagne. He owed his vast empire not to any conquests of his own but to an extraordinary series of royal marriages which made him heir to a great part of western Europe. These marriages had been arranged by his grandfather, Maximilian I, one of the most successful matchmakers that ever lived. Maximilian belonged to the House of Hapsburg, and in order to understand European history since 1500 we must learn something of Maximilian and the Hapsburg line.

714. Reasons why the German Kings failed to establish a Strong State. The German kings had failed to create a strong kingdom such as those over which Louis XI of France and Henry VII of England ruled. Their fine title of emperor had made them a great deal of trouble and done them no good, as we have seen (§§ 584, 585, 597, 599). Their attempts to keep Italy as well as Germany under their rule, and the alliance of the mighty bishop of Rome with their enemies, had well-nigh ruined them. Their position was further weakened by the fact that their office was not strictly hereditary. Although the emperors were often succeeded by their sons, each new emperor had to be *elected*, and those great vassals who controlled the election naturally took care to bind the candidate by solemn promises not to interfere with their privileges and independence. The result was that, after the downfall of the Hohenstaufens, Germany fell apart into a great number of practically independent states, of which none were very large and some were extremely small.

715. The Imperial Title Hereditary in the House of Austria. After an interregnum, Rudolf of Hapsburg had been chosen emperor in 1273 (§ 600). The original seat of the Hapsburgs, who were destined to play such a great part in European affairs, was in northern Switzerland, where the vestiges of their original castle may still be seen. Rudolf was the first prominent member of the family ; he established its position and influence by seizing the duchies of Austria and Styria, which became, under his successors, the nucleus of the extensive Austrian possessions.

About a century and a half after the death of Rudolf the German princes began regularly to choose as their emperor the ruler of the Austrian possessions, so that the imperial title became, to all intents and purposes, hereditary in the Hapsburg line. The Hapsburgs were, however, far more interested in adding to their family domains than in advancing the interests of the German Empire as a whole. Indeed, the Holy Roman Empire was nearly defunct, and, in the memorable words of Voltaire, it had ceased to be either holy, or Roman, or an empire.

716. Maximilian and the Hapsburg Marriages. Maximilian, while still a very young man, married Mary of Burgundy, the heiress to the Burgundian realms, which included what we now call Holland and Belgium and portions of eastern France. In this way the House of Austria got a hold on the shores of the North Sea. Mary died in 1482, and her lands were inherited by her infant son, Philip. Maximilian's next matrimonial move was to arrange a marriage between his son, Philip, and Joanna, the heiress to the Spanish kingdoms, and this makes it necessary for us to turn a moment to Spain, of which little or nothing has been said since we saw how the kingdom of the West Goths was overthrown by the Mohammedan invaders, over seven hundred years before Maximilian's time (§ 502).

717. Arab Civilization in Spain. The Mohammedan conquest served to make the history of Spain very different from that of the other states of Europe. One of its first and most important results was the conversion of a great part of the inhabitants to Mohammedanism. During the tenth century, which was so dark a period in the rest of Europe, the Arab civilization in Spain reached its highest development. Cordova, with its half million of inhabitants, its stately palaces, its university, its three thousand mosques, and its three hundred public baths, was perhaps unrivaled at that period in the whole world.

718. The Rise of New Christian Kingdoms in Spain. But the Christians were destined to reconquer the peninsula. As early as the year 1000[1] several small Christian kingdoms—Castile, Aragon, and Navarre—had come into existence in the northern part of Spain. Castile, in particular, began to push back the Mohammedans and, in 1085, reconquered Toledo from them. By 1250 the long war of the Christians against the Mohammedans, which fills the medieval annals of Spain, had been so successfully prosecuted that Castile extended to the south coast and included the great towns of Cordova and Seville. The Christian kingdom of Portugal was already as large as it is to-day.

The Moors, as the Spanish Mohammedans were called, held out for two centuries more in the mountainous kingdom of Granada, in the southern part of the peninsula. Not until 1492, after a long siege, was the city of Granada captured by the Christians and the last vestige of Mohammedan rule disappeared.

719. Spain becomes a European Power. The first Spanish monarch whose name need be mentioned here was Queen Isabella of Castile, who, in 1469, concluded an all-important marriage with Ferdinand, the heir of the crown of Aragon. It is with this union of Castile and Aragon that the great importance of Spain in European history begins. For the next hundred years Spain was to enjoy more military power than any other European state.

In the same year that the conquest of the peninsula was completed, the discoveries of Columbus, made under the auspices of Queen Isabella, opened up sources of undreamed-of wealth beyond

[1] See map above, p. 388.

the seas. The greatness of Spain in the sixteenth century was largely due to the riches derived from her American possessions. The shameless and cruel looting of the Mexican and Peruvian cities by Cortes and Pizarro (§ 678), and the silver mines of the New World, enabled Spain to assume, for a time, a position in Europe which her ordinary resources would never have permitted.

720. Revival of the Inquisition. Unfortunately, the most industrious, skillful, and thrifty among the inhabitants of Spain, that is, the Moors and the Jews, who well-nigh supported the whole kingdom by their toil, were bitterly persecuted by the Christians. So anxious was Isabella to rid her kingdom of the infidels that she revived the court of the Inquisition (§ 627). For several decades its tribunals arrested and condemned innumerable persons who were suspected of heresy, and thousands were burned at the stake during this period. These wholesale executions have served to associate Spain especially with the horrors of the Inquisition.

721. Charles and his Possessions. It was no wonder that the daughter and heiress of Ferdinand and Isabella seemed to Maximilian an admirable match for his son, Philip. Philip died, however, in 1506,— six years after his eldest son Charles was born, —and his poor wife, Joanna, became insane with grief and was thus incapacitated for ruling. So Charles could look forward to an unprecedented accumulation of glorious titles as soon as his grandfathers, Maximilian of Austria and Ferdinand of Aragon, should pass away.[1] He was soon to be duke of Brabant, margrave of Antwerp, count of Holland, archduke of Austria, count of Tyrol, king of Castile, Aragon, and Naples,[2] and of the vast Spanish possessions in America — to mention a few of his more important titles.

[1] Austria	Burgundy	Castile (America)	Aragon Naples, etc.
Maximilian I = (d. 1519)	Mary (d. 1482), dau. of Charles the Bold (d. 1477)	Isabella = (d. 1504)	Ferdinand (d. 1516)
Philip (d. 1506)	==	Joanna the Insane (d. 1555)	

Charles V (d. 1558) Ferdinand (d. 1564) = Anna, heiress to kingdoms
Emperor, 1519–1556 Emperor, 1556–1564   of Bohemia and Hungary

[2] Naples and Sicily were in the hands of the king of Aragon at this time (see note, p. 493, below).

Ferdinand died in 1516, and Charles, now a lad of sixteen, who had been born and reared in the Netherlands, was much bewildered when he first landed in his Spanish dominions. The Burgundian advisers whom he brought with him were distasteful

FIG. 128. CHARLES V AT THE AGE OF 48. (BY TITIAN)

to the haughty Spaniards, to whom, of course, they were foreigners; suspicion and opposition awaited him in each of his several Spanish kingdoms, for he found by no means a united Spain. Each kingdom demanded special recognition of its rights and proposed important reforms before it would acknowledge Charles as its king.

722. Charles elected Emperor (1519). It seemed as if the boy would have his hands full in asserting his authority as the first "king of Spain"; nevertheless, a still more imposing title and still more perplexing responsibilities were to fall upon his shoulders before he was twenty years old. It had long been Maximilian's ambition that his grandson should succeed him upon the imperial throne. After his death in 1519 the electors finally chose Charles as emperor — the fifth of that name — instead of the rival candidate, Francis I of France. By this election the king of Spain, who had not yet been in Germany and who never learned its language, became its ruler at a critical juncture, when the teachings of Luther (see next chapter) were adding a new kind of trouble to the old disorders.

II. How Italy became the Battleground of the European Powers

723. Charles VIII of France invades Italy. In order to understand the Europe of Charles V and the constant wars which occupied him all his life, we must turn back and review the questions which had been engaging the attention of his fellow kings before he came to the throne. It is particularly necessary to see clearly how Italy had suddenly become the center of commotion — the battlefield for Spain, France, and Germany.

Charles VIII of France (1483–1498) possessed little of the practical sagacity of his father, Louis XI (§ 580). He dreamed of a mighty expedition against the Turks and of the conquest of Constantinople. As the first step he determined to lead an army into Italy and assert his claim, inherited from his father, to the kingdom of Naples, which was in the hands of the House of Aragon.[1] While Italy had everything to lose by permitting a powerful foreign monarch to get a foothold in the South, there was no probability that the various little states into which the

---

[1] It will be remembered that the popes, in their long struggle with Frederick II and the Hohenstaufens, finally called in Charles of Anjou, the brother of St. Louis, and gave to him both Naples and Sicily (§ 599). Sicily revolted in 1282 and was united with the kingdom of Aragon, which still held it when Charles V came to the Spanish throne. Naples also was conquered by the king of Aragon, and was in his family when Charles VIII undertook his Italian expedition. Louis XI, although he claimed the right of the French to rule in Naples, had prudently refused to attempt to oust the Aragonese usurpers, as he had quite enough to do at home.

peninsula was divided would lay aside their animosities and combine against the invader. On the contrary, Charles VIII was urged by some of the Italians themselves to come.

The success of the French king seemed marvelous; he marched down the Italian peninsula without opposition. As he approached Florence the people, roused by the preaching of a famous Dominican friar, Savonarola, revolted against the rule of the Medici and established a republic. But the insignificant and ugly figure of the French king sadly disappointed them. So he soon deemed it wise to continue his way southward. Naples speedily fell into his hands. But he and his troops were demoralized by the wines and other pleasures of the South, and meanwhile his enemies at last began to form a combination against him. Ferdinand of Aragon was fearful lest he might lose Sicily, and Emperor Maximilian objected to having the French control Italy. Charles's situation became so dangerous that he may well have thought himself fortunate, at the close of 1495, to escape, with the loss of only a single battle, from the country he had hoped to conquer.

724. Results of Charles's Expedition. The results of Charles VIII's expedition appear at first sight trivial; in reality they were momentous. In the first place, it was now clear to Europe that the Italians had no real national feeling, however much they might despise the "barbarians" who lived north of the Alps. From this time down to the latter half of the nineteenth century, Italy was dominated by foreign nations, especially Spain and Austria. In the second place, the French learned to admire the art and culture of Italy (§§ 664–670, 699–701, 710–711). The nobles began to change their feudal castles, which since the invention of gunpowder were no longer impregnable, into luxurious palaces and country houses. The new scholarship of Italy also took root and flourished not only in France but in England and Germany as well, and Greek began to be studied outside of Italy. Consequently, just as Italy was becoming, politically, the victim of foreign aggressions, it was also losing, never to regain, that intellectual leadership which it had enjoyed since the revival of interest in Latin and Greek literature.

725. Francis I and his Attempt to conquer Northern Italy.
It would be wearisome and unprofitable to follow the attempts
of the French to get a foothold in northern Italy. Suffice it to
say that Charles VIII soon died and that his successor Louis XII
laid claim to the duchy of Milan in the north as well as to
Naples in the south. But he concluded to sell his claim to Naples

FIG. 129. FRANCIS I

to Ferdinand of Aragon and centered his attention on holding
Milan, but did not succeed in his purpose, largely owing to the
opposition of the Pope.

Francis I, who came to the French throne in 1515 at the age
of twenty, is one of the most famous of the French kings. He
was gracious and chivalrous in his ideas of conduct, and his
proudest title was "the gentleman king." Like his contemporaries, Pope Leo X, son of Lorenzo de' Medici, and Henry VIII
of England, he helped artists and men of letters and was interested
in fine buildings, of which a striking example is shown on the
following page (Fig. 130).

Francis opened his reign by a very astonishing victory. He led his troops into Italy, over a pass which had hitherto been regarded as impracticable for cavalry, and defeated the Swiss — who were in the Pope's pay — at Marignano. He then occupied Milan and opened negotiations with Leo X, who was glad to

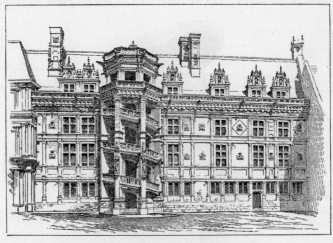

FIG. 130. COURT OF THE PALACE AT BLOIS

The expedition of Charles VIII to Italy called the attention of French architects to the beautiful Renaissance style used there. As cannon had by this time begun to render the old kind of castles with thick walls and towers useless as a means of defense, the French kings began to construct magnificent palaces of which several still exist. Charles VIII's successor, Louis XII, began a handsome structure at Blois, on the Loire River, and Francis I added a wing, the inner side of which is here reproduced. Its magnificent open staircase and wide, high windows have little in common with the old donjons of feudal times

make terms with the victorious young king. The Pope agreed that Francis should retain Milan, and Francis on his part acceded to Leo's plan for turning over Florence once more to the Medici, the family to which the Pope himself belonged. This was done, and some years later this wonderful republic became the grand duchy of Tuscany, governed by a line of petty princes under whom its former glories were never renewed.

726. Sources of Discord between France and the Hapsburgs.

Friendly relations existed at first between the two young sovereigns, Francis I and Charles V, but there were several circumstances which led to an almost incessant series of wars between them. France was clamped in between the northern and southern possessions of Charles and had at that time no natural boundaries. Moreover, there was a standing dispute over portions of the Burgundian realms. Charles also believed that, through his grandfather, Maximilian, he was entitled to Milan, which the French kings had set their hearts upon retaining. For a generation the rivals fought over these and other matters, and the wars between Charles and Francis were but the prelude to a conflict lasting over two centuries between France and the overgrown power of the House of Hapsburg.

727. Charles V goes to Germany.

In 1520 Charles V started for Germany to receive the imperial crown at Aix-la-Chapelle.

FIG. 131. THE WALLS OF ROTHENBURG

One town in Germany, Rothenburg on the little river Tauber, once a free imperial city, retains its old walls and towers intact and many of its old houses. It gives the visitor an excellent idea of how the smaller imperial towns looked two or three hundred years ago

On his way he landed in England with the purpose of keeping Henry VIII from forming an alliance with Francis. He then set sail for the Netherlands, where he was duly crowned king of the Romans. From there he proceeded, for the first time, to Germany, where he summoned his first diet at Worms.

III. Condition of Germany when Charles V became Emperor

728. The "Germanies" of the Sixteenth Century. In the time of Charles V there was no such Germany as that which precipitated the World War in 1914, but only what the French called the "Germanies"; that is, two or three hundred states, which differed greatly from one another in size and character. This one had a duke, that a count, at its head, while others were ruled over by archbishops, bishops, or abbots. There were many cities, like Nuremberg, Frankfort, and Cologne, just as independent as the great duchies of Bavaria, Würtemberg, and Saxony. Lastly there were the knights, whose possessions might consist of a single strong castle with a wretched village lying at its foot.

As for the emperor, he no longer had any power to control his vassals. He had neither money nor soldiers. At the time of Luther's birth the poverty-stricken Frederick III (Maximilian's father) might have been seen picking up a free meal at a monastery or riding behind a slow but economical ox team. The real power in Germany lay in the hands of the more important vassals, seven of whom were called the *electors*, because, since the thirteenth century, they had enjoyed the right to elect the emperor.

The towns, which had grown up since the great economic revolution that had brought in commerce and the use of money in the thirteenth century, were centers of culture in the north of Europe, just as those of Italy were in the south. Some of the towns were direct vassals of the emperor and were consequently independent of the particular prince within whose territory they were situated. These were called *free*, or *imperial*, cities and must be reckoned among the states of Germany.

The knights, who ruled over the smallest of the German territories, had earlier formed a very important class, but the introduction of gunpowder and new methods of fighting put them at a disadvantage, for they clung to their medieval traditions. Their tiny realms were often too small to support them, and they frequently turned to robbery for a living and proved a great nuisance to the merchants and townspeople whom they were accustomed to plunder now and then.

729. Neighborhood War. It is clear that these states, little and big, all tangled up with one another, would be sure to have frequent disputes among themselves. The emperor was not powerful enough to keep order, and each ruler had to defend himself if attacked. Neighborhood war was permitted by law if only some courteous preliminaries were observed. For instance, a prince or town was required to give warning three days in advance before attacking another member of the Empire.

Germany had a national assembly, called the *diet*, which met at irregular intervals, now in one town and now in another, for Germany had no capital city. The towns were not permitted to send delegates until 1487, long after the townspeople were represented in France and England. The restless knights and other minor nobles were not represented at all and consequently did not always consider the decisions of the diet binding upon them.

It was this diet that Charles V summoned to meet him on the Rhine, in the ancient town of Worms, when he made his first visit to Germany in 1520. The most important business of the assembly proved to be the consideration of the case of a university professor, Martin Luther, who was accused of writing heretical books, and who had begun what proved to be the first successful revolt against the powerful Medieval Church.

QUESTIONS

I. When and how did the House of Hapsburg become important? What marriages were arranged by Maximilian I which affected the history of Europe? How did Spain become a powerful kingdom? Over what countries did Ferdinand and Isabella rule? What was the extent of Charles V's dominions?

II. What were the results of the Italian expedition of Charles VIII? What were the causes of trouble between the French kings and the Hapsburgs? What are your impressions of Francis I?

III. Contrast Germany in Charles V's time with the German Empire before the World War. Who were the knights? the electors? What was the German diet? Why was the emperor unable to maintain order?

CHAPTER XXXII

MARTIN LUTHER AND THE REVOLT OF GERMANY AGAINST THE PAPACY

I. THE QUESTION OF REFORMING THE CHURCH: ERASMUS

730. Break-up of the Medieval Church into Catholics and Protestants. By far the most important event during the reign of Charles V was the revolt of a considerable portion of western Europe against the popes. The Medieval Church, which was described in a previous chapter, was in this way broken up, and *Protestant* churches appeared in various European countries which declared themselves entirely independent of the Pope and rejected a number of the religious beliefs which the Church had held previously.

With the exception of England all those countries that lay within the ancient bounds of the Roman Empire — Italy, France, Spain, Portugal, as well as southern Germany and Austria — continued to be faithful to the Pope and the Roman Catholic Church. On the other hand, the rulers of the northern German states, of England, Holland, Denmark, Norway, and Sweden, sooner or later became Protestants. In this way Europe was divided into two great religious parties, and this led to terrible wars and cruel persecutions which fill the annals of the sixteenth and seventeenth centuries.

731. Sources of Discontent with the Church. The revolt began in Germany. The Germans, while good Catholics, were suspicious of the popes, whom they regarded as Italians, bent upon getting as much money as possible out of the simple people north of the Alps. The revenue flowing to the popes from Germany was very large. The great German prelates, like the archbishops of Mayence, Treves, and Cologne, were each expected to contribute no less than ten thousand gold guldens to the papal treasury upon having their election confirmed by the Church authorities at Rome. The Pope enjoyed the right to fill many important church offices in Germany and frequently appointed Italians, who drew the revenue without going to Germany or performing the duties attached to the office. One person often held several church offices.

FIG. 132. PORTRAIT OF ERASMUS. (BY HOLBEIN)

This wonderful picture by Hans Holbein the Younger (1497–1543) hangs in the Louvre gallery at Paris. We have every reason to suppose that it is an excellent portrait, for Holbein lived in Basel a considerable part of his life and knew Erasmus well. The artist was, moreover, celebrated for his skill in catching the likeness when depicting the human face. He later painted several well-known Englishmen, including Henry VIII and his little son, Edward VI (see Fig. 135)

At first, however, no one thought of withdrawing from the Church or of attempting to destroy the power of the Pope. All that the Germans wanted was that the money which flowed toward Rome should be kept at home, and that the clergy should be upright, earnest men who should conscientiously perform their religious duties.

732. Erasmus (1465–1536). Among the critics of the Church in the early days of Charles V's reign the most famous and influential was Erasmus. He was a Dutchman by birth, but spent his life in various other countries — France, England, Italy, and Germany. He was a citizen of the world and in correspondence with literary men everywhere, so that his letters give us an excellent idea of the feeling of the times. He was greatly interested in the Greek and Latin authors, but his main purpose in life was to better the Church. He was well aware of the bad reputation of many of the clergymen of the time and he especially disliked the monks, for when he was a boy he had been forced into a monastery, much against his will.

One of his best-known books was his *Praise of Folly*, in which he held up to ridicule many of the practices and popular beliefs which Luther later attacked. He believed that superstition would certainly disappear as people became better educated.

It seemed to Erasmus that if everybody could read the Bible, especially the New Testament, for himself, it would bring about a great change for the better. He wanted to have the Gospels and the letters of Paul translated into the language of the people so that men and women who did not know Latin could read them and be helped by them.

Erasmus believed, moreover, that the time was favorable for reform. As he looked about him he beheld intelligent rulers on the thrones of Europe, men interested in books and art and ready to help scholars and writers. There were Henry VIII of England and Francis I of France. Then the Pope himself, Leo X, the son of Lorenzo the Magnificent, was a friend and admirer of Erasmus and doubtless sympathized with many of his views. The youthful Charles V had advisers who believed Erasmus to be quite right and were ready to work toward a reform of the Church. Charles was a devout Catholic, but he too agreed that there were many evils to be remedied. So it seemed to Erasmus that the prospects were excellent for a peaceful reform ; but, instead of its coming, his latter years were embittered by Luther's revolt and all the ill-feelings and dissensions that it created.

AETHERNA IPSE SVAE MENTIS SIMVLACHRA LVTHERVS
EXPRIMIT·AT VVLTVS CERA LVCAE OCCIDVOS
·M·D·X·X·

FIG. 133. LUTHER AS A MONK. (BY CRANACH, 1520)

None of the portraits of Luther are very satisfactory. His friend Cranach was not, like Holbein the Younger, a great portrait painter. This cut shows the reformer when his revolt against the Church was just beginning. He was thirty-seven years old and still in the dress of an Augustinian friar, which he soon abandoned

II. How Martin Luther revolted against the Papacy

733. Early Years of Luther. Martin Luther was born in 1483. He was the son of a poor miner, and he often spoke in later life of the poverty and superstition in which his boyhood was spent. His father, however, was determined that his son should be a lawyer, and so Martin was sent to the University of Erfurt. After he finished his college course and was about to take up the study of the law he had a deep religious experience and suddenly decided to become a monk.

He was much worried about his soul and feared that nothing he could do would save him from hell. He finally found comfort in the thought that in order to be saved he had only to *believe* sincerely that God would save him, and that he could not possibly save himself by trying to be good. He gained the respect of the head of the monastery, and when Frederick the Wise of Saxony was looking about for teachers for his new university at Wittenberg, Luther was recommended as a good person to teach Aristotle; so he became a professor.

As time went on, Luther began to be suspicious of some of the things that were taught in the university. He finally decided that Aristotle was after all only an ancient heathen who knew nothing about Christianity, and that the students had no business to study his works. He urged them to rely instead upon the Bible.

734. Luther's Idea of Salvation. Luther's main point was that man, through Adam's sin, had become so corrupt that he could, of himself, do nothing pleasing to God. He could only hope to be saved through *faith* in God's promise to save those who should repent. Consequently "good works," such as attending church, going on pilgrimages, repeating prayers, and visiting relics of the saints, could do nothing for a sinner if he was not already "justified by faith"; that is, made acceptable to God by his faith in God's promises. If he was "justified," then he might properly go about his daily duties, for they would be pleasing to God without what the Church was accustomed to regard as "good works."

Luther's teachings did not attract much attention until the year 1517, when he was thirty-four years old. Then something occurred to give him considerable prominence.

735. Indulgences. The fact has already been mentioned that the popes had undertaken the rebuilding of St. Peter's, the great central church of Christendom (§ 670). The cost of the enterprise was very great, and in order to collect contributions for the purpose Pope Leo X arranged for an extensive distribution of *indulgences* in Germany.

In order to understand the nature of indulgences and Luther's opposition to them, we must consider the teaching of the Catholic Church in regard to the forgiveness of sin. The Church taught that if one died after committing a serious ("mortal") sin which he had not repented and confessed, his soul would certainly be lost. If he sincerely repented and confessed his sin to a priest, God would forgive him and his soul would be saved, but he would not thereby escape punishment. This punishment might consist in fasting, saying certain prayers, going on a pilgrimage, or doing some other good work. It was assumed, however, that most men committed so many sins that even if they died repentant they had to pass through a long period in purgatory, where they would be purified by suffering before they could enter heaven.

Now an indulgence was a pardon, issued usually by the Pope himself, which freed the person to whom it was granted *from a part or all of his suffering in purgatory*. It did not forgive his sins or in any way take the place of true repentance and confession ; it only reduced the punishment which a truly contrite sinner would otherwise have had to endure, either in this world or in purgatory, before he could be admitted to heaven.[1]

The contribution to the Church which was made in return for indulgences varied greatly ; the rich were required to give a

[1] It is a common mistake of Protestants to suppose that the indulgence was forgiveness granted beforehand for sins to be committed in the future. There is absolutely no foundation for this idea. A person proposing to sin could not possibly be contrite in the eyes of the Church, and even if he had secured an indulgence it would, according to the theologians, have been quite worthless.

considerable sum, while the very poor were to receive these pardons gratis. The representatives of the Pope were naturally anxious to collect all the money possible and did their best to induce everyone to secure an indulgence, either for himself or for his deceased friends in purgatory. In their zeal they made many claims for the indulgences, to which no thoughtful churchman or even layman could listen without misgivings.

736. Luther's Theses on Indulgences. In October, 1517, Tetzel, a Dominican monk, began announcing indulgences in the neighborhood of Wittenberg and making claims for them which appeared to Luther wholly irreconcilable with Christianity as he understood it. He therefore, in accordance with the custom of the time, wrote out a series of ninety-five statements in regard to indulgences. These *theses*, as they were called, he posted on the church door and invited anyone interested in the matter to enter into a discussion with him on the subject, which he believed was very ill understood.

In posting these theses, Luther did not intend to attack the Church and had no expectation of creating a sensation. The theses were in Latin and addressed, therefore, only to learned men. It turned out, however, that everyone, high and low, learned and unlearned, was ready to discuss the nature of indulgences.

The theses were promptly translated into German, printed, and scattered abroad throughout the land. In these *Ninety-five Theses* Luther declared that the indulgence was very unimportant and that the poor man would better spend his money for the needs of his household. The truly repentant, he argued, do not flee punishment, but bear it willingly in sign of their sorrow. Faith in God, not the procuring of pardons, brings forgiveness, and every Christian who feels true sorrow for his sins will receive full remission of the punishment as well as of the guilt. Could the Pope know how his agents misled the people, he would rather have St. Peter's burn to ashes than build it up with money gained under false pretenses. Then, Luther adds, there is danger that the common man will ask awkward questions. For example, "If the Pope releases souls from purgatory for money, why not for charity's sake?" or, "Since the Pope is rich as Crœsus, why does he not build St. Peter's with his own money, instead of taking that of the poor man?"

737. Luther becomes Suspicious of the Papacy. Luther now began to read church history and reached the conclusion that the influence of the popes had not been very great until the times of Gregory VII (§§ 591–593), and therefore that they had not enjoyed their supremacy over the Church for more than four hundred years before his own birth. He was mistaken in this conclusion, but he had hit upon an argument that has been constantly urged by Protestants ever since. They assert that the power of the Medieval Church and of the papacy developed gradually and that the apostles knew nothing of Masses, indulgences, pilgrimages, purgatory, or the headship of the bishop of Rome.

The publication of Luther's theses brought him many sympathizers in Germany. Some were attracted by his protests against the ways in which the popes raised money, and others liked him for attacking Aristotle and the scholastic theologians. Erasmus' publisher at Basel agreed to publish Luther's books, of which he sent copies to Italy, France, England, and Spain, and in this way the Wittenberg monk began before long to be widely known outside of Germany as well as within it.

738. Contrast between Luther and Erasmus. But Erasmus himself, the mighty sovereign of the men of letters, refused to take sides in the controversy. Luther, he urged, would better be discreet and trust that as mankind became more intelligent they would outgrow their false ideas.

To Erasmus, man was capable of progress; cultivate him and extend his knowledge, and he would grow better and better. To Luther, on the other hand, man was utterly corrupt and incapable of a single righteous wish or deed. His will was enslaved to evil, and his only hope lay in the recognition of his absolute inability to better himself and in a humble reliance upon God's mercy. Only by *faith* and not by doing good works could he be saved.

Erasmus and many other thoughtful people of the time were willing to wait until everyone agreed that the Church should be reformed. Luther had no patience with an institution which seemed to him to be leading souls to destruction by inducing men to rely upon their good works. Erasmus declared that Luther, by scorning good works, had made his followers indifferent to their conduct, and that those who accepted Luther's teachings straightway became pert, rude fellows, who would not any longer take off their hats to him on the street.

739. Luther's *Address to the German Nobility*. By 1520 Luther, who gave way at times to his naturally violent disposition, had become threatening and abusive and suggested that the German rulers should punish the churchmen and force them to reform their conduct. "We punish thieves with the gallows, bandits with the sword, heretics with fire; why should we not, with far greater propriety, attack with every kind of weapon these very masters of perdition, the cardinals and popes?"

Of Luther's popular pamphlets, the first really famous one was his *Address to the German Nobility*, in which he calls upon the rulers of Germany, especially the knights, to reform the abuses themselves, since he believed that it was vain to wait for the Church to do so. He explains that there are three walls behind which the papacy had been wont to take refuge when anyone proposed to remedy its abuses. There was, first, the claim that the clergy formed a separate class, superior even to the civil rulers, who were not permitted to punish a churchman, no matter how bad he was. Secondly, the Pope claimed to be superior even to the great general assemblies of the Church, called councils, so that even the representatives of the Church itself might not correct him. And, lastly, the Pope assumed the sole right, when questions of belief arose, to interpret with authority the meaning of the Scriptures; consequently he could not be refuted by arguments from the Bible (§ 592).

Luther undertook to cast down these defenses by denying, to begin with, that there was anything especially sacred about a clergyman except the duties which he had been designated to perform. If he did not attend to his work, it should be possible to deprive him of his office at any moment, just as one would turn off an incompetent tailor or farmer, and in that case he should become a simple layman again. Luther claimed, moreover, that it was the right and duty of the rulers to punish a churchman who did wrong just as if he were the humblest layman.

The *Address to the German Nobility* closed with a long list of evils which must be done away with before Germany could become prosperous. Luther saw that his view of religion really implied a social revolution. He advocated reducing the monasteries to a tenth of their number and permitting those monks who were disappointed in the good they got from living in them freely to leave. He pointed out the evils of pilgrimages and of the numerous church holidays, which interfered with daily work. The clergy, he urged, should be permitted to marry and have families like other citizens. The universities should be reformed, and "the accursed heathen, Aristotle," should be cast out from them.

740. Luther Excommunicated. Luther had long expected to be excommunicated. But it was not until late in 1520 that John Eck, a personal enemy of his, arrived in Germany with a papal bull condemning many of Luther's assertions as heretical and giving him sixty days in which to recant. Should he fail to return to his senses within that time, he and all who adhered to or favored him were to be excommunicated, and any place which harbored him should fall under the interdict (§ 623). Now, since the highest power in Christendom had pronounced Luther a heretic, he should unhesitatingly have been delivered up by the German authorities. But no one thought of arresting him.

The bull irritated the German princes; whether they liked Luther or not, they decidedly disliked to have the Pope issuing commands to them. Then it appeared to them very unfair that Luther's personal enemy should have been intrusted with the publication of the bull. Even the princes and universities that were most friendly to the Pope published the bull with great reluctance. In many cases the bull was ignored altogether. Luther's own sovereign, the elector of Saxony, while no convert to the new views, was anxious that Luther's case should be fairly considered, and he continued to protect him. One mighty prince, however, the young Emperor Charles V, promptly and willingly published the bull; not, however, as emperor, but as ruler of the Austrian dominions and of the Netherlands.

741. Luther burns the Pope's Bull (1520). The Wittenberg professor felt himself compelled to oppose himself to both Pope and emperor. "Hard it is," he exclaimed, "to be forced to contradict all the prelates and princes, but there is no other way to escape hell and God's anger." Late in 1520 he summoned his students to witness what he called "a pious religious spectacle." He had a fire built outside the walls of Wittenberg and cast into it Leo X's bull condemning him, and a copy of the Laws of the Church, together with a volume of scholastic theology which he specially disliked.

Yet Luther dreaded disorder. He was certainly sometimes reckless and violent in his writings and often said that bloodshed could not be avoided. Yet he always opposed hasty reform. He was reluctant to make changes, except in belief. He held that so long as an institution did not actually mislead, it did no harm. He was, in short, no fanatic at heart.

III. The Diet at Worms (1520–1521)

742. Charles V's Want of Sympathy with the German Reformers. The Pope's chief representative in Germany, named Aleander, wrote as follows to Leo X about this time: "I am pretty familiar with the history of this German nation. I know their past heresies, councils, and schisms, but never were affairs so serious before. Compared with present conditions, the struggle between Henry IV and Gregory VII was as violets and roses. . . . Nine tenths of the Germans are shouting 'Luther,' and the other tenth goes so far at least as 'Death to the Roman curia.'"

Among the enemies of Luther and his supporters none was more important than the young emperor. It was toward the end of the year 1520 that Charles came to Germany for the first time (§ 729). After being crowned King of the Romans at Aix-la-Chapelle he assumed, with the Pope's consent, the title of emperor elect as his grandfather Maximilian had done. He then moved on to the town of Worms, where he was to hold his first diet and face the German situation.

Although scarcely more than a boy in years, Charles had already begun to take life very seriously. He had decided that Spain, not Germany, was to be the bulwark and citadel of all his realms. Like the more enlightened of his Spanish subjects he realized the need of reforming the Church, but he had no sympathy whatever with any change of religious belief. He proposed to live and die a devout Catholic of the old type, such as his orthodox ancestors had been.

743. Luther summoned to the Diet at Worms. Upon arriving at Worms the case of Luther was at once forced upon Charles's attention by Aleander, the papal representative, who exhorted him to outlaw the heretic without further delay. While Charles seemed convinced of Luther's guilt, he could not proceed against him without serious danger. The monk had become a sort of national hero and had the support of the powerful elector of Saxony. Other princes, who had ordinarily no wish to protect a heretic, felt that Luther's denunciation of the evils in the Church and of the actions of the Pope was very gratifying. After much discussion it was finally arranged, to the great disgust of the zealous Aleander, that Luther should be summoned to Worms and be given an opportunity to face the German nation and the emperor, and to declare plainly whether he was the author of the heretical books ascribed to him, and whether he still adhered to the doctrines which the Pope had condemned.

The emperor accordingly wrote the "honorable and respected" Luther a very polite letter, desiring him to appear at Worms and granting him a safe-conduct thither.

It was not, however, proposed to give Luther an opportunity to defend his beliefs before the diet. When he appeared he was simply asked if a pile of his Latin and German works were really his, and, if so, whether he revoked what he had said in them.

To the first question the monk replied in a low voice that he had written these and more. As to the second question, he asked that he might have a little while to consider.

The following day, in a Latin address which he repeated in German, he admitted that he had been overviolent in his attacks upon his opponents. But he said that he believed no one could deny that the Pope's decrees had often gone against the conscience of good Christians and that the German people had been robbed by the abuses of Church power. If, however, adequate arguments against his position could be found in the Scriptures, he said he would gladly and willingly recant.

744. The Edict of Worms (1521). There was now nothing for the emperor to do but to outlaw Luther, who had denied the binding character of the commands of the head of the Church. Aleander was accordingly assigned the agreeable duty of drafting the famous Edict of Worms.

This document declared Luther an outlaw on the following grounds : that he scorned and villified the Pope, despised the priesthood and stirred up the laity to dip their hands in the blood of the clergy, denied free will, taught licentiousness, despised authority, advocated a brutish existence, and was a menace to Church and State alike. Everyone was forbidden to give the heretic food, drink, or shelter, and was required to seize him and deliver him to the emperor.

Moreover, the decree provides that "no one shall dare to buy, sell, read, preserve, copy, print, or cause to be copied or printed, any books of the aforesaid Martin Luther, condemned by our holy father the Pope, as aforesaid, or any other writings in German or Latin hitherto composed by him, since they are foul, noxious, suspected, and published by a notorious and stiff-necked heretic."

So general was the disapproval of the edict that few were willing to pay any attention to it. Charles V immediately left Germany and for nearly ten years was occupied outside it with the government of Spain and a succession of wars.

IV. THE REVOLT AGAINST THE PAPACY BEGINS IN GERMANY

745. Luther begins a New Translation of the Bible. As Luther neared Eisenach upon his way home from Worms he was kidnaped by his friends and conducted to the Wartburg, a castle belonging to the elector of Saxony. Here he was concealed until any danger from the action of the emperor or diet should pass by. His chief occupation during several months of hiding was to begin a new translation of the Bible into German. He had finished the New Testament before he left the Wartburg in March, 1522.

Up to this time German editions of the Scriptures, while not uncommon, had been poor and obscure. Luther's task was a difficult one. He was anxious above all that the Bible should be put into language that would seem perfectly clear and natural to the common folk. So he went about asking the mothers and children and the laborers questions which might draw out the expression that he was looking for.

746. Pamphlets and Satires. Previous to 1518 there had been very few books or pamphlets printed in German. The translation of the Bible into language so simple that even the unlearned might read it was only one of the signs of a general effort to awaken the minds of the common people.

Hundreds of pamphlets, satires, and cartoons have come down to us which indicate that the religious and other questions of the day were often treated in somewhat the same spirit in which our comic papers deal with political problems and discussions now.

747. The Revolt Begins. Hitherto there had been a great deal of talk of reform, but as yet nothing had actually been done. There was no sharp line drawn between the different classes of reformers. All agreed that something should be done to better the Church ; few realized how divergent were the real ends in view. The rulers listened to Luther because they were glad of an excuse to get control of the church property and keep money from flowing to Rome. The peasants listened because he put the Bible into their hands and they found nothing there that proved that they ought to go on paying the old dues to their lords.

While Luther was quietly living in the Wartburg, translating the Bible, people began to put his teachings into practice. The monks and nuns left their monasteries in his own town of Wittenberg. Some of them married, which seemed a very wicked thing to all those that held to the old beliefs. The students and citizens tore down the images of the saints in the churches and even went so far as to oppose the celebration of the Mass, the chief Catholic ceremony.

Luther was greatly troubled by news of this disorderly reform. He did not approve of sudden and violent changes and left his hiding place to protest. He preached a series of sermons in Wittenberg in which he urged that all alterations in religious services and practices should be introduced by the *government* and not by the *people*. But his advice was not heeded.

748. The Peasant War. The conservative party, who were frankly afraid of Luther, received a terrible proof, as it seemed to them, of the noxious influence of his teachings. In 1525 the serfs rose, in the name of "God's justice," to avenge their wrongs. Luther was not responsible for the civil war which followed, though he had certainly helped to stir up discontent. He had asserted, for example, that the German feudal lords were hangmen, who knew only how to swindle the poor man. "Such fellows were formerly called rascals, but now must we call them 'Christian and revered princes.'" Yet in spite of his harsh talk about the princes, Luther really relied upon them to forward his movement, and he justly claimed that he had greatly increased their power by attacking the authority of the Pope and subjecting the clergy in all things to the government.

749. The "Twelve Articles." Some of the demands of the peasants were perfectly reasonable. The most popular expression of their needs was the dignified "Twelve Articles." In these they claimed that the Bible did not sanction any of the dues which the lords demanded of them, and that, since they were Christians like their lords, they should no longer be held as serfs. They were willing to pay all the old and well-established dues, but they asked to be properly remunerated for extra services demanded by the lord. They thought too that each community should have the right freely to choose its own pastor and to dismiss him if he proved negligent or inefficient.

There were, however, leaders who were more violent and who proposed to kill the "godless" priests and nobles. Hundreds of castles and monasteries were destroyed by the frantic peasantry, and some of the nobility were murdered with shocking cruelty. Luther tried to induce the peasants, with whom, as the son of a peasant, he was at first inclined to sympathize, to remain quiet ; but when his warnings proved vain he turned against them. He declared that they were guilty of the most fearful crimes and urged the government to put down the insurrection without pity.

750. The Peasant Revolt put down with Great Cruelty. Luther's advice was followed with terrible literalness by the German rulers, and the nobility took fearful revenge on the peasants. In the summer of 1525 their chief leader was defeated and killed, and it is estimated that ten thousand peasants were put to death, many with the utmost cruelty. Few of the rulers or landlords introduced any reforms, and the misfortunes due to the destruction of property and to the despair of the peasants cannot be imagined. The people concluded that the new gospel was not for them, and talked of Luther as "Dr. Lügner"; that is, liar. The old exactions of the lords of the manors were in no way lightened, and the situation of the serfs for centuries following the great revolt was worse rather than better.

V. DIVISION OF GERMANY INTO CATHOLIC AND PROTESTANT COUNTRIES

751. Religious Division of North and South Germany. Charles V was occupied at this time by his quarrels with Francis I (§ 726) and was in no position to return to Germany and undertake to enforce the Edict of Worms against Luther and his followers. Germany, as we have seen, was divided into hundreds of practically independent countries, and the various electors, princes, towns, and knights naturally could not agree as to what would best be done in the matter of reforming the Church. It became apparent not long after the Peasant War that some of the rulers were going to accept Luther's idea that they need no longer obey the Pope but that they were free to proceed to regulate the property and affairs of the churchmen in their domains without regard to the Pope's wishes. Other princes and towns agreed that they would remain faithful to the Pope if certain reforms were introduced, especially if the papal taxation were reduced. Southern Germany decided for the Pope and remains Catholic down to the present day. Many of the northern rulers, on the other hand, adopted the new teachings, and finally all of them fell away from the papacy and became Protestant.

Since there was no one powerful enough to decide the great question for the whole of Germany, the diet which met at Speyer in 1526 determined that pending the summoning of a church council each ruler should "so live, reign, and conduct himself as he would be willing to answer before God and His Imperial Majesty." For the moment, then, the various German governments were left to determine the religion of their subjects.

752. Origin of the Term "Protestants." The emperor, finding himself again free for a time to attend to German affairs, commanded the diet, which again met at Speyer in 1529, to order the enforcement of the Edict of Worms against the heretics.

The princes and towns that had accepted Luther's ideas drew up a *protest*, in which they claimed that the majority had no right to abrogate the edict of the former diet of Speyer, which had been passed unanimously, and which all had solemnly pledged themselves to observe. Those who signed this appeal were called from their action *Protestants*. Thus originated the name which came to be generally applied to those who do not accept the rule and teachings of the Roman Catholic Church.

753. Diet at Augsburg and the *Augsburg Confession*. Ever since the diet at Worms the emperor had resided in Spain, busied with a succession of wars carried on with the king of France. But in 1530 the emperor found himself at peace for the moment and came to Germany to hold a brilliant diet of his

German subjects at Augsburg in the hope of settling the religious problem, which, however, he understood very imperfectly. He ordered the Protestants to draw up a statement of exactly what they believed, which should serve as a basis for discussion. Melanchthon, Luther's most famous friend and colleague, who was noted for his great learning and moderation, was intrusted with this delicate task.

The *Augsburg Confession*, as his declaration was called, is a historical document of great importance for the student of the Protestant revolt.[1] Melanchthon's gentle disposition led him to make the differences between his belief and that of the old Church seem as few and slight as possible. He showed that both parties held the same fundamental views of Christianity. But he defended the Protestants' rejection of a number of the practices of the Roman Catholics, such as the celibacy of the clergy and the observance of fast days. There was little or nothing in the Augsburg Confession concerning the organization of the Church.

754. Charles V's Attempt at Pacification. Certain theologians who had been loud in their denunciations of Luther were ordered by the emperor to prepare a refutation of the Protestant views. The statement of the Catholics admitted that a number of Melanchthon's positions were perfectly orthodox; but the portion of the Augsburg Confession which dealt with the practical reforms introduced by the Protestants was rejected altogether.

Charles V declared the Catholic statement to be "Christian and judicious" and commanded the Protestants to accept it. They were to cease troubling the Catholics and were to give back all the monasteries and church property which they had seized. The emperor agreed, however, to urge the Pope to call a council to meet within a year. This, he hoped, would be able to settle all differences and reform the Church according to the views of the Catholics.

755. The Peace of Augsburg. For ten years after the emperor left Augsburg he was kept busy in southern Europe by

---

[1] It is still accepted as the creed of the Lutheran Church. Inexpensive copies of it in English may be procured from the Lutheran Publication Society, Philadelphia.

new wars ; and in order to secure the assistance of the Protestants he was forced to let them go their own way. Meanwhile the number of rulers who accepted Luther's teachings gradually increased. Finally there was a brief war between Charles and the Protestant princes, but there was little fighting done. Charles V brought his Spanish soldiers into Germany and captured both John Frederick of Saxony and his ally, Philip of Hesse, the chief leaders of the Lutheran cause, whom he kept prisoners for several years. Luther himself died in 1546.

These events did not, however, check the progress of the Protestants. The king of France, although he was persecuting heretics at home, promised them help against his enemy, the emperor, and Charles was forced to agree to a peace with the Protestants.

In 1555 the religious Peace of Augsburg was ratified. Its provisions are memorable. Each German prince and each town and knight directly under the emperor was to be at liberty to make a choice between the beliefs of the venerable Catholic Church and those embodied in the Augsburg Confession. If, however, an ecclesiastical prince — an archbishop, bishop, or abbot — declared himself a Protestant, he must surrender his possessions to the Church. Every German was either to conform to the religious practices of his particular state or emigrate from it. Everyone was supposed to be either a Catholic or a Lutheran, and no provision was made for any other belief.

This religious peace in no way established freedom of conscience, except for the rulers. Their power, it must be noted, was greatly increased, inasmuch as they were given the control of religious as well as of secular matters. This arrangement which permitted the ruler to determine the religion of his realm was more natural in those days than it would be in ours. The Church and the civil government had been closely associated with one another for centuries. No one as yet dreamed that every individual might safely be left quite free to believe what he would and to practice any religious rites which afforded him help and comfort.

QUESTIONS

I. What were the sources of discontent with the Church in Germany? What were the views of Erasmus in regard to church reform?

II. Tell something of Luther's life before he posted up his theses. What was an indulgence? Give some of Luther's views expressed in his Ninety-five Theses. Contrast the opinions of Erasmus and Luther. Discuss Luther's *Address to the German Nobility*. Why was Luther excommunicated? What was the fate of the papal bull directed against him?

III. Why did Charles V summon Luther at Worms? What did Luther say to the diet? What were the chief provisions of the Edict of Worms?

IV. Describe Luther's translation of the Bible. What was the state of public opinion in Germany after the diet at Worms? What was Luther's attitude toward reform? Why did the German peasants revolt? What did the Twelve Articles contain? What effect did the Peasant Revolt have on Luther?

V. What was the origin of the term "Protestant"? What was the Augsburg Confession? What were the results of the diet of Augsburg? What was the policy of Charles V in regard to the Protestants? What were the chief provisions of the Peace of Augsburg?

CHAPTER XXXIII

THE PROTESTANT REVOLT IN SWITZERLAND AND ENGLAND

I. ZWINGLI AND CALVIN

756. Origin of the Swiss Confederation. For at least a century after Luther's death the great issue between Catholics and Protestants dominates the history of all the countries with which we have to do, except Italy and Spain, where Protestantism never took permanent root. In Switzerland, England, France, and Holland the revolt against the Medieval Church produced discord, wars, and profound changes, which must be understood in order to follow the later development of these countries.

We turn first to Switzerland, lying in the midst of the great chain of the Alps which extends from the Mediterranean to Vienna. During the Middle Ages the region destined to be included in the Swiss Confederation formed a part of the Holy Roman Empire and was scarcely distinguishable from the rest of southern Germany. As early as the thirteenth century the three "forest" cantons on the shores of the winding Lake of Lucern formed a union to protect their liberties against the encroachments of their neighbors, the Hapsburgs (§ 715). It was about this tiny nucleus that Switzerland gradually consolidated. Lucern and the free towns of Zurich and Bern soon joined the Swiss league. By brave fighting the Swiss were able to frustrate the renewed efforts of the Hapsburgs to subjugate them.

Various districts in the neighborhood joined the Swiss union in succession, and even the region lying on the Italian slopes of the Alps was brought under its control. Gradually the bonds between the members of the Swiss union and the Empire were broken. In 1499 they were finally freed from the jurisdiction of the emperor, and Switzerland became a practically independent country. Although the original union had been made up of German-speaking people, considerable districts had been annexed in which Italian or French was spoken.[1] The Swiss did not,

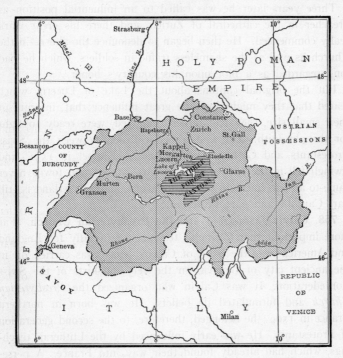

THE SWISS CONFEDERATION IN THE SIXTEENTH CENTURY

therefore, form a compact, well-defined nation, and consequently for some centuries their confederation was weak and ill-organized.

757. Zwingli leads Revolt against the Old Church. In Switzerland the first leader of the revolt against the Church was a young priest named Zwingli, who was a year younger than Luther. He lived in the famous monastery of Einsiedeln, near

[1] This condition has not changed; all Swiss laws are still proclaimed in three languages.

the Lake of Zurich, which was the center of pilgrimages on account of a wonder-working image. "Here," he says, "I began to preach the Gospel of Christ in the year 1516, before anyone in my locality had so much as heard the name of Luther."

Three years later he was called to an influential position as preacher in the cathedral of Zurich, and there his great work really commenced. He then began to denounce the abuses in the Church as well as the shameless traffic in soldiers, which he had long regarded as a blot upon his country's honor.[1]

But the original cantons about the Lake of Lucern, which feared that they might lose the great influence that, in spite of their small size, they had hitherto enjoyed, were ready to fight for the old faith. The first armed collision between the Swiss Protestants and Catholics took place at Kappel in 1531, and Zwingli fell in the battle. The various cantons and towns never came to an agreement in religious matters, and Switzerland is still part Catholic and part Protestant.

758. Calvin (1509–1564) and the Presbyterian Church. Far more important than Zwingli's teachings, especially for England and America, was the work of Calvin, which was carried on in the ancient city of Geneva, on the very outskirts of the Swiss Confederation. It was Calvin who organized the *Presbyterian Church* and formulated its beliefs. He was born in northern France in 1509; he belonged, therefore, to the second generation of Protestants. He was early influenced by the Lutheran teachings, which had already found their way into France. A persecution of the Protestants under Francis I drove him out of the country, and he settled for a time in Basel.

Here he issued the first edition of his great work, *The Institute of Christianity*, which has been more widely discussed than any other Protestant theological treatise. It was the first orderly exposition of the principles of Christianity from a Protestant

---

[1] Switzerland had made a business, ever since the time when Charles VIII of France invaded Italy, of supplying troops of mercenaries to fight for other countries, especially for France and the Pope. It was the Swiss who gained the battle of Marignano for Francis I (§ 725), and Swiss guards may still be seen in the Pope's palace, the Vatican.

standpoint and formed a convenient manual for study and discussion. The *Institute* is based upon the infallibility of the Bible
and rejects the infallibility of the Church and the Pope. Calvin
possessed a remarkably logical mind and a clear and admirable
style. The French version of his great work is the first example
of the successful use of that language in an argumentative treatise.

Calvin was called to Geneva about 1540 and intrusted with
the task of reforming the town, which had secured its independence of the duke of Savoy. Calvin intrusted the management of
church affairs to the ministers and the elders, or *presbyters*;
hence the name "Presbyterian." The Protestantism which found
its way into France was that of Calvin, not that of Luther, and
the same may be said of Scotland (see below, §§ 798–799).

II. How England fell away from the Papacy

759. Erasmus in England; More's *Utopia*. When Erasmus
(§ 732) came to England about the year 1500 he was delighted
with the people he met there. Henry VII was still alive. It will be
remembered that it was he that brought order into England after
the Wars of the Roses (§ 578). His son, who was to become the
famous Henry VIII, impressed Erasmus as a very promising boy.
We may assume that the intelligent men whom Erasmus met in
England agreed with him in regard to the situation in the Church
and the necessity of reform. He was a good friend of Sir Thomas
More, who is best known for his little book called *Utopia*, which
means "Nowhere." In it More pictures the happy conditions
in an undiscovered land where the government was perfect and
all the evils that he saw about him were done away.

760. Wolsey's Idea of the Balance of Power. Henry VIII
came to the English throne when he was eighteen years old. His
chief adviser, Cardinal Wolsey, deserves great credit for having
constantly striven to discourage his sovereign's ambition to take
part in the wars on the Continent. The cardinal's argument that
England could become great by peace better than by war was a
momentous discovery. Peace he felt would be best secured by

maintaining the *balance of power* on the Continent, so that no ruler should become dangerous by unduly extending his sway. For example, he thought it good policy to side with Charles V when Francis I was successful, and then with Francis after his terrible defeat at Pavia (1525) when he fell into the hands of Charles. This idea of the balance of power came to be recognized later by the European countries as a very important consideration

FIG. 134. HENRY VIII

in determining their policy. But Wolsey was not long to be permitted to put his enlightened ideas into practice. His fall and the progress of Protestantism in England are both closely associated with the notorious divorce case of Henry VIII.

761. Henry VIII's Divorce Case. Henry had married Catherine of Aragon, the aunt of Charles V. Only one of their children, Mary, survived to grow up. As time went on, Henry was very anxious to have a son and heir, for he was fearful lest a woman might not be permitted to succeed to the throne. Moreover, he had tired of Catherine, who was considerably older than he.

Catherine had first married Henry's older brother, who had died almost immediately after the marriage. Since it was a violation of the rule of the Church to marry a deceased brother's wife, Henry professed to fear that he was committing a sin by retaining Catherine as his wife and demanded to be divorced from her on the ground that his marriage had never been legal. His anxiety to rid himself of Catherine was greatly increased by the appearance at court of a black-eyed girl of sixteen, named Anne Boleyn, with whom the king fell in love.

Unfortunately for his case, his marriage with Catherine had been authorized by a dispensation from the Pope, so that Clement VII, to whom the king appealed to annul the marriage, could not, even if he had been willing to run the risk of angering the queen's nephew, Charles V, have granted Henry's request.

Wolsey's failure to induce the Pope to permit the divorce excited the king's anger, and with rank ingratitude for his minister's great services Henry drove him from office (1529) and seized his property. From a life of wealth which was fairly royal, Wolsey was precipitated into extreme poverty and soon died.

Henry induced Parliament to cut off some of the Pope's revenue from England ; but, as this did not bring Clement VII to terms, Henry lost patience and secretly married Anne Boleyn, relying on getting a divorce from Catherine later.

He then summoned an English church court which declared his marriage with Catherine null and void. He had persuaded Parliament to make a law providing that all lawsuits should be definitely decided within the realm and in this way cut off the possibility of the queen's appealing to the Pope (§ 618).

Parliament, which did whatever Henry VIII asked, also declared Henry's marriage with Catherine unlawful and that with Anne Boleyn legal. Consequently it was decreed that Anne's daughter, Elizabeth, born in 1533, was to succeed her father on the English throne instead of Mary, the daughter of Catherine.

762. How Henry VIII threw off the Papal Authority. In 1534 the English Parliament completed the revolt of the English Church from the Pope by assigning to the king the right to appoint all the English prelates and to enjoy all the income which had formerly found its way to Rome. In the Act of Supremacy, Parliament declared the king to be "the only supreme head in earth of the Church of England," and that he should enjoy all the powers which the title naturally carried with it.

Two years later every officer in the kingdom was required to swear to renounce the authority of the bishop of Rome. Refusal to take this oath was to be adjudged high treason. Many were unwilling to deny the Pope's headship merely because king and Parliament renounced it, and this legislation led to a persecution in the name of treason against the king which was even more horrible than that which had been carried on in the name of religion.

763. Henry VIII no Protestant. It must be carefully observed that Henry VIII was not a Protestant in the Lutheran sense of the word. He was led, it is true, by Clement VII's refusal to declare his first marriage illegal, to break the bond between the English and the Roman Church and to induce the English clergy and Parliament to acknowledge the king as supreme head in the religious as well as in the worldly interests of the country. Important as this was, it did not lead Henry to accept the teachings of Protestant leaders, like Luther, Zwingli, or Calvin.

Henry was anxious to prove that he was orthodox, especially after he had seized the property of the monasteries and the gold and jewels which adorned the receptacles in which the relics of the saints were kept. He presided in person over the trial of one who accepted the opinions of Zwingli, and he quoted Scripture to prove the contrary. The prisoner was condemned and burned as a heretic. Henry also authorized a new translation of the Bible into English. A fine edition of this was printed (1539), and every parish was ordered to obtain a copy and place it in the parish church, where all the people could readily make use of it.

764. Henry's Tyranny. Henry VIII was heartless and despotic. With a barbarity not uncommon in those days he allowed his old friend and adviser, Sir Thomas More, to be beheaded for refusing to pronounce the marriage with Catherine void. He caused numbers of monks to be executed for refusing to swear that his first marriage was illegal and for denying his title to supremacy in the Church. Others he permitted to die of starvation and disease in the filthy prisons of the time.

765. Dissolution of the English Monasteries. Henry wanted money; some of the English abbeys were rich, and the monks were quite unable to defend themselves against the charges which were brought against them. The king sent commissioners about to inquire into the state of the monasteries. A large number of scandalous tales were easily collected, some of which were undoubtedly true. The monks were doubtless often indolent and sometimes wicked. Nevertheless they were kind landlords, hospitable to the stranger, and good to the poor.

The royal commissioners took possession of the monasteries and sold every article upon which they could lay hands, including the bells and even the lead on the roofs. The picturesque remains of some of the great abbey churches are still among the chief objects of interest to the sight-seer in England. The monastery lands were, of course, appropriated by the king. They were sold for the benefit of the government or given to nobles whose favor the king wished to secure.

766. Destruction of Shrines and Images. Along with the destruction of the monasteries went an attack upon the shrines and images in the churches, which were adorned with gold and jewels. The shrine of St. Thomas of Canterbury (§ 548) was destroyed, and the bones of the saint were burned. These acts resembled the Protestant attacks on images which occurred in Germany, Switzerland, and the Netherlands. The main object of the king and his party was probably to get money, although the reason urged for the destruction was the superstitious veneration in which the relics and images were popularly held.

767. Henry's Third Marriage and the Birth of Edward VI. Henry's family troubles by no means came to an end with his marriage to Anne Boleyn. Of her, too, he soon tired, and three years after their marriage he had her executed on a series of monstrous charges. The very next day he married his third wife, Jane Seymour, who was the mother of his son and successor, Edward VI. Jane died a few days after her son's birth, and later Henry married in succession three other women who are historically unimportant since they left no children as claimants for the crown. Henry took care that his three children, all of whom were destined to reign, should be given their due place in the line of inheritance by act of Parliament.[1] His death in 1547 left the great problem of Protestantism and Catholicism to be settled by his son and daughters.

III. England becomes Protestant

768. Edward VI's Ministers introduce Protestant Practices. While the revolt of England against the papacy was carried through by the government at a time when the greater part of the nation was still Catholic, there was undoubtedly, under Henry VIII, an ever-increasing number of aggressive and ardent Protestants who approved the change. During the six years of the boy Edward's reign—he died in 1553 at the age of sixteen—those in charge of the government favored the Protestant party and did what they could to change the faith of all the people by bringing Protestant teachers from the Continent.

A general demolition of all the sacred images was ordered; even the beautiful stained glass, the glory of the cathedrals, was destroyed, because it often represented saints and angels. The king was to appoint bishops without troubling to observe the old forms of election (§§ 587–588), and Protestants began to be put into the high offices of the Church. Parliament turned over to the king the funds which had been established for the purpose of having Masses chanted for the dead, and decreed that thereafter the clergy should be free to marry.

---

[1] Henry VIII, m. (1) Catherine   m. (2) Anne Boleyn   m. (3) Jane Seymour

Mary (1553–1558)   Elizabeth (1558–1603)   Edward VI (1547–1553)

It was arranged that the son was to succeed to the throne. In case he died without heirs, Mary and then Elizabeth were to follow.

769. The Prayer Book and the "Thirty-nine Articles." A prayer book in English was prepared under the auspices of Parliament, not very unlike that used in the Church of England to-day (see below, § 797). Moreover, forty-two articles of faith were drawn up by the government, which were to be the standard of belief for the country. These, in the time of Queen Elizabeth, were revised and reduced to the famous "Thirty-nine Articles," which still constitute the creed of the Church of England.

The changes in the church services must have sadly shocked a great part of the English people, who had been accustomed to watch with awe and expectancy the various acts associated with the many church ceremonies and festivals. Earnest men who deplored the misrule of those who conducted Edward's government in the name of Protestantism must have concluded that the reformers were chiefly intent upon advancing their own interests by plundering the Church. We get

FIG. 135. EDWARD VI. (BY HOLBEIN)

This interesting sketch was made before Edward became king; he could have been scarcely six years old, as Holbein died in 1543

some idea of the desecrations of the time from the fact that Edward was forced to forbid "quarreling and shooting in churches" and "the bringing of horses and mules through the same, making God's house like a stable or common inn." Although many were heartily in favor of the recent changes, it is no wonder that after Edward's death there was a revulsion in favor of the old religion.

770. Queen Mary (1553-1558) and the Catholic Restoration. Edward VI was succeeded in 1553 by his half sister Mary, the daughter of Catherine, who had been brought up in the Catholic

faith and held firmly to it. Her ardent hope of bringing her kingdom back once more to her religion did not seem altogether ill-
founded, for the majority of the people were still Catholics at
heart, and many who were not Catholics disapproved of the policy
of Edward's ministers, who had removed abuses "in the devil's own way, by breaking in pieces."

FIG. 136. QUEEN MARY. (BY ANTONIO MORO)

This lifelike portrait, in the Madrid collection,
is by a favorite painter of Philip II, Mary's husband (see Fig. 138). It was painted about 1554,
and one gets the same impressions of Mary's
character from the portrait that one does from
reading about her. Moro had Holbein's skill in
painting faces

The Catholic cause appeared, moreover, to be strengthened by Mary's marriage with the Spanish prince, Philip II, the son of the orthodox Charles V. But although Philip later distinguished himself, as we shall see, by the merciless way in which he strove to put down heresy within his realms, he never gained any great influence in England. By his marriage with Mary he acquired the title of king, but the English took care that he should have no hand in the government nor by any means be permitted to succeed his wife on the English throne.

Mary succeeded in bringing about a nominal reconciliation between England and the Roman Church. In 1554 the papal legate
restored to the communion of the Catholic Church the "Kneeling"
Parliament, which theoretically, of course, represented the nation.

During the last four years of Mary's reign the most serious religious persecution in English history occurred. No less than two hundred and seventy-seven persons were put to death for denying the teachings of the Roman Church. The majority of the victims were humble artisans and husbandmen. The three most notable sufferers were the bishops Cranmer, Latimer, and Ridley, who were burned in Oxford.

It was Mary's hope and belief that the heretics sent to the stake would furnish a terrible warning to the Protestants and check the spread of the new teachings, but Catholicism was not promoted ; on the contrary, doubters were only convinced of the earnestness of the Protestants who could die with such constancy.[1]

QUESTIONS

I. How did the Swiss Confederation originate ? Describe the reforms begun by Zwingli. Who was Calvin and what are his claims to distinction ?

II. Mention the chief contemporaries of Erasmus. What was the policy of Wolsey ? Describe the divorce case of Henry VIII. In what way did Henry VIII break away from the papacy ? What reforms did he introduce ? What was the dissolution of the monasteries ?

III. What happened during the reign of Edward VI ? What was the policy of Queen Mary ?

[1] The Catholics, it should be noted, later suffered serious persecution under Elizabeth and James I, the Protestant successors of Mary. Death was the penalty fixed in many cases for those who obstinately refused to recognize the monarch as the rightful head of the English Church, and heavy fines were imposed for the failure to attend Protestant worship. Two hundred Catholic priests are said to have been executed under Elizabeth, Mary's sister, who succeeded her on the throne ; others were tortured or perished miserably in prison.

CHAPTER XXXIV

THE WARS OF RELIGION

I. The Council of Trent; the Jesuits

771. Council of Trent (1545–1563). In the preceding chapters we have seen how northern Germany, England, and portions of Switzerland revolted from the papacy and established independent Protestant churches. A great part of western Europe, however, remained faithful to the Pope and to the old beliefs which had been accepted for so many centuries. In order to consider the great question of reforming the Catholic Church and to settle disputed questions of religious belief a great church council was summoned by the Pope to meet in Trent, on the confines of Germany and Italy, in the year 1545. Charles V hoped that the Protestants would come to the council and that their ideas might even yet be reconciled with those of the Catholics. But the Protestants did not come, for they were too suspicious of an assembly called by the Pope to have any confidence in its decisions.

The Council of Trent was interrupted after a few sessions and did not complete its work for nearly twenty years after it first met. It naturally condemned the Protestant beliefs so far as they differed from the views held by the Catholics, and it sanctioned those doctrines which the Catholic Church still holds. It accepted the Pope as the head of the Church; it declared accursed anyone who, like Luther, believed that man would be saved by faith in God's promises alone, for the Church held that man, with God's help, could increase his hope of salvation by good works. It ratified all the seven sacraments, several of which the Protestants had rejected. The ancient Latin translation of the Bible — the Vulgate, as it is called — was proclaimed the standard of belief, and no one was to publish any views about the Bible differing from those approved by the Church.

772. The "Index." The Council suggested that the Pope's officials should compile a list of dangerous books which faithful Catholics might not read for fear that their faith in the old Church would be disturbed. Accordingly, after the Council broke up, the Pope issued the first "Index," or list of books which were not to be further printed or circulated on account of the false religious teachings they contained. Similar lists have since been printed from time to time. The establishment of this "Index of Prohibited Books" was one of the most famous of the Council's acts. It was hoped that in this way the spread through the printing press of heretical doctrines contrary to the teachings of the Roman Catholic Church and of immoral ideas could be checked.

773. Results of the Reform of the Catholic Church. Although the Council of Trent would make no compromises with the Protestants, it took measures to do away with certain abuses of which both Protestants and devout Catholics complained. All clergymen were to attend strictly to their duties, and no one was to be appointed who merely wanted the income from his office. The bishops were ordered to preach regularly and to see that only good men were ordained priests. A great improvement actually took place — better men were placed in office and many practices which had formerly irritated the people were permanently abolished.

774. Ignatius Loyola (1491–1556), **Founder of the Jesuits.** Among those who, during the final sessions of the Council, sturdily opposed every attempt to reduce in any way the exalted power of the Pope, was the head of a new religious society which was becoming the most powerful Catholic organization in Europe. The Jesuit order, or Society of Jesus, was founded by a Spaniard, Ignatius Loyola. He had been a soldier in his younger days, and while bravely fighting for his king, Charles V, had been wounded by a cannon ball (1521). Obliged to lie inactive for weeks, he occupied his time in reading the lives of the saints and became filled with a burning ambition to emulate their deeds. Upon recovering, he dedicated himself to the service of the Church, donned a beggar's gown, and started on a pilgrimage to Jerusalem.

Later he went to Paris and sought to influence his fellow students at the university; and finally, in 1534, seven of his companions agreed to follow him to Italy and devote themselves to the service of the Pope. When asked to what order they belonged, they replied, "To the Society of Jesus."

775. Rigid Discipline and Objects of the Jesuits. In 1538 Loyola summoned his followers to Rome, and there they worked out the principles of their order. When this had been done the Pope gave his sanction to the new society. Loyola had been a soldier, and he laid great and constant stress upon absolute and unquestioning obedience. This he declared to be the mother of all virtue and happiness. Not only were all the members of the new association to obey the Pope as Christ's representative on earth and to undertake without hesitation any journey, no matter how distant or perilous, which he might command, but each was to obey his superiors in the order as if he were receiving directions from Christ in person. He must have no will or preference of his own, but must be as the staff which supports and aids its bearer in any way in which he sees fit to use it. This admirable organization and incomparable discipline were the great secret of the later influence of the Jesuits.

The object of the society was to cultivate piety and the love of God, especially through example. The members were to pledge themselves to lead a pure life of poverty and devotion. A great number of the members were priests, who went about preaching, hearing confession, and encouraging devotional exercises. But the Jesuits were teachers as well as preachers and confessors. They clearly perceived the advantage of bringing young people under their influence; they opened schools and seminaries and soon became the schoolmasters of Catholic Europe. So successful were their methods of instruction that even Protestants sometimes sent their children to them.

776. Activities of the Jesuits. Before the death of Loyola over a thousand persons had joined the society. Under his successor the number was trebled, and it went on increasing for two centuries. The founder of the order had been, as we have seen, attracted to missionary work from the first, and the Jesuits rapidly spread not only over Europe but throughout the whole world. Francis Xavier, one of Loyola's original little band, went to Hindustan, the Moluccas, and Japan. Brazil, Florida, Mexico, and Peru were soon fields of active missionary work at a time when Protestants as yet scarcely dreamed of carrying Christianity

FIG. 137. PRINCIPAL JESUIT CHURCH IN VENICE

The Jesuits believed in erecting magnificent churches. This is a good example. The walls are inlaid with green marble in an elaborate pattern, and all the furnishings are very rich and gorgeous

to the heathen. We owe to the Jesuits' reports much of our knowledge of the condition of America when white men first began to explore Canada and the Mississippi valley, for the followers of Loyola boldly penetrated into regions unknown to Europeans and settled among the natives with the purpose of bringing the Gospel to them.

Dedicated as they were to the service of the Pope, the Jesuits early directed their energies against Protestantism. They sent their members into Germany and the Netherlands and even made strenuous efforts to reclaim England. Their success was most apparent in southern Germany and Austria, where they became the confessors and confidential advisers of the rulers. They not only succeeded in checking the progress of Protestantism but were able to reconquer for the Catholic Church some districts in which the old faith had been abandoned.

777. Accusations brought against the Jesuits. Protestants soon realized that the new order was their most powerful and dangerous enemy. Their apprehensions produced a bitter hatred which blinded them to the high purposes of the founders of the order and led them to attribute an evil purpose to every act of the Jesuits. The Jesuits' air of humility the Protestants declared to be mere hypocrisy under which they carried on their intrigues. They were popularly supposed to justify the most deceitful and immoral measures on the ground that the result would be "for the greater glory of God." The very obedience on which the Jesuits laid such stress was viewed by the hostile Protestant as one of their worst offenses, for he believed that the members of the order were the blind tools of their superiors and that they would not hesitate even to commit a crime if so ordered.[1]

II. Philip II and the Revolt of the Netherlands

778. Philip II, the Enemy of Protestantism. The chief ally of the Pope and the Jesuits in their efforts to check Protestantism in the latter half of the sixteenth century was the son of Charles V, Philip II. Like the Jesuits he enjoys a most unenviable reputation among Protestants. Certain it is that they had no more terrible enemy among the rulers of the day than he. He eagerly forwarded every plan to attack England's Protestant queen, Elizabeth, and finally manned a mighty fleet with the purpose of overthrowing

[1] As time went on, the Jesuit order degenerated just as the earlier ones had done. In the eighteenth century it undertook great commercial enterprises, and for this and other reasons lost the confidence and respect of even the Catholics. The king of Portugal was the first to banish the Jesuits from his kingdom; and then France, where they had long been very unpopular with an influential party of the Catholics, expelled them in 1764. Convinced that the order had outgrown its usefulness, the Pope abolished it in 1773. It was, however, restored in 1814, and now again has thousands of members.

her (§ 805). He resorted, moreover, to great cruelty in his attempts to bring back his possessions in the Netherlands to what he believed to be the true faith.

779. Division of the Hapsburg Possessions. Charles V, crippled with the gout and old before his time, laid down the cares of government in 1555–1556. To his brother, Ferdinand, who had acquired by marriage the kingdoms of Bohemia and Hungary, Charles had earlier transferred the German possessions of the Hapsburgs. To his son, Philip II (1556–1598), he gave Spain with its great American colonies, Milan, the kingdom of the Two Sicilies, and the Netherlands.[1]

780. The Netherlands. The Netherlands, which were to cause Philip his first and greatest trouble, included seventeen provinces which Charles V had inherited from his grandmother, Mary of Burgundy (§ 716). They occupied the position on the map where we now find the kingdoms of Holland and Belgium. Each of the provinces had its own government, but Charles V had grouped them together and arranged that the German Empire should protect them. In the north the hardy Germanic population had been able, by means of dikes which kept out the sea, to reclaim large tracts of lowlands. Here considerable cities had grown up— Harlem, Leyden, Amsterdam, and Rotterdam. To the south were the flourishing towns of Ghent, Bruges, Brussels, and Antwerp, which had for hundreds of years been centers of manufacture and trade.

---

[1] Division of the Hapsburg possessions between the Spanish and the German branches:

Maximilian I (d. 1519), m. Mary of Burgundy (d. 1482)

Philip (d. 1506), m. Joanna the Insane (d. 1555)

Charles V (d. 1558) Emperor, 1519–1556	Ferdinand (d. 1564), m. Anna, heiress to kingdoms of Bohemia and Hungary
Philip II (d. 1598) inherits Spain, the Netherlands, and the Italian possessions of the Hapsburgs	Maximilian II (d. 1576) Emperor, and inherits Bohemia, Hungary, and the Austrian possessions of the Hapsburgs

The map of Europe in the sixteenth century (see above, p. 496) indicates the vast extent of the combined possessions of the Spanish and German Hapsburgs.

781. Philip II's Harsh Attitude toward the Netherlands.
Philip's haughty manner made a disagreeable impression upon the
people at Brussels when his father first introduced him to them
as their future ruler. He was to them a Spaniard and a foreigner,
and he ruled them as such after he returned to Spain.

Instead of attempting to win them by meeting their legitimate
demands, he did everything to alienate all classes in his Burgundian realm and
to increase their
natural hatred and
lively suspicion of
the Spaniards. The
people were forced
to house Spanish
soldiers whose in-
solence drove them
nearly to despera-
tion.

What was still
worse, Philip pro-
posed that the In-
quisition (§ 627)
should carry on its
work far more ac-
tively than hitherto
and put an end to

FIG. 138. PHILIP II. (BY ANTONIO MORO)

the heresy which appeared to him to defile his fair realms.
The Inquisition was no new thing to the provinces. Charles V
had issued the most cruel edicts against the followers of
Luther, Zwingli, and Calvin. According to a law of 1550,
heretics who persistently refused to recant were to be burned
alive. Even those who confessed their errors and abjured their
heresy were, if men, to lose their heads ;. if women, to be buried
alive. In either case their property was to be confiscated. The
lowest estimate of those who were executed in the Netherlands
during Charles's reign is fifty thousand. Although these terrible

laws had not checked the growth of Protestantism, all of Charles's decrees were solemnly reënacted by Philip in the first month of his reign.

For ten years the people suffered Philip's rule; nevertheless their king, instead of listening to the protests of their leaders, who were quite as earnest Catholics as himself, appeared to be bent on the destruction of the land. So in 1566 some five hundred of the nobles ventured to protest against Philip's policy.

782. Alva's Cruel Administration (1567–1573). Thereupon Philip took a step which led finally to the revolt of the Netherlands. He decided to dispatch to the low countries the remorseless duke of Alva, whose conduct has made his name synonymous with blind and unmeasured cruelty.

The report that Alva was coming caused the flight of many of those who especially feared his approach. William of Orange, who was to be the leader in the approaching war against Spain, went to Germany. Thousands of Flemish weavers fled across the North Sea, and the products of their looms became before long an important article of export from England.

Alva brought with him a fine army of Spanish soldiers, ten thousand in number and superbly equipped. He appeared to think that the wisest and quickest way of pacifying the discontented provinces was to kill all those who ventured to criticize "the best of kings," of whom he had the honor to be the faithful servant. He accordingly established a special court for the speedy trial and condemnation of all those whose fidelity to Philip was suspected. This was popularly known as the Council of Blood, for its aim was not justice but butchery. Alva's administration from 1567 to 1573 was a veritable reign of terror.

783. William of Orange, called the Silent (1533–1584). The Netherlands found a leader in William, Prince of Orange and Count of Nassau. He is a national hero whose career bears a striking resemblance to that of Washington. Like the American patriot, he undertook the seemingly hopeless task of freeing his people from the oppressive rule of a distant king. To the Spaniards he appeared to be only an impoverished nobleman at the head of a handful of armed peasants and fishermen, contending against the sovereign of the richest realm in the world.

William had been a faithful subject of Charles V and would gladly have continued to serve his son after him had the oppression and injustice of the Spanish dominion not become intolerable. But Alva's policy convinced him that it was useless to send any more complaints to Philip. He accordingly collected a little army in 1568 and opened the long struggle with Spain.

William found his main support in the northern provinces, of which Holland was the chief. The Dutch, who had very generally accepted Protestant teachings, were purely German in blood, while the people of the southern provinces, who adhered (as they still do) to the Roman Catholic faith, were more akin to the population of northern France.

The Spanish soldiers found little trouble in defeating the troops which William collected. Like Washington, again, he seemed to lose almost every battle and yet was never conquered. The first successes of the Dutch were gained by the mariners, who captured Spanish ships and sold them in Protestant England. Encouraged by this, many of the towns in the northern provinces of Holland and Zealand ventured to choose William as their governor, although they did not throw off their allegiance to Philip. In this way these two provinces became the nucleus of the United Netherlands.

784. Both the Northern and Southern Provinces combine against Spain (1576). Alva recaptured a number of the revolted towns and treated their inhabitants with his customary cruelty ; even women and children were slaughtered in cold blood. But instead of quenching the rebellion he aroused the Catholic southern provinces to revolt.

After six years of this tyrannical and mistaken policy, Alva was recalled. His successor soon died and left matters worse than ever. The leaderless soldiers, trained in Alva's school, indulged in wild orgies of robbery and murder ; they plundered and partially reduced to ashes the rich city of Antwerp. The "Spanish fury," as this outbreak was called, together with the hated taxes, created such general indignation that representatives from all of Philip's Burgundian provinces met at Ghent in 1576 with the purpose of combining to put an end to the Spanish tyranny.

This union was, however, only temporary. Wiser and more moderate governors were sent by Philip to the Netherlands, and they soon succeeded in again winning the confidence of the southern Catholic provinces. So the northern provinces went their own way. Guided by William the Silent, they refused to consider the idea of again recognizing Philip as their king. In 1579 seven provinces, all lying north of the mouths of the Rhine and the Scheldt, formed the new and firmer Union of Utrecht. The articles of this union served as a constitution for the United Provinces which, two years later, at last formally declared themselves independent of Spain.

785. Assassination of William the Silent. Philip realized that William was the soul of the revolt and that without him it might, not improbably, have been put down. The king therefore offered to confer a title of nobility and a large sum of money on anyone who should make way with the Dutch patriot. After several unsuccessful attempts William, who had been chosen hereditary governor of the United Provinces, was shot in his house at Delft, 1584. He died praying the Lord to have pity upon his soul and "on this poor people."

786. Independence of the United Provinces. The Dutch had long hoped for aid from Queen Elizabeth or from the French, but had heretofore been disappointed. At last the English queen decided to send troops to their assistance. While the English rendered but little actual help, Elizabeth's policy so enraged Philip that he at last decided to attempt the conquest of England. The destruction of the "Armada," the great fleet which he equipped for that purpose (§ 805), interfered with further attempts to subjugate the United Provinces, which might otherwise have failed to maintain their liberty. Moreover, Spain's resources were being rapidly exhausted, and the State was on the verge of bankruptcy in spite of the wealth which it had been drawing from across the sea. But even though Spain had to surrender the hope of winning back the lost provinces, which now became a small but important European power, she refused formally to acknowledge their independence until 1648 (Peace of Westphalia, § 817).

III. The Huguenot Wars in France

787. Beginnings of Protestantism in France. The history of France during the latter part of the sixteenth century is little more than a chronicle of a long and bloody series of civil wars between the Catholics and Protestants.

Protestantism began in France in much the same way as in England. Those who had learned from the Italians to love the Greek language turned to the New Testament in the original and commenced to study it with new insight. Lefèvre, the most conspicuous of these Erasmus-like reformers, translated the Bible into French and began to preach justification by faith before he had ever heard of Luther.

The Sorbonne, the famous theological school at Paris, soon began to arouse the suspicions of Francis I against the new ideas. He had no special interest in religious matters, but he was shocked by an act of desecration ascribed to the Protestants, and in consequence forbade the circulation of Protestant books. About 1535 several adherents of the new faith were burned, and Calvin was forced to flee to Basel, where he prepared a defense of his beliefs which he published as a sort of preface to his famous *Institute of Christianity* (§ 758). Francis, before his death, became so intolerant that he ordered the massacre of three thousand defenseless peasants who dwelt on the slopes of the Alps, and whose only offense was adherence to the simple teachings of the Waldensians (see above, § 625).

Francis' son, Henry II (1547–1559), swore to extirpate the Protestants, and hundreds of them were burned. He was accidentally killed in a tourney and left his kingdom to three weak sons, the last scions of the house of Valois, who succeeded in turn to the throne during a period of unprecedented civil war and public calamity.

When his second son, Charles IX (1560–1574), came to the throne he was but ten years old, so that his mother, Catherine of Medici, of the famous Florentine family, claimed the right to conduct the government for her son until he reached manhood.

788. The Huguenots and their Political Aims. By this time the Protestants in France had become a powerful party. They were known as *Huguenots*[1] and accepted the religious teachings of their fellow countryman, Calvin. Many of them, including their great leader Coligny, belonged to the nobility. They had a strong support in the king of the little realm of Navarre, on the southern boundary of France. He belonged to a side line of the French royal house, known as the Bourbons, who were later to occupy the French throne (see genealogical table, p. 544). It was inevitable that the Huguenots should try to get control of the government, and they consequently formed a *political* as well as a *religious* party and were often fighting, in the main, for worldly ends.

Catherine tried at first to conciliate both Catholics and Huguenots, and granted a Decree of Toleration (1562) suspending the former edicts against the Protestants and permitting them to assemble for worship during the daytime and outside of the towns. Even this restricted toleration of the Protestants appeared an abomination to the more fanatical Catholics, and a savage act of the duke of Guise—a member of a very powerful family—precipitated civil war.

789. The Massacre of Vassy. As the duke was passing through the town of Vassy on a Sunday he found a thousand Huguenots assembled in a barn for worship. The duke's followers rudely interrupted the service, and a tumult arose in which the troops killed a considerable number of the defenseless multitude. The news of this massacre aroused the Huguenots and was the beginning of a war which continued, broken only by short truces, for over thirty years, until the last weak descendant of the house of Valois ceased to reign. As in the other religious wars of the time, both sides exhibited inhuman cruelty. France was filled

[1] The origin of this name is uncertain.

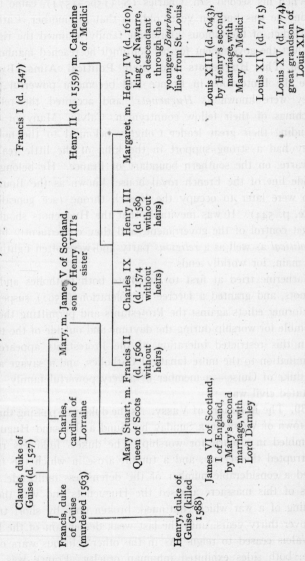

RELATIONS OF THE GUISES, MARY STUART, THE VALOIS, AND THE BOURBONS

Claude, duke of Guise (d. 1527)

Francis, duke of Guise (murdered 1563)

Charles, cardinal of Lorraine

Henry, duke of Guise (killed 1588)

Francis I (d. 1547)

Henry II (d. 1559), m. Catherine of Medici

Mary, m. James V of Scotland, son of Henry VIII's sister

Margaret, m. Henry IV (d. 1610), king of Navarre, a descendant through the younger, *Bourbon*, line from St. Louis

Mary Stuart, m. Francis II (d. 1560 without heirs) Queen of Scots

Charles IX (d. 1574 without heirs)

Henry III (d. 1589 without heirs)

Louis XIII (d. 1643), by Henry's second marriage, with Mary of Medici

James VI of Scotland, I of England, by Mary's second marriage, with Lord Darnley

Louis XIV (d. 1715)

Louis XV (d. 1774), great grandson of Louis XIV

for a generation with burnings, pillage, and barbarity. The leaders of both the Catholic and Protestant parties, as well as two of the French kings themselves, fell by the hands of assassins, and France renewed in civil war all the horrors of the English invasion in the fourteenth and fifteenth centuries.

790. Coligny's Influence. In 1570 a brief peace was concluded. The Huguenots were to be tolerated, and certain towns were assigned to them, where they might defend themselves in case of renewed attacks from the Catholics. For a time both Charles IX and his mother, Catherine of Medici, were on the friendliest terms with the Huguenot leader Coligny, who became a sort of prime minister. He was anxious that Catholics and Protestants should join in a great national war against France's old enemy, Spain.

791. Massacre of St. Bartholomew (1572). The strict Catholic party of the Guises frustrated this plan by a most fearful expedient. They easily induced Catherine of Medici to believe that she was being deceived by Coligny, and an assassin was engaged to put him out of the way ; but the scoundrel missed his aim and only wounded his victim. Fearful lest the young king, who was faithful to Coligny, should discover her part in the attempted murder, Catherine invented a story of a great Huguenot conspiracy. The credulous king was deceived, and the Catholic leaders at Paris arranged that not only Coligny but all the Huguenots, gathered in great numbers in the city to witness the marriage of the king's sister to the Protestant Henry of Navarre, should be massacred on the eve of St. Bartholomew's Day (August 23, 1572).

When the signal arranged was given, no less than two thousand persons were ruthlessly murdered in Paris before the end of the next day. The news of this attack spread into the provinces, and it is probable that, at the very least, ten thousand more Protestants were put to death outside of the capital.

792. Henry IV (1589–1610) accepts the Catholic Faith. Civil war again broke out and was accompanied by a complicated struggle between claimants of the throne of France, as a result of which the Huguenot Henry of Navarre ascended the throne as Henry IV in 1589.

The new king had many enemies, and his kingdom was devastated and demoralized by years of war. He soon saw that he must accept the religion of the majority of his people if he wished to reign over them. He accordingly asked to be readmitted to the Catholic Church (1593), excusing himself on the ground that "Paris was worth a Mass." He did not forget his old friends, however, and in 1598 he issued the Edict of Nantes.

793. The Edict of Nantes (1598). By this edict of toleration the Calvinists were permitted to hold services in all the towns and villages where they had previously held them, but in Paris and a number of other towns all Protestant services were prohibited. The Protestants were to enjoy the same political rights as Catholics and to be eligible to government offices. A number of fortified towns were to remain in the hands of the Huguenots, particularly La Rochelle, Montauban, and Nîmes. Henry's only mistake lay in granting the Huguenots the right to control fortified towns. In the next generation this privilege aroused the suspicion of the king's minister, Richelieu, who attacked the Huguenots, not so much on religious grounds as on account of their independent position in the state, which suggested that of the older feudal nobles.

FIG. 139. HENRY IV OF FRANCE

This spirited portrait of Henry of Navarre gives an excellent impression of his geniality and good sense

794. Ministry of Sully. Henry IV chose Sully, an upright and able Calvinist, for his chief minister. Sully set to work to reëstablish the kingly power, which had suffered greatly under the last three brothers of the house of Valois. He undertook to lighten the tremendous burden of debt which weighed upon the country. He laid out new roads and canals and encouraged agriculture and commerce ; he dismissed the useless noblemen and officers whom the government was supporting without any advantage to itself. Had his administration not been prematurely interrupted it might have brought France unprecedented power and prosperity ; but religious fanaticism put an end to his reforms.

In 1610 Henry IV, like William the Silent, was assassinated just in the midst of his greatest usefulness to his country. Sully could not agree with the regent, Henry's widow, and so gave up his position and retired to private life.

795. Richelieu. Before many years Richelieu, perhaps the greatest minister France has ever had, rose to power, and from 1624 to his death in 1642 he governed France for Henry IV's son, Louis XIII (1610–1643). Something will be said of his policy in connection with the Thirty Years' War (§§ 814–817).

IV. England under Queen Elizabeth

796. England under Elizabeth (1558–1603). The long and disastrous civil war between Catholics and Protestants, which desolated France in the sixteenth century, had happily no counterpart in England. During her long reign Queen Elizabeth succeeded not only in maintaining peace at home but in frustrating the conspiracies and attacks of Philip II, which threatened her realm from without. Moreover, by her interference in the Netherlands she did much to secure their independence of Spain.

797. Elizabeth establishes the Church of England. Upon the death of Catholic Mary (§ 770) and the accession of her half sister Elizabeth in 1558, the English government became once more Protestant. The new queen had a new revised edition issued of the Book of Common Prayer which had been prepared in the time of her half brother, Edward VI. This contained the services which the government ordered to be performed in all the churches of England. All her subjects were required to accept the queen's views and to go to church, and ministers were to use nothing but the official prayer book. Elizabeth did not adopt the Presbyterian system advocated by Calvin but retained many features of the Catholic Church, including the bishops and archbishops. So the Anglican Church followed a middle path halfway between the Lutherans and Calvinists on the one hand and the Catholics on the other.

FIG. 140. PORTRAIT OF QUEEN ELIZABETH

Elizabeth, the second woman to rule England, deemed herself a very handsome and imposing person. She was fond of fine clothes and doubtless had on her best when she sat for her portrait

The Roman Catholic churchmen who had held positions under Queen Mary were naturally dismissed and replaced by those who would obey Elizabeth and use her Book of Prayer. Her first Parliament gave the sovereign the *powers* of supreme head of the Church of England, although the *title*, which her father, Henry VIII, had assumed, was not revived.

The Church of England still exists in much the same form in which it was established in the first years of Elizabeth's reign, and the prayer book is still used; although Englishmen are no longer required to attend church and may hold any religious views they please without being interfered with by the government.

798. Presbyterian Church established in Scotland. While England adopted a middle course in religious matters Scotland became Presbyterian, and this led to much trouble for Elizabeth. There, shortly after her accession, the ancient Catholic Church was abolished, for the nobles were anxious to get the lands of the bishops into their own hands and enjoy the revenue from them. John Knox, a veritable second Calvin in his stern energy, secured the introduction of the Presbyterian form of faith and church government which still prevails in Scotland.

799. Mary Stuart, the Scotch Queen, the Hope of the Catholics. In 1561 the Scotch queen, Mary Stuart, whose French husband, Francis II,[1] had just died, landed at Leith. She was but nineteen years old, of great beauty and charm, and, by reason of her Catholic faith and French training, almost a foreigner to her subjects. Her grandmother was a sister of Henry VIII, and Mary claimed to be the rightful heiress to the English throne should Elizabeth die childless. Consequently the beautiful Queen of Scots became the hope of all those who wished to bring back England and Scotland to the Roman Catholic faith. Chief among these were Philip II of Spain and Mary's relatives the Guises (§§ 789 and 791) in France.

Mary quickly discredited herself with both Protestants and Catholics by her conduct. After marrying her second cousin, Lord Darnley, she discovered that he was a dissolute scapegrace and came to despise him. She then formed an attachment for a reckless nobleman named Bothwell. The house near Edinburgh in which Darnley was lying ill was blown up one night with gunpowder, and he was killed. The public suspected that both Bothwell and the queen were implicated. How far Mary was responsible for her husband's death no one can be sure. It is certain that she later married Bothwell and that her indignant subjects thereupon deposed her as a murderess. After fruitless attempts to regain her power she abdicated in favor of her infant son, James VI, and then fled to England to appeal to Elizabeth. While the prudent Elizabeth denied the right of the Scotch to

[1] Son of Henry II. See table, p. 544.

depose their queen, she was afraid of her claims and took good care to keep her rival practically a prisoner.

800. The Rising in the North (156) and Catholic Plans for deposing Elizabeth. As time went on, it became increasingly difficult for Elizabeth to adhere to her policy of moderation in the treatment of the Catholics. A rising in the north of England (1569) showed that there were many who would gladly reëstablish the Catholic faith by freeing Mary and placing her on the English throne. This was followed by the excommunication of Elizabeth by the Pope, who at the same time absolved her subjects from their allegiance to their heretical ruler. Happily for Elizabeth the rebels could look for no help either from Philip II or the French king. The Spaniards had their hands full, for the war in the Netherlands had just begun ; and Charles IX, who had accepted Coligny as his adviser, was at that moment in hearty accord with the Huguenots. The rising in the North was suppressed, but the English Catholics continued to look to Philip for help. They opened correspondence with Alva and invited him to come with six thousand Spanish troops to dethrone Elizabeth and make Mary Stuart queen of England in her stead. Alva hesitated, for he thought that it would be better to kill Elizabeth, or at least capture her. Meanwhile the plot was discovered and came to naught.

801. English Mariners capture Spanish Ships. Although Philip found himself unable to harm England, the English mariners caused great loss to Spain. In spite of the fact that Spain and England were not openly at war, Elizabeth's seamen extended their operations as far as the West Indies and seized Spanish treasure ships, with the firm conviction that in robbing Philip they were serving God. The daring Sir Francis Drake even ventured into the Pacific, where only the Spaniards had gone heretofore, and carried off much booty on his little vessel, the *Pelican*.

802. Relations between England and Catholic Ireland. One hope of the Catholics has not yet been mentioned, namely, Ireland, whose relations with England from very early times down to the present day form one of the most cheerless pages in the history of Europe. The population was divided into numerous clans, and their chieftains fought constantly with one another as well as with the English, who were vainly endeavoring to subjugate the island.

Several attempts were made by Catholic leaders to land troops in Ireland with the purpose of making the island the base for an attack on England. Elizabeth's officers were able to frustrate these enterprises, but the resulting disturbances greatly increased the misery of the Irish. In 1582 no less than thirty thousand people are said to have perished, chiefly from starvation.

803. Persecution of the English Catholics. As Philip's troops began to get the better of the opposition in the southern Netherlands, the prospect of sending a Spanish army to England grew brighter. Two Jesuits were sent to England in 1580 to strengthen the adherents of their faith and urge them to assist the foreign force against their queen, when it should come. Parliament now grew more intolerant and ordered fines and imprisonment to be inflicted on those who said or heard Mass or who refused to attend the English services. One of the Jesuit emissaries was cruelly tortured and executed for treason, the other escaped to the Continent.

In the spring of 1582 the first attempt by the Catholics to assassinate the heretical queen was made at Philip's instigation. It was proposed that when Elizabeth was out of the way an army should be sent to England to support the Catholics.

804. Execution of Mary Queen of Scots (1587). Mary Queen of Scots did not live to witness the attempt. She became implicated in another plot for the assassination of Elizabeth. Parliament now realized that as long as Mary lived Elizabeth's life was in constant danger; whereas, if Mary were out of the way, Philip II would have no interest in the death of Elizabeth, since Mary's son, James VI of Scotland, who would succeed Elizabeth on the English throne, was a Protestant. Elizabeth was therefore reluctantly persuaded by her advisers to sign a warrant for Mary's execution in 1587.

805. Destruction of the Spanish Armada (1588). Philip II, however, by no means gave up his project of reclaiming Protestant England. In 1588 he brought together a great fleet, including his best and largest warships, which was proudly called by the Spaniards the "Invincible Armada" (that is, fleet). This was to sail through the English Channel to the Netherlands and bring over the Spanish commander there and his veterans, who, it was expected, would soon make an end of Elizabeth's raw militia. The English ships were inferior to those of Spain in size although not in number, but they had trained commanders, such as Francis Drake and Hawkins.

These famous captains had long sailed the Spanish Main and knew how to use their cannon without getting near enough to the Spaniards to suffer from their short-range weapons. When the Armada approached it was permitted by the English fleet to pass up the Channel before a strong wind, which later became a storm. The English ships then followed, and both fleets were driven past the coast of Flanders. Of the hundred and twenty Spanish ships, only fifty-four returned home; the rest had been destroyed by English valor or by the gale, to which Elizabeth herself ascribed the victory. The defeat of the Armada put an end to the danger from Spain.

806. Failure of Philip II's Policy. As we look back over the period covered by the reign of Philip II, it is clear that it was a most notable one in the history of the Catholic Church. When he ascended the throne in 1556 Germany, as well as Switzerland and the Netherlands, had become largely Protestant. England, however, under his Catholic wife, Mary, seemed to be turning back to the old religion, while the French monarchs showed no inclination to tolerate the heretical Calvinists. Moreover, the new and enthusiastic order of the Jesuits promised to be a powerful agency in inducing the Protestants to accept once more the supremacy of the Pope and the doctrines of the Catholic Church as formulated by the Council of Trent. The tremendous power and apparently boundless resources of Spain itself, which were viewed by the rest of Europe with terror, Philip was prepared to dedicate to the destruction of Protestantism throughout western Europe. This he undoubtedly believed to be his chief duty.

But when Philip II died, in 1598, all was changed. England was permanently Protestant; the "Invincible Armada" had been miserably wrecked, and Philip's plan for bringing England once more within the fold of the Roman Catholic Church was forever frustrated. In France the terrible wars of religion were over, and a powerful king, lately a Protestant himself, was on the throne, who not only tolerated the Protestants but chose one of them for his chief minister and would brook no more meddling of Spain in French affairs. A new Protestant state, the United Netherlands (Holland), had actually appeared within the bounds of the realm bequeathed to Philip by his father. In spite of its small size Holland was destined to play, from that time on, quite as important a part in European affairs as the harsh Spanish stepmother from whose control it had escaped.

Spain itself had suffered most of all from Philip's reign. His domestic policy and his expensive wars had sadly weakened the country. The income from across the sea was bound to decrease as the mines were exhausted. After Philip II's death Spain sank to the rank of a secondary European power.

V. The Thirty Years' War

807. The Thirty Years' War really a Series of Wars. The last great conflict caused by the differences between the Catholics and Protestants was fought out in Germany during the first half of the seventeenth century. It is generally known as the Thirty Years' War (1618–1648), but there was in reality a series of wars; and although the fighting was done upon German territory, Sweden, France, and Spain played quite as important a part in the struggle as the various German states.

Just before the abdication of Charles V, the Lutheran princes had forced the emperor to acknowledge their right to their own religion and to the church property which they had seized. The religious Peace of Augsburg (§ 755) had, however, as we have seen, two great weaknesses. In the first place, only those Protestants who held the Lutheran faith were to be tolerated. The Calvinists, who were increasing in numbers, were not included in the peace. In the second place, the peace did not put a stop to the seizure of church property by the Protestant princes.

Protestantism, however, made rapid progress and invaded the Austrian possessions and, above all, Bohemia. So it looked for a time as if even the Catholic Hapsburgs were to see large portions of their territory falling away from the old Church. But the Catholics had in the Jesuits a band of active and efficient missionaries. They not only preached and founded schools but also succeeded in gaining the confidence of some of the German princes, whose chief advisers they became. Conditions were very favorable, at the opening of the seventeenth century, for a renewal of the religious struggle.

808. Opening of the Thirty Years' War (1618). The long war began in Bohemia in 1618. This portion of the Austrian possessions was strongly Protestant and decided that the best policy was to declare its independence of the Hapsburgs and set up a king of its own. It chose Frederick, the Elector of the Palatinate, a Calvinist who would, it was hoped, enjoy the support of his father-in-law, King James I of England.[1] So Frederick and his English wife moved from Heidelberg to Prague. But their stay there was brief, for the Hapsburg emperor (Ferdinand II) with the aid of the ruler of Bavaria put to flight the poor "winter king," as Frederick was called on account of his reign of a single season.

This was regarded by the Protestants as a serious defeat, and the Protestant king of Denmark decided to intervene. He remained in Germany for four years, but was so badly beaten by the emperor's able general, Wallenstein, that he retired from the conflict in 1629.

809. The Edict of Restitution (1629). The emperor was encouraged by the successes of the Catholic armies in defeating the Bohemian and Danish Protestant armies to issue that same

[1] James VI of Scotland, who succeeded Queen Elizabeth in 1603.

year an Edict of Restitution. In this he ordered the Protestants throughout Germany to give back all the church possessions which they had seized since the religious Peace of Augsburg (1555). Moreover, he decreed that only the Lutherans might hold religious meetings; the other "sects," including the Calvinists, were to be broken up. As Wallenstein was preparing to execute this decree in his usual merciless fashion, the war took a new turn.

810. Dismissal of Wallenstein; Gustavus Adolphus of Sweden (1594–1632). The Catholic League, which had been formed some time before, had become jealous of Wallenstein, who threatened to become too powerful, and it accordingly joined in the complaints, which came from every side, of the terrible extortions and incredible cruelty practiced by Wallenstein's troops. The emperor consented, therefore, to dismiss this most competent commander. Just as the Catholics were thus weakened, a new enemy arrived upon the scene who proved far more dangerous than any they had yet had to face; namely, Gustavus Adolphus, king of Sweden.

811. The Kingdom of Sweden. We have had no occasion hitherto to speak of the Scandinavian kingdoms of Norway, Sweden, and Denmark, which the northern German peoples had established about Charlemagne's time; but from now on they begin to take part in the affairs of central Europe. The Union of Calmar (1397) had brought these three kingdoms, previously separate, under a single ruler. About the time that the Protestant revolt began in Germany the union was broken by the withdrawal of Sweden, which became an independent kingdom. Gustavus Vasa, a Swedish noble, led the movement and was later chosen king of Sweden (1523). In the same year Protestantism was introduced. Vasa confiscated the church lands, got the better of the aristocracy,—who had formerly made the kings a great deal of trouble,—and started Sweden on its way toward national greatness.

812. Motives of Gustavus Adolphus. Gustavus Adolphus was induced to invade Germany for two reasons. In the first place, he was a sincere and enthusiastic Protestant and by far the most generous and attractive figure of his time. He was genuinely afflicted by the misfortunes of his Protestant brethren and anxious to devote himself to their welfare. Secondly, he undoubtedly hoped by his invasion not only to free his fellow Protestants from the oppression of the emperor and of the Catholic League but to gain a strip of German territory for Sweden.

813. Fate of Gustavus and Wallenstein. Gustavus was not received with much cordiality at first by the Protestant princes of the North, but they were brought to their senses by the awful destruction of Magdeburg by the troops of the Catholic League under General Tilly. Magdeburg was the most important town of northern Germany. When it finally succumbed after an obstinate and difficult siege, twenty thousand of its inhabitants were killed and the town burned to the ground. Although Tilly's reputation for cruelty is quite equal to that of Wallenstein, he was probably not responsible for the fire. After Gustavus Adolphus had met Tilly near Leipsic and victoriously routed the army of the League, the Protestant princes began to look with more favor on the foreigner.

The next spring Gustavus entered Bavaria and once more defeated Tilly (who was mortally wounded in the battle) and forced Munich to surrender. There seemed now to be no reason why he should not continue his progress to Vienna. At this juncture the emperor recalled Wallenstein, who collected a new army over which he was given absolute command. After some delay Gustavus met Wallenstein on the field of Lützen, in November, 1632, where, after a fierce struggle, the Swedes gained the victory. But they lost their leader and Protestantism its hero, for the Swedish king ventured too far into the lines of the enemy and was surrounded and killed.

The Swedes did not, however, retire from Germany, but continued to participate in the war, which now degenerated into a series of raids by leaders whose soldiers depopulated the land by their unspeakable atrocities. Wallenstein, who had long been detested even by the Catholics, was deserted by his soldiers and murdered (in 1634), to the great relief of all parties.

814. Richelieu renews the Struggle of France against the Hapsburgs. Just at this moment Richelieu (§ 795) decided that it would be to the interest of France to renew the old struggle with the Hapsburgs by sending troops against the emperor. France was still shut in, as she had been since the time of Charles V, by the Hapsburg lands. Except on the side toward the ocean her boundaries were in the main artificial ones and not those established by great rivers and mountains. She therefore longed to weaken her enemy and strengthen herself by winning Roussillon on the south and so make the crest of the Pyrenees the line of demarcation between France and Spain. She dreamed, too, of extending her sway toward the Rhine by adding the county of Burgundy (that is, Franche-Comté, as it

FIG. 141. PORTRAIT OF CARDINAL RICHELIEU. (FROM A CONTEMPORANEOUS PAINTING)

was often called) and a number of fortified towns which would afford protection against the Spanish Netherlands.

Richelieu declared war against Spain in May, 1635. He had already concluded an alliance with the chief enemies of the house of Austria. So the war was renewed, and French, Swedish, Spanish, and German soldiers ravaged an already exhausted country for a decade longer. The dearth of provisions was so great that the armies had to move quickly from place to place in order to avoid starvation. After a serious defeat by the Swedes the emperor (Ferdinand III, 1637–1657) sent a Dominican monk to expostulate with Cardinal Richelieu for his crime in aiding the German and Swedish heretics against Catholic Austria.

815. France succeeds Spain in Military Supremacy. The cardinal had, however, just died (December, 1642), well content with the results of his diplomacy. The French were in possession of Roussillon and of Lorraine and Alsace. The military exploits of the French generals, especially Turenne and Condé, during the opening years of the reign of Louis XIV (1643–1715), showed that a new period had begun in which the military and political supremacy of Spain was to give way to that of France (see below, Chapter XXXVI).

816. Close of the Thirty Years' War (1648). The participants in the war were now so numerous and their objects so various and conflicting that it is not strange that it required some years to arrange the conditions of peace, even after everyone was ready for it. It was agreed (1644) that France and the Empire should negotiate at Münster, and the emperor and the Swedes at Osnabrück—both of which towns lie in Westphalia. For four years the representatives of the several powers worked upon the difficult problem of satisfying everyone, but at last the treaties of Westphalia were signed late in 1648.

817. Provisions of the Treaties of Westphalia. The religious troubles in Germany were settled by extending the toleration of the Peace of Augsburg so as to include the Calvinists as well as the Lutherans. The Protestant princes were to retain the lands which they had in their possession in the year 1624, regardless of the Edict of Restitution, and each ruler was still to have the right to determine the religion of his state. The dissolution of the Holy Roman Empire was practically acknowledged by permitting the individual states to make treaties among themselves and with foreign powers ; this was equivalent to recognizing the practical independence which they had, as a matter of fact, already long enjoyed. While portions of northern Germany were ceded to Sweden, this territory did not cease to form a part of the Empire, for Sweden was thereafter to have three votes in the German diet.

The emperor also ceded to France three important towns— Metz, Verdun, and Toul—and all his rights in Alsace, although the city of Strassburg was to remain with the Empire. Lastly, the independence both of the United Netherlands and of Switzerland was acknowledged.

818. Disastrous Results of the War in Germany. The accounts of the misery and depopulation of Germany caused by the Thirty Years' War are well-nigh incredible. Thousands of villages were wiped out altogether; in some regions the population was reduced by one half, in others to a third, or even less, of what it had been at the opening of the conflict. The flourishing city of Augsburg was left with but sixteen thousand souls instead of eighty thousand. The people were fearfully barbarized by privation and suffering and by the atrocities of the soldiers of all the various nations. Until the end of the eighteenth century Germany remained too exhausted and impoverished to make any considerable contribution to the culture of Europe.

VI. The Beginnings of our Scientific Age

819. The New Science. The battles of the Thirty Years' War are now well-nigh forgotten, and few people are interested in Tilly and Wallenstein and Gustavus Adolphus. It seems as if the war did little but destroy men's lives and property, and that no great ends were accomplished by all the suffering it involved. But during the years that it raged certain men were quietly devoting themselves to scientific research which was to change the world more than all the battles that have ever been fought. These men adopted a new method. They perceived that the books of ancient writers, especially Aristotle, which were used as textbooks in the universities, were full of statements that could not be proved. They maintained that the only way to advance science was to set to work and try experiments, and by careful thought and investigation to determine the laws of nature without regard to what previous generations had thought.

820. The Discovery of Copernicus. The Polish astronomer Copernicus published a work in 1543 in which he refuted the old idea that the sun and all the stars revolved around the earth as a center, as was then taught in all the universities. He showed that, on the contrary, the sun was the center about which the earth and the rest of the planets revolved, and that the reason that the stars seem to go around the earth each day is because our globe revolves on its axis. Although Copernicus had been encouraged to write his book by a cardinal and had dedicated it to the Pope, the Catholic as well as the Protestant theologians declared that the new theory contradicted the teachings of the Bible, and they therefore rejected it. But we know now that Copernicus was right and the theologians and universities wrong.

821. Galileo. The Italian scientist Galileo (1564–1642), by the use of a little telescope he contrived, was able in 1610 to see the spots on the sun ; these indicated that the sun was not, as Aristotle had taught, a perfect, unchanging body, and showed also that it revolved on its axis, as Copernicus had guessed that the earth did. Galileo made careful experiments by dropping objects from the leaning tower of Pisa, which proved that Aristotle was wrong in assuming that a body weighing a hundred pounds fell a hundred times as fast as a body weighing but one. He wrote in Italian as well as in Latin. His opponents might have forgiven him had he confined his discussions to the learned who could read Latin, but they thought it highly dangerous to have the new ideas set forth in such a way that the people at large might come to doubt what the theologians and universities were teaching. Galileo was finally summoned before the Inquisition ; some of his theories were condemned, and he was imprisoned by the Church authorities.

822. Descartes. Just as the Thirty Years' War was beginning, a young Frenchman by the name of Descartes had finished his education at a Jesuit college and decided to get some knowledge of the world by going into the war for a short time. He did much more thinking than fighting, however. Sitting by the stove during the winter lull in hostilities, deep in meditation, it occurred to him one day that he had no reason for believing anything. He saw that everything that he accepted had come to him on the authority of someone else, and he failed to see any reason why the old authorities should be right. So he boldly set to work to think out a wholly new philosophy that should be entirely the result of his own reasoning. He decided, in the first place, that one

FIG. 142. GALILEO

thing at least was true. He was *thinking*, and therefore he must exist. This he expressed in Latin in the famous phrase *Cogito, ergo sum*, "I think, therefore I am." He also decided that God must exist and that He had given men such good minds that, if they only used them *carefully*, they would not be deceived in the conclusions they reached. In short, Descartes held that *clear* thoughts must be *true* thoughts.

Descartes not only founded modern philosophy, he was also greatly interested in science and mathematics. His most famous book, called *An Essay on Method*, was written in French and addressed to intelligent men who did not know Latin. He says

that those who use their own heads are much more likely to reach the truth than those who read old Latin books. Descartes wrote clear textbooks on algebra and that branch of mathematics known as analytical geometry, of which he was the discoverer.

823. Francis Bacon's *New Atlantis*. Francis Bacon, an English lawyer and government official, spent his spare hours in explaining how men could increase their knowledge. He too wrote in his native tongue as well as in Latin.

FIG. 143. RENÉ DESCARTES

He was the most eloquent representative of the new science which renounced *authority* and relied upon *experiment*. "We are the ancients," he declared, not those who lived long ago when the world was young and men ignorant. Late in life he began to write a little book, which he never finished, called the *New Atlantis*. It describes an imaginary state which some Europeans were supposed to have come upon in the Pacific Ocean. The chief institution was a "House of Solomon," a great laboratory for carrying on scientific investigation in the hope of discovering new facts and using them for bettering the condition of the inhabitants. This House of Solomon became a sort of model for the Royal Academy, which was established in London some fifty years after Bacon's death. It still exists and still publishes its proceedings regularly.

824. Scientific Societies Founded. The earliest societies for scientific research grew up in Italy. Later the English Royal Society and the French Institute were established, as well as similar associations in Germany. These were the first things of the kind in the history of the world — except perhaps the ancient *Museum* at Alexandria (§ 277). Their object was not, like that of the old Greek schools of

FIG. 144. FRANCIS BACON

philosophy and the medieval universities, mainly to hand down and explain the knowledge derived from the past, but to find out what had never been known before.

We have seen how in the thirteenth and fourteenth centuries new inventions were made, such as the compass, paper, spectacles, gunpowder, and, in the fifteenth century, the printing press. But in the seventeenth century progress began to be much more rapid, and an era of invention opened, in the midst of which we still live. The microscope and telescope made it possible to discover innumerable scientific truths that were hidden to the Greeks and Romans. In time this scientific advance produced a *spirit of reform*, also new in the world. This will be described in the following volume of this history.

QUESTIONS

I. What were the chief results of the Council of Trent? Why did the Protestants refuse to take part in it? Give an account of the life of Loyola. What were the objects of the Jesuit order? What accusations did the Protestants bring against the society?

II. What are your impressions of Philip II? How did it come about that the Netherlands belonged to Spain? Describe Philip's policy in dealing with the Netherlands. How did the United Netherlands gain their independence?

III. What were the religious conditions in France when Charles IX and Catherine of Medici came into power? What was the character of the Huguenot party? Describe the massacre of St. Bartholomew. How did Henry IV become king? What was the Edict of Nantes?

IV. What measures did Queen Elizabeth take in religious matters? How did the English Church originate? Tell the story of Mary Queen of Scots. What was the policy of Philip II in regard to Elizabeth? What were the general results of Philip II's reign?

V. What was the origin of the Thirty Years' War? What led the Swedish king to intervene? What did the Swedes gain by the intervention? Why did Richelieu send troops to fight in the war? What were the chief provisions of the treaties of Westphalia? What were the other results of the war?

VI. What is the difference between modern scientific research and the spirit of the medieval universities? Describe the discoveries of Copernicus. What did Galileo accomplish? Give the views of Descartes. What was the position of Francis Bacon in regard to scientific research? What was the "House of Solomon"? What societies were established for scientific investigation? Can you think of some of the effects that modern science has had on our lives?

BOOK VIII. THE SEVENTEENTH AND EIGHTEENTH CENTURIES

CHAPTER XXXV

STRUGGLE IN ENGLAND BETWEEN KING AND PARLIAMENT

I. James I and the Divine Right of Kings

825. Accession of James I of England (1603): the Stuarts.
On the death of Elizabeth in 1603, James I, the first of the
Scotch family of Stuart, ascended the throne. It will be remembered that he was the son of Mary Stuart, Queen of Scots, and
through her a descendant of Henry VII (see table, p. 544). In
Scotland he reigned as James VI; consequently the two kingdoms
were now brought together under the same ruler. This did not,
however, make the relations between the two countries much
more cordial than they had been in the past.

The chief interest of the period of the Stuarts, which began
with the accession of James I in 1603 and ended with the flight
from England of his grandson, James II, eighty-five years later,
is the long and bitter struggle between the kings and Parliament. The vital question was, Should the Stuart kings, who
claimed to be God's representatives on earth, do as they thought
fit, or should Parliament control them and the government of
the country?

826. The Attitude of the Tudors toward Parliament. We
have seen how the English Parliament originated in the time of
Edward I and how his successors were forced to pay attention
to its wishes (§§ 555–558, 567, 578). Under the Tudors—that
is, from the time of Henry VII to Elizabeth—the monarchs had
been able to manage Parliament so that it did, in general, just

what they wished. Henry VIII was a heartless tyrant, and his daughter Elizabeth, like her father, had ruled the nation in a high-handed manner, but neither of them had been accustomed to *say* much of their rights.

827. James I loved to discuss the King's Claims. James I, on the other hand, had a very irritating way of discussing his

claim to be the sole and divinely appointed ruler of England. "It is atheism and blasphemy," he declared, "to dispute what God can do ; . . . so it is presumption and high contempt in a subject to dispute what a king can do, or say that a king cannot do this or that." James was a learned man and was fond of writing books. Among those that he published was a work on monarchs, in which he claimed that the king could make any law he pleased without consulting Parliament ; that he was the master of every one of his subjects, high and low, and might put to death whom he pleased. A good king would act according to law, but is not bound to do so and has the power to change the law at any time to suit himself.

FIG. 145. JAMES I

828. The "Divine Right of Kings." These theories seem strange and very unreasonable to us, but James was only trying to justify the powers which the Tudor monarchs had actually exercised, and which the kings of France enjoyed down to the French Revolution of 1789. According to the theory of "the divine right of kings" it had pleased God to appoint the monarch the father of his people, who must obey him as they would God and ask no questions. The king was responsible to God alone, to whom he owed his powers, not to Parliament or the nation. These notions were supposed to be based on the teachings of the Bible.

It is unnecessary to follow the troubles between James I and Parliament, for his reign only forms the preliminary to the fatal experiences of his son, Charles I, who came to the throne in 1625.

829. Great Writers of James's Reign—Shakespeare, Bacon, Harvey. The writers of James's reign constituted its chief glory. They outshone those of any other European country. Shakespeare is generally admitted to be the greatest dramatist that the world has produced. While he wrote many of his plays before the death of Elizabeth, some of his finest—*Othello, King Lear*, and *The Tempest*, for example—belong to the time of James I.

During the same period Francis Bacon (§ 823) was writing his *Advancement of Learning*, which he dedicated to James I in 1605 and in which he urged that men should cease to rely upon the old textbooks, like Aristotle, and turn to a careful examination of animals, plants, and chemicals, with a view of learning about them and using the knowledge thus gained to improve the condition of mankind. Bacon's ability to write English is equal to that of Shakespeare, but he chose to write prose, not verse. It was in James's reign that the authorized English translation of the Bible was made which is still used in all countries where English is spoken. This was based on earlier translations made by Wycliffe (§ 637) and in the time of Henry VIII (§ 763).

An English physician of this period, William Harvey, examined the workings of the human body more carefully than any previous investigator and made the great discovery of the manner in which the blood circulates from the heart through the arteries and capillaries and back through the veins—a matter which had previously been entirely misunderstood. This discovery made a deep impression on Descartes, the great French philosopher (§ 822), who speaks of it in his *Essay on Method* as a fine example of what careful scientific study might accomplish.

II. How Charles I got along without Parliament

830. Charles I (1625–1649). Charles I, James I's son and successor, was somewhat more dignified than his father, but he was quite as obstinately set upon having his own way and showed no more skill in winning the confidence of his subjects. He did nothing to remove the disagreeable impressions of his father's reign and began immediately to quarrel with Parliament. When that body refused to grant him funds, mainly because they thought that these were likely to be wasted by his favorite, the duke of Buckingham, Charles attempted to raise money in irregular ways without the permission of Parliament.

The law prohibited him from asking for *gifts* from his people, but it did not forbid his asking them to *lend* him money, however little prospect there might be of his ever repaying it. Five gentlemen who refused to pay such a forced loan were imprisoned by the mere order of the king. This raised the question of whether the king had the right to send to prison those whom he wished without any legal reasons for their arrest.

831. The *Petition of Right*. This and other attacks upon the rights of his subjects aroused Parliament. In 1628 that body drew up the celebrated *Petition of Right*, which is one of the most important documents in the history of the English Constitution. In it Parliament called the king's attention to his unlawful exactions and to the acts of his agents who had in sundry ways molested and disquieted the people of the realm. Parliament therefore "humbly prayed" the king that no man need thereafter "make or yield any gift, loan, benevolence, tax, or such like charge" without consent of Parliament; that no free man should be imprisoned or suffer any punishment except according to the laws and statutes of the realm as presented in the Great Charter (§§ 553–555); and that soldiers should not be quartered upon the people on any pretext whatever. Very reluctantly Charles consented to this restatement of the limitations which the English had always, in theory at least, placed upon the power of their king.

The disagreement between Charles and Parliament was rendered much more serious by religious differences. The king had married a French Catholic princess, and the Catholic cause seemed to be gaining on the Continent. The king of Denmark had just been defeated by Wallenstein and Tilly (§ 808), and Richelieu had succeeded in depriving the Huguenots of their cities of refuge. Both James I and Charles I had shown their readiness to enter into agreements with France and Spain to protect Catholics in England, and there was evidently a growing inclination in England to revert to the older ceremonies of the Church, which shocked the more strongly Protestant members of the House of Commons. The communion table was again placed by many clergymen at the eastern end of the church and became fixed there as an altar, and portions of the service were once more chanted.

FIG. 146. CHARLES I OF ENGLAND

This portrait is by one of the greatest painters of the time, Anthony Van Dyck, 1599–1641 (see Fig. 148)

832. Charles dissolves Parliament (1629) and determines to rule by himself. These "popish practices" (as the more fanatical Protestants called them), with which Charles was supposed to sympathize, served to widen the breach between him and the Commons, which had been caused by the king's attempt to raise taxes on his own account. The Parliament of 1629, after a stormy session, was dissolved by the king, who determined to rule thereafter by himself. For eleven years no new Parliament was summoned.

Charles was not well fitted by nature to run the government of England by himself. He had not the necessary tireless energy. Moreover, the methods resorted to by his ministers to raise money without recourse to Parliament rendered the king more and more unpopular and prepared the way for the triumphant return of Parliament. For example, Charles applied to his subjects for "ship money." He was anxious to equip a fleet, but instead of requiring the various ports to furnish ships, as was the ancient custom, he permitted them to buy themselves off by contributing money to the fitting out of large ships owned by himself. Even those living inland were asked for ship money. The king maintained that this was not a tax but simply a payment by which his subjects freed themselves from the duty of defending their country.

833. John Hampden; William Laud. John Hampden, a squire of Buckinghamshire, made a bold stand against this illegal demand by refusing to pay twenty shillings of ship money which was levied upon him. The case was tried before the king's judges, and he was convicted, but by a bare majority. The trial made it tolerably clear that the country would not put up long with the king's despotic policy.

In 1633 Charles made William Laud archbishop of Canterbury. Laud declared that it was the part of good citizenship to conform outwardly to the services of the state church, but that everyone should be free to make up his own mind in regard to the interpretation to be given to the Bible. As soon as he became archbishop he began a series of visitations through his province. Every clergyman who refused to conform to the prayer book, or opposed the placing of the communion table at the east end of the church, or declined to bow at the name of Jesus, was, if obstinate, to be brought before the king's special Court of High Commission to be tried and, if convicted, to be deprived of his position.

834. The Different Sects of Protestants — High Church and Low Church. Laud's conduct was no doubt gratifying to the High Church party among the Protestants; that is, those who still clung to some of the ancient practices of the Roman Church, although they rejected the doctrine of the Mass and refused to regard the Pope as their head. The Low Church party, or *Puritans*, on the contrary, regarded Laud and his policy with aversion. While, unlike the Presbyterians, they did not urge the abolition of the bishops, they disliked all "superstitious

FIG. 147. JOHN HAMPDEN

usages," as they called the wearing of the surplice by the clergy, the use of the sign of the cross at baptism, the kneeling posture in partaking of the communion, and so forth. The Presbyterians, who are often confused with the Puritans, agreed with them in many respects, but went farther and demanded the introduction of Calvin's system of church government.

835. The Independents. Lastly, there was an ever-increasing number of Separatists, or Independents. These rejected both the organization of the Church of England and that of the Presbyterians, and desired that each religious community should organize itself independently. The government had forbidden these Separatists to hold their little meetings, which they called *conventicles*, and about 1600 some of them fled to Holland.

836. The Pilgrim Fathers. The community of them which established itself at Leyden dispatched the *Mayflower*, in 1620, with colonists — since known as the Pilgrim Fathers — to the New World across the sea.[1] It was these colonists who laid the foundations of a *New England* which has proved a worthy offspring of the mother country. The form of worship which they established in their new home is still known as Congregational.

III. How Charles I lost his Head

837. Charles I's Quarrel with the Scotch Presbyterians. In 1640 Charles found himself forced to summon Parliament, for he was involved in a war with Scotland which he could not carry on without money. There the Presbyterian system had been pretty generally introduced by John Knox in Elizabeth's time (see § 798). An attempt on the part of Charles to force the Scots to accept a modified form of the English prayer book led to the signing of the National Covenant in 1638. This pledged those who attached their names to it to reëstablish the purity and liberty of the Gospel, which, to most of the Covenanters, meant Presbyterianism.

838. The Long Parliament (1640). Charles thereupon undertook to coerce the Scots. Having no money, he bought on credit a large cargo of pepper, which had just arrived in the ships of the East India Company, and sold it cheap for ready cash. The soldiers, however, whom he got together showed little inclination to

---

[1] The name "Puritan," it should be noted, was applied loosely to the English Protestants, whether Low Churchmen, Presbyterians, or Independents, who aroused the antagonism of their neighbors by advocating a godly life and opposing popular pastimes, especially on Sunday.

fight the Scots, with whom they were in tolerable agreement on religious matters. Charles was therefore at last obliged to summon a Parliament, which, owing to the length of time it remained in session, is known as the Long Parliament.

The Long Parliament began by imprisoning Archbishop Laud in the Tower of London. They declared him guilty of treason,

Fig. 148. Children of Charles I

This very interesting picture, by the Flemish artist Van Dyck, was painted in 1637. The boy with his hand on the dog's head was destined to become Charles II of England. Next on the left is the prince who was later James II. The girl to the extreme left, the Princess Mary, married the governor of the United Netherlands, and her son became William III of England in 1688 (see below, § 853). The two princesses on the right died in childhood

and he was executed in 1645, in spite of Charles's efforts to save him. Parliament also tried to strengthen its position by passing the Triennial Bill, which provided that it should meet at least once in three years, even if not summoned by the king. In fact, Charles's whole system of government was done away with. Parliament drew up a "Grand Remonstrance," in which all of Charles's errors were enumerated and a demand was made that the king's ministers should thereafter be responsible to Parliament. This document Parliament ordered to be printed and circulated throughout the country.

Exasperated at the conduct of the Commons, Charles attempted to intimidate the opposition by undertaking to arrest five of its most active leaders, whom he declared to be traitors. But when he entered the House of Commons and looked around for his enemies, he found that they had taken shelter in London, whose citizens later brought them back in triumph to Westminster, where Parliament held its meetings.

839. The Beginning of Civil War (1642); *Cavaliers* and *Roundheads*. Both Charles and Parliament now began to gather troops for the inevitable conflict, and England was plunged into civil war. Those who supported Charles were called *Cavaliers*. They included not only most of the aristocracy and the Catholic party but also a number of members of the House of Commons who were fearful lest Presbyterianism should succeed in doing away with the English Church. The parliamentary party was popularly known as the *Roundheads*, since some of them cropped their hair close because of their dislike for the long locks of their more aristocratic and worldly opponents. The Cavaliers in turn scorned the Roundheads as a set of hypocrites, on account of their solemn ways and for liking to go to meeting and singing psalms instead of trying to have a good time.

840. Oliver Cromwell; Defeat of Charles's Armies at Marston Moor and Naseby. The Roundheads soon found a distinguished leader in Oliver Cromwell (b. 1599), a country gentleman and member of Parliament, who was later to become the most powerful ruler of his time. Cromwell organized a compact army of God-fearing men, who were not permitted to indulge in profane words or light talk, as is the wont of soldiers, but advanced upon their enemies singing psalms. The king enjoyed the support of northern England and also looked for help from Ireland, where the royal and Catholic causes were popular.

The war continued for several years, and a number of battles were fought which, after the first year, went in general against the Cavaliers. The most important of these were the battle of Marston Moor in 1644 and that of Naseby the next year, in which the king was disastrously defeated. The enemy came into possession of his correspondence, which showed them how their king had been endeavoring to bring armies from France and Ireland into England. This encouraged Parliament to prosecute the war with more energy than ever. The king, defeated on every hand, put himself in the hands of the Scotch army which had come to the aid of Parliament (1646), and the Scotch soon turned him over to Parliament. During the next two years Charles was held in captivity.

841. Pride's Purge. There were, however, many in the House of Commons who still sided with the king, and in December, 1648, that body declared for a reconciliation with the monarch, whom they had safely imprisoned in the Isle of Wight. The next day Colonel Pride, representing the army,—which constituted a party in itself and was opposed to all negotiations between the king and the Commons,—stood at the door of the House with a body of soldiers and excluded all the members who were known to take the side of the king. This outrageous act is known in history as "Pride's Purge."

842. Execution of Charles (1649). In this way the House of Commons was brought completely under the control of those most bitterly hostile to the king, whom they immediately proposed to bring to trial. They declared that the House of Commons, since it was chosen by the people, was supreme in England and the source of all just power, and that consequently neither king nor House of Lords was necessary. The mutilated House of Commons appointed a special High Court of Justice made up of Charles's sternest opponents, who alone would consent to sit in judgment on him. They passed sentence upon him, and on January 30, 1649, Charles was beheaded in front of his palace of Whitehall, London. It must be clear from the above account that it was not the nation at large which demanded Charles's death, but a very small group of extremists who claimed to be the representatives of the nation.

IV. Oliver Cromwell: England a Commonwealth

843. England becomes a Commonwealth, or Republic. The "Rump Parliament," as the remnant of the House of Commons was contemptuously called, proclaimed England to be thereafter a "commonwealth"; that is, a republic, without a king or House of Lords. But Cromwell, the head of the army, was nevertheless the real ruler of England. He derived his main support from the Independents; and it is very surprising that he was able to maintain himself so long, considering what a small portion of the English people was in sympathy with the religious ideas of that sect and with the abolition of kingship. Even the Presbyterians were on the side of Charles I's son, Charles II, the legal heir to the throne. Cromwell was a vigorous and skillful administrator and had a well-organized army of fifty thousand men at his command, otherwise the republic could scarcely have lasted more than a few months.

844. Ireland and Scotland Subdued. Cromwell found himself confronted by every variety of difficulty. The three kingdoms had fallen apart. The nobles and Catholics in Ireland proclaimed Charles II as king, and Ormond, a Protestant leader, formed an army of Irish Catholics and English royalist Protestants with a view of overthrowing the Commonwealth. Cromwell accordingly set out for Ireland, where, after taking Drogheda, he mercilessly slaughtered two thousand of the "barbarous wretches," as he called them. Town after town surrendered to Cromwell's army, and in 1652, after much cruelty, the island was once more conquered. A large part of it was confiscated for the benefit of the English, and the Catholic landowners were driven into the mountains. In the meantime (1650) Charles II, who had taken refuge in France, had landed in Scotland, and upon his agreeing to be a Presbyterian king the whole Scotch nation was ready to support him. But Scotland was subdued by Cromwell even more promptly than Ireland had been. So completely was the Scottish army destroyed that Cromwell found no need to draw the sword again in the British Isles.

845. The Navigation Act (1651). Although it would seem that Cromwell had enough to keep him busy at home, he had already engaged in a victorious foreign war against the Dutch, who had become dangerous commercial rivals of England. The ships which went out from Amsterdam and Rotterdam were the best merchant vessels in the world and had got control of the carrying trade

FIG. 149. OLIVER CROMWELL

This portrait is by Peter Lely and was painted in 1653

between Europe and the colonies. In order to put an end to this, the English Parliament passed the Navigation Act (1651), which permitted only English vessels to bring goods to England, unless the goods came in vessels belonging to the country which had produced them. This led to a commercial war between Holland and England, and a series of battles was fought between the English and Dutch fleets with indecisive results. This war is notable as the first example of the commercial struggles which were thereafter to take the place of the religious conflicts of the preceding period.

846. Cromwell dissolves the Long Parliament (1653) and is made Lord Protector. Cromwell failed to get along with Parliament any better than Charles I had done. The Rump Parliament had become very unpopular, for its members, in spite of their

Fig. 150. Great Seal of England under the Commonwealth, 1651

This seal is reduced considerably in the reproduction. It gives us an idea of the appearance of a session of the House of Commons when England was for a short period a republic. It is still to-day the custom for members to sit with their hats on, except when making a speech

boasted piety, accepted bribes and were zealous in the promotion of their relatives in the public service. At last Cromwell upbraided them angrily for their injustice and self-interest, which were injuring the public cause. On being interrupted by a member, he cried out, "Come, come, we have had enough of this? I'll put an end to this. It's not fit that you should sit here any longer," and calling in his soldiers he turned the members out of the House and sent them home. Having thus made an end of the Long Parliament (April, 1653), he summoned a Parliament of his own,

FIG. 151. DUTCH WAR VESSEL IN CROMWELL'S TIME

This vessel should be compared with the ship in Fig. 152 to realize the change that had taken place in navigation since the palmy days of the Hanseatic League. (See above, § 654)

made up of "God-fearing" men whom he and the officers of his army chose. This extraordinary body is known as Barebone's Parliament, from a distinguished member, a London merchant, with the characteristically Puritan name of Praisegod Barebone. Many of these godly men were unpractical and hard to deal with.

A minority of the more sensible ones got up early one winter morning (December, 1653) and, before their opponents had a chance to protest, declared Parliament dissolved and placed the supreme authority in the hands of Cromwell.

847. The Protector's Foreign Policy. For nearly five years Cromwell was, as Lord Protector,—a title equivalent to that of Regent,—practically king of England, although he refused actually to accept the royal insignia. He did not succeed in permanently organizing the government at home, but he showed remarkable ability in his foreign negotiations. He promptly formed an alliance with France, and English troops aided the French in winning a great victory over Spain. England gained thereby Dunkirk and the West Indian island of Jamaica. The French king, Louis XIV, at first hesitated to address Cromwell, in the usual courteous way of monarchs, as "my cousin," but soon admitted that he would have even to call Cromwell "father" should the English ruler wish it, as the Protector was undoubtedly the most powerful person in Europe. Indeed, Cromwell found himself forced to play the part of a monarch, and it seemed to many persons that he was quite as despotic as James I and Charles I.

FIG. 152. SHIP SUCH AS WAS USED IN THE TIME OF THE HANSEATIC LEAGUE

This is taken from a picture at Cologne, painted in 1409. It, as well as other pictures of the time, makes it clear that the Hanseatic ships were tiny compared with those used two hundred and fifty years later, when Cromwell fought the Dutch

848. Cromwell's Death (1658). In May, 1658, Cromwell fell ill, and as a great storm passed over England at that time, the Cavaliers asserted that the devil had come to fetch home the soul of the usurper. Cromwell was dying, it is true, but he was no instrument of the devil. He closed a life of honest effort for his fellow beings with a last touching prayer to God, whom he had consistently sought to serve : "Thou hast made me, though very unworthy, a mean instrument to do Thy people some good and Thee service : and many of them have set too high a value upon me, though others wish and would be glad of my death. Pardon such as desire to trample upon the dust of a poor worm, for they are Thy people too ; and pardon the folly of this short prayer, even for Jesus Christ's sake, and give us a good night, if it be Thy pleasure. Amen."

V. THE RESTORATION

849. The Restoration : Charles II. After Cromwell's death his son Richard, who succeeded him, found himself unable to carry on the government. He soon abdicated, and the remnants of the Long Parliament met once more. But the power was really in the hands of the soldiers. In 1660 George Monk, who was in command of the forces in Scotland, came to London with a view of putting an end to the anarchy. He soon concluded that no one cared to support the Rump, and that body peacefully disbanded of its own accord. Resistance would have been vain in any case with the army against it. The nation was glad to acknowledge Charles II, whom everyone preferred to a government by soldiers. A new Parliament, composed of both houses, was assembled, which welcomed a messenger from the king and solemnly resolved that, "according to the ancient and fundamental laws of this kingdom, the government is, and ought to be, by king, lords, and commons." Thus the Puritan revolution and the short-lived republic were followed by the *Restoration* of the Stuarts.

Charles II was quite as fond as his father of having his own way, but he was a man of more ability. He disliked to be ruled by Parliament, but, unlike his father, he was too wise to arouse the nation against him. He did not propose to let anything happen which would send him on his travels again. He and his courtiers led a gay life in sharp contrast to the Puritan ideas.

850. Religious Measures adopted by Parliament. Charles's first Parliament was a moderate body, but his second was made up almost wholly of Cavaliers, and it got along, on the whole, so well with the king that he did not dissolve it for eighteen years. It did not take up the old question, which was still unsettled, as to whether Parliament or the king was really supreme. It showed its hostility, however, to the Puritans by a series of intolerant acts, which are very important in English history. An effort was made to exclude Presbyterians and Independents from town offices. By the Act of Uniformity (1662) any clergyman who refused to accept everything in the Book of Common Prayer was to be excluded from holding his benefice. That many disagreed with the Anglican Church is shown by the fact that two thousand clergymen thereupon resigned their positions for conscience' sake.

These laws tended to throw all those Protestants who refused to conform to the Church of England into a single class, still known to-day as *Dissenters*. It included the Independents, the Presbyterians, and the newer bodies of the Baptists and the Society of Friends (commonly known as Quakers). These sects abandoned any idea of controlling the religion or politics of the country and asked only that they might be permitted to worship in their own way outside of the English Church.

851. Toleration favored by the King ; opposed by Parliament. Toleration found an unexpected ally in the king, who, in spite of his dissolute habits, had interest enough in religion to have secret leanings toward Catholicism. He asked Parliament to permit him to moderate the rigor of the Act of Uniformity by making some exceptions. He even issued a declaration in the interest of toleration, with a view of bettering the position of the Catholics and Dissenters. Suspicion was, however, aroused lest this toleration might lead to the restoration of "popery,"— as the Protestants called the Catholic beliefs,— and Parliament passed the harsh Conventicle Act (1664). Any adult attending a conventicle—that is to say, any religious meeting not held in accordance with the rules of the English Church—was liable to penalties which might culminate in deportation to some distant colony. Nevertheless, a few years later Charles II issued a declaration giving complete religious liberty to Roman Catholics as well as to Dissenters. Parliament not only forced him to withdraw this enlightened measure but passed the *Test Act*, which excluded everyone from public office who did not accept the views of the English Church and who would not take the communion according to its usage. This law excluding all but adherents of the English Church from office remained in force down into the nineteenth century.

852. War with Holland. The old war with Holland, begun by Cromwell, was renewed under Charles II, who was earnestly desirous to increase English commerce and to found new colonies. The two nations were very evenly matched on the sea, but in 1664 the English seized some of the West Indian Islands from the Dutch. And what was of much greater importance the English captured the Dutch settlement on Manhattan Island, which was renamed New York in honor of the king's brother, the Duke of York. In 1667 a treaty was signed by England and Holland which confirmed these conquests.

VI. THE REVOLUTION OF 1688

853. James II (1685–1688). Upon Charles II's death he was succeeded by his brother, James II, who was an avowed Catholic and had married, as his second wife, Mary of Modena, who was also a Catholic. He was a far more earnest man than the late king and was ready to reëstablish Catholicism in England regardless of what it might cost him. Mary, James's daughter by his first wife, had married her cousin, William III, Prince of Orange, the head of the United Netherlands, as Holland was called. The English nation might have tolerated James so long as they could look forward to the accession of his Protestant daughter. But when a son was born to his Catholic second wife, and James showed unmistakably his purpose of favoring the Catholics, messengers were dispatched by a group of Protestants to William of Orange, asking him to come and rule over them.

854. The Revolution of 1688 and the Accession of William III (1688–1702). William landed in November, 1688, and marched upon London, where he received general support from all the English Protestants, regardless of party. James II started to oppose William, but his army refused to fight and his courtiers deserted him. William was glad to forward James's flight to France, as he would hardly have known what to do with him had James insisted on remaining in the country. A new Parliament declared the throne vacant, on the ground that King James II,[1] " by the advice of the Jesuits and other wicked persons, having violated the fundamental laws and withdrawn himself out of the kingdom, had abdicated the government."

855. The Bill of Rights (1689). A Bill of Rights was then drawn up, condemning James's violation of the constitution and appointing William and Mary joint sovereigns. The Bill of Rights, which is an important monument in English constitutional history, once more stated the fundamental rights of the English nation and the limitations which the Petition of Right and the Great Charter of King John had placed upon the king. By this peaceful revolution of 1688 the English rid themselves of the Stuarts and their claims to rule by divine right; the rights of Parliament were once more asserted, and the Catholic question was practically settled by the dethroning of a king who openly favored the rule of the Pope.

The *Toleration Act* was passed by Parliament, which freed Dissenters from all penalties for failing to attend services in Anglican churches and allowed them to have their own meetings. Even Catholics, while not included in the act of toleration, were permitted to hold services undisturbed by the government.

[1] Charles I, m. Henrietta Maria of France
(1625–1649)

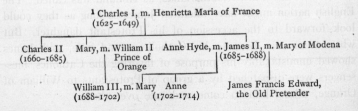

Charles II (1660–1685)   Mary, m. William II Prince of Orange   Anne Hyde, m. James II, m. Mary of Modena (1685–1688)

William III, m. Mary (1688–1702)   Anne (1702–1714)   James Francis Edward, the Old Pretender

QUESTIONS

I. What was the great issue during the period of the Stuarts? What were the views of kingship held by James I? Mention some of the books of his time.

II. What policy did Charles I adopt in regard to Parliament? What was the Petition of Right? What were the chief religious parties in England in the time of Charles I? Who was John Hampden? Mention some of the religious sects that date from that time which still exist in the United States.

III. What measures did the Long Parliament take against the king? Describe the civil war. What led to the execution of Charles I?

IV. What were the chief events during Cromwell's administration? What are your impressions of Cromwell?

V. What led to the restoration of the Stuarts? What was the attitude of Charles II toward the religious difficulties? Who were the Dissenters? What laws were passed in regard to them?

VI. Why was James II unpopular? Give an account of the revolution which put William and Mary on the English throne. What important acts were passed after the accession of William and Mary?

CHAPTER XXXVI

FRANCE UNDER LOUIS XIV

I. Position and Character of Louis XIV

856. France at the Accession of Louis XIV. Under the despotic rule of Louis XIV (1643–1715) France enjoyed a commanding influence in European affairs. After the wars of religion were over, the royal authority had been reëstablished by the wise conduct of Henry IV. Later, Richelieu had solidified the monarchy by depriving the Huguenots of the exceptional privileges granted to them for their protection by Henry IV; he had also destroyed the fortified castles of the nobles, whose power had greatly increased during the turmoil of the Huguenot wars. His successor, Cardinal Mazarin, who conducted the government during Louis XIV's boyhood, was able to put down a last rising of the discontented nobility.

857. What Richelieu and Mazarin had done for the French Monarchy. When Mazarin died, in 1661, he left the young monarch with a kingdom such as no previous French king had enjoyed. The nobles, who for centuries had disputed the power with the king, were no longer feudal lords but only courtiers. The Huguenots, whose claim to a place in the State beside the Catholics had led to the terrible civil wars of the sixteenth century, were reduced in numbers and no longer held fortified towns from which they could defy the king's officers. Richelieu and Mazarin had successfully taken a hand in the Thirty Years' War, and France had come out of it with enlarged territory and increased importance in European affairs.

858. The Government of Louis XIV. Louis XIV carried the work of these great ministers still farther. He gave that form to the French monarchy which it retained until the French Revolution. He made himself the very mirror of kingship. His marvelous court at Versailles became the model and the despair of other less rich and powerful princes, who accepted his theory of the absolute power of kings but could not afford to imitate his luxury. By his incessant wars he kept Europe in turmoil for over half a century. The distinguished generals who led his newly organized troops, and the wily diplomats who arranged his alliances and negotiated his treaties, made France feared and respected by even the most powerful of the other European states.

859. The Theory of the "Divine Right of Kings" in France. Louis XIV had the same idea of kingship that James I had tried in vain to induce the English people to accept (§§ 827–828). God had given kings to men, and it was His will that monarchs should be regarded as His lieutenants and

Fig. 153. Louis XIV

that all those subject to them should obey them absolutely, without asking any questions or making any criticisms; for in submitting to their prince they were really submitting to God Himself. If the king were good and wise, his subjects should thank the Lord; if he proved foolish, cruel, or perverse, they must accept their evil ruler as a well-deserved and just punishment which God had sent them for their sins. But in no case might they limit his power or rise against him.[1]

[1] Louis XIV does not appear to have himself used the famous expression "*I* am the *State*," usually attributed to him, but it exactly corresponds to his idea of the relation of the king and the State.

860. Different Attitude of English and French toward Absolute Monarchy. Louis XIV had two great advantages over James I. In the first place, the English nation has always shown itself far more reluctant than France to place absolute power in the hands of its rulers. By its Parliament, its courts, and its various declarations of the nation's rights, it had built up traditions which made it impossible for the Stuarts to establish their claim to be absolute rulers. In France, on the other hand, there was no Great Charter or Bill of Rights; the Estates General did not

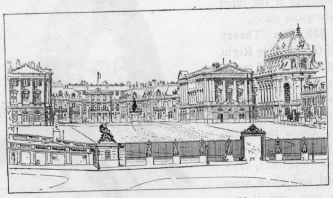

FIG. 154. FAÇADE OF THE PALACE OF VERSAILLES

hold the purse strings (§ 566), and the king was permitted to raise money without asking their permission or previously redressing the grievances which they chose to point out. They were therefore only summoned at irregular intervals. When Louis XIV took charge of the government, forty-seven years had passed without a meeting of the Estates General, and a century and a quarter was still to elapse before another call to the representatives of the nation was issued, in 1789.

Moreover, the French people placed far more reliance upon a powerful king than the English, perhaps because they were not protected by the sea from their neighbors, as England was. On every side France had enemies ready to take advantage of any weakness or hesitation which might arise from dissension between a parliament and the king. So the French felt it best, on the whole, to leave all in the king's hands, even if the nation suffered at times from his tyranny.

861. Personal Characteristics of Louis XIV. Louis had another great advantage over James. He was a handsome man, of elegant and courtly mien and the most exquisite perfection of manner ; even when playing billiards he is said to have retained an air of world mastery. The first of the Stuarts, on the contrary, was a very awkward man, whose slouching gait, intolerable manners, and pedantic conversation were utterly at variance with his lofty pretensions. Louis added, moreover, to his graceful exterior a sound judgment and quick apprehension. He said neither too much nor too little. He was, for a king, a hard worker and spent several hours a day attending to the business of government.

862. The Strenuous Life of a Despotic Ruler. It requires, in fact, a great deal of energy and application to be a real despot. In order thoroughly to understand and to solve the problems which constantly face the ruler of a great state, a monarch must, like Frederick the Great or Napoleon, rise early and toil late. Louis XIV was greatly aided by the able ministers who sat in his council, but he always retained for himself the place of first minister. He would never have consented to be dominated by an adviser, as his father had been by Richelieu. "The profession of the king," he declared, "is great, noble, and delightful if one but feels equal to performing the duties which it involves,"— and he never harbored a doubt that he himself was born for the business.

II. How Louis encouraged Art and Literature

863. The King's Palace at Versailles. Louis XIV was careful that his surroundings should suit the grandeur of his office. His court was magnificent beyond anything that had been dreamed of in the West. He had an enormous palace constructed at Versailles, just outside of Paris, with interminable halls and apartments and a vast garden stretching away behind it. About this a town was laid out, where those lived who were privileged to be near his Majesty or supply the wants of the royal court. This palace and its outlying buildings, including two or three less gorgeous residences for the king when he occasionally tired of the ceremony of Versailles, probably cost the nation about a hundred million dollars, in spite of the fact that thousands of peasants and soldiers were forced to turn to and work without pay. The furnishings and decorations were as rich and costly as the palace was splendid, and still fill the visitor with wonder. For over a

FIG. 155. ONE OF THE VAST HALLS OF VERSAILLES

century this magnificent "château" at Versailles continued to be the home of the French kings and the seat of their government.

864. Life at Louis XIV's Court. This splendor and luxury helped to attract the nobility, who no longer lived on their estates in well-fortified castles, planning how they might escape the royal control. They now dwelt in the effulgence of the king's countenance. They saw him to bed at night and in stately procession they greeted him in the morning. It was deemed a high honor to hand him his shirt as he was being dressed or, at dinner, to provide him with a fresh napkin. Only by living close to the king could the courtiers hope to gain favors, pensions, and lucrative offices for themselves and their friends, and perhaps

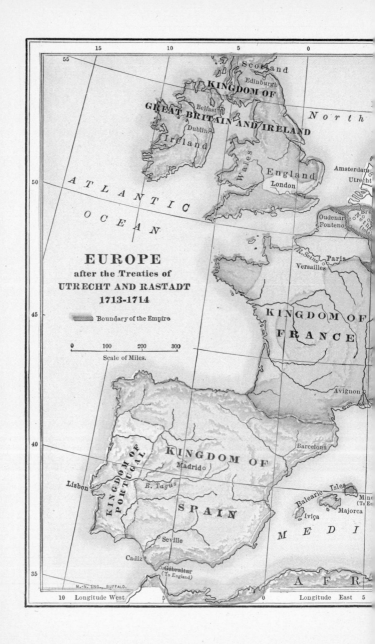

EUROPE
after the Treaties of
UTRECHT AND RASTADT
1713-1714

Boundary of the Empire

0   100   200   300
Scale of Miles.

Scotland
Edinburgh
KINGDOM OF
GREAT BRITAIN AND IRELAND
Belfast
Dublin
Ireland
Wales
England
London

North

Amsterdam
Utrecht

Bru
Oudenar
Fontenoy

R. Seine Paris
Versailles

KINGDOM OF
FRANCE

Avignon

ATLANTIC
OCEAN

KINGDOM OF PORTUGAL
Lisbon
KINGDOM OF
Madrid
R. Tagus
SPAIN
Seville
Cadiz
Gibraltar
(To England)

Barcelona

Balearic Isles
Mino
(To En
Majorca
Iviça

M E D I

A F R

M.N. ENG. BUFFALO.

10   Longitude West   Longitude   East   5

occasionally to exercise some little influence upon the policy of the government. For they were now entirely dependent upon the good will of their monarch.

865. The Reforms of Colbert. The reforms which Louis XIV carried out in the earlier part of his reign were largely the work of the great financier Colbert, to whom France still looks back with gratitude. He early discovered that the king's officials were stealing and wasting vast sums. The offenders were arrested and forced to disgorge, and a new system of bookkeeping was introduced, similar to that employed by business men. He then turned his attention to increasing the manufactures of France by establishing new industries and seeing that the older ones kept to a high standard, which would make French goods sell readily in foreign markets.

866. Art and Literature in the Reign of Louis XIV. It was, however, as a patron of art and literature that Louis XIV gained much of his celebrity. Molière, who was at once a playwright and an actor, delighted the court with comedies in which he delicately satirized the foibles of his time. Corneille, who had gained renown by the great tragedy of *The Cid* in Richelieu's time, found a worthy successor in Racine, the most distinguished, perhaps, of French tragic poets. The charming letters of Madame de Sévigné are models of prose style and serve at the same time to give us a glimpse into the more refined life of the court circle. In the famous memoirs of Saint-Simon the weaknesses of the king, as well as the numberless intrigues of the courtiers, are freely exposed with inimitable skill and wit.

Men of letters were generously aided by the king with pensions. Colbert encouraged the French Academy, which had been created by Richelieu. This body gave special attention to making the French tongue more eloquent and expressive by determining what words should be used. It is now the greatest honor that a Frenchman can obtain to be made one of the forty members of this association. A magazine which still exists, the *Journal des Savants*, was founded for the promotion of science at this time. Colbert had an astronomical observatory built at Paris ; and the Royal

Library, which possessed only about sixteen thousand volumes, began to grow into that great collection of two and a half million volumes — by far the largest in existence — which to-day attracts scholars to Paris from all parts of the world. In short, Louis XIV and his ministers believed one of the chief objects of any government to be the promotion of art, literature, and science, and the example they set has been followed by almost every modern state.

III. Louis XIV attacks his Neighbors

867. Louis XIV's Warlike Enterprises. Unfortunately for France, the king's ambitions were by no means exclusively peaceful. Indeed, he regarded his wars as his chief glory. He employed a carefully reorganized army and the skill of his generals in a series of inexcusable attacks on his neighbors, in which he finally squandered all that Colbert's economies had accumulated and led France to the edge of financial ruin.

Louis XIV's predecessors had had, on the whole, little time to think of conquest. They had first to consolidate their realms and gain the mastery of their feudal dependents, who shared the power with them; then the claims of the English Edwards and Henrys had to be met, and the French provinces freed from their clutches; lastly, the great religious dispute was settled only after many years of disintegrating civil war.

Louis XIV was, however, now at liberty to look about him and consider how he might best realize the dream of his ancestors and perhaps reëstablish the ancient boundaries which Cæsar reported that the Gauls had occupied. The "natural limits" of France appeared to be the Rhine on the north and east, the Jura Mountains and the Alps on the southeast, and to the south the Mediterranean and the Pyrenees. Richelieu had believed that it was the chief end of his ministry to restore to France the boundaries determined for it by nature. Mazarin had labored hard to win Savoy and Nice and to reach the Rhine on the north. Before his death France at least gained Alsace and reached the Pyrenees (§§ 815–817).

868. The Invasion of the Netherlands (1667). Louis XIV
first turned his attention to the conquest of the Spanish Netherlands, to which he laid claim through his wife, the elder sister
of the Spanish king, Charles II (1665–1700). He easily took a
number of towns on the border of the Netherlands and then
turned south and completely conquered Franche-Comté (§ 814).
This was an outlying province of Spain, isolated from her other
lands, and a tempting morsel for the hungry king of France.

These conquests alarmed Europe, and especially Holland, which
could not afford to have the barrier between it and France removed, for Louis XIV would be an uncomfortable neighbor.
A Triple Alliance, composed of Holland, England, and Sweden,
was accordingly organized to induce France to make peace with
Spain. Louis contented himself for the moment with the dozen
border towns that he had taken and which Spain ceded to him
on condition that he would return Franche-Comté.

869. Louis XIV breaks up the Triple Alliance. The success with which Holland had in general held her own against
the navy of England (§§ 845 and 852) and then brought the
proud king of France to a halt produced an elation on the part
of that tiny country which was very irritating to Louis XIV.
He was thoroughly vexed that he should have been blocked by
so trifling an obstacle as Dutch intervention. He consequently
conceived a strong dislike for the United Provinces, which was
increased by the protection that they afforded to writers who
annoyed him with their attacks. He broke up the Triple Alliance
by inducing Charles II of England to conclude a treaty which
pledged England to help France in a new war against the Dutch.

870. Louis XIV's Invasion of Holland (1672). Louis XIV
then startled Europe again by seizing the duchy of Lorraine, which
brought him to the border of Holland. At the head of a hundred
thousand men he crossed the Rhine (1672) and easily conquered
southern Holland. For the moment the Dutch cause appeared
to be lost. But William of Orange showed the spirit of his great
ancestor William the Silent ; the sluices in the dikes were opened
and the country flooded, so the French army was checked before

it could take Amsterdam and advance into the north. The emperor sent an army against Louis, and England deserted him and made peace with Holland.

When a general peace was concluded at the end of six years, the chief provisions were that Holland should be left intact and that France should this time retain Franche-Comté, which had been conquered by Louis XIV in person. This bit of the Burgundian heritage thus became at last a part of France, after France and Spain had quarreled over it for a century and a half. For the ten years following there was no open war, but Louis seized the important free city of Strassburg and made many other less conspicuous but equally unwarranted additions to his territory. The emperor was unable to do more than protest against these outrageous encroachments, for he was fully occupied with the Turks, who had just laid siege to Vienna.

IV. LOUIS XIV AND HIS PROTESTANT SUBJECTS

871. Situation of the Huguenots at the Beginning of Louis XIV's Reign. Louis XIV exhibited as woeful a want of statesmanship in the treatment of his Protestant subjects as in the prosecution of disastrous wars. The Huguenots, deprived of their former military and political power, had turned to manufacture, trade, and banking; "as rich as a Huguenot" had become a proverb in France. There were perhaps a million of them among fifteen million Frenchmen, and they undoubtedly formed by far the most thrifty and enterprising part of the nation. The Catholic clergy, however, did not cease to urge the complete suppression of heresy.

872. Revocation of the Edict of Nantes and its Results. Louis XIV had scarcely taken the reins of government into his own hands before the perpetual nagging and injustice to which the Protestants had been subjected at all times took a more serious form. Upon one pretense or another their churches were demolished. Children were authorized to renounce Protestantism when they reached the age of seven. Rough dragoons were quartered upon the Huguenots with the hope that the insulting behavior of the soldiers might frighten the heretics into accepting the religion of the king.

At last Louis XIV was led by his officials to believe that practically all the Huguenots had been converted by these harsh measures. In 1685, therefore, he revoked the Edict of Nantes, and the Protestants thereby became outlaws and their ministers subject to the death penalty. Thousands of the Huguenots succeeded in eluding the vigilance of the royal officials and fled, some to England, some to Prussia, some to America, carrying with them their skill and industry to strengthen France's rivals. This was the last great and terrible example in western Europe of that fierce religious intolerance which had produced the Albigensian Crusade, the Spanish Inquisition, and the Massacre of St. Bartholomew.

873. Louis's Operations in the Rhenish Palatinate. Louis XIV now set his heart upon conquering the Palatinate, a Protestant land, to which he easily discovered that he had a claim. The rumor of his intention and the indignation occasioned in Protestant countries by the revocation of the Edict of Nantes resulted in an alliance against the French king headed by William of Orange. Louis speedily justified the suspicions of Europe by a frightful devastation of the Palatinate, burning whole towns and destroying many castles, including the exceptionally beautiful one of the elector at Heidelberg. Ten years later, however, Louis agreed to a peace which put things back as they were before the struggle began. He was preparing for the final and most ambitious undertaking of his life, which precipitated the longest and bloodiest war of all his warlike reign.

V. War of the Spanish Succession

874. The Question of the Spanish Succession. The king of Spain, Charles II, was childless and brotherless, and Europe had long been discussing what would become of his vast realms when his sickly existence should come to an end. Louis XIV had married one of his sisters, and the emperor, Leopold I, another, and these two ambitious rulers had been considering for some time how they might divide the Spanish possessions between the Bourbons and the Hapsburgs. But when Charles II died, in 1700, it was discovered that he had left a will in which he made Louis's younger grandson, Philip, the heir to his twenty-two crowns, but on the condition that France and Spain should never be united.

875. Louis's Grandson, Philip, becomes King of Spain. It was a weighty question whether Louis XIV should permit his grandson to accept this hazardous honor. Should Philip become king of Spain, Louis and his family would control all of south-western Europe from Holland to Sicily, as well as a great part of North and South America. This would mean the establishment of an empire more powerful than that of Charles V. It was clear that the disinherited emperor and the ever-watchful William of Orange, now king of England (§ 854), would never permit this unprecedented extension of French influence. They had already shown themselves ready to make great sacrifices in order to check far less serious aggressions on the part of the French king. Nevertheless, family pride and personal ambition led Louis criminally to risk the welfare of his country. He accepted the will and informed the Spanish ambassador at the French court that he might salute Philip V as his new king. The leading French newspaper of the time boldly proclaimed that the Pyrenees were no more.

876. The War of the Spanish Succession. King William soon succeeded in forming a new Grand Alliance (1701) in which Louis's old enemies, England, Holland, and the emperor, were the most important members. William himself died just as hostilities were beginning, but the long War of the Spanish Succession was carried on vigorously by the great English general, the duke of Marlborough, and the Austrian commander, Eugene of Savoy. The conflict was more general than the Thirty Years' War; even in America there was fighting between French and English colonists, which passes in American histories under the name of Queen Anne's War. All the more important battles went against the French, and after ten years of war, which was rapidly ruining the country by the destruction of its people and its wealth, Louis XIV was willing to consider some compromise, and after long discussion a peace was arranged in 1713.

877. The Treaty of Utrecht (1713). The Treaty of Utrecht changed the map of Europe as no previous treaty had done, not even that of Westphalia. Each of the chief combatants got his share of the Spanish booty over which they had been fighting. The Bourbon Philip V was permitted to retain Spain and its colonies on condition that the Spanish and French crowns should never rest on the same head. To Austria fell the Spanish Netherlands, hereafter called the Austrian Netherlands, which continued to form a barrier between Holland and France. Holland received certain fortresses to make its position still more secure. The Spanish possessions in Italy, that is, Naples and Milan, were also given to Austria, and in this way Austria got the hold on Italy which it retained until 1866. From France, England acquired Nova Scotia, Newfoundland, and the Hudson Bay region, and so began the expulsion of the French from North America. Besides these American provinces she received the rock and fortress of Gibraltar, which still gives her command of the narrow entrance to the Mediterranean.

878. The Development of International Law. The period of Louis XIV is remarkable for the development of international law. The incessant wars and great alliances embracing several powers made increasingly clear the need of well-defined rules governing states in their relations with one another both in peace and in war. It was of the utmost importance to determine, for instance, the rights of ambassadors and of the vessels of neutral powers not engaged in the war, and what should be considered fair conduct in warfare and in the treatment of prisoners.

The first great systematic treatise on international law was published by Grotius in 1625, when the horrors of the Thirty Years' War were impressing men's minds with the necessity of finding some means other than war of settling disputes between nations. While the rules laid down by Grotius and later writers have, as we must sadly admit, by no means put an end to war, they have prevented many conflicts by increasing the ways in which nations may, without recourse to arms, come to an understanding with one another through their ambassadors.

879. France in the Eighteenth Century. Louis XIV outlived his son and his grandson and left a sadly demoralized kingdom to his five-year-old great-grandson, Louis XV (1715–1774). The national treasury was depleted, the people were reduced in numbers and were in a miserable state, and the army, once the finest in Europe, was in no condition to gain further victories.

Something will be said in the following chapters of the wars in which France became involved in the eighteenth century and how she lost her colonies in both India and America. When the great French Revolution began in 1789 France became once more the great cause of agitation in Europe. The general conditions and the spirit of reform in France and elsewhere which led to the French Revolution will be taken up at the beginning of the following volume.

QUESTIONS

I. What did Richelieu accomplish in strengthening the French monarchy? What were Louis XIV's ideas of kingship? Why did the French view the "divine right of kings" differently from the English? Contrast Louis XIV with James I.

II. Describe the palace of Versailles. What were the chief reforms of Colbert? Mention some of the great writers of Louis XIV's time. How did the government aid scholarship and science?

III. What led Louis XIV to attack his neighbors? What are the "natural" boundaries of France? What country did Louis first attack? What additions did he make to French territory?

IV. What was the policy of Louis XIV toward the Huguenots? Who were Louis XIV's chief enemies?

V. What were the causes of the War of the Spanish Succession? What were the chief changes provided for in the Treaty of Utrecht?

CHAPTER XXXVII

RUSSIA AND PRUSSIA BECOME EUROPEAN POWERS

I. BEGINNINGS OF RUSSIA

880. Emergence of Two New European Powers. While much has been said in the preceding chapters of France, England, Spain, the Germanies, and the Netherlands, it has not been necessary hitherto to speak of either Russia or Prussia. During the past two hundred years these two states have played a great and terrible rôle in the affairs of Europe and of the world. The aggressions of Prussia finally united most of the civilized nations of the globe against her in the World War, and then the Bolshevik revolution in Russia seemed to many to threaten the whole existing order. We must, accordingly, now turn from the Rhine and the Pyrenees to the shores of the Baltic and the vast plains of eastern Europe in order to see how these two states grew up and became actors in the great drama of humanity.

While the long War of the Spanish Succession had been in progress, due to Louis XIV's anxiety to add Spain to the possessions of his family, another conflict was raging in the North, and changes were taking place there comparable in importance to those which were ratified by the Peace of Utrecht. Russia, which had hitherto faced eastward, was turning toward the West, upon which she was destined to exert an ever-increasing influence, extending even to our own country. The newly founded kingdom of Prussia was gathering its forces for those warlike enterprises which have characterized its history and which ultimately led to a disaster so great that it is impossible for the human imagination fully to appreciate the tragedy.

881. The Slavic Peoples. We have had little occasion hitherto, in dealing with the history of western Europe, to refer to the Slavic peoples, to whom the Russians, Poles, Bohemians, and many other nations of eastern Europe belong. Together they form the most numerous race in Europe, but only recently has their history begun to merge into that of the world at large. In the eighteenth century Russia first began to take an increasingly important part in European affairs. Before the World War, which began in 1914, the realms of the Tsar which lay in Europe exceeded in extent those of all the other rulers of the continent put together, and yet they were scarcely more than a quarter of his whole dominion, which embraced northern and central Asia— an empire nearly three times the size of the United States.

The Slavs were settled along the Dnieper, Don, and Vistula Rivers long before the Christian Era. After the East Goths had penetrated into the Roman Empire (§ 458) the Slavs followed their example and invaded, ravaged, and conquered the Balkan Peninsula, which they held for some time. When the German Lombards went south into Italy, about 569 (§ 465), the Slavs pressed behind them into the eastern Alps, where they still live to the north of the Adriatic Sea. Other Slavic hordes had driven the Germans across the Oder and the upper Elbe. Later the German emperors, beginning with Charlemagne, began to push them back, but the Bohemians and Moravians, who are Slavs, still hold an advanced position close on the borders of Germany.

882. Beginnings of Russia. In the ninth century some of the Northmen invaded the districts to the east of the Baltic, while their relatives were causing grievous trouble in France and England (§§ 520, 537, 540). It is generally supposed that one of their leaders, Rurik, was the first to consolidate the Slavic tribes about Novgorod into a sort of state, in 862. Rurik's successor extended the bounds of the new empire to the south as far as the Dnieper River. The word "Russia" is probably derived from *Rous*, the name given by the neighboring Finns to the Norman adventurers. Before the end of the tenth century the Greek form of Christianity was introduced and the Russian ruler was baptized. The frequent intercourse with Constantinople might have led to rapid advance in civilization had it not been for a great disaster which put Russia back for centuries.

883. The Tartar Invasion. Russia is geographically nothing more than an extension of the vast plain of northern Asia, which the Russians were destined finally to conquer. It was therefore exposed to the great invasion of the Tartars, or Mongols, who swept in from the east in the thirteenth century. The powerful Tartar ruler, Genghis Khan (1162–1227), conquered northern China and central Asia, and the mounted hordes of his successors crossed into Europe and overran Russia, which had fallen apart into numerous principalities. The Russian princes became the dependents of the Great Khan and had frequently to seek his far-distant court, some three thousand miles away, where he freely disposed of both their crowns and their heads. The Tartars exacted tribute of the Russians but left them undisturbed in their laws and religion.

884. Influence of the Tartar Occupation on Russia. Of the Russian princes who went to prostrate themselves at the foot of the Great Khan's throne, none made a more favorable impression upon him than the prince of Moscow, to whose advantage the Khan was wont to decide all cases of dispute between the prince and his rivals. When the Mongol power had begun to decline in strength and the princes of Moscow had grown stronger, they ventured, in 1480, to kill the Mongol ambassadors sent to demand tribute and thus freed themselves from the Mongol yoke. But the Tartar occupation had left its mark, for the princes of Moscow imitated the Khans rather than the Western rulers, of whom, in fact, they knew nothing. In 1547 Ivan the Terrible assumed the title of "Tsar," [1] which was the Russian equivalent of the title "king," or "emperor." The costumes and etiquette of the court were also Asiatic. The Russian armor suggested that of the Chinese, and their headdress was a turban. It was the task of Peter the Great to Europeanize Russia.

[1] The word "Tsar," or "Czar," is derived from "Cæsar" (German, *Kaiser*), but was used in Slavic books for the title of the kings of antiquity as well as for the Roman emperors. Peter the Great called himself "Imperator"; that is, "emperor." The Tsar was also known as "Autocrat of all the Russias."

II. PETER THE GREAT

885. Peter the Great (1672–1725). At the time of Peter's accession, in 1672, Russia, which had grown greatly under Ivan the Terrible and other enterprising rulers, still had no outlet to the sea. In manners and customs the kingdom was Asiatic, and its government was like that of a Tartar prince. Peter had no objection to the despotic power which fell to him, but he knew that Russia was very much behind the rest of Europe and that his crudely equipped soldiers could never make head against the well-armed and well-disciplined troops of the West. He had no seaport and no ships, and without these Russia could never hope to take part in the world's affairs. His two great tasks were therefore to introduce Western

FIG. 156. PETER THE GREAT

Peter was a tall, strong man, impulsive in action, sometimes vulgarly familiar, but always retaining an air of command. When he visited Louis XV of France in 1717 he astonished the court by taking the seven-year-old king under the arms and hoisting him up in the air to kiss him. The courtiers were much shocked at his conduct

habits into his barbarous realms and to "make a window," as he expressed it, through which Russia might look abroad.

886. Peter's Travels in Europe. In 1697–1698 Peter himself visited Germany, Holland, and England with a view to investigating every art and science of the West, as well as the most approved methods of manufacture, from the making of a man-of-war to the etching of an engraving. Nothing escaped the keen eyes of this rude, half-savage Northern giant. For a week he put on the wide breeches of a Dutch laborer and worked in the shipyard at Zaandam near Amsterdam. In England, Holland, and Germany he engaged artisans, scientific men, architects, ship captains, and those versed in artillery and in the training of troops—all of whom he took back with him to aid in the reform and development of Russia.

887. Peter's Reform Measures. Peter was called home by the revolt of Russian nobles and churchmen who were horrified at his desertion of the habits and customs of his forefathers. They hated what they called "German ideas," such as short coats, tobacco smoking, and shaven faces. Peter took a fearful revenge upon the rebels and is said to have himself cut off the heads of many of them. Like the barbarian that he was at heart he left their heads and bodies lying about all winter, unburied, in order to make the terrible results of revolt against his power quite plain to all.

Peter's reforms extended through his whole reign. He made his people give up their cherished oriental beards and long flowing garments. He forced the women of the richer classes, who had been kept in a sort of oriental harem, to come out and meet the men in social assemblies, such as were common in the West. He invited foreigners to settle in Russia and sent young Russians abroad to study. He reorganized the government officials on the model of a Western kingdom and made over his army in the same way.

888. Founding of St. Petersburg. Finding that the old capital, Moscow, clung persistently to its ancient habits, Peter prepared to found a new capital for his new Russia. He selected for this purpose a bit of territory on the Baltic which he had conquered from Sweden—very marshy, it is true, but where he might hope to construct Russia's first real port. Here he built St. Petersburg[1] at enormous expense and colonized it with Russians and foreigners. Russia was at last becoming a European power.

[1] Changed to *Petrograd* during the war with Germany in 1914 so that the Russian capital should no longer be called by a German name.

889. Russia gains on the Baltic. The next problem was to get control of the provinces lying between the Russian boundary and the Baltic Sea. These belonged to Sweden, which happened to have at that time a very warlike young monarch, Charles XII. He filled Europe with astonishment for a time by engaging in war with Denmark, Poland, and Russia and gaining many surprising victories. But his attempt to penetrate into Russia proved as fatal to him as a similar attempt did to Napoleon a century later. His prowess only served to set back Russia's plans for the moment. Three years after his death, which occurred in 1718, Peter forced Sweden to cede to him Livonia, Esthonia, and other Swedish territory which had previously cut Russia off from the sea.

890. Peter's Attempt to reach the Black Sea. Peter looked with longing eyes on the possessions of the Turks to the south of him, and he made vain attempts to extend the Russian control as far as the Black Sea. He did not succeed in this, but it had become evident that if the Turks were to be driven from Europe, Russia would prove a mighty rival of the other European powers in the division of the spoils.

For a generation after the death of Peter the Great, Russia fell into the hands of incompetent rulers. It only appears again as a European state when the great Catherine II came to the throne, in 1762. From that time on, the Western powers had always to consider the vast Slavic empire in all their great struggles. They had also to consider a new kingdom in northern Germany, which was just growing into a great power as Peter began his work. This was Prussia, whose beginnings we must now consider.

III. Origin of the Kingdom of Prussia

891. Brandenburg and the Hohenzollerns. The electorate of Brandenburg had figured on the map of Germany for centuries, and there was no particular reason to suppose that it was to become one day the dominant state in Germany and, finally, a great menace to the world. Early in the fifteenth century the

old line of electors had died out, and Emperor Sigismund had sold
Brandenburg to a hitherto unimportant house, the Hohenzollerns,
which is known to us now through such names as those of Frederick the Great, of William I, the first German emperor, and of
his grandson, the notorious "kaiser," William II. Beginning
with a strip of territory extending some ninety or a hundred miles
to the east and to the west of the little town of Berlin, the successive representatives of the line gradually extended their boundaries until the kingdom of Prussia embraced nearly two thirds

TERRITORIES OF THE GREAT ELECTOR OF BRANDENBURG

of Germany. Of the earlier little annexations nothing need be
said. While it has always been the pride of the Hohenzollern
family that almost every one of its reigning members has added
something to what his ancestors handed down to him, no great
extension took place until just before the Thirty Years' War.
About that time the electors of Brandenburg inherited Cleves
and Mark and thus got their first hold on the Rhine district.

892. Prussia acquired by the Elector of Brandenburg. What
was quite as important, a few years later the electors of Brandenburg won, far to the east, the duchy of Prussia, which was separated from Brandenburg by Polish territory. "Prussia" was
originally the name of a region on the Baltic inhabited by heathen
Slavs. These had been conquered in the thirteenth century by
one of the orders of crusading knights (the Teutonic order), who,

when the conquest of the Holy Land was abandoned, in the thirteenth century (§ 612), looked about for other occupation.

After the German knights had conquered Prussia it began to fill up with German colonists. In Luther's day (1525) the knights were converted to Protestantism and dissolved their order. They then formed their lands into the duchy of Prussia, and their Grand Master, who was a relative of the elector of Brandenburg, became their first duke. About a hundred years later (1618) this branch of the Hohenzollerns died out, and the duchy then fell to the elector of Brandenburg.

893. The Territories of the Great Elector (1640–1688). Notwithstanding this substantial territorial gain, there was little promise that the hitherto obscure electorate would ever become a formidable power when, in 1640, Frederick William, known as the Great Elector, came to the throne of Brandenburg. His territories were scattered from the Rhine to the Vistula, his army was of small account, and his authority was disputed by powerful nobles. The center of his domain was Brandenburg. Far to the west was Mark, bordering on the Rhine valley, and Cleves, lying on both banks of that river. Far to the east, beyond the Vistula, was the duchy of Prussia (see map, p. 605).

The Great Elector was, however, well fitted for the task of welding these domains into a powerful state. He was coarse by nature, heartless in destroying opponents, treacherous in diplomatic negotiations, and entirely devoid of the refinement which distinguished his contemporary, Louis XIV, and his court. He resolutely set to work to increase his territories and his power.

By shrewd tactics during the closing days of the Thirty Years' War he managed to secure, by the Treaty of Westphalia (§ 817), the bishoprics of Minden and Halberstadt and the duchy of Farther Pomerania, which gave him a good shore line on the Baltic.

894. Reforms of the Great Elector. Knowing that the interests of his house depended on military strength, he organized, in spite of the protests of the taxpayers, an army out of all proportion to the size and wealth of his dominions, and this was the beginning of that great Prussian war machine which was developed as time went on and showed its tremendous strength in the conflict which began in 1914. He succeeded in creating an absolute monarchy on the model furnished by Louis XIV. He joined with England and Holland in their alliances against Louis, and the army of Brandenburg began to be known and feared.

FIG. 157. MILITARY PUNISHMENT

The armies of the old régime were mostly made up of hired soldiers or serfs, and the officers maintained discipline by cruel punishments. In this picture of a Prussian regiment one soldier is being flogged while half suspended by his wrists; another is forced to walk between two files of soldiers who must beat his bared back with heavy rods. It has been said that these soldiers found war a relief from the terrors of peace, since in war time the punishments were lessened

Though a good Protestant, the Great Elector permitted religious freedom to a remarkable degree. He made Catholics eligible to office and, on the other hand, gave asylum to the persecuted Huguenots of France (§§ 788 ff.), even offering them special inducements to settle in his realms. As Frederick the Great said of him, he was his own prime minister and his own commander in chief.

895. Brandenburg becomes the Kingdom of Prussia (1701). It was accordingly a splendid legacy which the Great Elector left in 1688 to his son, Frederick III, and although the career of the latter was by no means so brilliant as that of his father, he induced the emperor to permit him to change his title from "elector" to "king" and so to transform his *electorate* into a *kingdom*.[1] The title "King in Prussia"[2] was deemed preferable to the more natural "King of Brandenburg" because Prussia lay wholly without the bounds of the empire, and consequently its ruler was not in any sense subject to the emperor but was entirely independent.

896. Militarism of Frederick William I (1713–1740). The second ruler of the new kingdom, Frederick William I, the father of Frederick the Great, was a rough and boorish king who devoted himself entirely to governing his realm, collecting tall soldiers, drilling his battalions, hunting wild game, and smoking strong tobacco. He was passionately fond of military life from his childhood. He took special pride in stalwart soldiers and collected them at great expense from all parts of Europe. He raised the Prussian army, which numbered twenty-seven thousand in the days of the Great Elector, to eighty-four thousand, making it almost equal to that maintained by France or Austria. He was constantly drilling and reviewing his men, whom he addressed as "my blue children."

Moreover, by constant management, miserly thrift, and entire indifference to luxury, Frederick William treasured up a huge sum of money. He discharged a large number of court servants, sold at auction many of the royal jewels, and had a great part of the family table silver coined into money. Consequently he was able to leave to his son, Frederick II, not only an admirable army but an ample supply of gold. Indeed, it was his toil and economy that made possible the achievements of his far more distinguished son.

---

[1] As king of Prussia his title was, of course, Frederick I.

[2] He was not king of all of Prussia. Frederick the Great changed it to "King of Prussia" after the incorporation of the rest, in the partition of Poland.

IV. The Wars of Frederick the Great

897. Accession of Frederick II, called "the Great" (1740–1786). In his early years Frederick II grieved and disgusted his boorish old father by his dislike for military life and his interest in books and music. He was a particular admirer of the French and preferred their language to his own. No sooner had he become king, however, than he suddenly developed marvelous energy and skill in warlike enterprises. Chance favored his designs.

898. Frederick's Attack upon Silesia. The Emperor Charles VI, the last representative of the direct male line of the Hapsburgs, died in 1740, just a few months before Frederick ascended the throne, leaving only a daughter, Maria Theresa, to inherit his vast and miscellaneous dominions. He had induced the other European powers to promise to accept the "pragmatic sanction," or solemn will, in which he left everything to the young Maria Theresa; but she had no sooner begun to reign than her greedy neighbors prepared to seize her lands. Her greatest enemy was the newly crowned king of Prussia, who at first pretended friendship for her. Frederick determined to seize Silesia, a strip of Hapsburg territory lying to the southeast of Brandenburg. He accordingly marched his army into the coveted district and occupied the important city of Breslau without declaring war or offering any excuse except a vague claim to a portion of the land.[1]

899. The War of the Austrian Succession. France, stimulated by Frederick's example, joined with Bavaria in the attack upon Maria Theresa. It seemed for a time as if her struggle to keep her realm intact would be vain, but the loyalty of all the various peoples under her scepter was roused by her extraordinary courage and energy. The French were driven back, but

---

[1] As no woman had ever been elected empress, the duke of Bavaria managed to secure the Holy Roman Empire, as Emperor Charles VII. Upon his death, however, in 1745, Maria Theresa's husband, Francis, duke of Lorraine, was chosen emperor. Their son, Joseph II, succeeded his father in 1765, and upon his death, in 1790, his brother Leopold II was elected. When he died, in 1792, the empire fell to his son Francis II, who was the last of the "Roman" emperors but assumed the new title "Emperor of Austria."

Maria Theresa was forced to grant Silesia to Frederick in order to induce him to retire from the war. Finally, England and Holland joined in an alliance for maintaining the balance of power, for they had no desire to see France annex the Austrian Netherlands. A few years later (1748) all the powers, tired of the war,— which is known as the War of the Austrian Succession,—laid down their arms and agreed to what is called in diplomacy the *status quo ante bellum*, which simply means that things were to be restored to the condition in which they had been before the opening of hostilities.

FIG. 158. FREDERICK THE GREAT

900. Policy of Frederick the Great. Frederick was, however, permitted to keep Silesia, which increased his dominions by about one third of their former extent. He now turned some of his attention to making his kingdom richer by draining the swamps, promoting industry, and drawing up a new code of laws. He found time, also, to gratify his interest in men of letters and invited Voltaire, the famous French writer, to make his home at Berlin. It will not seem strange to anyone who knows anything of the character of these two men that they quarreled after two or three years and that Voltaire left the Prussian king with very bitter feelings. (See also § 915.)

901. The Seven Years' War; the Alliance between France and Austria. Maria Theresa was by no means reconciled to the loss of Silesia, and she began to lay her plans for expelling the perfidious Frederick and regaining her lost territory. This led to one of the most important wars in modern history, in which not only almost every European power joined but which involved the whole world, from the Indian rajahs of Hindustan to the colonists of Virginia and New England. This Seven Years' War (1756–1763) will be considered in its broader aspects in the next chapter (§§ 943–946). We shall mention here only the part played in it by the king of Prussia.

Maria Theresa's ambassador at Paris was so skillful in his negotiations with the French court that in 1756 he induced it, in spite of its two hundred years of hostility to the House of Hapsburg, to enter into an alliance with Austria against Prussia. Russia, Sweden, and Saxony also agreed to join in a concerted attack on Prussia. Their armies, coming as they did from every point of the compass, threatened the complete annihilation of Austria's rival. It seemed as if Frederick's armies might be wiped out and the new kingdom of Prussia might disappear altogether from the map of Europe.

902. Frederick's Victorious Defense. However, it was in this war that Frederick earned his title of "the Great" and showed himself the equal of the ablest generals the world has seen, from Alexander to Napoleon. Undaunted by the overwhelming numbers of his enemies and by the loss of several battles, Frederick defeated the French and his German enemies in the most famous, perhaps, of his battles, at Rossbach in 1757. A month later he routed the Austrians brilliantly at Leuthen, not far from Breslau. Thereupon the Swedes and the Russians retired from the field and left Frederick for the moment master of the situation.

England now engaged the French and left Frederick at liberty to deal with his other enemies. Money paid him by the English government helped him to stay in the field, but for a time it looked as if he might, after all, be vanquished. But the accession of a new Tsar, who was an ardent admirer of Frederick, led Russia to conclude peace with Prussia, whereupon Maria Theresa reluctantly agreed to give up once more her struggle with her inveterate enemy. Shortly afterwards England and France came to terms, and a general settlement was made at Paris in 1763 (see below, § 946).

V. Three Partitions of Poland, 1772, 1793, and 1795

903. Question of West Prussia. Frederick's success in seizing and holding one of Austria's finest provinces did not satisfy him. The central portions of his kingdom — Brandenburg, Silesia, and Pomerania — were completely cut off from East Prussia by a considerable tract known as West Prussia, which belonged to the kingdom of Poland. The upper map on the opposite page will show how great must have been Frederick's temptation to fill this gap, especially as he well knew that Poland was in no condition to defend its possessions.

904. Weakness of Poland. With the exception of Russia, Poland was the largest kingdom in Europe. It covered an immense plain with no natural boundaries, and the population, which was very thinly scattered, belonged to several races. Besides the Poles themselves there were Germans in the cities of West Prussia and Russians in Lithuania. The Jews were very numerous everywhere, forming half of the population in some of the towns. The Poles were usually Catholics, while the Germans were Protestants and the Russians adhered to the Greek Church. These differences in religion, added to those of race, created endless problems and dissensions and explain many of the difficulties involved in the attempt to reëstablish an independent Polish republic after the great World War.

The government of Poland was the worst imaginable. Instead of having developed a strong monarchy, as her neighbors — Prussia, Russia, and Austria — had done, she remained in a state of feudal anarchy, which the nobles had taken the greatest pains to perpetuate by binding their kings in such a way that they had no power either to maintain order or to defend the country from attack. The king could not declare war, make peace, impose taxes, or pass any law, without the consent of the diet. As the diet was composed of representatives of the nobility, any one of whom could freely veto any measure,— for no measure could pass that had even one vote against it,— most of the diets broke up without accomplishing anything.

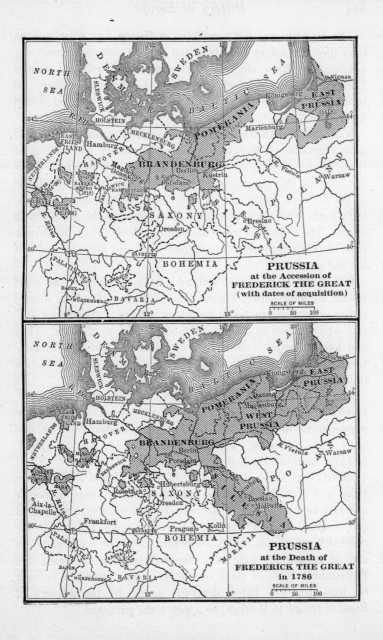

PRUSSIA
at the Accession of
FREDERICK THE GREAT
(with dates of acquisition)

SCALE OF MILES
0   50   100

PRUSSIA
at the Death of
FREDERICK THE GREAT
in 1786

SCALE OF MILES
0   50   100

The kingship was not hereditary in Poland, but whenever the ruler died the nobles assembled and chose a new one, commonly a foreigner. These elections were tumultuous, and the various European powers regularly interfered, by force or bribery, to secure the election of a candidate whom they believed would favor their interests.

905. The Polish Nobles and Peasants. The nobles in Poland were numerous. There were perhaps a million and a half of them, mostly very poor, owning only a trifling bit of land. There was a saying that the poor noble's dog, even if he sat in the middle of his master's estate, was sure to have his tail upon a neighbor's land. There was no middle class except in the few German towns. The peasants were miserable indeed. They had sunk from serfs to slaves over whom their lords had even the right of life and death.

906. First Partition of Poland (1772). It required no great insight to foresee that Poland was in danger of falling a prey to her greedy and powerful neighbors, Russia, Prussia, and Austria, who clamped in the unfortunate kingdom on all sides. They had long shamelessly interfered in its affairs and had actually taken active measures to oppose all reforms of the constitution in order that they might profit by the chronic anarchy.

The ruler of Russia was the famous Catherine II (see below, § 916), who arranged with Frederick the Great to prevent any improvement in Poland and to keep up and encourage the disorder. Finally, Poland's kind neighbors, including Austria, agreed, in 1772, each to take a slice of the unhappy kingdom.

Austria was assigned a strip inhabited by almost three million Poles and Russians and thus added two new kinds of people and two new languages to her already varied collection of races and tongues. Prussia was given a smaller piece, but it was the coveted West Prussia, which she needed to fill out her boundaries, and its inhabitants were to a considerable extent Germans and Protestants. Russia's strip, on the east, was inhabited entirely by Russians. The Polish diet was forced, by the advance of Russian troops to Warsaw, to approve the partition.

907. Revival of Poland (1772–1791). Poland seemed at first, however, to have learned a great lesson from the disaster. During the twenty years following its first dismemberment there was an extraordinary revival in education, art, and literature. Historians and poets sprang up to give distinction to the last days of Polish independence. The constitution which had made Poland the

FIG. 159. A CARTOON OF THE PARTITION OF POLAND

Catherine II, Joseph II, and Frederick II are pointing out the part of the map of Poland they each propose to take. The king of Poland is trying to hold his crown from falling off his head. What is left of Poland on the map?

laughingstock and the victim of its neighbors was abolished, and an entirely new one worked out. It did away with the free veto of the nobles, made the crown hereditary, and established a parliament somewhat like that of England.

Russia had no desire that Poland should become a strong monarchy, and it sent soldiers to help the enemies of the new constitution on the ground that Russia could not bear to see any changes in the government "under which the Polish commonwealth had flourished for so many centuries." Russia and Prussia, having secured the continuance of disorder in Poland, declared that they could not put up with such a dangerous neighbor and proceeded to a second partition in 1793.

908. Second Partition (1793). Prussia cut deep into Poland, added a million and a half of Poles to her subjects, and acquired the towns of Thorn, Danzig, and Posen. Russia's gains were three millions of people, who at least belonged to her own race. On this occasion Austria was put off with the promises of her confederates, Russia and Prussia, that they would use their good offices to secure Bavaria for her in exchange for the Austrian Netherlands.

909. Revolt of Kosciusko (1794). At this juncture the Poles found a national leader in the brave Kosciusko, who had fought under Washington for American liberty. With the utmost care and secrecy he organized an insurrection in the spring of 1794 and summoned the Polish people to join his standard of national independence. The Poles who had been incorporated into the Prussian monarchy thereupon rose and forced Prussia to withdraw its forces.

910. Third and Final Partition (1795). Russia was ready, however, to crush the patriots. Kosciusko was wounded and captured in battle, and by the end of the year Russia was in control of Warsaw. The Polish king was compelled to abdicate, and the remnants of the dismembered kingdom were divided, after much bitter contention, among Austria, Russia, and Prussia. In the three partitions which blotted out the kingdom of Poland from the map of Europe, Russia received nearly twice the combined shares of Austria and Prussia.

VI. The Austrian Realms: Maria Theresa and Joseph II

911. The Hapsburgs in Austria. While the Hohenzollerns of Prussia from their capital at Berlin had been extending their power over northern Germany, the great house of Hapsburg, established in the southeastern corner of Germany, with its capital at Vienna, had been grouping together, by conquest or inheritance, the vast realm over much of which it ruled down to the end of the World War, in 1918. It will be remembered that Charles V, shortly after his accession, ceded to his brother, Ferdinand I, the German or Austrian possessions of the house of Hapsburg (§ 779), while he himself retained the Spanish, Burgundian, and Italian dominions. Ferdinand, by a fortunate marriage with the heiress of the kingdoms of Bohemia and Hungary, greatly augmented his territory. Hungary was, however, almost completely conquered by the Turks at that time, and till the end of the seventeenth century the energies of the Austrian rulers were largely absorbed in a long struggle against the Mohammedans.

912. Conquests of the Turks in Europe. A Turkish tribe from western Asia had, at the opening of the fourteenth century, established themselves in western Asia Minor under their leader, Othman (d. 1326). It was from him that they derived their name of Ottoman Turks, to distinguish them from the Seljuk Turks, with whom the crusaders had come into contact. The leaders of the Ottoman Turks showed great energy. They not only extended their Asiatic territory far toward the east, and later into Africa, but they gained a footing in Europe as early as 1353. They gradually conquered the Slavic peoples in Macedonia and occupied the territory about Constantinople, although it was a hundred years before they succeeded in capturing the ancient capital of the Eastern Empire.

This advance of the Turks naturally aroused grave fears in the states of western Europe lest they too might be deprived of their independence. The brunt of the defense against the common foe devolved upon Venice and the German Hapsburgs, who carried on an almost continuous war with the Turks for nearly two centuries. As late as 1683 the Mohammedans collected a large force and besieged Vienna, which might very well have fallen into their hands had it not been for the timely assistance which the city received from the king of Poland. From this time on, the power of the Turks in Europe rapidly decreased, and the Hapsburgs were able to regain the whole territory of Hungary and

Transylvania. Their possession of these lands, which they held until 1918, was recognized by the Sultan in 1699.

913. Heterogeneous Population under the Hapsburgs. The conquest of Silesia by Frederick the Great was more than a severe blow to the pride of Maria Theresa; for, since it was inhabited by Germans, its loss lessened the Hapsburg power inside the empire. In extent of territory the Hapsburgs more than made up for it by the partitions of Poland, but since the Poles were an alien race they added one more difficulty to the very difficult problem of ruling so many various peoples, each of whom had a different language and different customs and institutions. The Hapsburg possessions were inhabited by Germans in Austria proper, a Slav people (the Czechs) mixed with Germans in Bohemia and Moravia, Poles in Galicia, Hungarians or Magyars along with Rumanians and smaller groups of other peoples in Hungary; Croats and Slovenes (both Slavs) in the south, Italians in Milan and Tuscany, and Flemish and Walloons in the Netherlands.

FIG. 160. MARIA THERESA

The problems which confronted Maria Theresa and her son Joseph II were much more difficult than those of France or England. Poles, Italians, Magyars, and Germans could never be united into one state by such common interests as Englishmen or Frenchmen have felt so keenly in the last two centuries. Instead of fusing together to form a nation, the peoples ruled over by the Hapsburgs have been on such bad terms with each other that with the terrible disasters of the World War they finally split apart, forming separate nations. Moreover, since some of its peoples, especially the Slavs, Poles, and Rumanians, lived in neighboring states as well, the Hapsburg monarchy was always much concerned in what happened outside its borders. The immediate cause of the terrible conflict which began in 1914 was trouble between Austria and her neighbor Serbia. So if one hopes to understand the great questions of our own time he must follow carefully the complicated history of Austria and her ever-changing realms.

VII. Reforms of Frederick II, Catherine II, and Joseph II

914. The "Benevolent Despots." The monarchs whose wars we have been following — Frederick the Great, Catherine the Great, Maria Theresa, and Emperor Joseph II — are commonly known as the "enlightened" or "benevolent" despots. They were no doubt more "enlightened" than the older kings ; at least they all read books and associated with learned men. But they were not more "benevolent" than Charlemagne, or Canute, or St. Louis, or many other monarchs of earlier centuries, who had believed it their duty to do all they could for the welfare of their people. On the other hand, the monarchs of the eighteenth century were certainly despots in the full sense of the word. They held that all the powers of the State were vested in them, and had no idea of permitting their subjects any share in the government. Moreover, they waged war upon one another as their predecessors had done, and were constantly trying, as we have seen, to add to their own territories by robbing their neighbors.

915. Attitude of Frederick the Great. When Frederick the Great became king he devoted himself less to music and philosophy and more to the practical problems of government. He allowed the people no part in the government, it is true, but he worked very hard himself. He rose early and was busy all day. He was his own prime minister and the real head of all branches of the government, watching over the army and leading it in battle, attending to foreign affairs, guarding the finances, overseeing the courts, journeying up and down the land investigating the conduct of his officials and examining into the condition of his people.

In religious matters Frederick was extremely tolerant; he held that his subjects should be allowed to worship God in any way they pleased. His kingdom had long been Protestant, but there were many Catholics in various parts of it. He welcomed Huguenots and Jesuits with equal cordiality and admitted Catholics as well as Protestants to his service. "I stand neutral between Rome and Geneva," he once said; "he who wrongs his brother of a different faith shall be punished; were I to declare for one or the other creed I should excite party spirit and persecution; my aim, on the contrary, is to show the adherents of the different churches that they are all fellow citizens."

916. Catherine II, Empress of Russia (1762–1796). In Russia, Peter the Great had been a genuine "benevolent despot," although the benevolence was more apparent to later generations than to his own half-Asiatic subjects.[1] But in the days of Frederick the Great the ruler of all the Russias was a German woman, Catherine II, who is one of the most picturesque and interesting figures in history. She was the daughter of one of Frederick the Great's officers and had been selected by him in 1743, at the request of the Tsarina Elizabeth, Peter's younger daughter, as a suitable wife for her nephew, the heir to the throne. At the age of fourteen this inexperienced girl found herself in the midst of the intrigues of the court at St. Petersburg; she joined the Greek Church, exchanged her name of Sophia for that of Catherine, and, by zealous study of both books and men, prepared to make her new name famous. Her husband, who ruled for six months as Peter III, proved to be a worthless fellow, who early began to neglect and maltreat her. Catherine won over the imperial guard and had herself proclaimed empress. Peter was forced to abdicate and was carried off by some of Catherine's supporters, who put him to death, probably with her tacit consent.

---

[1] Peter was succeeded in 1725 by his widow, Catherine, who ruled ably for two years. His son Alexis had been tortured to death in prison for rebellion, and Alexis' son Peter II, who followed Catherine, was reactionary. Under Anne (1730–1740), niece of Peter I, German influence triumphed. Then came Elizabeth (1741–1762), Peter's younger daughter, referred to in the text. She hated Frederick II for his personal remarks about her and aided Maria Theresa against him.

917. Character of Catherine the Great. In the spirit of Peter the Great, Catherine determined to carry on the Europeanizing of Russia and extend her empire. She was thoroughly unscrupulous and hypocritical, but she was shrewd in the choice and management of her ministers and was herself a hard worker. She rose at six o'clock in the morning, hurried through her toilet, prepared her own light breakfast, and turned to the exacting and dull business of government, carefully considering the reports laid before her relating to the army, the navy, finances, and foreign affairs.

FIG. 161. CATHERINE II

Catherine II showed herself almost as interested in the French philosophers and reformers of the time [1] as did Frederick. In her frequent letters to Voltaire she explained to him her various plans for reform.

918. Catherine maintains Serfdom but seizes the Church Lands. There was some talk of abolishing serfdom in Russia, but Catherine rather increased than decreased the number of serfs, and she made their lot harder than it had been before by forbidding them to complain of the treatment they received at the hands of their masters. She appropriated the vast property of the churches and monasteries, using the revenue to support the clergy and monks, and such surplus as remained she devoted to schools and hospitals.

919. Rash Reforms of Joseph II (1765–1790). It is clear that while Frederick and Catherine expressed great admiration for the

---

[1] The views of the reformers who preceded the French Revolution will be considered in the second volume of this history.

reformers, they did not attempt to make any sweeping changes in the laws or the social order. Emperor Joseph II, who, after the death of his mother, Maria Theresa, in 1780, became ruler of the Austrian dominions, had, however, the courage of his convictions. He proposed to transform the scattered and heterogeneous territories over which he ruled into a well-organized state in which disorder, confusion, prejudice, fanaticism, and intellectual bondage should disappear and all his subjects be put in possession of their "natural" rights. Germans, Hungarians, Italians, Poles, Bohemians, and Belgians were all to use the German language in official communications. The old irregular territorial divisions were abolished and his realms divided into thirteen new provinces. All the ancient privileges enjoyed by the towns and the local assemblies were done away with and replaced by a uniform system of government in which his own officials enjoyed the control.

He attacked the Church, which was so powerful in his realms. He was heartily opposed to the monks; he consequently abolished some six hundred of their monasteries and used their property for charitable purposes and to establish schools. He appointed the bishops without consulting the Pope and forbade money to be sent to Rome. Marriage was declared to be merely a civil contract and so was taken out of the control of the priests. Lutherans, Calvinists, and other heretics were allowed to worship in their own way.

Joseph II sought to complete his work by attacking the surviving features of feudalism and encouraging the development of manufactures. He freed the serfs in Bohemia, Moravia, Galicia, and Hungary, transforming the peasants into tenants; elsewhere he reduced the services due from them to the lord. He taxed nobles and clergy without regard to their claims to exemption and supplanted the confused and uncertain laws by a uniform system which is the basis of Austrian law to-day.

Naturally Joseph met opposition on every hand. The clergy abhorred him as an oppressor, and all who were forced to sacrifice their old privileges did what they could to block his reforms, however salutary they might be. Joseph died in 1790, a sadly disappointed man. He had been forced to undo almost all that he had hoped to accomplish, and his reforms left few permanent results.

920. General Policy of the Benevolent Despots. It has become clear, as we have reviewed the activities of these benevolent despots, that all of them were chiefly intent upon increasing their own power ; they were more despotic than they were benevolent. They opposed the power of the Pope and brought the clergy under their own control. In some cases they took a portion of the property of the churches and monasteries. They tried to improve the laws and do away with the existing contradictions and obscurities. They endeavored to "centralize" the administration and to place all the power in the hands of their own officials instead of leaving it with the nobles or the old local assemblies. They encouraged agriculture, commerce, and industries in various ways. All these measures were undertaken primarily with a view to strengthening the autocratic power of the ruler and increasing the revenue and the military strength of his government, for none of these energetic monarchs showed any willingness to admit the people to a share in the government, and only Joseph II ventured to attempt to free the serfs.

QUESTIONS

I. In what portions of eastern Europe were the Slavs settling during the barbarian invasions ? What is supposed to be the origin of the name "Russia"? Give some of the results of the domination of Russia by the Mongols.

II. What were the boundaries of Russia upon the accession of Peter the Great ? What territories did he add ? What were some of Peter's reforms ?

III. Explain how the elector of Brandenburg came to have the title of "King of Prussia." Mention some of the chief rulers of the Hohenzollern line. What had been accomplished toward making Prussia a great European power before the accession of Frederick the Great ?

IV. Give an account of the War of the Austrian Succession. What were the chief events of the Seven Years' War ? What have you learned of Frederick the Great ? Why was he a great admirer of the French ?

V. Describe the conditions in Poland in the eighteenth century. How was the first partition of Poland arranged? When did the second partition take place and why was Austria left out? Under what conditions did the third partition take place?

VI. Explain the relations of Austria and the Turks. What was the extent of the Hapsburg dominions when Maria Theresa came to the throne. Mention as many as you can of the peoples under the rule of Maria Theresa. Why are the former Austrian dominions specially interesting to us to-day?

VII. Who were the "benevolent" despots and why are they so called? In what ways did Frederick the Great attempt to reform his kingdom? Who was Catherine the Great? Describe her policy. Mention the reforms of Joseph II.

CHAPTER XXXVIII

HOW ENGLAND BECAME QUEEN OF THE OCEAN

I. ENGLAND AFTER THE REVOLUTION OF 1688

921. England establishes her Supremacy on the Sea. In the last chapter we reviewed the progress of affairs in eastern Europe and noted the development of two new European powers, Prussia and Russia, which have for the past two centuries played a great part in the affairs of the world. In the West, England was rapidly becoming the most important state. While she did not greatly influence the course of the wars on the Continent she was already beginning to make herself mistress of the seas— a position which she still holds, owing to her colonies and her unrivaled fleet.

At the close of the War of the Spanish Succession her navy was superior to that of any other power, for both France and Spain had been greatly weakened by the long conflict. Fifty years after the Treaty of Utrecht, England had succeeded in driving out the French both from North America and from India and in laying the foundations of her vast empire beyond the seas, which still gives her the commercial supremacy of the world.

922. Questions settled by the Accession of William and Mary. With the accession of William and Mary in 1688 (§ 854) England may be said to have practically settled the two great questions that had produced such serious dissensions during the previous fifty years. In the first place, the nation had clearly shown that it proposed to remain Protestant in spite of the Catholic sympathies of her former Stuart kings ; and the relations between the Church of England and the dissenters were gradually being satisfactorily adjusted. In the second place, the powers of the king had been carefully defined, and from the opening of the eighteenth century to the present time no English monarch has ventured to veto an act of Parliament.[1]

923. The Union of England and Scotland (1707). William III was succeeded in 1702 by his sister-in-law, Anne, a younger daughter of James II. Far more important than the war which her generals carried on against Spain was the final union of England and Scotland. As we have seen, the difficulties between the two countries had led to much bloodshed and suffering ever since Edward I's futile attempt to conquer Scotland (§ 562).

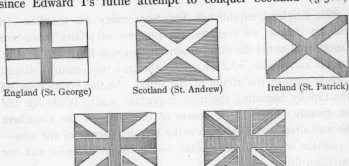

England (St. George)   Scotland (St. Andrew)   Ireland (St. Patrick)

Great Britain   Great Britain and Ireland

FIG. 162. THE UNION JACK[2]

The two countries had, it is true, been under the same ruler since the accession of James I, but each had maintained its own independent parliament and system of government. Finally, in 1707, both nations agreed to unite their governments into one. Forty-five members of the British House of Commons were to be chosen thereafter in Scotland, and sixteen Scotch lords were to be added to the English House of Lords. In this way the whole island of Great Britain was placed under a single government, and the occasions for strife were thereby greatly reduced.

1 The last instance in which an English ruler vetoed a measure passed by Parliament was in 1707.

2 The flag of Great Britain, combining the crosses of St. George and St. Andrew, was called the Union Jack from *Jacques*, the French form of James I, the first king of Great Britain. The cross of Ireland was added upon its union with Great Britain in 1801. Upright lines indicate red; horizontal lines, blue.

924. Accession of George I (1714–1727) of Hanover. Since none of Anne's children survived her, she was succeeded, according to an arrangement made before her accession, by the nearest Protestant heir. This was the son of James I's granddaughter Sophia. She had married the elector of Hanover[1]; consequently the new king of England, George I, was also elector of Hanover and a member of the Holy Roman Empire.[2]

925. England and the "Balance of Power." William of Orange had been a continental statesman before he became king of England, and his chief aim had always been to prevent France from becoming overpowerful. He had joined in the War of the Spanish Succession in order to maintain the "balance of power" between the various European countries.[3] During the eighteenth century England continued, for the same reason, to engage in the struggles between the continental powers, although she had no expectation of attempting to extend her sway across the Channel. The wars which she waged in order to increase her own

[1] Originally there had been seven electors (§ 728), but the duke of Bavaria had been made an elector during the Thirty Years' War, and in 1692 the father of George I had been permitted to assume the title of "Elector of Hanover."

[2] James I (1603–1625)

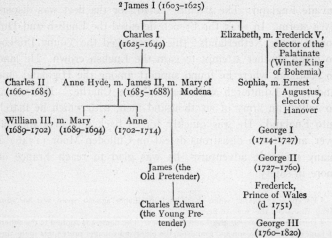

[3] Wolsey, it will be recalled, advanced the same reason in Henry VIII's time for England's intervention in continental wars (§ 760).

power and territory were carried on in distant parts of the world and more often on sea than on land.

926. Walpole's Policy of Peace. For a quarter of a century after the Treaty of Utrecht, England enjoyed peace.[1] Under the influence of Sir Robert Walpole, who for twenty-one years directed the government, peace was maintained within and without. Not only did Walpole avoid going to war with other countries but he was careful to prevent the ill feeling at home from developing into civil strife. His principle was to "let sleeping dogs lie"; so he strove to conciliate the dissenters and to pacify the Jacobites,[2] as those were called who still desired to have the Stuarts return.

927. "Prince Charlie," the Young Pretender, in Scotland. When, in 1740, Frederick the Great and the French attacked Maria Theresa (§§ 898, 899), England's sympathies were with the injured queen. As elector of Hanover, George II (who had succeeded his father in 1727) led an army of German troops against the French and defeated them on the river Main. Frederick then declared war on England; and France sent the grandson of James II,[3] the Young Pretender, as he was called, with a fleet to invade England. The attempt failed, for the fleet was dispersed by a storm. In 1745 the French defeated the English and Dutch forces in the Netherlands; this encouraged the Young Pretender to make another attempt to gain the English crown. He landed in Scotland, where he found support among the Highland chiefs, and even Edinburgh welcomed "Prince Charlie." He was able to collect an army of six thousand men, with which he marched into England. He was quickly forced back into Scotland, however, and after a disastrous defeat on Culloden Moor (1746) and many romantic adventures, he was glad to reach France once more in safety.

---

[1] Except in 1718-1720, when she joined an alliance against Spain, and her admiral, Byng, destroyed the Spanish fleet.

[2] Derived from *Jacobus*, the Latin for James. The name was applied to the adherents of James II and of his son and grandson, the elder and younger pretenders to the throne.

[3] The children of James II by his second and Catholic wife, Mary of Modena, had been excluded from the throne at the accession of William and Mary.

Soon after the close of the War of the Austrian Succession in 1748, England entered upon a series of wars which were destined profoundly to affect not only her position but also the fate of distant portions of the globe. But before considering these we must see what changes were taking place in the English government in the eighteenth century.

II. THE ENGLISH LIMITED MONARCHY IN THE EIGHTEENTH CENTURY AND GEORGE III

928. Limited Monarchy of England. In striking contrast to the absolute rule of the "benevolent despots" on the Continent, the island of Britain was, as we have seen, governed by its Parliament. There the king, from the Revolution of 1688 on, had owed his crown to Parliament and admitted that he was limited by the constitution, which he had to obey. This did not prevent at least one English king from trying to have his own way in spite of the restrictions placed upon him, as we shall see.

929. Whigs and Tories. There were two great political parties in England — the Whigs, successors of the Roundheads, who advocated the supremacy of Parliament and championed toleration for the Dissenters ; and the Tories, who, like the earlier Cavaliers (§ 839), upheld the divine right of kings and the supremacy of the Anglican, or Established, Church. After the death of Anne many of the Tories favored calling to the throne the son of James II (popularly called "the old Pretender"), whereupon the Whigs succeeded in discrediting their rivals by denouncing them as Jacobites and traitors. They made the new Hanoverian king, George I, believe that he owed everything to the Whigs, and for a period of nearly fifty years, under George I and George II, they were able to control Parliament.

930. Robert Walpole, Prime Minister (1721-1742). George I himself spoke no English, was ignorant of English politics, and was much more interested in Hanover than in his new kingdom. He did not attend the meetings of his ministers, as his predecessors had done, and turned over the management of affairs to the Whig leaders. They found a skillful "boss" and a judicious statesman in Sir Robert Walpole, who maintained his own power and that of his party by avoiding war and preventing religious dissensions at home. He used the king's funds to buy the votes necessary to maintain the Whig majority in the House of Commons and to get his measures through that body. He was England's first "prime minister."

931. Development of the Cabinet and the Office of Prime Minister. The existence of two well-defined political parties standing for widely different policies forced the king to choose all his ministers from either one or the other. The more prominent among his advisers came gradually to form a little group who resigned together if Parliament refused to accept the measures they advocated. In this way the "cabinet government," begun under William III, developed, with a prime minister, or premier, at its head. Under weak monarchs the prime minister would naturally be the real ruler of the kingdom.

932. The Position of the King. It was still possible, to be sure, for the king to profit by the jealousies of rival statesmen and by favoring first one, then another, to keep the upper hand. This was especially the case after the Tories gave up hope of restoring the Stuarts, upon the failure of Prince Charles in 1745 (§ 927), so that the Hanoverian kings no longer needed to rely upon the Whigs as the one loyal party.

933. George III and Parliament. Finally, George III, who came to the throne in 1760, succeeded in getting a party of his own, known as the "King's Friends," and with their aid, and a liberal use of what would now be regarded as bribery and graft, ran the government much as he wanted to. His mother, a German princess, had taught him that he ought to be a king like those on the Continent; and, in spite of the restrictions of Parliament, he did rule in a high-handed and headstrong way. During the war with the American colonies, which soon broke out, he was practically his own prime minister.

934. Growing Demand for Reform. The really weak spot in the English constitution, however, was less the occasional high-handedness of the king than the fact that Parliament did not represent the nation as a whole. Already in the eighteenth century there was no little discontent with the monopoly which the landed gentry and the rich enjoyed in Parliament. There was an increasing number of writers to point out to the people the defects in the English system. They urged that every man should have the right to participate in the government by casting his vote and that the unwritten constitution of England should be written down and so made clear and unmistakable. Political clubs were founded, which entered into correspondence with political societies in France ; newspapers and pamphlets poured from the press in enormous quantities, and political reform found champions in the House of Commons.

935. The Younger Pitt. This demand for reform finally induced the younger Pitt, son of the Earl of Chatham, who was prime minister from 1783 to 1801, to introduce bills into the House of Commons for remedying some inequalities in representation. But the violence and disorder accompanying the French Revolution, which began in 1789, involved England in a long and tedious war and discredited reform with Englishmen who had formerly favored change, to say nothing of the Tories, who regarded with horror any proposal looking toward an extension of popular government.

936. England had a Modern Free Government but not a Democracy. It is clear that England possessed the elements of a modern free government, for her king was master of neither the persons nor the purses of his subjects, nor could he issue arbitrary laws. Political affairs were discussed in newspapers and pamphlets, so that weighty matters of government could not be decided secretly in the king's closet without the knowledge of his subjects. Nevertheless it would be far from correct to regard the English system as democratic.

A hereditary House of Lords could block any measure introduced in the House of Commons, and the House of Commons itself represented not the nation but a small minority of landowners and traders. Government offices were monopolized by members of the Established Church, and the poor were oppressed by cruel criminal laws administered by officials chosen by the king. Workingmen were prohibited from forming associations to promote their interests. It was more than a century after the accession of George III before the English peasant could go to the ballot box and vote for members of Parliament.

III. How Europe began to extend its Commerce over the Whole World

937. Vast Extent of the European Colonial Dominion. The long and disastrous wars of the eighteenth century were much more than merely quarrels of monarchs. They were caused also by commercial and colonial rivalries, and they extended to the most distant parts of the world. In the War of the Spanish Succession the trade of Spain was at stake as well as the throne. From the seventeenth century on, the internal affairs of each country have been constantly influenced by the demands of its merchants, and the achievements of its sailors and soldiers, fighting rival nations or alien peoples thousands of miles from London, Paris, or Vienna. The great manufacturing towns of England— Leeds, Manchester, and Birmingham—owe their prosperity to India, China, and Australia. Liverpool, Amsterdam, and Triest, with their long lines of docks and warehouses and their fleets of merchant vessels, would dwindle away if their trade were confined to the demands of their European neighbors.

Europe includes scarcely a twelfth of the land upon the globe, and yet over three fifths of the world is to-day either occupied by peoples of European origin or ruled by European states. The possessions of France in Asia and Africa exceed the entire area of Europe; even the little kingdom of the Netherlands administers a colonial dominion three times the size of Germany. The British Empire, of which the island of Great Britain is but a hundredth part, includes one fifth of the world's dry land. Moreover, European peoples have populated the United States (which is nearly as large as all of Europe), Mexico, and South America.

The widening of the field of European history is one of the most striking features of modern times. Though the Greeks and Romans carried on a large trade in silks, spices, and precious stones with India and China, they really knew little of the world beyond southern Europe, northern Africa, and western Asia, and much that they knew was forgotten during the Middle Ages. Slowly, however, the interest in the East revived, and travelers began to add to the scanty knowledge handed down from antiquity.

938. Colonial Policy of Portugal, Spain, and Holland. The voyages which had brought America and India within the ken of Europe during the fifteenth and early sixteenth centuries were, as we know, mainly undertaken by the Portuguese and the Spaniards. Portugal was the first to realize the advantage of extending her commerce by establishing stations in India after Vasco da Gama rounded the Cape of Good Hope in 1498 (§ 673) ; and later by founding posts on the Brazilian coast of South America ; then Spain laid claim to Mexico, the West Indies, and a great part of South America. These two powers later found a formidable rival in the Dutch, who succeeded in expelling the Portuguese from a number of their settlements in India and the Spice Islands and brought Java, Sumatra, and other tropical regions under Dutch control.

939. The French and English in North America. In North America the chief rivals were England and France, both of which succeeded in establishing colonies in the early part of the seventeenth century. Englishmen settled at Jamestown in Virginia (1607), then in New England, Maryland, Pennsylvania, and elsewhere. The colonies owed their growth in part to the influx of refugees,— Puritans, Catholics, and Quakers,— who exiled themselves in the hope of gaining the right freely to enjoy their particular forms of religion. On the other hand, many came in order to better their fortunes in the New World, and thousands of bond servants and slaves were brought over as laborers.

Just as Jamestown was being founded by the English the French were making their first successful settlement in Nova Scotia and at Quebec. Although England made no attempt to oppose it, the

French occupation of Canada progressed very slowly. In 1673 Marquette, a Jesuit missionary, and Joliet, a merchant, explored a part of the Mississippi River. La Salle sailed down the great stream and named the new country which he entered, Louisiana, after his king. The city of New Orleans was founded, near the mouth of the river, in 1718, and the French established a chain of forts between it and Montreal.

The contest between England and France for the supremacy in North America was responsible for almost continuous border war, which burst out more fiercely with each war in the Old World. Finally, England was able, by the Treaty of Utrecht, to establish herself in the northern regions, for France thereby ceded to her Newfoundland, Nova Scotia, and the borders of Hudson Bay (§ 877). While the English in North America at the beginning of the Seven Years' War numbered over a million, the French did not reach a hundred thousand.

IV. The Contest between France and England for Colonial Empire

940. Extent of India. The rivalry of England and France was not confined to the wildernesses of North America, occupied by half a million of savage red men. At the opening of the eighteenth century both countries had gained a firm foothold on the borders of the vast Indian empire, inhabited by two hundred millions of people and the seat of an ancient and highly developed civilization. One may gain some idea of the extent of India by laying the map of Hindustan upon that of the United States. If the southernmost point, Cape Comorin, be placed over New Orleans, Calcutta will lie nearly over New York City, and Bombay in the neighborhood of Des Moines, Iowa.

941. The Mongolian Emperors of Hindustan. A generation after Vasco da Gama rounded the Cape, a Mongolian conqueror, Baber, had established his empire in India. The dynasty of Mongolian rulers which he founded was able to keep the whole country under its control for nearly two centuries; then after the death

of the Great Mogul Aurungzeb, in 1707, their empire began to
fall apart in much the same way as that of Charlemagne had
done. Like the counts and dukes of the Carolingian period, the
emperor's officials, the subahdars and nawabs (nabobs), and the
rajahs (Hindu princes who had been subjugated by the Mongols)
had gradually got the power in their respective districts into their

FIG. 163. THE TAJ MAHAL

This mausoleum of princes was built at Agra, India, in 1632. It has been
described as "the most splendidly poetic building in the world . . . a dream
in marble, which justifies the saying that the Moguls designed like Titans
but finished like jewelers." The entire building is of white marble, inlaid
with precious stones. Although this is regarded as the most perfect monument, India has many others of great magnificence, witnesses of the power
and wealth of her princes

own hands. Although the emperor, or Great Mogul, as the English called him, continued to maintain himself in his capital of
Delhi, he could no longer be said to rule the country at the opening of the eighteenth century, when the French and English were
beginning to turn their attention seriously to his coasts.

942. English and French Settlements in India. In the time
of Charles I (1639) a village had been purchased by the English

East India Company on the southeastern coast of Hindustan, which grew into the important English station of Madras. About the same time posts were established in the district of Bengal, and later Calcutta was fortified. Bombay was already an English station. The Mongolian emperor of India at first scarcely deigned to notice the presence of a few foreigners on the fringe of his vast realms, but before the end of the seventeenth century hostilities began between the English East India Company and the native rulers, which made it plain that the foreigners would be forced to defend themselves.

The English had to face not only the opposition of the natives but that of a European power as well. France also had an East India Company, and at the opening of the eighteenth century Pondicherry was its chief center, with a population of sixty thousand, of which two hundred only were Europeans. It soon became apparent that there was little danger from the Great Mogul ; moreover, the Portuguese and Dutch were out of the race, so the native princes and the French and English were left to fight among themselves for the supremacy.

943. England Victorious in the Struggle in America (1756–1763). Just before the clash of European rulers, known as the Seven Years' War, came, in 1756 (§ 901), the French and English had begun their struggle in both America and India. In America the so-called French and Indian War began in 1754 between the English and French colonists. General Braddock was sent from England to capture Fort Duquesne, which the French had established to keep their rivals out of the Ohio valley. Braddock knew nothing of border warfare, and he was killed and his troops routed. Fortunately for England, France, as the ally of Austria, was soon engaged in a war with Prussia that prevented her from giving proper attention to her American possessions. A famous statesman, the elder Pitt,[1] was now at the head of the English ministry. He was able not only to succor the hard-pressed king of Prussia with money and men but also to support the militia of the thirteen American colonies in their attacks upon the French. The

---

[1] So called to distinguish him from his son, prime minister later (see § 935).

French forts at Ticonderoga and Niagara were taken; Quebec was won in Wolfe's heroic attack, 1759; and the next year all Canada submitted to the English. England's supremacy on the sea was demonstrated by three admirals, each of whom destroyed a French fleet.

944. Dupleix and Clive in India. In India conflicts between the French and the English had occurred during the War of the Austrian Succession. The governor of the French station of Pondicherry was Dupleix, a soldier of great energy, who proposed to drive out the English and firmly establish the power of France over Hindustan. His chances of success were greatly increased by the quarrels among the native rulers, some of whom belonged to the earlier Hindu inhabitants and some to the Mohammedan Mongolians who had conquered India in 1526. Dupleix had very few French soldiers, but he began the enlistment of the natives, a custom eagerly adopted by the English. These native soldiers, whom the English called Sepoys, were taught to fight in the manner of Europeans.

945. Clive renders English Influence Supreme in India. But the English colonists, in spite of the fact that they were mainly traders, discovered among the clerks in Madras a leader equal in military skill and energy to Dupleix himself. Robert Clive, who was but twenty-five years old at this time, organized a large force of Sepoys and gained a remarkable ascendancy over them by his astonishing bravery.

At the moment that the Seven Years' War was beginning, bad news reached Clive from the English settlement of Calcutta, about a thousand miles to the northeast of Madras. The nawab of Bengal had seized the property of some English merchants and imprisoned one hundred and forty-five Englishmen in a little room,—the "black hole" of Calcutta,—where most of them died of suffocation before morning. Clive hastened to Bengal, and with a little army of nine hundred Europeans and fifteen hundred Sepoys he gained a great victory at Plassey, in 1757, over the nawab's army of fifty thousand men. Clive then replaced the nawab of Bengal by a man whom he believed to be friendly to the English. Before the Seven Years' War was over, the English had won Pondicherry and deprived the French of all their former influence in the region of Madras.

946. England's Gains in the Seven Years' War. When the Seven Years' War was brought to an end, in 1763, by the Treaty of Paris, it was clear that England had gained far more than any other power. She was to retain her two forts commanding the Mediterranean — Gibraltar, and Port Mahon on the island of Minorca; in America, France ceded to her the vast region of Canada and Nova Scotia, as well as several of the islands in the West Indies. The region beyond the Mississippi was ceded to Spain by France, who thus gave up all her claims to North America. In India, France, it is true, received back the towns which the English had taken from her, but she had permanently lost her influence over the native rulers, for Clive had made the English name greatly feared among them.

V. Revolt of the American Colonies from England

947. England long left her Colonies very Free. England had, however, no sooner added Canada to her possessions and driven the French from the broad region which lay between her dominions and the Mississippi than she lost the better part of her American empire by the revolt of the irritated colonists, who refused to submit to her interference in their government and commerce.

The English settlers had been left alone, for the most part, by the home government and had enjoyed *far greater freedom* in the management of their affairs than had the French and Spanish colonists. Virginia established its own assembly in 1619 and Massachusetts became almost an independent commonwealth. Regular constitutions developed, which were later used as the basis for those of the several states when the colonies gained their independence. By the end of the Seven Years' War (1763) the colonists numbered over two millions. Their rapidly increasing wealth and strength, their free life in a new land, the confidence they had gained in their successful conflict with the French,—all combined to render interference of the home government intolerable to them.

948. Navigation Laws. England had, like Spain, France, and other colonizing countries, enacted a number of navigation and trade laws by which she tried to keep all the benefits of colonial trade and industry to herself. The early navigation laws passed under Cromwell and Charles II were specially directed against the enterprising Dutch traders. They provided that all products grown or manufactured in Asia, Africa, or America should be imported into England or her colonies only in English ships. Thus if a Dutch merchant vessel laden with cloves, cinnamon, teas, and silks from the Far East anchored in the harbor of New York, the inhabitants could not lawfully buy of

FIG. 164. THE ELDER PITT

Pitt, Earl of Chatham, more than any other one man, was responsible for the victories of England in the Seven Years' War. A great orator, as well as a shrewd statesman, he inspired his country with his own great ideals. He boldly upheld in Parliament the cause of the American colonists, but died in 1778 before he could check the policy of the king

the ship's master, no matter how much lower his prices were than those offered by English shippers. Furthermore, another act provided that no commodity of European production or manufacture should be imported into any of the colonies without being shipped through England and carried in ships built in England or the colonies. So if a colonial merchant wished to buy French wines or Dutch watches, he would have to order through English merchants. Again, if a colonist desired to sell to a European merchant such products as the law permitted him to sell to foreigners, he had to export them in English ships and even send them by way of England.

949. Trade Laws. Certain articles in which the colonists were interested, such as sugar, tobacco, cotton, and indigo, could be sold only in England. Other things they were forbidden to export at all, or even to produce. For instance, though they possessed the finest furs in abundance, they could not export any caps or hats to England or to any foreign country. The colonists had built up a lucrative lumber and provision trade with the French West Indies, from which they imported large quantities of rum, sugar, and molasses, but in order to keep this trade within British dominions, the importation of these commodities was forbidden.

950. The Colonists evade the English Restrictions. The colonists naturally evaded these laws as far as possible; they carried on a flourishing smuggling trade and built up industries in spite of them. Tobacco, sugar, hemp, flax, and cotton were grown and cloth was manufactured. Furnaces, foundries, nail and wire mills supplied pig and bar iron, chains, anchors, and other hardware. It is clear that where so many people were interested in both manufacturing and commerce a loud protest was sure to be raised against any attempts of England to restrict the business of the colonists in favor of her own merchants.

But previous to 1763 the navigation and trade laws had been loosely enforced and business men of high standing in their communities ventured to neglect them and engage in illegal trade, which from the standpoint of the mother country constituted "smuggling." English statesmen had been busy during the previous century with the great struggle at home and with the wars stirred up by Louis XIV. After the Peace of Utrecht, Walpole for twenty years prudently refused to interfere with the independence of the colonies.

951. Change in English Colonial Policy after 1763. With the close of the successful Seven Years' War, and the conquest of Canada and the Ohio valley, arrangements had to be made to protect the new territories and meet the expenses incident to the great enlargement of the British Empire. The home government naturally argued that the prosperous colonists might make some contribution in the form of taxes to the expenses of the late war and the maintenance of a small body of troops for guarding the new possessions.

952. The Stamp Act. This led to the passage of the Stamp Act, which taxed the colonists by requiring them to pay the English government for the stamps which had to be used on leases, deeds, and other legal documents in order to make them binding. This does not appear to modern historians to have been a tyrannical act, and it was certainly perfectly legal. But it stirred up some of the leaders among the colonists, who declared that they had already borne the brunt of the recent war and that Parliament had no right to tax them since they were not represented directly in that body. They forgot that large classes in the mother country and in the colonies themselves were no more represented directly than they were in Parliament. Whatever may have been the merits of their arguments, representatives of the colonies met in New York in 1765 and denounced the Stamp Act as indicating "a manifest tendency to subvert the rights and liberties of the colonists."

The unpopular stamp tax was repealed, in spite of the opposition of King George III, who, with some of the Tory party in Parliament, thought that the colonists should be punished rather than conciliated. Many of the Whigs were very friendly to them and a proposal was made to permit the colonists to tax themselves, but Benjamin Franklin, then in England, sadly admitted that they would not consent to do so. Parliament then decided to raise a certain amount by duties on glass, paper, and tea, and a board was established to secure a stricter enforcement of the old and hitherto largely neglected navigation laws and other restrictions. The protests of the colonists led Parliament, however, to remove all the duties except that on tea, which was retained owing to the active lobbying of the East India Company, whose interests were at stake.

953. The Boston Tea Party (1773) ; **Attitude of Parliament toward the Colonists.** The effort to make the Americans pay a very moderate duty on tea and to force upon the Boston markets the Company's tea at a very low price produced trouble in 1773. Those who had supplies of "smuggled" tea to dispose of and who were likely to be undersold even after the small duty was paid raised a new cry of illegal taxation, and a band of young men was got together in Boston who seditiously boarded a tea ship in the harbor and threw the cargo into the water. This so-called Boston Tea Party fanned the slumbering embers of discord between the colonies and the mother country.

A considerable body in Parliament were opposed to coercing the colonists. Burke, perhaps the most able member of the House of Commons, urged the ministry to leave the Americans to tax themselves, but George III, and the Tory party in Parliament, could not forgive the colonists for their opposition. They believed that the trouble was largely confined to New England and could easily be overcome. In 1774 acts were passed prohibiting the landing and shipping of goods at Boston ; and the colony of Massachusetts was deprived of its former right to choose its judges and the members of the upper house of its legislature, who were thereafter to be selected by the king.

954. The Continental Congresses. These measures, instead of bringing Massachusetts to terms, so roused the apprehension of the rest of the colonists that a congress of representatives from all the colonies was held at Philadelphia in 1774 to see what could be done. This congress decided that all trade with Great Britain should cease until the grievances of the colonies had been redressed. The following year the Americans attacked the British troops at Lexington and made a brave stand against them in the battle of Bunker Hill. The second congress decided to prepare for war and raised an army which was put under the command of George Washington, a Virginia planter who had gained some distinction in the late French and Indian War.

955. Declaration of Independence (July 4, 1776). Up to this time few people had openly advocated the separation of the colonies from the mother country, but the proposed compromises came to nothing, and in July, 1776, Congress declared that "these United States are, and of right ought to be, free and independent."

The party which favored an attempt to gain independence were a minority of the population. The so-called "Tories" who opposed separation from England were perhaps as numerous as the "patriots" who advocated the American Revolution; and the other third of the colonists appear to have been indifferent.

956. The United States receives Aid from France. The Declaration of Independence naturally excited great interest in France. The outcome of the Seven Years' War had been most lamentable for that country, and any trouble which came to her old enemy, England, could not but be a source of congratulation to the French. The United States therefore regarded France as their natural ally and immediately sent Benjamin Franklin to Versailles in the hope of obtaining the aid of the new French king, Louis XVI. The king's ministers were uncertain whether the colonies could long maintain their resistance against the overwhelming strength of the mother country. It was only after the Americans had defeated Burgoyne at Saratoga that France, in 1778, concluded a treaty with the United States in which the independence of the new republic was recognized. This was equivalent to declaring war upon England. The French government aided the colonies with loans, and enthusiasm for the Americans was so great in France that a number of the younger nobles, the most conspicuous of whom was the Marquis of Lafayette, crossed the Atlantic to fight as volunteers in the American army.

957. Success of the Revolution. There was so much difference of opinion in England in regard to the expediency of the war and so much sympathy in Parliament for the colonists that the military operations were not carried on with much vigor. Nevertheless the Americans found it no easy task to win the war. In spite of the skill and heroic self-sacrifice of Washington, they lost more battles than they gained. It is extremely doubtful whether they would have succeeded in bringing the war to a favorable close, by forcing the English general, Cornwallis, to capitulate at

Yorktown (1781), had it not been for the aid of the French fleet. The chief result of the war was the recognition by England of the independence of the United States, whose territory was to extend to the Mississippi River. To the west of the Mississippi the vast territory of Louisiana still remained in the hands of Spain, as well as Florida, which England had held since 1763 but now gave back.

Spain and Portugal were able to hold their American possessions a generation longer than the English, but in the end practically all of the Western Hemisphere, with the exception of Canada, completely freed itself from the domination of the European powers. Cuba, one of the very last vestiges of Spanish rule in the West, gained its independence with the aid of the United States in 1898.

958. Great Extension of England's Colonial Possessions. England had lost her American colonies as a result of the only important and successful revolt that has ever taken place in her great empire. This led to the creation of a sister state speaking her own language and destined to occupy the central part of the North American continent from the Atlantic to the Pacific. She still retained Canada, however, and in the nineteenth century added a new continent in the southern hemisphere, Australia, to her vast colonial empire. In India she had no further rivals among European nations and gradually extended her influence over the whole region south of the Himalayas.

959. France in the Eighteenth Century. As for France, she had played a rather pitiful rôle during the long reign of Louis XIV's great-grandson, Louis XV (1715–1774). She had, however, been able to increase her territory by the addition of Lorraine (1766) and, in 1768, of the island of Corsica. A year later a child was born in the Corsican town of Ajaccio, who one day, by his military genius, was to make France the center for a time of an empire rivaling that of Charlemagne in extent. When the nineteenth century opened, France was no longer a monarchy, but a republic; and her armies were to occupy in turn every European capital from Madrid to Moscow. The marvelous transformations produced by the French Revolution and the wars of

Napoleon, the great changes of the nineteenth century, and the causes and course of the recent World War will form the subject of the next volume of this history.

QUESTIONS

I. What important questions did the accession of William and Mary settle? When and on what terms were England and Scotland united? When and why did the House of Hanover come to the English throne? What do you understand by the "balance of power"? Who was the Young Pretender and what attempts did he make to gain the English throne?

II. Contrast the limited monarchy of England with the benevolent despotism of the Continent. Discuss the two great political parties of England. Who was Sir Robert Walpole? Describe the origin of the cabinet. Explain the position of the king during the eighteenth century. What was the great cause of dissatisfaction with parliamentary government in England in the eighteenth century?

III. Why must we study the European colonies in order to understand European history? What countries preceded England in acquiring colonies? Give the possessions of Spain, England, and France in North America previous to the Seven Years' War.

IV. Tell something of the extent and population of India. How did England get its first foothold in India? Where were the French settlements? What was the result of the French and Indian War in America? in India? Enumerate England's colonial possessions at the end of the war.

V. Describe England's navigation and trade laws. Give the chief events leading to the revolt of England's colonies in America. Were the English unanimously in favor of coercing the American colonies? Why did France favor the colonies? What were the chief results of the American Revolution?

BIBLIOGRAPHY

It is not the aim of this bibliography to mention all of even the important books in various languages that relate to the periods in question. The writers are well aware that teachers are busy people, and that high-school libraries and local public libraries usually furnish at best only a few historical works. It is therefore most important that those books should be given prominence in this list which the teacher has some chance of procuring and finding the time to use. It not infrequently happens that the best account of a particular period or topic is in a foreign language or in a rare publication, such as a doctor's dissertation, which could only be found in one of our largest libraries. All such titles, however valuable, are omitted from this list. They can be found mentioned in all the more scholarly works in the various fields.

The part of this bibliography which relates to ancient and classical times has been arranged to facilitate the selection of a small high-school library. The particularly good and available books which on an average would not cost more than $1.50 or $2.00 are indicated with a dagger (†) before the title. From these a selection can be made. Books deemed especially valuable are in some cases indicated by the double dagger (††). All books with a star (*) are suited chiefly for the teacher and are rather advanced for the high-school student. Where a book is referred to often, the star or dagger usually appears only with the first mention.

The authors would urge upon the teachers the importance of illustrative material, especially in dealing with the ancient and the Greek and Roman periods. The references to BREASTED'S *Ancient Times* have been inserted largely because of its wealth of illustrations.

CHAPTER I

General Accounts. *SOLLAS, *Ancient Hunters* (second edition). †TYLOR, *Primitive Culture.* †HOERNES, *Primitive Man.* †MYRES, *The Dawn of History*, chaps. i–ii, vii–xi. An excellent little book in which only the traditional Babylonian chronology needs revision. *SIR JOHN LUBBOCK (LORD AVEBURY), *Prehistoric Times.* *OSBORN, *Men of the Old Stone Age.* A very valuable and sumptuously illustrated presentation of Early Stone Age life. †BREASTED, *Ancient Times*, chap. i.

CHAPTER II

A. Histories. BREASTED, *History of Egypt.* †BREASTED, *History of the Ancient Egyptians.* *HALL, *The Ancient History of the Near East*, chaps. i–iv, vi–viii. BREASTED, *Ancient Times*, chaps. ii–iii.

B. **Art and Archæology.** †MASPERO, *Art in Egypt.* A useful little manual in *Ars una — species mille.* (Hachette & Cⁱᵉ, and Scribner's, New York.) *MASPERO, *Manual of Egyptian Archæology.* (Last edition, 1914. Putnam's.) †HEDWIG FECHHEIMER, *Die Plastik der Aegypter* (156 beautiful plates showing the finest examples of Egyptian sculpture. The best series to be had, and very low priced).

C. **Mythology and Religion.** *BREASTED, *The Development of Religion and Thought in Ancient Egypt.*

D. **Social Life.** †ERMAN, *Life in Ancient Egypt.*

E. **Excavation and Discovery.** †EDWARDS, *Pharaohs, Fellahs, and Explorers.* *PETRIE, *Ten Years' Digging in Egypt.* WEIGALL, *Treasury of the Nile.* Two quarterly journals begun in 1914, called *Ancient Egypt* (edited by Petrie; $2.00 a year; subscriptions taken by Dr. W. C. Winslow, 525 Beacon Street, Boston, Mass.) and *Journal of Egyptian Archæology* (published by the Egypt Exploration Fund). Both report discoveries in Egypt as fast as made.

F. **Original Sources in English.** *BREASTED, *Ancient Records of Egypt,* Vols. I–V. †PETRIE, *Egyptian Tales.* †MASPERO, *Popular Stories of Ancient Egypt* (translated from the French by Mrs. C. H. W. Johns).

G. **The Monuments as they are To-day.** The Underwood & Underwood series of Egyptian views, edited by †BREASTED, *Egypt through the Stereoscope: a Journey through the Land of the Pharaohs* (100 views with explanatory volume and set of maps). †(Selected views, with explanations printed on the backs, may be secured at moderate cost. The most useful fifteen on Egypt are Nos. 17, 27, 29, 30, 31, 42, 48, 52, 57, 60, 62, 69, 82, 89, 97.)

H. **Wall Maps and Geography.** BREASTED-HUTH, *Ancient History Maps.* (Denoyer-Geppert Co., 460 E. Ohio St., Chicago, Ill.) Maps B 1 and B 3; *Teacher's Manual* (accompanying these maps), pp. 13–19, 33–40.

CHAPTER III

A. **Histories.** KING, **History of Sumer and Akkad* and **History of Babylonia.* †GOODSPEED, *History of the Babylonians and Assyrians.* Recent discoveries have greatly altered the chronology. †C. H. W. JOHNS, *Ancient Babylonia* (Cambridge Manuals). †C. H. W. JOHNS, *Ancient Assyria* (Cambridge Manuals). *HALL, *The Ancient History of the Near East,* chaps. v, x, xii. *OLMSTEAD, *Sargon of Assyria.* *ROGERS, *A History of Babylonia and Assyria.* BREASTED, *Ancient Times,* chaps. iv–v.

B. **Art and Archæology.** There is no handbook corresponding to Maspero's *Art in Egypt.* *HANDCOCK, *Mesopotamian Archæology.* *HALL, *The Ancient History of the Near East.* *JASTROW, *Civilization of the Babylonians and Assyrians.*

C. **Mythology and Religion.** *JASTROW, *Aspects of Religious Belief and Practice in Babylonia and Assyria.* See also his *Civilization.*

D. **Social Life.** †SAYCE, *Babylonian and Assyrian Life and Customs.* *JASTROW, *Civilization.*

E. **Excavation and Discovery.** *ROGERS, A History of Babylonia and Assyria,* Vol. I. There is no journal reporting discoveries in Babylonia and Assyria (like *Ancient Egypt* above), but see the new journal of the American Archæological Institute, called *Art and Archæology* ($2.00 a year; subscriptions taken by The Macmillan Company, 64–66 Fifth Avenue, New York), which reports discovery in the whole field of ancient man.

F. **Original Sources in English.** *R. F. HARPER (Ed.), *Assyrian and Babylonian Literature.* †BOTSFORD, *A Source Book of Ancient History,* chap. iii. *SAYCE (Ed.), *Records of the Past* (First Series, 12 vols.; Second Series, 6 vols.). †C. H. W. JOHNS, *Oldest Code of Laws in the World* (Laws of Hammurapi). *KING, *Letters of Hammurapi.*

G. **The Monuments as they are To-day.** The buildings surviving in Babylonia and Assyria are in a very ruinous state. Photographs are now available in the excellent series by Underwood & Underwood on Mesopotamia.

H. **Wall Maps and Geography.** BREASTED-HUTH, *Ancient History Maps,* Maps B 2 and B 3. *Teacher's Manual,* pp. 40–45.

CHAPTER IV

A. **Histories.** There is no good modern history of Persia in English based on the sources, but see : †BENJAMIN, *Story of Persia* (Story of the Nations Series). MEYER, "Persia," in *Encyclopædia Britannica.* RAWLINSON, *Five Great Monarchies : Persia.* BREASTED, *Ancient Times,* chaps. vi–viii. *HALL, *The Ancient History of the Near East,* chaps. ix and xii. *GEORGE ADAM SMITH, *The Historical Geography of the Holy Land.* The most valuable of the many books on Palestine, but a little advanced for high-school pupils. *HENRY PRESERVED SMITH, *Old Testament History.* *CORNILL, *History of the People of Israel.* †KENT, *History of the Hebrew People.* †KENT, *History of the Jewish People.* †MACALISTER, *A History of Civilization in Palestine* (Cambridge Manuals).

B. **Art and Archæology.** *PERROT and CHIPIEZ, *History of Art : Persia.* RAWLINSON, *Monarchies.*

C. **Mythology and Religion.** MEYER, "Persia," in *Encyclopædia Britannica.* RAWLINSON, *Monarchies.* *BUDDE, *The Religion of Israel to the Exile.* *CHEYNE, *Jewish Religious Life after the Exile.* †J. M. POWIS SMITH, *The Prophet and his Problems* (Scribner's).

D. **Exploration and Discovery.** †JACKSON, *Persia, Past and Present.* This valuable book is the best introduction to the subject of Persia as a whole and contains much information on all the above subjects. †MICHAELIS, *A Century of Archæological Discovery.* HILPRECHT, *Recent Research in Bible Lands.* †MACALISTER, *A History of Civilization in Palestine* (Cambridge Manuals). Current reports will be found in *Journal of the Palestine Exploration Fund* and in *Art and Archæology* (see above).

E. **Original Sources in English.** †TOLMAN, *The Behistan Inscription of King Darius.* The Persian monuments are not numerous, and this inscription of Behistun (or Behistan) is the most important. A considerable part of it will be found quoted in BOTSFORD, *A Source Book of Ancient History*, pp. 57–59. The *Avesta* will be found in the series called Sacred Books of the East. The Old Testament in the Revised Version. †MOORE, *The Literature of the Old Testament.* *CORNILL, *Introduction to the Canonical Books of the Old Testament.* *ROGERS, *Cuneiform Parallels to the Old Testament.* †BOTSFORD, *A Source Book of Ancient History*, chap. iv.

F. **Palestine, its People and Monuments as they are To-day.** The Underwood & Underwood stereoscopic photographs (edited by HURLBUT), *Traveling in the Holy Land through the Stereoscope* (100 views with guidebook and maps). †(A selection of the best ten would include Nos. 8, 9, 18, 25, 39, 40, 41, 47, 61, 71.) GEORGE ADAM SMITH, *The Historical Geography of the Holy Land.* PATON, *Guide to Jerusalem.*

G. **Wall Maps and Geography.** BREASTED-HUTH, *Ancient History Maps,* Maps B 2 and B 4. *Teacher's Manual*, pp. 37, 45–50.

CHAPTER V

A. **Histories.** †BOTSFORD, *Hellenic History*, chaps. i–iii. †WESTERMANN, *Ancient Nations*, pp. 43–50, chaps. vii–viii. †GOODSPEED, *Ancient World*, pp. 65–87. BREASTED, *Ancient Times*, chaps. viii–x. ††MYRES, *Dawn of History*, chaps. viii–ix. †KIMBALL-BURY, *Students' Greece*, chaps. i–ii. ††BURY, *History of Greece*, second edition, chap. i. ††REINACH, *Story of Art*, pp. 26–32. HAWES, *Crete the Forerunner of Greece.* †BAIKIE, *Sea Kings of Crete.* *MOSSO, *Dawn of Mediterranean Civilization.* *HALL, *Ancient History of the Near East*, pp. 31–62. †ZIMMERN, *Greek Commonwealth* (second edition). †GREENIDGE, *Greek Constitutional History*, chap. ii. ††CAPPS, *Homer to Theocritus*, pp. 14–128. †KELLER, *Homeric Life.* *SEYMOUR, *Homeric Age.* *SANDYS, *Companion to Greek Studies.*

B. **Sources and Source Selections.** †BOTSFORD, *Source Book of Ancient History*, chaps. vii–ix. †THALLON, *Readings in Greek History*, chap. i. ††BOTSFORD and SIHLER, *Hellenic Civilization*, chap. ii.

C. **Maps and Geography.** BREASTED-HUTH, *Ancient History Maps*, Maps B 3, B 5, and B 6. *Teacher's Manual*, pp. 17–24, 48–55.

CHAPTER VI

A. **Histories.** BOTSFORD, *Hellenic History*, chap. iv. WESTERMANN, *Ancient Nations*, chap. ix. GOODSPEED, *Ancient World*, pp. 79–82, 87–92, 100–101. BREASTED, *Ancient Times*, chap. xi. KIMBALL-BURY, *Students' Greece*, chap. iii. BURY, *Greece*, chap. ii. †ALLCROFT, *History of Sicily*, chaps. i–ii. GREENIDGE, *Greek Constitutional History*, chaps. ii–iii. CAPPS, *Homer to Theocritus*, pp. 129–140. KELLER, *Colonization*, pp. 26–50. ZIMMERN, *Greek Commonwealth.* SANDYS, *Companion.*

B. **Sources and Source Selections.** BOTSFORD and SIHLER, *Hellenic Civilization*, chap. iii. BOTSFORD, *Source Book*, chap. xi. *Herodotus* (RAWLINSON), IV, 150–159. *Hesiod and Theognis* (COLLINS). *Hesiod* (MAIR). THALLON, *Readings*, chaps. ii–iv.

C. **Wall Maps and Geography.** BREASTED-HUTH, *Ancient History Maps*, Maps B 6 and B 7. *Teacher's Manual*, pp. 51–60.

CHAPTER VII

A. **Histories.** BOTSFORD, *Hellenic History*, chaps. vi–ix. WESTERMANN, *Ancient Nations*, chap. x. GOODSPEED, *Ancient World*, pp. 101–108, 115–125. BREASTED, *Ancient Times*, chap. xii. KIMBALL-BURY, *Students' Greece*, pp. 79–89 and chaps. v–vi. GREENIDGE, *Greek Constitutional History*, pp. 135–187. BURY, *Greece*, pp. 144–162 and chaps. iv–v. CAPPS, *Homer to Theocritus*, chaps. vi–vii. ††BENN, *Ancient Philosophy*, chaps. i–ii. REINACH, *Story of Art*, pp. 33–41. †MAHAFFY, *Social Life in Greece*, chaps. iv–v. ZIMMERN, *Greek Commonwealth*. SANDYS, *Companion*.

B. **Sources and Source Selections.** BOTSFORD and SIHLER, chap. iv. BOTSFORD, *Source Book*, chaps. x, xii–xiv. †*Aristotle's Constitution of Athens* (KENYON or POSTE), chaps. i–xxii. †*Plutarch's Lives of Theseus and Solon.* †*Herodotus*, I, 29–33, 59–64; III, 39–46, 120–125. THALLON, *Readings*, chaps. iv and vi.

C. **Wall Maps and Geography.** BREASTED-HUTH, *Ancient History Maps*, Maps B 6 and B 8. *Teacher's Manual*, pp. 56–61.

CHAPTER VIII

A. **Histories.** BOTSFORD, *Hellenic History.* WESTERMANN, *Ancient Nations*, chaps. xi–xiii. GOODSPEED, *Ancient World*, pp. 109–155, 168–173. BREASTED, *Ancient Times*, chaps. xiii–xiv. KIMBALL-BURY, *Students' Greece*, chaps. vii–x, pp. 64–74. ALLCROFT, *History of Sicily*, chaps. iii ff. BURY, *Greece*, chaps. vi–viii. HALL, *Near East*, chap. xii. †HOGARTH, *Ancient East*, pp. 120–186. *ABBOTT, *Pericles*, chap. iii. *GRUNDY, *Great Persian War.* †SEIGNOBOS, *Ancient Civilization*, chap. xi. GREENIDGE, *Greek Constitutional History*, pp. 78–120, 189–207. †GRANT, *Greece in the Age of Pericles*, chaps. v–vii. *ABBOTT, *Pericles*, chaps. iv–viii. ZIMMERN, *Greek Commonwealth*. SANDYS, *Companion*.

B. **Sources and Source Selections.** BOTSFORD and SIHLER, pp. 162–172 and chaps. vi–vii. †FLING, *Source Book of Greek History*, chap. v. BOTSFORD, *Source Book*, chaps. xv–xvii. *Herodotus*, Bks. VI–IX, especially VII, 140–233. *Plutarch's Lives of Aristides, Themistocles, Pausanias, Cimon, Lycurgus.* †*Æschylus' Persians*, especially lines 355–520. THALLON, *Readings*, chaps. v, vii–ix. *Xenophon's State of the Lacedæmonians.* *Aristotle's Athenian Constitution*, chaps. xxiii–xxvii. †*Thucydides* (JOWETT), I, 98–103, 127–139.

C. **Wall Maps and Geography.** BREASTED-HUTH, *Ancient History Maps*, Maps B 7, B 8, and B 9. *Teacher's Manual*, pp. 65–69 (Map A).

CHAPTER IX

A. **Histories.** BOTSFORD, *Hellenic History.* WESTERMANN, *Ancient Nations,* chaps. xiv–xv. GOODSPEED, *Ancient World,* 156–169. BREASTED, *Ancient Times,* chap. xv. KIMBALL-BURY, *Students' Greece,* chap. xi. SEIGNOBOS, *Ancient Civilization,* chap. xiv. BURY, *Greece,* chap. ix. GRANT, *Age of Pericles,* chaps. vii–x, xii. BENN, *Ancient Philosophy,* chap. iii. ††TARBELL, *History of Greek Art,* chaps. iii, vii, and viii. CAPPS, *Homer to Theocritus,* chaps. viii–xii. †MONROE, *History of Education,* pp. 28–59. MAHAFFY, *Social Life in Greece,* chaps. vi ff. ABBOTT, *Pericles,* chaps. xvi–xviii. ZIMMERN, *Greek Commonwealth.* SANDYS, *Companion.*

B. **Sources and Source Selections.** BOTSFORD and SIHLER, chaps. viii–xi. BOTSFORD, *Source Book,* chap. xviii. *Plutarch's Pericles.* THALLON, *Readings,* chap. ix.

C. **Wall Maps and Geography.** BREASTED-HUTH, *Ancient History Maps,* Map 8. *Teacher's Manual,* pp. 61–64.

CHAPTER X

A. **Histories.** BOTSFORD, *Hellenic History.* WESTERMANN, *Ancient Nations,* chap. xvi. GOODSPEED, *Ancient World,* pp. 174–199. BREASTED, *Ancient Times,* chap. xvi. KIMBALL-BURY, *Students' Greece,* chaps. xii and xiv. BURY, *Greece,* chaps. x–xi. ALLCROFT, *Sicily.* GRANT, *Age of Pericles,* chap. xi. ABBOTT, *Pericles,* chaps. xiv–xv. *FERGUSON, *Greek Imperialism,* Lect. II. *WHIBLEY, *Political Parties in Athens.* ZIMMERN, *Greek Commonwealth.*

B. **Sources and Source Selections.** BOTSFORD and SIHLER, chap. vi. BOTSFORD, *Source Book,* chaps. xix–xx. FLING, *Source Book,* chap. vii. *Plutarch's Lives of Alcibiades, Nicias, Lysander.* Thucydides (JOWETT), Selections. THALLON, *Readings,* chaps. x–xii.

C. **Wall Maps and Geography.** BREASTED-HUTH, *Ancient History Maps,* Maps B 9 and B 6. *Teacher's Manual,* pp. 69–70 (Map B).

CHAPTER XI

A. **Histories.** BOTSFORD, *Hellenic History.* WESTERMANN, *Ancient Nations,* chap. xvii, pp. 193–198. GOODSPEED, *Ancient World,* pp. 184–189, 200–220. BREASTED, *Ancient Times,* chaps. xvii–xviii. KIMBALL-BURY, *Students' Greece,* chaps. xv–xvii. ALLCROFT, *History of Greece, 404–362 B.C.* BURY, *Greece,* chaps. xii–xiv. ALLCROFT, *Sicily.* CAPPS, *Homer to Theocritus,* pp. 330–338, chaps. xv–xvii. †SANKEY, *Spartan and Theban Supremacies.* MAHAFFY, *Social Life in Greece,* chaps. vi ff. BENN, *Ancient Philosophy,* chaps. iv–vi. REINACH, *Story of Art,* pp. 50–58, 66–74. MONROE, *History of Education,* pp. 59–72. TARBELL, *Greek Art,* chap. ix. FERGUSON, *Greek Imperialism,* Lect. III. †TAYLOR, *Plato.* *MAUTHNER, *Aristotle.* SANDYS, *Companion.*

***B.* Sources and Source Selections.** BOTSFORD, *Source Book*, chaps. xxii–xxiii.
†*Xenophon's Anabasis*, IV, 7 ff.; *Xenophon's Agesilaos* (DAKYNS). *Nepos's Epaminondas. Plutarch's Lives of Pelopidas and Timoleon.* THALLON, *Readings*, chaps. xiii–xiv. BOTSFORD and SIHLER, chaps. xii–xv. FLING, *Source Book*, chap. viii. THALLON, *Readings*, pp. 513–516, 532–558. *Xenophon's Economics* (DAKYNS). *Plato's Apology.* Selections from *Euripides* in †APPLE-TON, *Greek Poets*, and in †GOLDWIN SMITH, *Specimens of Greek Tragedy. Aristophanes' Acharnians and Birds* (FRERE in Everyman's).

***C.* Wall Maps and Geography.** BREASTED-HUTH, *Ancient History Maps*, Map B 9. *Teacher's Manual*, pp. 70–72 (Map C).

CHAPTER XII

***A.* Histories.** BOTSFORD, *Hellenic History.* WESTERMANN, *Ancient Nations*, pp. 187–193, chaps. xix–xxii. GOODSPEED, *Ancient World*, pp. 220–269. BREASTED, *Ancient Times*, chaps. xix–xxi. KIMBALL-BURY, *Students' Greece*, chaps. xviii–xx. ALLCROFT, *History of Greece, 362–323 B.C.* BURY, *Greece*, chaps. xvi–xviii. †HOGARTH, *Ancient East*, pp. 186–251. FERGUSON, *Greek Imperialism*, Lects. IV–VII. CAPPS, *Homer to Theocritus*, chaps. xiv, xviii. †CURTEIS, *Macedonian Empire.* †WHEELER, *Alexander.* *GARDNER, *New Chapters in Greek History*, chap. xv. †SHUCKBURGH, *Greek History*, pp. 235–310. GREENIDGE, *Greek Constitutional History*, chap. vii. MAHAFFY, *Problems in Greek History*, chap. ix; † *Progress of Hellenism*, Lects. II–V; **Greek Life and Thought*, chaps. i–xvi; *Alexander's Empire*, chaps. xiv, xx, and xxiii. MONROE, *History of Education*, pp. 73–78. †TUCKER, *Life in Ancient Athens*, chap. ix. TARBELL, *Greek Art*, chap. x. †TILLYARD, *Agathocles.* *TARN, *Antigonos Gonatas.*

***B.* Sources and Source Selections.** BOTSFORD and SIHLER, chaps. xvi–xix. BOTSFORD, *Source Book*, chaps. xxiv–xxvii. *Plutarch's Lives of Demosthenes, Phocion, Alexander.* †*Arrian's Anabasis* (selections). JUSTIN, *History*, Bk. IX (Bohn). *Demosthenes's Crown* and *Third Philippic.* THALLON, *Readings*, chap. xv. DAVIS, *Readings*, I, chaps. ix–x. *Plutarch's Lives of Aratus, Demetrius, Pyrrhus, Agis, Cleomenes, Eumenes.* FLING, *Source Book*, chap. xiii. †*Polybius's Histories.* (SHUCKBURGH) Selections, especially those on the Achæan League.

***C.* Wall Maps and Geography.** BREASTED-HUTH, *Ancient History Maps*, Map B 10. *Teacher's Manual*, pp. 74–79.

CHAPTER XIII

***A.* Histories.** BOTSFORD, *History of Rome*, chaps. i–iv. WESTERMANN, *Ancient Nations*, chaps. xxiii–xxv. GOODSPEED, *Ancient World*, pp. 276–325, 331–342. BREASTED, *Ancient Times*, chap. xxii. †BRYANT, *Short History of Rome*, chaps. i–vii. †FOWLER, *Rome*, pp. 7–54. ††MYRES, *Dawn*, chap. x. MOSSO, *Dawn of Civilization*, chaps. xxi–xxii, xxiv–xxv. JONES, *Companion* to *Roman History*, pp. 1–12. †HEITLAND, *Short History of the Roman Republic*, pp. 1–82. †HOW and LEIGH, *History of Rome*, pp. 1–131. †PELHAM, *Outlines*, pp. 45–67. ††ABBOTT, *Roman Political Institutions*, chap. iv. †CARTER, *Religion of Numa*. *FRANK, *Roman Imperialism*.

B. Sources and Source Selections. BOTSFORD, *Story of Rome*, chaps. i–iv; *Source Book*, chaps. xxix–xxxi. MUNRO, *Source Book*, chaps. i, ii, iv, and v. *Plutarch's Lives of Romulus, Numa, Pyrrhus, Camillus.* DAVIS, *Source Readings*, II, pp. 1–40.

C. Wall Maps and Geography. BREASTED-HUTH, *Ancient History Maps*, Maps B 11 and B 12. *Teacher's Manual*, pp. 13–17, 25–32 (Italy), 80–96.

CHAPTER XIV

A. Histories. BOTSFORD, *History of Rome*, chap. v. WESTERMANN, *Ancient Nations*, pp. 275–276, 279–284, chaps. xxvi–xxvii. GOODSPEED, *Ancient World*, pp. 326–354. BREASTED, *Ancient Times*, chaps. xxiii–xxiv. BRYANT, *Short History*, pp. 67–79 and chaps. ix–xi. FOWLER, *Rome*, pp. 55–110. HEITLAND, *Short History*, pp. 82–97. †LIDDELL, *Student's Rome*, pp. 218–229, 256–320. *GREENIDGE, *Roman Public Life*, chap. vii. HOW and LEIGH, *Rome*, pp. 131–244. †SMITH, *Carthage and the Carthaginians*. FRANK, *Roman Imperialism*. *HAVELL, *Republican Rome*, pp. 156–274. HEITLAND, *Short History*, pp. 98–145. *MORRIS, *Hannibal*.

B. Sources and Source Selections. BOTSFORD, *Story of Rome*, pp. 101–124; *Source Book*, chaps. xxxii–xxxiii. MUNRO, *Source Book*, chaps. iii and vi. DAVIS, *Source Readings*, II, pp. 41–50 and chap. iii. *Polybius*, I, 56–62; III, 49–56. †*Livy*, xxi, 32–38. *Plutarch's Lives of Fabius and Marcellus*.

C. Wall Maps and Geography. BREASTED-HUTH, *Ancient History Maps*, Maps B 13 (A) and B 14 (A–D). *Teacher's Manual*, pp. 97–100, 106–109.

CHAPTER XV

A. Histories. BOTSFORD, *History of Rome*, pp. 116–150. WESTERMANN, *Ancient Nations*, chaps. xxix–xxx. GOODSPEED, *Ancient World*, pp. 354–363, 365–392. BREASTED, *Ancient Times*, chap. xxv. BRYANT, *Short History*, chaps. xii–xiv. FOWLER, *Rome*, pp. 110–135. †MASOM, *Rome*, *133–78 B.C.*, chap. i. †ALLCROFT and MASOM, *Rome*, *202–133 B.C.*, chaps. x–xiv. †DAVIS, *Influence of Wealth in Imperial Rome*, chap. ii. ABBOTT, *Roman Political Institutions*, chap. v. GREENIDGE, *Roman Public Life*, chap. viii; *Roman History*, Vol. I, chap. i. *DUFF, *Literary History of Rome*, pp. 92–117. PELHAM, *Outlines*, pp. 149–198. HEITLAND, *Short History*, pp. 146–248. †ABBOTT, *Society and Politics in Ancient Rome*, pp. 22–40.

B. Sources and Source Selections. BOTSFORD, *Story of Rome*, pp. 125–126 and chap. vi; *Source Book*, chaps. xxxiv–xxxv. DAVIS, *Source Readings*, II, pp. 85–104. MUNRO, *Source Book*, chaps. vii and xii. *Livy*, xxxiv, 1–8; xlv, 10–12. *Plutarch's Lives of Cato the Censor, Flaminius, Æmilius Paulus.*

C. **Wall Maps and Geography.** BREASTED-HUTH, *Ancient History Maps*, Map B 14 (E). *Teacher's Manual*, pp. 109–111.

CHAPTER XVI

A. **Histories.** BOTSFORD, *History of Rome*, chaps. vii–viii. WESTERMANN, *Ancient Nations*, chaps. xxxi–xxxiv and pp. 379–382. GOODSPEED, *Ancient World*, pp. 392–428. BREASTED, *Ancient Times*, chap. xxvi. BRYANT, *Short History*, chaps. xv–xxvi. FOWLER, *Rome*, pp. 136–186. HEITLAND, *Short History*, pp. 249–512. †ABBOTT, *Common People of Ancient Rome*, pp. 235–286. PELHAM, *Outlines*, pp. 201–258, 398–469. ABBOTT, *Roman Political Institutions*, chaps. vi–vii. HOW and LEIGH, *Rome*, pp. 331–551. †PRESTON and DODGE, *Private Life of the Romans*, chap. v. †ALLCROFT, *Rome, 78–31 B.C.* FRANK, *Roman Imperialism.* *JONES, *Companion to Roman History.* *FOWLER, *Cæsar.* *STRACHAN-DAVIDSON, *Cicero.*

B. **Sources and Source Selections.** BOTSFORD, *Story of Rome*, chaps. vii–viii; *Source Book*, chaps. xxxvi–xxxvii. MUNRO, *Source Book*, pp. 180–185 and chap. viii. DAVIS, *Source Readings*, II, pp. 105–162. *Plutarch's Lives of Tiberius and Gaius Gracchus, Marius, Sulla, Crassus, Pompey, Cicero, Cæsar, Sertorius.* †*Cæsar's Gallic War*, I, 42–47. *Sallust's Jugurthine War* (Bohn).

C. **Wall Maps and Geography.** BREASTED-HUTH, *Ancient History Maps*, Maps B 14 (E, F, G) and B 15. *Teacher's Manual*, pp. 109–122.

CHAPTER XVII

A. **Histories.** BOTSFORD, *History of Rome*, pp. 204–232. WESTERMANN, *Ancient Nations*, pp. 382–403. GOODSPEED, *Ancient World*, pp. 428–451. BREASTED, *Ancient Times*, chap. xxviii. FOWLER, *Rome*, pp. 187–211. CAPES, *Early Empire.* *JONES, *Roman Empire*, chaps. i–iii. †BURY, *Students' Roman Empire*, chaps. i–xii. ABBOTT, *Roman Political Institutions*, chap. xii. DAVIS, *Influence of Wealth*, chap. vii. PELHAM, *Outlines*, pp. 357–509. *FIRTH, *Augustus.* †FOWLER, *History of Roman Literature*, Bk. II. ††MACKAIL, *Roman Literature*, Bk. II, chaps. i–v. †TUCKER, *Life in the Roman World*, chap. v. *ARNOLD, *Roman Provincial Administration.*

B. **Sources and Source Selections.** BOTSFORD, *Story of Rome*, chaps. ix–x; *Source Book*, chaps. xxxviii–xxxix. MUNRO, *Source Book*, chaps. ix and xi. DAVIS, *Source Readings*, II, pp. 163–196. †LAING, *Masterpieces of Latin Literature* (selections). † *The Deeds of Augustus* (Fairley's translation in the *Pennsylvania Translations and Reprints*), Vol. V, No. 1. *Suetonius's Lives of the Cæsars* (selections). †*Tacitus's Annals*, XV, 38–45, 60–65. †*Roman Farm Management, by a Virginia Farmer* (Fairfax Harrison).

C. **Wall Maps and Geography.** BREASTED-HUTH, *Ancient History Maps*, Maps B 13 (B) and B 16. *Teacher's Manual*, pp. 100–104, 123.

CHAPTER XVIII

A. **Histories.** BOTSFORD, *History of Rome*, pp. 232–266. WESTERMANN, *Ancient Nations*, pp. 403–435. GOODSPEED, *Ancient World*, pp. 451–482. BREASTED, *Ancient Times*, chap. xxviii. FOWLER, *Rome*, pp. 211–251. PELHAM, *Outlines*, pp. 509–541. REINACH, *Story of Art*, pp. 75–83. †PELLISON, *Roman Life in Pliny's Time*, chap. ix. *MAU and KELSEY, *Pompeii*, chaps. vii–viii, xii–xxii, xlvi–xlviii, lvi–lix. TUCKER, *Roman Life*, chaps. i–iii, xix–xxi. GREEN-IDGE, *Roman Public Life*, chap. xi. *HARDY, *Studies in Roman History*, Series I, chaps. i–v. JONES, *Roman Empire*, chaps. iv–vi. DAVIS, *Influence of Wealth*, chaps. iii–vi. BURY, *Students' Roman Empire*. *CUMONT, *Oriental Religions in Roman Paganism* (an epoch-making work). *GLOVER, *Conflict of Religions in the Early Roman Empire* (a valuable account of the rivals of Christianity).

B. **Sources and Source Selections.** BOTSFORD, *Story of Rome*, chap. xi; *Source Book*, chap. xl. DAVIS, *Source Readings*, II, pp. 196–287. MUNRO, *Source Book*, pp. 162–171, 176–179. *Letters of Pliny* (FIRTH). New Testament, The Acts.

C. **Wall Maps and Geography.** BREASTED-HUTH, *Ancient History Maps*, Maps B 13 (B) and B 16. *Teacher's Manual*, pp. 123–128.

CHAPTER XIX

A. **Histories.** BOTSFORD, *History of Rome*, chap. xii. WESTERMANN, *Ancient Nations*, chaps. xl–xli. GOODSPEED, *Ancient World*, pp. 483–501. BREASTED, *Ancient Times*, chap. xxix. JONES, *Roman Empire*, chaps. vii–xi. OMAN, *Byzantine Empire*, chap. ii. ABBOTT, *Roman Political Institutions*, chap. xvi. *WRIGHT, *Palmyra and Zenobia*, chaps. xi–xv. SEIGNOBOS, *Ancient Civilization*, pp. 332–346. DAVIS, *Outline History*, pp. 130–183. PELHAM, *Outlines*, pp. 577–586. †CUTTS, *St. Jerome*. JONES, *Companion to Roman History*. *COTTERILL, *Medieval Italy*, pp. 21–54. DAVIS, *Influence of Wealth*, chap. viii. *UHLHORN, *Conflict of Christianity with Heathenism*, pp. 420–479. *FIRTH, *Constantine*. *DILL, *Roman Society in the Last Century of the Western Empire* (excellent).

B. **Sources and Source Selections.** BOTSFORD, *Source Book*, chaps. xli–xliii, xlv. DAVIS, *Source Readings*, II, pp. 287–389. MUNRO, *Source Book*, pp. 171–174. †ROBINSON, *Readings in European History*, Vol. I, pp. 14–27. *The Notitia Dignitatum* (*Pennsylvania Translations and Reprints*).

C. **Wall Maps and Geography.** BREASTED-HUTH, *Ancient History Maps*, Map B 16 (Insert). *Teacher's Manual*, pp. 128–130.

CHAPTER XX

A. **General Reading.** The best short accounts of the barbarian invasions are EMERTON, *Introduction to the Middle Ages*, chaps. i–vii, and THORNDIKE, *History of Medieval Europe*, chaps. iii and v. OMAN, *The Dark Ages*, gives a somewhat fuller narrative of the events. ADAMS, G. B., *Civilization during the Middle Ages*, chaps. i, ii, iv, and v, discusses the general conditions and results.

B. **Source Material.** The textbook and the collateral reading should always be supplemented by examples of contemporaneous material. ROBINSON, *Readings in European History*, Vol. I (from the barbarian invasions to the opening of the sixteenth century) and Vol. II (from the opening of the sixteenth century to the present day), arranged to accompany chapter by chapter ROBINSON'S *Introduction to the History of Western Europe*, will be found especially useful in furnishing extracts which reënforce the narrative together with extensive bibliographies and topical references.

For extracts relating to the barbarian invasions, see ROBINSON, *Readings*, Vol. I, pp. 28–55. OGG, *A Source Book of Mediæval History*, chaps. i–iv. Much more extensive are the extracts given in HAYES, C. H., *An Introduction to the Sources relating to the Germanic Invasions*, 1909 (Columbia University Studies in History, Economics, and Public Law, Vol. XXXIII, No. III). See also THATCHER and MCNEAL, *A Source Book for Mediæval History*.

C. **Historical Atlases.** Constant use should be made of good historical atlases. By far the best and most convenient for the high school is SHEPHERD, WM. R., *Historical Atlas*, 1911 (see maps 43, 45, 48, 50–52). DOW, EARLE E., *Atlas of European History*, 1907, also furnishes clear maps of the chief changes.

D. **Additional Reading.** HODGKIN, the author of an extensive work in eight volumes on *Italy and her Invaders*, has written two small works, *Dynasty of Theodosius* and *Theodoric the Goth*. SERGEANT, *The Franks*, may be recommended. Every historical student should gain some acquaintance with the celebrated historian GIBBON. Although his *Decline and Fall of the Roman Empire* was written about a century and a half ago, it is still of great interest and importance and is incomparable in its style. The best edition is published by The Macmillan Company, with corrections and additions by a competent modern historian, J. B. BURY. *The Cambridge Mediæval History*, by various writers, now in course of publication, devotes its first volume to the period in question.

E. **Guide to the Study of the Middle Ages.** An admirable syllabus, guide, and exhaustive bibliography for the study of the Middle Ages may be found in the compilation of PAETOW, L. J., *A Guide to the Study of Mediæval History*, 1917. This is indispensable to anyone making a serious study of the period.

CHAPTER XXI

***A*. General Reading.** For short accounts of the development of the papacy, see THORNDIKE, *History of Mediæval Europe*, chap. vi; FLICK, *The Rise of the Mediæval Church*; and WALKER, *The History of the Christian Church*. Church histories are usually written either by Catholics or Protestants, who naturally differ in their interpretation of events. One may refer to FISHER, *History of the Christian Church* (Protestant), or ALZOG, *Manual of Universal Church History* (Catholic). MILMAN, *History of Latin Christianity*, although old, is scholarly and readable and to be found in many good libraries. *Cambridge Mediæval History*, Vol. I, chaps. iv, vi. NEWMAN, *Manual of Church History*, Vol. I (Protestant).

***B*. Source Material.** ROBINSON, *Readings*, Vol. I, pp. 14–27 and chap. iv. By far the best collection of illustrative sources is to be found in AYER, J. C., *A Source Book of Ancient Church History*, 1913.

CHAPTER XXII

***A*. General Reading.** THORNDIKE, *History of Mediæval Europe*, chaps. ix–x. WORKMAN, *Evolution of the Monastic Ideal*. TAYLOR, HENRY O., *Classical Heritage of the Middle Ages*, — admirable chapter on Monasticism. HARNACK, *Monasticism*, a little book by a very distinguished church historian. Accounts of the rise of the monks will be found in all the church histories referred to in the bibliography for Chapter XXI.

***B*. Source Material.** ROBINSON, *Readings*, chap. v. There is a *Life of St. Columban*, written by one of his companions, which, although short and simple in the extreme, furnishes a better idea of the Christian spirit of the sixth century than the longest treatise by a modern writer. This life may be found in *Translations and Reprints*, Vol. II, No. 7, translated by Professor Munro. The chief portions of the Benedictine Rule may be found in HENDERSON, E. F., *Select Historical Documents of the Middle Ages*, pp. 74 ff., and in THATCHER and McNEAL, *A Source Book for Mediæval History*, pp. 432 ff. There is an excellent translation by Brehaut of GREGORY OF TOURS, *History of the Franks*. See map, pp. 46–47, in SHEPHERD, *Historical Atlas*, showing spread of Christianity in Europe.

***C*. Additional Reading.** *Cambridge Mediæval History*, Vol. II, chap. xvi. The most complete history of the monks is by the French writer MONTALEM-BERT, *The Monks of the West from St. Benedict to St. Bernard*, which has been translated into English (6 vols.). The writer's enthusiasm and excellent style make the work very attractive.

***D*. Mohammed and his Followers.** For Mohammed and the Saracens, see THATCHER and SCHWILL, *Europe in the Middle Age*, chap. xv. GILMAN, *The Saracens*. GIBBON has a famous chapter on Mohammed and another on the conquests of the Arabs. These are the fiftieth and fifty-first of his great work. *Cambridge Mediæval History*, Vol. II, chaps. x–xii.

E. **Source Material.** It is not hard to find a copy of one of the English translations of the Koran. See brief extracts in ROBINSON, *Readings*, and in OGG, *Source Book of Mediæval History*, pp. 97 ff. STANLEY LANE-POOLE, *Speeches and Table Talk of Mohammed*, is very interesting.

F. **Additional Reading.** MUIR, *Life of Mohammed*. AMEER ALI, *The Life and Teachings of Mohammed, a Short History of the Saracens*, by one who sympathizes with them.

CHAPTER XXIII

A. **General Reading.** EMERTON, *Introduction to the Middle Ages*, chaps. xii–xiv. THORNDIKE, *History of Medieval Europe*, chaps. xi–xii. BRYCE, *Holy Roman Empire*, chaps. iv–v. HENDERSON, *History of Germany in the Middle Ages*, chaps. iv–v. OMAN, *Dark Ages*, chaps. xix–xxii.

B. **Source Material.** ROBINSON, *Readings*, pp. 120–125 and chap. vii. DUNCALF and KREY, *Parallel Source Problems in Mediæval History*, pp. 3–26.

C. **Additional Reading.** HODGKIN, *Charles the Great*, a small volume. MOMBERT, *A History of Charles the Great*, the most extensive treatment in English. *Cambridge Mediæval History*, Vol. II, chaps. xviii–xix.

CHAPTER XXIV

A. **General Reading.** EMERTON, *Introduction to the Middle Ages*, chap. xv. THORNDIKE, *History of Medieval Europe*, chaps. xiii–xiv. OMAN, *Dark Ages*, chaps. xxiii–xxv. EMERTON, *Mediæval Europe*, chap. xiv. ADAMS, *Civilization during the Middle Ages*, chap. ix.

B. **Source Material.** ROBINSON, *Readings*, chaps. viii–ix. OGG, *Source Book of Mediæval History*, chap. x. THATCHER and MCNEAL, *A Source Book for Mediæval History*, pp. 341–417.

C. **Additional Reading.** SEIGNOBOS, *Feudal Régime* (excellent). See " Feudalism," in *Encyclopædia Britannica*, 11th ed. INGRAM, *History of Slavery and Serfdom*, especially chaps. iv–v. CHEYNEY, *Industrial and Social History of England*. *Cambridge Mediæval History*, Vol. II, chap. xx. MUNRO and SELLERY, *Mediæval Civilization*, pp. 159–212.

CHAPTER XXV

A. **General Reading.** There are a number of convenient general histories of England during the Middle Ages which can be used to supplement the short account here given: CHEYNEY, *Short History of England*; GREEN, *Short History of the English People*; CROSS, A. L., *A History of England and Greater Britain*, chaps. iv–xviii; ANDREWS, CHARLES M., *History of England*;

TERRY, *History of England*; and a number of others. For France, ADAMS, G. B., *Growth of the French Nation*; DURUY, *History of France*; and a more recent treatment by DAVIS, W. S., *The History of France*.

B. Source Material. ROBINSON, *Readings*, chaps. xi, xx. There are several source books of English history: CHEYNEY, *Readings in English History*, chaps. iv–xii; COLBY, *Selections from the Sources of English History*; LEE, *Source-Book of English History*; KENDALL, *Source Book of English History*.

C. Additional Reading. There is, of course, a great deal more available in English relating to English history than to the history of the continental countries. One will find plenty of references to the more extensive works in any of the books mentioned above. Especially valuable are the great series edited by OMAN, HUNT, and POOLE, on the political history of England, and TRAILL and MANN, *Social England*. The indispensable guide to a study of the Magna Carta (Great Charter) is McKECHNIE, *Magna Carta.*

CHAPTER XXVI

A. General Reading. EMERTON, *Mediæval Europe*, chaps. iii–x. HENDERSON, E. F., *History of Germany in the Middle Ages*. A clear and scholarly account of the whole period. THORNDIKE, *History of Medieval Europe*, chap. xv. DAVIS, H. W. C., *Medieval Europe*, chaps. v–vii.

B. Source Material. ROBINSON, *Readings*, Vol. I, chaps. xii–xiv. DUNCALF and KREY, *Parallel Source Problems in Mediæval History*, Problem II (Canossa). THATCHER and McNEAL, *A Source Book for Mediæval History*, Section III, pp. 132–259.

C. Additional Reading. TOUT, *The Empire and the Papacy*, with chief attention to the strictly political history. BRYCE, *Holy Roman Empire*, chaps. viii–xi. Excellent maps for the period will be found in SHEPHERD, *Historical Atlas*.

CHAPTER XXVII

A. General Reading. EMERTON, *Mediæval Europe*, chap. xi. TOUT, *The Empire and the Papacy*, chaps. vii, viii, xiii, xiv, xix. THORNDIKE, *History of Medieval Europe*, chap. xvi. DAVIS, *Medieval Europe*, chap. viii. MUNRO and SELLERY, *Mediæval Civilization*, pp. 240–276. ADAMS, *Civilization during the Middle Ages*, chap. xi, for discussion of general results.

B. Source Material. ROBINSON, *Readings*, chap. xv. THATCHER and McNEAL, *A Source Book for Mediæval History*, Section IX, pp. 510–544. *Translations and Reprints*, published by the Department of History of the University of Pennsylvania, Vol. I, Nos. 2, 4, and Vol. III, No. 1.

C. Additional Reading. ARCHER and KINGSFORD, *The Crusades.* GIBBON, *Decline and Fall of the Roman Empire*, chaps. lviii–lix. See " Crusades," in *Encyclopædia Britannica*, 11th ed.

CHAPTER XXVIII

A. **General Reading.** The available material on this important subject is rather scattered. In ROBINSON'S *Western Europe*, chaps. xvi, xvii, xxi, a somewhat fuller account of the Church is given. See EMERTON, *Mediæval Europe*, chap. xvi. The works of Flick and Walker referred to under Chapter XXI above are useful brief treatments. Special topics can be looked up in the *Encyclopædia Britannica*, the *Catholic Encyclopædia*, or any other good encyclopedia.

B. **Source Material.** ROBINSON, *Readings*, Vol. I, chaps. xvi, xvii, xxi. THATCHER and McNEAL, *A Source Book for Mediæval History*, contains many important documents relating to the Church.

C. **Additional Reading.** CUTTS, *Parish Priests and their People.* The opening chapter of LEA, *A History of the Inquisition of the Middle Ages*, gives a remarkable account of the medieval Church and the abuses which prevailed. The first volume also contains chapters upon the origin of both the Franciscan and Dominican orders. For St. Francis the best work is SABATIER, *St. Francis of Assisi.* See also GASQUET, *English Monastic Life*; JESSOPP, *The Coming of the Friars, and Other Historic Essays*; CREIGHTON, *History of the Papacy*, introductory chapter.

CHAPTER XXIX

A. **General Reading.** EMERTON, *Mediæval Europe*, chap. xv. DAVIS, *Mediæval Europe*, chap. ix. THORNDIKE, *History of Medieval Europe*, chaps. xvii–xix, xxxi–xxxii. HULME, *Renaissance and Reformation.* EMERTON, *The Beginnings of Modern Europe*, chaps. iv–v, ix–x.

Historians are so accustomed to deal almost exclusively with political events that one looks to them in vain for much information in regard to town life in the Middle Ages and is forced to turn to special works: GIBBINS, *History of Commerce*, best short account with good maps; CUNNINGHAM, *Western Civilization in its Economic Aspects*, Vol. II; CHEYNEY, *Industrial and Social History of England*; GIBBINS, *Industrial History of England*; DAY, C., *History of Commerce*; LUCHAIRE, *Social Life in the Time of Philip Augustus.* SYMONDS, *Age of Despots*, gives a charming account of town life in Italy in its more picturesque aspects. HAMLIN, *History of Architecture*, good introduction. Good account of early discoveries in *Cambridge Modern History*, Vol. I, chaps. i–ii.

B. **Source Material.** ROBINSON, *Readings*, Vol. I, chap. xviii. OGG, *A Source Book of Mediæval History*, chap. xx. THATCHER and McNEAL, *A Source Book for Mediæval History.* Section X, pp. 545–612, gives many interesting documents. Marco Polo's account of his travels is easily had in English. The best edition of *Travels of Sir John Mandeville* is that published by The Macmillan Company, because it contains the accounts on which the anonymous writer of the travels depended for his information.

CHAPTER XXX

A. **General Reading.** EMERTON, *Mediæval Europe*, chap. xiii. THORNDIKE, *History of Medieval Europe*, chaps. xx–xxii. MUNRO and SELLERY, *Mediæval Civilization*, pp. 277–357, 458–490. HULME, *Renaissance and Reformation*. RASHDALL, *History of the Universities in the Middle Ages*, introductory chapters.

B. **Source Material.** ROBINSON, *Readings*, Vol. I, chap. xix. STEELE, *Mediæval Lore*, extracts from an encyclopedia of the thirteenth century. The *Song of Roland* is translated into spirited English verse by O'Hagan. The reader will find a beautiful example of a French romance of the twelfth century in an English translation of *Aucassin and Nicolette.* Mr. Steele gives charming stories of the twelfth and thirteenth centuries in *Huon of Bordeaux*, *Renaud of Montauban*, and *The Story of Alexander.* MALORY, *Mort d'Arthur*, a collection of the stories of the Round Table made in the fifteenth century for English readers, is the best place to turn for these famous stories. ROBINSON and ROLFE, *Petrarch* (new enlarged edition, 1914), a collection of his most interesting letters. WHITCOMB, *Literary Source Book of the Italian Renaissance.* COULTER, *Mediæval Garner*, a collection of selections from the literary sources.

C. **Additional Reading.** The best treatment of medieval intellectual history is TAYLOR, H. O., *The Mediæval Mind*, 2 vols. SAINTSBURY, *Flourishing of Romance*, a good introduction to medieval literature. WALSH, *The Thirteenth, the Greatest of Centuries* (rather too enthusiastic in its claims). SMITH, JUSTIN H., *The Troubadours at Home.* CORNISH, *Chivalry.* DEVINNE, *Invention of Printing.* PUTNAM, *Books and their Makers during the Middle Ages.* BURCKHARDT, *The Civilization of the Renaissance in Italy.* VAN DYCK, *The History of Painting.*

CHAPTER XXXI

A. **General Reading.** HAYES, C. J. H., *Political and Social History of Modern Europe*, Vol. I, chaps. i, iii (excellent brief account). JOHNSON, *Europe in the Sixteenth Century*, chaps. i–ii. *Cambridge Modern History*, Vol. I, chaps. iv, xi. See "Charles V," in *Encyclopædia Britannica.* DURUY, *History of France*, Ninth and Tenth Periods.

B. **Source Material.** ROBINSON, *Readings*, Vol. II, chap. xxiii.

C. **Additional Reading.** *Cambridge Modern History*, Vol. II, chap. ii. DYER and HASSALL, *Modern Europe* (a political history of Europe in 6 vols.), Vol. I. CREIGHTON, *History of the Papacy.* PASTOR, *History of the Popes*, Vol. V. BRYCE, *Holy Roman Empire*, chap. xiv.

CHAPTER XXXII

A. **General Reading.** HAYES, *Modern Europe*, Vol. I, chap. iv. HENDERSON, E. F., *Short History of Germany.* JOHNSON, *Europe in the Sixteenth Century*, chaps. iii–v. A good recent discussion of the period is contained in HULME,

Renaissance and Reformation. LINDSAY, *History of the Reformation*, Vol. I. See "Reformation," in *Encyclopædia Britannica*, 11th ed.

B. Source Material. ROBINSON, *Readings*, Vol. I, chap. xxi, and Vol. II, chaps. xxiv–xxvi. WACE and BUCHHEIM (Editors), *Luther's Primary Works* and *The Augsburg Confession.* WHITCOMB, *Source Book of the German Renaissance.* HAZLITT, *Luther's Table Talk.* SMITH, PRESERVED, *Luther's Correspondence and other Contemporary Letters.*

C. Additional Reading. McGIFFERT, *Martin Luther.* BEARD, *Martin Luther*, especially introductory chapters on general conditions. CREIGHTON, *History of the Papacy*, Vol. VI. *Cambridge Modern History*, Vol. I, chaps. ix, xix, and Vol. II, chaps. iv–viii. JANSSEN, *History of the German People*, Vols. I–II. EMERTON, *Desiderius Erasmus*, very interesting. SMITH, PRESERVED, *The Life and Letters of Martin Luther.* BÖHMER, *Luther in the Light of Recent Research.* PEARSON, KARL, *The Ethic of Freethought*, chap. ix, on the intellectual aspects of Luther's teachings and policy.

CHAPTER XXXIII

A. General Reading. JOHNSON, *Europe in the Sixteenth Century*, pp. 272 ff. See "Zwingli" and "Calvin," in *Encyclopædia Britannica.* Chapters on the changes under Henry VIII and Edward VI will be found in all general histories of England; for example, POLLARD, A. F., *History of England* (Home University Library), chap. iv; CHEYNEY, *Short History of England*, chap. xii; CROSS, *A History of England*, chaps. xx–xxii; GREEN, *Short History of the English People*, chaps. vi–vii.

B. Source Material. ROBINSON, *Readings*, chap. xxvii. GEE and HARDY, *Documents Illustrative of English Church History*, pp. 145 ff., very useful and full. CHEYNEY, *Readings in English History*, chap. xii.

C. Additional Reading. *Cambridge Modern History*, Vol. II, chaps. x–xi, xiii–xv. JACKSON, S. M., *Huldreich Zwingli.* LINDSAY, *History of the Reformation*, Vol. II, Bk. III, chaps. i–iii, and Bk. IV. GASQUET, *The Eve of the Reformation.* POLLARD, *Henry VIII*; and, by the same, *History of England from the Accession of Edward VI to the Death of Elizabeth*, — two admirable works by one of the most stimulating of modern English historians.

CHAPTER XXXIV

A. General Reading. JOHNSON, *Europe in the Sixteenth Century*, chaps. vii–ix. HAYES, *Modern Europe*, Vol. I, chaps. v–vi (excellent). WAKEMAN, *European History, 1598–1715*, chaps. i–v. The portion of the chapter dealing with English affairs can be readily supplemented by means of the general histories of England, CHEYNEY, CROSS, GREEN, GARDINER, TERRY, etc.

B. Source Material. ROBINSON, *Readings*, Vol. II, chaps. xxviii, xix. CHEYNEY, *Readings in English History*, chap. xiii.

C. **Additional Reading.** *Cambridge Modern History*, Vol. II, chaps. ix, xvi, xviii–xix; Vol. III, chaps. i, vi–x, xv, xx; Vol. IV, chaps. i, iii–vi, xiii–xiv. LINDSAY, *History of the Reformation*, Vol. II, Bk. III, chaps. iv–v, and Bk. VI. PUTNAM, RUTH, *William the Silent.* PAYNE, *Voyages of Elizabethan Seamen to America*, Vol. I. MOTLEY, *Rise of the Dutch Republic.* GINDELY, *History of the Thirty Years' War.*

CHAPTER XXXV

A. **General Reading.** POLLARD, *History of England*, chap. v. CHEYNEY, *Short History of England*, chaps. xiv–xvi. HAYES, *Modern Europe*, Vol. I, chap. viii. CROSS, *A History of England*, chaps. xxvii–xxxv. GREEN, *Short History of the English People*, chaps. viii–ix. GARDINER, *Students' History of England*, Pts. VI–VIII.

B. **Source Material.** ROBINSON, *Readings*, chap. xxx. CHEYNEY, *Readings in English History*, chaps. xiv–xvi. LEE, *Source Book of English History*, Pt. VI; COLBY, *Selections from the Sources of English History*, Pt. VI, the Stuart Period. GEE and HARDY, *Documents Illustrative of English Church History*, pp. 508–664.

C. **Additional Reading.** *Cambridge Modern History*, Vol. III, chap. xvii; Vol. IV, chaps. viii–xi, xv, xix; Vol. V, chaps. v, ix–xi. MORLEY, *Oliver Cromwell.* MACAULAY, Essay on Milton. GARDINER, *The First Two Stuarts and the Puritan Revolution.* PEASE, *The Leveller Movement.*

CHAPTER XXXVI

A. **General Reading.** *Cambridge Modern History*, Vol. V, chaps. i–ii, xiii–xiv. HAYES, *Modern Europe*, Vol. I, chap. vii. WAKEMAN, *Europe from 1598 to 1715*, chaps. ix–xi, xiv–xv. DURUY, *History of France*, Thirteenth Period. ADAMS, *Growth of the French Nation.*

B. **Source Material.** ROBINSON, *Readings*, Vol. II, chap. xxxi. Memoirs of the period are often obtainable in translation at reasonable prices. The greatest of these, those of Saint Simon, are condensed to a three-volume English edition.

C. **Additional Reading.** PERKINS, *France under the Regency*, one of several valuable books by this author. TAINE, *The Ancient Régime*, a brilliant picture of life in France in the eighteenth century. LOWELL'S *Eve of the French Revolution* is also general; it is less picturesque but gives a fairer idea of conditions.

CHAPTER XXXVII

A. **General Reading.** *Cambridge Modern History*, Vol. V, chaps. xvi, xx–xxi; Vol. VI, chap. xx. HAYES, *Modern Europe*, Vol. I, chaps. xi–xii. HENDERSON, *A Short History of Germany*, Vol. I, pp. 148–218. RAMBAUD, *History of Russia*, Vols. I–II, the best treatment of Russia. SCHWILL, *Modern Europe,* pp. 215–247, good outline. MARRIOTT and ROBERTSON, *Evolution of Prussia* (excellent). BEAZLEY, and others, *History of Russia*. MAVOR, *Economic History of Russia*. TUTTLE, *History of Prussia*, 4 vols.

B. **Source Material.** ROBINSON, *Readings*, Vol. II, chap. xxxii. ROBINSON and BEARD, *Readings in Modern European History*, Vol. I, chap. iv.

C. **Additional Reading.** BRIGHT, *Maria Theresa*. CARLYLE, *Frederick the Great*, a classic. EVERSLEY, *The Partitions of Poland*. PHILLIPS, *History of Poland*, good short account in Home University Library. HASSALL, *European History, 1757–1789*. KLUCHEVSKY, *A History of Russia*, 3 vols. SCHEVILL, *The Making of Modern Germany*. SCHUYLER, *Peter the Great*, standard English biography. WALISZEWSKI, *Life of Peter the Great*. LEWINSKI-CORWIN, *A Political History of Poland*.

CHAPTER XXXVIII

A. **General Reading.** HAYES, *Modern Europe*, Vol. I, chaps. ix–x. BECKER, *The Beginnings of the American People*. VAN TYNE, *The American Revolution*. *Cambridge Modern History*, Vol. V, chap. xxii; Vol. VI, chaps. vi, xv. CROSS, *A History of England and Greater Britain*, chap. xli, detailed manual. EGERTON, *A Short History of British Colonial Policy*, best treatment. MUIR, R., *The Expansion of Europe*, chaps. i–iv. CHEYNEY, *A Short History of England*, chap. xvii. GIBBINS, *History of Commerce in Europe*. LYALL, *The Rise of British Dominion in India*. POLLARD, *Factors in Modern History*, chap. x, a most suggestive treatment of the rise of nationalism in modern England. WOODWARD, *A Short History of the Expansion of the British Empire*, best introduction. ALTSCHUL, *The American Revolution in our School Textbooks*, excellent compilation illustrating the prevailing bias against Great Britain.

B. **Source Material.** ROBINSON, *Readings*, Vol. II, chap. xxxiii. ROBINSON and BEARD, *Readings in Modern European History*, Vol. I, chaps. vi–vii. CHEYNEY, *Readings in English History*, chaps. xiii, xvii. MUZZEY, *Readings in American History*. HART, *American History told by Contemporaries*, Vol. I.

C. **Additional Reading.** CHEYNEY, *European Background of American History*, an excellent survey. EDGAR, *The Struggle for a Continent*. HUNTER, *A Brief History of the Indian Peoples*. LUCAS, *A Historical Geography of the British Colonies*, 5 vols., the most extensive treatment. MACAULAY, *Essay on Clive*. MAHAN, *The Influence of Sea-Power upon History, 1660–1783*, a classic. MORRIS, *A History of Colonization*, 2 vols. Parkman, *A Half-Century of Conflict*, 2 vols. SEELEY, *The Expansion of England*, a well-known general survey. Three indispensable books for the teacher in furnishing a proper background for an interpretation of the Revolution are ALVORD, *The Mississippi Valley in British Politics*; SCHLESINGER, *The Colonial Merchants and the American Revolution*; and FISHER, *The Struggle for American Independence*. THWAITES, *The Colonies*. TRAILL, *Social England*, Vol. V.

INDEX

Marked letters sound as in fär, prudent, möve, *French* boṅ

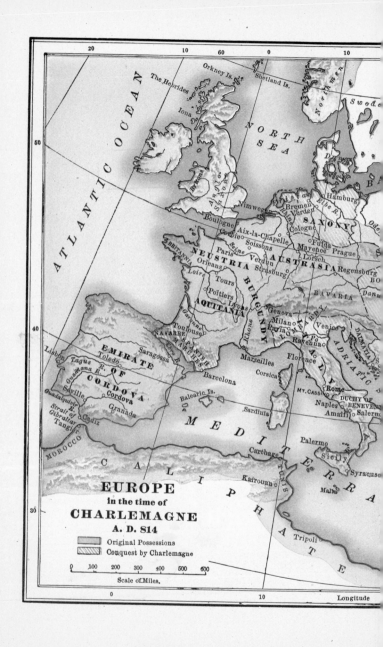

EUROPE
in the time of
CHARLEMAGNE
A. D. 814

Original Possessions
Conquest by Charlemagne

0   100   200   300   400   500   600
Scale of Miles.

SLAVONIC

RACES

Novgorod

Kief

Dnieper R.

(Magyars)

Hungarians

Danube

Cherson

BLACK SEA

CASPIAN SEA

BULGARIA

Adrianople

Constantinople

Nicæa

ROUMELIA

Angora

Trapezus

Araxes

Tigris

PHRYGIA.

Iconium

Edessa

MESOPOTAMIA

Antioch

Rhodes

Cyprus

Crete

MEDITERRANEAN SEA

Sidon
Tyre
Acre

Damascus
Nazareth

Ascalon

Jaffa

Jerusalem

BAGDAD

Alexandria

Pelusium

F

EGYPT

W.-N. ENG., BUFFALO.

Greenwich   30   40

30   40   60 50   60

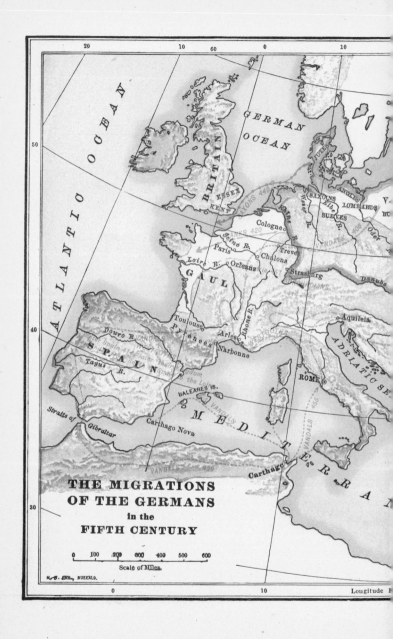

THE MIGRATIONS
OF THE GERMANS
in the
FIFTH CENTURY

0   100   200   300   400   500   600
Scale of Miles.

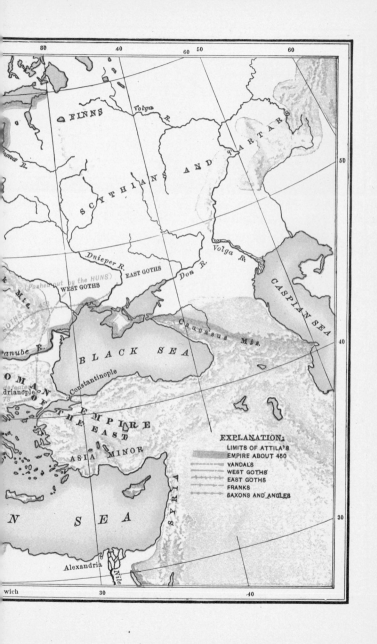

FINNS

Volga R.

SCYTHIANS AND TARTAR

Dnieper R.

(Pushed out by the HUNS)

WEST GOTHS

EAST GOTHS

Don R.

Volga R.

CASPIAN SEA

Caucasus Mts.

BLACK SEA

Constantinople

drianople

ROM

ON THE EAST EMPIRE

ASIA MINOR

Danube R.

Alexandria

Nile

SYRIA

N SEA

EXPLANATION:
LIMITS OF ATTILA'S
EMPIRE ABOUT 450
VANDALS
WEST GOTHS
EAST GOTHS
FRANKS
SAXONS AND ANGLES

wich

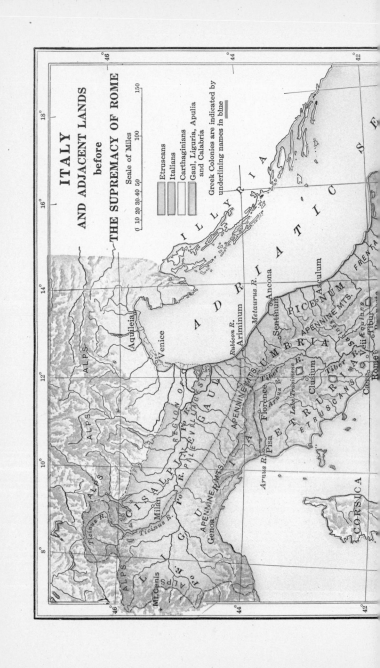

ITALY
AND ADJACENT LANDS
before
THE SUPREMACY OF ROME

Scale of Miles
0 10 20 30 40 50   100   150

Etruscans
Italians
Carthaginians
Gaul, Liguria, Apulia
and Calabria

Greek Colonies are indicated by
underlining names in blue

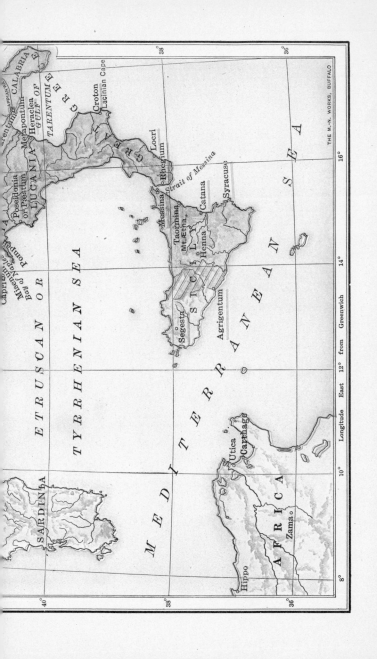

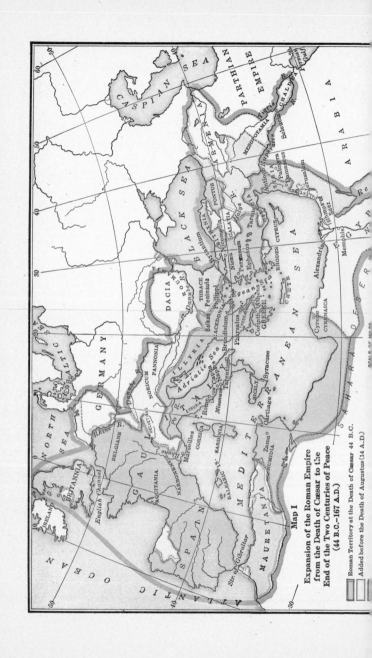

Map I

Expansion of the Roman Empire
from the Death of Cæsar to the
End of the Two Centuries of Peace
(44 B.C.–167 A.D.)

Roman Territory at the Death of Cæsar 44 B.C.

Added before the Death of Augustus (14 A.D.)

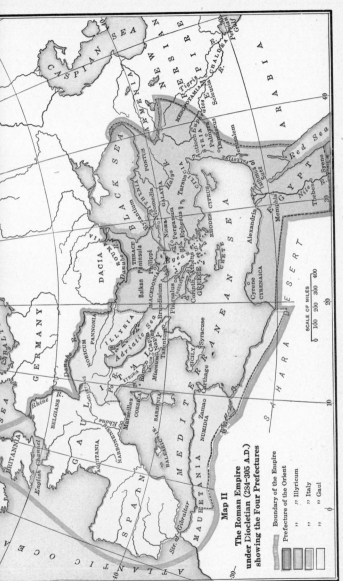

Map II

**The Roman Empire
under Diocletian (284-305 A.D.)
showing the Four Prefectures**

Boundary of the Empire
,,   ,, Illyricum
,,   ,, Italy
,,   ,, Gaul
Prefecture of the Orient

SCALE OF MILES
0   100   200   300   400

SEQUENCE MAP SHOWING TERRITORIAL GAINS AND LOSSES OF THE ROMAN EMPIRE FROM THE DEATH OF
CÆSAR (44 B.C.) TO THE DEATH OF DIOCLETIAN (305 A.D.)

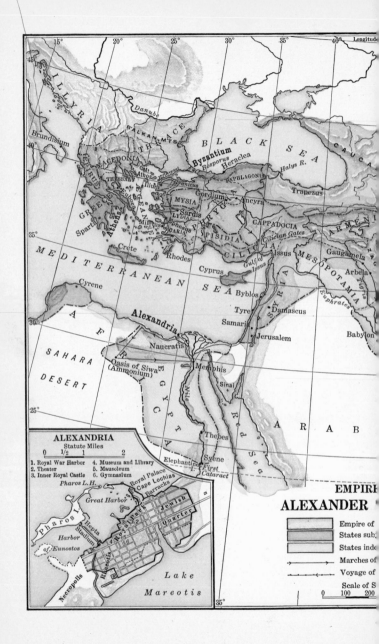

EMPIRE of
ALEXANDER

Empire of
States subj
States inde
Marches of
Voyage of
Scale of S

0   100   200

ALEXANDRIA

Statute Miles

0   1/2   1   2

1. Royal War Harbor   4. Museum and Library
2. Theater   5. Mausoleum
3. Inner Royal Castle 6. Gymnasium

Pharos L. H.
Royal Palace
Great Harbor   Cape Lochias
Hepta   Barracks
Stadium   Jewish
Harbor   Quarter
of Eunostos
Necropolis
Lake
Mareotis

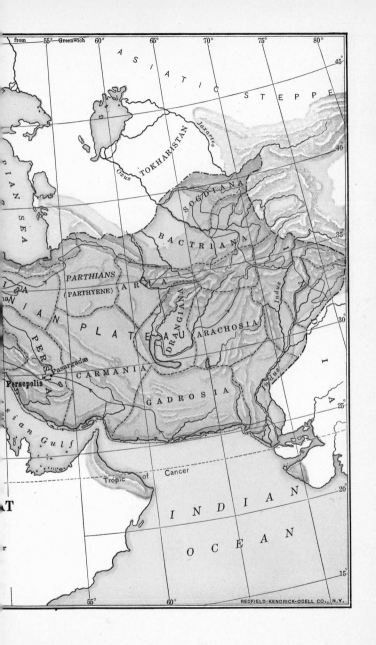

45°

A S I A T I C

S T E P P E

40°

Oxus

Jaxartes

TOKHARISTAN

SOGDIANA

35°

BACTRIANA

CASPIAN SEA

PARTHIANS

(PARTHYENE) A R I A

ana

DRANGIANA

P L A T E A U

ARACHOSIA

30°

PERSIA

Indus

Pasargadæ

CARMANIA

Persepolis

GADROSIA

25°

Persian Gulf

Indus

I N D I A

Tropic of Cancer

20°

AT

r

I N D I A N

O C E A N

15°

55° 60°

GERMANY
ABOUT 1550.

— Boundary of Empire
Habsburg Territories
Hohenzollern Territories
Ecclesiastical Territories
Imperial Cities

0 10 20 30 40 50   100

Scale of Miles.

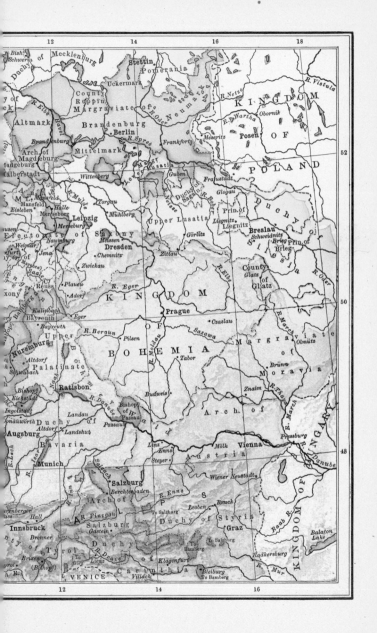

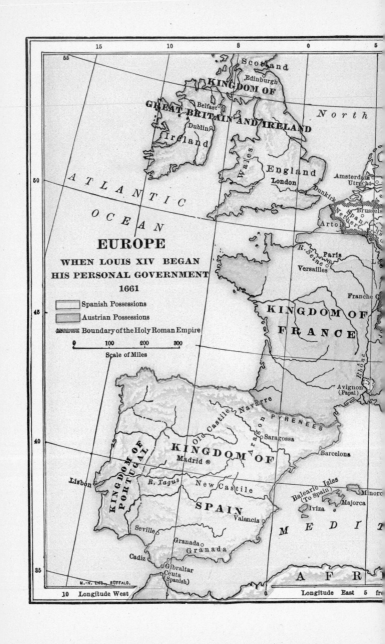

EUROPE

WHEN LOUIS XIV BEGAN

HIS PERSONAL GOVERNMENT

1661

Spanish Possessions

Austrian Possessions

Boundary of the Holy Roman Empire

0   100   200   300

Scale of Miles

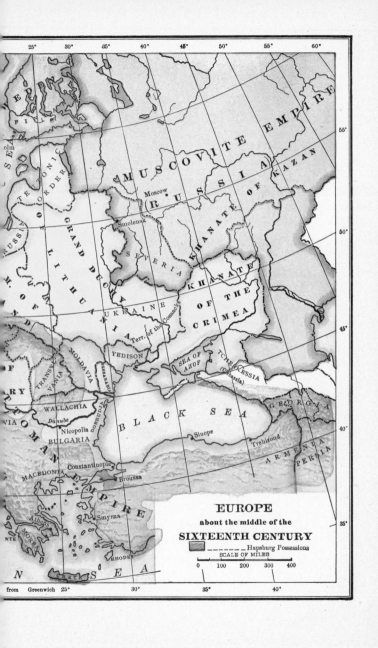

EUROPE

about the middle of the

SIXTEENTH CENTURY

▨ _ _ _ _ _ _ Hapsburg Possessions

SCALE OF MILES

0   100   200   300   400

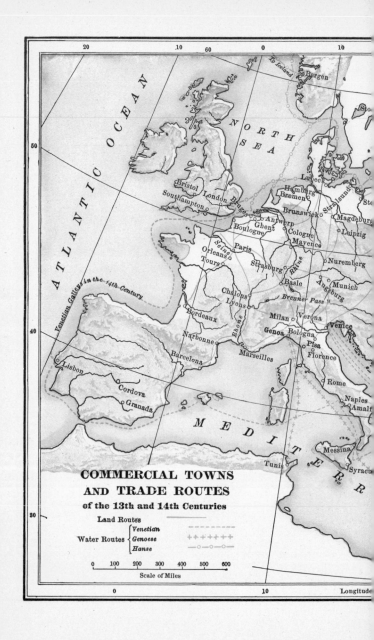

**COMMERCIAL TOWNS
AND TRADE ROUTES
of the 13th and 14th Centuries**

Land Routes

Water Routes { Venetian / Genoese / Hanse }

0   100   200   300   400   500   600
Scale of Miles

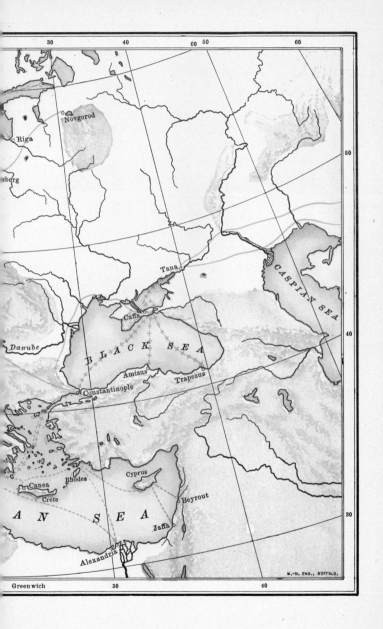

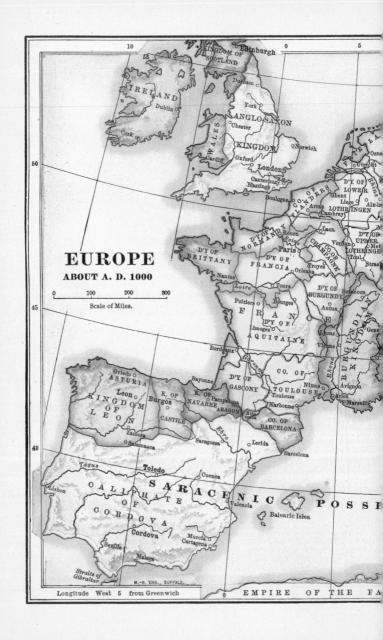

EUROPE

ABOUT A. D. 1000

0   100   200   300

Scale of Miles.

KINGDOM OF SCOTLAND

Edinburgh

IRELAND

Durham

Dublin

York

ANGLO-SAXON

Cork

WALES

Chester

Norwich

Cardiff

Oxford

London

Canterbury

Hastings

Boulogne

FRIESLA

Osne

Utrecht

D'Y OF LOWER LOTHRINGEN

Ghent

Liege

Aix-la-

Arras

Cambray

D'Y OF NORMANDY

Rouen

Paris

Laon

Verdun

Met

D'Y OF UPPER LOTHRINGEN

Tul

Stras

D'Y OF BRITTANY

D'Y OF FRANCIA

Orleans

Troyes

CHAMPAGNE

Nantes

Loire

Tours

Bourges

D'Y OF BURGUNDY

Besancon

Gene

Poitiers

F R A N C E

Autun

D'Y OF AQUITAINE

Limoges

Lyons

Vienne

BURGUNDIAN KINGDOM

Bordeaux

Garonne

CO. OF

Rhone

Bayonne

D'Y OF GASCONY

Nimes

Avignon

Oviedo

ASTURIA

K. OF NAVARRE

Toulouse

Arles

Marseill

Leon

Burgos

Pampelona

Narbonne

KINGDOM OF LEON

CASTILE

ARAGON

Ribagona

CO. OF BARCELONA

Zamora

Ebro

Saragossa

Lerida

Barcelona

Salamanca

Tagus

Toledo

Cuenca

Lisbon

C A L I P H A T E

S A R A C E N I C

P O S S I

OF

CORDOVA

Valencia

Balearic Isles

Cordova

Murcia

Seville

Cartagena

Malaga

Straits of Gibraltar

M.-N. ENG., BUFFALO.

EMPIRE   OF   THE   FA

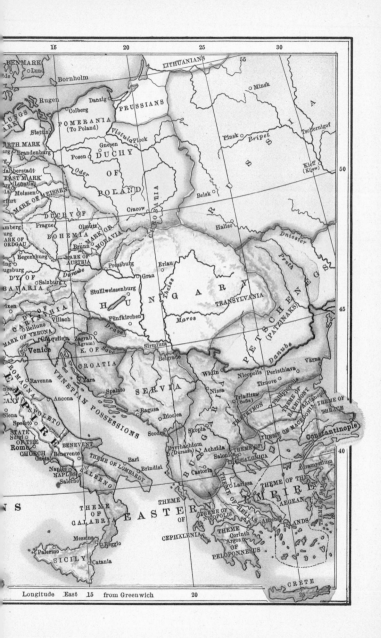

DENMARK
Lund
Bornholm
Rugen
Danzig
Colberg
PRUSSIANS
POMERANIA
(To Poland)
Stettin
URTH MARK
Brandenburg
Vistula
Plock
Gnesen
Posen
DUCHY
Oder
OF
POLAND
Belsk
Cracow
DUCHY OF
BOHEMIA
Prague
Olmutz
Brunn
MARK OF
MORAVIA
MARK OF MEISSEN
Meissen
EAST MARK
(Lusatia)
Halberstadt
Regenburg
MARK OF
AUSTRIA
Salzburg
Pressburg
Gran
Erlau
Stuhlweissenburg
Theiss
H U N G A R Y
Funfkirchen
Maros
TRANSYLVANIA
Minsk
Pinsk
Bripet
Tschernigof
R
U
S
S
I
A
Kieff
(Kijew)
Halics
Dniester
R
U
S
Pruth
P
E
T
S
C
H
E
N
E
G
S
(PATZINAKS)
Danube
Varna
BAVARIA
D'Y OF
D'Y OF
CARINTHIA
Belluno
Villach
Aquileia
Zagrab
(Agram)
Drave
Save
Sirmium
Belgrade
K. OF
CROATIA
SERVIA
Widin
Nissa
Nicopolis
Peristhlava
Tirnovo
MARK OF VERONA
Venice
Ravenna
Zara
VENETIAN POSSESSIONS
Spalato
Ancona
Ragusa
Dioclea
Scodra
Skopla
Triaditza
(Sofia)
Philippopolis
THEME OF MACEDONIA
THEME OF STRYMON
THEME OF
THRACE
Constantinople
OMAGN
CANY
Siena
Spoleto
STATE
OF
ROME
STATE OF THE
CHURCH
Gaeta
D'Y OF
SPOLETO
BENEVENT
Benevento
Bari
Brindisi
THEME OF LOMBARDY
SALERNO
Salerno
NAPLES
Napoli
Dyrrhachium
(Durazzo)
Achrida
Castoria
B U L G A R I A
THEME OF
SALONICA
Salonica
Adramyttium
THEME OF THE
EMPIRE
AEGEAN
Larissa
THEME
OF
CALABRIA
E A S T E R N
THEME
OF
CEPHALENIA
Messina
Reggio
Palermo
SICILY
Catania
THEME OF HELLAS
Athens
THEME OF
NICOPOLIS
THEME
OF
PELOPONNESUS
Corinth
Argos
ISLANDS
THEME
C R E T E

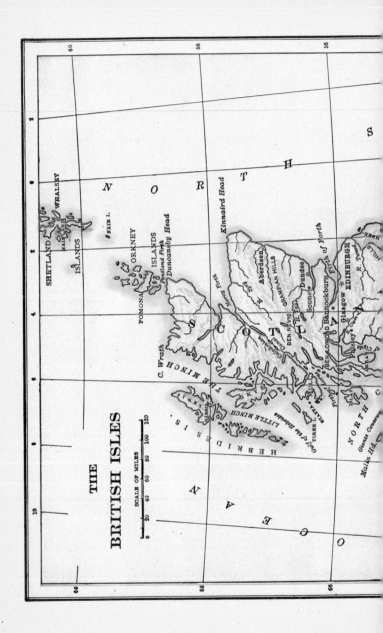

THE
BRITISH ISLES

SCALE OF MILES
0   20   40   60   80   100 120

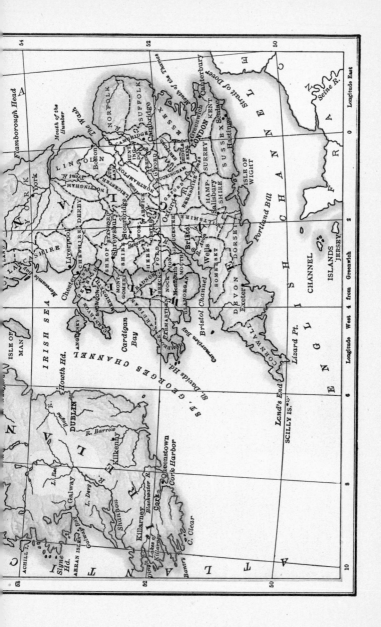

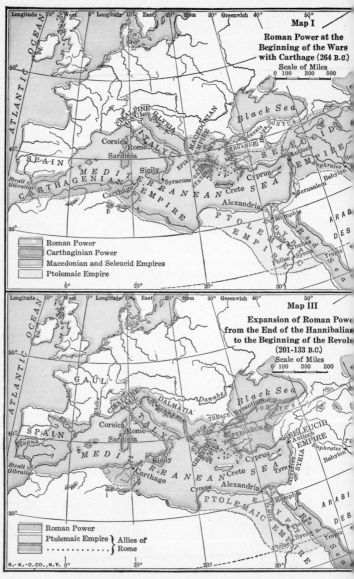

SEQUENCE MAP SHOWING THE EXPANSION OF THE ROMAN
TO THE DE

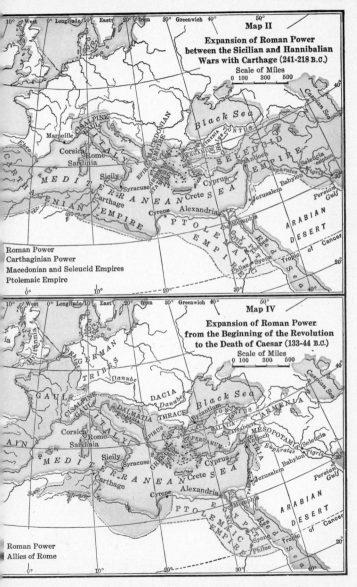

Map II

Expansion of Roman Power between the Sicilian and Hannibalian Wars with Carthage (241-218 B.C.)

Scale of Miles
0   100   300   500

Roman Power
Carthaginian Power
Macedonian and Seleucid Empires
Ptolemaic Empire

Map IV

Expansion of Roman Power from the Beginning of the Revolution to the Death of Caesar (133-44 B.C.)

Scale of Miles
0   100   300   500

Roman Power
Allies of Rome

THE BEGINNING OF THE WARS WITH CARTHAGE (264 B.C.)
R (44 B.C.)

Venice

HUNGARY

45

DALMATIA

ADRIATIC SEA

Raymond of Toulouse

Godfrey of Bouillon

River

BULGARIA

MACEDONIA

EASTERN

APULIA

Naples

Bari

North French

Durazzo

Fdk. Barbarossa

Brindisi

Normans

Otranto

EPIRUS

Thessalonica

40

Philip Augustus

Richard

CALABRIA

IONIAN

SEA

HELLAS

AEGEAN SEA

Rhegium

SICILY

MALTA

Richard and Philip Augustus — 1191

35

CRETE

MEDITERRANEA

M.-N. ENG., BUFFALO.

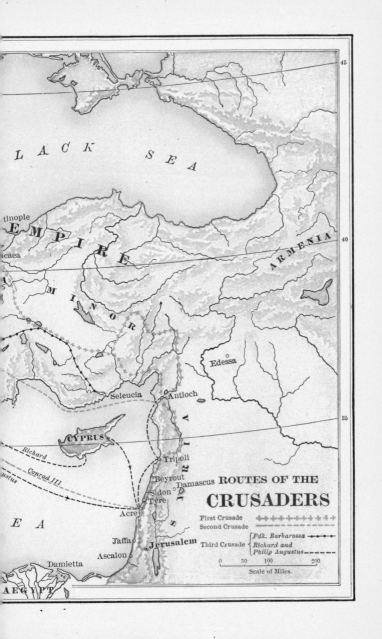

ROUTES OF THE
CRUSADERS

First Crusade
Second Crusade
Third Crusade { Fdk. Barbarossa
Richard and
Philip Augustus

0   50   100   200
Scale of Miles.